LEGAL METHODS AND SYSTEMS:
TEXT AND MATERIALS

Fourth Edition

CARL F. STYCHIN, B.A., J.D., LL.M., LL.D.
Professor of Law and Social Theory, University of Reading

LINDA MULCAHY, LL.B., LL.M., Ph.D.
Professor of Law, London School of Economics, London University

SWEET & MAXWELL

THOMSON REUTERS

First edition	1999	by Carl F Stychin
Second impression	2000	
Third impression	2001	
Second edition	2003	by Carl F Stychin and Linda Mulcahy
Second impression	2005	
Third edition	2007	by Carl F Stychin and Linda Mulcahy
Fourth edition	2010	by Carl F Stychin and Linda Mulcahy

Published in 2010 by Thomson Reuters (Legal) Ltd
(Registered in England & Wales, Company No 1679046.
Registered Office and address for service: 100 Avenue Road, London, NW3 3PF)
trading as Sweet & Maxwell

Typeset by Servis Filmsetting Ltd, Stockport, Cheshire
Printed and bound in Great Britain by Ashford Colour Printers

For further information on our products and services, visit
www.sweetandmaxwell.co.uk

No natural forests were destroyed to make this product; only farmed timber was used and re-planted

A CIP catalogue record for this book is available from the British Library

ISBN 9780414041837

Thomson Reuters and the Thomson Reuters logo are trademarks of Thomson Reuters
Sweet & Maxwell ® is a registered trademark of Thomson Reuters (Legal) Limited

PREFACE

Previous editions of this text have emerged from courses in legal method and legal system taught by the authors at Keele University, Reading University and Birkbeck University of London. The aim of those courses has been to introduce students, not only to the "traditional" foundations of legal reasoning, but also to more socio-legal and theoretical scholarship, including feminist and critical legal theories. This text carries on that approach. We have sought to provide students with a firm grounding in the canon as well as providing them with a range of materials which will encourage them to critique approaches which privilege the statute and case report. The aim is not to indoctrinate, but to stimulate lively debate and scepticism about legal authorities (including the casebook itself!).

In this fourth edition, we have sought to reflect on ongoing debate about human rights, the reform of the tribunal system and the ways in which the insights of comparative lawyers have resonance in our multi-cultural society. We have also tried to make the text more user-friendly and engaging for the reader by the introduction of mind maps. We have aimed to create a sourcebook of materials and commentary, along with questions suitable for tutorials and essays. Each chapter contains sufficient material for a tutorial or seminar and poses a series of questions or exercises which aim to guide students in their reading and focus their attention on key points.

Finally we would like to use this opportunity to express our gratitude to all the students we have taught who have engaged with the materials in this book and brought fresh insights to it.

Carl F. Stychin and Linda Mulcahy
London
April 2010

CONTENTS

ACKNOWLEDGEMENTS

Grateful acknowledgement is made to the following authors and publishers for their permission to quote from their works:

ABEL-SMITH, B. and STEVENS, R.: *In Search of Justice: Society and the Legal System* (London: Penguin, 1968) © Brian Abel-Smith and Robert Stevens, 1968. Reproduced by permission of Penguin Books Ltd

ABRAMCZYK, J.: "The tyranny of the majority: liberalism in legal education", *Canadian Journal of Women and the Law*, 1992, Vol.5 at 442, p.451. Reprinted by permission of University of Toronto Press Incorporated (*http://www.utpjournals.com*)

ALLISON, J.W.F.: "Theoretical and institutional underpinnings of a separate administrative law", in Michael Taggart (ed), *The Province of Administrative Law* (Oxford: Hart Publishing, 1997). Reprinted with permission of Hart Publishing, Oxford

ALTMAN, A.: *Critical Legal Studies: A Liberal Critique* (Princeton, New Jersey: Princeton University Press) © 1990 Princeton University Press, 1993 paperback edition. Reprinted by permission of Princeton University Press

ARMSTRONG, N.: "Making tracks" in A.A.S. Zuckerman and Ross Cranston, (eds), *Reform of Civil Procedure: Essays on "access to justice"* (Oxford: Clarendon Press, Oxford, 1995) © By permission of Oxford University Press

ATIYAH, P.S.: *Law and Modern Society*, 2nd edn (Oxford: Oxford University Press, 1995) © By permission of Oxford University Press

BAILEY, S.H., CHING, J., GUNN M.J., and ORMEROD, D.: *Smith, Bailey and Gunn on the Modern English Legal System*, 4th edn (London: Sweet and Maxwell, 2002)

BAKER, J.H.: "Statutory interpretation and parliamentary intention" (1993) 52 *Cambridge Law Journal* 353 Cambridge University Press.

BALE, C.G.: "Parliamentary Debates and Statutory Interpretation: Switching on the Light or Rummaging in the Ashcans of the Legislative Process" (1995) 74 *Canadian Bar Review* 1, Canadian Bar Association. © Canadian Bar Review and C.G. Bale

BANAKAS, S.: "The contribution of comparative law to the harmonisation of European private law" in Andrew Harding and Esin Orucu (eds), *Comparative Law in the 21st century*, (London/The Hague/New York: Kluwer, 2002)

BELL, J.: *French Legal Cultures* (London: Butterworths, 2001) By permission of Cambridge University Press

BELL, J. and ENGLE, SIR G.: *Cross on Statutory Interpretation,* 3rd edn (London: Butterworths, 1995) © By permission of Oxford University Press

BOON, A.: "History is past politics: a critique of the legal skills movement in England and Wales", *Journal of Law and Society* v25.i1, reprinted by permission of Blackwell Publishing

BOON, A., DUFF L., AND SHINER, M.: "Career paths and choices in a highly differentiated profession: the position of newly qualified solicitors" (2001) v64i4, reprinted by permission of Blackwell Publishing

BRADLEY, A.W.: "The sovereignty of parliament—form or substance?" in Jeffrey Jowell and Dawn Oliver (eds), *The Changing Constitution*, 5th edn (Oxford: Oxford University Press, 2004) © By permission of Oxford University Press

BROWN, H. and MARRIOTT A.: *ADR Principles and Practice*, 1st edn (London: Sweet and Maxwell, 1996)

BURNS, ROBERT P.: *A Theory of the Trial* (Princeton and Oxford: Princeton University Press) © 1999, Princeton University Press. Reprinted by permission of Princeton University Press

BUSH, R. and FOLGER, J.: *The Promise of Mediation* Copyright © Jossey-Bass, San Francisco, 1994. Reprinted with permission of John Wiley & Sons, Inc

CANE, P.: *The Anatomy of Tort Law* (Oxford: Hart Publishing, 1997). Reprinted with permission of Hart Publishing, Oxford

CAPPELLETTI, M.: "Alternative Dispute Resolution Processes within the Framework of the World-wide Access-to-justice Movement" (1993) 56 *Modern Law Review* 282, reprinted by permission of Blackwell Publishing

COLLINS, H.: *Marxism and Law* (Oxford: Clarendon Press, 1982) © By permission of Oxford University Press

CONAGHAN, J.: "Feminist perspectives on the law of tort" in *The Critical Lawyers Handbook 2*, Paddy Ireland and Per Laleng (eds) (London: Pluto Press, 1997)

COTTERRELL, R.: *The Politics of Jurisprudence*, 2nd edn (Oxford: Oxford University Press, 2003) © By permission of Professor R. Cotterrell;
The Sociology of Law: An Introduction, 2nd edn (London: Butterworths, 1992) © By permission of Professor R. Cotterrell

COWNIE, F., BRADNEY, A. and BURTON, M.: *English Legal System in Context*, 4th edn (Oxford: Oxford University Press, 2007) ©By permission of Oxford University Press

CRAIG, P.: "Formal and Substantive Conceptions of the Rule of Law: an Analytical Framework" (1997) Public Law 467 (London: Sweet and Maxwell, 1997)

CRAIG, P. and DE BÚRCA, G.: *EU Law: Text, Cases and Materials*, 4th edn (Oxford: Oxford University Press, 2008) © By permission of Oxford University Press

CROSS R. and HARRIS, J.W.: *Precedent in English Law*, 4th edn (Oxford: Clarendon Press, 1991) © By permission of Oxford University Press

DARBYSHIRE, P: *Darbyshire on the English Legal System*, 8th edn (London: Sweet & Maxwell, 2005); *Eddey on the English Legal System*, 7th edn (London: Sweet & Maxwell, 2001)

DENNING, LORD: *The Discipline of Law* (London: Butterworths, 1979) © By permission of Oxford University Press

DICEY, A.V.: *An Introduction to the Law of the Constitution*, 8th edn (London: Macmillan, 1915)

DOWNES, T.A.: *Textbook on Contract*, 5th edn (London: Blackstone Press, 1997) © By permission of Oxford University Press

DWORKIN, R.: *Law's Empire* (HarperCollins, 1985) Reprinted by permission of HarperCollins Publishers Ltd. © (Ronald Dworkin) (1985)
US rights: Reprinted by permission of the publisher from THE ALCHEMY OF RACE AND RIGHTS: DIARY OF A LAW PROFESSOR by Patricia S. Williams, pp12–13, Cambridge, Mass.: Harvard University Press, Copyright © 1991 by the President and Fellows of Harvard College

ELLIOTT, C., QUINN, F.: *English Legal System*, 3rd edn © Longman 2000. Reprinted by permission of Pearson Education Limited

EWING, K.D.: "The Human Rights Act and parliamentary democracy" (1999) 62 *Modern Law Review* 79, reprinted by permission of Blackwell Publishing

EWING, K.D. and THAM, J.: "The Continuing Futility of the Human Rights Act" (2008) *Public Law* 668 (London: Sweet and Maxwell, 2008)

FARRAR, J.D., DUGDALE, A.M.: *Introduction to Legal Method*, 3rd edn (London: Sweet & Maxwell, 1990)

FIRTH, G.: "The rape trial and sexual history evidence—*R v A* and the (un)worthy complainant" *Northern Ireland Quarterly*, 2006, Vol (57)(3) at 442, pp.451–453, 454–456, 461–463

FISS, O.M.: "Against settlement" (1984) 93 *Yale Law Journal* 1073 Reprinted by permission of the Yale Law Journal

FLETCHER, G.P.: *Basic Concepts of Legal Thought* (New York: Oxford University Press, 1996) © By permission of Oxford University Press, Inc

FRANK, J.: *Law and the Modern Mind* (Gloucester, MA : Peter Smith Publisher, Inc, 1970) By permission of Transaction Publishers

GEARTY, C.: "11 September 2001, counter-terrorism and the Human Rights Act" (2005) 23 *Journal of Law and Society* 18 reprinted by permission of Blackwell Publishing

GELDART, W.: *Introduction to English Law*, 11th edn (Oxford: Oxford University Press, 1995) ©By permission of Oxford University Press

GENN. H.: "Access to just settlements: the case of medical negligence" in A.A.S. Zuckerman and Ross Cranston (eds) *Reform of Civil Procedure: Essays on "access to justice"* (Oxford: Clarendon Press, Oxford, 1995) © By permission of Oxford University Press; *Judging Civil Justice, The Hamlyn Lectures 2008* (Cambridge: Cambridge University Press, 2010); *Mediation in Action: Resolving Court Disputes without Trial*, published by the Calouste Gulbenkian Foundation

GLENN, H.P.: *Legal Traditions of the World: Sustainable Diversity in Law*, 2nd edn (Oxford: Oxford University Press, 2004) © By permission of Oxford University Press

GOODRICH, P.: *Reading the Law* (Oxford: Blackwell, 1986). Reprinted by permission of Blackwell Publishing

GRAYCAR, R.: "The gender of judgments: an introduction:" in Margaret Thornton (ed) *Public Private: Feminist Legal Debates* (Melbourne: Oxford University Press, 1995). Reproduced by permission of Oxford University Press Australia from *Public Private Feminist Legal Debates* 1995, Thornton © Oxford University Press, *http://www.oup.com.au*

GRIFFITH, J.A.G.: *The Politics of the Judiciary*, 4th edn (London: Harper Collins 1991). © (J.A.G. Griffith) (1991) Reprinted by permission of HarperCollins Publishers Ltd. By permission of the Authors Licensing & Collecting Society Lt on behalf of J.A.G. Griffith, the author of *'The Politics of the Judiciary'*

GRILLO, T.: "The medication alternative: process dangers for woman" (1991) 100 *Yale Law Journal* 1545. Reprinted by permission of the Yale Law Journal

HARRIS, P.: *An Introduction to Law*, 6th edn (London: Butterworths, 2002). Reprinted by permission of Cambridge University Press

HARTLEY, T.C.: "Five forms of uncertainty in European Community Law" (1996) 55 *Cambridge Law Journal* 265. Cambridge University Press. By permission of the author

HARRINGTON, J.A. and MANJI, A.: "Mind with mind and spirit with spirit: Lord Denning and African legal systems" (2003) 30 *Journal of Law and Society* 376, reprinted by permission of Blackwell Publishing

HERMAN, D.: "'An unfortunate coincidence': Jews and Jewishness in twentieth-century English judicial discourse" (2006) 33 *Journal of Law and Society* 277, reprinted by permission of Blackwell Publishing

HEUSTON, R.F.V.: "*Donoghue v Stevenson* in retrospect" (1957) 20 *Modern Law Review* 1, reprinted by permission of Blackwell Publishing

HIBBITS, BERNARD J.: "The politics of principle: Albert Venn Dicey and the rule of law" (1994) 23 *Anglo-American Law Review* 25 now called Common Law World Review. Reproduced with the kind permission of Vathek Publishers

HOWARTH, D.: *Textbook on Tort* (London: Butterworths, 1995) © By permission of Oxford University Press

HORWITZ, M.: "The rule of law: an unqualified human good?" (1977) 86 *Yale Law Journal* 561. Reprinted by permission of The Yale Law Journal

JOHNSTONE, G.: *Restorative Justice: Ideas, Values and Debates* (Devon: Willan Publishing, 2002)

JOWELL, J.: "Parliamentary Sovereignty Under the new Constitutional Hypothesis" (2006) *Public Law* 562 at 578–579 (London: Sweet and Maxwell, 2006);
"The Rule of Law Today" in Jeffrey Jowell and Dawn Oliver (eds) *The Changing Constitution*, 5th edn (Oxford: Oxford University Press, 2004) © By permission of Oxford University Press

KAIRYS, D.: *Politics of Law: A Progressive critique*, 3rd edn (USA: Basic Books, 1990). Copyright © 1998 David Kairys. Reprinted by permission of Basic Books, a member of the Perseus Books Group

KAVANAGH, A.: "*Pepper v Hart* and matters of constitutional principle" (2005) 121 L.Q.R. 98 (London: Sweet and Maxwell, 2005)

KLUG, F.: "The long road to human rights compliance" *Northern Ireland Quarterly* 2006, Vol 57(1) at 186, pp.195–198. By permission of Queen's University Belfast

KWAW, E.: *The Guide to Legal Analysis, Lethal Methodology and Legal Writing* (Toronto: Emond Montgomery Publications, 1992). Reproduced with permission of Emond Montgomery Publications

LANGBEIN, J.H.: *The Origins of the Adversary Criminal Trial* (Oxford: Oxford University Press, 2003) © By permission of Oxford University Press

LEWIS, G.: *Lord Atkin*, (Oxford: Hart Publishing, 1999). Reprinted with permission of Hart Publishing, Oxford

LLEWELLYN, K.N.: *The Bramble Bush* (New York: Oceana Publications, 1996) © By permission of Oxford University Press, Inc

LORD GRIFFITHS: "The History and Future of the Jury" (1987) 18 *Cambrian Law Review* 5, Department of Law and Criminology, University of Wales Aberystwyth

LORD LESTER OF HERNE HILL QC: "Human rights and the British constitution", in Jeffrey Jowell and Dawn Oliver (eds) *The Changing Constitution*, 5th edn (Oxford: Oxford University Press, 2004) © By permission of Oxford University Press

MACCORMICK, N.: *Legal Reasoning and Legal Theory* (Oxford: Clarendon Press, 1978 reprinted 1995) © By permission of Oxford University Press

MANCHESTER, C., SALTER, D.: *Exploring the Law: The dynamics of precedent and statutory interpretation*, 3rd edn (London: Sweet & Maxwell, 2006)

MANSELL, W.: "Goodbye to all that: the rule of law, international law, the United States, and the use of force" (2004) 31 *Journal of Law and Society* 433, reprinted by permission of Blackwell Publishing

MANSELL, W., METEYARD, B. and THOMSON, R.: *A Critical Introduction to Law*, 3rd edition Copyright (© 2004) Cavendish, London. Reproduced by permission of Taylor & Francis Books UK

MARKESINIS, B.S.: "A Matter of Style" (1994) 110 L.Q.R. 607 (London: Sweet and Maxwell, 1994)

MARSHALL, G.: "Interpreting interpretation in the Human Rights Bill" (1998) *Public Law* 167 (London: Sweet and Maxwell, 1998)

McEWAN, J.: "Ritual, Fairness and Truth: The Adversarial and Inquisitorial models of Criminal Trial", in Anthony Duff, Lindsay Farmer, Sandra Marshall and Victor Tadros (eds) *The Trial on Trial, Vol 1: Truth and Due Process* (Oxford and Portland, Oregon: Hart Publishing, 1994). Reprinted with permission of Hart Publishing, Oxford

MENKEL-MEADOW, C.: "Lawyer negotiations: theories and realities—What we learn from mediation" (1993) 56 M.L.R. 361 *Modern Law Review*. Reprinted by permission of Blackwell Publishing

McLEOD, I.: *Legal Method* (Basingstoke: Palgrave, 2009)

MENSKI, W.: *Comparative Law in a Global Context*, 2nd edn (Cambridge: Cambridge University Press, 2006). Reprinted by permission of the W. Merenski and Cambridge University Press

MOSSMAN, M.J.: "Feminism and legal method: the difference it makes", Copyright (© 1991) from *At the Boundaries of Law* by Martha Albertson Fineman and Nancy Sweet Thomadsen (eds) (New York: Routledge). Reproduced by permission of Routledge, a division of the Taylor & Francis Group

MULCAHY, L.: "Feminist fever? Cultures of adversarialism in the aftermath of the Woolf reforms" in *Current Legal Problems* Vol 58 (2005) edited by Holder, J. and O'Cinneide, C. © By permission of Oxford University Press;
"Can Leopards change their spots? An Evaluation of the Role of Lawyers in Medical Negligence Meditation" (2001) 8(3) *International Journal of the Legal Profession* (Online) 203. Reprinted by permission of the publisher (Taylor & Francis Group, *http://www.informaworld.com*)

Nicholas, B.: *The French Law of Contract*, 2nd edn (Oxford: Clarendon Press, 1992) © By permission of Oxford University Press

NOBLES, R. and SCHIFF, D.: "The Criminal Cases Review Commission: reporting success" (2001) 64 *Modern Law Review* 280. Reprinted by permission of Blackwell Publishing

PARTINGTON, M.: *An Introduction to the English Legal System*, 3rd edn (Oxford: Oxford University Press, 2006) © By permission of Oxford University Press

RACKLEY, E.: "Difference in the House of Lords" in *Social and Legal Studies* (2006) 15 at 163. Reprinted by permission of Sage Publications

RIFKIN, J.: "Mediation from a feminist perspective: promise and problems" (1984) 2 *Law and Inequality* 21 University of Minnesota Law School. By permission of Janet Rifkin

RT HON LADY JUSTICE ARDEN: "The interpretation of UK domestic legislation in the light of European Convention on Human Rights jurisprudence" *Statute Law Review*, 2004, Vol 25(3), at 165, pp.170–179, by permission of Oxford University Press

SAMUELS, A.: "Human Rights Act 1998 Section 3: A New Dimension to Statutory Interpretation?" (2008) 29 *Statute Law Review* 130. Oxford University Press

SHACHAR, A.: "Privatising Diversity: A Cautionary Tale from Religious Arbitration in Family Law" (2008) 9 *Theoretical Inquiries in Law* 573. By permission from *Theoretical Inquiries in Law*, Tel Aviv University

SHELDON, S.: *Beyond Control: Medical Power and Abortion Law* (London: Pluto Press, 1997)

SMART, C.: *Feminism and the Power of Law* Copyright © 1989, London: Routledge. Reproduced by permission of Taylor & Francis Books UK

STEYN, J.: *"Pepper v Hart*; A Re-examination" *Oxford Journal of Legal Studies*, Spring 2001, Vol 21(1) at 59, pp.60–72, by permission of Oxford University Press

STREET, H.: *Justice in the Welfare State*, 2nd edn (London: Steven & Sons, 1975) by permission of Sweet and Maxwell

SUGARMAN, D.: "A Hatred of Disorder": Legal Science, Liberalism and Imperialism" in Peter Fitzpatrick (ed) *Dangerous Supplements* (London: Pluto Press, 1991)

SZYSZCZAK and CYGAN: *Understanding Law* (London: Sweet & Maxwell, 2005)

THOMPSON, E.P.: *Whigs and Hunters*, (London: Penguin, 1990) Copyright © E.P. Thompson, 1975. Reproduced by permission of Penguin Books Ltd and *The Essential E.P. Thompson* Compilation © 2001 by Dorothy Thompson. Published by The New Press, New York, 2001, *http://www.thenewpress.com*

TOMKINS, A.: "Introduction: on being sceptical about human rights", in *Sceptical Essays on Human Rights*, T.Campbell, K.D. Ewing and A. Tomkins (eds) (Oxford: Oxford University Press, 2001) © By permission of Oxford University Press

VAGO, S.: *Law and Society*, 7th edn (New Jersey: Prentice Hall, 2003)

VANDEVELDE, K.J.: *Thinking Like A Lawyer* (Boulder: Westview Press, 1996). Copyright © 1996 Kenneth J Vandevelde. Reprinted by permission of Westview Press, a member of the Perseus Books Group

WALDRON, J.: *The Law* Copyright (© 1990), London: Routledge. Reproduced by permission of Taylor & Francis Books UK

WARD, R. and AKHTAR, A.: *Walker & Walker's English Legal System*, 9th edn (Oxford University Press, 2005) © By permission of Oxford University Press

WERRO, F.: *Notes of the Purpose and Aims of Comparative Law*, originally published in 75 TUL. L. REV. 1225–1233 (2001). Reprinted with the permission of the Tulane Law Review Association, which holds the copyright

WILLIAMS, P.J.: *The Alchemy of Race and Rights: Diary of a Law Professor*, pp.12–13. Cambridge, Mass.: Harvard University Press, Copyright © 1991 by the President and Fellows of Harvard College. Reprinted by permission of the publisher: Harvard University Press

Woodhouse, D.: "The Constitutional Reform Act 2005—Defending Judicial Independence the English Way" (2007) 5 *International Journal of Constitutional Law* 153. Oxford University Press and New York School of Law

Zweigert K. and Kötz, H.: *Introduction to Comparative Law*, 3rd edn (Oxford: Clarendon Press, 1998) © By permission of Oxford University Press

While every care has been taken to establish and acknowledge copyright, and contact the copyright owners, the publishers tender their apologies for any accidental infringement. They would be pleased to come to a suitable arrangement with the rightful owners in each case.

TABLE OF CASES

All references are to page numbers

TABLE OF STATUTES

All references are to page numbers

TABLE OF STATUTORY INSTRUMENTS

All references are to page numbers

1

INTRODUCTION TO LEGAL METHODS: APPROACHES TO LAW AND LEGAL REASONING

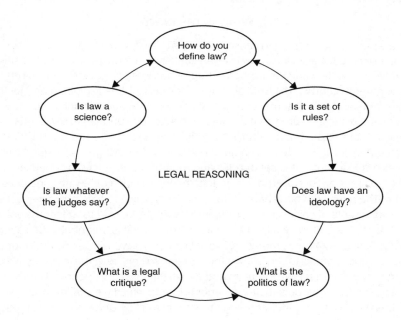

In this chapter, we begin with a brief introduction to legal reasoning and analysis. As in all the other chapters, we provide you with extracts from important books and articles in the field. Our commentary and questions help to guide you around these writings. The advantage of a cases and materials book over and above a sole-authored text is that it exposes you to a range of different ideas about law which have been espoused by a variety of authors associated with very different schools of thought. By the end of this chapter, you should:

- appreciate the various perspectives from which legal methods and legal systems can be studied;

- identify some of the problems involved in claiming that a value-free approach to the subject is possible.

Some of the readings we have selected apply ways of thinking developed in other academic disciplines—such as sociology—to legal analysis. This type of academic work is known as "interdisciplinary", because it involves bringing the ideas and understandings which have been developed in one field of inquiry to the study of law. This material is important because it can provide students of law with a broader and deeper understanding of the way law operates in practice and the devices which are sometimes used to privilege the interests of some sections of society over others.

Many of the selections we have made might be characterised as critical, because of the ways in which the authors interrogate assumptions about the functions of law and its effectiveness. The authors argue that the way in which students are taught—and what they are taught—is highly political, but that the politics of law is often disguised and made to appear politically neutral and objective. For example, law students are taught that there is a "method" to legal reasoning but you should also ask yourself, even while you are learning this method, whether there are not other methods of analysing problems which are equally as valid. Thus, one of the aims of this chapter is to provoke you to think critically about law, legal reasoning, and the way in which law is taught to students in universities.

I. What is the Law?

If you begin by asking yourself what we mean by the term "law", you will probably assume that it presupposes the existence of a society. Law is often conceived, by lawyers and others alike, as a set of rules which govern a society and create a structure of authority or government to run the social order. In the seventeenth century, the English writer Thomas Hobbes explained and justified the existence of rules and authority in terms of a "social contract". In our original state, Hobbes argued, we lived without rules, which ensured that life was (in his famous phrase) nasty, brutish, and short. In time, people came to realise that an alternative might be preferable, and they entered into agreements with each other; creating rules which governed their relationships. He argued that law might be understood as a social contract, a set of rules and regulations enforced by political institutions, which we refer to as the state or government. In this theory, the idea of law also includes the notion of enforcement of the rules with punishments (or *sanctions*) which follow from the disobedience of rules. Thus, for proponents of social contract theory, law might be said to reflect the values of the population, and this value system, which the legal system advances, might also be called an *ideology*, made up of political, economic, moral and social values. As we will see throughout this book, most of us never *actually* agreed to the laws in force in this society, and the ideology which underpins the legal system may well reflect the interests and beliefs of only some people. But the idea that there is an ideology which underpins the legal order is one to which we shall frequently return. We will also see in this chapter that understanding law simply as a set of rules does not fully answer the question of what constitutes law.

Questions

1. We will begin with an historical consideration of the question of what law is but before doing so we would like you to attempt to define law for yourself. You have probably been asked why you want to study law. Reflecting on the answers you have given, try to analyse what it is that you imagine when you think about law. Does your definition of law involve people, places, things, processes or concepts?

2. Where do the ideas that fuel law come from? What is the source of its authority?

In the following extract, Peter Goodrich makes an important distinction between the ideas that shape law and the places it is made.

Peter Goodrich, *Reading the Law* (Oxford: Blackwell, 1986), pp.3–13:

"One of the most longstanding and intractable of the debates surrounding the study of law concerns the nature and definition of the term law itself. At different times and in different cultures the term law may be taken to refer to institutions as radically different as magic, song-contests, vendetta (feuding), trial by ordeal and the rules of war. Even within the relative homogeneity of the western legal tradition, law has taken very diverse forms and has been derived from very distinct sources. At different stages in the development of western law it has been said variously that law 'comes from' God, from nature or the 'natural order of things', from the monarch, from the various forms of commonwealth or sovereignty, from the 'spirit of the people' or from custom and social usage, to name but a few of the more acceptable or prevalent views. Obviously the way in which we define law will, in terms of the examples given, make a considerable difference to the requisite manner of its study; if law comes from God then it would be best to be theologians or priests for the purposes of studying it professionally, whereas if it is really self-help or vendetta then skill with an axe or a gun is more likely to be useful than any knowledge of rules or texts or any ability to argue. The question posed by the difficulty of defining law is a serious practical problem for students and practitioners of the law, and it raises directly important issues of how law is to be differentiated from other social phenomena. Such issues go to the very heart of the professional status of law as a discipline and indeed of lawyers as its interpreters. [Here] we shall outline the traditional modes of defining law by reference to its ideational (conceptual) and institutional (legal) sources and shall then comment more broadly upon the practical meaning of the status law. . . .

To claim that law is a distinct enterprise, that it is independent of other forms of social control and requires institutions and experts, indeed a science, for its proper organization and functioning, is a fairly constant claim within the western legal tradition. Despite the apparent diversity of both the form and the content of law during the course of its lengthy history and of the very different social, political and economic roles played by the law, the legal institution itself has maintained a virtually uninterrupted doctrinal belief in the distinctiveness of law, a belief in its unity and its separation from other phenomena of social control. The two claims, those of unity and of separation, have traditionally been closely linked in legal doctrine; law is kept separate and distinct from other institutions and forms of control precisely by virtue of being a unity, by virtue of having an 'essential' characteristic which distinguishes law from all else."

Many of the legal problems we will focus on in this text should make you sceptical about whether legal reasoning can be separated from moral or political arguments, and whether legal method is, in any sense, a scientific or objective inquiry which is "value-free". In the remainder of this chapter, we outline the ideas of the modern proponents of the view that legal reasoning is inextricably intertwined with politics and morality. In particular, we introduce you to the ideas of legal realism and its various offshoots.

David Kairys, *The Politics of Law: A progressive critique*, 3rd edn (New York: Basic Books, 1998), pp.2–4:

"The separation of law from politics is supposedly accomplished and ensured by a number of perceived attributes of the legal decision-making process, including judicial subservience to the Constitution, statutes, and precedent; the quasi-scientific, objective nature of legal analysis; and the technical expertise of judges and lawyers. Together, these attributes constitute an idealized decision-making process in which (1) the law on a particular issue is preexisting, predictable, and available to anyone with reasonable legal skill; (2) the facts relevant to disposition of a case are ascertained by objective hearing and evidentiary rules that reasonably ensure that the truth will emerge; (3) the result in a particular case is determined by a rather routine application of the law to the facts; and (4) except for the occasional bad judge, any reasonably competent and fair judge will reach the 'correct' decision.

Of course, there are significant segments of the bar, trends in legal scholarship, and popularly held beliefs that repudiate this idealized model. The school of jurisprudence known as Legal Realism long ago exposed its falsity. Later jurisprudential developments, such as theories resting the legitimacy of law on the existence of widely shared values, at least implicitly recognize the social and political content of law. Explicit consideration by judges of values in certain forms, such as 'public policy' and 'social utility', is generally acknowledged as appropriate. And it is commonly known that the particular judge assigned to a case has a significant bearing on the outcome. For many, the law's malleability is a matter of common knowledge, not a surprise or a cause for alarm.

But most of this thinking is either limited to law journals or compartmentalized, existing alongside and often presented as part of the idealized process. Despite the various scholarly trends and the open consideration of social policy and utility, legal decisions are expressed and justified in terms of the idealized process. The explicit or implicit theme of almost every judicial opinion is 'the law made me do it'. And this is how the courts as well as their decisions are depicted and discussed throughout society. Even the cynical views one often hears about the law, such as 'the system is fixed' or 'it's all politics', are usually meant to describe departures from, rather than characteristics of, the legal process.

The underlying conception envisions a legal process that, if not perverted by bias, corruption, or stupidity, will produce distinctly legal, fair rules and results untainted by politics or anyone's social values. While this perception is not monolithic or static (at various times substantial segments of society have come to question the idealized model), it has fairly consistently had more currency in the United States than in any other country.

Public debate over judicial decisions usually focuses on whether courts have deviated from the idealized decision-making process rather than on the substance of decisions or the nature and social significance of judicial power. Perceived deviations undermine the legitimacy and power of the courts, and are usually greeted with a variety of institutional and public challenges, including attacks by politicians and the press, proposals for statutory or constitutional change, and, occasionally, threats or attempts to impeach judges.

Dissatisfaction with the courts and their decisions is usually expressed in terms of this notion of deviation from the idealized model. Thus, the conservative criticism that the courts have overstepped their bounds—going beyond or outside legal reasoning and the idealized process—is now commonplace, as is the accompanying plea for judicial restraint and less intrusive government.

[We] reject the idealized model and the notion that a distinctly legal mode of reasoning or analysis determines legal results. The problem is not that courts deviate from legal reasoning. There is no legal methodology or process for reaching particular, correct results. This understanding of the law has been recently most closely associated with Critical Legal Studies and . . . before that with Legal Realism."

Cownie, Bradney and Burton build on this understanding of alternative approaches to the study of law by giving us a brief summary of the origins of legal realism. Proponents of this approach have provided us with another perspective from which to view the legitimacy of law. Rather than looking to legal texts they have focused on the extent to which legitimacy can be judged by level of compliance with legal rules and the respect in which the law is held. This approach is most simply characterised by the term "law in action".

Fiona Cownie, Anthony Bradney and Mandy Burton, *English Legal System in Context*, 4th edn (Oxford: Oxford University Press, 2007), pp.14–15:

"Awareness of the importance of looking at the actual operation of legal systems owes much to studies by a number of American jurists, now known as American Legal Realists, working mainly at Harvard University in the early decades of the twentieth century. In terms of the legal system, the Realists were concerned not primarily with legal rules, cases and statutes, but with what actually happened when the legal system was at work. A classic statement of the concerns of Legal Realism is that made in a book review by one of the leading Realists, Karl Llewellyn. He wrote:

'The reviewer holds that the time has passed when the study of law could be profitably centred on legal doctrine. At the present juncture, the only serviceable focus of law study is law in action not only in the sense of . . . what the courts and all quasi-judicial bodies actually do; but also [in the sense of] the actual ordering of men's actions.'

American Legal Realism shifted its focus of enquiry firmly away from traditional study of legal rules. This thesis can be illustrated by examining some of the work of Jerome Frank, regarded as one of the more extreme practitioners of Legal Realism.

Frank was heavily critical of the work of Christopher Columbus Langdell, the American legal academic who is best known for introducing the 'case method' of teaching law into American law schools. Langdell viewed law as a science, which could be practised very simply by applying legal rules mechanically to specific cases recorded in the law reports. Langdell's method rested heavily on the positivistic notion that law resided solely in the reports of decided cases or in statutes. Jerome Frank criticised this, arguing that Langdellian legal science had very little to do with law, because it overlooked such things as the lawyer–client relationship and the role of the jury. He argued that Langdell's attitude towards law was typical of what he termed 'the basic legal myth'; lawyers promote the myth that legal rules can be applied in a mechanical way because they, like all human beings, are constantly looking for certainty. The purpose of Realism, on the other hand, was to expose this myth. This concern with what Frank saw as law in action, rather than with the 'legal myth' of the law in the books, was typical of the concerns expressed by members of the Legal Realist movement. Given the nature of Frank's work it is not surprising that Legal Realism 'has sometimes been seen as part of a general movement in American social thought called 'the revolt against formalism'."

In the UK, legal realism has expressed itself in two different movements: socio-legal studies and critical legal studies. Although distinctions might be drawn between the methodologies employed by these two groups or the extent to which they are motivated by particular political beliefs, they share many of the same concerns about the liberal models of law espoused earlier in this chapter. The socio-legal community represents a "broad church". Socio-legal researchers undertake library-based theoretical work, empirical work which leads to the development of grounded theory, as well as more policy-orientated studies which feed directly into the policy-making process. What binds the socio-legal community is an approach to the study of legal phenomena which is multi- or interdisciplinary in its approach. Their theoretical perspectives and methodologies are informed by research undertaken in many other disciplines. Traditionally socio-legal scholars have bridged the divide between law and sociology, social policy, and economics. But there is increasing interest in law and disciplines within the field of humanities. Within the UK, socio-legal study has tended to be characterised by its involvement in undertaking empirical work which focuses on the operation of law in practice. Empirical work involves studying groups who are affected by, or in regular contact with, the law, courts or law enforcers. Much of this work has been influential in encouraging policy makers to reform existing laws so that they are more sensitive to the needs of those using them. Whilst there is increasingly more dialogue between the offspring of legal realism, critical legal scholars have been more vociferous in their criticisms of the ideological foundations of the current legal system. In the following extract, Vago provides us with a rather upbeat analysis of this movement's achievements.

Steven Vago, *Law and Society*, 7th edn (New Jersey: Prentice Hall, 2003), pp.65–67:

"Critical Legal Studies (CLS but also referred to as CRITS) is a vibrant, refreshing, controversial and enduring addition to the ongoing jurisprudential debate on law, legal education and the role of lawyers in society. It is widely considered, by critics and followers alike, to comprise some of the most exciting . . . scholarship around, and one sociologist of law described it as being 'where the action is'. The movement began with a group of junior faculty members and law students at Yale in the late 1960s who have since moved to other places. In 1977, the group organized itself into the Conference on Critical Legal Studies, which has over 400 members and holds an annual conference that draws more than 1,000 participants . . .

Legal realists in the 1920s and 1930s argued against the nineteenth-century belief that the rule of law was supreme. They contended, because a good lawyer could argue convincingly either side of a given case, there was actually nothing about the law that made any judicial decision inevitable. Rather, they pointed out, the outcome of a case depended largely, if not entirely, on the predilections of the judge who happened to be deciding it. Thus, far from being a science, the realists argued, law was virtually inseparable from politics and economics.

Proponents of the movement reject the idea that there is anything distinctly legal about legal reasoning. As with any other kind of analysis, legal reasoning, they maintain, cannot operate independently of the personal biases of lawyers and judges, or of the social context in which they are acting. Furthermore, law is so contradictory that it allows the context of a case to determine the outcome. That attribute of law—its inability to cover all situations—is called indeterminancy. Because law consists of a variety of contradictions and inconsistencies, judicial decisions cannot be self-contained models of reasoning as they claim to be. Decisions rest on grounds outside of formal legal doctrine which are inevitably political.

Critical scholars also reject law as being value-free and above political, economic, and social considerations. Laws only seem neutral and independent, even those that reflect the dominant values in society. Therefore, laws legitimate the status quo. They maintain that law is actually part of the system of power in society rather than a protection against it.

Although proponents of the movement insist that their ideas are still tentative and evolving, their attacks on law and legal training have created a good deal of criticism. The movement has been called Marxist, utopian, hostile to rules, and incoherent. Critical legal scholars have been accused of favoring violence over bargaining, of advocating the inculcation of leftist values in legal education, and of being preoccupied with 'illegitimate hierarchies' such as the bar; their approach to law is 'nihilistic', and they teach cynicism to their students, which may result in 'the learning of the skills of corruption'. Nihilist law teachers with a proclivity for revolution are likely to train criminals, and they have, therefore 'an ethical duty to depart from law school'. It is unlikely that the controversy between proponents and opponents of the movement will be settled in the foreseeable future. Further, although the movement has been fairly successful in questioning the validity of the Western legal system, it has failed . . . its major objective of developing and gaining broader support for new legal doctrines that are more representative of class, gender and race differences. So far, the most useful function of the movement is indicating the extent to which politics influences the legal system."

It is clear from this extract that the growth of critical legal studies has been far from uncontroversial. The challenge it poses to liberal jurisprudence is taken up by Andrew Altman.

Andrew Altman, *Critical Legal Studies: A liberal critique* (Princeton, New Jersey: Princeton University Press, 1993), pp.13–15:

"There are three main prongs to the CLS attack on the liberal embrace of the rule of law, three main elements to the CLS charge that the rule of law, as liberal theory conceptualizes it, is a myth. . . . a preliminary characterization of them is possible at this stage.

The first prong hinges on the claim that the rule of law is not possible in a social situation where the kind of individual freedom endorsed by the liberal view reigns. Such a situation would be characterized by a pluralism of fundamentally incompatible moral and political viewpoints. The establishment of the rule of law under the conditions of pluralism would require some mode of legal reasoning that could be sharply distinguished from moral and political deliberation and choice. There would have to be a sharp distinction, so the argument goes, between law, on one side, and both morals and politics, on the other. Without such a distinction, judges and other individuals who wield public power could impose their own views of the moral or political good on others under the cover of law. Such impositions, however, would destroy the rule of law and the liberal freedom it is meant to protect.

Thus, the liberal view requires that legal reasoning—that is, reasoning about what rights persons have under the law and why—be clearly distinguished from reasoning about political or ethical values. Legal reasoning is not to be confused with deciding which party to a case has the best moral or political argument. Yet it is precisely this kind of legal reasoning that is impossible in a setting of moral and political pluralism, according to CLS. The law-politics distinction collapses, and legal reasoning becomes tantamount to deciding which party has the best moral or political argument. Karl Klare puts the CLS position concisely: 'This [liberal] claim about legal reasoning—that it is autonomous from political and ethical choice—is a falsehood.'

Duncan Kennedy is even more blunt, but the essential point is the same:

> 'Teachers teach nonsense when they persuade students that legal reasoning is distinct, as a method for reaching correct results, from ethical or political discourse in general . . . There is never a "correct legal solution" that is other than the correct ethical or political solution to that legal problem.'

The second prong of the CLS attack on the rule of law revolves around the claim that the legal doctrines of contemporary liberal states are riddled by contradictions. The contradictions consist of the presence of pairs of fundamentally incompatible norms serving as authoritative elements of legal doctrine in virtually all departments of law. These contradictions are thought to defeat the notion that the rule of law actually reigns in those societies that most contemporary liberal philosophers regard as leading examples of political societies operating under the rule of law. Kennedy contends that the contradictions are tied to the fact that legal doctrine does not give us a coherent way to talk about the rights of individuals under the law: 'Rights discourse is internally inconsistent, vacuous, or circular. Legal thought can generate plausible rights justifications for almost any result.' Klare echoes Kennedy's claim: 'Legal reasoning is a texture of openness, indeterminacy, and contradiction.'

As Klare and Kennedy suggest, the CLS view is that the consequence of these doctrinal contradictions is pervasive legal indeterminacy—that is, the widespread inability of the authoritative rules and doctrines to dictate a determinate outcome to legal cases. The contradictions enable lawyers and judges to argue equally well for either side of most legal cases, depending on which of two contradictory legal norms they choose to rely upon. Moreover, the existence of indeterminacy is tied to the collapse of the distinction between law and politics. Judges can and do covertly rely on moral and political considerations in deciding which of two incompatible legal norms they will base their decisions upon. In existing liberal states, we have not the rule of law but the rule of politics. Joseph Singer sums up this phase of the CLS attack on the rule of law nicely:

> 'While traditional legal theorists acknowledge the inevitability and desirability of some indeterminacy, traditional legal theory requires a relatively large amount of determinacy as a fundamental premise of the rule of law. Our legal system, however, has never satisfied this goal.'

Closely associated with the first two prongs of the CLS attack on the rule of law is the thesis that the very idea of the rule of law serves as an instrument of oppression and domination. David Kairys expresses the general idea in a manner characteristic of much CLS writing:

> 'The law is a major vehicle for the maintenance of existing social and power relations. . . . The law's perceived legitimacy confers a broader legitimacy on a social system . . . characterized by domination. This perceived legitimacy of the law is primarily based . . . on the distorted notion of government by law, not people.'

In the CLS view, then, the idea that our political society operates under the rule of law serves to perpetuate illegitimate relations of power. Exposing the rule of law as a myth is thought of in the CLS movement as an essential part of a strategy designed to undermine those relations of power."

Questions

1. It can be seen from this extract that the critique of Anglo-American models of law provided by critical legal scholars is much more damning of Western ideals of law than other texts included in this chapter. The vision of lawyers as amoral agents choosing between contradictory legal norms is a powerful one. To what extent does this tally with your personal view about the role of lawyers in society? Give reasons for your response.

2. In what ways could you argue that the law is capable of serving as an instrument of oppression and domination? Can you think of any examples?

In a similar vein, Carol Smart has argued that another of law's functions is to make claims as to the "truth" of things. Law is a form of knowledge which sometimes disqualifies other ways of thinking: namely, those in which someone is not "thinking like a lawyer". According to Smart, legal method is the means through which law (and practitioners of the law) construct law and legal *discourse* as a privileged way of understanding. Smart's analysis should be remembered in those moments in your legal education when you may feel that you are being "indoctrinated" into a particular way of thinking; a way of thinking which seems to run counter to other ways of analysing problems and of viewing society.

Carol Smart, *Feminism and the Power of Law* (London: Routledge, 1989), pp.10–13:

"[L]aw sets itself above other knowledges like psychology, sociology, or common sense. It claims to have the method to establish the truth of events. The main vehicle for this claim is the legal method which is taught in law schools. . . . A more 'public' version of this claim, however, is the criminal trial which, through the adversarial system, is thought to be a secure basis for findings of guilt and innocence. Judges and juries can come to correct legal decisions; the fact that other judges in higher courts may overrule some decisions only goes to prove that the system ultimately divines the correct view.

Law's claim to truth is not manifested so much in its practice, however, but rather in the ideal of law. In this sense it does not matter that practitioners may fall short of the ideal. If we take the analogy of science, the claim to scientificity is a claim to exercise power, it does not matter that experiments do not work or that medicine cannot find a cure for all ills. The point is that we accord so much status to scientific work that its truth outweighs other truths, indeed it denies the possibility of others. We do not give quite such a status to law, although we operate as if the legal system does dispense justice (i.e. correct decisions), and we certainly give greater weight to a judge's pronouncement of guilt than a defendant's proclamation of innocence. Indeed there are those who would say that 'law is what the judges say it is'. The judge is held to be a man of wisdom, a man of knowledge, not a mere technician who can ply his trade.

If we accept that law, like science, makes a claim to truth and that this is indivisible from the exercise of power, we can see that law exercises power not simply in its material effects (judgements) but also in its ability to disqualify other knowledges and experiences. Non-legal knowledge is therefore suspect and/or secondary. Everyday experiences are of little interest in terms of their meaning for individuals. Rather these experiences must be translated into another form in order to become 'legal' issues and before they can be processed through the legal system. For the system to run smoothly, whether it is criminal or civil, the ideal is that all parties are legally represented and that the parties say as little as possible (i.e. they are mute). The problem for the lawyer is that the litigant may bring in issues which are not, in legal terms, pertinent to the case, or s/he might inadvertently say something that has a legal significance unknown to her/him. So the legal process translates everyday experience into legal relevances, it excludes a great deal that might be relevant to the parties, and it makes its judgements on the scripted or tailored account. . . .

Law sets itself outside the social order, as if through the application of legal method and rigour, it becomes a thing apart which can in turn reflect upon the world from which it is divorced. Consider the following quotation from Lord Denning, written when he was Master of the Rolls (i.e. head of the Court of Appeal).

'By a series of Acts of Parliament, however, starting in 1870, all the disabilities of wives in regard to property have been swept away. A married woman is now entitled to her own property and earnings, just as her husband is entitled to his. Her stocks and shares remain hers. Her wedding presents are hers. Her earnings are hers. She can deal with all property as fully as any man. . . . No longer is she dependent on her husband. She can, and does, go out to work and earn her own living. Her equality is complete.'

In this conceptualisation it is law that has given women equality (accepting for the moment that they do have formal equality). In this way law is taken to be outside the social body, it transcends it and acts upon it. Indeed the more it is seen as a unified discipline that responds only to its own coherent, internal logic, the more powerful it becomes. It is not simply that in this passage Denning omits to point out how many women chained themselves to railings, demonstrated and lobbied in Parliament to change the law, nor that he ignores the dramatic changes to women's economic position which occurred quite independently of law, it is rather that he constructs law as a kind of sovereign with the power to give or withhold rights. . . . Linked to this idea, law is constructed as a force of linear progress, a beacon to lead us out of darkness. . . .

Lastly in this section on truth and knowledge, I want to consider how law extends itself beyond uttering the truth of law, to making such claims about other areas of social life. What is important about this tendency is that the framework for such utterances remains legal—and hence retains the mantle of legal power. To put it figuratively, the judge does not remove his wig when he passes comment on, for example, issues of sexual morality in rape cases. He retains the authority drawn from legal scholarship and the 'truth' of law, but he applies it to non-legal issues. This is a form of legal imperialism in which the legitimacy law claims in the field of law extends to every issue in social life. Hence Lord Denning states:

> 'No matter how you may dispute and argue, you cannot alter the fact that women are quite different from men. The principal task in the life of women is to bear and rear children: . . . He is physically the stronger and she the weaker. He is temperamentally the more aggressive and she the more submissive. It is he who takes the initiative and she who responds. These diversities of function and temperament lead to differences of outlook which cannot be ignored. But they are, none of them, any reason for putting women under the subjection of men.'

Here Denning is articulating a Truth about the natural differences between women and men. He combines the Truth claimed by socio-biology (i.e. a 'scientific' truth) with the Truth claimed by law. He makes it clear that there is no point in argument; anyone who disagrees is, by definition, a fool. Hence the feminist position is constructed as a form of 'disqualified knowledge', whilst the naturalistic stance on innate gender differences acquires the status of a legal Truth. In this passage both law and biological determinism are affirmed, whilst law accredits itself with doing good."

Questions

1. Imagine that you have been asked to give a short presentation in your seminar group about major legal schools of thought which have influenced our response to the question "what is law?". Make some brief notes on how you would explain the approaches outlined in this chapter.

2. What do you think these groups are able to tell us about the operation of formal law and its effectiveness?

3. Carol Smart and others have sought to analyse the functions of law from a sociological perspective. Is there value in looking at legal methods and legal systems from the perspective of other disciplines? Give reasons for your answer.

2

CONSTITUTIONAL ASPECTS OF LEGAL METHOD: THE RULE OF LAW AND THE SUPREMACY OF PARLIAMENT

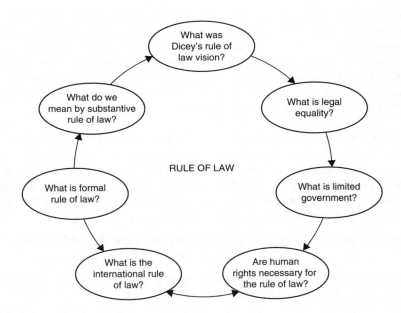

In this chapter we look at key constitutional concepts and doctrines which are relevant to the way in which legal reasoning is carried out. We focus on two central ideas: the rule of law and the supremacy of Parliament. By the end of this chapter, you should:

- have an appreciation of the varied meanings of rule of law;

- recognise the political character of the concept of the rule of law;

- be able to understand the rule of law in an historical context;

- understand the contemporary relevance of the rule of law;

- appreciate the tension between the rule of law and the supremacy of Parliament;
- recognise the relevance of the Human Rights Act 1998 to both the rule of law and the supremacy of Parliament.

I. THE RULE OF LAW

If you were to conduct a poll on any street in the United Kingdom, and ask the so-called "average person" if he or she was subject to the "rule of law", you would probably be told unequivocally, "yes". However, if you also asked what is meant by the phrase "rule of law", you would likely get a great variety of responses. On one level, to claim that a society is subject to the rule of law is simply to say that it is governed by fixed rules set down in law, rather than by the arbitrary force of a dictator. But, of course, a society governed by rules will also be governed by individuals who make, change, and enforce the law. Moreover, the simple fact that a society is governed by rules—even lots of rules—may mean that it is subject to the rule of law, but it certainly does not in itself ensure that the society qualifies as a "just" or fair one.

Wade Mansell, Belinda Meteyard and Alan Thomson, *A Critical Introduction to Law*, 3rd edn (London: Cavendish, 2004), pp.149–150:

"There is, of course, no necessary causal link between the Rule of Law and the restraint of the powerful. Apartheid South Africa always claimed to be a Rule of Law state even while 4.5 million white people ruled 28 million disenfranchised black people and also owned 87% of the land. Apartheid South Africa also executed more people than any comparable state (in fact, no other state was comparable) and yet, because of the appearance of safeguards for defendants, was able to claim that this practice too was consistent with the Rule of Law. Certainly in some ways it was the Rule of Law ideology which provided the clothes with which the state attempted to hide the nakedness of government aggression."

The example of apartheid in South Africa suggests that the rule of law may be a rather empty concept, capable of being deployed to justify the most terrible violations of individual and group dignity and self-determination. In fact, some might argue that given the *types* of laws which characterised apartheid, it is inappropriate to describe that regime as governed by the rule of law. At this point, we can make another observation about the rule of law: it means different things to different people, and the concept is a difficult one to pin down with an easy definition.

George P. Fletcher, *Basic Concepts of Legal Thought* (New York: Oxford University Press, 1996), pp.11–13:

"Of all the dreams that drive men and women into the streets, from Buenos Aires to Budapest, the 'rule of law' is the most puzzling. We have a pretty good idea what we mean by 'free markets' and 'democratic elections'. But legality and the 'rule of law' are ideals that present themselves as opaque even to legal philosophers. Many American jurists treat the rule of law as though it were no more than governance by rules. Thus we find Justice Scalia arguing explicitly that the rule of law is no more than the law of rules. And philosophers, such as Friedrich Hayek and Joseph Raz, make the same assumption that the rule of law means that the government 'is bound by rules fixed and announced beforehand.' Playing by the rules is, in some dubious contexts, a great achievement, but once societies have minimized graft and arbitrary rule, the 'rule of law' seems to promise more than blindly playing the game. After all, the rules of the game might be horribly unjust.

There are in fact two versions of the rule of law, a modest version of adhering to the rules and a more lofty ideal that incorporates criteria of justice. We shuffle back and forth between them because we are unsure of the import of the term 'law' in the expression 'rule of law.' . . . Do we mean rule by the laws laid down—whether the legal rules are good or bad? Or do we mean 'rule by Law,' by the right rules, by the rules that meet the tests of morality and justice? Because we have only one word for law in place of the two commonly found in other legal systems, we suffer and perhaps cultivate this ambiguity."

Paul Craig, "Formal and substantive conceptions of the rule of law: an analytical framework" [1997] P.L. 467 at 467:

"Formal conceptions of the rule of law do not however seek to pass judgment upon the actual content of the law itself. They are not concerned with whether the law was in that sense a good law or a bad law, provided that the formal precepts of the rule of law were themselves met. Those who espouse substantive conceptions of the rule of law seek to go beyond this. They accept that the rule of law has the formal attributes mentioned above, but they wish to take the doctrine further. Certain substantive rights are said to be based on, or derived from, the rule of law. The concept is used as the foundation for these rights, which are then used to distinguish between 'good' laws, which comply with such rights, and 'bad' laws which do not."

Question

Explain what is meant by the claim that there are two versions of the rule of law.

The tension between *formal* and *substantive* conceptions of the rule of law is central to the confusion over its meaning. It suggests that there are at least two different versions of the rule of law. Nevertheless, it has long been claimed that the English legal system is characterised by the rule of law, most famously in the late nineteenth century by the law professor Albert Venn Dicey. According to Dicey, the rule of law was a key feature which distinguished the English *constitution* (or fundamental structure of government) from those of continental Europe. While "foreigners" might be subject to the exercise of *arbitrary* power, the English, by contrast, were protected by the rule of law. It is hardly surprising that Dicey is characterised as a thoroughly chauvinistic "anti-European"!

Albert Venn Dicey, *An Introduction to the Law of the Constitution*, 8th edn (London: Macmillan, 1915), pp.183–197:

"When we say that the supremacy of the rule of law is a characteristic of the English constitution, we generally include under one expression at least three distinct though kindred conceptions.

We mean, in the first place, that no man is punishable or can be lawfully made to suffer in body or goods except for a distinct breach of law established in the ordinary legal manner before the ordinary Courts of the land. In this sense the rule of law is contrasted with every system of government based on the exercise by persons in authority of wide, arbitrary, or discretionary powers of constraint.

Modern Englishmen may at first feel some surprise that the 'rule of law' (in the sense in which we are now using the term) should be considered as in any way a peculiarity of English institutions, since, at the present day, it may seem to be not so much the property of any one nation as a trait common to every civilised and orderly state. Yet, even if we confine our observation to the existing condition of Europe, we shall soon be convinced that the 'rule of law' even in this narrow sense is peculiar to England, or to those countries which, like the United States of America, have inherited English traditions. In almost every continental community the executive exercises far wider discretionary authority in the manner of arrest, of temporary imprisonment, of expulsion from its territory, and the like, than is either legally claimed or in fact exerted by the government in England; and a study of European politics now and again reminds English readers that wherever there is discretion there is room for arbitrariness, and that in a republic no less than under a monarchy discretionary authority on the part of the government must mean insecurity for legal freedom on the part of its subjects. . . .

We mean in the second place, when we speak of the 'rule of law' as a characteristic of our country, not only that with us no man is above the law, but (what is a different thing) that here every man, whatever be his rank or condition, is subject to the ordinary law of the realm and amenable to the jurisdiction of ordinary tribunals.

In England the idea of legal equality, or of the universal subjection of all classes to one law administered by the ordinary Courts, has been pushed to its utmost limit. With us every official, from the Prime Minister down to a constable or a collector of taxes, is under the same responsibility for every act done without legal justification as any other citizen. The Reports abound with cases in which officials have been brought before the Courts, and made, in their personal capacity, liable to punishment, or to the payment of damages, for acts done in their official character but in excess of their lawful authority. A colonial governor, a secretary of state, a military officer, and all subordinates, though carrying out the commands of their official superiors, are as responsible for any acts which the law does not authorise as is any private and unofficial person. Officials, such for example as soldiers or clergymen of the Established Church, are, it is true, in England as elsewhere, subject to laws which do not affect the rest of the nation, and are in some instances amenable to tribunals which have no jurisdiction over their fellow countrymen; officials, that is to say, are to a certain extent governed under what may be termed official law. But this fact is in no way inconsistent with the principle that all men are in England subject to the law of the realm; for though a soldier or a clergyman incurs from his position legal liabilities from which other men are exempt, he does not (speaking generally) escape thereby from the duties of an ordinary citizen. . . .

There remains yet a third and a different sense in which the 'rule of law' or the predominance of the legal spirit may be described as a special attribute of English institutions. We may say that the constitution is pervaded by the rule of law on the ground that the general principles of the constitution (as for example the right to personal liberty, or the right of public meeting) are with us the result of judicial decisions determining the rights of private persons in particular cases brought before the Courts; whereas under many foreign constitutions the security (such as it is) given to the rights of individuals results, or appears to result, from the general principles of the constitution. . . .

There is in the English constitution an absence of those declarations or definitions of rights so dear to foreign constitutionalists. Such principles, moreover, as you can discover in the English constitution are, like all maxims established by judicial legislation, mere generalisations drawn either from the decisions or dicta of judges, or from statutes which, being passed to meet special grievances, bear a close resemblance to judicial decisions, and are in effect judgments pronounced by the High Court of Parliament. To put what is really the same thing in a somewhat different shape, the relation of the rights of individuals to the principles of the constitution is not quite the same in countries like Belgium, where the constitution is the result of a legislative act, as it is in England, where the constitution itself is based upon legal decisions. In Belgium, which may be taken as a type of country possessing a constitution formed by a deliberate act of legislation, you may say with truth that the rights of individuals to personal liberty flow from or are secured by the constitution. In England the right to individual liberty is part of the constitution, because it is secured by the decisions of the Courts . . . [I]n Belgium individual rights are deductions drawn from the principles of the constitution, whilst in England the so-called principles of the constitution are inductions or generalisations based upon particular decisions pronounced by the Courts as to the rights of given individuals. . . .

The fact, again, that in many foreign countries the rights of individuals, e.g. to personal freedom, depend upon the constitution, whilst in England the law of the constitution is little else than a generalisation of the rights which the Courts secure to individuals, has this important result. The general rights guaranteed by the constitution may be, and in foreign countries constantly are, suspended. They are something extraneous to and independent of the ordinary course of the law. . . . [W]here the right to individual freedom is a result deduced from the principles of the constitution, the idea readily occurs that the right is capable of being suspended or taken away. Where, on the other hand, the right to individual freedom is part of the constitution because it is inherent in the ordinary law of the land, the right is one which can hardly be destroyed without a thorough revolution in the institutions and manners of the nation."

It is essential that you recognise that Dicey was writing at a particular historical period, and more importantly, he was writing from a political perspective that saw the maintenance of individual property and freedom to use that property as the most important value to be protected. He was opposed to any increase in activity by the state. He clearly thought that law should ignore differences that existed between people in terms of wealth and power, and should treat them all the same (*formally equal*), rather than the government taking steps to increase equality of opportunity (*substantive equality*). Yet he was also opposed to the movement for women's suffrage (a demand for *formal equality*).

Since Dicey's time, most lawyers have come to realise many inadequacies in his limited (and often incorrect) concept of the rule of law. Today, governments do have wide powers, and most people would agree that governments do need *discretion* to operate effectively. That is, ensuring that officials of government only act in accordance with strict *rules* may prove too inflexible in the implementation of public policies. Instead, officials need flexibility and discretion in applying law and policy to fit individual circumstances. However, while we increasingly have come to recognise the importance of discretion on the part of officials of the state, there are also situations in which clear rules and guidelines—the rule of law—may seem important as a way to limit the power of officials to act in ways which are perceived as *arbitrary* or unfair. Thus, it might be argued that although discretion is not inconsistent with the rule of law, discretion should also be exercised in accordance with general principles of law. The actions of state officials thereby should be constrained by the law so that they do not act unreasonably. This historical tension between clear rules and discretion has been described by Jowell, along with other criticisms of Dicey's rule of law vision.

Jeffrey Jowell, "The Rule of Law Today", in Jeffrey Jowell and Dawn Oliver (eds) *The Changing Constitution*, 5th edn (Oxford: Oxford University Press, 2004), pp.7–14:

"The second and third of Dicey's meanings of the Rule of Law display a concern not to allow the British to go the way of other countries, such as France, where a separate system of public law is administered by separate courts dealing with cases between the state and the individual. In 1928 William Robson wrote his celebrated book *Justice and Administrative Law*, in which he roundly criticized Dicey for his misinterpretation of both the English and French systems on that matter. He pointed out that there were in England 'colossal distinctions' between the rights and duties of private individuals and those of the administrative organs or government even in Dicey's time. Public authorities possessed special rights and special exemptions and immunities, to the extent that the citizen was deprived of a remedy against the state 'in many cases where he most requires it'. Robson also convincingly showed how Dicey had misinterpreted French law, where the *droit administratif* was not intended to exempt public officials from the rigour of private law, but to allow experts in public administration to work out the extent of official liability. Robson also noted the extent of Dicey's misrepresentation that disputes between officials and private individuals in Britain were dealt with by the ordinary courts. He pointed to the growth of special tribunals and inquiries that had grown up to decide these disputes outside the courts, and was in no doubt that a 'vast body of administrative law' existed in England.

The attack on Dicey continued a few years later with W. Ivor Jennings's *The Law and the Constitution*, which appeared in 1933. Repeating many of Robson's criticisms of Dicey's second and third meanings of the Rule of Law, Jennings also delivered a withering, and almost fatal, attack upon Dicey's first meaning—his claim that wide discretionary power had no place under the Rule of Law. It should be remembered here that Dicey was a trenchant critic of notions of 'collectivism'. . . .

Jennings felt that the Rule of Law implicitly promoted Dicey's political views. He equated Dicey's opposition to state regulation with that of the 'manufacturers who formed the backbone of the Whig Party', who 'wanted nothing which interfered with profits, even if profits involved child labour, wholesale factory accidents, the pollution of rivers, of the air, and of the water supply, jerry-built houses, low wages, and other incidents of nineteenth-century industrialism'. . . .

The Second World War then provided compelling reasons to centralize power, an opportunity further built upon by the Labour government of 1945. As Robson wrote in the second edition of his book in 1947, increasingly Parliament had given powers to resolve disputes between the citizen and the state not to the courts—to Dicey's 'ordinary law'—but to specialized organs of adjudication such as administrative tribunals and inquiries. This was not 'due to a fit of absentmindedness' but because these bodies would be speedier and cheaper, and would possess greater technical knowledge and have 'fewer prejudices against government' than the courts. Here he may have been echoing the words of Aneurin Bevan, Minister of Health in the 1945 Labour government and architect of the National Health Service, who caused a stir in the House of Commons by establishing tribunals in the Health Service, divorced from 'ordinary courts', because he greatly feared 'judicial sabotage' of socialist legislation.

Despite this onslaught on Dicey's revision of the Rule of Law, its epitaph refused to be written. Two particularly strong supporters wrote in its favour in the 1940s. F.A. Hayek's *The Road to Serfdom* in 1943 graphically described that road as being paved with governmental regulations. C.K. Allen, with less ideological fervour, pleaded for the legal control of executive action. Not much heed was paid to these pleas until the late 1950s when the Franks Committee revived interest in Diceyan notions by suggesting judicial protections over the multiplying tribunals and inquiries of the growing state. It was in the 1960s, however, that disparate groups once again started arguing in favour of legal values. Some of these groups were themselves committed to a strong governmental role in providing social welfare, but objected to the manner in which public services were carried out. Recipients of Supplementary Benefit, for example, objected to the fact that benefits were administered by officials in accordance with a secret code (known as the 'A Code') and asked instead for publication of a set of welfare 'rights'. They also objected to the wide discretion allowed their case-workers to determine the level of their benefits. The heirs of Jennings and his followers, such as Professor Richard Titmus, opposed this challenge to the free exercise of official discretion and objected strongly to a 'pathology of legalism' developing in this area.

Another plea for the Rule of Law came at about the same time from individuals who were being displaced from their homes by programmes of urban redevelopment. While not asking for a catalogue of 'rights', their claim was for participation in decisions by which they were affected. Their plea did not primarily concern the substance of the law. Just as the welfare recipients were not simply arguing for higher benefits, but for fair procedures to determine the benefits, local amenity groups directed their demands for the Rule of Law less at the content of the decisions ultimately taken than at the procedures by which they were reached. They were by no means adopting the undiluted Diceyan view that all discretionary power is bad. Nevertheless, they recognized the value of legal techniques to control the exercise of official power. . . .

An official possessed of discretion frequently has a choice about how it should be operated: whether to keep it open-textured, maintaining the option of a variety of responses to a given situation, or to confine it by a rule or standard—a process of legalisation. For example, officials administering welfare benefits could provide them on a case-by-case basis according to their conception of need, or they could announce precise levels of benefit for given situations. Similarly, laws against pollution could be enforced by a variable standard whereby the official must be satisfied that the polluter is achieving the 'best practicable means' of abatement. Alternatively, levels of pollution could be specified in advance, based on the colour of smoke emission, or the precise quantities of sulphur dioxide. A policy of promoting safe driving could, similarly, be legalised by a rule specifying speeds of no more than 30 miles per hour on given streets.

Now for Dicey, and particularly for Hewart and Hayek, who mistrusted the grant of virtually any official discretion, the virtue of rule-bound conduct was principally that it allowed affected persons to know the rules before being subjected to them retrospectively. This helped businesses plan their investments in a free market. However, it was also a principle of justice under which no person should be condemned without a presumed knowledge of the rule alleged to have been breached. This assumes a penal law or criminal regulation of one form or another, and is understandable in that context where the lack of rules would involve risky guesses with serious consequences for non-compliance. It is fairer to a person prosecuted for a tax offence to have been made aware of the precise tax required than for the levels to be determined at the discretion of an official.

This argument, however, has a somewhat different compulsion when one is dealing not with penalties but with regulation involving the allocation of scarce resources. Should an applicant for a university place be entitled, out of fairness, to know the precise grades required for entrance? Should the applicant for welfare benefits be entitled to know the rules about allocations of winter fuel supplements? In cases such as these the argument in favour of rules over discretion is an argument less from certainty than from *accountability*. This argument has two facets, the first being a concern to provide a published standard against which to measure the legality of official action and thus to allow individual redress against official action that does not accord with the rule or standard. An announced level of resources to qualify for welfare assistance ought to allow redress to a person who qualifies but is refused assistance. The second facet of accountability refers to the fact that the actual process of making rules and their publication generates *public assessment* of the fidelity of the rule to legislative purpose. Many statutes confer powers on officials to further the policy of the Act in question in accordance with wide discretion. The power may be to allocate housing, or to provide for the needy, or to diminish unacceptable pollution of the air or water. The process of devising a points system for housing allocation, benefits for the needy, and acceptable emission levels of pollution thus forces the official into producing a formal operational definition of purpose. . . .

The virtues of rules, as we have seen, include their qualities of legality, certainty, consistency, uniformity, congruence to purpose, and accountability loosely so called. All these play an important part in the control of official discretion and may be seen as concrete manifestations of the Rule of Law. . . .

Officials are well aware of the benefit of rules to their own efficiency. Rules announce or clarify official policies to affected persons, and thus facilitate obedience. They may also allow routine treatment of cases, thus increasing the speed of decision-making. A zoning system in planning, a list of features of 'substandard' housing, and a list of grades for university admission all allow decisions to be taken more quickly than a system that requires constant reappraisal of each case on its merits. Rules therefore reduce the anxiety and conserve the energy needed to reach decisions on a case-by-case basis. The portrayal by the sociologist Max Weber of his ideal-type bureaucrat applying rules '*sine ira et studio*—without hatred or passion, and hence without affection or enthusiasm'—alludes to the non-affective approach to legalized framework, to the possibility of insulating the decisionmaker from the pressure of constant reconsideration. Despite the fact that rules may promote criticism, they also, in the short run at least, provide a shield behind which officials may hide, pleading consistent and uniform justice in response to criticism that the individual's case is unique.

So here we have the tension: the virtues of rules—their objective, even-handed features—are opposed to other administrative benefits, especially those of flexibility, individual treatment, and responsiveness. The virtue of rules to the administrator (routine treatment) may be a defect to the client with a special case (such as the brilliant applicant for a university place who failed to obtain the required grades because of a family upset or illness just before the examination). The administrator's shield may be seen as an unjustified protection from the client's sword. Officials themselves may consider that a task requires flexibility, or genuinely want to help a particular client, but feel unable to do so. Hence the classic bureaucratic response: 'I'd like to help you—but there is this rule.' . . .

Before leaving the costs and benefits of rule-based official action, we should note that the existence of a rule does not automatically ensure its implementation. Nor is it always desirable that rules be enforced. The existence of a rule outlawing a speed of over 30 miles per hour, for example, will not necessarily mean that people who speed are automatically prosecuted. Sometimes the prosecuting official will lack the resources to prosecute some offenders, or lack the will. Occasions may exist, however, when a policy of full enforcement could, for example, mean that a doctor narrowly exceeding the limit of 30 miles per hour on a deserted street late at night while speeding to the scene of an accident would be prosecuted. That prosecution makes no sense in furthering the goal of preventing unsafe driving. Full enforcement would in this case play no part in the achievement of fidelity to purpose. On other occasions laws may not be enforced in order to further other values in society. For example, studies have shown that assault laws may not be enforced in a situation of marital violence as police will not wish to exacerbate poor relationships or cause deprivation for children. The objective of the law prohibiting violence is in these situations considered secondary to a value which seeks to preserve the well-being of the family unit.

This last example shows that even the most clear-cut rule may or should not be enforced. Most law-enforcers weigh the cost in damages of the prohibited act against the cost of abating the act. An example is the regulation of pollution, where the damage of the polluter to the environment is, according to a number of studies, measured against the costs of abatement: the firm may be forced out of business, or may locate else-where, causing damage to the local economy and unemployment. Or the cost of abatement may be passed on to the ultimate consumer of a needed product."

Questions

1. To what extent is the rule of law compatible with the exercise of discretion by officials and agencies of the state? Give examples.

2. Should a lecturer's decision whether to grant someone an extension on his or her essay dead-line be governed by clear rules or the exercise of a broad discretion tailored to the particular circumstances?

Dicey's "rule of law" vision has been widely criticised for many decades on a range of different grounds. It is important to recognise that, while the "rule of law" as a concept may continue to be useful and important, Dicey's understanding of it obviously does not retain a great deal of relevance.

Bernard J. Hibbitts, "The politics of principle: Albert Venn Dicey and the rule of law" (1994) 23 Anglo-American Law Review, pp.25–26, 29:

"The first element of the Rule . . . corresponded with Dicey's fears that a socialist–collectivist Parliament would seek to displace the common law and the common courts by the creation of alternative adjudicative standards and bodies, so as to achieve its political ends more conveniently. The second element of the Rule corresponded with his desire to ensure that in legal disputes the state and the individual were equal, and that the state would not be able, at least in the context of the judicial forum, to take advantage of its overwhelming power. The third element of the Rule corresponded with an underlying conviction that fundamental individual rights (such as the right to personal freedom, the right to freedom of discussion and the right of public assembly) had to be put beyond the reach of governments which might seek to curtail them to facilitate broader social and economic goals . . .

   At the end of the day there is little about the rule of law that is sacred. . . . the Rule as Dicey formulated it was very much the expression of one man's political, philosophical and professional concerns. To the extent that one shares Dicey's opinions and attitudes the Rule is supportable; to the extent one holds contrary views, it is not."

Although Dicey's understanding of the "rule of law" may have been informed by his nineteenth-century world view, some of the concepts to which he referred, such as "equality before the law", continue to have relevance. Waldron places the rule of law in a more modern context in which the idea of equality and the rule of law continues to have political and legal importance.

Jeremy Waldron, The Law (London: Routledge, 1990), pp.29–42:

PEDRO v DISS "Late one night in 1979, a man called Ya Ya Pedro was standing by the door of his brother's house in London. Another man, Martin Diss, came up to him, identified himself as a police officer, and asked Pedro what he was doing there. Pedro walked away without answering. When Constable Diss repeated his question, Pedro told him to 'fuck off'. Eventually he allowed himself to be searched, but when the policeman began to question him about some keys that he found in his pockets, Pedro walked away again. Constable Diss grabbed him by the arm and said, 'Do you live here?' Pedro replied with another obscenity and swung backwards, striking the constable in his chest with an elbow. As he did this, the constable took hold of his cloth-ing, and Pedro punched him. He was eventually restrained with the assistance of two other officers, and they arrested Pedro and charged him with assaulting a constable in the execution of his duty.

   When Pedro appeared before the Highbury magistrates, he was convicted and fined £50. But he appealed to the High Court, and the Chief Justice, Lord Lane, with one other judge, overturned the conviction and sentence.

They said that when Pedro punched Constable Diss, the officer was *not* acting in the lawful execution of his duty. The police, said Lord Lane, do not have an unlimited power to detain people for questioning: their powers of legitimate detention and arrest are set down and governed by law. If they go beyond those powers, the person they have got hold of is entitled to strike back in self defence, just as he may resist *any* other person who attacks him. Lord Lane went on:

> 'It is a matter of importance, therefore, to a person at the moment when he is first physically detained by a police officer, to know whether that physical detention is or is not regarded by that officer as a formal arrest or detention. That is one of the reasons why it is a matter of importance that the arresting or detaining officer should make known to the person in question the fact that, and the grounds on which, he is being arrested or detained.'

Constable Diss claimed that he had thought Pedro was a burglar, and that he was authorized by Section 66 of the Metropolitan Police Act 1839 to 'stop, search and detain any person who may be reasonably suspected of having or conveying in any manner anything stolen or unlawfully obtained'. The problem was he didn't tell Pedro that that was what he was doing; he didn't say this was the power he was exercising and these were the grounds of his suspicion. So Pedro had no way of distinguishing the situation from one in which he was being unlawfully attacked. That was why Lord Lane held that he was entitled to defend himself, even against a police officer.

It is tempting to say that Pedro got off on a 'technicality'. In some countries, you are not allowed to resist a police officer even if his attempt to detain you is unjustified; moreover the officer has no obligation to say why you are being detained and you certainly have no entitlement to resist him if he does not. I don't want to argue that the rule in *Pedro v Diss* is necessarily better. But the case illustrates a couple of broader points of principle.

First, it involves a determination to subject members of the police force, as far as possible, to the same basic rules of law as every other citizen. Ordinary members of the public are not normally allowed to detain one another forcibly and they are entitled to resist anyone who tries to do that to them. The police are subject to that basic framework of rules along with everyone else.

Second, it embodies a particular attitude towards any *special* powers that may be thought necessary for the police to be able to do their job. The special powers of the police are to be limited and governed by rules—not just any rules, but rules which are known and publicized rather than hidden away in the Police Training Manual. Indeed, the striking thing about the case is the judges' insistence that Diss ought to have told Pedro the particular rule on which he was relying. Members of the public shouldn't have to submit to a general sense that the police are simply 'special' and can interfere with their lives in ways in which they may not interfere with one another. They are entitled to know what's going on, and to know by what authority the constable is acting in what would otherwise be an objectionable (and resistible) way. Otherwise they will be at the mercy of unpredictable arbitrary power. . . .

One law for all

Think back for a moment to Ya Ya Pedro and Constable Diss. Diss grabs hold of Pedro, and Pedro punches him in the struggle to free himself. The magistrates say he is guilty of assault. On appeal, the High Court says (in effect): 'No. Unless the arrest is lawful, Pedro is entitled to defend himself against Martin Diss just as if he were any other citizen who tried to grab hold of him. Once they go beyond their specified powers, the police have no special privileges. The ordinary rules of self-defence apply. If it's wrong for me to attack Pedro, it's also wrong for Constable Diss to attack Pedro. The law is the same for everyone.'

This requirement of universality—the idea of 'one law for all'—is a prominent feature of the normative ideal of the rule of law. But why is universality a good thing? Why is it desirable that there should be one law for everyone, irrespective of who they are, or what their official status?

One obvious application of universality is that we don't, on the whole, allow personalized laws; we don't have laws that make exceptions for particular people. In medieval England, there used to be things called 'Bills of

Attainder', announcing that someone in particular (the Earl of Warwick, or the king's brother for example) was thereby banished from the realm and his estates confiscated. The idea of the rule of law is that the state should not use personalized mechanisms of that sort.

Moral philosophers link this requirement of universality with morality and with rationality. They say that if you make a moral judgement about someone or something, your judgement can't be based simply on that person or that incident in particular, or if it is, it's arbitrary. It must be based on some feature of the person or action—something *about* what they did, something that might in principle be true of another person or another situation as well. In other words it must be based on something that can be expressed as a universal proposition. For example, if I want to say, 'It is all right for Diss to defend himself', I must say that because I think self defence is all right in general in that sort of case, not merely because I want to get at Pedro or say something special about Diss. So I must also be prepared to say that it would be all right for Pedro to defend himself in a similar circumstance. Unless I can point to some clearly relevant difference between the two cases, then I must accept that the same reasoning applies to both.

Another way of putting it is that universalizability expresses an important principle of justice: it means dealing even-handedly with people and treating like cases alike. If I am committed to treating like cases alike, then I ought to be able to state my principles in a universal form. If I cannot—that is, if I can't find a way to eliminate references to particular people from my legislation—that is probably a good indication that I am drawing arbitrary distinctions based on bias or self-interest or something of that sort.

As well as these philosophical reasons, there are also pragmatic arguments in favour of universality. We are less likely to get bad laws or oppressive laws, if the burden of any law falls as much on those who make it as on the rest of the population. The king might think twice about banning tobacco, if it means that he can't have a cigarette. An MP may be reluctant to impose heavy penalties on adultery when he remembers what he was doing last week. If our legislators are human in their inclinations and temptations, they may be less likely to enact laws that are inhumanly demanding if they know that the legislation may be applied to their conduct as well.

Now I say you are *less* likely to get oppressive laws. There are no guarantees. An ascetic sovereign may be perfectly willing to subject his own conduct to the same harsh discipline he imposes on his subjects. When the Iranian parliament enacted amputation as a penalty for repeated offences of theft, its members presumably welcomed the possibility that they too should have their hands cut off if they offend against Allah in that way. The idea of the rule of law usefully prohibits legislation which singles somebody out for special treatment. But being singled out is only one way of being oppressed. People may be oppressed as members of a group or because they possess some general characteristic, such as being a black or being a woman, and it is much more difficult to rule out this sort of legislation on the basis of the ideal of the rule of law. As soon as we recognize that, then we recognize that the idea of universality—the idea of 'one law for all'—is not nearly as straightforward as it looks. It rules out one type of discrimination: discrimination against (or in favour of) named individuals. But it doesn't rule out discrimination against (or in favour of) certain *types* of people. It doesn't, for example, rule out the sort of discrimination that we find in the [former] South African Group Areas Act, since that discrimination is stated in terms that make no reference whatever to particular individuals. It is true of course that the Group Areas Act treats different people differently: apartheid applies one set of standards to blacks and another set of standards to whites. But if that *by itself* were enough to rule out apartheid legislation, it would also rule out an awful lot of legislation which we regard as desirable and necessary.

The trouble with the purely formal idea of 'one law for all' is that, if it is interpreted absolutely literally, it becomes really far too simple to capture the requirements of good legislation in a modern state. When you think about it, it seems crazy to say we should apply literally the *same* legal rules to everyone in all circumstances. Do we want to enforce the same standards of cleanliness in a paint-shop as in a restaurant? Is there to be one law to govern children and adults? Must ambulance drivers observe the same speed limits as the rest of us? No-one thinks that ought to be the case. . . . We don't want our commitment to universality to blind us to those distinctions and discriminations that are morally or pragmatically justified.

Special rules for officials?

As a matter of fact, this point has important implications for the way law applies to politics. The simple idea with which we began was that the same rules should apply to officials like Constable Diss as apply to citizens like Ya Ya Pedro. There should be one law for all, and no special law for officials of the state. But now, if it is reasonable to apply different standards of hygiene to paint-shops and restaurants, if it is reasonable to allow a higher speed limit for ambulances than for private motorists, why isn't it also reasonable to apply rules of behaviour to police officers that are different from the ones we apply to ordinary citizens? After all, don't the police—like ambulance drivers—have a *special* job to do?

It is amazing what a grip the simple idea of 'one law for all' has had in British law and legal theory. For a long time, it was fashionable to pretend that a police officer was nothing but 'a citizen in uniform'—that his powers to question suspects and arrest felons were no greater than that of the ordinary 'man in the street'. It was simply that he did this for a living, and was trained at it, whereas the ordinary citizen had better things to do. This has long since become a fiction. The police have a whole array of powers to arrest people, to detain them for questioning, to break, enter and search their homes, and so on, which are conferred on them specifically by legislation. And the same is true of many other state officials—from the VAT-man to the social worker. They have a job to do, and Parliament has given them special powers to do it. These special powers may or may not be excessive; the issue is politically controversial. But few deny that state officials need *some* special powers (and also *some* special protections) if they are to be able to do their job.

Equally important, we may also want to say that state officials need to have special *restrictions* on their conduct (that are different from, and additional to, the ones that apply to the rest of us), as well as special powers. I will use a case to illustrate this point.

In a 1979 case, *Malone v Metropolitan Police Commissioner*, an antiques dealer, James Malone, who was suspected of handling stolen property, sued for an injunction [an order to stop someone from doing something] to restrain the London police from tapping his telephone. The judge refused to give an injunction. He held that the police had a perfect right to do it, not because there was any specific legal authorization, but simply because telephone-tapping did not involve any trespass or other unlawful act. 'The subscriber speaks into his telephone, and the process of tapping appears to be carried out by Post Office officials making recordings, with Post Office apparatus on Post Office premises, of the electrical impulses on Post Office wires provided by Post Office electricity. There is no question of there being any trespass on [Malone's] premises for the purpose of attaching anything either to the premises themselves or to anything on them: all that is done is done within the Post Office's own domain.'

In other words, since the ordinary law of trespass has not been violated here, the action of the officials does not require any specific authorization. Malone's case, the judge said, rested on the assumption 'that nothing is lawful that is not positively authorized by law'. But England has always been a country where anything not expressly forbidden by the law is permitted: that is the basis of our liberty. It seems to follow that, since there is no law on the matter, the police have the right to tap telephones.

We have already seen the absurdity of holding that the police should have no more powers than the ordinary citizen. Now we are seeing the absurdity of the converse proposition—that the police should not be subject to any special restrictions that don't apply to other people. They should have as much freedom as the rest of us. That proposition is absurd, because the power (both legal and physical) that the police have makes them especially dangerous *as well as* especially useful. Acting within the state apparatus, officials can do things to citizens which are quite different in character from the sort of things citizens can do to one another. It is a mistake for us to think that the laws we use to deal with one another will necessarily be adequate for our dealings with the officials of the state. . . .

In other words, we might talk in terms of a *modified* 'rule of law' doctrine to be applied to the conduct of officials. The simple principle of 'one law for all' holds that state officials should be bound by exactly the same rules as everyone else. That's the version we have to give up. The modified version, however, insists that official conduct should be governed by *the same sort* of legal rules, even if they are not literally the same rules, as the rest of us. We may take the simple version as our default position. State officials (police officers, etc.) are to be governed by the ordinary law of the land, unless there is a specific legal provision to the contrary. If, however, there is a need for a special provision (because the police, for example, have a special job to do), we should not simply make an exception in the ordinary law of the land; we should lay down *rules* to govern the conduct of the officials."

Questions

1. What is meant by the claim that the rule of law includes a requirement of universality? Does that mean that the law should not be used to draw distinctions between people? When, if ever, are such distinctions justifiable?

2. How does the rule of law apply to the conduct of officials? Are state officials governed by the same rules as everyone else?

The rule of law is capable of encompassing a wide range of ideas. For example, it has been argued that the rule of law requires that laws generally should be *prospective* and not *retrospective*. What this means is that Parliament should not enact laws which seek to regulate (and make illegal) events which have already occurred, and which were permitted at that time. Furthermore, the rule of law sometimes is said to include the idea that laws should be published and reasonably intelligible to those who are required to regulate their conduct in accordance with them. In other words, people need to be able to understand the law. A judiciary which is independent of the other branches of government is also sometimes described as central to the rule of law, as is the openness of the courts to the general public. Further elements of the rule of law might be said to include: the fact that new laws should be enacted only after publicity, opportunity for debate and consultation; and that warning should be given to the public before the law is changed (so that behaviour can be changed to meet the new legal situation).

For some commentators, the range of constraints on the exercise of the power of the state, which are contained within the concept of the rule of law, make it an inherently positive and important ideal. Despite its limitations, it is a valuable concept.

E.P. Thompson, *Whigs and Hunters* (London: Penguin Books, 1990), p.266:

"[T]he rule of law itself, the imposing of effective inhibitions upon power and the defence of the citizen from power's all-intrusive claims, seems to me to be an unqualified human good. To deny or belittle this good is, in this dangerous century when the resources and pretensions of power continue to enlarge, a desperate error of intellectual abstraction."

Other commentators, especially on the political left, argue that the rule of law is not an "unqualified human good", because its limited scope does not advance the cause of social justice or *substantive* equality. Moreover, the underlying philosophy of the rule of law, especially in the form expressed by Dicey, positively discourages progressive social change because of its conservative focus on rules, formal equality, and rights under law. In other words, while the rule of law may constrain the exercise of state power, it does not recognise how the power of the state might be used positively to create a more just, equal society. Horwitz has made this point in a direct response to Thompson.

Morton Horwitz, "The rule of law: an unqualified human good?" (1977) 86 *Yale Law Journal* 561 at 566:

"I do not see how a man of the left can describe the rule of law as an 'unqualified human good'! It undoubtedly restrains power, but it also prevents power's benevolent exercise. It creates formal equality—a not inconsiderable virtue—but it *promotes* substantive inequality by creating a consciousness that radically separates law from politics, means from ends, processes from outcomes. By promoting procedural justice it enables the shrewd, the calculating, and the wealthy to manipulate its forms to their own advantage. And it ratifies and legitimates an adversarial, competitive and atomistic conception of human relations."

Finally, the rule of law is based upon an assumption about the character of human relationships; namely, that law (and its "rule") is necessary to the maintenance of civilised society. The assumption here is that without the rule of law, society would degenerate into chaos. Marxists criticise this idea because, they argue, it gives too much power to law, and it ignores the way in which the rule of law actually serves to legitimate the political and economic system as it currently stands.

Hugh Collins, *Marxism and Law* (Oxford: Clarendon Press, 1982), pp.12–13:

"Few would doubt the important role of law in preventing the disintegration of social order or restricting authoritarian governments. Yet Marxists claim that legal fetishism embodies a distorted image of reality which must be unmasked. To begin with, the notion that society rests on law is too simplistic. It is implausible to think that without law everyone would be at each other's throat, or would use superior physical force to take another's possessions. It is much more likely that informal standards of behaviour based on reciprocity would permit an elementary form of stable community to exist. Clearly there is a subtle relationship between the function of laws and informal customs in constituting the normative basis for a peaceful and prosperous society which will not be revealed if an assumption about the necessity and priority of law is adopted. Growing from that insight, Marxists portray the heavy dependence of organizations of power in modern society upon law as the result of a specific historic conjuncture of circumstances, and argue that the important role of law today in maintaining social order is not an immutable feature of human civilization in the future."

The rule of law has also been invoked to describe relations between states in the international arena. Specifically, in the period since the Second World War, it has been argued that the rule of *force* should be constrained by the rule of international law. This can be a very politically controversial subject, as demonstrated by the intense feelings generated by the question of whether the war in Iraq was legal. As Mansell shows, this can also be understood as a rule of law issue and whether there remains a rule of law which controls the actions of the powerful in international relations.

Wade Mansell, "Goodbye to all that: the rule of law, international law, the United States, and the use of force" (2004) 31 *Journal of Law and Society* 433 at 434–439:

"With regard to intervention in Iraq, many international lawyers concluded that the matter could be resolved by recourse to what was argued to be clear international law. A brief letter to a national newspaper in the United Kingdom by the Good and the Great international legal academics of Great Britain spelt out this position. Readers were curtly informed:

> We are teachers of international law. On the basis of the information publicly available, there is no justi-fication under international law for the use of military force against Iraq. The UN charter outlaws the use of force with only two exceptions: individual or collective self defence in response to an armed attack and action authorised by the security council as a collective response to a threat to the peace, breach of the peace or act of aggression. There are currently no grounds for a claim to use such force in self-defence. The doctrine of pre-emptive self-defence against an attack that might arise at some hypothetical future time has no basis in international law. Neither security council resolution 1441 nor any prior resolution authorises the proposed use of force in the present circumstances.
>
> Before the military action can lawfully be undertaken against Iraq, the security council must have indicated its clearly expressed assent. It has not yet done so. A vetoed resolution could provide no such assent. The prime minister's assertion that in certain circumstances a veto becomes 'unreasonable' and may be disregarded has no basis in international law. The UK has used its security council veto on 32

occasions since 1945. Any attempt to disregard these votes on the ground that they were 'unreasonable' would have been deplored as an unacceptable infringement of the UK's right to exercise a veto under UN charter article 27.

A decision to undertake military action in Iraq without proper security council authorisation will seriously undermine the international rule of law. Of course, even with that authorisation, serious questions would remain. A lawful war is not necessarily a just, prudent or humanitarian war.

The conclusion was thus inevitable. Because Article 2(4) of the United Nations Charter proscribes the use of force except pursuant to Article 51 (allowing self defence), or pursuant to a Security Council Resolution under Chapter VII of the Charter, (the Council having been persuaded of the reality of a 'threat to the peace, breach of the peace, or act of aggression') an invasion of Iraq could not be lawful. QED.

So strong, clear, and seemingly incontrovertible was this position that when the United Kingdom government sought to justify intervention, it purported to accept that legal analysis while finding room for manoeuvre within it. Advice accepted by the government argued the legality of the intervention because of non-compliance by Iraq with Chapter VII resolutions which had authorized the use of force. In the United Kingdom, the government accepted the need for its actions to be legal, accepted the constraints upon the use of force arising from the UN Charter, and argued within that circumscription. Thus, in the United Kingdom, the governance by the UN of the use of force was accepted as representing international law and any illegality was denied. . . .

Recently it has become clear that this position is not necessarily shared in the United States of America. Events there, in the aftermath of September 2001, have apparently led to quite dramatic reconsideration of international law, particularly concerning the use of force. I say 'apparently' because contrary to common opinion there is a great deal of evidence which suggests that a reconsideration of international law and the use of force has been under way in the United States at least since the end of the Cold War in 1990. During the Clinton administration, many of those who were to become key figures in the administration of George W. Bush (now often referred to as the 'neo-conservatives') were actively promoting a new role for the United States, with dramatic and drastic implications for international law, and indeed for the United States itself. This promotion came in the form of submissions to the Clinton administration, the activities of 'think tanks', and also in academic writings. All were concerned to redefine the legitimacy of international actions by the United States aimed at protecting United States' interests in a world with but one super-power. . . .

Great emphasis is placed upon the constraints on United States sovereignty which international law might sustain, rendering it impotent in the face of threats perceived as real, both to its security and to its political and economic interests. It is not always clear . . . whether the argument being made is that international law is generally and fundamentally flawed, or whether the unique wealth, military power, and wisdom of the United States means that it alone should be exempt from rules applicable to lesser nations."

Questions

1. Do you think there is an international rule of law that governs relations between states? Give examples from current events to support your answer.

2. Do you think that the detention of prisoners in Guantánamo Bay raised issues concerning the rule of law?

At this point, you should recognise that the rule of law is not a neutral concept, but rather, that it is thoroughly political. This means that *your* politics inevitably will impact upon *your* views of the politics of the rule of law. As a student, the most important point is to think *critically* about any claim to speak the "truth" about the rule of law (or anything else!).

II. THE SUPREMACY OF PARLIAMENT

Returning again to Dicey's analysis of the English constitution, the rule of law was only one of two fundamental elements; the other was the supremacy of Parliament. The tension between the rule of law and parliamentary supremacy has been particular to the British parliamentary system of government. According to Dicey, the essence of the law of the constitution was that Parliament has the right to make or unmake any law whatever. This means that no person or body is recognised as having a right to override or set aside legislation. Parliament is the supreme law-making body, its legislative power is unrestricted, and the laws it passes cannot be set aside by the courts. The role of judges, in relation to laws enacted by Parliament, is to interpret and apply them, rather than to pass judgment on whether they are good or bad laws. This fact distinguishes the British constitutional structure historically from that found in many other jurisdictions, in which a written constitutional document—such as a Bill of Rights—is the fundamental law which provides the basis for courts to invalidate legislation on constitutional grounds, should it contradict, for example, the rights and freedoms guaranteed in the constitution. However, as we will see later, this historic principle of British constitutionalism is now altered by virtue of membership in the legal order of the European Union.

Parliamentary supremacy also includes the idea that no Parliament can force itself or a future Parliament to retain any particular law now on the books, for to do so would mean that the Parliament in the future was not supreme. Thus, any law, no matter how fundamental, in theory can be repealed by ordinary parliamentary procedure at any time in the future. You might think, therefore, that parliamentary supremacy, as a constitutional principle, has the potential easily to undermine the ideal of the rule of law, which we have already examined. The fact that Parliament conceivably can do just about anything would seem extremely dangerous to the idea of a society governed by law. Dicey sought to answer such concerns, and claimed that the rule of law and parliamentary supremacy (or sovereignty, as he referred to it) in fact were complementary.

Albert Venn Dicey, *An Introduction to the Law of the Constitution*, 8th edn (London: Macmillan, 1915), pp.402–409:

"The sovereignty of Parliament and the supremacy of the law of the land—the two principles which pervade the whole of the English constitution—may appear to stand in opposition to each other, or to be at best only counterbalancing forces. But this appearance is delusive; the sovereignty of Parliament, as contrasted with other forms of sovereign power, favours the supremacy of the law, whilst the predominance of rigid legality throughout our institutions evokes the exercise, and thus increases the authority, of Parliamentary sovereignty.

The sovereignty of Parliament favours the supremacy of the law of the land.

That this should be so arises in the main from two characteristics or peculiarities which distinguish the English Parliament from other sovereign powers.

The first of these characteristics is that the commands of Parliament (consisting as it does of the Crown, the House of Lords, and the House of Commons) can be uttered only through the combined action of its three constituent parts, and must, therefore always take the shape of formal and deliberate legislation. The will of Parliament can be expressed only through an Act of Parliament.

This is no mere matter of form; it has most important practical effects. It prevents those inroads upon the law of the land which a despotic monarch, such as Louis XIV, Napoleon I, or Napoleon III, might effect by ordinances or decrees, or which the different constituent assemblies of France, and above all the famous Convention, carried out by sudden resolutions. The principle that Parliament speaks only through an Act of Parliament greatly increases the authority of the judges. A Bill which has passed into a statute immediately becomes subject to judicial interpretation, and the English Bench have always refused, in principle at least, to interpret an Act of Parliament otherwise than by reference to the words of the enactment. . . .

The second of these characteristics is that the English Parliament as such has never, except at periods of revolution, exercised direct executive power or appointed the officials of the executive government.

No doubt in modern times the House of Commons has in substance obtained the right to designate for appointment the Prime Minister and the other members of the Cabinet. But this right is, historically speaking, of recent acquisition, and is exercised in a very roundabout manner; its existence does not affect the truth of the assertion that the Houses of Parliament do not directly appoint or dismiss the servants of the State; neither the House of Lords nor the House of Commons, nor both Houses combined, could even now issue a direct order to a military officer, a constable, or a tax-collector; the servants of the State are still in name what they once were in reality—'servants of the Crown'; and, what is worth careful notice, the attitude of Parliament towards government officials was determined originally, and is still regulated, by considerations and feelings belonging to a time when the 'servants of the Crown' were dependent upon the King, that is, upon a power which naturally excited the jealousy and vigilance of Parliament.

Hence several results all indirectly tending to support the supremacy of the law. Parliament, though sovereign, unlike a sovereign monarch who is not only a legislator but a ruler, that is, head of the executive government, has never hitherto been able to use the powers of the government as a means of interfering with the regular course of law; and what is even more important, Parliament has looked with disfavour and jealousy on all exemptions of officials from the ordinary liabilities of citizens or from the jurisdiction of the ordinary Courts. Parliamentary sovereignty has been fatal to the growth of 'administrative law.' The action, lastly, of Parliament has tended as naturally to protect the independence of the judges, as that of other sovereigns to protect the conduct of officials. It is worth notice that Parliamentary care for judicial independence has, in fact, stopped just at that point where on a priori grounds it might be expected to end. The judges are not in strictness irremovable; they can be removed from office on an address of the two Houses; they have been made by Parliament independent of every power in the State except the Houses of Parliament. . . .

The fact that the most arbitrary powers of the English executive must always be exercised under Act of Parliament places the government, even when armed with the widest authority, under the supervision, so to speak, of the Courts. Powers, however extraordinary, which are conferred or sanctioned by statute, are never really unlimited, for they are confined by the words of the Act itself, and, what is more, by the interpretation put upon the statute by the judges. Parliament is supreme legislator, but from the moment Parliament has uttered its will as lawgiver, that will becomes subject to the interpretation put upon it by the judges of the land, and the judges, who are influenced by the feelings of magistrates no less than by the general spirit of the common law, are disposed to construe statutory exceptions to common law principles in a mode which would not commend itself either to a body of officials, or to the Houses of Parliament, if the Houses were called upon to interpret their own enactments. In foreign countries, and especially in France, administrative ideas—notions derived from the traditions of a despotic monarchy—have restricted the authority and to a certain extent influenced the ideas of the judges. In England judicial notions have modified the action and influenced the ideas of the executive government. By every path we come round to the same conclusion, that Parliamentary sovereignty has favoured the rule of law, and that the supremacy of the law of the land both calls forth the exertion of Parliamentary sovereignty, and leads to its being exercised in a spirit of legality."

According to Dicey, then, the concepts of rule of law and parliamentary supremacy were actually complementary. Both acted as a way to control officials of the state (the "executive" branch of government). The government of the day always needs the support of Parliament to act, and judges, in their role as interpreters of law, can ensure that the powers of government, as granted by Parliament, have not been exceeded. Finally, the ultimate political supremacy, according to Dicey, rested with the electorate. Once again, Dicey's constitutional vision is informed by a political ideology; one in which government should have a *limited* role, and where individualism and individual rights to private property are central.

Despite being grounded in a particularly nineteenth-century view of the world, the idea of parliamentary supremacy as central to the British constitutional structure has continued to be of vital importance.

A.W. Bradley, "The sovereignty of parliament—form or substance?", in Jeffrey Jowell and Dawn Oliver (eds) *The Changing Constitution*, **5th edn (Oxford: Oxford University Press, 2004), pp.29–31:**

The essence of parliamentary sovereignty as a legal doctrine

"Nevertheless, not only since the publication in 1885 of A.V. Dicey's *The Law of the Constitution* but also before this, the sovereignty of Parliament has been accepted as one of the fundamental doctrines of constitutional law in the United Kingdom. In 1689, after the overthrow of James II, but before the union of the English and Scottish Parliaments in 1707, the Earl of Shaftesbury wrote:

> The Parliament of England is that supreme and absolute power, which gives life and motion to the English Government.

The significance of Dicey's analysis is that, despite the extensive political and social changes that have occurred since 1885, and despite criticism which his work received from constitutional lawyers such as Sir Ivor Jennings, his statement of the doctrine has retained a remarkable influence on both legal and political thinking about Parliament. Dicey summarized his views in this way:

> The principle of parliamentary sovereignty means neither more nor less than this, namely, that Parliament [defined as the Queen, the House of Lords, and the House of Commons, acting together] . . . has, under the English constitution, the right to make or unmake any law whatever; and, further, that no person or body is recognised by the law as having a right to override or set aside the legislation of Parliament.

The principle, 'looked at from its positive side', ensures that any Act of Parliament will be obeyed by the courts. The same principle, 'looked at from its negative side', ensures that there is no person or body of persons who can make rules which override or derogate from an Act of Parliament or which, 'to express the same thing in other words', will be enforced by the courts in contravention of an Act of Parliament.

A further implication drawn from the sovereignty of Parliament is that a sovereign Parliament is not bound by the Acts of its predecessors, and thus that no Parliament can bind its successors. This facet of sovereignty has arisen in part because the courts, when faced with two conflicting statutes on the same subject, have applied the rule that the later Act of Parliament prevails. By the doctrine of implied repeal, the later Act repeals the earlier Act to the extent that the later Act is inconsistent with provisions in the earlier Act. This doctrine has been pressed into service to sustain the proposition that the one rule of the common law that Parliament may not change is the rule that the courts must always apply the latest Act of Parliament on the subject. But this view ought not to be taken as axiomatic and a contrary view is examined below.

The source of legislative sovereignty

Discussion of the source of legislative sovereignty necessarily raises fundamental questions about the relationship between courts and Parliament and the source of that relationship. It would be attractive if we could identify the legal source of the doctrine of sovereignty, but this is not an easy task. Could the source of the sovereignty of Parliament be found in an Act of Parliament itself? A well-known, but possibly over-simple, answer to this question was given by the New Zealand jurist, Sir John Salmond:

> No statute can confer this power upon Parliament for this would be to assume and act on the very power that is to be conferred.

But Parliament might be entitled to make such an assumption if over many years it had enacted a wide variety of statutes without its authority to legislate being questioned. Indeed, this leads directly to the next question, whether the legal source of authority for the doctrine of sovereignty may be found in decisions of the courts. Decisions of the courts are authoritative in determining the common law. Thus the sovereignty of Parliament can be said to be based upon decisions of the courts in applying Acts of Parliament, since, if the courts apply

Acts of Parliament and say that they must do so because they are bound by *all* such Acts, then the courts are declaring a fundamental rule, namely that effect must be given to Acts of Parliament, whatever their content.

A third and intermediate possibility, rather than attributing the source of legislative sovereignty to Parliament or to the courts acting separately, is to examine the past and present relationship between the courts, the legislature, and other holders of office in the state, looking at what the courts and the legislature have done in relation to each other, and also at the stance of other key actors in the political system (such as ministers of the Crown). Such an explanation looks at past institutional behaviour and assumes that this can be expected to continue. However, if the rule of legislative sovereignty came about from a historical process, rather than as a result of a 'big bang' creation of a fundamental rule, can we be certain that this area of constitutional evolution has come to a full stop? On this basis, changes in the relationship may occur over time. Indeed, such changes may happen more rapidly where the incentive to change is created by an event such as a radical initiative taken by the legislature. In this situation the courts might respond to such an initiative in a manner for which there was no direct precedent, and in a manner that the new legislation might not have expressly invited."

This historical relationship between Parliament and the courts, in which Parliament is supposedly supreme, and the courts apply laws enacted by Parliament, is demonstrated by a case decided by the House of Lords (which, until recently, was the highest court in the United Kingdom). Decisions of the Law Lords generally include many judgments, and portions of three of those judgments (all of which agreed in the result) illustrate how the Lords in this case sought to respect the principle of parliamentary supremacy.

British Railways Board and another v Pickin [1974] 1 All E.R. 609, HL.

[The Bristol and Exeter Railway Co. was incorporated (created) by statute in 1836 to make a railway from Bristol to Exeter with branch lines to Bridgwater and Tiverton. The Act provided that if the line was abandoned, the lands acquired by the company to build the railways would return to the owners of the land on either side of the railway. In the 1960s, the line fell into disuse. The land adjacent was sold to George Pickin. Meanwhile, Parliament, at the behest of the British Railway Board (the successor to the Bristol and Exeter Railway Co.), enacted the British Railways Act 1968, which provided that provisions such as the one governing the reversion of the land on either side of the Bristol and Exeter railway, would not apply to land vested in the British Railway Board. Pickin commenced action against the Board claiming, amongst other things, that the Board had misled Parliament in its promotion of the Bill, and that the court should declare him owner of the adjacent land. The portions of the judgments in the House of Lords of interest to us concern the claim that Parliament was misled into enacting the statute].

Lord Reid

[Lord Reid recited the facts of the case and the issues raised]:

". . . The respondent's [Pickin's] alternative ground of action is not easy to state concisely. He appears to allege that in obtaining the enactment of s.18 of the 1968 Act in their favour the board fraudulently concealed certain matters from Parliament and its officers and thereby misled Parliament into granting this right to them. . . .

The function of the court is to construe and apply the enactments of Parliament. The court has no concern with the manner in which Parliament or its officers carrying out its standing orders perform these functions. Any attempt to prove that they were misled by fraud or otherwise would necessarily involve an enquiry into the manner in which they had performed their functions in dealing with the bill which became the British Railways Act 1968.

In whatever form the respondent's case is pleaded he must prove not only that the board acted fraudulently but also that their fraud caused damage to him by causing the enactment of s.18. He could not prove that without an examination of the manner in which the officers of Parliament dealt with the matter. So the court would, or at least might, have to adjudicate on that.

For a century or more both Parliament and the courts have been careful not to act so as to cause conflict between them. Any such investigations as the respondent seeks could easily lead to such a conflict, and I would only support it if compelled to do so by clear authority. But it appears to me that the whole trend of authority for over a century is clearly against permitting any such investigation.

The respondent is entitled to argue that s.18 should be construed in a way favourable to him and for that reason I have refrained from pronouncing on that matter. But he is not entitled to go behind the Act to shew that s.18 should not be enforced. Nor is he entitled to examine proceedings in Parliament in order to shew that the board by fraudulently misleading Parliament caused him loss. . . ."

Lord Morris of Borth-Y-Gest:

". . . The question of fundamental importance which arises is whether the court should entertain the proposition that an Act of Parliament can so be assailed in the courts that matters should proceed as though the Act or some part of it had never been passed. I consider that such doctrine would be dangerous and impermissible. It is the function of the courts to administer the laws which Parliament has enacted. In the processes of Parliament there will be much consideration whether a bill should or should not in one form or another become an enactment. When an enactment is passed there is finality unless and until it is amended or repealed by Parliament. In the courts there may be argument as to the correct interpretation of the enactment: there must be none as to whether it should be on the statute book at all. . . ."

Lord Simon of Glaisdale:

". . . The system by which, in this country, those liable to be affected by general political decisions have some control over the decision-making is parliamentary democracy. Its peculiar feature in constitutional law is the sovereignty of Parliament. This involves that, contrary to what was sometimes asserted before the 18th century, and in contradistinction to some other democratic systems, the courts in this country have no power to declare enacted law to be invalid. . . ."

III. A Note on the Constitution

The Law Lords in several places in their judgments in *Pickin* refer to the constitution and constitutional law. Although you will take at least one course in constitutional and administrative law, a few notes on the constitution are needed now in order for you to understand its implications for legal reasoning and legal method. The term constitution refers to the fundamental rules and limitations under which the power of the state is exercised. The constitution establishes institutions of government and divides powers between them; it limits the power of the state; and sometimes, it sets out rights held by citizens. The constitution is the fundamental framework of the legal and political system. In some countries, such as the United States, that constitutional framework is easy to identify. It is written down in a document called the "Constitution", and it includes a "Bill of Rights". But, in the United Kingdom, the constitution is more difficult to find. It is sometimes referred to as an "unwritten" constitution, because it is not set down in a single, comprehensive document. Rather, the British constitution consists of a variety of rules, customs, and understandings which empower and limit government. We would say, for example, that the idea of parliamentary supremacy and the rule of law are elements of our constitution. The constitutional framework can be "found" in a variety of places: in ordinary law enacted by Parliament, which deals with matters which are considered to be fundamental; in laws created by judges in the course of deciding cases before them (which is known as the "common law"); and the rules which Parliament has set down to govern its own internal procedures ("the law and custom of Parliament").

It is also of constitutional significance that the United Kingdom is a constitutional monarchy. This means that government is still conducted in the name of the Queen, which signifies the ultimate governing authority. Our structure of government is also characterised by a bicameral Parliament. This means that Parliament is composed of two "houses": a lower house (the House of Commons) chosen through popular election, and an upper house (the House of Lords), which is partly hereditary and partly appointed (although this might be subject to reform in the future). We also characterise our system as an example of "responsible government", in that the government of the day (the executive) is accountable to the House of Commons (the legislature) and can be defeated on the floor of the House in a vote. We also would describe the United Kingdom as a unitary, rather than a federal state, in that ultimate power rests with a central government in London (although some powers have been decentralised to Scotland, Wales, and Northern Ireland through the policy of the devolution of power). Finally, the British constitution might be described in terms of the principle of "limited government", to the extent that government can only do what it is empowered under law to perform. This idea was central to Dicey's ideal of the rule of law.

Also of constitutional significance is what Dicey referred to as "conventions of the constitution", which he acknowledged were sometimes more important in constitutional terms than the law itself. These are simply practices or customs which have become so fundamental as to be considered of constitutional significance. They include the fact that the Queen assents to all laws passed by both Houses of Parliament (this is called the "Royal Assent"); the Queen acts only on the advice of her ministers, and ministers exercise the prerogatives (rights) which have been retained by the Crown; ministers are responsible to Parliament; members of the government are collectively responsible to Parliament; and the Prime Minister must be a member of the House of Commons rather than the House of Lords.

These conventions are not written down. They are simply practices of constitutional government which have grown up over time. Most importantly, disobedience of a convention means that it ceases to exist. If the Prime Minister was chosen from the House of Lords (and he or she chose to stay a member of the Lords) then the convention would no longer be a convention. This is what distinguishes convention from law: disobedience of a law does not mean that the law no longer exists. Moreover, unlike law, there is no *sanction*, other than potentially a political one at the ballot box, for violating a convention. Thus, a convention may be recognised as part of the constitution, but it is not *enforceable* by the courts. It is politically, rather than *legally*, binding.

For Dicey, writing at the end of the nineteenth century, Britain's constitutional structure—the rule of law, supremacy of Parliament, and conventions of the constitution—was a *model* of constitutional government, superior to anything offered in other countries with written constitutions contained in a single document. Central to that balanced constitutional structure was the role of the courts. The courts' job was to uphold the intention of Parliament in the interpretation of legislation, but the role of the courts also was to review the actions of the executive branch of government (the cabinet and civil service) to ensure that its actions were within the lawful authority granted by Parliament. In this way, the courts upheld the rule of law, because they protected the individual against the potential for the arbitrary exercise of power by the executive.

However, in the twentieth century, that model of a balanced and harmonious constitution (if it ever really existed) increasingly has come unstuck. The House of Commons has become dominant, while the role of the House of Lords has been constricted both by legislation and the political environment in which an unelected body is seen as illegitimate. In this way, the upper house becomes less of a "check" on the actions of the Commons. Nor does the Royal Assent act as a "check" on legislation, because of the convention that the Queen acts only on the advice of ministers and does not withhold her consent (which also was the case in Dicey's time). Moreover, because of the development of the system of political parties, the individual Member of Parliament has less and less of a role in independently scrutinising legislation proposed by the government (although there are still instances where this effectively occurs).

As a result of these developments, the government of the day dominates the legislative and executive functions of government. Moreover, the principle of parliamentary supremacy limited the power of the courts to act as a means of controlling government in that, as we have seen, they could not invalidate legislation. This relationship between Parliament, the executive branch of government, and the courts is often referred to as the doctrine of *separation of powers*. This term refers to the three primary functions of government: legislative (the making of laws); executive (the execution of laws, or putting laws into operation); and judicial (the interpretation of laws), and the degree to which those functions are distributed amongst different people. The classic example of a pure separation of powers is found in the United States, where the legislative function is the task of Congress; the executive function is the job of the President and his or her cabinet, who are not members of Congress; and the judicial function is the task of judges. That degree of separation of powers is absent in the United Kingdom. In part, this is because the Prime Minister and his or her cabinet are Members of Parliament; they are part of the legislature as well as being the head of the executive branch. Consequently, we say that the legislative and executive branches are largely *fused* together.

VI. THE HUMAN RIGHTS ACT 1998 AND THE SUPREMACY OF PARLIAMENT

We will consider the impact of the Human Rights Act 1998 in connection with the principles of statutory interpretation in Ch.7, but it is also important with respect to the principle of parliamentary supremacy. The Act *empowers* the judiciary to uphold certain rights of the individual from being infringed by the state, while also, at the same time, remaining true to the supremacy of Parliament—even if parliamentary law undermines those fundamental rights. In other words the courts can declare laws to be *incompatible* with our human rights, but the courts cannot refuse to apply these laws in the end. The Act protects a number of rights enshrined in the European Convention on Human Rights, and the relationship between the Act, the Convention, Parliament and the courts is a complex one.

Lord Lester of Herne Hill Q.C., "Human rights and the British constitution", in Jeffrey Jowell and Dawn Oliver (eds) *The Changing Constitution*, 5th edn (Oxford: Oxford University Press, 2004), pp.63–64, 65–67, 68–69, 73, 75–76, 80, 81–82:

"The earlier concepts of 'fundamental rights', and of a 'fundamental' constitutional law taking precedence over ordinary laws, became eclipsed at the end of the seventeenth century by the concept of absolute parliamentary sovereignty. In the early part of the century, the judges had struggled not only for independence from undue Executive interference but also for the right to withhold effect from laws that they regarded as unconscionable or as contrary to a higher, fundamental natural law. The judges won the struggle for independence against the Crown's claim to rule by prerogative, but the price paid by the common lawyers for their alliance with Parliament against the divine right of kings was that the common law could be changed by Parliament as it pleased. The 'glorious bloodless' revolution of 1688 was won by Parliament, and although the Bill of Rights of 1688–9 and the Act of Settlement of 1700 recognized some important personal rights and liberties, the terms of the constitutional settlement were mainly concerned with the rights and liberties of Parliament. The alliance of Parliament and the common lawyers ensured that the supremacy of the law would mean the supremacy of Parliament; more realistically, it came to mean, between general elections, the supremacy of the government in Parliament. The doctrine of the supremacy of Parliament, described by Lord Hailsham of St Marylebone as operating in practice as an 'elected dictatorship', became the keystone of the British Constitution. . . .

   Although the ideology of fundamental rights was rejected by successive generations of British governments and constitutional thinkers on the political left and right, it has been a potent force across the world. American and French concepts of human rights and judicial review shaped systems of government subject to binding constitutional codes in Europe and beyond. The conquests of Napoleon's armies spread through the European continent not only the Code Civil but also the public philosophy and public law of the United States and France. These ideas and systems were also spread to other continents. Today, the many countries whose legal systems are based upon the civil law have legally binding constitutional guarantees of fundamental human rights derived from seventeenth-century England and the eighteenth-century enlightenment. In the common law world, as the colonies of the British Empire gained independence, Bills of Rights were introduced giving constitutional protection to human rights.

The human rights-based philosophy also became profoundly influential in creating a new international legal order in the wake of the horrors of the Second World War. In December 1948, the UN General Assembly adopted the Universal Declaration of Human Rights, recognizing certain rights as basic human entitlements: free speech as much as freedom from torture. In 1966, two International Covenants were opened for signature, a Covenant on Civil and Political Rights, and a Covenant on Economic, Social and Cultural Rights. The two Covenants came into force in 1976, and are reinforced by several UN human rights conventions, for example, against torture, race and sex discrimination, and protecting the rights of the child.

Meanwhile, in Western Europe, a second terrible war in half a century and the barbarous atrocities of the Nazi Holocaust convinced European politicians and jurists of the need to forge a new Europe. The need to guard against the rise of new dictatorships, to avoid the risk of relapse into another disastrous European war, and to provide a beacon of hope for the peoples of Central and Eastern Europe living under Soviet totalitarian regimes, inspired the foundation, in 1949, of the Council of Europe. Members of the Council of Europe are obliged to accept the principles of the rule of law and the enjoyment by everyone within their jurisdiction of human rights and fundamental freedoms.

One of the Council of Europe's first tasks was to draft a human rights convention for Europe, conferring enforceable rights upon individuals against sovereign states. It was a revolutionary enterprise. The master builders of the European Convention knew why human rights protection had to transcend national boundaries, nationality, and citizenship. They saw the need to link positive law with ethical values, and to protect individuals and minorities against the misuse of power by elected governments and unelected public officials in periods of emergency and normal times. The inventors of the European Convention were determined never again to permit state sovereignty to shield from international liability the perpetrators of crimes against humanity, never again to allow governments to shelter behind the traditional argument that what a state does to its own citizens or to the stateless is within its exclusive jurisdiction and beyond the reach of the international community. So they resolved to create a binding international code of human rights with effective legal safeguards for all victims of violations by contracting states.

For the first time, individuals would be able to exercise personally enforceable rights under international law, before an independent and impartial tribunal—the European Court of Human Rights—against the public authorities of their own states. No matter whether the violation occurred because of an administrative decision by a minister or civil servant, or because of the judgment of a national supreme court, or because of legislation enacted by a national parliament; there would be no privilege or immunity enabling state authorities automatically to shield themselves against supra-national European judicial scrutiny. . . .

The Convention guarantees basic civil and political rights to everyone within the jurisdiction of the Contracting States: the right to life (Article 2); the prohibition of torture and inhuman or degrading treatment or punishment (Article 3); the prohibition of slavery and forced labour (Article 4); the right to liberty (Article 5); the right to a fair trial (Article 6); no punishment without law (Article 7); respect for private and family life (Article 8); freedom of thought, conscience, and religion (Article 9); freedom of expression (Article 10); freedom of assembly and association (Article 11); the right to marry and found a family (Article 12); the right to an effective national remedy (Article 13); and non-discrimination in the enjoyment of Convention rights (Article 14).

The United Kingdom ratified the First Protocol to the Convention, on 3 November 1952, which added the right to the protection of property (Article 1); the right to Education (Article 2); and the right to free elections (Article 3). The United Kingdom ratified the Sixth Protocol to the Convention on 27 January 1999, abolishing the death penalty.

In December 1965, the first Wilson Government decided to accept the right of individual petition and the jurisdiction of the European Court of Human Rights to rule on cases brought by individuals against the United Kingdom. It was to prove to be a momentous decision, for it meant that, in fact if not in a formal sense, political (if not legal) sovereignty was henceforth to be shared with the European institutions created by the Convention. . . .

In all there have been some one hundred and thirty judgments of the European Court finding breaches by the UK, many of them controversial and far-reaching. They include: the inhuman treatment of suspected terrorists in Northern Ireland; inadequate safeguards against telephone tapping by the police; unfair discrimination against British wives of foreign husbands under immigration rules; unjust restrictions upon prisoners' correspondence and visits; corporal punishment in schools; corporal punishment by a stepfather; criminal sanctions against private homosexual conduct; the exclusion of homosexuals from the armed services; the lack of legal recognition of transsexuals; ineffective judicial protection for detained mental patients, or would-be immigrants, or individuals facing extradition to countries where they risk being exposed to torture or inhuman treatment, or homosexuals whose private life is infringed; the dismissal of workers because of the oppressive operation of the closed shop; interference with free speech by unnecessarily maintaining injunctions restraining breaches of confidence, or because of a jury's award of excessive damages for libel, or by punishing a journalist for refusing to disclose his confidential source; the right to have a detention order under the Mental Health Act reviewed; parental access to children; access to child care records; review of the continuing detention of those serving discretionary life sentences and mandatory life sentences; access to legal advice for fine and debt defaulters; unfair court martial procedures; lack of availability of legal aid in some criminal cases; and lack of access to civil justice. . . .

The Human Rights Act is a first major step towards a full British Bill of Rights. The Act is an essential element in the constitutional resettlement of the different nations and regions of the United Kingdom, and the recognition of people of the United Kingdom as citizens endowed with basic human rights. Half a century after the European Convention on Human Rights was drafted, it creates a direct link between Convention rights and the laws of the UK, enabling British courts to give direct effect to Convention rights. The Act is no ordinary law. It is a fundamental, constitutional measure of greater contemporary significance to the protection of human rights than any previous constitutional measure. . . .

Section 3 case law is evolving, and different courts have given it a different emphasis. In the House of Lords in *Re S (Care Order: Implementation of Care Plan)*, Lord Nicholls of Birkenhead stated that section 3 is 'a powerful tool whose use is obligatory. It is not an optional canon of construction. Nor is its use dependent on the existence of ambiguity.' Lord Bingham of Cornhill approved *Re S* in *R (Anderson)* v. *Secretary of State for the Home Department* but warned that section 3 allowed for judicial interpretation but not 'judicial vandalism' so as to give the statutory provision 'an effect quite different from that which Parliament intended'. Lord Steyn examined the interpretative obligation of section 3 in the rape shield case, *R* v. *A (No 2)*, and concluded that,

> in accordance with the will of Parliament as reflected in section 3 it will sometimes be necessary to adopt an interpretation which linguistically may appear strained. The techniques to be used will not only involve the reading down of express language in a statute but also the implication of the provisions. A declaration of incompatibility is a measure of last resort. It must be avoided unless it is plainly impossible to do so. If a *clear* limitation on Convention rights is stated *in terms*, such an impossiblity will arise. . . .

The declaration of incompatibility is essential in bringing the problem to the attention of the Executive and the Legislature, and acting as trigger for amending legislation by means of a remedial order. Despite its incompatibility with Convention rights, the offending legislation will remain valid and effective, unless and until legislative amendments are made. Parliamentary sovereignty is maintained and Parliament's legislative powers remain intact in deciding whether to remove the incompatibility. However, failure to make such amendment to remedy the domestic court's declaration of incompatibility will lead to a complaint to the European Court of Human Rights in Strasbourg, with a high probability that the European Court will come to a similar conclusion. This will be a powerful incentive to the government to introduce, and for Parliament to approve, the necessary remedial order. . . .

The fact that courts and tribunals have a duty to act compatibly with the Convention is significant because of the Act's potential 'horizontal effect'. The main focus of the Convention is upon protecting the individual against the abuse of power by the public authorities of the state. However, like other national constitutional charters of human rights, it is necessary to extend protection beyond the state and its agents to 'private governments'—those bodies which are private in form but public in substance. The courts have a duty of acting compatibly with the Convention, not only in cases involving other public authorities in this extended sense, but also in developing the common law when deciding cases between private persons. This is especially the case where the Convention imposes positive obligations on the state to protect individuals against breaches of their rights."

Some might argue that the Human Rights Act 1998 is an imperfect attempt at protecting individual rights because of its deference to the principle of parliamentary supremacy. Ewing, by contrast, argues that this is the great strength of the legislation.

K.D. Ewing, "The Human Rights Act and Parliamentary democracy" (1999) 62 M.L.R. 79 at 79, 98–99:

"The Human Rights Act 1998 is the culmination of an aggressive campaign for the incorporation into domestic law of the European Convention on Human Rights, a campaign in which the judges joined forces with other political activists. Variously described as 'brilliant'; 'a masterly exposition of the parliamentary draftsman's art'; and even 'a thing of intellectual beauty'; the Act has also been greeted as an 'ingenious compromise' between the 'maximalists' and 'minimalists', the former supporting a judicial power to invalidate legislation, as is the case in Canada. But although it is purported to reconcile in 'subtle' form the protection of human rights with the sovereignty of Parliament (a claim even more credible after an important but unsung Commons amendment), the Act also represents an unprecedented transfer of political power from the executive and legislature to the judiciary, and a fundamental re-structuring of our 'political constitution'. As such it is unquestionably the most significant formal redistribution of political power in this country since 1911, and perhaps since 1688 when the Bill of Rights proclaimed loudly that proceedings in Parliament ought not to be questioned or impeached in any court or any other place.

[For] all that, the inevitable incorporation of the Convention has been secured in a manner which subordinates Convention rights to constitutional principle and democratic tradition. We should not diminish the importance of the fact that the Human Rights Act does not give the courts the power to strike down legislation. Nor should we diminish the reasons why the government withheld this power from the courts, grounded as they were in a desire to ensure that 'no court in this land, not even the Judicial Committee of the House of Lords, can place itself in the position of sovereignty over the High Court of the elected Parliament'. The government appeared particularly concerned to preserve 'the fundamental position established in our constitution: the sovereignty of Parliament', said to be 'one of the profound strengths of our system'. This is a refreshing position to have adopted, if only because the sovereignty of Parliament is something which should not really be conceded, acting as it does as a constitutional and legal principle which has metamorphosed in a dynamic constitution, to give effect to one of the first political principles of democratic self-government. This is the principle of popular sovereignty whereby the elected and accountable representatives of the people should be empowered by the authority of a mandate to give effect without restraint to what used to be called the General Will.

This is not to deny that the Human Rights Act confers a significant political power on the courts, or indeed that it enables the courts formally to set the agenda on human rights questions. Nor is it to deny that in the 'overwhelming majority of cases', a declaration of incompatibility will be accepted by the government and Parliament of the day, thereby ensuring that the elected branch will in practice defer to the unelected branch. But the government appears genuinely to anticipate the possibility that this will not always be so, and there may well be cases (such as abortion) where Parliament will assert its political and legal authority over the courts. In this way the sovereignty of Parliament will be preserved both in principle and in practice, even though it is unquestionably the case that Parliament's position would have been stronger politically and constitutionally if incorporation of the ECHR had stopped short of giving the courts the power to challenge primary legislation."

After the events of September 11, 2001, Parliament enacted the Anti-terrorism, Crime and Security Act 2001, which included extended powers for the Home Secretary to order the indefinite detention of a suspected (non-UK-citizen) terrorist, without the right to trial. In order to enable this measure, the government "derogated" from art.5(1) of the European Convention in this case (the right to *liberty*).

However, the House of Lords was not prepared to grant extreme *deference* to the government when a case came before it on the legislation. Gearty summarises the Law Lords' decision in *A v Secretary of State for the Home Department* [2004] UKHL 563, in which the Law Lords found that the derogation was insufficiently broad to uphold the legislation, given its impact both on the right to liberty and non-discrimination as between nationals and non-citizens:

Conor Gearty, "11 September 2001, counter-terrorism and the Human Rights Act" (2005) 23 *Journal of Law and Society* 18 at 29:

"The House of Lords agreed by the overwhelming margin of 8–1, when the case came before it that not even the deference rightly given in the field of national security could permit the indefinite detention of suspected non-national (but not national) terrorists. Their lordships ruled that the derogation was not valid and, at the same time, made a declaration of incompatibility in relation to the detention provisions of the 2001 Act, on the ground that these breached both Articles 5 and 14 of the Convention. In making these rulings, the Lords have gone some way towards redeeming the reputation of the courts in the field of civil liberties."

Finally, a key aspect of the rule of law has always been that individuals should not be subjected to torture. A case went to the House of Lords which raised the question whether evidence that an individual was a terrorist and a threat to national security, pursuant to the Anti-Terrorism, Crime and Security Act 2001, could be used even if it had been produced through torture by non-British officials. The House of Lords was unanimous in its conclusion that such evidence could not be admitted in a court. For our purposes, of interest is the way in which the Law Lords turn to their understanding of the rule of law to justify their conclusion. These extracts from some of the judgments give a sense of their Lordships' strength of feeling.

A and Others v Secretary of State for the Home Department (No. 2) [2005] UKHL 71.

Lord Bingham of Cornhill:

"My Lords, may the Special Immigration Appeals Commission (SIAC), a superior court of record established by statute, when hearing an appeal under s 25 of the Anti-terrorism, Crime and Security Act 2001 by a person certified and detained under ss 21 and 23 of the Act, receive evidence which has or may have been procured by torture inflicted, in order to obtain evidence, by officials of a foreign state without the complicity of the British authorities? That is the central question which the House must answer in these appeals. The appellants, relying on the common law of England, on the European Convention for the Protection of Human Rights and Fundamental Freedoms 1950 (the European Convention) and on principles of public international law, submit that the question must be answered with an emphatic negative. The Secretary of State agrees that this answer would be appropriate in any case where the torture had been inflicted by or with the complicity of the British authorities. He further states that it is not his intention to rely on, or present to the SIAC or to the Administrative Court in relation to control orders, evidence which he knows or believes to have been obtained by a third country by torture. This intention is, however, based on policy and not on any acknowledged legal obligation. Like any other policy it may be altered, by a successor in office or if circumstances change. The admission of such evidence by the SIAC is not, he submits, precluded by law. Thus he contends for an affirmative answer to the central question stated above. The appellants' case is supported by written and oral submissions made on behalf of 17 well-known bodies dedicated to the protection of human rights, the suppression of torture and the maintenance of the rule of law. . . .

The Secretary of State is right to submit that the SIAC is a body designed to enable it to receive and assess a wide range of material, including material which would not be disclosed to a body lacking in special characteristics. And it would of course be within the power of a sovereign Parliament (in breach of international law) to confer power on the SIAC to receive third party torture evidence. But the English common law has regarded torture and its fruits with abhorrence for over 500 years, and that abhorrence is now shared by over 140 countries which have acceded to the Torture Convention. I am startled, even a little dismayed, at the suggestion (and the acceptance by the Court of Appeal majority) that this deeply-rooted tradition and an international obligation solemnly and explicitly undertaken can be overridden by a statute and a procedural rule which make no mention of torture at all. Counsel for the Secretary of State acknowledges that during the discussion on Pt 4 the subject of torture was never the subject of any thought or any allusion. The matter is governed by the principle of legality very clearly explained by my noble and learned friend Lord Hoffmann in *R v Secretary of State for the Home Dept, ex p Simms* [1999] 2 All ER 400 at 412, [2000] 2 AC 115 at 131:

> Parliamentary sovereignty means that Parliament can, if it chooses, legislate contrary to fundamental principles of human rights. The Human Rights Act 1998 will not detract from this power. The constraints upon its exercise by Parliament are ultimately political, not legal. But the principle of legality means that Parliament must squarely confront what it is doing and accept the political cost. Fundamental rights cannot be overridden by general or ambiguous words. This is because there is too great a risk that the full implications of their unqualified meaning may have passed unnoticed in the democratic process. In the absence of express language or necessary implication to the contrary, the courts therefore presume that even the most general words were intended to be subject to the basic rights of the individual. In this way the courts of the United Kingdom, though acknowledging the sovereignty of Parliament, apply principles of constitutionality little different from those which exist in countries where the power of the legislature is expressly limited by a constitutional document.

It trivialises the issue before the House to treat it as an argument about the law of evidence. The issue is one of constitutional principle, whether evidence obtained by torturing another human being may lawfully be admitted against a party to proceedings in a British court, irrespective of where, or by whom, or on whose authority the torture was inflicted. To that question I would give a very clear negative answer.

I accept the broad thrust of the appellants' argument on the common law. The principles of the common law, standing alone, in my opinion compel the exclusion of third party torture evidence as unreliable, unfair, offensive to ordinary standards of humanity and decency and incompatible with the principles which should animate a tribunal seeking to administer justice. But the principles of the common law do not stand alone. Effect must be given to the European Convention, which itself takes account of the all but universal consensus embodied in the Torture Convention. The answer to the central question posed at the outset of this opinion is to be found not in a governmental policy, which may change, but in law."

Lord Nicholls of Birkenhead:

"My Lords, torture is not acceptable. This is a bedrock moral principle in this country. For centuries the common law has set its face against torture. In early times this did not prevent the use of torture under warrants issued by the King or his Council. But by the middle of the seventeenth century this practice had ceased. In 1628 John Felton assassinated the Duke of Buckingham. He was pressed to reveal the names of his accomplices. The King's Council debated whether 'by the Law of the Land they could justify the putting him to the Rack'. The King, Charles I, said that before this was done 'let the Advice of the Judges be had therein, whether it be Legal or no'. The King said that if it might not be done by law 'he would not use his Prerogative in this Point'. So the judges were consulted. They assembled at Serjeants' Inn in Fleet Street and agreed unanimously that Felton 'ought not by the Law to be tortured by the Rack, for no such Punishment is known or allowed by our Law'. . . .

Torture attracts universal condemnation, as amply demonstrated by my noble and learned friend Lord Bingham of Cornhill. No civilised society condones its use. Unhappily, condemnatory words are not always matched by conduct. Information derived from sources where torture is practised gives rise to the present problem. The context is cross-border terrorism. Countering international terrorism calls for a flow of information between the security services of many countries. Fragments of information, acquired from various sources, can be pieced together to form a valuable picture, enabling governments of threatened countries to take preventative steps. What should the security services and the police and other executive agencies of the country do if they know or suspect information received by them from overseas is the product of torture? Should they discard this information as 'tainted', and decline to use it lest its use by them be regarded as condoning the horrific means by which the information was obtained?

The intuitive response to these questions is that if use of such information might save lives it would be absurd to reject it. If the police were to learn of the whereabouts of a ticking bomb it would be ludicrous for them to disregard this information if it had been procured by torture. No one suggests the police should act in this way. Similarly, if tainted information points a finger of suspicion at a particular individual: depending on the circumstances, this information is a matter the police may properly take into account when considering, for example, whether to make an arrest.

In both these instances the executive arm of the state is open to the charge that it is condoning the use of torture. So, in a sense, it is. The government is using information obtained by torture. But in cases such as these the government cannot be expected to close its eyes to this information at the price of endangering the lives of its own citizens. Moral repugnance to torture does not require this.

The next step is to consider whether the position is the same regarding the use of this information in legal proceedings and, if not, why not. In my view the position is not the same. The executive and the judiciary have different functions and different responsibilities. It is one thing for tainted information to be used by the executive when making operational decisions or by the police when exercising their investigatory powers, including powers of arrest. These steps do not impinge upon the liberty of individuals or, when they do, they are of an essentially short-term interim character. Often there is an urgent need for action. It is an altogether different matter for the judicial arm of the state to admit such information as evidence when adjudicating definitively upon the guilt or innocence of a person charged with a criminal offence. In the latter case repugnance to torture demands that proof of facts should be found in more acceptable sources than information extracted by torture."

Lord Hoffman:

"My Lords, on 22 August 1628 George Villiers, Duke of Buckingham and Lord High Admiral of England, was stabbed to death by John Felton, a naval officer, in a house in Portsmouth. The 35-year-old duke had been the favourite of King James I and was the intimate friend of the new King Charles I, who asked the judges whether Felton could be put to the rack to discover his accomplices. All the judges met at Serjeants' Inn. Many years later Blackstone recorded their historic decision: 'The judges, being consulted, declared unanimously, to their own honour and the honour of the English law, that no such proceeding was allowable by the laws of England.'

That word honour, the deep note which Blackstone strikes twice in one sentence, is what underlies the legal technicalities of this appeal. The use of torture is dishonourable. It corrupts and degrades the state which uses it and the legal system which accepts it. When judicial torture was routing all over Europe, its rejection by the common law was a source of national pride and the admiration of foreign writers such as Voltaire and Beccaria. In our own century, many people in the United States, heirs to that common law tradition, have felt their country dishonoured by its use of torture outside the jurisdiction and its practice of extra-legal 'rendition' of suspects to countries where they would be tortured. . . .

Just as the writ of habeas corpus is not only a special (and nowadays infrequent) remedy for challenging unlawful detention but also carries a symbolic significance as a touchstone of English liberty which influences the rest of our law, so the rejection of torture by the common law has a special iconic importance as the touchstone of a human and civilised legal system. Not only that: the abolition of torture, which was used by the state in Elizabethan and Jacobean times to obtain evidence admitted in trials before the court of Star Chamber, was achieved as part of the great constitutional struggle and civil war which made the government subject to the law. Its rejection has a constitutional resonance for the English people which cannot be overestimated.

During the last century the idea of torture as a state instrument of special horror came to be accepted all over the world, as is witnessed by the international law materials collected by my noble and learned friend Lord Bingham of Cornhill. Among the many unlawful practices of state officials, torture and genocide are regarded with particular revulsions: crimes against international law which every state is obliged to punish wherever they may have been committed."

Lord Hope of Craighead:

"Torture, one of the most evil practices known to man, is resorted to for a variety of purposes and it may help to identify them to put this case into its historical context. The lesson of history is that, when the law is not there to keep watch over it, the practice is always at risk of being resorted to in one form or another by the executive branch of the government. The temptation to use it in times of emergency will be controlled by the law wherever the rule of law is allowed to operate. But where the rule of law is absent, or is reduced to a mere form of words to which those in authority pay no more than lip service, the temptation to use torture is unrestrained. The probability of its use will rise or fall according to the scale of the perceived emergency.

In the first place, torture may be used on a large scale as an instrument of blatant repression by totalitarian governments. That is what was alleged in *R* v. *Bow Street Metropolitan Stipendiary Magistrate, ex p Pinochet Ugarte (No 3)* [1999] 2 All ER 97, [2000] 1 AC 147, where the picture presented by the draft charges against Senator Pinochet which had been prepared by the Spanish judicial authorities was of a conspiracy. It was a conspiracy of the most evil kind—to commit widespread and systematic torture and murder to obtain control of the government and, having done so, to maintain control of government by those means for so long as might be necessary. Or it may be used in totalitarian states as a means of extracting confessions from individuals whom the authorities wish to put on trial so that they can be used against them in evidence.

The examples I have just mentioned are of torture as an instrument of power. But the use of torture to obtain confessions was also sanctioned by the judiciary in many civil law jurisdictions, and it remained part of their criminal procedure until the latter part of the seventeenth century. This was never part of English criminal procedure and, as there was no need for it, its use for this purpose was prohibited by the common law."

The Government also enacted the Prevention of Terrorism Act 2005 which attempted to deal with all terrorist activity, no matter the nationality of the individuals involved. It also included a different system of detention known as "control orders". Further legislation, the Terrorism Act 2006, extended the period of detention without charge for terrorist suspects and created the criminal offence of glorifying terrorism. The compatibility of control orders with the Human Rights Act was considered by the House of Lords and the result is analysed by Ewing and Tham.

K.D. Ewing and Joo-Cheong Tham, "The Continuing Futility of the Human Rights Act" [2008] *Public Law* 668 at 669–670; 681–682; 688; 693.

"Detention and internment were replaced by a new regime of restraint, in the form of control orders introduced by the Prevention of Terrorism Act 2005, authorising what is sometimes pejoratively referred to as house arrest. This regime has now also been subject to intense judicial scrutiny in three cases decided on the same day,[1] but on this occasion the House of Lords appears to have beaten a retreat. Perhaps the first sign of retreat is that

---

[1]   *Secretary of State for the Home Department v JJ* [2007] UKHL 45, [2007] 3 W.L.R. 642; *Secretary of State for the Home Department v MB and AF* [2007] UKHL 46, [2007] 3 W.L.R. 681; and *Secretary of State for the Home Department v E* [2007] UKHL 47, [2007] 3 W.L.R. 720.

the level of intensity of that judicial scrutiny was much diminished, in the sense that there was no procession of nine judges to consider the issues, which were dealt with by a more standard Bench of five. This, however, is overshadowed by the second and much more important (but perhaps concealed) sign of judicial retreat, which is that—unlike the indefinite detention powers they replaced--the control order regime has survived largely unscathed. The decisions are thus remarkably paradoxical, in the sense that while two of the three applications to challenge the control order regime were successful, the rulings are more important for what they appeared to permit rather than what they purported to prohibit. So although the decisions were initially welcomed as another step towards the 'normalisation' of terrorism laws, and a positive exercise of judicial power, others were making different headlines and emphasising that 'Judges Back Control Orders'. . . .

It is our contention that the control order cases reveal a deep and paradoxical respect for traditional constitutional principle, in terms of a commitment to the sovereignty of Parliament in particular, but a commitment to only a weak conception of the rule of law, giving rise to unease and concern if—as some judges now claim—'the rule of law enforced by the courts is the controlling principle upon which our constitution is based'. The weak commitment to the rule of law which the cases appear to reveal has important implications for the judicial protection of human rights, with a weak conception of the rule of law leading inexorably to low levels of protection of human rights, of which the control order decisions provide some further evidence. . . . Although we would readily concede that too much should not be made of three cases decided on the same day, these cases nevertheless represent not only sharp differences of judicial opinion about the nature of human rights protection, but also what may be the centre of judicial gravity about the place of the HRA in the contemporary constitution. The surprising vigour of parliamentary sovereignty not only provides evidence for the deep roots and unshakeable strength of the principle, but also raises questions about the most effective way of protecting human rights under the British constitution. . . .

The control order cases are important for a host of reasons, but not least because they provide us with further evidence of the nature of human rights protection, litigation and jurisprudence as we approach the 10th anniversary of the enactment of the HRA. For although the applicants succeeded in two of the three cases, as already suggested the real story about these decisions lies not in what they prohibited but in what they appeared to permit. Most notably, they continue to permit the making of control orders, which involve detention for long periods of time and restrictive non-curfew conditions, which mean that the subject is never free from severe restraint. The most striking feature of the litigation, however, is that no one thought it appropriate to argue that the regime of non-derogating control orders, as distinct from particular orders, was incompatible with human rights; that no attempt was made to secure a declaration of incompatibility on the substance of the law; and that such an attempt was made only in relation to the extreme procedural limitations under which individuals laboured before control orders were made against them . . . This failure to address control orders on the high plains of s. 4—after a flurry of excitement and misplaced optimism caused by the declaration of incompatibility in the *A* case—provides further evidence, if any were needed, of the enduring influence of the principle of parliamentary sovereignty, from which it seems impossible to break free. This failure to engage with s.4 on the substance of the control orders is thus not exceptionable, with the report of the House of Lords Constitution Committee in 2007 informing us that only one post-2000 statute had been declared incompatible by the Lords, which had also overturned a number of declarations of incompatibility made by lower courts. Despite individual judges claiming a democratic mandate to make such declarations, and despite bold rhetoric about the rule of law trumping parliamentary sovereignty, the reality is very different. . . .

What might be referred to as a diluted commitment to the rule of law thus has serious implications for the nature of the protection for human rights under the HRA. Indeed, the commitment to only a weak conception of the rule of law sees a correspondingly weak commitment to the substance of human rights. The judges have only shaved the worst features of the control order regime, and have helped to forge a regime that can only with some bewilderment be said to be one in which the human rights of the individuals in question are fully respected. On one side of the human rights balance sheet, it is true that the House of Lords has held that indefinite detention of foreign nationals without trial is not consistent with Convention rights, and that evidence obtained by torture is not admissible if the suspect is able to convince a court that on a balance of probabilities torture has been used. On the same side, it has also been held that 18-hour house arrest is not permissible and that individuals who are subject to a control order must have some knowledge of the case against them to enable them to contest the application. But as we celebrate these advances, we should also look at the other side of the balance sheet and ask what has been achieved for the individuals who were successful in these different cases. Although we cannot be sure because of the anonymity of the parties involved, it remains possible that individuals who started on this long journey of litigation some seven years ago remain in detention, albeit under house arrest in an 'open prison' rather than internment in a closed institution (albeit one with three walls in the memorably shocking analysis of the government's lawyers in the *Belmarsh* case). Although it may be argued that house arrest for fixed periods of indefinite number is better than indefinite imprisonment, what has been secured in terms of the quality of detention has been surrendered in terms of the breadth of detention, with the control orders applying to British as well as non-British nationals. While it is also true that the courts also managed to reduce detention under control orders from 18 to 16 hours a day, the settlement on 16 hours as being a permissible period during which people can be detained in accordance with their human rights emboldened the government perversely to consider 'strengthening some existing orders' with a view to increasing the period of detention of those who were being detained for less. . . .

So after the excitement following the *Belmarsh* case, normal service appears thus to have been resumed, in terms of the approach of the courts. The approach is not necessarily improper or inappropriate, but so profound is the respect by the judges for the continuing sovereignty of Parliament that even parliamentary institutions appear unhappy with the approach of the Bench, which indicates the limitations of the strategy of protection of human rights by the HRA. The prevailing pull of parliamentary sovereignty and the corresponding weakness of the rule of law which these cases reveal, have implications for public policy on the development of human rights protection. If the courts are to continue to defer to the sovereignty of Parliament and if the rule of law is to be a fairly 'weak reed' in this 'dismal swamp', it makes sense to focus attention on Parliament rather than the courts as a source of restraint on the executive. The problem of liberty in the British constitution is a symptom of the problem of institutional power, which will not be addressed by rights, lawyers or judges, heretical to some though such claims may be. The problem of institutional power is a political problem rather than a legal one, and it is a problem of how best to constrain the power of the executive by building up the countervailing power of Parliament, with strategies that will enable Parliament more easily politically to use the legal powers at its disposal. As ministers have made clear, although we have the JCHR and although MPs and peers may make use of the HRA and decisions there under, the government acts on its own legal advice, and not on the legal advice it receives from Parliament or its committees, however eminent their membership. As a result, the HRA only marginally adds to the power of Parliament, which is more likely to be moved by human rights concerns based on principle rather than legality, hardly surprising in view of the contested nature of Convention rights (as the control order cases vividly demonstrate). In any event, as we have seen, it is unlikely that the HRA or the JCHR will lead to a major change of policy on human rights grounds. The control order cases strongly suggest also that the HRA cannot adequately protect human rights, with a divided and now unpredictable court. Intoxicated by the heady brew of rights talk, some have argued that this shows we need even more rights; a more sober response might be that, on the contrary, it shows nothing of the kind; rather, it shows a need instead for less loose talk about 'rights', and more serious talk about how to create powerful representative institutions."

Questions

1. Does the Human Rights Act strike the right balance between rights of individuals and the supremacy of Parliament?

2. Do you think that the Law Lords have appropriately upheld the rule of law in their response to anti-terrorism legislation? Should the Law Lords have *deferred* to the "wisdom" of Parliament in the area of national security? Should they have been less deferential?

3. Do you think "control orders" in themselves are incompatible with the protection of human rights?

Finally, we return to the reform of the judiciary which has been a result largely of the Human Rights Act. This is a recent development, as Darbyshire explains.

Penny Darbyshire, *Darbyshire on the English Legal System*, 9th edn, (London: Sweet and Maxwell, 2008), pp.157–158; 165–166:

"The Constitutional Reform Act replace[d] the House of Lords Appellate Committee with a Supreme Court for the United Kingdom in 2009. . . . [T]his Act results from the Government announcement in 2003 that it was determined to reform the constitution, by abolishing the Lord Chancellor, reforming judicial appointments and moving the law lords into a Supreme Court. Their aim was, according to the Lord Chancellor, Lord Falconer, to 'put the relationship between Parliament, the Government and judges on a modern footing. We will have a proper separation of powers and we will further strengthen the independence of the judiciary. . . . The time has come to cease asking the law lords to try to fulfil two increasingly incompatible roles.'

The problem with the law lords, apart from their inclusion of the Lord Chancellor . . . was their place in the legislature and consequent danger that they could be involved in debates on Bills which they might later have to have to interpret and apply in court. Further, despite the constitutional convention that law lords should not take part in political debates in the House of Lords chamber, some law lords had done so. Both in reality and in appearance, the law lords breached the separation of judicial and legislative power required by the European Convention on Human Rights. Senior Law Lord Tom Bingham and his eminent colleague Johan Steyn had both advocated the establishment of a Supreme Court in prominent 2001–2002 speeches and elsewhere.

Although they acknowledged that they represented a minority opinion among the law lords in 2003, the Government was persuaded by their arguments. Lord Steyn invoked the words of the famous constitutional-ist Walter Bagehot, that 'the Supreme Court of the English people . . . ought not to be hidden beneath the robes of a legislative assembly'. He was alarmed at the confusion of functions in the eyes of the public and foreign observers, reminding us that when the law lords delivered their judgments in the first *Pinochet* case, in the Lords' chamber, foreign television viewers thought that Lady Thatcher was part of the dissenting minor-ity, opposing the extradition of General Pinochet in 1998. Acknowledging that law lords now seldom spoke in House of Lords debates, he argued that their privilege to do so was no longer defensible. We needed an inde-pendent Supreme Court which would 'in the eyes of the public carry a badge of independence and neutrality . . . a potent symbol of the rule of law' . . .

Part 3 of the Constitutional Reform Act 2005 provides for a new Supreme Court, and transfers to it the judicial functions of the appellate committee of the House of Lords and the devolution jurisdiction of the Judicial Committee of the Privy Council. . . . The Court consists of 12 judges appointed by her Majesty, under letters patent. The number can be increased by Order in Council. The Court will have a President and Deputy President and the others are to be called Justices of the Supreme Court. The Act provides that the existing Lords of Appeal, law lords, will be the first Justices of the Supreme Court. Selection and appointment of new Justices is provided for in some detail, in Part 3 of the Act. . . . The bench should generally consist of an uneven number of judges and a minimum of three. Acting judges may be appointed, to supplement the permanent Justices, drawn from the CA or equivalent in Scotland and Northern Ireland and from a supplementary panel consisting effectively of the same people who could have sat as Lords of Appeal. The Court may appoint and hear from a special adviser. The Court's rules are to be made by the President, with a view to securing that the Court is "accessible fair and efficient" and they must be 'both simple and simply expressed'. They have already been drafted, after consultation. The Lord Chancellor must appoint a Chief Executive, in consultation with the President of the Supreme Court, and the President may appoint other staff. The CE has already been appointed. The Lord Chancellor is responsible for providing an appropriate building and resources. The selected building is Middlesex Guildhall, across Parliament Square from the Palaces of Westminster. It is very contentious, since the law lords wanted a dedicated new building, not a converted Crown Court. Also, it has annoyed building histo-rians and conservationists since they consider its interiors to have been one of the most important examples of gothic revivalist architecture.

The Act lays down the rules as to precedent. An appeal from one jurisdiction in the UK will not be binding on the courts of another UK jurisdiction so a Scottish appeal would not be binding on England and Wales. In devolution proceedings, however, all cases are binding throughout the UK, except on the Court itself.

The statute is silent on the details of procedure and, indeed, on the court's power to select cases it wishes to hear so the Justices will be free to devise their own practice. . . .

As a final reminder, it is important to understand that this is not a Supreme Court like that of the US, with power to strike down unconstitutional legislation, although some of the Court's decisions in Community law and human rights will inevitably have that effect."

The Importance of the independence of the judiciary as the rationale for the new Supreme Court is explored by Woodhouse. Note, though, that independence is a relative concept in terms of the judiciary's relationship with the other branches of government.

Diana Woodhouse, "The Constitutional Reform Act 2005—Defending Judicial Independence the English Way" (2007) 5 *International Journal of Constitutional Law* 153 at 156–159; 163–164:

"In most modern democratic societies the need for judicial independence tends to be taken as a constitutional given, and the phrase is used as if there were consensus about its meaning and requirements. Most would agree that its purpose is to ensure that judges can fulfill their two functions of (*a*) protecting citizens from the arbitrary use of power by government and (*b*) impartially resolving disputes, whether between individuals or between individuals and the state. Even so, there are differences in emphasis. In countries where judges undertake constitutional review, the primary importance of judicial independence may lie in ensuring that governments act in accordance with a constitution. In the U.K., the focus tends to be on the courts' autonomy in upholding the rule of law and, more recently, in protecting human rights, and in 'preserv[ing]' the judge's impartiality whatever the case in which he or she has to deal and whatever the circumstances.' Regardless of the weight accorded to any one specific aspect, judicial independence is not something to which judges can lay claim to as a privilege for themselves; it is, rather, 'a right of the people and of a person and a duty of the judiciary and a judge.' In addition to serving the interests of the individual case, such independence serves the wider purpose of maintaining public confidence in the system of justice and in the system of government. Thus, judicial independence may be seen more appropriately as a means to several ends rather than as an end in itself, with its constitutional value deriving from those ends.

From this it follows that the meaning and requirements of judicial independence will vary according to the settings in which it is exercised. Major differences will emerge depending on the changing judicial context; for example, between a court of first instance, where the judge is deciding questions of fact and applying the law according to precedent, and the highest appellate court, where the judge decides questions of public policy and creates binding precedent, as the new Supreme Court will do. There are differences, as well, between civil and criminal courts, with the latter generally regarded as endowed with the highest degree of independence. Moreover, the meaning of judicial independence will vary with the prevailing judicial culture. Because there is no one ideal model to which all subscribe, determining 'what the principle means in a given country during a specific period requires attention to the historical and political context in which it operates.'

In the U.K., the present context is very different from that of fifty years ago, say, and is changed further by the CRA. The debate around the act's passage put on display a lack of agreement regarding the role of judges and their relationship with the other arms of government, both of which are factors that determine how much and what kind of judicial independence is required and that inform the mechanisms appropriate for its defense. Against this background, it is not surprising that, in common with constitutional and legislative provisions elsewhere, the CRA provides no definition of judicial independence. Section 1, which seeks to protect judges from politicians' attempts to interfere with or otherwise influence particular decisions, implies that this protection attaches primarily to the judge hearing a case, although the degree of independence possessed by the individual judge making a decision is—again unsurprisingly—not articulated and thus open to interpretation and dispute.

What is clear is that the act does not support the notion that judicial independence requires institutional autonomy. The new Supreme Court will, like all other courts in England and Wales, depend on the Department of Constitutional Affairs not only for its funding but also for the full range of administrative support and services, including human resources, property management, and IT. This contrasts, for instance, with the High Court of Australia, which, while still reliant upon the government for its budget, is self-administering and undertakes these functions for itself. Within the confines of the resources allocated, Australia's Court therefore has greater autonomy than is intended for the U.K.'s new court. The CRA does recognize the need for adequate funding and for judicial consultation on matters concerning the administration of justice, and, in a new move, it provides for judicial concerns on these issues to be reported to Parliament by the lord chief justice; nonetheless, the model of judicial independence the act presents is limited, particularly when compared with arrangements in some other jurisdictions, such as Australia.

The act is also silent as to what constitutes a threat to judicial independence or how to conduct a defense against such a threat. There is a range of generally accepted measures intended to protect judges from potentially dangerous pressures, including, most obviously, provisions relating to appointment, tenure, and remuneration, which, in England as elsewhere, have long been provided by legislation.

However, many of the U.K. protections, including those that police the boundary between the executive and the judiciary and govern the external activities of judges, rely on understandings, conventions, and guidance rather than statutory provisions and enforceable codes. Thus, these protections depend on a commonality of purpose and shared values across various political, institutional, and judicial cultures. Assuming this commonality exists, such mechanisms may be more effective in protecting judicial independence than more formal structures, and in the past this may have been the case. However, developments in government–such as the emphasis on public management and efficiency, changes in the role and focus of the judiciary making it more outward-looking, and increased public expectations coupled with a decline in public trust–mean that the relationships that have promoted a sharing of values are changing. Commonality of purpose can no longer be assumed. This became evident in the late 1980s when senior judges publicly opposed some of the reforming policies of the lord chancellor and, more recently, when they spoke out against the lord chancellor's intention to abolish his own office, as originally proposed in the Constitutional Reform Bill. For their part, lords chancellor have expressed disquiet about the way in which the courts are interpreting the Human Rights Act 1998 and have called for judges to exercise restraint. . . .

As for the English situation, requiring lord chancellors to defend judicial independence as it relates to the core requirements–appointment, tenure, and salaries–is one matter, although there may still be disputes in this area. To expect them to defend judges from political criticism, on the basis that such criticism undermines judicial independence, is quite another, not only because of the transformed office of lord chancellor but also because of questions as to when such a defense is needed. In the U.K., as in Australia, there is the possibility, even probability, of disagreement in this regard between lord chancellors and judges; moreover, one will likely see lord chancellors seeking to limit their role, as the Australian attorney general did, to circumstances they see as exceptional, whatever the judges' characterization of the circumstances might be. Indeed, section 1(4)(a) allows for this, in its stipulation that lord chancellors should 'have regard' for the need to defend judicial independence. This is not the same as requiring them to defend it, and their perception of 'need' may be very different from that of the members of the judiciary.

The CRA would seem, therefore, to afford less statutory protection than has been portrayed by the government; the judges may find that they themselves will have to take some responsibility for the defense of their independence. The CRA provides a mechanism through which such a defense could operate, as it confers on the lord chief justice, as head of the judiciary, the right to bring matters of concern relating to the administration of justice to the attention of Parliament. The effect on judicial independence of politicians' public criticism of judges could presumably be just such a matter of concern, although this has yet to be proved.

The best defense for judicial independence, however, may be greater accountability and openness. Calls by politicians, the media, and academics for judges to be more accountable have increased as the judicial role has expanded. Mechanisms that provide for managerial and financial accountability, personal accountability, process accountability, and–most controversially–for content or substantive accountability are, to varying degrees, already in place. To be subject to public criticism by elected representatives, even when that criticism is unfair, may also be seen as a way of holding tenured judges to account, rather than as an attack on judicial independence.

In addition, the CRA establishes a 'judicial appointments and conduct ombudsman,' an office that will strengthen the complaints system already in existence. It also provides for the new Supreme Court to be more accountable than the House of Lords, requiring the Court's chief executive to produce an annual report. While the focus of that exercise will be on administrative efficiency, the judges will, nevertheless, be implicated in their Court's performance, particularly where this relates to the throughput of cases, which they could be under pressure from the government and the public to improve. This requirement, in itself, could be portrayed as an interference with their independence, there being a thin line between efficiency—about which the government and the public should have opinion—and the discretion of the Court to determine how best to dispose of the case in front of it. More controversially, because the new Court will be separate from the legislature and the lord chancellor will no longer be head of the judiciary and thus answerable to Parliament for matters relating to the judges, the Supreme Court could be under pressure for its president to appear before a committee of Parliament, perhaps alongside the lord chief justice, to answer questions about trends and developments in the law and the administration of justice. Such accountability and transparency, which are not provided for in the CRA, have the potential for proving a better protection of judicial independence than that offered by a government minister whose loyalty is first and foremost to the government and his or her cabinet colleagues."

Question

Do you think that the creation of the Supreme Court enhances judicial independence? In what ways? Is this adequate? Was there a problem in the first place?

Useful website addresses

Ministry of Justice, Human Rights, *http://www.justice.gov.uk/about/human-rights.htm* [Accessed May 12, 2010]

Supreme Court of the United Kingdom, *http://www.supremecourt.gov.uk* [Accessed May 12, 2010]

European Court of Human Rights, *http://www.echr.coe.int* [Accessed May 12, 2010]

National Council for Civil Liberties, *http://www.liberty-human-rights.org.uk* [Accessed May 12, 2010]

Justice, the British Section of the International Commission of Jurists, *http://www.justice.org.uk* [Accessed May 12, 2010]

Electoral Commission, *http://www.electoralcommission.gov.uk* [Accessed May 12, 2010]

The Electoral Reform Society, *http://www.electoral-reform.org.uk* [Accessed May 12, 2010]

The Hansard Society, *http://www.hansard-society.org.uk* [Accessed May 12, 2010]

3

CONSTITUTIONAL ASPECTS OF LEGAL METHOD: JUDICIAL REVIEW

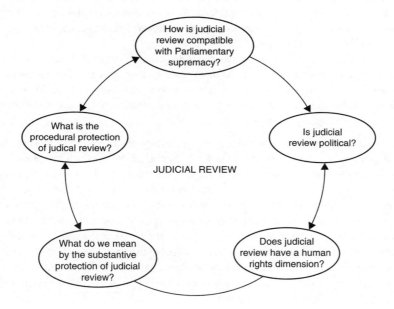

This chapter looks at judicial review, one of the fundamental constitutional doctrines. In order to understand our legal method and system, a basic comprehension of the idea of judicial review is important. It is one of the principal ways in which judges control the actions of the government, ensuring that it acts in accordance with the law. By the end of this chapter, you should:

- understand the basic concept of judicial review and how it fits within the rule of law;
- recognise why judicial review has sometimes appeared to undermine the actions of democratically elected governments;
- appreciate why judicial review can be politically controversial;
- understand the difficulty of reconciling the principle of Parliamentary supremacy with judicial review and the rule of law;
- recognise that the Human Rights Act has created new opportunities for judges to review the actions of the government;
- appreciate the difficulty of distinguishing between public and private actors and functions.

I. JUDICIAL REVIEW AND THE RULE OF LAW

The basis for judicial review can be found in the fundamental tenets of the rule of law. For Dicey, the role of the judiciary was to ensure that power was not exercised by governments in an arbitrary, "lawless" fashion. Judicial review, it is argued, is the means by which judges ensure that power is exercised in conformity with the authority granted by Parliament under statute.

Jeffrey Jowell, "The rule of law today" in Jeffrey Jowell and Dawn Oliver (eds), *The Changing Constitution*, **5th edn (Oxford: Oxford University Press, 2004), pp.19–23:**

"How does the Rule of Law operate in practice in the United Kingdom? Let us first note that our courts have not, outside of directly effective European Law, felt themselves able to review the validity of primary legislation. This means that a principle like the Rule of Law *can* be expressly overridden by Parliament. But the absence of judicial review of primary legislation is by no means fatal to the Rule of Law. As a constitutional principle it still serves as a basis for evaluation of laws and a critical focus for public debate. A British government may succeed in introducing detention without trial, or retroactive legislation, but strong justification is needed for such a law to withstand the Rule of Law's moral strictures.

While the sovereignty of Parliament prevails over the Rule of Law the courts will not permit the Rule of Law to stand in the way of Parliament's clear intent. However, the courts will seek to reconcile the two constitutional principles where it is possible to do so. They do this by assuming that Parliament intended to abide by the Rule of Law which it may only override by clear words or by necessary implication. This approach upholds what has been called the 'principle of legality'. Lord Hoffman put it thus:

> Parliamentary sovereignty means that Parliament can, if it chooses, legislate contrary to fundamental principles of human rights. The Human Rights Act 1998 will not detract from this power. The constraints upon its exercise by Parliament are ultimately political, not legal. But the principle of legality means that Parliament must squarely confront what it is doing and accept the political cost. Fundamental rights cannot be overridden by general or ambiguous words. This is because there is too great a risk that the full implications of their unqualified meaning may have passed unnoticed in the democratic process. In the absence of express language or necessary implication to the contrary, the courts therefore presume that even the most general words were intended to be subject to the basic rights of the individual. In this way the courts of the United Kingdom, though acknowledging the sovereignty of Parliament, apply principles of constitutionality little different from those which exist in countries where the power of the legislature is expressly limited by a constitutional document.

The practical implementation of the Rule of Law takes place primarily through judicial review of the actions of public officials. It is elaborated and given specific content when courts evaluate the exercise of discretionary powers conferred by Parliament on the executive and others exercising public functions. What have emerged as the three principal 'grounds' of judicial review themselves rest in large part on the Rule of Law. The first ground, that of 'illegality', is designed to ensure that officials act within the scope of their lawful powers. The courts ensure that the official decisions do not stray beyond the 'four corners' of a statute by failing to take into account 'relevant' considerations (that is, considerations which the law requires), or by taking into account 'irrelevant' considerations (that is, considerations outside the object and purpose that Parliament intended the statute to pursue). This exercise is a clear instance of the implementation of the Rule of Law, whereby the courts act as guardians of Parliament's true intent and purpose.

The second ground of review, that of 'procedural propriety', requires decision-makers to be unbiased and to grant a fair hearing to claimants before depriving them of a right or significant interest (such as an interest in livelihood or reputation). We have seen that the right not to be condemned unheard is a central feature of the Rule of Law, which the courts presume Parliament to respect. Even where a statute is silent on the matter, the courts will insist that the 'justice of the common law' (which incorporates the principle of the Rule of Law) supplies the omission of the legislature.

Over the past few years, the courts have implied a requirement of a fair hearing even where the claimant does not possess a threatened right or interest. A hearing will be required where a 'legitimate expectation' has been induced by the decisionmaker. In such a case the claimant has, expressly or impliedly, been promised either a hearing or the continuation of the benefit. The courts will not sanction the disappointment of such an expectation unless the claimant is permitted to make representations on the matter. The notion of the legitimate expectation is itself rooted in that aspect of the Rule of Law which requires legal certainty.

The third ground of judicial review, 'irrationality' or 'unreasonableness', is more difficult to fit into the Rule of Law in so far as it governs the substance and not merely the procedure of official action. Suppose the police charge only bearded drivers, or drivers of a particular race, with traffic offences? Suppose an education authority chose to dismiss all teachers with red hair? Suppose a prison officer refused to permit a prisoner to communicate with his lawyer? Suppose a minister raised the minimum sentence of a prisoner, having earlier told him that the sentence would be set at a lower level? Would these decisions offend the Rule of Law? If so, the Rule of Law becomes a substantive doctrine and not merely procedural. Our courts, through judicial review, tread warily in this area, carefully deferring to the primary decision maker and interfering only if, on the authority of the *Wednesbury* case, the decision was manifestly unreasonable. Nowadays, where human rights are in issue, the courts may adopt stricter scrutiny of the decision, but in general judges are cautious about second-guessing administrators on matters where they possess limited expertise.

The practical implementation of the Rule of Law over the years makes it clear that it is a substantive and not merely a procedural principle. A local authority which withdrew the licence of a rugby club whose members had visited South Africa during the apartheid regime fell foul of the principle in the form of the doctrine that there should be no punishment where there was no law (since sporting contacts with South Africa were not then prohibited). Access to justice has been upheld in a case where a prison governor had refused a prisoner access to his lawyer. The Lord Chancellor's imposition of substantial court fees were held unlawfully to impede access to the courts. The legitimate expectation has been upheld in its substantive form (grounding a right not merely to a fair hearing but to a promised benefit itself). For example, in the case of *Pierson*, it was held that, despite the fact that the Home Secretary had discretion to set a prisoner's tariff (the minimum sentence prior to parole), the decision to increase the tariff retrospectively—contrary to an earlier indication that the lesser sentence would be imposed—offended the Rule of Law in its substantive sense. Lord Steyn in that case said:

> Parliament does not legislate in a vacuum. Parliament legislates for a European liberal democracy based upon the tradition of the common law . . . and . . . unless there is the clearest provision to the contrary, Parliament must not be presumed to legislate contrary to the Rule of Law.

In a more recent case it was held that a local authority, which promised the claimants a 'home for life' in an institution for the chronically sick, was not permitted to disappoint the resultant legitimate expectation.

Cases such as these demonstrate the inherent elasticity of the Rule of Law. A recent case raised a novel point. It concerned the legal effect of a decision which had not been communicated to the person affected. The relevant legislation permitted an asylum-seeker's right to income support to be terminated once his or her asylum had been refused by a 'determination' of the Home Secretary. The refusal in this case was recorded only in an internal file note in the Home Office and communicated to the Benefits Agency, which promptly denied the appellant future income support. The determination was not, however, communicated to the appellant.

The appellant in this case could not easily invoke the normal requirement of the Rule of Law in her favour. The decision did not take effect retrospectively; ignorance of the law does not normally excuse its application, and the doctrine of prior notice normally applied only to permit the appellant to make representations on the case to the primary decisionmaker (here the Home Secretary). Nevertheless, the House of Lords, by majority, held that the decision violated 'the constitutional principle requiring the Rule of Law to be observed'.

Lord Steyn, with whom the majority of their Lordships concurred, based his argument both upon legal certainty ('surprise is the enemy of justice') and upon accountability: the individual must be informed so 'she can decide what to do' and 'be in a position to challenge the decision in the courts' (this being an aspect of the principle of the right of access to justice).

The House of Lords had no truck with the notion that the Home Secretary's determination had strictly been made. This was 'legalism and conceptualism run riot', which is reminiscent of the state described by Kafka 'where the rights of an individual are overridden by hole in the corner decisions or knocks on doors in the early hours'.

The Rule of Law does, therefore, possess substantive content. It is a principle that promotes certainty, regularity, and access to justice, as well as the virtues of official rationality and integrity. It thus advances procedural as well as substantive goals. Being a principle rather than a specific rule, it requires elaboration in the light of the practical reason of each generation and the developing imperatives of contemporary democracy."

Question

How does judicial review forward both a procedural and a substantive conception of the rule of law?

Jowell hints at the possibility that judicial review, at times, may appear to involve the judiciary substituting its view of appropriate public policy for that which has been implemented by officials of government. In those situations, the judiciary appears to be exercising a highly *political* function. Moreover, the politics of the judiciary has sometimes appeared to be very conservative. A "classic" example of judicial review which seemed to tread very close to party politics occurred in the early 1980s:

Bromley London Borough Council v Greater London Council and another [1982] 1 All E.R. 129, CA.

[This case was a judicial review of the action of the Greater London Council (GLC) in attempting to reduce fares on London Transport by 25 per cent. Bromley London Borough Council brought the proceedings, asking the courts to stop the implementation of the policy (which required substantial increases in rates) on the grounds that it was beyond the powers of the GLC as defined by the relevant statutes of Parliament or, alternatively, that the policy implementation was an invalid exercise of the GLC's discretion provided under statute. The Divisional Court refused the application, but the Borough Council appealed to the Court of Appeal.]

Lord Denning M.R.:

Introduction in outline
"On 7 May 1981 there was an election for the Greater London Council (the GLC). In advance of the election, the Labour Party issued a manifesto. In it they promised that, if they won, they would within six months cut the fares on London's buses and tubes by 25%. They did win the election. They kept their promise. They told the London Transport Executive (the LTE) to cut the fares by 25%. The travelling public were well pleased with the gift. It meant millions of pounds in their pockets instead of in the ticket machines. But not the ratepayers of London. They were required to contribute £69m to pay for it. In order to enforce payment, the GLC made a supplementary precept. This was an order directed to all the 35 London boroughs commanding them to raise the necessary funds. They were to do it by making a supplementary rate on all the ratepayers. The London boroughs have most reluctantly obeyed. They have made the supplementary rate and have required their ratepayers to pay it. But meanwhile one London borough, Bromley, has challenged the validity of the whole procedure. They apply to the courts for an order of certiorari to quash the supplementary precept.

At the outset I would say that all three members of this court are interested on all sides. We are all fare-paying passengers on the tubes and buses and benefit from the 25% cut in fares. My wife and I also have the benefit of senior citizens to travel free. We are all ratepayers in the area of Greater London and have to pay the increase in rates imposed by the supplementary precept. No objection is taken by any party to our hearing the case. Any Court of Appeal would be likewise placed.

Now for the detail

The manifesto

In March 1981 the Greater London Labour Party issued a manifesto headed 'Socialist Policy for the GLC'. It filled a printed book of some 180 pages containing detailed proposals and promises. At the same time they issued a summarised version headed 'Vote Labour in London May 7th'. It was priced at 30p. It filled a printed booklet of 14 pages of close print. It said in the foreword: 'All candidates are committed to the proposals and pledges contained in the manifesto.' It set out proposals for action on jobs, on housing, on transport, on the environment, on safety and on recreation. On transport it made this pledge:

'*Fares*. Within six months of winning the election, Labour will cut fares on London Transport buses and tubes by an average of 25%. At the same time a much simpler system of fares will be introduced, one which will be easy to understand, will allow faster boarding and will ease the burden on transport workers. There will then be a freeze on fares for four years. The existing system of free travel for senior citizens on London's buses will be extended to the tubes and British Rail services within London.'

There was a paragraph dealing with the cost of all the proposals, taken together. It was headed '*Paying for the Programme*':

'Labour presents this programme in the full knowledge of its financial implications. As more than half of the GLC's rate revenue comes from the commercial sector, individual householders will only be paying about £1 a week more by 1983/4 for cheaper fares, better public transport services, less congestion, better housing, more jobs, and a safer, cleaner environment. For example, regular users of London Transport will benefit by £1.50 a week.'

The effect of the election

At the election of 7 May 1981 the Labour Party won by a small majority of seats. This was interpreted by their spokesmen on many occasions as giving them a 'clear mandate' from the people of London to cut the fares by 25%. Not only as giving them a mandate but also as a 'promise' and also a 'commitment' by which they promised and committed themselves to implementing a reduction in fares by 25% overall.

The leader of the council gives instructions

The election was on Thursday, 7 May. They lost no time. On Tuesday, 12 May 1981 there was a meeting between Mr Kenneth Livingstone, the leader of the council, and Sir Peter Masefield, the chairman of the LTE. There is no record of what took place, but Dunn LJ inferred, and certainly reasonably inferred, that 'the leader told Sir Peter that the GLC intended to put into immediate effect the policy of overall reduction of fares of 25% and asked him to produce proposals for a new fare structure to implement the policy and a revised budget for 1981'.

This inference is supported by a report of 2 June which recorded that:

'The Leader of the Council has instructed London Transport to submit to the Transport Committee at their meeting on 1 July 1981 fares proposals which incorporate a proposal for an immediate reduction in London Transport fares of 25%.'

That is the very word, 'instructed': 'The Leader of the Council has instructed London Transport . . .'

Those instructions were duly carried out. On 9 June 1981 London Transport submitted a memorandum and issued a press release saying that the GLC had made a '*requirement* of a 25 per cent overall cut' and put forward alternative methods of implementing that requirement. I stress again the words 'requirement of the GLC'.

The block grant

Whilst the LTE was arranging for the 25% cut, the officers of the GLC were looking into the effect on the rates. They then drew to the attention of the GLC that the ratepayers would suffer a heavy penalty. It would lose the block grant which the government gave it. So they would have to pay not only for the cut in fares but also for the loss of the grant. That was pointed out on 23 June 1981 by the comptroller of finance. In a report of that date he said:

'. . . The Council faces a loss of block grant of £91 million under the block grant system for a decision to finance £110 million revenue costs from rates instead of fares. Therefore, the Council has to decide not only how to finance the operating shortfall in 1981–82 but whether rate payers should pay a heavy penalty . . . the Council is faced with the fact that . . . the rate payers will pay heavily . . .'

This was nothing more nor less than a plea by the officers that the ratepayers should be considered. But it fell on deaf ears. Notwithstanding the clear warning, the GLC decided at a meeting on 7 July 1981 to implement the cut in full regardless of the heavy penalty on the ratepayers. It had before it a report saying that it was necessary to 'implement the *commitment* to reduce fares by an overall 25 per cent'. This meant the levy of a supplementary rate precept. The whole was to take effect by 4 October 1981. That recommendation was approved by a majority of 43 to 33.

The final steps are taken

On 21 July 1981 the GLC did all that was necessary to complete the cut and to issue a supplementary precept. In advance of it, it issued a press release which is most illuminating. It put all the blame on the government. I will quote two sentences from it:

'The bill to ratepayers for the GLC's cutting of bus and Tube fares by 25 per cent and keeping London Transport out of the red will be a 6.1p rate—"as predicted during the GLC election campaign", announced Dr. Tony Hart, Chairman of the Council's Finance and General Purposes Committee, today. But "vindictive" Government policies over local council grants will double the cost to ratepayers without any benefit to Londoners.'

The press release is worth reading in full. All I would say is that it shows that the Labour Party in their manifesto had reckoned only on a 6.1p increase in the rates; but also that in point of fact it would have to be 11.9p in the rates. So their calculations during the course of the election have all been falsified by events since the election in regard to the block grant. Nevertheless they determined to press on with their cut and the precept, regardless of the penal blow it would inflict on the ratepayers. It was carried by 42 to 38 on 21 July 1981.

The supplementary precept is issued

On 22 July 1981 the GLC issued to all the London boroughs a supplementary precept for 1981–82. It said:

'The Greater London Council hereby require you to levy in respect of the current year the rates specified below:
    General London Purposes at 6.1 new pence in the pound (chargeable on the whole of Greater London).'

Then there is this significant addition about the loss of the block grant:

'The supplementary precepts issued are gross precepts and therefore take no account of the GLC or ILEA block grant losses consequent on the issue of the supplementary precepts. Authorities are therefore recommended to levy an additional rate for grant loss . . . .'

The London Borough of Bromley received that precept on 28 July. They took legal advice and decided to challenge it. They telephoned the GLC on 10 August and told it so. Then on 11 September they issued proceedings in the courts.

The law

This brings me to the law. It was divided in the argument in two parts. First, the statutory powers of the GLC. Second, the way it exercised its powers.

The statutory powers of the GLC

We have studied in detail the provisions of the Transport (London) Act 1969. I will state the result. The LTE is a statutory corporation, a body corporate. It is entrusted with the task of running the buses and tubes of London. It is its duty to run it on business lines. It must manage its income and expenditure so as to break even so far as practicable. If it cannot pay its way, the GLC can make grants to it to keep it going. The GLC have a degree of control over it, but it is of a limited character. The GLC can give it general directions on matters of policy (see s.11(1)) but it cannot interfere with the day-to-day running of its affairs. But even those matters of policy are not open-ended. They are confined to policies which will 'promote the process of integrated, efficient and economic transport facilities and services for Greater London' (see s.1(1)). This includes the objectives of quick, frequent, reliable services, and reasonable fares. But it does not include the promotion of social or philanthropic or political objectives. It does not include free travel for all. It does not include a reduction in fares which is completely uneconomic. The word 'economic' is significant. It means what we all mean when we say of a financial proposal, 'That is not an economic proposition,' meaning that under it expenditure will exceed the income. It certainly does not warrant the instruction given here to cut fares by 25%.

Apart from this fundamental point, the statute contains specific provisions about fares. The LTE is the charging authority, not the GLC. The LTE has in the first instance to settle the general level and structure of the fares to be charged. These are subject to the approval of the GLC. If the GLC approve, they are to be published. If the GLC disapprove, then there is this important provision in s.11(3):

> '. . . the Council may direct the Executive to submit proposals for an alteration in the Executive's fare arrangements to achieve any object of general policy specified by the Council in the direction.'

Any such direction has by s.41(3) to be in writing. No such direction was given in this case.

Furthermore, when the LTE is settling the general level and structure of fares, it must consider the position of those parts of its undertaking which fall outside the London area. It must consult the county councils concerned and see if they are prepared to make any contribution to the cost. No such consultation was held in this case.

In view of these considerations, I am of opinion that the GLC had no power whatever to give instructions to the LTE as it purported to do. The leader had no right whatever to go to Sir Peter Masefield and tell him to cut the fares by an overall 25%; nor had Sir Peter any business to accede to it. The GLC itself had no power to make resolutions to enforce a 25% cut. That was a completely uneconomic proposition done for political motives, for which there is no warrant; including the supplementary precept. It was beyond its powers. It is ultra vires and void. It cannot be allowed to stand.

The way it exercised its powers

In case I am wrong on that point, I go on to consider whether the GLC exercised its powers properly.

It appears to me that the GLC owed a duty both to the travelling public and to the ratepayers. Its duty to the travelling public is to provide an integrated, efficient and economic service at reasonable fares. Its duty to the ratepayers is to charge them as much as is reasonable and no more. In carrying out those duties, the members of the GLC have to balance the two conflicting interests: the interest of the travelling public in cheap fares and the interest of the ratepayers in not being overcharged. The members of the GLC have to hold the balance between these conflicting interests. They have to take all relevant considerations into account on either side. They must not be influenced by irrelevant considerations. They must not give undue weight to one consideration over another, lest they upset the balance. They must hold the balance fairly and reasonably. If they come to a decision which is, in all the circumstances, unjust and unreasonable, then the courts can and should interfere. . . .

[T]he majority of the GLC gave altogether undue weight to the following consideration. They had issued a manifesto in which they had promised to cut the fares on London Transport by 25%. They regarded the election result as giving them a *mandate* to fulfil that promise. They regarded themselves as *committed* to the implementation of that promise. They were determined to 'honour' that commitment, come what may. They afterwards discovered that it would injure the ratepayers severely, far more severely than they had realised when they made the promise. It would injure the ratepayers because of the loss of the block grant. This loss has doubled the burden on the ratepayers. But nevertheless the majority of the GLC determined to go ahead with the cut of 25% irrespective of the penalising hardship on the ratepayers.

In giving such weight to the manifesto, I think the majority of the GLC were under a complete misconception. A manifesto issued by a political party, in order to get votes, is not to be taken as gospel. It is not to be regarded as a bond, signed, sealed and delivered. It may contain, and often does contain, promises or proposals that are quite unworkable or impossible of attainment. Very few of the electorate read the manifesto in full. A goodly number only know of it from what they read in the newspapers or hear on television. Many know nothing whatever of what it contains. When they come to the polling booth, none of them vote for the manifesto. Certainly not for every promise or proposal in it. Some may be influenced by one proposal. Others by another. Many are not influenced by it at all. They vote for a party and not for a manifesto. I have no doubt that in this case many ratepayers voted for the Labour Party even though, on this item alone, it was against their interests. And vice versa. It seems to me that no party can or should claim a mandate and commitment for any one item in a long manifesto. When the party gets into power, it should consider any proposal or promise afresh, on its merits, without any feeling of being obliged to honour it or being committed to it. It should then consider what is best to do in the circumstances of the case and to do it if it is practicable and fair.

Another thing is that the figure of 25% was not explained in any way whatever. No councillor has given evidence or has made an affidavit before the courts at all. It is acknowledged by the GLC that the statute does not empower it to abolish fares altogether, or to give free travel for all. But in principle I see no difference between abolishing fares altogether and cutting them by one-half or one-quarter. It is a gift to the travelling public at the expense of the general body of ratepayers. There seems to be no financial reason for choosing 25%. Why not 20% or 30% or even 50%? It seems to me that the figure of 25% was an arbitrary figure clutched from the air in order to be attractive to the electorate.

In the result I hold the GLC did not hold the balance fair. The 25% was more than fair to the travelling public and less than fair to the ratepayers. Millions of passengers on the buses and tubes come from far outside the London area. They come every day. They get the benefit of the 25% cut in fares without paying a penny on their rates at home. That is more than fair to them. It is a gift indeed to them, given without paying a penny for it. Whereas thousands of ratepayers in London who pay the rates never use the buses or tubes at all. Bromley, for instance, has no tubes. It is less than fair to them. It is positively penal. It is not fair to make these ratepayers pay for these gifts to people who come from far afield. The employees of London Transport see the 'cut' as equivalent to a money gift. They get free travel anyway. They each claimed, and got, an extra £50 because the free travel was worth less after the 'cut'. It cost £3m, all to be paid by the ratepayers.

Conclusion

My conclusion is that the actions here of the GLC went beyond its statutory powers and are null and void. Even if they were within their statutory powers, they were distorted by giving undue weight to the manifesto and by the arbitrary and unfair nature of the decision. The supplementary precept must be quashed, and a declaration made accordingly.

I realise that this must cause much consternation to the GLC and the LTE. They will be at their wits' end to know what to do. But it is their own fault. They were very foolish not to take legal advice before they embarked on this sequel to their election. Even after legal proceedings were intimated to them in August, they went ahead with their plans and put them into operation on 4 October 1981. They must unscramble the affair as best they can. At any rate, they cannot burden the ratepayers of London with this supplementary precept.

I would allow the appeal accordingly."

[Oliver L.J. and Watkins L.J. delivered separate reasons, concurring in the result reached by Lord Denning M.R. The case was appealed by the GLC to the House of Lords, which affirmed, on varied grounds, the result reached by the Court of Appeal.]

The *Bromley* decision was harshly criticised. This is because it appeared to many people to be wrong for judges to intervene in matters best left to the judgment of *elected* representatives. As well, the judiciary did not seem to appreciate the concerns which gave rise to the policy in the first place.

J.A.G. Griffith, *The Politics of the Judiciary*, 4th edn (London: HarperCollins, 1991), pp.130–131:

"In this case, the Law Lords chose to say that the GLC had not adequately taken into account the interests of the ratepayers and that the interests of the users of public transport had been unduly preferred. Such an argument can logically be applied whenever public authorities spend the ratepayers' (or the taxpayers') money to further some statutory purpose. Particular public expenditure can always be criticized on the ground that it is excessive or wrongly directed, whether on defence or education or the building of motorways or any other public service. The constitutional reply is that public authorities, being directly or indirectly elected, are the representatives of the public interest and that their function is precisely that of making such decisions. The criticism is then seen as being political and if the electors of Greater London disapprove of what is being done in their name by their representatives, the remedy lies in their hands at the next election. Nor is this merely constitutional or political theory, divorced from reality, for without doubt the election in 1985 for the GLC would have turned very largely on this issue and on the view taken of the controversial Labour administration at County Hall during its four years in office. It is surely no more the function of the judiciary to tell the GLC where the public interest lay in its spending of public money than it is the function of the judiciary to make similar arguments about spending by the Departments of the central government."

J.A.G. Griffith, *The Politics of the Judiciary*, 4th edn (London: HarperCollins, 1991), pp.302–304:

"The judgments delivered in the Court of Appeal and the House of Lords in *Bromley v GLC* demonstrate how ill-suited is judicial review to the examination of administrative policies. They show how the narrow approach of the courts to the interpretation of statutes leads to a misunderstanding of the purpose of legislation. . . .

The crisis in urban transport received popular recognition in the publication in 1963 of Colin Buchanan's *Traffic in Towns*. This was followed in 1966 by the white paper on *Transport Policy*. This emphasized the 'severe discomforts' brought by the growth of road traffic: congestion, the misery of commuter travel, noise, fumes, danger, casualties and the threat to the environment; and the need to plan, as a whole, for the related needs of industry, housing and transport. The paper drew attention to the mutually contradictory objectives of providing adequate services and self-financing.

In January 1968, the London Transport Joint Review was published and was followed in July by the white paper *Transport in London*. The Review found that the major factor underlying London Transport's recurrent financial deficit was the imbalance between peak and off-peak demand. The Review was somewhat ambiguous about the need for financial viability, but it certainly envisaged some form of grant and emphasized the social benefits of controlling the level of fares while providing proper services. *Transport in London* went further in emphasizing the need of the transport system to take account of 'the social as well as the economic needs of the country'. Subsidization through the local rates was one of the means adopted by the Transport Act 1968 for conurbations outside London and this was intended to enable the transport authorities to achieve, in part, the purpose of developing transport as a social service.

The Transport (London) Act 1969 was seen by ministers as taking this approach further. For the first time in London, the responsibility for transport was given to a directly elected local authority acting through an Executive appointed by itself. Comparison has been made with a nationalized industry operating the day-to-day management under the general directions of a minister. But the control by the GLC over the LTE was much tighter than that of a minister over the coal, gas or electricity authorities. The GLC was not merely empowered but required by section 1 'to develop policies, and to encourage, organize and, where appropriate, carry out measures'. The LTE existed to implement policies of the GLC (section 4(1)) and to act 'in accordance with principles laid down or approved by the GLC' (section 5(1)). Additionally, the GLC might give the LTE general directions in relation to functions which the GLC was under a duty to perform (section 11(1)). There were also other more detailed provisions emphasizing the powers of the GLC. Above all, the GLC's primary duty was to promote 'the provision of integrated, efficient and economic transport facilities and services for Greater London'. Finally, the LTE was required to submit to the GLC for their approval the general level and structure of the fares to be charged and the GLC might 'direct the Executive to submit proposals for an alteration in the Executive's fare arrangements to achieve any object of general policy specified by the Council in the direction' (section 11(3)). . . .

Bromley v GLC raises all the questions about the nature, the function, and the limits of judicial review. The whole method of adjudication as presently adopted by the courts is inappropriate to the consideration of political decisions affecting the distribution of costs between the tax and rate-paying public, on the one hand, and the users of public services, on the other."

Following the decision of the House of Lords in Bromley v GLC, fares doubled, and the GLC produced a new scheme, in which it directed the LTE to cut fares by 25 per cent, with an accompanying grant from the Council to the LTE to make up the lost revenues. The LTE objected, and the case was heard by the Divisional Court, which concluded that the scheme was valid because the grant allowed the LTE to balance its revenue account, and because the GLC had now considered its statutory duties. Griffith commented:

> "The new scheme, upheld by the Divisional Court in the later case, was made under the same statute and did not appreciably hold a different balance between ratepayers and transport users. The decision of the Divisional Court bears the marks of a rescue operation, seeking to save some sanity for transport policy in London and for the right of statutory authorities to exercise statutory powers within the statutory terms given to them."[1]

Questions

1. Was Lord Denning's *substantive* approach to judicial review in *Bromley v GLC* justifiable or was it illegitimate? Defend your answer.

2. Does Lord Denning's judgment seem more "political" than "legal"? Could a judgment have been written in this case which did not seem political?

3. In 1984 the Conservative Government announced its intention to introduce legislation to abolish the GLC, and under the Local Government Act 1985 the abolition took effect on April 1, 1986. Do you think that decision is consistent with the rule of law?

In some cases, by contrast, the judiciary has been careful to avoid questioning the actions of the government, particularly in those cases where executive action is justified on the basis of "national security".

Council of Civil Service Unions and others v Minister for the Civil Service [1984] 3 All E.R. 935, HL.

Lord Fraser of Tullybelton:

"My Lords, Government Communications Headquarters (GCHQ) is a branch of the public service under the Foreign and Commonwealth Office, the main functions of which are to ensure the security of the United Kingdom military and official communications, and to provide signals intelligence for the government. These functions are of great national importance and they involve handling secret information which is vital to the national security. The main establishment of GCHQ is at Cheltenham, where over 4,000 people are employed. There are also a number of smaller out-stations, one of which is at Bude in Cornwall.

Since 1947, when GCHQ was established in its present form, all the staff employed there have been permitted, and indeed encouraged, to belong to national trade unions, and most of them did so. Six unions were represented at GCHQ. They were all members, though not the only members, of the Council of Civil Service Unions

---

[1]   J.A.G. Griffiths, *The Politics of the Judiciary*, 4th edn (London: Harper Collins, 1991) pp.135–136.

(CCSU), the first appellant. The second appellant is the secretary of CCSU. The other appellants are individuals who are employed at GCHQ and who were members of one or other of the unions represented there. A departmental Whitley Council was set up in 1947 and, until the events with which this appeal is concerned, there was a well-established practice of consultation between the official side and the trade union side about all important alterations in the terms and conditions of employment of the staff.

On 25 January 1984 all that was abruptly changed. The Secretary of State for Foreign and Commonwealth Affairs announced in the House of Commons that the government had decided to introduce with immediate effect new conditions of service for all staff at GCHQ, the effect of which was that they would no longer be permitted to belong to national trade unions but would be permitted to belong only to a departmental staff association approved by the director. The announcement came as a complete surprise to the trade unions and to the employees at GCHQ, as there had been no prior consultation with them. The principal question raised in this appeal is whether the instruction by which the decision received effect, and which was issued orally on 22 December 1983 by the respondent (who is also the Prime Minister), is valid and effective in accordance with Art.4 of the Civil Service Order in Council 1982. The respondent maintains that it is. The appellants maintain that it is invalid because there was a procedural obligation on the respondent to act fairly by consulting the persons concerned before exercising her power under Art.4 of the Order in Council, and she had failed to do so. Underlying that question, and logically preceding it, is the question whether the courts, and your Lordships' House in its judicial capacity, have power to review the instruction on the ground of a procedural irregularity, having regard peculiarly to the facts (a) that it was made in the exercise of a power conferred under the royal prerogative and not by statute and (b) that it concerned national security.

It is necessary to refer briefly to the events which led up to the decision of 22 December 1983. Between February 1979 and April 1981 industrial action was taken at GCHQ on seven occasions. The action took various forms: one-day strikes, work to rule and overtime bans. The most serious disruption occurred on 9 March 1981, when about 25% of the staff went on one-day strike and, according to Sir Robert Armstrong, the Secretary to the Cabinet, who made an affidavit in these proceedings, parts of the operations at GCHQ were virtually shut down. The appellants do not accept the respondent's view of the seriousness of the effects of industrial action on the work at GCHQ. But clearly it must have had some adverse effect, especially by causing some interruption of the constant day and night monitoring of foreign signals communications. The industrial action was taken mainly in support of national trade unions, when they were in dispute with the government about conditions of service of civil servants generally, and not about local problems at GCHQ. In 1981 especially it was part of a campaign by the national trade unions, designed to do as much damage as possible to government agencies including GCHQ. Sir Robert Armstrong in his affidavit refers to several circular letters and 'campaign reports' issued by CCSU and some of its constituent unions, which show the objectives of the campaign. . . ."

[The first and second appellants obtained leave from Glidewell J. to bring proceedings for judicial review on the basis that the instruction of December 22, 1983 was invalid. Glidewell J. found it to be invalid on the basis of a procedural irregularity in failing to consult before issuing the instruction. The Court of Appeal reversed the judge's decision and dismissed the application for judicial review. Lord Fraser considered the first issue—the reviewability of the exercise of prerogative powers, leaving the question open. He then considered the national security issue, but only after finding that, in the absence of a pressing matter of national security, a duty to consult the trade unions would be found on the basis of a legitimate expectation based on prior practice.]

"The question is one of evidence. The decision on whether the requirements of national security outweigh the duty of fairness in any particular case is for the government and not for the courts; the government alone has access to the necessary information, and in any event the judicial process is unsuitable for reaching decisions on national security. . . .

The evidence in support of this part of the respondent's case came from Sir Robert Armstrong in his first affidavit . . . . [I]t does set out the respondent's view that to have entered into prior consultation would have served to bring out the vulnerability of areas of operation to those who had shown themselves ready to organise disruption. That must be read along with the earlier parts of the affidavit in which Sir Robert had dealt in some detail with the attitude of the trade unions which I have referred to earlier in this speech. The affidavit, read as a whole, does in my opinion undoubtedly constitute evidence that the minister did indeed consider that prior consultation would have involved a risk of precipitating disruption at GCHQ. I am accordingly of the opinion that the respondent has shown that her decision was one which not only could reasonably have been based, but was in fact based, on considerations of national security, which outweighed what would otherwise have been the reasonable expectation on the part of the appellants for prior consultation."

[All of the Law Lords dismissed the appeal. Lords Scarman, Diplock and Roskill found that powers exercised directly under the prerogative are not automatically immune from judicial review. Rather, the issue was the justiciability of its subject matter. But the Lords agreed that once a minister produced evidence that her decision was taken for reasons of national security, the question became non-justiciable because the executive alone was sole judge of what national security required.]

Questions

1. In light of the decision of the House of Lords in *CCSU v Minister for the Civil Service*, what advice would you give a government minister as to how to ensure that his or her decisions are not subject to judicial review?

2. Compare the level of deference given to the executive in *Bromley* and *CCSU* by the judiciary. How would you explain the difference?

3. Do you think that judges should avoid questioning the actions of government ministers in cases which concern "national security"? Try to support your answer using the example of the Government's response to the threat of terrorism.

Another famous example of judicial review was also highly politically charged, and generated much criticism of the judiciary's decision that the local council had misused its power.

Wheeler and others v Leicester City Council [1985] 2 All E.R. 1106, HL.

Lord Roskill:

"My Lords, this is an appeal by members of the Leicester Football Club suing on their own behalf and on behalf of all other members of the club. In reality it is an appeal by the club and I shall so treat it. It is brought by leave of the Court of Appeal. That court on 14 March 1985 by a majority (Ackner L.J. and Sir George Waller, Browne-Wilkinson L.J. dissenting) dismissed an appeal by the club against the refusal of Forbes J. on 27 September 1984 to grant the club judicial review of a decision by the respondents, Leicester City Council, made on 21 August 1984. That decision is recorded in minute no 46 of the council's policy and resources committed in the following terms:

'RESOLVED: that the Leicester Football Club be suspended from using the Welford Road recreation ground for a period of 12 months and that the situation be reviewed at the end of that period in the light of the club's attitude to sporting links with South Africa.'

As a result of the passing of that resolution, the club applied for a judicial review of the decision for the purpose of quashing it, for a declaration that it was of no effect and for an injunction preventing, inter alia, the implementation of the resolution. On 10 September 1984 Otton J. gave the club leave to move for judicial review and, pending the hearing of the motion, granted the injunction sought. As already stated, Forbes J. refused the relief sought and since the appeal to the Court of Appeal failed, the club has remained banned from the use of the Welford Road recreation ground save for training purposes, this last by virtue of a concession later made by the council in circumstances to which I will refer in due course.

My Lords, the background to this unfortunate dispute between a rugby football club of renown, now over a century old, and the council is fully stated in the judgments below. I gratefully adopt those statements for in truth the relevant facts are not in dispute. But some reference to the facts is essential for the proper understanding of the issues involved.

The story starts with the announcement of the Rugby Football Union (the RFU) on 30 March 1984 that they had accepted an invitation to take a touring side to South Africa. On 19 April 1984 the membership of this side was announced. The membership included three well-known members of the club. All three were regular England players. It should be mentioned that the club does not have any direct representation of the RFU. It has one representative on the Leicestershire Rugby Union and the latter body has one representative on the main committee of the RFU.

On 1 April 1984, Mr John Allen, the secretary and former captain of the club, was telephoned by the assistant chief executive of the council and asked if representatives of the club would attend a meeting with Mr Soulsby, the leader of the council, in connection with the projected tour and the participation of the club's three members.

That meeting took place on 12 April 1984. Mr Soulsby read out four questions. These four questions have been recorded in writing but no copies were given to the club representatives at the meeting. Since I attach importance to the content of these four questions, both individually and collectively, I record them in full:

'1. Does the Leicester Football Club support the Government opposition to the tour? 2. Does the Leicester Football Club agree that the tour is an insult to the large proportion of the Leicester population? 3. Will the Leicester Football Club press the Rugby Football Union to call off the tour? 4. Will the Leicester Football Club press the players to pull out of the tour?'

Mr Allen told Mr Soulsby he would take the questions back to the committee of the club and would return for a further meeting on 8 May 1984. At that latter meeting it was made plain by Mr Soulsby (Mr Allen's affidavit was not contradicted on this matter) that 'the club's response would only be acceptable if in effect all four questions were answered in the affirmative'.

On 14 May 1984, Mr Allen again wrote to Mr Soulsby and handed him a written statement of the club's response:

'Leicester Football Club have always enjoyed cordial relations with Leicester City Council on a strictly non-political basis and seek to continue that relationship. The club join with the council in condemning apartheid but recognise that there are differences of opinion over the way in which the barriers of apartheid can be broken down. The government have not declared sporting contacts illegal or even applied sanctions against those involved in tours. Their opposition is on an advisory basis, similar to the advice to athletes at the time of the Moscow Olympics, leaving the decision to the individuals concerned. The decision by the Rugby Football Union to approve the tour was taken by a large majority of their committee, but the club had forwarded to the Leicestershire Rugby Union, the club's constituent body, the anti-apartheid case against the tour, which merits serious consideration. Rugby Union players as amateur sportsmen have individual choice as to when and where they play, subject only to the constraints of R.F.U. rules and club loyalty. However, the club, having read the memorandum to the R.F.U. prepared by the anti-apartheid movement, and accepting the serious nature of its contents, have supplied copies to the tour players and asked them to seriously consider the contents before finally reaching a decision whether to tour. The club are and always have been multi-racial and will continue that principle for the benefit of Leicester and rugby football.'

Mr Soulsby said he noted the club's response but added that he did not think 'it would have gone far enough to satisfy the membership of the controlling Labour group on the council'.

This meeting was followed by various statements through the media and elsewhere that the council were considering sanctions against the club for what the council regarded as the club's failure to discourage its members from taking part in the South African tour.

No solution was found during the ensuing weeks. On 21 August 1984 the resolution banning the club from the use of the Welford Road recreation ground was passed in the terms which I have already mentioned. This resolution was subsequently notified to the club. Mr Small, the club's solicitor and also one of its members wrote on 30 August 1984 to ask whether the ban included a ban on using the recreation ground for training. A brief reply, dated 31 August 1984, indicated that the ban was intended to be total. The letter, over the signature of the assistant chief executive, included these sentences:

'It was and is the council's intention to prevent members of the Tigers [ie the club] training on the recreation ground in the evenings as well as banning the use of the rugby pitch for the club matches. For the ban on training the council would seek to rely on Byelaw 16 of the Parks Byelaws and would maintain that the use of the recreation ground by the Tigers would per se interfere with other use of the recreation ground.'

Mr Small (whose evidence on this matter was not contradicted) was subsequently told by Mr Stephenson that if the club tried to train on the ground the floodlighting would be discontinued and this would be effective to prevent training.

By the time the matter was before Forbes J. it was recognised that this reliance on byelaw 16 was indefensible. I say no more about it save to express regret that the contention should ever have been advanced. Any defence of the council's action based on the Race Relations Act 1976, however well founded, could not possibly have extended to justify a ban on training, as Forbes J. pointed out.

The reasons for the imposition of the ban are clearly set out in para 13 of Mr Soulsby's affidavit. I quote that paragraph in full:

'I refute any suggestion that the purported sanction against the club was imposed in response to the actions of their players. I wish to make it clear that the action taken by the council was in response to the attitude taken by the club in failing to condemn the tour and to discourage its members from playing. The council has taken its steps therefore because of what the club did or did not do. It was always recognised that the club were not in the position of employers and could not instruct their players. However, the club is, as the applicants' evidence shows, a premier rugby football club and an influential member of the Rugby Football Union. At no time was the club asked to do anything by the city council which was beyond their powers to do. The steps taken by the city council have not been taken in order to penalise the club for having members who went to South Africa, still less, to penalise the club in order to penalise the players.'

It is important to emphasise that there was nothing illegal in the action of the three members in joining the tour. The government policy recorded in the well-known Gleneagles agreement made in 1977 between the Commonwealth heads of government, has never been given the force of law at the instance of any government, whatever its political complexion, and a person who acts otherwise than in accordance with the principles of the agreement commits no offence even though he may by his action earn the moral disapprobation of his fellow citizens. That the club condemns apartheid, as does the council, admits of no doubt. But the council's actions against the club were not taken, as already pointed out because the club took no action against its three members. They were taken, according to Mr Soulsby, because the club failed to condemn the tour and to discourage its members from playing. The same point was put more succinctly by counsel for the council: 'The club failed to align themselves wholeheartedly with the council on a controversial issue.' The club did not condemn the tour. They did not give specific affirmative answers to the first two questions. Thus, so the argument ran, the council, legitimately bitterly hostile to the policy of apartheid, were justified in exercising their statutory discretion to determine by whom the recreation ground should be used so as to exclude those, such as the club, who would not support the council's policy on the council's terms. The club had, however, circulated to those involved the powerfully reasoned and impressive memorandum which had been sent to the RFU on 12 March 1984 by the anti-apartheid movement. Of the club's own opposition to apartheid as expressed in its memorandum which was given to Mr Soulsby, there is no doubt. But the club recognised that those views, like those of the council, however passionately held by some, were by no means universally held, especially by those who sincerely believed that the evils of apartheid were enhanced rather than diminished by a total prohibition of sporting links with South Africa.

The council's main defence rested on s.71 of the Race Relations Act 1976. That section appears as the first section of Pt X of the Act under the cross-heading 'supplemental'. For ease of reference I will set out the section in full:

> 'Without prejudice to their obligation to comply with any other provision of this Act, it shall be the duty of every local authority to make appropriate arrangements with a view to securing that their various functions are carried out with due regard to the need—(a) to eliminate unlawful racist discrimination; and (b) to promote equality of opportunity, and good relations, between persons of different racial groups.'

My Lords, it was strenuously argued on behalf of the club that this section should be given what was called a 'narrow' construction. It was suggested that the section was only concerned with the actions of the council as regards its own internal behaviour and was what was described as 'inward looking'. The section had no relevance to the general exercise by the council or indeed of any local authority of their statutory functions, as for example in relation to the control of open spaces or in determining who should be entitled to use a recreation ground and on what terms. It was said that the section was expressed in terms of 'duty'. But it did not impose any duty so as to compel the exercise by a local authority of other statutory functions in order to achieve the objectives of the 1976 Act.

My Lords, in respectful agreement with both courts below, I unhesitatingly reject this argument. I think the whole purpose of this section is to see that in relation to matters other than those specifically dealt with, for example, in Pt II (employment) and in Pt III (education) local authorities must in relation to 'their various functions' make 'appropriate arrangements' to secure that those functions are carried out 'with due regard to the need' mentioned in the section.

It follows that I do not doubt that the council were fully entitled in exercising their statutory discretion under, for example, the Open Spaces Act 1906 and the various Public Health Acts, which are all referred to in the judgments below, to pay regard to what they thought was in the best interests of race relations.

The only question is, therefore, whether the action of the council of which the club complains is susceptible of attack by way of judicial review. It was forcibly argued by counsel on behalf of the council that once it was accepted, as I do accept, that s.71 bears the construction for which the council contended, the matter became one of political judgment only, and that by interfering the courts would be trespassing across that line which divides a proper exercise of statutory discretion based on a political judgment, in relation to which the courts must not and will not interfere, from an improper exercise of such a discretion in relation to which the courts will interfere. . .

I do not for one moment doubt the great importance which the council attach to the presence in their midst of a 25% population of persons who are either Asian or Afro-Caribbean in origin. Nor do I doubt for one moment the sincerity of the view expressed in Mr Soulsby's affidavit regarding the need for the council to distance itself from bodies who hold important positions and do not actively discourage sporting contacts with South Africa. Persuasion, even powerful persuasion, is always a permissible way of seeking to obtain an objective. But in a field where other views can equally legitimately be held, persuasion, however powerful, must not be allowed to cross that line where it moves into the field of illegitimate pressure coupled with the threat of sanctions. The four questions, coupled with the insistence that only affirmative answers to all four would be acceptable, are suggestive of more than powerful persuasion. The second question is to my mind open to particular criticism. What, in the context, is meant by 'the club'? The committee? The playing members? The 4,300 non-playing members? It by no means follows that the committee would all have agreed on an affirmative answer to the question and still less that a majority of their members, playing or non-playing, would have done so. Nor would any of these groups of members necessarily have known whether 'the large proportion', whatever the phrase may mean in the context, of the Leicester population would have regarded the tour as 'an insult' to them.

None of the judges in the courts below have felt able to hold that the action of the club was unreasonable or perverse in the *Wednesbury* sense. They do not appear to have been invited to consider whether those actions, even if not unreasonable on *Wednesbury* principles, were assailable on the grounds of procedural impropriety or unfairness by the council in the manner in which, in the light of the facts which I have outlined, they took their decision to suspend for 12 months the use by the club of the Welford Road recreation ground.

I would greatly hesitate to differ from four learned judges on the *Wednesbury* issue but for myself I would have been disposed respectfully to do this and to say that the actions of the council were unreasonable in the *Wednesbury* sense. But even if I am wrong in this view, I am clearly of the opinion that the manner in which the council took that decision was in all the circumstances unfair within the third of the principles stated in *Council of Civil Service Unions v Minister for Civil Service*. The council formulated those four questions in the manner of which I have spoken and indicated that only such affirmative answers would be acceptable. They received reasoned and reasonable answers which went a long way in support of the policy which the council had accepted and desired to see accepted. The views expressed in these reasoned and reasonable answers were lawful views and the views which, as the evidence shows, many people sincerely hold and believe to be correct. If the club had adopted a different and hostile attitude, different considerations might well have arisen. But the club did not adopt any such attitude.

In my view, therefore, this is a case in which the court should interfere because of the unfair manner in which the council set about obtaining its objective. . . .

Since preparing this speech I have had the advantage of reading in draft the speech of my noble and learned friend Lord Templeman with which I find myself in complete agreement.

I would, therefore, allow the appeal and order certiorari to issue to quash the council's decision of 21 August 1984, the terms of which I have already set out. I do not think that the declaration or the injunction sought is necessary at this juncture, but lest they become so, I would remit the matter to the High Court with liberty to the club to apply for such further relief as may be thought necessary to protect their rights. The council must pay the costs in this House and both courts below."

[Lord Templeman delivered separate reasons in which he agreed with Lord Roskill. Lords Bridge of Harwich, Lord Brightman and Lord Griffiths also agreed.]

Question

Was the decision of the council a matter of political judgment on which the courts should have intervened? What responsibility did the council have in this situation?

II. PARLIAMENTARY SUPREMACY AND JUDICIAL REVIEW

The *Bromley v GLC* and *Wheeler v Leicester City Council* cases did not directly raise the issue of parliamentary supremacy. The councils had limited powers which had been granted under statutes enacted by Parliament. The issue was whether they had exceeded their powers or exercised their discretion unreasonably. In that sense, the judges saw the cases as directly raising "rule of law" issues about the importance of ensuring that officials of the state exercise only those powers granted to them under statute, and do so in a reasonable, rather than arbitrary, fashion.

However, the principle of parliamentary supremacy, as we saw in Ch.2, demands that Parliament, provided its procedural rules are followed, has unlimited scope in terms of the substance of the laws it wishes to enact. For example, Parliament could have specifically and explicitly empowered the GLC to cut fares, had it so wanted. Moreover, Parliament has frequently attempted to prevent the courts from judicially reviewing the exercise of discretionary powers by officials of the state, by including provisions within the empowering statutes, known as *ouster clauses* (designed to "oust" the judiciary from reviewing government actions). An ouster clause is an attempt by the legislature explicitly to exclude review of a decision by judicial review, within the terms of the relevant statute. Given the principle of parliamentary supremacy, we might think that such clauses—if they are clear and unambiguous in their language—should ensure that judges do not review the decisions made by officials. However, courts in general have interpreted ouster clauses narrowly, and have jealously guarded their ability to judicially review, on the basis of the importance of this supervisory role for the judiciary in ensuring the legality of executive actions.

The House of Lords has also suggested that there may be points at which the principle of parliamentary supremacy might be limited by the rule of law. We have already touched upon this issue in Ch.2. In *Jackson v Attorney General*, the Law Lords upheld the Hunting Act 2004, which made the hunting with dogs of wild animals unlawful. However, in so doing, some of the Law Lords made clear that the judiciary might be prepared to place limits on what Parliament could do in order to protect the basic constitutional structure and institutions of the country.

R. [Jackson and others] v Attorney General [2005] UKHL 56.

Lord Steyn:

"The classic account given by Dicey of the doctrine of the supremacy of Parliament, pure and absolute as it was, can now be seen to be out of place in the modern United Kingdom. Nevertheless, the supremacy of Parliament is still the *general* principle. If that is so, it is not unthinkable that circumstances could arise where the courts may have to qualify a principle established on a different hypothesis of constitutionalism. In exceptional circumstances involving an attempt to abolish judicial review or the ordinary role of the courts, the Appellate Committee of the House of Lords or a new Supreme Court may have to consider whether this is constitutionally fundamental which even a sovereign Parliament acting at the behest of a complaisant House of Commons cannot abolish. It is not necessary to explore the ramifications of this question in this opinion. No such issues arise on the present appeal."

Lord Hope of Craighead:

"My Lords, I start where my learned friend, Lord Steyn, has just ended. Our constitution is dominated by the sovereignty of Parliament. But Parliamentary sovereignty is no longer, if it ever was, absolute. It is not uncontrolled in the sense referred to by Lord Birkenhead LC in *McCawley v The King* [1920] AC 691, 720. It is no longer right to say that its freedom to legislate admits of no qualification whatsoever. Step by step, gradually but surely, the English principle of the absolute legislative sovereignty of Parliament which Dicey derived from Coke and Blackstone is being qualified. . . .

Nor should we overlook the fact that one of the guiding principles that were identified by Dicey at p 35 was the universal rule or supremacy throughout the constitution of ordinary law. Owen Dixon, "The Law and Constitution" (1935) 51 LQR 590, 596 was making the same point when he said that it is of the essence of supremacy of the law that the courts shall disregard as unauthorised and void the acts of any organ of government, whether legislative or administrative, which exceed the limits of the power that organ derives from the law. In its modern form, now reinforced by the European Convention on Human Rights and the enactment by Parliament of the Human Rights Act 1998, this principle protects the individual from arbitrary government. The rule of law enforced by the courts is the ultimate controlling factor on which our constitution is based. The fact that your Lordships have been willing to hear this appeal and to give judgment upon it is another indication that the courts have a part to play in defining the limits of Parliament's legislative sovereignty."

The significance of the House of Lords decision for the supremacy of Parliament was considered by Jowell in terms of a "new constitutional hypothesis".

Jeffrey Jowell, "Parliamentary Sovereignty under the New Constitutional Hypothesis" [2006] Public Law 562 at 578–579:

"It can no longer be doubted that one of the preconditions of any constitutional democracy, properly so-called, is respect for certain rights that neither the executive nor the legislature, representative as it may be, should be able to deny with impunity. But how convincing is the claim of the supporters of parliamentary sovereignty that its demise would have the effect of simply transferring unfettered power from the elected legislature to the unelected judiciary? That claim is misleading. It ignores the fact that the spheres of the judiciary and the legislature are distinct. For a start, even under the model of a rights-based democracy, legislative authority inevitably contains a wide area of discretion to make social and economic policy, over which the courts have no dominium. It is not for the judges to second-guess the legislature on utilitarian calculations of the social good. Their role is strictly confined to the limited issue of whether the various inherent elements of democracy have been infringed by other branches of government and therefore cannot be sustained. Even within the bounds of parliamentary sovereignty, as we have seen, the courts already exercise this role to some degree. The historic dialogue and process of iteration and self-correction between Parliament and the courts has allowed the development of public law rights and duties to which both the legislature and judiciary have contributed.

If parliamentary sovereignty were to be discarded as our prime constitutional principle, it is true that 'the last word' would pass from the legislature to the courts--but only on the question whether the legislature has strayed beyond the line of its democratic confines. The assertion of this authority would require of the courts a boldness to interpret constitutional principles as they ought to be. However, it will also require a modest appreciation of their own limitations. There will be issues on the margins of legal principle and socio-economic policy which will inevitably invite the charge of judicial overreach. Parliament, however, is not in a position to judge these matters in its own cause. And there is much to be said for having these decisions made by those who are insulated from the necessity to respond to the perceived opinion of the moment.

If a future Parliament were to pass a law which infringed the rule of law or other constitutional fundamentals, it may be that our judges will feel that they still lack sufficient authority to strike it down on the ground that it subverts the implied conditions—the essential features—of our constitutional democracy. However, some of those conditions, such as free and regular elections, underlie the legitimacy of the principle of parliamentary sovereignty itself. Others, such as access to justice, are necessary requirements of a modern hypothesis of constitutionalism. Some of the dicta in *Jackson* confirm the real possibility that, in the words of Lord Hope: 'The rule of law enforced by the courts is the ultimate controlling factor on which our constitution is based'."

Questions

1. Do you think that there are some limits on what Parliament can do, even if it is "supreme"? What might those limits be?

2. Are these limitations on Parliament's ability to act properly seen as "political" or "legal"? Is it easy to distinguish between the two? Can you think of some examples?

III. Defining "The State"

It is important to recognise that the ability of the judiciary to review those actions of officials of the state through judicial review depends, by definition, on those officials being part of *the state*. In other words, they must be *public* officials. For Dicey and his followers, the fear of arbitrary power and the defence of the "rule of law" was exclusively focused upon the dangers that the state posed to the individual. The doctrine of judicial review is the response to those fears. However, that raises the question whether "the state" is always to be feared, or whether it should be seen as able to exercise power positively. Moreover, since the 1980s, many commentators would argue that, in some respects at least, the state has "shrunk", with many of its functions no longer clearly being exercised by "public" officials. This is because of government policies such as privatisation of nationalised industries. As a consequence, the line between "public" and "private" is not always bright and clear. Finally, we might question Dicey's premise that it is always the exercise of discretion by public officials that we need to fear. Should we not also be concerned (or more concerned) about "privately" employed individuals who may have been granted wide discretionary powers that can have a severe impact upon the citizen? The definition of the "public", for the purposes of administrative law, is a very complicated issue, and Allison provides a good introduction to how it has increased in complexity.

John W.F. Allison, "Theoretical and institutional underpinnings of a separate administrative law", in Michael Taggart (ed), *The Province of Administrative Law* (Oxford: Hart Publishing, 1997), pp.82–83:

"Identifying the state and its administration has not been facilitated by the privatisation schemes of the last two decades. . . .

First, statutes, such as the British Aerospace Act 1980 and the Telecommunications Act 1984, sought to roll back the frontiers of the state, but the state's former role, together with its continuing role chiefly through regulation, contributes to the vague sense that a public function is still being performed by the privatised industry. A commentator in *The Economist* observed: '[m]any of the once-nationalised companies do retain much of the feel of state behemoths'. The contraction of the state administration, like its earlier extension, obscures its distinctness.

Secondly, after initially attempting to reduce the number of hybrid institutions, central government increased expenditure on them, created new agencies [institutions related to central government but not part of government] (e.g. OFTEL and OFGAS) to regulate the privatised industries, and hived off more executive functions to quasi-governmental agencies (e.g., the Housing Action Trusts) and to the many new semi-autonomous departmental agencies envisaged by the Next Steps Programme.

Thirdly, although central government has preferred regulation as the formal corrective to privatisation, it has nevertheless continued, in fact, to bargain with the privatised industries and has also effectively promoted the 'contracting-out' of numerous service functions. . . .

In short, privatisation has not resulted in a clearly-defined core of government or minimal state administration. Woolf and Jowell rightly conclude that the:

'legal relationships that arise out of . . . new forms of service provision (e.g. through contracting out and the "hiving off" of central departmental responsibilities to new agencies) are neither wholly "public" or "private".'[2]

Questions

1. Can you think of examples in which it is unclear whether an official operates as part of the state or should be considered "private"? If you were a judge, how would you try to make the determination of when an official is part of the state?

2. If judicial review was unavailable to review the actions of an official—because he or she was exercising a private function—are there legal remedies that might be useful? Could the law of contract be helpful?

---

2   S.A. Smith, Lord Woolf and J. Jowell, *Judicial Review of Administrative Action* (5th ed., Sweet and Maxwell, London, 1995) p. 165

IV. The Human Rights Act 1998 and Judicial Review

The Human Rights Act 1998 expands the role and scope of judicial review because the state is placed under a legal obligation to act in accordance with European Convention rights. As McLeod explains:

> "Section 6 of the Act makes it unlawful for a public authority (which is defined as *excluding* both Houses of Parliament but as *including* courts and tribunals, as well as 'any person certain of whose functions are functions of a public nature') to act in a way which is incompatible with Convention rights. (The phrase 'functions of a public nature' is likely to import into this area of law the principles which the courts have developed to help them identify the distinction between public and private law for the purposes of judicial review generally.) . . . The effect of s.7 of the Act is that a person who wishes to establish that there has been a breach of the duty under s.6, may do so proactively by claiming judicial review, or reactively by way of defence to proceedings brought by, or at the instigation of, the public authority." (Ian McLeod, *Legal Method*, 5th edn, Basingstoke: Palgrave, 2005, p.98.)

This brings us back to the difficult question—one which courts are now forced to deal with—of what exactly are "functions of a public nature", as opposed to private acts. Although the public/private divide appears central to the Human Rights Act 1998, this may be somewhat misleading. The relationship between individual and the state (the "public function") is often described as the *vertical* effect of the Act (the state being conceived as *above* the individual). By contrast, the legal relationship of private individuals to each other (conceived as being side-by-side), is the *horizontal* effect of the Act. The *horizontal* impact of the Human Rights Act has been a contentious issue as McLeod explains.

Ian McLeod, *Legal Method*, 7th edn (Basingstoke: Palgrave, 2009), pp.112–113:

"The fact that the Human Rights Act places a duty on public authorities to act in a way which is compatible with Convention rights, without imposing a similar duty on anyone else, might seem to make the Act enforceable only against the state and its emanations, or to use the terminology which has been developed in relation to Community law . . . vertically but not horizontally. Furthermore, this view might appear to be supported by a contribution which the Lord Chancellor made to the Committee stage in the House of Lords, when he said that 'the Convention had its origins in a desire to protect people from the misuse of power by the state, rather than from the actions of individuals' and therefore s.6 of the Act 'does not impose a liability on organizations which have no public functions at all.'

However, some eleven days later, he said:

> 'We . . . believe that it is right as a matter of principle for the courts to have the duty of acting compatibly with the Convention not only in cases involving other public authorities but also in developing the common law in deciding cases between individuals.'

Reading these two statements carefully, it is clear that the Lord Chancellor's view was that there is nothing in the Act to create any new causes of action against private individuals and organizations; and, therefore, borrowing the terminology of Community law again, the Act has no horizontal *direct* effect. On the other hand, the status of the courts as public authorities means that they have a duty to develop *existing* causes of action in the light of Convention rights. In other words, the intention was that in cases brought against private individuals and organizations, any relevant Convention rights would (borrowing the terminology of Community law yet again) have horizontal *indirect* effect. Furthermore, the courts have agreed that this was not only the intention of the Act but also its effect (see, for example, *Douglas v Hello Ltd (No 3)* [2005] EWCA Civ, 596, [2005] 4 All ER 128)."

Questions

1. Explain the importance of the concepts of the "public" and "private" in judicial review. Why do those concepts prove so difficult to apply?

2. What impact has the Human Rights Act 1998 had on the role and scope of judicial review?

Useful website addresses

Ministry of Justice, Human Rights, *http://www.justice.gov.uk/about/human-rights.htm* [Accessed May 12, 2010]

4

CONSTITUTIONAL ASPECTS OF LEGAL METHOD: THE IMPACT OF MEMBERSHIP IN THE EUROPEAN UNION

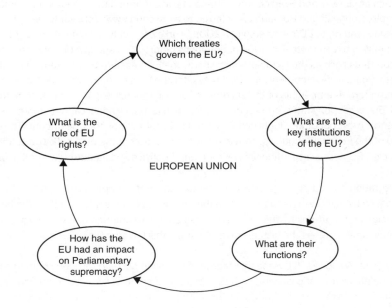

In this chapter we examine the impact on our legal method and system of membership in the European Union (EU). You will study the EU in much greater detail in other courses in your degree. Nevertheless, you need a basic knowledge at this early stage. By the end of this chapter, you should:

- have an appreciation of the historical development and the institutional structure of the EU;

- recognise the significant impact of the EU on the principle of parliamentary supremacy;

- be aware of the important role of the rights of individuals protected by European Law.

I. THE HISTORICAL SIGNIFICANCE OF THE EU

In order to understand the importance of the EU, it is first helpful to gain an appreciation of its historical significance and evolution.

Erika Szyszczak and Adam Cygan, *Understanding Law* (London: Sweet and Maxwell, 2005), pp.1–2, 4–5:

"European Union (EU) law cannot be understood without considering the geopolitical relationships that prevail within the European continent, and examining the EU's interaction with the wider world. The EU dominates the geopolitical area of the continent of Europe and following the 2004 enlargement consists of twenty-five Member States and a population of over 450M citizens. This makes the EU the world's largest supranational trading bloc in terms of population. The geographic land mass of the EU spans from the Arctic Circle in Finland to the Azores in the Atlantic Ocean. Yet following the 2004 enlargement, many European countries remain outside the process of EU integration. One consequence of the 2004 enlargement is that the centre of gravity of the EU has shifted eastwards and its surface area has increased by a quarter. In particular, this means that for the first time the EU shares a border with countries of the former Soviet Union.

The continent of Europe can be divided into those countries inside the EU and those situated on its periphery. For some, such as Norway and Switzerland referenda have confirmed their intention to remain outside. Others, for example, Romania and Bulgaria are referred to as 'second wave applicants' and are engaged in a process of accession leading to EU membership in 2009.[1] Turkey, the only non-Christian country to seek EU membership, is unlikely to complete accession negotiations before 2015 and can be categorised as a 'third wave applicant'. Yet countries such as the Ukraine, which shares the EU's eastern border, remain outside the formal accession process. Political developments in 2004 may alter the EU's relations with the Ukraine, though in the medium to long term membership of the EU remains an aspiration. Despite being outside the governance structures of the EU, accession states, and even countries such as the Ukraine, cannot ignore the consequences of having the world's most populous single economic and political zone as their neighbour. The day-to-day decision-making of the EU's neighbours is influenced by the spill over of the EU's policy objectives. In addition to economic policies, EU norms also influence environmental policies and increasingly immigration and human rights strategies. . . .

European integration is not a post-war twentieth-century concept. European history up to the mid twentieth century is categorised by military expansionists from the Romans to Napoleon and Hitler, who have pursued aggressive campaigns through which attempts were based on the assumption that military superiority would create and maintain an empire. As the history books illustrate, this forced integration has, sooner or later, ended in failure.

Consequently, post-World War II European integration has been pursued through creating a political consensus amongst political elites and citizens, with the objective of creating a shared European identity.

The roots of the EU lie in the Second World War. Since 1945 European cooperation and integration has taken place at various levels and is characterised by a desire to avoid conflict. Jean Monnet, described as the architect of European integration, argued that only a federal Europe could avoid future military conflict. The Council of Europe, in 1948, was the first formal cooperation in post war Europe. The genesis of the Council of Europe can be traced back to Winston Churchill's Zurich University speech in 1946. Here he spoke of a 'common European home' and 'united states of Europe' which required Franco–German reconciliation. The most notable and enduring achievement of the Council of Europe has been the European Convention on the Protection of Human Rights and Fundamental Freedoms (ECHR). The jurisprudence of the European Court of Human Rights, which has interpreted the principles of the ECHR, has provided uniform minimum standards of human rights norms for all signatories.

---

[1]   In fact, Romania and Bulgaria were allowed to join the European Union on 1 January 2007, bringing the total number of member states to twenty-seven.

The process of reconciliation began with the French Foreign Minister Robert Schuman advocating the eponymous Schuman Plan on May 9, 1950. In this post-war period, Europe was still reliant upon the Marshall Aid programme which the United States had provided since 1945 to assist European regeneration. Schuman was advocating that Marshall Aid be replaced with a distinct European renaissance. At the core was a belief that economic integration would deliver prosperity for individuals. The plan would require nation states to work within a formal supranational institutional framework. Schuman viewed his plan as a blueprint for economic, political and military co-operation in Europe. But from 1950 to the early 1960s the Cold War would dominate European politics and provide a diversion and barrier to wider European integration.

A feature of European cooperation in the early 1950s is that it lacked trust and commitment from those involved. France, still wary of recent events, remained cautious of Germany and was unenthusiastic about military cooperation. The French Parliament refused to ratify the European Defence Community Treaty in 1952. Although some military cooperation existed in the form of the Western European Union, the North Atlantic Treaty Organisation (NATO) signed in 1949 overshadowed this informal cooperation. Ironically, despite the desire for an independent European identity, NATO has remained dominated by the USA and suggests that military cooperation requires a strong transatlantic relationship. The Western European Union did evolve in the 1980s and was formally absorbed in to the EU under the CFSP.

The UK was a reluctant participant in the early years of European integration, primarily because it remained distrustful of political cooperation with France. The UK participated in NATO and was closer to the USA in strategic terms. This tense relationship with its European neighbours would see the UK outside the formal framework of European integration until 1973."

Richard Ward and Amanda Akhtar, *Walker & Walker's English Legal System*, 10th edn (Oxford: Oxford University Press, 2008), pp.110–114:

"On 1 January 1973 the UK became a Member State of the European Communities. There were originally three communities: the European Coal and Steel Community (ECSC), the European Atomic Energy Community (Euratom), and the European Economic Community (EEC). The EEC, which was by far the most ambitious and significant of the three projects, was officially renamed 'the European Community' (EC) by the Treaty on European Union in 1992. The ECSC expired on 23 July 2002, leaving Euratom and the European Community as the two remaining elements of the European Communities.

Created in 1957 by the Treaty of Rome, the European Community (or the EEC as it then was) initially comprised six members, but has since expanded to its current composition of twenty-seven Member States. The Treaty reflected a post-war desire to achieve stability through European unity, and the aim set out in the Preamble was to create an 'ever closer union' amongst the peoples of Europe. This was to be achieved through common action in the economic field. The Community was to have its own institutions, along with laws that could regulate the powers and obligations of Members States in economic matters.

The Single European Act and the Treaty on European Union
The Community has now developed far beyond the original aims set by the Treaty of Rome. Not only has its membership increased, its role has expanded beyond the economic into social, financial, and political areas of competence. In 1987 the Single European Act was adopted, and in addition to strengthening the institutional position of the European Parliament, it established the objective of making 'concrete progress towards European unity'. It sought to achieve this by amending the Treaty of Rome.

The process of amendment and reform was continued by the Treaty on European Union, which is more commonly referred to as the Maastricht Treaty. The UK ratified this treaty in 1993 after considerable political controversy, and it was given effect in law by the European Communities (Amendment) Act 1993. Not only did the Maastricht Treaty formally re-name the EEC as the 'European Community', it also radically amended the Treaty of Rome in order to achieve its aims. These aims are stated in the Preamble to be a continuation of the process of 'ever closer union', economic and monetary union, the development of a single currency, common citizenship, common foreign and defence policies, and the enhancement of the democratic functions of Community institutions.

The effects of the Maastricht Treaty were significant. Firstly, it extended the area of legal competence of the Community: it created a common citizenship, expanded existing rights of movement and voting, increased co-ordination of general economic policy, established a Central Bank, and increased the rights of workers. Secondly, the Treaty established a European Union (EU), founded on the existing Members States of the European Communities. The EC and its body of laws formed one of the three pillars of the European Union, the other two being concerned with (a) establishing a common foreign and security policy, and (b) achieving co-operation in justice and home affairs. These other two pillars did not form part of the EC framework, with the result that decisions made under them have thus far been made at a political level and have not been subject to the jurisdiction of the European Court of Justice. This position is now changing as a result of the Treaty of Amsterdam.

The Treaty of Amsterdam

The next significant step in the development of the EC and EU was the signing of the Treaty of Amsterdam in 1997. The Treaty came into force on 1 May 1999 and made substantive amendments to both the EC Treaty and the Treaty on European Union. It also made specific commitments to a number of important non-economic goals, including human rights, environmental protection, and equality. Another important objective was to simplify the existing treaties by removing obsolete provisions: an obvious consequence of this is that most of the provisions in the earlier treaties were renumbered. The position of the European Parliament was also strengthened.

Economic co-operation still lies at the heart of the 'closer Europe' objective, but this is now balanced against other important aims. Thus Article 2 of the amended EC Treaty states that in addition to 'establishing a common market and an economic and monetary union,' the Community shall also have the task of promoting:

> '[A] harmonious, balanced and sustainable development of economic activities, a high level of employ-
> ment and of social protection, equality between men and women, sustainable and non-inflationary
> growth, a high degree of competitiveness and convergence of economic performance, a high level of
> protection and improvement of quality of life, and economic and social cohesion and solidarity among
> Member States.'

An amended Article 3 identifies a wide range of activities permissible in order to achieve the Community's goals. These now include policies relating to education, health, consumer protection, tourism, civil protection, the environment, and 'the flowering of cultures', along with the original concerns of common agricultural policies, the elimination of trade barriers, and the free movement of workers, goods and services. In addition to the specific provisions of the Treaty, Article 94 (ex 100) provides for:

> 'the approximation of such laws, regulation or administrative provisions of the Member States as directly
> affect the establishment or functioning of the common market.'

From a legal perspective, one of the most important changes brought about by the Treaty of Amsterdam was the re-drawing of the boundaries between the EC and the EU. The Justice and Home Affairs pillar of the EU was re-titled 'Police and Judicial Co-operation in Criminal Matters', and a large part of it was brought within the framework of the EC pillar, making it susceptible to the jurisdiction of the European Court of Justice. Another EU provision which was expressly made justiciable by the Treaty of Amsterdam is the new Article 6(2) (ex Art F(2)). This provides that:

> 'The Union shall respect fundamental rights as guaranteed by the European Convention on Human Rights
> and Fundamental Freedoms . . . as general principles of Community law.'

However, the second EU pillar—the Common Foreign and Security Policy—still lies beyond the jurisdiction of the Court of Justice.

The Treaty of Nice and the Charter of Fundamental Rights

The Treaty of Nice was signed by the Members States on 26 February 2001 but it did not come into force until 1 February 2003. Unlike its predecessors this Treaty was primarily concerned with institutional reform, and it paved the way for the number of Member States to be increased from fifteen to twenty-seven. In anticipation of the likelihood that achieving unanimity will become more difficult as the EU gets bigger, it also amended the existing treaties to allow more measures to be adopted by qualified majority.

Another important document to be agreed when the European Council met in Nice was the Charter of Fundamental Rights of the European Union. The Charter sets out a number of economic and social rights of the kind that one might expect from an organization founded on an economic agenda. Thus it includes the right to education, the right to engage in work, the right not to be dismissed unjustifiably, and the right to collective bargaining. However, it also includes many of the civil and political rights found in most other international human rights agreements, along with more novel ones such as the right to protection of family data. The civil and political rights correspond closely with those found in the ECHR, and to avoid any inconsistency in interpretation the Charter states that:

> 'In so far as this Charter contains rights which correspond to rights guaranteed by the Convention for the Protection of Human Rights and Fundamental Freedoms, the meaning and scope of those rights shall be the same as those laid down by the said Convention. This provision shall not prevent Union law providing more extensive protection.'

The Charter was signed in December 2000. At that time it was not expressed to be legally binding, but the Treaty of Lisbon has since provided for a new Article 6(1) to be added to the Treaty on European Union. This will give the rights, freedoms and principles set out in the Charter the same legal value as the Treaties, meaning that they will be binding on EU institutions as well as on the Member States when they are implementing EU law. The UK and Poland, however, have negotiated exemptions.

The Treaty of Lisbon: A Constitution in All But Name?

In 2004, almost three years after the idea was first accepted in principle, the Heads of State and Government formally signed the EU Constitutional Treaty. The intention was that this document should replace the four major treaties on which the Union is founded, and that the EU should be given a distinct legal personality. The idea was to formally merge the EU with the EC and abolish its pillar structure, in addition to incorporating the Charter of Fundamental Rights into the main body of European Law. The Constitution was also intended to make the EU more democratic, and to this end many of its provisions were concerned with institutional reform.

The Constitution was an ambitious and controversial project, and despite being ratified by several member States, it was effectively derailed by rejection in national referenda in both France and the Netherlands. The UK's referendum plans were postponed indefinitely, and the President of the European Commission acknowledged that the Constitution had probably been dealt a fatal blow:

> 'It is difficult to see what a renegotiation would achieve. It is highly unlikely it would produce a radically different or better document. The Constitution is already the best possible compromise. It represents a delicate balance of competing views, which contains many improvements to the way in which the EU carries out its business. That is why there is no plan B'.

A 'plan B' eventually did emerge in the shape of the Treaty of Lisbon, and although billed as an 'amending' treaty it will bring about many of the changes intended by the ill-fated Constitution. It will significantly amend both the Treaty on European Union and the Treaty of Rome (to be known in future as the Treaty on the Functioning of the European Union), and as stated previously, it will give legal effect to the Charter of Fundamental Rights. It provides for the EU to formally replace and succeed the EC, and it will give the EU a distinct legal personality. It also incorporates many of the institutional and democratic changes originally set out in the Constitution: it will, for example, reduce the size of the European Commission, redistribute the seats within the European Parliament, and give the Parliament an enhanced role. National Parliaments will also have a greater role, as they will have the opportunity to consider proposals for new EU legislation directly. The EU will be forced to reconsider any proposed laws which are deemed by at least a third of national Parliaments to infringe the principle of subsidiarity, and if a majority of national Parliaments oppose a proposal it may be struck down altogether.

The Treaty was signed by representatives from each Member State in December 2007, but it will not take effect until all twenty-seven states have ratified it."

II. Institutional Structure of the EU

When the United Kingdom joined the EU (which was then the European Economic Community), it signed up to a political and economic *union* of nation states. It is hardly surprising that there are a wide range of institutions which govern relations between the members.

Richard Ward and Amanda Akhtar, *Walker & Walker's English Legal System*, 10th edn (Oxford: Oxford University Press, 2008), pp.116–119:

"The EC and the EU operate through four main institutions, though these institutions have only a limited role with regard to foreign and security policy and certain other aspects of EU business. These institutions are the Council, the Commission, the Court of Justice, and the European Parliament.

The Council
The Council of the European Union, formerly known as the Council of Ministers, is the EC's main legislative and decision-making body. Article 202 of the EC Treaty states that its task is to ensure that the Treaty's objectives are obtained, and that the general economic policies of the Member States are co-ordinated. It also empowers the Council to 'take decisions', which primarily means approving legislation proposed by the Commission. The Council is also responsible for negotiating with non-EU states, approving the EU budget and making decisions under the Union's second and third pillars.

The Council is composed of the ministers for each Member State, with the precise composition at any given time being determined by the matter under discussion. For example, a Council meeting to discuss environmental issues would be attended by the environment Minister from each state and it would be referred to as 'the Environment Council'. For the purposes of continuity, a permanent committee of officials (COREPAR) conducts much of the routine work of the Council, for later ratification. The Presidency of the Council is held by each State in turn for a period of six months. The main functions of the Presidency are to convene and chair meetings of the Council, and also to determine agendas.

The Treaty requires decisions on matters such as immigration policy and taxation to be unanimous, but in most other matters the Council operates on the basis of qualified majority voting (QMV). Each Member State is entitled to cast a certain number of votes, with the numbers being weighted to give the most votes to the most populous countries. The current QMV rules date from 2004, when the EU was expanded from fifteen states. The UK, France, Germany, and Italy now have twenty-nine votes each, followed by Spain and Poland with twenty-seven. The least populous state, Malta, has just three. A qualified majority requires at least 72 per cent of the available votes and the approval of a majority (or sometimes a two-thirds majority) of the Member States. In addition, a Member State can ask for confirmation that the votes cast in favour represent at least 62 per cent of the EU's population. This means that if a handful of large countries act together, they will be able to veto measures which have the support of the remaining states.

The Treaty of Lisbon provides for QMV to become the default method of decision-making within the Council, and this means that it will be extended to a whole new range of policy areas. From 2014 a new system of 'double majority voting' will be phased in. Under this system, a qualified majority will require at least 55 per cent of the members of the Council (i.e. fifteen out of the twenty-seven states) to vote in favour of a measure. Those voting in favour will also have to represent at least 65 per cent of the EU's population.

The Commission

The powers of the Commission are set out in Article 211 (ex 155) of the EC Treaty and they principally concern the formulation of legislative proposals and the implementation and enforcement of measures adopted by the institutions. It can investigate potential breaches of Community law and may refer them to the European Court of Justice, although frequently it is able to resolve such issues through political negotiations. The Commission can even impose its own sanctions where it finds breaches of the EC's competition laws, fining states and large companies which are found to have engaged in anti-competitive behaviour. Finally, the Commission is also responsible for managing the EU budget, and acting together with the Council it is able to represent the EU at an international level.

The Commissioners hold office for a renewable term of five years, with each one being responsible for a particular policy area. There is currently one Commissioner per country, but the Treaty of Lisbon provides for this number to be reduced from 2014 onwards. In future only two-thirds of Member States will have a Commissioner at any given time, based on a system of equal rotation.

The Parliament

Although originally comprising members nominated by Member States, the European Parliament has been directly elected since 1979. Elections are held every five years, with the total number of MEPs now standing at 785. The Treaty of Lisbon provides for the total number of MEPs to be capped at 751 (including the President), and when this comes into effect each state will be represented by between six and ninety-six MEPs. The Parliament holds plenary sessions in both Strasbourg and Brussels, although much of the preparatory work is done by committees. The General Secretariat and its departments are based in Luxembourg.

In the original Article 137 of the EC Treaty (now 189), the role of the Parliament was stated to be advisory and supervisory. Its position has since been considerably strengthened and it now has much greater involvement in the legislative process. It also has important roles in approving the Community budget and scrutinizing the other institutions. There are different legislative procedures for different areas of EC law, and many of them now require the approval or involvement of the Parliament. The most significant of these is the co-decision procedure established under Article 251, which, although rather complicated, effectively gives the Parliament a power of veto in a wide range of matters. The range of measures made by this procedure will increase considerably if the European Constitution is ever adopted: so much so that it will be known in future as the 'ordinary legislative procedure'. Despite this welcome development however, the European Parliament will still lack the power to legislate independently.

In addition to its legislative role, the Parliament can ask questions of the Commission and Council, and it can even censure the Commission and remove it on a motion passed by a two-thirds majority. Though the power of censure was once regarded as a largely theoretical sanction, a significant milestone was reached in 1999 when the *threat* of a vote of no confidence forced the entire Commission to resign. This action followed a damning report into accusations of maladministration and fraud, in matters for which the Commission had overall responsibility. Had the Commission not resigned of its own accord, the Parliament would undoubtedly have forced it to do so by passing a motion of no confidence.

The Court of Justice

The Court of Justice consists of one judge from each Member State, assisted by eight Advocates-General. It can sit either in chambers of three or five judges, in a Grand Chamber of thirteen judges, or exceptionally, in plenary session. It has a crucial role in enforcing Community obligations and in ensuring the uniform interpretation of European law throughout the Community. Cases reach the Court either through direct actions or through references from national courts on points of Community law. Member States are obliged to apply its principles within their own jurisdictions, and the UK gives effect to this obligation by virtue of the European Communities Act 1972.

A Court of First Instance was created in 1988, to ease the problems of workload and delay which had bedevilled the Court of Justice. The Court of First Instance deals with disputes between the Community and its servants, along with actions for judicial review brought by natural or other legal persons. Since the Treaty of Nice came into force on 1 February 2003, it has also been able to deal with some references from national courts under the Article 234 procedure."

III. THE EU AND PARLIAMENTARY SUPREMACY

The impact of the EU on the principle of parliamentary supremacy is important for your understanding of our legal method and system today. The key questions can be stated in the following way:

"Now, given that European law takes precedence over the domestic law of the member states, it can happen that a legal rule of the EC is in direct conflict with a rule of domestic law. What is the consequence of this for English law, and the constitutional doctrine of the supremacy of Parliament? Can we still, in Britain, speak of the constitutional 'sovereignty' of our own Parliament, given the relationships between our law and legislation and those of the European Community?"[2]

The answer to that question has been explored by Bradley.

AW Bradley, "The Sovereignty of Parliament—Form or Substance" in Jeffrey Jowell and Dawn Oliver (eds) *The Changing Constitution*, 5th edn (Oxford: Oxford University Press, 2004), pp.42–46:

"[t]he European Union, of which the European Community forms part, is a unique, grouping of states created in 1993 by the Maastricht Treaty. The European Economic Community (the precursor of the present Community) was created by the Treaty of Rome in 1957. The United Kingdom acceded to the EEC by the Treaty of Brussels 1972, which was implemented in the United Kingdom by the European Communities Act 1972. What is distinctive about the Community compared with other international organizations is that broad executive, legislative, and fiscal powers are vested in organs of the Community. The European Court of Justice at Luxembourg (together with the Court of First Instance) exercises judicial powers in applying and enforcing Community law. Regulations made by the Council of Ministers are directly applicable in all member states as soon as they have been promulgated by the Council. Treaty provisions and other Community measures may have direct effect in member states, i.e. they may create rights that are directly enforceable by individuals in national courts, without needing to be implemented by national legislation. As the Court of Justice said in 1963:

'the Community constitutes a new legal order of international law, *for the benefit of which the states have limited their sovereign rights*, albeit within limited fields, and the subjects of which comprise not only Member States but also their nationals.'

From the perspective of the Court of Justice, it is essential that the main rules of Community law should have direct effect in the legal systems of the member states:

'The binding force of the Treaty [of Rome] and of measures taken in application of it must not differ from one state to another as a result of internal measures, lest the functioning of the Community system should be impeded and the achievement of the aims of the Treaty placed in peril.'

Community law cannot be overridden by domestic legal provisions 'without being deprived of its character as Community law and without the legal basis of the Community being called into question'. Community law thus creates obligations upon member states, and also individual rights enforceable in national courts.

The Community legal order is plainly inconsistent with the sovereignty of Parliament. Dicey asserted that 'no person or body is recognised by the law of England as having a right to override or set aside the legislation of Parliament'. In fact, United Kingdom law now recognizes that Community organs have the right to make

---

[2]   Phil Harris, *Introduction to Law* (6th ed., Butterworths, London, 2002), p.231.

decisions and issue regulations which may override legislation by Parliament. The supremacy or primacy of Community law within the economic or social areas with which it deals was already a significant aspect of the Community system during the 1960s, but it does not stand comfortably beside structures of constitutional law based on national frontiers. While the problem takes a special form in the United Kingdom, other member states have experienced comparable difficulties in adjusting their systems of constitutional law to take account of Community law. The Court of Justice has repeatedly emphasized that the application of Community law may not be delayed by obstacles in national law, even where these arise from constitutional considerations, such as concern for the protection of fundamental rights. As the court said in 1978:

> 'A national court which is called on within the limits of its jurisdiction, to apply provisions of Community law is under a duty to give full effect to these provisions, if necessary refusing of its own motion to apply any conflicting provisions of national legislation, even if adopted subsequently, and it is not necessary for the court to request or await the prior setting aside of such provisions by legislative or other constitutional means.'

When Denmark, the Republic of Ireland, and the United Kingdom acceded to the European Community together in 1973, each was required to take steps to accommodate Community law within their legal systems. In Denmark and Ireland, formal constitutional amendments were necessary. This course of action was not open to the United Kingdom, but it was essential that Parliament should authorize the reception of Community law. Legal effect had to be given not only to existing but also to future rules of Community law.

Given this necessity, the sovereignty of Parliament was 'at once an advantage and a source of difficulty'. The advantage was that no constitutional amendment was necessary. It took only a few lines in an Act of Parliament to give effect to a massive body of Community law and to equip the British government with additional powers to handle Community affairs. The difficulty came so far as the future was concerned: could a guarantee be given or an undertaking entrenched that Parliament would in the future neither legislate to leave the Community nor (whether by accident or design) legislate in a manner which conflicted with Community law?

The view of the government in 1972 was that no absolute legislative undertaking by Parliament could or should be given, since a future Parliament could disregard such an undertaking. Instead, the European Communities Act 1972 went so far as was thought possible in instructing British courts how to apply Community law in the future.

Section 2(1) of the 1972 Act gave effect in the United Kingdom to all rules of Community law that have direct application or direct effect within member states. This applied both to existing and to future Community rules. By section 2(2), the Government acquired very wide powers of making regulations to implement the United Kingdom's Community obligations and to give effect to rights arising under Community law. These powers included power to amend Acts of Parliament.

By section 2(4), it was provided that 'any enactment passed or to be passed, other than one contained in this part of the Act, shall be construed and shall have effect subject to the foregoing provisions of this section'— subject, in other words, to the comprehensive reception of existing and future Community law made by section 2(1). By section 3, questions of Community law were to be decided by the European Court of Justice or in accordance with the decisions of that Court, and all national courts were in future to take judicial note of such decisions. It was, however, section 2(4) that was the subject of most discussion. In form a new rule of construction, it appeared to require all legislation, both existing and future, to have effect subject to the rules of Community law that operated in national law under section 2(1). Arguably, the rule went far beyond being a rule of construction by declaring that, within the post-accession 'hierarchy of norms', Community law would be superior to any Act of Parliament, whenever enacted.

When these provisions were debated in Parliament, it was widely agreed that they did not exclude the possibility that Parliament might one day wish to repeal the Act and thus prevent the continued operation of Community law within the United Kingdom. The ultimate sovereignty of Westminster was thus not affected, as ministers admitted, though they refused to allow a statement to this effect to be included in the Act. But there was for many years uncertainty about a less extreme situation, namely what the position would be if an Act passed after 1972 were found to contain a provision that was impossible to reconcile with a rule of Community law. In this situation, we have already seen that the European Court would insist that Community law must prevail. Should the British courts adopt the same position, as sections 2 and 3 of the 1972 Act might indicate was their duty, or does the later Act of Parliament override these sections of the 1972 Act, to the extent of requiring the later Act to prevail?

In 1972, since it was impossible to undertake that no such conflict would arise in future, the government accepted that a later Act might prevail over the European Communities Act 1972 to the extent of the conflict.

The initial response of British judges to the questions posed by the 1972 Act showed a preference for resolving potential clashes and inconsistencies by interpretation, and they were reluctant to reach the sovereignty question. Thus in a much quoted dictum, Lord Denning MR said that the incoming tide of Community law could not be held back. 'Parliament has decreed that the Treaty is henceforward to be part of our law. It is equal in force to any statute.' The crucial question, however, was not whether Community law has the same force as any statute, but whether it has greater force than a statute by prevailing over subsequent Acts which conflict with it. There occurred a succession of difficult cases in which United Kingdom law on sex discrimination and employment protection was called into question by the application of Community rules that required equal treatment of men and women as regards their conditions of employment and pay."

As Bradley suggests, British courts have faced a number of claims by female workers seeking to enforce their rights to equal pay under European law. These cases are useful for us because they show how the principle of parliamentary supremacy was altered to reflect the reality of the new European legal order. The *Garland* case is a good example.

Garland v British Rail Engineering Ltd [1982] 2 All E.R. 402, ECJ and HL.

[The appellant, a married woman, complained to an industrial tribunal that her employer, British Rail, was discriminating against her because of sex contrary to s.6(2) of the Sex Discrimination Act 1975 by continuing to provide male employees after they retired with non-contractual concessionary travel facilities for themselves and their wives and dependent children. When female employees retired the provision of such facilities for their families was withdrawn. The industrial tribunal dismissed the complaint on the ground that s.6(4) of the Act exempts "a provision in relation to . . . retirement" (i.e. such provisions are outside of the purview of the Sex Discrimination Act) and, therefore, the discrimination was not unlawful. An appeal to the Employment Appeal Tribunal was upheld on the basis that the continuation of the privilege after retirement was not "a provision in relation to . . . retirement". The Court of Appeal then restored the decision of the industrial tribunal on the grounds that the statutory phrase "a provision in relation to . . . retirement" included any provision about retirement. The appellant then appealed to the House of Lords, which referred to the European Court of Justice the question whether the discrimination was contrary to Art.119 [now 141] of the EEC (now EC) Treaty (which reads "each Member State shall . . . maintain the application of the principle that men and women should receive equal pay for equal work"), and if so, whether the article conferred enforceable Community rights on individuals.]

European Court of Justice

[After reviewing the facts and questions raised, the Court ruled]:

"It follows from those considerations that rail travel facilities such as those referred to by the House of Lords fulfil the criteria enabling them to be treated as pay within the meaning of article 119 [now 141] of the EEC Treaty.

The argument that the facilities are not related to a contractual obligation is immaterial. The legal nature of the facilities is not important for the purposes of the application of article 119 [now 141] provided that they are granted in respect of the employment.

It follows that where an employer (although not bound to do so by contract) provides special travel facilities for former male employees to enjoy after their retirement this constitutes discrimination within the meaning of article 119 [now 141] against former female employees who do not receive the same facilities. . . ."

[Following receipt by the House of Lords of the judgment of the European Court of Justice, the matter was reconsidered:]

Lord Diplock

[Lord Diplock reviewed the facts, legislation, and the ruling of the Court of Justice]:

". . . My Lords, even if the obligation to observe the provisions of article 119 [now 141] were an obligation assumed by the United Kingdom under an ordinary international treaty or convention and there were no question of the treaty obligation being directly applicable as part of the law to be applied by the courts in this country without need for any further enactment, it is a principle of construction of United Kingdom statutes, now too well established to call for citation of authority, that the words of a statute passed after the treaty has been signed and dealing with the subject matter of the international obligation of the United Kingdom, are to be construed, if they are reasonably capable of bearing such a meaning, as intended to carry out the obligation and not to be inconsistent with it. A fortiori is this the case where the treaty obligation arises under one of the Community treaties to which s.2 of the European Communities Act 1972 applies."

[The other Law Lords concurred, and the appeal was allowed.]

The *Garland* case stands for the proposition that judges should interpret, if possible, domestic legislation in such a way as to be consistent with obligations entered into by the United Kingdom government under international treaties. This is especially true with respect to the treaties of the European Union, which are part of United Kingdom law. Given that this principle deals only with the *interpretation* of domestic legislation (i.e. how broadly or narrowly it is read), it can be argued that it does not directly undermine the principle of parliamentary supremacy. Lord Diplock undoubtedly would say that we must *assume* that Parliament intended to abide by its international obligations, and judges must interpret legislation accordingly. This has proven to be an important principle in widening the scope of sex discrimination provisions in British law.

Although EU law has been important in increasing employment protection, particularly for women, it was not perceived as challenging the principle of the supremacy of Parliament. Rather, the impact of the European legal order on parliamentary supremacy was demonstrated by a different legal struggle, known simply as the *Factortame* decisions. Atiyah sets the scene for us.

P.S. Atiyah, *Law and Modern Society*, 2nd edn (Oxford: Oxford University Press, 1995), pp.96–97:

"The profound effects of membership of the Community on the sovereignty of Parliament were not fully demonstrated until the dramatic *Factortame* case, when it first became apparent that English courts now had the power to declare Acts of Parliament to be void or invalid because they contravened European Community law. In this case the Community had allocated fishery quotas to its members, but a number of Spanish fishermen attempted to evade the effect of the quotas by registering companies in England, and then transferring their trawlers into the names of these companies, which were thus English companies. Their trawlers fished in British waters, but continued to land their catch in Spain. Not surprisingly, the British government thought that this was an evasion of the whole system of quotas and they introduced into Parliament a Bill which was in due course enacted as the Merchant Shipping Act 1988. Under this Act the companies, though registered in England, were to be treated as Spanish companies because their owners were Spanish. This Act of Parliament was then challenged as invalid on the ground that it contravened one of the basic corner-stones of European Community law, namely, that member states were not allowed to *discriminate* against nationals of other states. In this particular case the non-discrimination principle was invoked in a highly technical way, and because the fishery quotas had actually been agreed by the Community, it was obviously somewhat unfair that the Spanish fishermen were able to invoke it. But that is not really relevant to the crucial importance of the case. What happened when the case first reached the House of Lords was that it was held that as a matter of English law it was impossible to challenge the validity of the Merchant Shipping Act, and it was not even possible to suspend the operation of the Act while the case was referred to the European Court. But the matter was referred to the European Court, which decided that since

European Community rights were at stake (the right not to be discriminated against) the English courts *had* to have the power to suspend the operation of the Act pending a full hearing of the issue at the European Court."

Factortame Ltd and others v Secretary of State for Transport (No. 2) [1991] 1 All E.R. 70, ECJ and HL.

European Court of Justice:

". . . In accordance with the case law of the court, it is for the national courts, in application of the principle of co-operation laid down in article 5 of the EEC Treaty, to ensure the legal protection which persons derive from the direct effect of provisions of Community law. . . .

The court has also held that any provision of a national legal system and any legislative, administrative or judicial practice which might impair the effectiveness of Community law by withholding from the national court having jurisdiction to apply such law the power to do everything necessary at the moment of its application to set aside national legislative provisions which might prevent, even temporarily, Community rules from having full force and effect are incompatible with those requirements, which are the very essence of Community law . . . .

It must be added that the full effectiveness of Community law would be just as much impaired if a rule of national law could prevent a court seised of a dispute governed by Community law from granting interim relief in order to ensure the full effectiveness of the judgment to be given on the existence of the rights claimed under Community law. It follows that a court which in those circumstances would grant interim relief, if it were not for a rule of national law, is obliged to set aside that rule. . . .

Consequently, the reply to the question raised should be that Community law must be interpreted as meaning that a national court which, in a case before it concerning Community law, considers that the sole obstacle which precludes it from granting interim relief is a rule of national law must set aside that rule."

[Upon receipt of the opinion of the Court of Justice, the House of Lords granted an interim injunction restraining the enforcement of legislation pending a decision in the case. In so doing, Lord Bridge commented on the relationship between EC law and parliamentary supremacy:]

Lord Bridge of Harwich:

". . . Some public comments on the decision of the Court of Justice, affirming the jurisdiction of the courts of member states to override national legislation if necessary to enable interim relief to be granted in protection of rights under Community law, have suggested that this was a novel and dangerous invasion by a Community institution of the sovereignty of the United Kingdom Parliament. But such comments are based on a misconception. If the supremacy within the European Community of Community law over the national law of member states was not always inherent in the EEC Treaty it was certainly well established in the jurisprudence of the Court of Justice long before the United Kingdom joined the Community. Thus, whatever limitation of its sovereignty Parliament accepted when it enacted the European Communities Act 1972 was entirely voluntary. Under the terms of the 1972 Act it has always been clear that it was the duty of a United Kingdom court, when delivering final judgment, to override any rule of national law found to be in conflict with any directly enforceable rule of Community law. Similarly, when decisions of the Court of Justice have exposed areas of United Kingdom statute law which failed to implement Council directives, Parliament has always loyally accepted the obligation to make appropriate and prompt amendments. Thus there is nothing in any way novel in according supremacy to rules of Community law in those areas to which they apply and to insist that, in the protection of rights under Community law, national courts must not be inhibited by rules of national law from granting interim relief in appropriate cases is no more than a logical recognition of that supremacy."

A full hearing of the European Court of Justice subsequently declared that the Merchant Shipping Act did indeed violate Community law, and it was eventually invalidated by the High Court. The offending sections were removed by Parliament through amending legislation. The significance of the decision is considered by Atiyah.

P.S. Atiyah, *Law and Modern Society*, 2nd edn (Oxford: Oxford University Press, 1995), pp.97–100:

"In one sense this decision was little more than a practical necessity. If national courts could not declare their own national law to be invalid when it conflicted with European Community law, the practical working of the European Community legal system would be immensely cumbersome. It would mean that any conflict of this kind would have to be decided in defiance of Community law, the government would then be obliged to intro-duce amending legislation, and in the meantime, anyone whose rights had been adversely affected would be entitled to compensation, but there would be no machinery by which that compensation could be secured in an English court. So it would take years to enforce rights accorded by Community law, and if governments dragged their heels, the whole system would collapse into chaos. In this connection, it must be appreciated that conflicts between our national law and Community law are potentially very common, far more common than conflicts with international law or ordinary treaties. Even though the UK government has one of the best records among members of the Community in giving effect to Community Directives and other decisions, it has become increasingly apparent that many conflicts arise because our ministers and their advisers have not fully appreci-ated the way in which the European Court was likely to interpret Community law. So, in a practical sense it is really imperative that national courts should recognize the precedence of Community law over national laws, and the courts of all other member states in the Community in fact do recognize this. It must also be said that this is an absolute prerequisite of a federal state, and although the Community is not yet a federal state, it may eventually evolve into one. Without the *Factortame* decision it is doubtful if that could be done.

So the *Factortame* decision was a practical necessity. But at the same time it was, in a legal sense, a revo-lutionary decision. It was the first time for more than 300 years that an English Court had declared an Act of Parliament to be unenforceable in law. What this means, therefore, is that English law is now subject to European Community law. If there is a conflict between them, the English law may, and sometimes *must*, be declared invalid by English courts. In a sense, therefore, we have now acquired a written constitution—con-sisting of the various European Treaties—and laws contrary to the constitution will in future be invalid. So the sovereignty of Parliament seems to have been dethroned from its pivotal point at the centre of English constitutional law with very little appreciation of that fact by Parliament, politicians, or the public.

How has this happened? Many lawyers thought that the sovereignty of Parliament was the centre-piece of our unwritten constitution, and was something which simply could not be surrendered or abandoned. Every Parliament was traditionally thought to be legally sovereign and so capable of altering any previous law simply by passing a new Act. Why therefore was the Merchant Shipping Act of 1988 not treated simply as altering all previous law and, if necessary, the European Communities Act itself? If this had been done, the UK government would have been in breach of the Treaties and would have been under an obligation to amend or repeal the Merchant Shipping Act, but at least the traditional doctrine of Parliamentary sovereignty would have been pre-served. In fact, the judges in the House of Lords did not deny that this *could have been done*. Parliament could have phrased the Merchant Shipping Act to make it quite clear that it was to be applied whether or not it was in conformity with European law. In that case, said the judges in the House of Lords, they would have obeyed the Act, and so the sovereignty of Parliament would have been respected. But of course the government and Parliament did not *want* to pass an Act which violated European law. They thought that the Act they passed was good in law, but it turned out that they were mistaken. So the judges in the House of Lords thought that they should look at the Merchant Shipping Act as though Parliament had said at the beginning of the Act: 'The following Act is passed on the assumption that it is not in violation of European Community law; if it is contrary to Community law, do not enforce it.'

In this way the traditional respect for Parliamentary sovereignty was to some degree reconciled with the practical need to recognize the supremacy of European Community law.

In one sense this reconciliation may seem pretty empty. It now seems quite clear that we shall see many Acts of Parliament challenged in future as contrary to European law, and some of these challenges will be upheld. Moreover, it will not, of course, be open to Parliament to overrule these decisions by passing another Act, unless

Parliament chooses openly to defy the Community Treaties—which could only provoke a political crisis of the first order. So, to a limited extent, we shall have what many politicians (and perhaps the public and the press) intensely dislike, 'government by judges'. On the other hand, there is also reality in the way the House of Lords approached this problem, because it is very unlikely that Parliament will ever pass an Act which is clearly and plainly invalid as contrary to European law. Where it happens at all, it will nearly always happen by accident or mistake, and it may well accord with Parliament's intent that if the Act is found to conflict with Community law, it should not be enforced.

It must not be thought that all this means that English law can be challenged as invalid because (for instance) it is contrary to French or German law. It is only invalid if it is contrary to European Community law, which is the central law of the Community. In this respect the Community increasingly resembles a federal system of law, like that of the USA or Canada or Australia, where there is a federal government and a federal legislature, on the one hand, and state governments and state legislatures on the other. There are two sets of laws, each perfectly valid within its own sphere, but state laws which conflict with (valid) federal laws are invalid. In a strict legal sense, the situation in the European Community is thus similar to that of a federal state."

Questions

1. How does our membership in the EU *directly* impact upon the principle of parliamentary supremacy?

2. Do you think Parliament is still "supreme"? Do you think this is a legal or a political question (or both)? Explain.

3. Why was the *Factortame* case so important?

IV. THE IMPACT OF THE EU ON THE PROTECTION OF INDIVIDUAL RIGHTS

Finally, in this chapter, we turn to how developments in the EU have altered the principle of parliamentary supremacy with a particular focus on individual rights. We have already considered the role of rights in the context of the Human Rights Act 1998 and the European Convention on Human Rights. The Convention should not be confused with those obligations which arise by virtue of our membership in the European Union.

In fact, the law of the European Union legal order increasingly is proving a source of legally enforceable rights for individuals. The *Garland* case, which we have already examined, exemplifies how European rights of equal pay and equal treatment in employment and social security, on the basis of sex, will be enforced by the judiciary. The *Factortame* case exemplifies the enforcement of rights of free movement of nationals within the European Union, which again was enforced by the courts directly against the British Government. Moreover, the European Court of Justice has recognised that European law confers rights on individuals which can be enforced against other *individuals*, rather than the state. This is a complex area of European law, and one which you will look at in much greater detail in courses on the law of the European Union. For our purposes, these developments highlight the extent to which important social and economic rights are no longer solely within the power of Parliament to grant. Instead, the sources of these rights are the treaties, regulations, and directives of the European Union, and will be enforced by the European Court of Justice as well as by domestic courts.

The recognition of rights cannot be separated from broader social and political questions; issues with which Parliament might not be prepared to deal. Thus, it might be argued that the recognition of European rights is an important means for the furtherance of social change—for altering the norms and values of society as a whole. The relationship between legal and social change is complex, but the following case illustrates that there have been limits on the extent to which the European Court of Justice has been prepared to go in its furtherance of the "equal pay" principle.

Grant v South-West Trains Ltd [1998] All E.R. 193, ECJ.

European Court of Justice:

"1.   By decision of 19 July 1996, received at the Court of Justice of the European Communities on 22 July 1996, the Industrial Tribunal, Southampton, referred to the Court of Justice for a preliminary ruling under art.177 [now 234] of the EC Treaty six questions on the interpretation of art.119 [now 141] of that Treaty, Council Directive (EEC) 75/117 on the approximation of the laws of the member states relating to the application of the principle of equal pay for men and women (OJ 1975 L45 p. 19), and Council Directive (EEC) 76/207 on the implementation of the principle of equal treatment for men and women as regards access to employment, vocational training and promotion, and working conditions (OJ 1976 L39 p.40).

2.   Those questions were raised in proceedings between Ms Grant and her employer South-West Trains Ltd (SWT) concerning the refusal by SWT of travel concessions for Ms Grant's female partner.

3.   Ms Grant is employed by SWT, a company which operates railways in the Southampton region.

4.   Clause 18 of her contract of employment, entitled 'Travel facilities', states:

'You will be granted such free and reduced rate travel concessions as are applicable to a member of your grade. Your spouse and depend[a]nts will also be granted travel concessions. Travel concessions are granted at the discretion of [the employer] and will be withdrawn in the event of their misuse.'

5.   At the material time, the regulations adopted by the employer for the application of those provisions, the Staff Travel Facilities Privilege Ticket Regulations, provided in cl 8 ('Spouses') that:

'Privilege tickets are granted to a married member of staff . . . for one legal spouse but not for a spouse legally separated from the employee . . . Privilege tickets are granted for one common law opposite sex spouse of staff . . . subject to a statutory declaration being made that a meaningful relationship has existed for a period of two years or more.'

6.   The regulations also defined the conditions under which travel concessions could be granted to current employees (cls 1 to 4), employees having provisionally or definitively ceased working (cls 5 to 7), surviving spouses of employees (cl 9), children of employees (cls 10 and 11) and dependent members of employees' families (cl 12).

7.   On the basis of those provisions Ms Grant applied on 9 January 1995 for travel concessions for her female partner, with whom she declared she had had a 'meaningful relationship' for over two years.

8.   SWT refused to allow the benefit sought, on the ground that for unmarried persons travel concessions could be granted only for a partner of the opposite sex.

9.   Ms Grant thereupon made an application against SWT to the Industrial Tribunal, Southampton, arguing that that refusal constituted discrimination based on sex, contrary to the Equal Pay Act 1970, art.119 [now 141] of the EC Treaty and/or Directive 76/207. She submitted in particular that her predecessor in the post, a man who had declared that he had had a meaningful relationship with a woman for over two years, had enjoyed the benefit which had been refused her. . . .

13.   As a preliminary point, it should be observed that the court has already held that travel concessions granted by an employer to former employees, their spouses and dependents, in respect of their

employment are pay within the meaning of art.119 [now 141] of the Treaty (see, to that effect the judgment in *Garland v. British Rail Engineering Ltd* 12/81 [1982] 2 All ER 402). . . .

15. In view of the wording of the other questions and the grounds of the decision making the reference, the essential point raised by the national tribunal is whether an employer's refusal to grant travel concessions to the person of the same sex with whom an employee has a stable relationship constitutes discrimination prohibited by art.119 [now 141] of the Treaty and Directive 75/117, where such concessions are granted to an employee's spouse or the person of the opposite sex with whom an employee has a stable relationship outside marriage.

16. Ms Grant submits, first, that such a refusal constitutes discrimination directly based on sex. She submits that her employer's decision would have been different if the benefits in issue in the main proceedings had been claimed by a man living with a woman, and not by a woman living with a woman.

17. Ms Grant argues that the mere fact that the male worker who previously occupied her post had obtained travel concessions for his female partner, without being married to her, is enough to identify direct discrimination based on sex. In her submission, if a female worker does not receive the same benefits as a male worker, all other things being equal, she is the victim of discrimination based on sex (the 'but for' test).

18. Ms Grant contends, next, that such a refusal constitutes discrimination based on sexual orientation, which is included in the concept of 'discrimination based on sex' in art.119 [now 141] of the Treaty. In her opinion, differences in treatment based on sexual orientation originate in prejudices regarding the sexual and emotional behaviour of persons of a particular sex, and are in fact based on those persons' sex. . . .

19. Ms Grant claims, finally, that the refusal to allow her the benefit is not objectively justified. . . .

26. The refusal to allow Ms Grant the concessions is based on the fact that she does not satisfy the conditions prescribed in those regulations, more particularly on the fact that she does not live with a 'spouse' or a person of the opposite sex with whom she has had a 'meaningful' relationship for at least two years.

27. That condition, the effect of which is that the worker must live in a stable relationship with a person of the opposite sex in order to benefit from the travel concessions, is, like the other alternative conditions prescribed in the undertaking's regulations, applied regardless of the sex of the worker concerned. Thus travel concessions are refused to a male worker if he is living with a person of the same sex, just as they are to a female worker if she is living with a person of the same sex.

28. Since the condition imposed by the undertaking's regulations applies in the same way to female and male workers, it cannot be regarded as constituting discrimination directly based on sex.

29. Second, the court must consider whether, with respect to the application of a condition such as that in issue in the main proceedings, persons who have a stable relationship with a partner of the same sex are in the same situation as those who are married or have a stable relationship outside marriage with a partner of the opposite sex.

30. Ms Grant submits in particular that the laws of the member states, as well as those of the Community and other international organisations, increasingly treat the two situations as equivalent.

31. While the European Parliament, as Ms Grant observes, has indeed declared that it deplores all forms of discrimination based on an individual's sexual orientation, it is nevertheless the case that the Community has not as yet adopted rules providing for such equivalence.

32. As for the laws of the member states, while in some of them cohabitation by two persons of the same sex is treated as equivalent to marriage, although not completely, in most of them it is treated as equiv-

alent to a stable heterosexual relationship outside marriage only with respect to a limited number of rights, or else is not recognised in any particular way. . . .

35. It follows that, in the present state of the law within the Community, stable relationships between two persons of the same sex are not regarded as equivalent to marriages or stable relationships outside marriage between persons of opposite sex. Consequently, an employer is not required by Community law to treat the situation of a person who has a stable relationship with a partner of the same sex as equivalent to that of a person who is married to or has a stable relationship outside marriage with a partner of the opposite sex.

36. In those circumstances, it is for the legislature alone to adopt, if appropriate, measures which may affect that position. . . .

50. Accordingly, the answer to the national tribunal must be that the refusal by an employer to allow travel concessions to the person of the same sex with whom a worker has a stable relationship, where such concessions are allowed to a worker's spouse or to the person of the opposite sex with whom a worker has a stable relationship outside marriage, does not constitute discrimination prohibited by art.119 [now 141] of the Treaty or Directive 75/117."

Questions

1. We could describe the approach of the ECJ as judicial restraint, in that it explicitly throws the issue over to the legislatures, and the political institutions of the European Union. Do you think that such an approach to rights is justifiable? Why do you think the Court did not adopt a more *activist* stance, as it had done in other cases, such as *Garland*?

2. Should "spouses" (or "partners" or *whatever*) of employees be entitled to benefits such as these? Why?

3. Do you think that the ECJ might have been worried that a result in favour of Lisa Grant would have been out of step with thinking in some EU countries at that time? Is that concern justifiable? How should judges approach the relationship between progressive law reform through claims to individual rights, and more socially conservative attitudes which may be present in the general population? Is there only one perspective on these issues across the EU? How would you resolve such an issue if you were a judge on the ECJ?

Although the European Court of Justice in *Grant* was *deferential* to the Member States, subsequent developments have demonstrated the complex and contradictory story of the entrenchment of human rights in EC law.

Paul Craig and Gráinne de Búrca, *EU Law: Text, Cases and Materials*, 4th edn (Oxford: Oxford University Press, 2008), pp.408–409:

"Undoubtedly the most significant source of EC competence in the field of human rights protection within the EU . . . has been that introduced by the Amsterdam Treaty into Article 13 of the EC Treaty, supplementing the existing range of EU gender equality policies. Article 13 provides that the Community legislature may, within the limits of the Community's powers, take 'appropriate action to combat discrimination based on sex, racial or ethnic origin, religion or belief, disability, age or sexual orientation'. Hitherto, discrimination on grounds of sex and nationality was expressly prohibited by Community law, although the basis for adopting general legislation in these fields was for some time unclear. While the case of *P v S* appeared to suggest that a more general prohibition on discrimination extending beyond sex and nationality to embrace transsexuality and other grounds was *already* part of the 'great value of equality' and one of the fundamental principles underlying EC law, the ECJ in *Grant v South West Trains* beat a hasty retreat from that position.

In *Grant* the Court ruled, in a case concerning an employee who had been refused travel benefits for her same-sex partner, that EC law did not currently cover discrimination on the basis of sexual orientation. The Court in *Grant* confined the ruling in *P v S* to discrimination based 'essentially' on the sex of the person, which did not, in its view, apply to discrimination on the grounds of sexual orientation of the kind at issue in *Grant*. In making reference to Article 13 EC concerning sexual orientation which was not yet in force at the time, the ECJ argued that it was not for the Court to extend Community law beyond the scope provided for in the Treaty.

Its more expansive judicial approach to prohibiting discrimination against transsexuals under EC sex equality law, on the other hand, was confirmed in *K.B. v NHS*, where the ECJ drew support from the ECtHR to give a somewhat convoluted ruling on the incompatibility of British law with EC equal pay law. The Court ruled that the inability of a woman to obtain a survivor's pension as the widow of her post-operative transsexual partner amounted to unequal treatment in violation of Article 141 on equal pay between men and women, where that inability was due to the fact that under UK law, a couple whose birth certificates show they are of the same sex could not marry and a birth certificate could not be legally altered to reflect a sex change. Although this did not amount to discrimination between men and women, it did amount to discrimination as between transsexuals (who could not legally marry someone of their original sex) and non-transsexual persons. The complicated logic of the ECJ's ruling seems to proceed in three stages: (i) because the refusal to permit a birth certificate to be altered in these circumstances was a violation of the right to private life under the ECHR, it followed (ii) that the legal condition which prevented her from qualifying for the right to equal treatment under EC law was a violation of the ECHR, and consequently (iii) this brought her case within the scope of EC equal pay law.

However, the more restrictive approach in *Grant* to the issue of sexual-orientation discrimination (as compared with discrimination against transsexuals) was reinforced in the case of *D v Council*, which concerned unequal benefits for an EU employee whose relationship with a same-sex partner had been granted formal status as a registered partnership under Swedish law. While the case on its facts clearly concerns an indirect form of discrimination on grounds of sexual orientation, since traditional marriage with the access to financial benefits which it brings was not open to same-sex couples—just as the legal barrier to marriage in *K.B.* concerned an indirect discrimination of the same kind against transsexuals—the ECJ based its reasoning on an acceptance of the non-equivalence of a traditional marriage and a nationally recognized registered partnership. Further, just as in *Grant*, the ECJ emphasized its own unfitness, as a judicial institution, to bring about a positive change which was more properly to be enacted by legislation.

This clearly represents a retreat from the strong principle of equality as a fundamental right, and a deferential judicial stance in a situation where the exercise of positive legislative competence has been made possible under the Treaty and under staff regulations, but not yet exercised. Further, although no legislative move had been made to give registered partnerships a position equivalent to marriage, an amendment to the Staff Regulations which had not come into force at the time of the case provided for equal treatment of officials irrespective of their sexual orientation."

Finally, you should be aware that the EU has developed another important rights document, the Charter of Fundamental Rights which contains a number of fundamental human rights. The legal status of the Charter remains ambiguous, as Criag and de Búrca explain.

Paul Craig and Gráinne de Búrca, *EU Law: Text, Cases and Materials*, 4th edn (Oxford: Oxford University Press, 2008), pp.26:

"The Cologne European Council in 1999 launched another initiative of major constitutional significance, in establishing a 'body' which included national parliamentarians, European parliamentarians, and national government representatives to draft a Charter of fundamental rights for the EU. This body, which renamed itself a 'Convention', began work early in 2000 and drew up a Charter before the end of the same year. The Convention worked in an unusually open and transparent way, posting documents, materials, and drafts on a specially dedicated website, and holding its meetings openly. The Charter was 'solemnly proclaimed' by the Commission, Parliament and Council and received the political approval of the Member States at the European Council meeting in Nice in December 2000, but a decision on its legal status and specifically the question of its possible integration into the Treaties was placed on the so-called 'post-Nice agenda' and postponed until the 2004 IGC.

The Charter was a significant development. In substantive terms, despite criticisms of its content, the document was largely welcomed as a step forward for the legitimacy, identity, and human rights commitment of the EU. In terms of process, the mode by which it was drafted and adopted also attracted positive comment as a considerable improvement on the method by which treaties and other agreements have traditionally been negotiated and drawn up at EU level."

Questions

1. Do you think that the decision in *Grant* may be partly responsible for the subsequent developments described by Craig and de Búrca?

2. Are there reasons why the collective actions by Member State governments may be preferable to decisions of the European Court of Justice in advancing human rights in the European Union?

3. "There is little reason to trust judges as arbiters of controversial political issues. They will generally interpret law and facts from the standpoint of dominant groups in society." Discuss, with particular reference to the decisions in *Grant v South West Trains*, *Garland*, *CCSU*, *GLC v Bromley* and *Wheeler*.

Useful website addresses

Gateway to the European Union, *http://europa.eu* [Accessed May 12, 2010]

Portal to the law of the European Union, *http://eur-lex.europa.eu/RECH_legislation.do?ihmlang=en* [Accessed May 12, 2010]

Home page of the Court of Justice of the European Communities, *http://curia.europa.eu/jcms/j-6/* [Accessed May 12, 2010]

5

STATUTORY INTERPRETATION: INTRODUCTION TO LEGISLATION

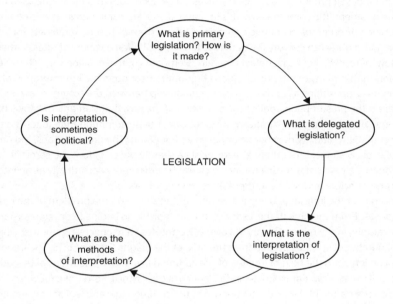

In this chapter, our focus shifts to the interpretation of legislation by the judiciary.
By the end of this chapter, you should:

- appreciate the historically important relationship between the common law and legislation;

- be aware of the primary steps in the process by which legislation is created;

- recognise the difficulties inherent in the process of statutory interpretation;

- be able to apply "rules" of statutory interpretation and to recognise the limitations of all such rules;

- appreciate that statutory interpretation raises contentious issues regarding the politics of judging;

- be aware of the distinction between "fact" and "law".

I. THE RELATIONSHIP BETWEEN LEGISLATION AND COMMON LAW

Although our legal system is referred to as a common law system, we will see in this chapter that it is legislation created by Parliament which is increasingly at the centre of our legal world. The historical relationship between these two pillars of the legal order provides a starting point for understanding the way in which statutes are handled by the judiciary.

Peter Goodrich, *Reading the Law* (Oxford: Blackwell, 1986), pp.40–44:

"In historical terms the primary source of law within the English legal system is unwritten law. Whilst in this respect it does not differ significantly from the early history of vernacular local legal systems in the rest of Europe, it does differ from those legal systems in that the unwritten law has retained its position as a significant source of law. Unwritten law (common law) is defined as custom derived from time immemorial. Written law is seen as a subsequent development. It has since medieval times been seen as a technique used to strengthen, interpret, regulate or amend the common law. This image of the relationship between written and unwritten law has persisted even through the economic transformations of the eighteenth and nineteenth centuries, and Blackstone in the mid-eighteenth century refers to legislation as fulfilling a variety of roles, 'either declaratory of the common law, or remedial of some defects therein'. Remnants of this position can still be seen in operation contemporarily in that many of the presumptions brought to bear upon the interpretation of legislation have their basis in presuppositions as to the historical relationship between the common law and legislation. For example, there is the presumption against the alteration of the law, that Parliament knows the law and only consciously changes the law. More substantively, we would cite the presumption that, following the common law principles of culpability, liability may not be imposed without fault. The presumptions, too numerous to be here detailed, collectively suggest that there already exists a seamless web of law, the common law, which may be changed but only as a result of a conscious act which will be interpreted accordingly as an interference with pre-existing law and principle and will be interpreted restrictively in its effects. . . .

With the separation of the judicial and legislative roles of the sovereign the problem of the relative status of the two sources arises. From the time of the Tudor monarchs legislation begins to develop as a major source of new law. For example, in the reign of Henry VIII over 600 statutes were enacted, a number which probably exceeds the total number of statutes passed from the time of the Magna Carta of 1215. The importance of legislation and its incursion upon the field of interest of the common law and the activities of the judiciary at this time is also reflected in case law. For example, in *Dr Bonham's Case* (1610), Lord Coke provides one of the earliest reflections upon the nature of the distinction between the common law and legislation and it is also from this period that one of the earliest rules of statutory interpretation was formulated, the rule in *Heydon's Case* (1584), suggesting the growing importance of statutory law. The importance of legislation and the development of the power of the House of Commons continues throughout the Restoration until the crisis which culminated with the 'Glorious Revolution' of 1688 and led to the enactment of the Bill of Rights which provides a formal statement of the new balance of power within the State, establishing the supremacy of the two Houses of Parliament over the monarch.

The importance of Parliament and the primary status of its legislative statements was consolidated in the political and jurisprudential traditions arising from the seventeenth century through to the nineteenth century in the work of Hobbes, Bentham, Austin and Dicey, works which may generally be characterized as emphasizing the written law of the sovereign institution, Parliament, as the supreme source of law. The impact of the concept of the 'supremacy' of Parliament is to be found increasingly acknowledged in the contemporary decisions of the common-law courts, as for example, in *Edinburgh and Dalkeith Railway v. Wauchope* [1842] 8 Cl & F 710, and in *Lee v. Bude and Torrington Railway* [1971] LR CP 577, 582, where it was acknowledged that although natural equity represented the 'law of laws' or the 'immutable law of nature', the substantive principles of such law stand 'as a warning, rather than [as] authority to be followed. We sit here as servants of the Queen and the legislature. Are we to act as regents over what is done by Parliament with the consent of the Queen, Lords and Commons? I deny that any such authority exists. . . . The proceedings here are judicial not autocratic'; and the judiciary are correspondingly the servants and not the judges of the content of legislation. The effect of this ideological tradition is that in the last instance legislation must supersede all previous law, be it previous enactments or the established common law."

The excerpt from Goodrich illustrates the historical development of the principle of parliamentary supremacy, as legislation enacted by Parliament came to have priority both over the common law and earlier inconsistent statutes. The role of the judges, in relation to legislation, thus became *interpretive* in that they *interpreted* statute law to cases brought before them. Before we further consider the precise role of judges in relation to statutes, however, it is important for you to have a basic understanding of how legislation is made.

II. THE LEGISLATIVE PROCESS

Penny Darbyshire, *Darbyshire on the English Legal System*, 8th edn (London: Sweet and Maxwell, 2005), pp.21–28:

"The most obvious source of codified law is an Act of Parliament, the UK Parliament. In the British constitution, a fundamental doctrine is that of parliamentary sovereignty which recognises that supreme power is vested in Parliament and that there is no limit in law to the law-making capacity of that institution. This is now massively tempered by membership of the Common Market, now European Union, since 1973 and the importation of the European Convention on Human Rights by the Human Rights Act 1998, in 2000. Nevertheless, unless it conflicts with Community law or the Convention, what Parliament passes in the form of an Act will be put into effect by the courts. . . .

This acceptance by the courts of parliamentary supremacy is entirely a matter of history derived directly from the seventeenth century conflict between the Stuart Kings and Parliament. In that conflict, the courts took the side of Parliament and one result of their joint success was that, thereafter, the courts have been prepared to acknowledge the supremacy of Parliament within its own sphere, whilst Parliament has readily allowed the independence of the judiciary to become an acknowledged factor in the constitution. The contrast with countries with a written constitution (most countries) is, however, very marked in that their Supreme Courts have the power to overrule legislation as being 'unconstitutional.' No such power exists in the English legal system. In *British Railways Board v Pickin* (1974) an unsuccessful attempt was made to persuade the courts to intervene on the grounds that the Board had obtained powers in a private Act of Parliament by misleading Parliament. The only role of the courts is to 'interpret' the statutory provisions to the circumstances of any given case. If there is an element of human rights in issue, they must, where possible, interpret Acts so as to give effect to Convention rights and they are obliged to recognise Community law as supreme, if it conflicts with English law.

Another unsuccessful attempt to overturn an Act was made in 2005, in *R. (Jackson) v Attorney-General* [2005] EWCA Civ 126. In this case, pro-hunt supporters challenged the validity of the Hunting Act 2004, arguing that it was invalid because it was passed under a procedure laid down by the Parliament Act 1949 which was in itself invalid. The 2004 Act, banning foxhunting, had been hotly controversial. The Government had used their powers under the 1949 Act to pass the Bill through the House of Commons only, without the consent of the House of Lords, who had rejected a previous version. The 1949 Act had amended the Parliament Act 1911, which permitted a Bill to be passed by the Commons alone, under certain circumstances, provided a two year period had elapsed. The 1949 Act reduced the period to one year. Lord Woolf C.J. in the Court of Appeal (CA) remarked that it was very rare for the courts to entertain a challenge to an Act of Parliament but the Administrative Court, below, had been correct to admit the challenge. The 1911 Act was very unusual. The House of Lords, House of Commons and the King had used the machinery of legislation to make a fundamental change to the constitution. It was 'perfectly appropriate' for the courts to consider the issue since they were helping Parliament and the public by clarifying the legal position when such clarification was obviously necessary. The Court held that the constitution could be amended by the legislature and it was clear that such an amendment was intended by the 1911 Act but that did not mean it was intended that the 1911 Act could not be amended by the 1949 Act.

The Queen in Parliament

The UK Parliament is made up of three constituent elements: the monarch; the House of Lords; and the House of Commons. An Act of Parliament normally has approval of all three elements. Under certain conditions, it can be passed without the approval of the Lords, using the Parliament Acts 1911 and 1949. This has only been done a few times and occurred in 2004 with the Hunting Act.

The monarch's place in Parliament is a formality. She attends the opening of each new session of Parliament, as she does each autumn and after each General Election when a new government is elected, such as in 2005. She reads the speech from the throne, which is the Government's statement of its legislative proposals for the coming session of Parliament. The speech is written by the Prime Minister and does not in any way reflect her personal views. All legislation must receive the Royal Assent before it becomes law. It has not been refused since the reign of Queen Anne in 1707 and will never be refused; such is the strength of the constitutional convention that the monarchy does not interfere in politics.

Procedure

An Act of Parliament starts off as a Bill. Most Bills are Government Bills. Their clauses will have been agreed by the 'sponsoring' department which has instructed parliamentary counsel to draft the Bill.

Before the Bill becomes an Act of Parliament, and the clauses become sections, it must undergo five stages in each House. It may start off in the Commons or Lords. Once the Bill with any amendments has been approved by the House of Commons and, normally, the House of Lords, it needs only the Royal Assent to become an Act of Parliament. It comes into immediate effect unless it contains its own starting date, or it has a provision which allows different parts of the Act to be brought into force at different times, by a minister making a statutory instrument to that effect. For instance, different parts of the Criminal Justice Act 2003 are now being brought into force, in 2005, the time of writing. The Human Rights Act 1998 came into force in 2000, to give the courts, public bodies and the public time to prepare. . . .

The Form of an Act of Parliament (Statute)

Language

Statutory language must be precise. Every Act must relate to existing legislation on the subject so clauses often amend old Acts or cross-refer to others. Further, although the modern aim is to draft the law in plain English, the endeavour to close loopholes also makes Acts complex. . . . Controversial or big Bills suffer many amendments, especially by the Government who introduced them. It is said that there is a tendency to introduce Bills in outline and fill in the details as they pass through Parliament. These factors combine to make statutes complicated and notoriously difficult for the lay person to understand. Although the earliest statutes had long titles and preambles, since the Short Titles Act 1896, Acts of Parliament have been given a short title and preambles have become the exception.

Citation

From 1963 every Act is given a Chapter number for the year in which it receives the Royal Assent. This abolishes the centuries-old system by which Acts were given a Chapter number for the session of the parliament in question designated by the regnal year of the monarch. This system could produce difficulties. For instance, 1937 under the former system was cited as '1 Edw. 8 and 1 Geo. 6.' The present system is to refer to an Act by its short title and Chapter number for the year in questions: for example The Gender Recognition Act 2004 (c.7).

Acts are published by the Office of Public Sector Information (OPSI). It operates as part of the Cabinet Office. In practice, OPSI makes new legislation available for sale to the public as soon as it has been given the Royal Assent. It is available free online from the OPSI, with all public Acts from 1988.

Public Bills and Private Bills

A Public Bill is legislation which affects the public at large, and applies throughout England and Wales. Most Bills are Public and sponsored by the Government. A Private Bill is legislation which affects a limited section of the population, either by reference to locality or by reference to a particular family or group of individuals. These are known respectively as Local and Personal Bills. A Private Member's Bill is a Public Bill introduced by a back-bench Member of Parliament, who has been successful in the ballot. A Hybrid Bill may cover work of national importance but in a local area. Examples are the Channel Tunnel Bills of the 1970s and 1980s.

Consolidation, codification and statute law revision

Consolidation is the process by which provisions in a number of Acts of Parliament are brought together and re-enacted as one Act. It is not a method for changing the law but it does make the law easier to find. In order to ease the passage of such measures, they go through Parliament in a special procedure. In 2000, for example, the legis-lation concerning sentencing was consolidated in the Powers of the Criminal Courts (Sentencing) Act 2000.

Codification is the term used of an Act of Parliament which brings together all the existing legislation and case law and forms a complete restatement of the law. It can involve changes in the law and is thus one method of law reform. Recently, Lord Chief Justice Bingham, as he then was, added his weight to the academ-ics' increasingly impatient demand for a codification of the criminal law and Professor Spencer added a persua-sive and reasoned argument for codifying criminal procedure and the Government included plans for a code in its legislative proposals announced in its 2001 white paper, *Criminal Justice: The Way Ahead*. . . .

The Law Commission, which was set up under the Law Commissions Act 1965, has, as one of its respon-sibilities, to keep under review all the law with a view to its systematic development and reform including, in particular, the codification of the law. It is consequently working at the present time on possible legislation which will, at some future time, codify particular branches of the law. The Law Commission also has overall responsibility for advising the repeal of obsolete and unnecessary enactments. Since 1993/94, a Special Public Bill Committee 'fast-track' procedure has been used for legislation proposed by the Law Commission and other non-contentious Bills. This 'Jellicoe procedure' employs a committee of specialists (*e.g.* judges and lawyers on the Arbitration Bill 1996) instead of a committee of the whole House. Lord Chancellor Mackay's ill-fated Domestic Violence Bill 1995 was supposed to be one such Bill. Unfortunately, it proved to be very controversial and was lost. . . .

Delegated legislation

This is the name given to the law made in documentary form by subordinate authorities acting under law-making powers delegated by Parliament or the sovereign, acting under her prerogative. Parliament does not have time or expertise to fill in the details or technicalities of the law so most big Bills are mere frameworks. The big difference between Acts of Parliament (primary legislation) and subordinate or delegated legislation is that the courts can quash the latter if it is outside the remit of delegated power (substantively *ultra vires*) or has not been made in a procedurally correct way (procedurally *ultra vires*). The CA confirmed that it was entitled to review subordinate legislation on the grounds of illegality, procedural impropriety or *Wednesbury* unreasonableness, even where it had been debated and approved by affirmative resolution of both Houses of Parliament. The Court was entitled to assess for itself the facts presented to Parliament as supporting the legality of the subordinate legislation. The extent to which a statutory power was open to judicial review on the ground of irrationality depended critically on the nature and purpose of the enabling legislation: *R. (Javed) v SS for Home Department* and joined cases [2001] EWCA Civ 789.

Such legislation can take the following forms.

Orders in Council

Parliament sometimes permits the Government through Her Majesty in Council to make law by way of an Order in Council. This is particularly true where an emergency is imminent. Orders in Council are sometimes issued under a prerogative power, as was the Order in Council concerned in the case of *CCSU v Minister for the Civil Service* (1984), otherwise known as 'the GCHQ case', which Margaret Thatcher used to issue a ban on trade union membership in GCHQ. An Order in Council requires the formality of a meeting of the Privy Council in the presence of the Queen. Practically, the decision to use prerogative power in this way is made by the Cabinet, or a small section thereof.

Statutory Instruments

A more common form of delegated legislation is the power frequently given to ministers to make law for a specified purpose. The document containing this law is called a statutory instrument and thousands are issued every year. As each one is published it is given a number for the year, for example, the Greenhouse Gas Emissions Trading Scheme (Amendment) Regulations (SI 2004/3390). Statutory instruments have become of major importance as a source of law. Much more law is contained in them than in Acts. Almost all Community law comes into English law via statutory instruments like the one just mentioned.

Byelaws

Parliament delegates to local authorities and other public bodies the power to make local laws or laws limited to their particular functions. Thus local authorities can make town laws, or byelaws, for their areas. For instance, there are often rules governing behaviour in parks or leisure centres. Even so the authority has to obtain confirmation of the byelaws from the named central government minister before the byelaws take effect. The power to make byelaws also belongs to public bodies such as the British Airports Authority. Byelaws can be quashed on judicial review by the Divisional Court of the Queen's Bench Division if they are *ultra vires*, or their illegality can be used as a defence where someone is prosecuted for infringing them. This happened to Lindis Percy, a protester against US defence forces in this country. She appealed to the Crown Court against her conviction for breach of byelaws by repeatedly entering a secure defence installation and the Crown Court upheld her appeal, holding the byelaws to be *ultra vires* the Military Lands Act 1892, the enabling Act (facts in *SS for Defence v Percy* (1999, HC)). Another example is *Boddington v British Transport Police* (1998, HL), where B sought to defend himself on the ground that the posting of no smoking notices by Network South Central was *ultra vires*. He was convicted and the House of Lords dismissed his last appeal.

Welsh Law

Wales gained considerable autonomy in making delegated legislation for Wales, from 1999. Under the Government of Wales Act 1998 and subsequent legislation, this includes substantial areas of government, such as agriculture, planning and the environment, health and social services, education and industry, housing and local government, sport and leisure and the Welsh language. In turn, the Assembly has delegated many of its powers to its First Minister, who leads the Welsh Assembly Government. . . .

Comment on delegated legislation

Since the mid-point of the twentieth century, there has been increasing concern that Acts are mere frameworks, giving substantial powers to Ministers to fill in the details through delegated powers, usually using statutory instruments. For instance, the Access to Justice Act 1999 provides a new framework for the provision of legal services but leaves it up to the Lord Chancellor to devise a funding code to say what types of litigation will be publicly funded and leaves it up to regional bodies to allocate priorities in spending their budget. Concern has repeatedly been expressed that too much legislative power is being given to the executive. The Lords raised this concern in a debate in 1991, citing the Child Support Act, which gave over 100 regulation-making powers to the Minister and others, most of which were subjected to the negative procedure, by which a statutory instrument automatically becomes law unless concerns about it are positively raised in Parliament.

In recent years there has been concern over the frequent use of 'Henry VIII' sections in Acts which permit a Minister to amend primary legislation, an Act, through a statutory instrument. In *Thorburn v Sunderland City Council* [2002] EWHC 195 imperial heroes challenged the validity of delegated legislation to amend the Weights and Measures Act 1985. It implemented an EC Metrication Directive and made it illegal to sell loose goods by the pound. The statute contained a 'Henry VIII clause', allowing itself to be amended by subordinate legislation. The High Court dismissed the argument that Henry VIII clauses should only be used to make minor amendments to Acts. They also dismissed the argument founded on the doctrine of implied repeal, that the 1985 Act had impliedly repealed s.2(2) of the European Communities Act 1972.

A power for a Minister to 'fast-track' an amendment to a piece of legislation which has been declared by the courts to be incompatible with the European Convention on Human Rights is contained in the Human Rights Act 1998. This caused concern in the passage of the Bill through the Lords."

III. An Introduction to Interpretation

We now turn to the *interpretation* of legislation by judges. After a statute successfully completes the parliamentary process, it enters the statute book. However, questions about the scope, meaning, and applicability of legislation to particular factual situations may arise. This is where the judiciary may be called upon, within a legal dispute, to *interpret* the meaning of a statute. We refer to this as statutory interpretation. We will see that, while the creation of law is the role of Parliament, the function of interpretation leaves the judiciary, in some cases, with a considerable degree of freedom in determining what that legislation *means*. This task often involves highly controversial *choices* which judges are forced to make. Good examples of the problems faced by judges in interpretation are provided by Dworkin.

Ronald Dworkin, *Law's Empire* (London: HarperCollins, 1986), pp.15–23:

Elmer's case

"Elmer murdered his grandfather—he poisoned him—in New York in 1882. He knew that his grandfather's existing will left him the bulk of the estate, and he suspected that the old man, who had recently remarried, would change the will and leave him nothing. Elmer's crime was discovered; he was convicted and sentenced to a term of years in jail. Was he legally entitled to the inheritance his grandfather's last will provided? The residuary legatees under the will, those entitled to inherit if Elmer had died before his grandfather, were the grandfather's daughters. Their first names are not reported, so I will call them Goneril and Regan. They sued the administrator of the will, demanding that the property now go to them instead of Elmer. They argued that since Elmer had murdered the testator, their father, the law entitled Elmer to nothing.

The law pertaining to wills is for the most part set out in special statutes, often called statutes of wills, which stipulate the form a will must take to be considered valid in law: how many and what kinds of witnesses must sign, what the mental state of the testator must be, how a valid will, once executed, may be revoked or changed by the testator, and so forth. The New York statute of wills, like most others in force at that time, said nothing explicit about whether someone named in a will could inherit according to its terms if he had murdered the testator. Elmer's lawyer argued that since the will violated none of the explicit provisions of the statute it was valid, and since Elmer was named in a valid will he must inherit. He said that if the court held for Goneril and Regan, it would be changing the will and substituting its own moral convictions for the law. The judges of the highest court of New York all agreed that their decision must be in accordance with the law. None denied that if the statute of wills, properly interpreted, gave the inheritance to Elmer, they must order the administrator to give it to him. None said that in that case the law must be reformed in the interests of justice. They disagreed about the correct result in the case, but their disagreement—or so it seems from reading the opinions they wrote—was about what the law actually was, about what the statute required when properly read.

How can people who have read the text of a statute in front of them disagree about what it actually means, about what law it has made? We must draw a distinction between two senses of the word 'statute.' It can describe a physical entity of a certain type, a document with words printed on it, the very words congressmen or members of Parliament had in front of them when they voted to enact that document. But it can also be used to describe the law created by enacting that document, which may be a much more complex matter. Consider the difference between a poem conceived as a series of words that can be spoken or written and a poem conceived as the expression of a particular metaphysical theory or point of view. Literary critics all agree about what the poem 'Sailing to Byzantium' is in the first sense. They agree it is the series of words designated as that poem by

W.B. Yeats. But they nevertheless disagree about what the poem is in the second sense, about what the poem really says or means. They disagree about how to construct the 'real' poem, the poem in the second sense, from the text, the poem in the first sense.

In much the same way, judges before whom a statute is laid need to construct the 'real' statute—a statement of what difference the statute makes to the legal rights of various people—from the text in the statute book. Just as literary critics need a working theory, or at least a style of interpretation, in order to construct the poem behind the text, so judges need something like a theory of legislation to do this for statutes. This may seem evident when the words in the statute book suffer from some semantic defect; when they are ambiguous or vague, for example. But a theory of legislation is also necessary when these words are, from the linguistic point of view, impeccable. The words of the statute of wills that figured in Elmer's case were neither vague nor ambiguous. The judges disagreed about the impact of these words on the legal rights of Elmer, Goneril, and Regan because they disagreed about how to construct the real statute in the special circumstances of that case.

The dissenting opinion, written by Judge Gray, argued for a theory of legislation more popular then than it is now. This is sometimes called a theory of 'literal' interpretation, though that is not a particularly illuminating description. It proposes that the words of a statute be given what we might better call their acontextual meaning, that is, the meaning we would assign them if we had no special information about the context of their use or the intentions of their author. This method of interpretation requires that no context-dependent and unexpressed qualifications be made to general language, so Judge Gray insisted that the real statute, constructed in the proper way, contained no exceptions for murderers. He voted for Elmer.

Law students reading his opinion now are mostly contemptuous of that way of constructing a statute from a text; they say it is an example of mechanical jurisprudence. But there was nothing mechanical about Judge Gray's argument. There is much to be said (some of which he did say) for his method of constructing a statute, at least in the case of a statute of wills. Testators should know how their wills will be treated when they are no longer alive to offer fresh instructions. Perhaps Elmer's grandfather would have preferred his property to go to Goneril and Regan in the event that Elmer poisoned him. But perhaps not: he might have thought that Elmer, even with murder on his hands, was still a better object for his generosity than his daughters. It might be wiser in the long run for judges to assure testators that the statute of wills will be interpreted in the so-called literal way, so that testators can make any arrangements they wish, confident that their dispositions, however amusing, will be respected. Besides, if Elmer loses his inheritance just because he is a murderer, then that is a further punishment, beyond his term in jail, for his crime. It is an important principle of justice that the punishment for a particular crime must be set out in advance by the legislature and not increased by judges after the crime has been committed. All this (and more) can be said on behalf of Judge Gray's theory about how to read a statute of wills.

Judge Earl, however, writing for the majority, used a very different theory of legislation, which gives the legislators' *intentions* an important influence over the real statute. 'It is a familiar canon of construction,' Earl wrote, 'that a thing which is within the intention of the makers of a statute is as much within the statute as if it were within the letter; and a thing which is within the letter of the statute is not within the statute, unless it be within the intention of the makers.' (Notice how he relies on the distinction between the text, which he calls the 'letter' of the statute, and the real statute, which he calls the 'statute' itself.) It would be absurd, he thought, to suppose that the New York legislators who originally enacted the statute of wills intended murderers to inherit, and for that reason the real statute they enacted did not have that consequence.

We must take some care in stating what Judge Earl meant about the role intention should play in constructing statutes. He did not mean that a statute can have no consequence the legislators did not have in mind. This is plainly too strong as a general rule: no legislator can have in mind all the consequences of any statute he votes for. The New York legislators could not have contemplated that people might bequeath computers, but it would be absurd to conclude that the statute does not cover such bequests. Nor did he mean only that a statute can contain nothing that the legislators intended that it not contain. This seems more plausible, but it is too weak to be of any use in Elmer's case. For it seems likely that the New York legislators did not have the case of murderers in mind at all. They did not intend that murderers inherit, but neither did they intend that they should not. They had no active intention either way. Earl meant to rely on a principle we might call intermediate between these excessively strong and weak principles: he meant that a statute does not have any consequence the legislators would have rejected if they had contemplated it.

Judge Earl did not rely only on this principle about legislative intention; his theory of legislation contained another relevant principle. He said that statutes should be constructed from texts not in historical isolation but against the background of what he called general principles of law: he meant that judges should construct a statute so as to make it conform as closely as possible to principles of justice assumed elsewhere in the law. He offered two reasons. First, it is sensible to assume that legislators have a general and diffuse intention to respect traditional principles of justice unless they clearly indicate the contrary. Second, since a statute forms part of a larger intellectual system, the law as a whole, it should be constructed so as to make that larger system coherent in principle. Earl argued that the law elsewhere respects the principle that no one should profit from his own wrong, so the statute of wills should be read to deny inheritance to someone who has murdered to obtain it.

Judge Earl's views prevailed. They attracted four other judges to his side, while Judge Gray was able to find only one ally. So Elmer did not receive his inheritance. . . .[T]he dispute about Elmer was not about whether judges should follow the law or adjust it in the interests of justice. At least it was not if we take the opinions I described at face value and (as I shall argue later) we have no justification for taking them any other way. It was a dispute about what the law was, about what the real statute the legislators enacted really said.

The Snail Darter case

I now describe a much more recent case, though more briefly, in order to show that this kind of dispute continues to occupy judges. In 1973, during a period of great national concern about conservation, the United States Congress enacted the Endangered Species Act. It empowers the secretary of the interior to designate species that would be endangered, in his opinion, by the destruction of some habitat he considers crucial to its survival and then requires all agencies and departments of the government to take 'such action necessary to insure that actions authorized, funded, or carried out by them do not jeopardize the continued existence of such endangered species.'

A group of conservationists based in Tennessee had been opposing dam construction projects of the Tennessee Valley Authority, not because of any threat to species but because these projects were altering the geography of the area by converting free-flowing streams into narrow, ugly ditches to produce an unneeded increase (or so the conservationists believed) in hydroelectric power. The conservationists discovered that one almost finished TVA dam, costing over one hundred million dollars, would be likely to destroy the only habitat of the snail darter, a three-inch fish of no particular beauty or biological interest or general ecological importance. They persuaded the secretary to designate the snail darter as endangered and brought proceedings to stop the dam from being completed and used.

The authority argued that the statute should not be construed to prevent the completion or operation of any project substantially completed when the secretary made his order. It said the phrase 'actions authorized, funded, or carried out' should be taken to refer to beginning a project, not completing projects begun earlier. It supported its claim by pointing to various acts of Congress, all taken after the secretary had declared that completing the dam would destroy the snail darter, which suggested that Congress wished the dam to be completed notwithstanding that declaration. Congress had specifically authorized funds for continuing the project after the secretary's designation, and various of its committees had specifically and repeatedly declared that they disagreed with the secretary, accepted the authority's interpretation of the statute, and wished the project to continue.

The Supreme Court nevertheless ordered that the dam be halted, in spite of the great waste of public funds. (Congress then enacted a further statute establishing a general procedure for exemption from the act, based on findings by a review board). Chief Justice Warren Burger wrote an opinion for the majority of the justices. He said, in words that recall Judge Gray's opinion in Elmer's case, that when the text is clear the Court has no right to refuse to apply it just because it believes the results silly. Times change, however, and the chief justice's opinion was in one respect very different from Judge Gray's. Burger recognized the relevance of congressional intention to the decision what statute Congress had made. But he did not accept Earl's principle about the *way* in which congressional intention is relevant. He refused to consider the counterfactual test that Earl's analysis made decisive. 'It is not for us,' he said, 'to speculate, much less act, on whether Congress would have altered its stance had the specific events of this case been anticipated.'

Instead he adopted what I called, in discussing Earl's opinion, the excessively weak version of the idea that judges constructing a statute must respect the legislature's intentions. That version comes to this: if the acontextual meaning of the words in the text is clear—if the words 'carry out' would normally include continuing as well as beginning a project—then the Court must assign those words that meaning unless it can be shown that the legislature actually intended the opposite result. The legislative history leading up to the enactment of the Endangered Species Act did not warrant that conclusion, he said, because Congress plainly wanted to give endangered species a high order of protection even at great cost to other social goals, and it is certainly possible, even if not probable, that legislators with that general aim would want the snail darter saved even at the amazing expense of a wasted dam. He rejected the evidence of the later committee reports and the actions of Congress in approving funding for the continuation of the dam, which might have been thought to indicate an actual intention not to sacrifice the dam to this particular species. The committees that had reported in favour of the dam were not the same as the committees that had sponsored the act in the first place, he said, and congressmen often vote on appropriations without fully considering whether the proposed expenditures are legal under past congressional decisions.

Justice Lewis Powell wrote a dissent for himself and one other justice. He said that the majority's decision constructed an absurd real statute from the text of the Endangered Species Act. 'It is not our province,' he said, 'to rectify policy or political judgments by the Legislative Branch, however egregiously they may disserve the public interest. But where the statutory and legislative history, as in this case, need not be construed to reach such a result, I view it as the duty of this Court to adopt a permissible construction that accords with some modicum of common sense and the public weal.' This states yet another theory of legislation, another theory of how the legislature's intentions affect the statute behind the text, and it is very different from Burger's theory. Burger said that the acontextual meaning of the text should be enforced, no matter how odd or absurd the consequences, unless the court discovered strong evidence that Congress actually intended the opposite. Powell said that the courts should accept an absurd result only if they find compelling evidence that it was intended. Burger's theory is Gray's, though in a less rigid form that gives some role to legislative intention. Powell's theory is like Earl's, though in this case it substitutes common sense for the principles of justice found elsewhere in the law.

Once again, if we take the opinions of these two justices at face value, they did not disagree about any historical matters of fact. They did not disagree about the state of mind of the various congressmen who joined in enacting the Endangered Species Act. Both justices assumed that most congressmen had never considered whether the act might be used to halt an expensive dam almost completed. Nor did they disagree over the question of fidelity. Both accepted that the Court should follow the law. They disagreed about the question of law; they disagreed about how judges should decide what law is made by a particular text enacted by Congress when the congressmen had the kind of beliefs and intentions both justices agreed they had in this instance."

The examples outlined by Dworkin raise issues central to statutory interpretation, including whether words can have a "literal" meaning, how the purpose of a statute should be determined, and how the intention of the legislature should be discovered. These are important questions, and students, lawyers, legal academics and judges spend a good deal of their time determining what statutes mean in particular factual settings. The first rule for engaging in interpretation is a simple one: START WITH THE WORDS OF THE STATUTE! After all, statutes operate in a *mandatory* fashion. That is, if the words of a statute clearly do apply to a situation, then courts cannot disregard the operation of a statute, given the fundamental principle of the supremacy of Parliament. So too, if the facts do not fall within the words of the statute, then the statute does not apply. The problem of statutory interpretation arises in those cases where the facts are neither clearly within or outside the language of the statute. Generally speaking, that uncertainty is a product of the language of the statute—either it is found to be uncertain or vague.

However, sometimes statutory language may give rise to issues of interpretation even when that language *appears* to be perfectly clear, as the following cases demonstrate.

Fisher v Bell [1960] 3 All E.R. 731, QBD.

Lord Parker C.J.:

"This is an appeal by way of Case Stated by justices for the City and County of Bristol, before whom an information was preferred by the appellant, a chief inspector of police, against the respondent that he on a certain day in a shop unlawfully did offer for sale a knife which was to use ordinary terms, a flick knife, contrary to s.1 of the Restriction of Offensive Weapons Act, 1959. Section 1(1) of the Act provides:

> 'Any person who manufactures, sells or hires or offers for sale or hire or lends or gives to any other person—(a) any knife which has a blade which opens automatically by hand pressure applied to a button, spring or other device in or attached to the handle of the knife, sometimes known as a "flick knife". . . . shall be guilty of an offence. . . .'

The justices, without deciding whether the knife in question was a knife of the kind described in the statute, decided that the information must be dismissed on the ground that there had not been an offer for sale.

The short facts are these. The respondent keeps a retail shop in Bristol and, in October, 1959, a police constable, walking past the shop, saw in the window, amongst other articles, one of the knives. Behind the knife in the window was a ticket with the words 'Ejector knife—4s.' The police officer went in and informed the respondent that he would be reported for offering for a sale such knife, and the respondent replied: 'Fair enough'.

The sole question is whether the exhibition of that knife in the window with the ticket constituted an offer for sale within the statute. I think that most lay people would be inclined to the view (as, indeed, I was myself when I first read these papers), that if a knife were displayed in a window like that with a price attached to it, it was nonsense to say that that was not offering it for sale. The knife is there inviting people to buy it, and in ordinary language it is for sale; but any statute must be looked at in the light of the general law of the country, for Parliament must be taken to know the general law. It is clear that, according to the ordinary law of contract, the display of an article with a price on it in a shop window is merely an invitation to treat. It is in no sense an offer for sale the acceptance of which constitutes a contract. That is clearly the general law of the country. Not only is that so, but it is to be observed that, in many statutes and orders which prohibit selling and offering for sale of goods, it is very common, when it is so desired, to insert the words 'offering or exposing for sale', 'exposing for sale' being clearly the words which would cover the display of goods in a shop window. Not, only that, but it appears that under several statutes—we have been referred in particular to the Prices of Goods Act, 1939, and the Goods and Services (Price Control) Act, 1941—Parliament, when it desires to enlarge the ordinary meaning of those words, has a definition section enlarging the ordinary meaning of 'offer for sale' to cover other matters including, be it observed, exposure of goods for sale with the price attached.

In those circumstances I, for my part, though I confess reluctantly, am driven to the conclusion that no offence was here committed. At first sight it appears absurd that knives of this sort may not be manufactured, they may not be sold, they may not be hired, they may not be lent, they may not be given, but apparently they may be displayed in shop windows; but even if this is a *casus omissus*—and I am by no means saying that it is—it is not for this court to supply the omission. . . .

For my part, approaching this matter apart from authority, I find it quite impossible to say that an exhibition of goods in a shop window is itself an offer for sale. We were, however, referred to several cases, one of which is *Keating v Horwood*, a decision of this court. There, a baker's van was being driven on its rounds. There was bread in it that had been ordered and bread in it that was for sale, and it was found that that bread was under weight, contrary to the Sale of Food Order, 1921. That order was an order of the sort to which I have referred already and which prohibited the offering or exposing for sale. In giving his judgment, Lord Hewart, C.J., said:

> 'The question is whether, on the facts, there were (i) an offering, and (ii) an exposure, for sale. In my opinion there were both.'

Avory, J., agreed. Shearman, J., however, said:

> 'I am of the same opinion. I am quite clear that this bread was exposed for sale, but have had some doubt whether it can be said to have been offered for sale until a particular loaf was tendered to a particular customer.'

There are three matters to observe on that case. The first is that the order plainly contained the words 'expose for sale', and, on any view, there was in that case an exposing for sale. Therefore, the question whether there was an offer for sale was unnecessary for decision. Secondly, the principles of general contract law were referred to; and thirdly, albeit all part of the second ground, the respondents were not represented and there was, in fact, no argument. For my part, I cannot take that as an authority for the proposition that the display here in a shop window was an offer for sale. . . .

Accordingly, I have come to the conclusion in this case that the justices were right, and this appeal must be dismissed.

Ashworth, J.: I agree.

Elwes, J.: I also agree.

Appeal dismissed."

Smith v Hughes [1960] 1 W.L.R. 830, QBD.

Lord Parker C.J.:

"These are six appeals by way of case stated by one of the stipendiary magistrates sitting at Bow Street, before whom informations were preferred by police officers against the defendants, in each case that she 'being a common prostitute, did solicit in a street for the purposes of prostitution, contrary to section 1(1) of the Street Offences Act, 1959.' The magistrate in each case found that the defendant was a common prostitute, that she had solicited and that the solicitation was in a street, and in each case fined the defendant.

The facts, to all intents and purposes, raise the same point in each case; there are minute differences. The defendants in each case were not themselves physically in the street but were in a house adjoining the street. In one case the defendant was on a balcony and she attracted the attention of men in the street by tapping and calling down to them. In other cases the defendants were in ground-floor windows, either closed or half open, and in another case in a first-floor window.

The sole question here is whether in those circumstances each defendant was soliciting in a street or public place. The words of section 1(1) of the Act of 1959 are in this form: 'It shall be an offence for a common pros- titute to loiter or solicit in a street or public place for the purpose of prostitution.' Observe that it does not say there specifically that the person who is doing the soliciting must be in the street. Equally, it does not say that it is enough if the person who receives the solicitation or to whom it is addressed is in the street. For my part, I approach the matter by considering what is the mischief aimed at by this Act. Everybody knows that this was an Act intended to clean up the streets, to enable people to walk along the streets without being molested or solicited by common prostitutes. Viewed in that way, it can matter little whether the prostitute is soliciting while in the street or is standing in a doorway or on a balcony, or at a window, or whether the window is shut or open or half open; in each case her solicitation is projected to and addressed to somebody walking in the street. For my part, I am content to base my decision on that ground and that ground alone. I think the magistrate came to a correct conclusion in each case, and that these appeals should be dismissed."

[Hilbery J. and Donovan J. agreed].

Questions

1. In *Smith v Hughes*, Lord Parker, having found the language of the statute to be ambiguous, turned to the statute's purpose in order to determine whether it applied to the conduct of the defendants. But can we criticise Lord Parker on the basis that, even though that may have been the intention of the legislature, it is not what the legislature actually wrote in the statutory provision? Should a defendant be found guilty of a criminal offence on the basis of an ambiguous statute? As we will see shortly, the judiciary often claims that "penal statutes" (those which punish the individual for his or her acts) should be construed "narrowly". This means that ambiguities are resolved in favour of the individual. Why do you think that "rule" of interpretation was not applied in *Smith v Hughes*?

2. Why does it appear that that same rule *was* applied in *Fisher v Bell*? Why does one defendant get the benefit of the rule while the other does not?

The issue of prostitution in the criminal law has given rise to other questions of statutory interpretation, one of which involved the meaning of "common prostitute".

R. v McFarlane [1994] 2 All E.R. 283, CA.

Lord Taylor of Gosforth C.J.

[Lord Taylor of Gosforth C.J. delivered the following judgment of the court:]
"On December 16, 1991 in the Crown Court at Knightsbridge, the appellant was convicted of living on the earnings of prostitution. He was sentenced to four months' imprisonment. This appeal involves a point of law as to the meaning of prostitution which surprisingly has not been the subject of judicial decision with any finality prior to this.

The appellant lived as man and wife with Miss Josephs who, on the judge's ruling, was a prostitute. She maintained she was not a prostitute but a clipper—one who offers sexual services for reward and pockets the reward in advance never intending to provide the service. She said that she engaged in this occupation four or five nights a month, earning up to £400 on a good night. There was evidence, and it was accepted by the appellant and Miss Josephs, that he lived at least partly on her earnings in that they shared their living expenses. The main issue in the case was whether he was thus living on the earnings of prostitution knowingly. The prosecution pointed to the fact that he had lived with her for eleven years, the past five of which she had on her own account been engaged on this business. It was pointed out that he must have been aware of the pattern of her life, the fact that she had more money than could be accounted for by the £50 a week job as a cloakroom attendant which she said she told him she did.

Further, on 16 January 1990 the appellant was seen taking Miss Josephs and her sister into the court at Bow Street where they both appeared on charges of loitering for the purposes of prostitution. There was also evidence from two police officers who kept observation on the appellant between 29 January and 6 February 1991. Those observations tended to show that he assisted her in her occupation. At 10 pm on 30 January he drove Miss Josephs in his car to the West End of London. Later that night, in the same area, Miss Josephs offered one of the police officers sexual intercourse for £40 (which of course was not accepted). On 4 February the appellant drove Miss Josephs to Rupert Street and left her there. In Wardour Street she offered the other officer in the case sexual intercourse for £40. He too did not accept it. At 11.30 pm on 5 February the appellant drove Miss Josephs to the top end of Rupert Street and left her there. He met her an hour later in Shaftesbury Avenue. She took something from her shoe which she gave to the appellant. At 10.15 pm on 6 February the appellant again drove Miss Josephs to the same area and waited in the car in Rupert Street. At 10.40 pm she went off with someone in a taxi, returning to the appellant an hour later.

Whether or not that was an occasion of 'clipping' or the real thing is a matter which we need not consider in any depth.

The defence case was that the appellant knew nothing of Miss Joseph's activities. She gave evidence that she told him she worked as a cloakroom girl and also behind the bar at a club. She kept her real occupation secret from him. She used to go out to make it look as if she was at the job which she told him she did. She told him the money for items she bought for the home came from her mother. As regards the attendance at Bow Street Magistrates' Court, the appellant said that he had not stayed for the hearing, and Miss Josephs told him that it concerned a deception charge of which she was acquitted. As regards the observation evidence, essentially the appellant and Miss Josephs, together with her sister, challenged the evidence of observations, maintaining that it was all lies.

A submission was made to the learned judge that acting as a clipper did not amount to acting as a prostitute. Although at that stage counsel both for the prosecution and the defence supported that view, the learned judge rejected it. When the appeal came on before another constitution of this court, counsel then appearing for the Crown (not counsel who has appeared for the Crown today) again supported the appellant's submission that the learned judge's ruling was wrong. However, the court itself took the view that the matter should be fully argued, saying: 'There was a substantial argument in favour of the view taken by the trial judge.' It is most convenient therefore to deal first with what the learned judge said both in giving his ruling and in directing the jury. In his ruling he said:

> 'The question of whether someone offering themselves, but intending—and it has to be intending—firmly never, ever to make good that offer—it has to go that far—it has never, so far as I can see, been adjudicated upon. My view is that the indications in the textbooks—and I have looked at *Blackstone's Criminal Practice* and it is not so obvious, but again it speaks of offering—the dictionary, and decided cases say that as soon as you are offering yourself for lewdness for reward, you are indulging in prostitution and that is how I propose to direct the jury.'

When it came to the summing up, the learned judge said this to the jury:

> 'She has told you she is not a prostitute, she is a clipper. But, a prostitute is a person who offers her body for lewdness for reward. Put in slightly more 'with it' words, such as Sarah Tuckey [that is the sister] used, 'offers sexual services'. I am bound to say that I prefer the directness of the old Anglo-Saxon, but there it is. Miss Josephs said, 'Yes, I do offer sexual services, but I do not mean to make that offer good.' And she suggests to you that for that reason she is not a prostitute. But, members of the jury, she has made the offer. It is at that point that she is a prostitute. The fact that the offer is bogus, rather than genuine, if it was, is neither here nor there. There are not two categories—a clipper and a prostitute. There are prostitutes who are honest and prostitutes who are dishonest. Miss Josephs tells you that she is a dishonest prostitute. But she is a prostitute, members of the jury.'

The issue on this appeal is whether, as a matter of law, the judge was correct to rule and direct the jury that a woman who offers herself for sexual services, takes the money and fails to provide the services, is engaging in prostitution within the meaning of s.30 of the Sexual Offences Act 1956. Section 30, so far as is relevant, provides as follows:

> '(1) It is an offence for a man knowingly to live wholly or in part on the earnings of prostitution . . .'

Mr Carne for the appellant submits that to be a prostitute a woman must not only offer sexual services, but must provide them, or be prepared to do so. For the Crown, Mr Carter-Manning Q.C. submits the essence of the offence is the offer of the sexual services in return for reward.

The word 'prostitute' and 'prostitution' are not defined in any statute. Our attention was drawn to dictionary definitions and to three decided cases. The *Concise Oxford Dictionary* defines a prostitute as: 'A woman who offers her body to promiscuous sexual intercourse esp. For payment . . .'. *The Shorter Oxford English Dictionary* defines a prostitute as: 'A woman who is devoted, or (usu.) [who] offers her body to indiscriminate sexual inter- course, esp. for hire; a common harlot . . .'. Mr Carne points to the definition of 'offer' in *The Shorter Oxford English Dictionary*, and to one meaning given there: 'To give, make presentation of . . . To tender for acceptance or refusal . . .'. However, another meaning within the same dictionary is: 'To make the proposal, suggest . . . To propose, or express one's willingness (to do something), conditionally on the assent of the person addressed.' . . ."

[Lord Taylor then considered the relevant case law on the definition of prostitution, and concluded:]

"In our judgment both the dictionary definitions and the cases show that the crucial feature in defining pros- titution is the making of an offer of sexual services for reward. Mr Carne submits that the true offence here was not one of living off immoral earnings, and that the woman in question, Miss Josephs, was not acting by way of prostitution. She was acting dishonestly and she could have been proceeded against, he submits, for obtaining money by false pretences. It may be that the appellant could have been proceeded against for conspiring with her to do so, or of aiding and abetting her. But it is submitted that the offence of living off immoral earnings is not made out. Mr Carne also submits that the mischief against which s.30 of the Sexual Offences Act 1956 is directed is the exploitation of women. Here, the appellant was not exploiting Miss Josephs sexually, only dishonestly. . . .

We have no doubt that the ruling of the learned judge was both robust and correct (to adopt the phrase used by Mr Carter-Manning in his submission). For a man to live off the earnings of a woman who offers sexual serv- ices, takes the money and then reneges on the offer, if she does, is in our view to live off the earnings of prostitu- tion, or, as it used to be termed, immoral earnings. Indeed, most people would consider such earnings doubly immoral. This appeal is dismissed."

Questions

1. Does the Court of Appeal's definition of prostitution accord with a "common sense" understand- ing of the term? Would most people agree that prostitution is the offer of sexual services for compensation?

2. The appellant was convicted of the offence which is commonly known as being a "pimp". What evidence was there that he was a pimp? Is living with someone who sells sexual services sufficient to constitute living off the earnings of prostitution?

3. The appellant in this case argued that he should have been charged with a different offence, namely, aiding and abetting the offence of obtaining money by false pretences, or conspiracy to do so. Why do you think the appellant was not charged with that offence?

4. This case also involves a "penal statute". Why was an apparent ambiguity not resolved in favour of the appellant, in accordance with the "rule" that penal statutes should be strictly construed?

5. Can a man be a "common prostitute"? For the answer, see *DPP v Bull* [1994] 4 All E.R. 411, QB.

Although judges will rarely admit that the process of statutory interpretation is "political", in the sense of involving important *choices* concerning social issues of widespread concern, they are some- times required to make such decisions. Moreover, the language which judges use is often itself politi- cally charged. A classic example is the judgment of Lord Denning in *Royal College of Nursing v DHSS*. The case concerned the interpretation of the Abortion Act 1967. Pay close attention to the language which Lord Denning uses to describe the termination of a pregnancy.

Royal College of Nursing of the United Kingdom v Department of Health and Social Security [1981] 1 All E.R. 545, QBD, CA & HL.

Lord Denning M.R.:

"Abortion is a controversial subject. The question for us today is this: when a pregnancy is terminated by medical induction, who should do the actual act of termination? Should it be done by a doctor? Or can he leave it to the nurses? The Royal College of Nursing say that the doctor should do the actual act himself and not leave it to the nurses. The Department of Health take a different view. They say that a doctor can initiate the process and then go off and do other things, so long as he is 'on call'. The controversy is so acute that it has come before us for decision.

Throughout the discussion I am going to speak of the unborn child. The old common lawyers spoke of a child *en ventre sa mère*. Doctors speak of it as the fetus. In simple English it is an unborn child inside the mother's womb. Such a child was protected by the criminal law almost to the same extent as a new-born baby. If anyone terminated the pregnancy, and thus destroyed the unborn child, he or she was guilty of a felony and was liable to be kept in penal servitude for life (see the Offences against the Person Act 1861), unless it was done to save the life of the mother. Likewise anyone who assisted or participated in the abortion was guilty, including the mother herself. I have tried several cases of 'backstreet abortions', where the mother died or was made seriously ill. I have passed severe sentences of imprisonment for the offence.

The Abortion Act 1967

The approach to the subject was revolutionised by the Abortion Act 1967. It legalised abortion if it was done so as to avoid risk to the mother's health, physical or mental. This has been interpreted by some medical practitioners so loosely that abortion has become obtainable virtually on demand. Whenever a woman has an unwanted pregnancy, there are doctors who will say it involves a risk to her mental health. But the Act contains some safeguards. It provided that, in order for the abortion to be lawful, it was subject to three conditions. (1) The woman had to get two doctors to give a certificate. (2) The abortion had to be done in hospital. (3) The pregnancy had to be 'terminated by a registered medical practitioner'. It is this last condition which comes up for consideration today. It arises because of the advance in medical science.

The material words of the 1967 Act, in s.1(1), are that '. . . a person shall not be guilty of an offence under the law relating to abortion when a pregnancy is terminated by a registered medical practitioner . . .'

At the time that the Act was passed, and for five years afterwards, there was no difficulty of interpretation. All abortions then, at any rate when the mother was three months pregnant or more, were done by surgical methods. The knife with the cutting edge was operated by a registered medical practitioner. He used it to remove the unborn child. The knife was never handled by a nurse. She was not a registered medical practitioner.

Medical induction

Since 1972 a new method has been used. It is called medical induction. It does not involve a knife. It started quite simply in ordinary full-time births, so as to induce labour a few hours early, to save the mother the stress of waiting, or for the convenience of doctors and staff. But it is now becoming much used to effect abortions, when the mother is pregnant for three months or more. It is done by pumping a chemical fluid into the mother's womb. It is called prostaglandin. This fluid so affects the muscles and shape of the mother's inside that it forces her into labour prematurely, so that the unborn child is expelled from the body, usually dead, but sometimes at the point of death.

There are two distinct stages in this process. The first stage is done by a doctor, a registered medical practitioner. The mother is taken from the ward to the operating theatre. She is given a general anaesthetic. The doctor inserts a fine catheter into her body so as to reach a particular part of her womb. But no fluid is pumped into her at that stage. She is then taken back to the ward. She is left there until she recovers from the anaesthetic. The doctor writes out a few notes telling the nurse what to do. He then goes off, saying, 'Give me a call if there is any difficulty'.

The second stage is done by the nurses. When the mother comes round from the anaesthetic, they get a flexible tube and connect up the catheter to a pump which is electrically driven; or to a dripping device. They then get the special fluid called prostaglandin. They have to see that it is of the right concentration. They have it in a bottle, and pump the fluid into the woman's body. They have to regulate the dose and control the intake, by speed and amount, as occasion requires. If need be, they have to get another bottle. They have to watch the woman and note her reactions; and take such steps as occasion requires. Labour is induced. The unborn child is expelled from the woman's body. The process make take 18 hours, or even up to 30 hours. If the unborn child is not expelled by that time, the process is stopped. The child is allowed to live on, to await normal delivery later.

Here I would stop for a moment to point out that the first stage (done by the doctor) does nothing to terminate the pregnancy. The insertion of the catheter is only a preparatory act. It is the second stage (done by the nurses) which terminates the pregnancy. There is an agreed statement of facts which shows that the causative factor is the administration of prostaglandin. . . .

The Royal College's objection

I can quite understand that many nurses dislike having anything to do with these abortions. It is a soul-destroying task. The nurses are young women who are dedicated by their profession and training to do all they can to preserve life. Yet here they are called on to destroy it. It is true that the statute gives them an escape clause. They can refuse to participate in any treatment to which they have a 'conscientious objection': see s.4 of the 1967 Act. But the report of Dame Elizabeth Lane and her colleagues (Report of the Committee on the Working of the Abortion Act) shows that many nurses do not take advantage of this 'escape clause': because it means that other nurses will have to do this heart-rending task; and they feel it may be held against them by their superiors. So they take part in it, much against their will.

It is against this background that the Royal College of Nursing ask the question: is it lawful for nurses to be called on to terminate pregnancy in this way? The Royal College say No, it is not lawful; it is not a nurse's job to terminate a pregnancy. The Department of Health and Social Security say Yes, it is lawful. They have issued a circular in which they presume to lay down the law for the whole of the medical profession. They say that it is no offence if the pregnancy is terminated by a suitably qualified person in accordance with the written instructions of a registered medical practitioner. This is the wording of the circular:

> 'However, the Secretary of State is advised that the termination can properly be said to have been terminated by the registered medical practitioner provided it is decided upon by him, initiated by him, and that he remains throughout responsible for its overall conduct and control in the sense that any actions needed to bring it to conclusion are done by appropriately skilled staff acting on his specific instructions but *not necessarily in his presence.*'

Note those words 'not necessarily in his presence'. They are crucial.

The interpretation of the 1967 Act
The lawfulness depends on the true interpretation of the statute; but, before going into it, I would say a word or two about the approach to it.

(i)   Abortion is a subject on which many people feel strongly. In both directions. Many are for it. Many against it. Some object to it as the destruction of life. Others favour it as the right of the woman. Emotions run so high on both sides that I feel that we as judges must go by the very words of the statute, without stretching it one way or the other, and writing nothing in which is not there.

(ii)   Another thing to remember is that the statute is directed to the medical profession, to the doctors and nurses who have to implement it. It is they who have to read it and to act on it. They will read it, not as lawyers, but as laymen. So we should interpret it as they would.

(iii) If there should ever be a case in the courts, the decision would ultimately be that of a jury. Suppose that during the process the mother died or became seriously ill, owing to the nurse's negligence in administering the wrong chemical fluid, and the nurse was prosecuted under the 1861 Act for unlawfully administering to her a noxious thing or using other means with intent to procure her miscarriage. The nurse would have no defence unless the pregnancy was 'terminated by a registered medical practitioner'. Those are simple English words which should be left to a jury to apply, without the judge attempting to put his own gloss on them. I should expect the jury to say that the pregnancy was not terminated by a registered medical practitioner but by a nurse.

(iv)   If in such a case there were a claim for damages, the nurse might not be covered by insurance because she would not be engaged in 'nursing professional services acceptable to the Royal College of Nursing'.

(v)   Statutes can be divided into two categories. In the first category Parliament has expressly said 'by a registered medical practitioner or by a person acting in accordance with the directions of any such practitioner', or words to that effect. In the second category Parliament has deliberately confined it: '*by* a fully registered medical practitioner' omitting any such words as 'or by his direction'. This statute is in the second category.

(vi)   Woolf J. tested the statute by supposing that a registered medical practitioner performed an abortion operated on a woman whom he believed to be pregnant but who was not so in fact. The 1967 Act would give him no defence to a charge under the 1861 Act.[1] That is such a fanciful instance that I do not think it throws any light on the true construction of this statute.

(vii)   The Solicitor General emphasised the word 'treatment' in ss.1(3), 3(1)(a) and (c) and 4(1). He suggested that s.1(1) should be read as if it said that a person should not be guilty of an offence 'when the treatment (for termination of a pregnancy) is by a registered medical practitioner'. He submitted that, whenever the registered medical practitioner did what the Department of Health advised, it satisfied the statute, because the treatment, being initiated by him and done under his instructions, was 'by' him. I cannot accept this interpretation. I think the word 'treatment' in those sections means 'the actual act of terminating the pregnancy'. When the medical induction method is used, this means the continuous act of administering prostaglandin from the moment it is started until the unborn child is expelled from the mother's body. This continuous act must be done by the doctor personally. It is not sufficient that it is done by a nurse when he is not present.

Conclusion

Stress was laid by the Solicitor General on the effect of this ruling. The process of medical induction can take from 18 to 30 hours. No doctor can be expected to be present all that time. He must leave it to the nurses: or not use the method at all. If he is not allowed to leave it to the nurses, the result will be either that there will be fewer abortions or that the doctor will have to use the surgical method with its extra hazards. This may be so. But I do not think this warrants us departing from the statute. The Royal College of Nursing have advised their nurses that under the statute they should not themselves terminate a pregnancy. If the doctor advises it, he should do it himself, and not call on the nurses to do it.

    I think that the Royal College are quite right. If the Department of Health want the nurses to terminate a pregnancy, the Minister should go to Parliament and get the statute altered. He should ask them to amend it by adding the words 'or by a suitably qualified person in accordance with the written instructions of a registered medical practitioner'. I doubt whether Parliament would accept the amendment. It is too controversial. At any rate, that is the way to amend the law and not by means of a departmental circular.

    I would allow the appeal accordingly."

[Brightman L.J. and Sir George Baker delivered separate reasons, allowing the appeal].

The case was then appealed to the House of Lords. The Law Lords divided 3:2, and the majority allowed the appeal from the Court of Appeal, restoring the original judgment of Woolf J. The analysis offered by Lord Diplock is in sharp contrast with that of Lord Denning.

---

[1]   Woolf, J. the trial judge in this case was making the point that this anomaly would result from a narrow interpretation of the 1967 Act, from which he concluded that overly narrow interpretations should be eschewed.

Lord Diplock:

". . . Subsection (1) although it is expressed to apply only 'when a pregnancy is terminated by a registered medical practitioner' . . . also appears to contemplate treatment that is in the nature of a team effort and to extend its protection to all those who play a part in it. The exoneration from guilt is not confined to the registered medical practitioner by whom a pregnancy is terminated, it extends to any person who takes part in the treatment for its termination.

What limitation on this exoneration is imposed by the qualifying phrase, 'when a pregnancy is terminated by a registered medical practitioner'? In my opinion, in the context of the Act, what it requires is that a registered medical practitioner, whom I will refer to as a doctor, should accept responsibility for all stages of the treatment for the termination of the pregnancy. The particular method to be used should be decided by the doctor in charge of the treatment for termination of the pregnancy; he should carry out any physical acts, forming part of the treatment, that in accordance with accepted medical practice are done only by qualified medical practitioners, and should give specific instructions as to the carrying out of such parts of the treatment as in accordance with accepted medical practice are carried out by nurses or other members of the hospital staff without medical qualifications. To each of them, the doctor, or his substitute, should be available to be consulted or called on for assistance from beginning to end of the treatment. In other words, the doctor need not do everything with his own hands; the requirements of the subsection are satisfied when the treatment for termination of a pregnancy is one prescribed by a registered medical practitioner carried out in accordance with his directions and of which a registered medical practitioner remains in charge throughout."

Questions

1. Give examples, drawn from Lord Denning's judgment, where the words which he uses to describe abortion, mirrors the language which is often used by anti-abortion campaigners. What alternative phrases and sentences could have been employed to convey the ideas which he expressed, but which would be less inflammatory?

2. What evidence does Lord Denning provide for his assertion that abortion "on demand" is now available in the United Kingdom because of the willingness of doctors to certify that a woman's health is endangered by the continuation of her pregnancy? Is this part of the judgment relevant to the issue before the Court?

3. In his judgment at trial, Woolf J. made clear that the position of the Royal College of Nursing was "neutral" towards the issue in this case, but that they merely wanted clarification of the law. Does Lord Denning portray their position in that way?

4. Is Lord Diplock's analysis of the termination procedure as the work of a team of medical personnel more convincing than Lord Denning's analysis of the potential liability of nurses for carrying out their duties?

The decision of the House of Lords in *Royal College of Nursing v DHSS* might seem a victory for the right of women to have safe, medical abortions. However, the decision can be read as more complex in its political meanings, as Sheldon explains.

Sally Sheldon, *Beyond Control: Medical power and abortion law* (London: Pluto Press, 1997), pp.97–98:

"This case is notable for several reasons. Perhaps its most striking feature is the extent to which those judges who found for the DHSS are prepared to stretch an interpretation of the terms of the Abortion Act in order to reach an acceptable decision. The decision which the House of Lords eventually comes to is the common-sense verdict and no doubt accords with 'the obvious intention of the Act', yet it is one that is squared with the actual wording of the statute only with great difficulty. When the doctor's actual involvement in the termination is limited to the insertion of the catheter—an act preparatory to the administration of the postaglandins which cause the uterus to contract and expel the foetus—it involves a rather creative interpretation to see the doctor as terminating the pregnancy rather than the nursing staff who do everything else. Explicitly underlying this decision is a refusal to interfere with 'good medical practice'.

. . . Whilst nurses are hereby authorised to carry out certain actions in this kind of termination, they can still do so only under the control of the doctor who retains the ultimate responsibility for the operation. This strict hierarchy of the relationship between doctors and nurses is thus reproduced in the legal assessment and the doctors' monopoly over the performance of abortions is reasserted. . . .

The RCN case demonstrates again how the reluctance of law to interfere with medical discretion and good medical practice can benefit women by protecting the provision of abortion services. It also emphasises, however, how this goes hand in hand with an entrenchment of doctors' control over such services."

IV. Methods of Statutory Interpretation

We turn now to the so-called "rules" of statutory interpretation: the literal rule; the golden rule; and the mischief rule. Most lawyers today would readily agree that these approaches to interpretation have been misnamed as "rules", for they provide at best guidance to different judicial approaches. Alternatively, they are justifications for decisions which have been reached by judges on other, unarticulated grounds. The "rules" themselves do not dictate the outcomes of the cases. As Goodrich explains, the rules of interpretation also reflect different approaches to the judicial process itself.

Peter Goodrich, *Reading the Law* (Oxford: Blackwell, 1986), pp.54–57:

"On numerous occasions judges, during the course of giving judgment in a dispute, have taken the opportunity to make statements as to how they approach the task of interpretation, not only to justify their own conclusions as to the meaning of statutory provisions under consideration, but also to provide models of behaviour for others to follow. The content and the taxonomy of the techniques is a reflection of many of the matters relating to the relationship between the legislature and the judiciary and the distinction between the written law and unwritten law discussed earlier. The methods of interpretation embody a vast collection of frequently overlapping and on occasion conflicting rules, principles and presumptions which have accumulated over several centuries.

The general approach which is said to be the primary method of common-law statutory interpretation is usually referred to as the literal approach. The classic statement of this technique is found in *The Queen v Judge of the City of London Court* [1892] 1 QB 273: 'If the words of an Act are clear, you must follow them, even though they lead to a manifest absurdity. The Court has nothing to do with the question whether the legislature has committed an absurdity.' The literal approach demands that the court apply the ordinary, natural meaning of the words used. . . .

An adaptation of this first approach is often referred to as the Golden Rule. Its concern is to provide an alternative approach in the face of an absurdity resulting from the literal interpretation. The rule, however, is inadequate in that it provides little guidance as to how interpretation is to proceed beyond the conclusion of absurdity. The classic exposition of the rule is to be found in *River Wear Commissioners v Adamson* [1877] 2 AC 743, where Lord Blackburn stated:

'But it is to be borne in mind that the office of the Judge is not to legislate, but to declare the expressed intention of the legislature even if that expressed intention appeared to the court to be injudicious; and I believe that it is not disputed that what Lord Wensleydale used to call the Golden rule is right viz. That we are to take the whole statute together and construe it all together, giving the words their ordinary significance unless when so applied they produce an inconsistency or an absurdity or inconvenience so great as to convince the court that the intention could not have been to use them in their ordinary signification and to justify the court in putting on them some other significance which though less proper is one which the court thinks the words will bear.' (763)

The third and oldest statement relating to techniques of interpretation is found in the rule known as the Mischief Rule or the Rule in *Heydon's Case* [1584] 3 Co Rep 7. This rule emphasizes the interrelationship between the status quo prior to the legislation and the objectives of the new law: 'four things are to be discussed and considered: 1. What was the common law before the making of the Act; 2. What was the mischief and defect for which the common law did not provide; 3. What remedy the Parliament hath resolved and appointed to cure the disease of the commonwealth; and 4. The true reason for the remedy.' In following this line of approach the ultimate objective is to interpret the law in such a fashion that the objectives of the enactment are realized.

Finally, a technique which is reminiscent of the rule in *Heydon's Case* is referred to as the *purposive approach*. It embodies the general ethos of the previous method in that it stresses the need to interpret the enactment in such a way that the objectives (purposes) of the statute are realized. It differs from Heydon's formulation in that it does not locate the approach purely in the context of the common law, nor does it confine objectives to their historical origin though this may be one source of information about the objectives. In *Royal College of Nursing v DHSS* [1981] AC 800, Lord Diplock discusses the interrelationship of approaches with respect to the interpretation of the Abortion Act 1967: 'whatever may be the technical imperfections of its draftsmanship, however, its purpose in my view becomes clear if one starts by considering what was the state of the law relating to abortion before the passing of the Act, what was the mischief that required amendment, and in what respect was the existing law unclear'. The historical, social and economic aspects to abortion were then examined as well as the more obvious features of its moral and legal history to the conclusion that 'the wording and the structure of the section are far from elegant, but the policy of the Act, it seems to me, is clear. There are two aspects to it: the first is to broaden the grounds upon which abortions may be lawfully obtained; the second is to ensure that the abortion is carried out with all proper skill and in hygienic conditions.'

The relative importance of these styles of interpretation is itself a source of considerable controversy which raises the theoretical and substantive issues about the role of the judge, the law-making dimension of interpretation and the threat this poses to the abstract supremacy of written law. The controversy can be reduced, for present purposes, to two positions which have both a descriptive and a prescriptive quality. The first represents the judge as a passive actor in the process of interpretation, merely giving the words of the Act their natural meaning and applying that meaning to the situation in the dispute. It stresses a mechanical representation of interpretation, emphasizing the impartiality involved in adjudication. The model is most sympathetic to the adoption of the literalist style of interpretation. The second model rejects the notion that this can be the only role-model for a judge. This model represents the judge as a party who necessarily undertakes an active role in the task of interpretation. Whilst the judge is not a completely free agent, this model stresses the role of the judge as an active participant in the process of creating legal meaning and the need for the judge to resort to the whole range of resources within the legal culture which may lead variously to references to social policy, economics, and other broad-ranging administrative and political considerations of the 'consequences' of the rules to be applied. This model suggests a dynamic role for the judiciary. It is most sympathetic to those techniques of interpretation which seek to realize the purpose and objectives of legislation, the Mischief Rule and the purposive style of interpretation in particular. The first model, on the other hand, provides no threat to the law-making role of the legislature, as the judge is the passive servant merely reading the written law and applying it. The second model potentially threatens the superiority of the written law in that the judge may be seen as a law-maker with the capacity to change or even to undermine the supremacy of the written law by resorting to sources and materials outside the statutory provision, and thereby threatening its status.

Judicial observations on the merits and demerits of the various styles of role-model are numerous. One of the most quoted examples is found in a confrontation between Lord Denning when in the Court of Appeal and Viscount Simonds in the House of Lords in the case of *Magor and St Mellons Rural District Council v Newport*

District Council [1952] AC 189. A more recent example of the controversy, and one which provides a clearer expression of the political considerations which underpin the debate is to be found in the judgment of Lord Diplock in *Duport Steels Ltd v Sirs and Others* [1980] 1 WLR 142:

> 'When Parliament legislates to remedy what the majority of its members at the time perceive to be a defect or a lacuna in the law (whether it be written law enacted by existing statutes or the unwritten common law as it has been expounded by the judges in decided cases), the role of the judiciary is confined to ascertaining from the words that Parliament has approved as expressing its intention, what the intention was, and to giving effect to it. Where the meaning of the statutory words is plain and unambiguous it is not for the judge to invent fancied ambiguities as an excuse for failing to give effect to its plain meaning because they themselves consider that the consequences of doing so would be inexpedient or even unjust or immoral.'

> A statute passed to remedy what is perceived by Parliament to be a defect in the existing law may in actual operation turn out to have injurious consequences that Parliament did not anticipate at the time the statute was passed. . . . [I]t is for Parliament, not for the judiciary, to decide whether any changes should be made to the law as stated in the Acts . . .

> It endangers continued public confidence in the political impartiality of the judiciary, which is essential to the continuance of the rule of law, if judges, under the guise of interpretation, provide their own preferred amendments to statutes which experience of their operation has shown to have had consequences that members of the court before whom the matter comes consider to be injurious to the public interest."

First-year law students frequently assume that the three "rules" of statutory interpretation are binding on judges; and that courts mechanically move between them to resolve issues of statutory interpretation. This is not the way in which judges approach their task. As Lord Reid explained:

> "They are not rules in the ordinary sense of having some binding force. They are our servants not our masters. They are aids to construction, presumptions or pointers. Not infrequently one 'rule' points in one direction, another in a different direction. In each case we must look at all relevant circumstances and decide as a matter of judgment what weight to attach to any particular 'rule.' "[2]

In that same case, Lord Simon of Glaisdale outlined an approach to interpretation which tried to bring together the various rules, and which provides a useful description of the way in which courts go about the task of statutory interpretation:

> "It is sometimes put that, in statutes dealing with ordinary people in their everyday lives, the language is presumed to be used in its primary ordinary sense, unless this stultifies the purpose of the statute, or otherwise produces some injustice, absurdity, anomaly or contradiction, in which case some secondary ordinary sense may be preferred, so as to obviate the injustice, absurdity, anomaly or contradiction, or fulfil the purpose of the statute: while, in statutes dealing with technical matters, words which are capable of both bearing an ordinary meaning and being terms of art in the technical matter of the legislation will presumptively bear their primary meaning as such terms of art (or, if they must necessarily be modified, some secondary meaning as terms of art). . . .

> But, in fact, these two statutory situations—dealing with ordinary people in their everyday lives, on the one hand, and dealing with technical branches of the law, on the other—are only two extreme situations. Statutory language, like all language, is capable of an almost infinite

---

[2]   *Mansell v Olins* [1975] 1 All E.R. 16 at 18, HL.

gradation of 'register'—*i.e.* it will be used at the semantic level appropriate to the subject-matter and to the audience addressed (the man in the street, lawyers, merchants, etc). It is the duty of a court of construction to tune in to such register and so to interpret the statutory language as to give to it the primary meaning which is appropriate in that register (unless it is clear that some other meaning must be given in order to carry out the statutory purpose or to avoid injustice, anomaly, absurdity or contradiction). In other words, statutory language must always be given presumptively the most natural and ordinary meaning which is appropriate in the circumstances.

It is essential that this 'golden' rule is adhered to. An English court of construction must put itself in the place of the draftsman, and ascertain the meaning of the words used in the light of all the circumstances known by the draftsman—especially the 'mischief' which is the subject-matter of the statutory remedy."[3]

The determination of the "ordinary" meaning of legislation and the "mischief" at which it was aimed can be a controversial job for judges. The following two cases demonstrate how the application of "rules" of interpretation is sometimes far from straightforward.

R. (on the application of Quintavalle) v Secretary of State for Health [2003] UKHL 13.

Lord Bingham of Cornhill:

"My Lords, the issues in this appeal are whether live human embryos created by cell nuclear replacement (CNR) fall outside the regulatory scope of the Human Fertilisation and Embryology Act 1990 and whether licensing the creation of such embryos is prohibited by s 3(3)(D) of that Act. . . .

This case is not concerned with embryos created in the ordinary way as a result of sexual intercourse. Nor is it directly concerned with the creation of live human embryos in vitro where the female egg is fertilised by the introduction of male sperm outside the body. CNR, a very recent scientific technique, involves neither of those things. In the Court of Appeal and in the House the parties were content to adopt the clear and succinct explanation given by the judge of what CNR means and involves ([2001] 4 All ER 1013):

'In the ovary the egg is a diploid germ (or reproductive) cell. It is described as "diploid" because its nucleus contains a full set of 46 chromosomes. By the process of meiotic division the nucleus divides into two parts. Only one of these, a pronucleus containing only 23 chromosomes (described as "haploid"), plays any further part in the process. Fertilisation begins when the male germ cell, the sperm, whose pronucleus contains 23 chromosomes, meets the haploid female germ cell and is a continuous process taking up to 24 hours. As part of the process the male and female pronuclei fuse to form one nucleus with a full complement of 46 chromosomes, a process known as syngamy. The one-cell structure that exists following syngamy is the zygote. At this stage it is generally referred to as an embryo. At about 15 days after fertilisation a heaping-up of cells occurs which is described as the "primitive streak".

Fertilisation may of course take place in the normal way or in vitro.

CNR is a process by which the nucleus, which is diploid, from one cell is transplanted into an unfertilised egg, from which . . . the nucleus has been removed. The [replacement] nucleus is derived from either an embryonic foetal or an adult cell. The cell is then treated to encourage it to grow and divide, forming first a two-cell structure and then developing in a similar way to an ordinary embryo.

CNR is a form of cloning. Clones are organisms that are genetically identical to each other. When CNR is used, if the embryo develops into a live individual, that individual is genetically identical to the nucleus transplanted into the egg. There are other methods of cloning, for example, embryo splitting, which may occur naturally or be encouraged. Identical twins are the result of embryo splitting.

---

[3] *Mansell v Olins* [1975] 1 All E.R. 16 at 25–26, HL.

The famous Dolly the sheep was produced by CNR. Live young have since been produced by CNR in some other mammals. It has not yet been attempted in humans.

. . . CNR of the kind under consideration does not . . . involve fertilisation.'

The Act

The 1990 Act was passed 'to make provision in connection with human embryos and any subsequent development of such embryos; to prohibit certain practices in connection with embryos and gametes; to establish a Human Fertilisation and Embryology Authority', and for other purposes. The sections at the heart of this appeal are ss 1 and 3, which I should quote in full:

'Principal terms used

1.—(1) In this Act, except where otherwise stated—(a) embryo means a live human embryo where fertilisation is complete and (b) references to an embryo include an egg in the process of fertilisation, and, for this purpose, fertilisation is not complete until the appearance of a two cell zygote.

(2) This Act, so far as it governs bringing about the creation of an embryo, applies only to bringing about the creation of an embryo outside the human body; and in this Act—(a) references to embryos the creation of which was brought about *in vitro* (in their application to those where fertilisation is complete) are to those where fertilisation began outside the human body whether or not it was completed there, and (b) references to embryos taken from a woman do not include embryos whose creation was brought about *in vitro*.

(3) This Act, so far as it governs the keeping or use of an embryo, applies only to keeping or using an embryo outside the human body.

(4) References in this Act to gametes, eggs or sperm, except where otherwise stated, are to live human gametes, eggs or sperm but references below in this to gametes or eggs do not include eggs in the process of fertilisation . . .

3.—(1) No person shall—(a) bring about the creation of an embryo, or (b) keep or use an embryo, except in pursuance of a licence.

(2) No person shall place in a woman—(a) a live embryo other than a human embryo, or (b) any live gametes other than human gametes.

(3) A licence cannot authorise—(a) keeping or using an embryo after the appearance of the primitive streak, (b) placing an embryo in any animal, (c) keeping or using an embryo in any circumstances in which regulations prohibit its keeping or use, or (d) replacing a nucleus of a cell of an embryo with a nucleus taken from a cell of any person, embryo or subsequent development of any embryo.

(4) For the purposes of subsection (3)(a) above, the primitive streak is to be taken to have appeared in an embryo not later than the end of the period of 14 days beginning with the day when the gametes are mixed, not counting any time during which the embryo is stored.'

The Act imposes three levels of control. The highest is that contained in the Act itself. As is apparent, for example from s3(2) and (3), the Act prohibits certain activities absolutely, a prohibition fortified by a potential penalty of up to ten years' imprisonment (s 4(1)). The next level of control is provided by the Secretary of State, who is empowered to make regulations for certain purposes subject (so far as relevant here) to an affirmative resolution of both Houses of Parliament (s45(1), (4)). Pursuant to s 3(3)(c) the Secretary of State may make regulations prohibiting the keeping or use of an embryo in specified circumstances. The third level of control is that exercised by the Authority. Section 3(1) prohibits the creation, keeping or use of an embryo except in pursuance of a licence, and the Act contains very detailed provisions governing the grant, revocation and suspension of licences and the conditions to which they may be subject: see, among other references, ss 11–22 and Sch 2 to the Act. A power is also conferred on the Authority to give binding directions: ss 23–24.

The first argument of the appellant is squarely based on the wording of s 1(1)(a) of the Act, fortified by that of sub-s (1)(b). It hinges on the words 'where fertilisation is complete'. That makes clear, it is argued, that the live human embryos to which the Act applies are such embryos as are the product of fertilisation, for the obvious reason that if there is no fertilisation there can be no time when fertilisation is complete (and there is never an egg in the process of fertilisation). Therefore the Act does not apply to embryos created by CNR, unsurprisingly since in 1990 the creation of live human embryos was unknown to Parliament. The second argument of the appellant is put as an alternative: if embryos created by CNR are, contrary to the first argument, embryos within the scope of the Act, then the CNR process is specifically prohibited by s 3(3)(d) and cannot be licensed.

The approach to interpretation

By the end of the hearing it appeared that the parties were divided less on the principles governing interpretation than on their application to the present case. Since, however, the Court of Appeal were said to have erred in their approach to construction , it is necessary to address this aspect, if relatively briefly.

Such is the skill of Parliamentary draftsmen that most statutory enactments are expressed in language that is clear and unambiguous and gives rise to no serious controversy. But these are not the provisions which reach the courts, or at any rate the appellate courts. Where parties expend substantial resources arguing about the effect of a statutory provision it is usually because the provision is, or is said to be, capable of bearing two or more different meanings, or to be of doubtful application to the particular case which has now arisen, perhaps because the statutory language is said to be inapt to apply to it, sometimes because the situation which has arisen is one which the draftsman could not have foreseen and for which he has accordingly made no express provision.

The basic task of the court is to ascertain and give effect to the true meaning of what Parliament has said in the enactment to be construed. But that is not to say that attention should be confined and a literal interpretation given to the particular provisions which give rise to difficulty. Such an approach not only encourages immense prolixity in drafting, since the draftsman will feel obliged to provide expressly for every contingency which may possibly arise. It may also (under the banner of loyalty to the will of Parliament) lead to the frustration of that will, because undue concentration on the minutiae of the enactment may lead the court to neglect the purpose which Parliament intended to achieve when it enacted the statute. Every statute other than a pure consolidating statute is, after all, enacted to make some change, or address some problem, or remove some blemish, or effect some improvement in the national life. The court's task, within the permissible bounds of interpretation, is to give effect to Parliament's purpose. So the controversial provisions should be read in the context of the statute as a whole, and the statute as a whole should be read in the historical context of the situation which led to its enactment.

There is, I think, no inconsistency between the rule that statutory language retains the meaning it had when Parliament used it and the rule that a statute is always speaking. If Parliament, however long ago, passed an Act applicable to dogs, it could not properly be interpreted to apply to cats; but it could properly be held to apply to animals which were not regarded as dogs when the Act was passed but are so regarded now. The meaning of 'cruel and unusual punishments' has not changed over the years since 1689, but many punishments where were not then thought to fall with that category would now be held to do so. . . .

The background to the Act

The birth of the first child resulting from in vitro fertilisation in July 1978 prompted much ethical and scientific debate which in turn led to the appointment in July 1982 of a Committee of Inquiry under the chairmanship of Dame Mary Warnock to—

> 'consider recent and potential developments in medicine and science related to human fertilisation and embryology; to consider what policies and safeguards should be applied, including the consideration of the social, ethical and legal implications of these developments; and to make recommendations.'

The committee reported in July 1984 (*Report of the Inquiry into Human Fertilisation and Embryology* (Cmnd 9314) (the Warnock Report). A White Paper was published in November 1987 *Human Fertilisation and Embryology: A Framework for Legislation* (cm 259) when the Department of Health and Social Security recognised (para 6) 'the particular difficulties of framing legislation on these sensitive issues against a background of fast-moving medical and scientific development'.

There is no doubting the sensitivity of the issues. There were those who considered the creation of embryos, and thus of life, in vitro to be either sacrilegious or ethically repugnant and wished to ban such activities altogether. There were others who considered that these new techniques, by offering means of enabling the infertile to have children and increasing knowledge of congenital disease, had the potential to improve the human condition, and this view also did not lack religious and moral arguments to support it. Nor can one doubt the difficulty of legislating against a background of fast-moving medical and scientific development. It is not often that Parliament has to frame legislation apt to apply to developments at the advanced cutting edge of science.

The solution recommended and embodied in the 1990 Act was not to ban all creation and subsequent use of live human embryos produced in vitro but instead, and subject to certain express prohibitions of which some have been noted above, to permit such creation and use subject to specified conditions, restrictions and time limits and subject to the regimes of control briefly described . . . above. The merits of this solution are not a matter for the House in its judicial capacity. It is, however, plain that while Parliament outlawed certain grotesque possibilities (such as placing a live animal embryo in a woman or a live human embryo in an animal), it otherwise opted for a strict regime of control. No activity within this field was left unregulated. There was to be no free for all.

Section 1(1)(a)

It is against this background that one comes to interpret s 1(1)(a). At first reading Mr Gordon's construction has an obvious attraction: the Act is dealing with live human embryos 'where fertilisation is complete', and the definition is a composite one including the last four words. But the Act is only directed to the creation of embryos in vitro, outside the human body (s 1(2)). Can Parliament have been intending to distinguish between live human embryos produced by fertilisation of a female egg and live human embryos produced without such fertilisation? The answer must certainly be negative, since Parliament was unaware that the latter alternative was physically possible. This suggests that the four words were not intended to form an integral part of the definition of embryo but were directed to the time at which it should be treated as such. . . .

Bearing in mind the constitutional imperative that the courts stick to their interpretative role and do not assume the mantle of legislators, however, I would not leave the matter there. . . . (1) Does the creation of live human embryos by CNR fall within the same genus of facts as those to which the expressed policy of Parliament has been formulated? In my opinion, it plainly does. An embryo created by in vitro fertilisation and one created by CNR are very similar organisms. The difference between them as organisms is that the CNR embryo, if allowed to develop, will grow into a clone of the donor of the replacement nucleus which the embryo produced by fertilisation will not. But this is a difference which plainly points towards the need for regulation, not against it. (2) Is the operation of the 1990 Act to be regarded as liberal and permissive in its operation or restrictive and circumscribed? This is not an entirely simple question. The Act intended to permit certain activities but to circumscribe the freedom to pursue them which had previously been enjoyed. Loyalty to the evident purpose of the Act would require regulation of activities not distinguishable in any significant respect from those regulated by the Act, unless the wording or policy of the Act shows that they should be prohibited. (3) Is the embryo created by CNR different in kind or dimension from that for which the Act was passed? Plainly not: as already pointed out the organisms in question are, as organisms, very similar. While it is impermissible to ask what Parliament would have done if the facts had been before it, there is one important questions which may permissibly be asked: it is whether Parliament, faced with the taxing task of enacting a legislative solution to the difficult religious, moral and scientific issues mentioned above, could rationally have intended to leave live human embryos created by CNR outside the scope of regulation had it known of them as a scientific possibility. There is only one possible answer to this question and it is negative. . . .

Section 3(3)(d)

It seems to me quite clear that CNR does not involve 'replacing a nucleus of a cell of an embryo' because there is no embryo until the nucleus of the recipient cell is replaced by the nucleus of the donor cell. I accordingly conclude that s 3(3)(d), which cannot have been drafted to prohibit CNR, does not, almost fortuitously, have that result. The target of s 3(3)(d) is in my opinion plain by para 12.14 of the Warnock Report, which need not be quoted but which was directed to a particular form of genetic manipulation, replacement of the nucleus of a fertilised human egg. The White Paper (para 36) referred to 'techniques aimed at modifying the genetic constitution of an embryo', and proposed that legislation 'should clearly prohibit all such activities, but with a power for Parliament itself, by affirmative resolution, to make exceptions to these prohibitions if new developments made that appropriate'. Section 3(3)(d) was, I infer, enacted to give effect to this recommendation. If, as Mr Gordon contended, Parliament intended to ban all cloning by s 3(3)(d), it would have been possible so to provide; but it is clear that Parliament did not intend to prohibit embryo-splitting, which creates clones, and to which the Warnock Report referred in para 12.11. In my opinion, the subsection cannot be interpreted to prohibit CNR.

For these reasons I would dismiss the appeal with costs."

[Lords Steyn, Hoffmann, Millett and Scott concurred with Lord Bingham in separate reasons.]

Questions

1. Why was the literal rule not followed by Lord Bingham in this case? To what outcome would that rule have led?

2. What does Lord Bingham mean when he states that: "There is, I think, no inconsistency between the rule that statutory language retains the meaning it had when Parliament used it and the rule that a statute is always speaking"? Are you convinced?

3. Why does Lord Bingham speak of the "constitutional imperative that the courts stick to their interpretative role and do not assume the mantle of legislators"? Why do you think this point concerns Lord Bingham?

4. How did this case end up in the courts? Who is the appellant, Quintavalle? Do you think it was right for the Law Lords to be asked to consider this issue?

R. v Z [2005] UKHL 35.

Lord Bingham of Cornhill:

"My Lords, in an indictment dated 11 June 2003, four defendants were charged (among other counts) with belonging 'to a proscribed organisation, namely the Real Irish Republican Army', contrary to s 11(1) of the Terrorism Act 2000. They objected that the Real Irish Republican Army (to which I shall for convenience refer as the Real IRA) was not a proscribed organisation within the meaning of s 11(1). Girvan J, sitting in the Crown Court at Belfast, upheld the objection for reasons given in a judgment delivered on 25 May 2004 and acquitted the defendants on those counts. The acquittals prompted the Attorney General for Northern Ireland to refer the following point of law for the opinion of the Court of Appeal in Northern Ireland under s 15 of the Criminal Appeal (Northern Ireland) Act 1980:

'Does a person commit an offence contrary to s 11(1) of the Terrorism Act 2000 if he belongs or professes to belong to the Real Irish Republican Army?'

The Court of Appeal (Kerr LCJ, Nicholson and Campbell LJJ) ([2004] NICA 23, [2005] NI 106), for reasons given by Kerr LCJ in a judgment of 30 June 2004, differed from the judge and answered that question in the affirmative. In this appeal, the acquitted person (anonymized as Z) contends that the question should be answered negatively.

The statutory provision most directly in issue in the appeal is s 3 of the 2000 Act, which provides:

'3. *Proscription*—

    (1) For the purposes of this Act an organisation is proscribed if—(a) it is listed in Schedule 2, or (b) it operates under the same name as an organisation listed in that Schedule.

    (2) Subsection (1)(b) shall not apply in relation to an organisation listed in Schedule 2 if its entry is the subject of a note in that Schedule.

    (3) The Secretary of State may by order—(a) add an organisation to Schedule 2; (b) remove an organisation from that Schedule; (c) amend that Schedule in some other way.

    (4) The Secretary of State may exercise his power under subsection (3)(a) in respect of an organisation only if he believes that it is concerned in terrorism.

    (5) For the purposes of subsection (4) an organisation is concerned in terrorism if it—(a) commits or participates in acts of terrorism, (b) prepares for terrorism, (c) promotes or encourages terrorism, or (d) is otherwise concerned in terrorism.'

Section 11 creates the offence of belonging or professing to belong to a proscribed organisation. Other sections create other offences related to proscribed organisations. In s 121 'organisation' is defined to include 'any association or combination of persons'. Schedule 2 to the Act, entitled 'Proscribed organisations', lists a number of such organisations, of which the first 14 have an Irish or Northern Irish provenance. First on the list is 'The Irish Republican Army' (henceforward, for convenience, the IRA). One of these listed organisations, the Orange Volunteers, is the subject of a note in the Schedule:

> 'The entry for The Orange Volunteers refers to the organisation which uses that name and in the name of which a statement described as a press release was published on 14th October 1998.'

The IRA entry is not the subject of any note. The Real IRA is not, as such, listed. Hence the simple submission made for the acquitted person that the Real IRA is not a proscribed organisation for purposes of the 2000 Act. . . .

    In argument before the House, as in the Court of Appeal, . . . Mr Macdonald realistically accepted that the Real IRA is a terrorist organisation deserving of proscription and that the intention of Parliament was that it should be proscribed. But he insisted that the task of the court is to interpret the provision which Parliament has enacted and not to give effect to an inferred intention of Parliament not fairly to be derived from the language of the statute. For this proposition he was able to cite a wealth of familiar but powerful authority . . . Mr Macdonald also relied on the important principle of legal policy . . . that a person should not be penalised except under a clear law, should not (as is sometimes said) be put in peril on an ambiguity . . . Thus Mr Macdonald submitted that, whatever Parliament may have wished or intended, the Real IRA is not an organisation listed in Sch 2 and no process of construction, properly so called, could lead to the conclusion that it is. Similarly, the Real IRA does not operate under the same name as an organisation listed in that Schedule: it operates under a name which is different, and intentionally different because chosen to convey that the Real IRA is a body separate in its membership and distinct in its aims from the IRA.

    The Attorney General in his argument did not take radical issue with the principles of construction on which Mr Macdonald relied, and I would not for my part wish to throw doubt upon them. But the interpretation of a statute is a far from academic exercise. It is directed to a particular statute, enacted at a particular time, to address (almost invariably) a particular problem or mischief. . . .

    In the present case the historical context seems to me to be of fundamental, and in the end conclusive, importance.

    All the Westminster and Stormont statutes to which I have referred above, whether taking effect in Northern Ireland or Great Britain, were directed to a common end: the elimination of Irish-related terrorism. . . . The object of all these statutes, with the exception of the 1998 Sentences Act, was to suppress such terrorism by stifling the organisations which were dedicated to violence for political ends. By criminalising membership or professed membership of such bodies and other more active acts of participation, it was intended if possible to close them down but at least to impede their functioning. For nearly half a century after 1922 references to the IRA were unproblematical since, however shadowy and secretive that body might be, there was never more than one body bearing, or claiming to bear, that name or any part or variant of it.

By 1973, when the first in the modern series of statutes was enacted, that was no longer so. Nor, importantly, was it thought to be so. As the Court of Appeal recorded, the existence of two groups, the Official IRA and the Provisional IRA, each claiming to be the true embodiment of the IRA, loyal to its aims and ideals, was a known fact. In designing a proscription regime to counter the formidable threat which terrorism then presented, there was no doubt a choice of legislative techniques, one particular, one general. The particular approach would have proscribed the Provisional but not the Official IRA. The general approach was to proscribe the IRA using a blanket description to embrace all emanations, manifestation and representations of the IRA, whatever their relationship to each other, including the Provisional IRA. One course which would, if considered, have been rejected out of hand would have been to proscribe the IRA, meaning only the original IRA if it still existed or the Official IRA if it did not, since it would have been entirely futile to proscribe a body believed to have foresworn terrorism and omit a body believed to present a potent terrorist threat. . . .

It may very well be that the Real IRA and other groups within the IRA family are separate in their member-ship and distinct in their aims, but this is precisely the type of unfathomable enquiry which sub-ss (1)(a) and (b) of s 3, read together, were intended to preclude. It would invite an almost theological inquiry, as in deciding whether the Old Believers in Russia or the Old Catholics in the Netherlands, Germany, Austria, Switzerland, Poland and elsewhere are the true keepers of the faith. Subsections (1)(a) and (b), although expressed in differ-ent language, in my opinion reproduce the effect of the formula first enacted in s 19(3) of the 1973 Act, and it imposes a single composite test: is this the body listed in the Schedule or a part or emanation of it or does it in any event operate under the name of an organisation listed in the Schedule? To that question the only possible answer on the admitted facts of the present case is the affirmative answer which the Court of Appeal gave. . . .

For these reasons I would answer the referred question in the affirmative and dismiss the appeal. In accord-ance with the ordinary practice, the acquitted person will receive his costs of the appeal to the House out of central funds and the Attorney General will bear his own costs."

[Lords Woolf, Rodger, Carswell and Brown concurred with Lord Bingham in separate reasons.]

Questions

1. Why does Lord Bingham avoid a literal approach to interpretation in this case? What does he mean when he states that "interpretation of a statute is a far from academic exercise"?

2. Can you foresee any difficulties with the determination that the "Real IRA" is a proscribed organisation even though it is not listed as such?

3. Does Lord Bingham strengthen his analysis when he states that "it may very well be that the Real IRA and other groups within the IRA family are separate in their membership and distinct in their aims"?

4. How did counsel for Z seek to rely upon the "rule of law" in support of his client? Why do you think the Law Lords were unsympathetic to this argument?

V. The Distinction Between Fact and Law

We now turn our attention to what has been described as "one of the most vexed questions in the whole topic of legal classification".[4] This is the distinction between questions of fact and law. It is an issue of particular importance in administrative law because a decision of an administrative tribunal

---

4   Ian McLeod, *Legal Method*, 5th edn (Basingstoke: Macmillan, 2005), p.33.

is more easily challengeable on judicial review if it is characterised as an issue of law rather than fact. This is because it is assumed that the tribunal is in the best position to make determinations on questions of fact, but that the role of courts is to ensure that questions of law have been properly decided by the original decision maker. The classic statement of the distinction between fact and law was provided by Denning L.J.:

> "It is important to distinguish between primary facts and the conclusions from them. Primary facts are facts which are observed by witnesses and proved by oral testimony or facts proved by the production of a thing itself, such as original documents. Their determination is essentially a question of fact for the tribunal of fact, and the only question of law that can arise on them is whether there was any evidence to support the finding. The conclusions from primary facts are, however, inferences deduced by a process of reasoning from them. If, and in so far as, those conclusions can as well be drawn by a layman (properly instructed on the law) as a lawyer, they are conclusions of fact for the tribunal of fact: and the only questions of law which can arise on them are whether there was a proper direction in point of law; and whether the conclusion is one which could reasonably be drawn from the primary facts. . . . If, and in so far, however, as the correct conclusion to be drawn from primary facts requires, for its correctness, determination by a trained lawyer—as, for instance, because it involves the interpretation of documents or because the law on the point cannot properly be understood or applied except by a trained lawyer—the conclusion is a conclusion of law."[5]

The distinction between questions of fact and law has also proven important in the context of the interpretation of statutes. Is the interpretation of a word or phrase in a statute a question of fact (and therefore a matter primarily for the determination of the original decision maker) or a question of law (and, as a consequence, readily open to judicial review or appeal)? The law in this area is far from clear, but a succinct explanation of the distinction has been provided by Vandevelde.

Kenneth J. Vandevelde, *Thinking Like a Lawyer* (Boulder: Westview Press, 1996), pp.11–12:

"Because there are only three things to be decided in a dispute, there are only three types of issues that can arise in legal reasoning. These are issues of fact, issues of law, and issues requiring application of law to fact.

Issues of fact all pose essentially the same basic question: What is the situation to which the law must be applied? In other words, what events have occurred to create the dispute?

Issues of law also pose essentially one basic question: What are the rules of law governing this situation?

Issues requiring the application of law to fact similarly pose one general question: What rights or duties exist between the parties under the governing law in this situation? These issues are sometimes called mixed questions of law and fact.

A single dispute may present all three types of issues or any combination of them. For example, assume that a man sues a physician claiming that she was negligent in failing to administer a particular diagnostic test to him and that, as a result, he sustained injuries three years later that would have been preventable had his disease been diagnosed earlier.

The physician may put at issue some of the plaintiff's factual allegations. She may raise as issues of fact two questions: Would the diagnostic test actually have revealed that the patient was suffering from the disease? Would the disease have been less injurious had it been discovered earlier?

The parties may also disagree on the applicable law. For example, the physician may raise this question as an issue of law: Does the statute of limitations for negligence claims against a medical practitioner require the claims to be filed within two years of the time the negligence occurred or within two years of the time the

---

[5] *British Launderers' Association v Central Middlesex Assessment Committee and Hendon Rating Authority* [1949] 1 All E.R. 21 at 25–26.

negligence was discovered? If the law requires the claim to be filed within two years of the time the negligence occurred, then the patient would have no right to compensation from the physician.

In addition, the parties may disagree about the application of the law to the facts. For example, the parties may present another question to the court as a mixed issue of law and fact: In this situation, did the physician's failure to administer the test constitute negligence? This is a mixed question of law and fact because it requires the court to apply the legal definition of negligence to the facts to determine whether the physician's conduct constitutes negligence. If the physician was not negligent, then the patient has no right to compensation."

The courts in this country have grappled with the distinction between fact and law, and the results at times have been far from clear, as the next case demonstrates.

Brutus v Cozens [1972] 2 All E.R. 1297, HL.

Lord Reid:

"My Lords, the charge against the appellant is that on 28 June 1971, during the annual tournament at the All England Lawn Tennis Club, Wimbledon, he used insulting behaviour whereby a breach of the peace was likely to be occasioned, contrary to section 5 of the Public Order Act 1936, as amended.

While a match was in progress on no 2 court he went on to the court, blew a whistle and threw leaflets around. On the whistle being blown nine or ten others invaded the court with banners and placards. I shall assume that they did this at the instigation of the appellant although that is not made very clear in the case stated by the justices. Then the appellant sat down and had to be forcibly removed by the police. The incident lasted for two or three minutes. This is said to have been insulting behaviour.

It appears that the object of this demonstration was to protest against the apartheid policy of the government of South Africa. But it is not said that that government was insulted. The insult is said to have been offered to or directed at the spectators. The spectators at no 2 court were upset; they made loud shouts, gesticulated and shook their fists and while the appellant was being removed some showed hostility and attempted to strike him. The justices came to the conclusion that the appellant's behaviour was not insulting within the terms of the offence alleged. They did not consider the other points raised in argument but dismissed the information without calling on the appellant.

On a case stated a Divisional Court set aside the judgment of the justices and remitted the case to them to continue the hearing of the case. They certified as a point of law of general public importance:

'Whether conduct which evidences a disrespect for the rights of others so that it is likely to cause their resentment or give rise to protests from them is insulting behaviour within the meaning of s.5 of the Public Order Act 1936.'

Section 5 is in these terms:

'Any person who in any public place or at any public meeting—(a) uses threatening, abusive or insulting words or behaviour . . . with intent to provoke a breach of the peace or whereby a breach of the peace is likely to be occasioned, shall be guilty of an offence.'

Subsequent amendments do not affect the question which we have to consider.

It is not clear to me what precisely is the point of law which we have to decide. The question in the case stated for the opinion of the court is 'Whether, on the above statements of facts, we came to a correct determination and decision in point of law'. This seems to assume that the meaning of the word 'insulting' in s.5 is a matter of law. And the Divisional Court appear to have proceeded on that footing.

In my judgment that is not right. The meaning of an ordinary word of the English language is not a question of law. The proper construction of a statute is a question of law. If the context shows that a word is used in an unusual sense the court will determine in other words what that unusual sense is. But here there is in my opinion no question of the word 'insulting' being used in any unusual sense. It appears to me . . . to be intended to have its ordinary meaning. It is for the tribunal which decides the case to consider, not as law but as fact, whether in the whole circumstances the words of the statute do or do not as a matter of ordinary usage of the English language cover or apply to the facts which have been proved. If it is alleged that the tribunal has reached a wrong decision then there can be a question of law but only of a limited character. The question would normally be whether their decision was unreasonable in the sense that no tribunal acquainted with the ordinary use of language could reach that decision. . . .

We were referred to a number of dictionary meanings of 'insult' such as treating with insolence or contempt or indignity or derision or dishonour or offensive disrespect. Many things otherwise unobjectionable may be said or done in an insulting way. There can be no definition. But an ordinary sensible man knows an insult when he sees or hears it. . . . If the view of the Divisional Court was that in this section the word 'insulting' has some special or unusually wide meaning, then I do not agree. Parliament has given no indication that the word is to be given any unusual meaning. Insulting means insulting and nothing else.

If I had to decide, which I do not, whether the appellant's conduct insulted the spectators in this case, I would agree with the justices. The spectators may have been very angry and justly so. The appellant's conduct was deplorable. Probably it ought to be punishable. But I cannot see how it insulted the spectators.

I would allow the appeal with costs."

[Lord Morris of Borth-y-Gest, Viscount Dilhorne, Lord Diplock, and Lord Kilbrandon agreed that the appeal should be allowed.]

Questions

1. Why does Lord Reid state that he does not have to decide whether the appellant's conduct was "insulting"?

2. Do you think that the appellant's strategy of drawing attention to the apartheid regime in South Africa was successful? Why or why not? Remember that these events occurred in 1971, before there was widespread protest in this country against apartheid.

3. It is interesting that no mention is made in the judgments of the South African regime against which the protest was aimed. It is perhaps ironic that the appellant's behaviour is described as deplorable, when its impact was simply to interrupt a tennis game for a few minutes in an attempt to gain international publicity regarding a government widely viewed as deplorable. Do you think that Lord Reid should have discussed the South African Government's policy openly in his judgment?

VI. Case Study on Statutory Interpretation: the Race Relations Act

The best way of understanding how courts approach statutory interpretation is through examples. In this section, we examine one controversial instance of statutory interpretation in which the courts were sharply divided: the Race Relations Act. We begin with what is now a "classic" case, *Mandla v Dowell Lee*, in which the Court of Appeal and House of Lords differed sharply on the interpretation of the word "ethnic" in the context of Sikhs in Britain. We will then compare the way in which the Court of Appeal subsequently applied the reasoning of the House of Lords in *Mandla* to what appears to be a very similar set of facts in *Dawkins v Department of the Environment*.

Mandla v Dowell Lee and another [1982] 3 All E.R. 1108, CA.

Lord Denning M.R.:

"How far can Sikhs in England insist on wearing their turbans? A turban is their distinctive headgear. They do not cut their hair but plait it under their turbans. Some of them feel so strongly about it that, when they are motorcyclists, they do not wear crash helmets; and when they are barristers they do not wear wigs.

Sewa Singh Mandla is a Sikh and rightly proud of it. He is a solicitor of the Supreme Court, practising in Birmingham. In 1978 he applied to send his son Gurinder to a private school in Birmingham called the Park Grove School. Gurinder was then aged 13. The school was very suitable for him. It had a high reputation. It took boys of all races. There were 305 boys altogether. Over 200 were English, but there were many others. Five were Sikhs, 34 Hindus, 16 Persians, six Negroes, seven Chinese and about 15 from European countries.

Mr Mandla took his son to see the headmaster. Both he and his son were wearing their turbans. The headmaster felt that it might give rise to difficulties if Gurinder wore his turban in school. He asked the father: 'Will you consent to his removing his turban and cutting his hair?' The father said: 'No. That is completely out of the question.' The headmaster said that he would think about it. Then on 24 July 1978 he wrote:

> 'Thank you for bringing your son to see me. As I promised, I have given much thought to the problem and I have reluctantly come to the conclusion that on balance it would be unwise to relax the School Rules with regard to uniform at the moment. I do not see any way in which it would be possible to reconcile the two conflicting requirements. May I wish you well in your efforts to promote harmony and peace, and I hope you find a suitable school for Gurinder without difficulty.'

Mr Mandla did find another school for Gurinder where he is allowed to wear his turban. So all is now well with them. But Mr Mandla reported the headmaster to the Commission for Racial Equality. They took the matter up with the headmaster. On 19 September 1978 the headmaster wrote this letter:

> 'To make my position quite clear, the boy was not rejected because he was a Sikh since we do not make racial distinctions and we have several Sikhs in the School. It was the turban that was rejected, and I believe your Acts cover people, not clothes.'

The commission, however, did not let the matter rest. They pursued the headmaster relentlessly. They interviewed him. They demanded information from him. Eventually they decided to assist Mr Mandla in legal proceedings against him. With their assistance in money and advice Mr Mandla issued proceedings against the headmaster of the school in the Birmingham County Court. He claimed damages limited to £500 and a declaration that the defendants had committed an act of unlawful discrimination. The county court judge heard the case for five days in February and June 1980, with many witnesses and much argument. The judge dismissed the claim. The Commission for Racial Equality, in Mr Mandla's name, appeal to this court.

The headmaster appeared before us in person. He has not the means to instruct counsel and solicitors. He put his case moderately and with restraint. He has himself done much research in the India Office library and elsewhere. It must have taken him many hours and many days. Now we have to consider what it all comes to.

The Law

The case raises this point of great interest: what is a 'racial group' within the Race Relations Act 1976? If the Sikhs are a 'racial group' no one is allowed to discriminate against any of their members in the important fields of education and employment and so forth. No matter whether the discrimination is direct or indirect, it is unlawful. But, if they are not a 'racial group' discrimination is perfectly lawful. So everything depends on whether they are a 'racial group' or not.

The statute in s.3(1) of the 1976 Act contains a definition of 'racial group'. It means a 'group of persons defined by reference to colour, race, nationality or ethnic or national origins'. That definition is very carefully framed. Most interesting is that it does not include religion or politics or culture. You can discriminate for or against Roman Catholics as much as you like without being in breach of the law. You can discriminate for or against Communists as much as you please, without being in breach of the law. You can discriminate for or against the 'hippies' as much as you like, without being in breach of the law. But you must not discriminate against a man because of his colour or of his race or of his nationality, or of 'his ethnic or national origins'. It is not suggested that the Sikhs are a group defined by reference to colour or race or nationality. Nor was much stress laid on national origins. But it is said most persuasively by counsel for the [claimants] that the Sikhs are a group of persons 'defined by reference to ethnic origins'. It is so important that I will consider each word of that phrase.

'Ethnic'

The word 'ethnic' is derived from the Greek word 'ἐθνός' which meant simply 'nation'. It was used by the 72 Palestinian Jews who translated the Old Testament from Hebrew into Greek (in the Septuagint). They used it to denote the non-Israelitish nations, that is, the Gentiles. When the word 'ethnic' was first used in England, it was used to denote peoples who were not Christian or Jewish. This was the meaning attached to it in the great *Oxford English Dictionary* itself in 1890.

But in 1934 in the *Concise Oxford Dictionary* it was given an entirely different meaning. It was given as: 'pertaining to race, ethnological'. And 'ethnological' was given as meaning: 'corresponding to a division of races'. That is the meaning which I, acquiring my vocabulary in 1934, have always myself attached to the word 'ethnic'. It is, to my mind, the correct meaning. It means 'pertaining to race'.

But then in 1972 there was appended a second supplement of the *Oxford English Dictionary*. It gives a very much wider meaning than that which I am used to. It was relied on by counsel for the [claimants]:

> 'Also, pertaining to, or having common racial, cultural, religious or linguistic characteristics, especially designating a racial or other group within a larger system; hence (U.S. colloquial), foreign, exotic.'

As an example of this new meaning, the second supplement refers to a book by Huxley and Haddon called *We Europeans* (1935). It mentions 'the non-committal terms *ethnic group*' and refers to the 'special type of *ethnic* grouping of which the Jews form the best-known example' (my emphasis). This reference to the Jews gives us a clue to the meaning of ethnic.

Why are 'the Jews' given as the best-known example of 'ethnic grouping'? What is their special characteristic which distinguishes them from non-Jews? To my mind it is a racial characteristic. The *Shorter Oxford Dictionary* describes a Jew as 'a person of Hebrew race'. Some help too can be found in our law books. . . . If a man desires that his daughter should only marry 'a Jew' and cuts her out of his will if she should marry a man who is not 'a Jew', he will find that the court will hold the condition void for uncertainty. The reason is because 'a Jew' may mean a dozen different things. It may mean a man of the Jewish faith. Even if he was a convert from Christianity, he would be of the Jewish faith. Or it may mean a man of Jewish parentage, even though he may be a convert to Christianity. It may suffice if his grandfather was a Jew and his grandmother was not. The Jewish blood may have become very thin by intermarriage with Christians, but still many would call him 'a Jew'. All this leads me to think that, when it is said of the Jews that they are an 'ethnic group', it means that the group as a whole share a common characteristic which is a racial characteristic. It is that they are descended, however remotely, from a Jewish ancestor. When we spoke of the 'Jewish regiments' which were formed and fought so well during the war, we had in mind those who were of Jewish descent or parentage. When Hitler and the Nazis so fiendishly exterminated 'the Jews', it was because of their racial characteristics and not because of their religion.

There is nothing in their culture of language or literature to mark out Jews in England from others. The Jews in England share all of these characteristics equally with the rest of us. Apart from religion, the one characteristic which is different is a racial characteristic.

'Origins'

The statute uses the word 'ethnic' in the context of 'origins'. This carries the same thought. I turn once again to the *Shorter Oxford Dictionary*. When the word 'origin' is used of a person it means 'descent, parentage'. I turn also to the speech of Lord Cross in *Ealing London Borough v. Race Relations Board* [1972] 1 All ER 15 at 117, [1972] AC 342 at 365:

> 'To me it suggests a connection subsisting at the time of birth . . . The connection will normally arise because the parents or one of the parents of the individual in question are or is identified by descent . . .'

So the word 'origins' connotes a group which has a common racial characteristic.

'Ethnic Origins'

If I am right in thinking that the phrase 'ethnic origins' denotes a group with a common racial characteristic, the question arises: why is it used at all? The answer is given by Lord Cross in the *Ealing London Borough* case ([1972] 1 All ER 15 at 117–118, [1972] AC 342 at 366):

> 'The reason why the word "ethnic or national origins" were added to the words "racial grounds" which alone appear in the long title was, I imagine, to prevent argument over the exact meaning of the word "race".'

In other words, there might be much argument whether one group or other was of the same 'race' as another, but there was thought to be less whether it was a different 'ethnic group'.

'Racial Group'

This brings me back to the definition in the statute of a 'racial group'. It means 'a group of persons defined by reference to colour, race, nationality or ethnic or national origins'.

The word 'defined' shows that the group must be distinguished from another group by some definable characteristic. English, Scots or Welsh football teams are to be distinguished by their national origins. The Scottish clans are not distinguishable from one another either by their ethnic or national origins, but only by their clannish or tribal differences. French Canadians are distinguished from other Canadians by their ethnic or national origins. Jews are not to be distinguished by their national origins. The wandering Jew has no nation. He is a wanderer over the face of the earth. The only definable characteristic of the Jews is a racial characteristic. I have no doubt that, in using the words 'ethnic origins', Parliament had in mind primarily the Jews. There must be no discrimination against the Jews in England. Anti-Semitism must not be allowed. It has produced great evils elsewhere. It must not be allowed here.

But the words 'ethnic origins' have a wider significance than the Jews. The question before us today is whether they include the Sikhs.

The Sikhs

The word 'Sikh' is derived from the Sanskrit 'Shishya', which means 'disciple'. Sikhs are the disciples or followers of Guru Nanak, who was born on 5 April 1469. There are about 14 m Sikhs, most of whom live in the part of the Punjab which is in India. Before the partition of the province in 1947 half of them lived in that portion which is now Pakistan; but on the partition most of them moved into India. There was tragic loss of life.

There is no difference in language which distinguishes the Sikhs from the other peoples in India. They speak Punjabi or Hindi or Urdu, or whatever the vernacular may be. There is no difference in blood which distinguishes them either. The people of India are largely the product of successive invasions that have swept into the country. They have intermingled to such an extent that it is impossible now to separate one strain from the other. The Sikhs do not recognise any distinction of race between them and the other peoples of India. They freely receive converts from Hinduism, or vice versa. Not only from outside, but even within the same family. The outstanding distinction between the Sikhs and the other peoples of India is in their religion, Sikhism, and its accompanying culture.

This is so marked that Dr Ballard, who is a lecturer in race relations in the University of Leeds, thought it was an ethnic difference. But, if you study his evidence, it is plain that he was using the word 'ethnic' in a special sense of his own. For him it did not signify any racial characteristic at all. These are some illuminating passages from his evidence:

> 'Sikhs, most obviously, are not a race in biological terms. Their origins are extremely diverse, probably more diverse than us English . . . I think they are a classic example of an ethnic group because of their distinctive cultural traditions . . . We are busy coining lots of new words here. I think ethnicity is the proper word to coin . . .'

The evidence shows that Sikhs as a community originate from the teaching of Guru Nanak. About the fifteenth century he founded the religious sect. There were a series of Gurus who followed Nanak, but the tenth and last is most important. Early in the nineteenth century he instituted major social and cultural reforms and turned the Sikhs into a community. He laid down the rules by which the hair was not to be cut and it was to be covered by a turban. By adopting this uniform Sikhs made their communal affiliation very clear, both to each other and to outsiders. But they remained at bottom a religious sect.

It is sometimes suggested that the Sikhs are physically a different people. But that is not so. In an important book on *The People of Asia* (1977) p.327 Professor Bowles of Syracuse University, New York, says:

> 'The difference [between Muslims, Sikhs and Hindus] are mainly cultural, not biological. Much has been written about the tallness . . . and excellent physique of the Sikh, qualities often attributed to their well-balanced vegetarian diet. In part this may be true, but the Sikhs are matched in physique by several other Punjab populations—meat-eating as well as vegetarian. Muslims as well as Hindus. Some of the neighbouring Pathan tribesmen are even taller. The Sikh physique is probably due to the fact that many have entered professions that have given them an economic advantage over their compatriots, Indians or Pakistanis. A correlation between nutrition and physique holds throughout the entire subcontinent, but it may be more noticeable in the Punjab, where there is such a variety of merchants and traders . . .'

On all this evidence, it is plain to me that the Sikhs, as a group, cannot be distinguished from others in the Punjab by reference to any racial characteristic whatever. They are only to be distinguished by their religion and culture. That is not an ethnic difference at all.

Conclusion

I have dealt with the evidence at length because of the differences on the point in the lower courts and tribunals. In our present case the evidence has been more fully canvassed than ever before. It has been most well and carefully considered by His Honour Judge Gosling here. I agree with his conclusion that Sikhs are not a racial group. They cannot be defined by reference to their ethnic or national origins. No doubt they are a distinct community, just as many other religious and cultural communities. But that is not good enough. It does not enable them to complain of discrimination against them.

You must remember that it is perfectly lawful to discriminate against groups of people to whom you object, so long as they are not a racial group. You can discriminate against the Moonies or the skinheads or any other group which you dislike or to which you take objection. No matter whether your objection to them is reasonable or unreasonable, you can discriminate against them, without being in breach of the law.

No doubt the Sikhs are very different from some of those groups. They are a fine community upholding the highest standards, but they are not a 'racial group'. So it is not unlawful to discriminate against them. Even though the discrimination may be unfair or unreasonable, there is nothing unlawful in it.

In our present case the headmaster did not discriminate against the Sikhs at all. He has five Sikh boys in his school already. All he has done is to say that, when the boy attends school, he must wear the school uniform and not wear a turban. The other Sikh boys in the school conform to this requirement. They make no objection. Mr Mandla is, I expect, strictly orthodox. He feels so strongly that he insists on his son wearing his turban at all times. But that feeling does not mean that the headmaster was at fault in any way. He was not unfair or unreasonable. It is for him to run his school in the way he feels best. He was not guilty of any discrimination against the Sikhs, direct or indirect.

I cannot pass from this case without expressing some regret that the Commission for Racial Equality thought it right to take up this case against the headmaster. It must be very difficult for educational establishments in this country to keep a proper balance between the various pupils who seek entry. The statutes relating to race discrimination and sex discrimination are difficult enough to understand and apply anyway. They should not be used so as to interfere with the discretion of schools and colleges in the proper management of their affairs.

In the circumstances I need say nothing as to the contentions about the word 'can' or 'justifiable' in the statutes. They do not arise.

I would dismiss the appeal."

Oliver L.J.:

[Oliver L.J. delivered separate concurring reasons, and concluded with some comments on the actions of the Commission for Racial Equality in this case.]

". . . In the result, I agree that the appeal fails. I would add only this. Without in any way minimising the great assistance which counsel for the plaintiffs have given the court in this difficult case, it is right that some tribute should be paid to the courtesy, skill and patience with which Mr Dowell Lee has conducted in person a case which must have caused him immense personal distress and anxiety. I cannot help observing that the events of which complaint have been made took place as long ago as the summer of 1978, four years ago. Throughout Mr Dowell Lee appears to have behaved with the greatest courtesy and restraint. After an entirely courteous correspond-ence with the first [claimant], he found himself the subject of a visitation from a representative of the Commission for Racial Equality and the papers before us contain the notes of an interview with him at which he appears to have been deliberately interrogated with a view to extracting admissions of racial bias and at which barely con-cealed threats of 'investigation' were made unless he modified the stance which he had adopted. Thereafter he, whose proper business was running his school in a way which to him seemed most suited to the needs of his students, found himself involved in an action fostered and supported by the commission. The proceedings were commenced two years later and have throughout been maintained by the commission in the name of better race relations, although it emerged, ironically, at the trial that the first [claimant] would not, if the matter of his son's entry had been pursued, have been willing in any event for him to go to a school where he would have been expected to attend religious classes of the Christian faith as part of the normal curriculum. There is, and this should be made, I think, entirely clear, absolutely no foundation, in my judgment, for the suggestion that Mr Dowell Lee is seeking or has sought to exclude children from the school either on racial or religious grounds. . . . Mr Dowell Lee's objection to the wearing of the turban at school is precisely, as I understand it, because he feels that it would tend to accentuate those very religious and social distinctions which it is his desire to minimise in trying to effect a homogenous school community. Whether that is an objection which all or any of the members of this court would equally feel is immaterial. It is, in my judgment, a perfectly respectable viewpoint and is the sincerely held and responsible opinion of a man who is running a multiracial school in a difficult area. I have to say that, speaking entirely for myself, I regard it as lamentable that Mr Dowell Lee's entire livelihood and the future of his school should have been put at risk at the instance of a publicly financed body designed to foster better racial relations. Anything less likely to achieve that result than this case I find it difficult to imagine. As it is Mr Dowell Lee has been compelled to waste a great deal of his time and the resources of the school in defending himself against charges which could hardly have been levelled at any target less deserving of them. He has been dragged through two courts at enormous expense in order, apparently, to establish a point which no doubt is a difficult and important one, but is now entirely academic for both [claimants]. It seems to me a great pity that it should have been thought necessary to test it at the expense of an entirely blameless individual who has done no more than to seek in the best way that he knows how to run his own business in his own way. What makes it, perhaps, particularly ironic is the evidence of the plaintiffs' expert Mr Indarijit Singh:

'Tolerance is the willingness, and a Sikh should be willing, to fight in every way including, if need be, eventu-ally to give his life, to upholding the next person's right to determine his own particular way of life.'

For my part, I find it regrettable that this unimpeachable sentiment should not have been applied here and that machinery designed specifically for the protection of the weak and disadvantaged should have operated as, it seems to me, it has in this case, albeit no doubt with the loftiest of motives, as an engine of oppression.

I should only add that, in saying this, I am making no criticism whatever of counsel for the [claimant] or those instructing him, who have conducted the appeal in accordance with their clients' instructions with the most punctilious fairness and propriety.

I too would dismiss the appeal."

Kerr L.J.:

[Kerr L.J. delivered concurring reasons, concluding with the following comment.]

". . . I would add my disquiet to what Lord Denning M.R. and Oliver L.J. have already said about the events which have led up to these proceedings. The Commission for Racial Equality is clearly highly motivated and does useful work in cases where there is clear evidence, or real ground for suspicion, that racial discrimination exists and is practised. But this is not such a case. This school was demonstrably conducted harmoniously on a multiracial basis. I have read in this evidence the notes of the interview of the headmaster by an official of the commission. In parts this reads more like an inquisition than an interview, and I can see no basis whatever for what I can only describe as harassment of this headmaster. All that the commission has achieved in this case, as it seems to me, is to create racial discord where there was none before."

Questions

1. Consider Lord Denning's description of the ethnic mix of the school. What does he mean by "English" students? Can you see any problem with describing the student body in this way?

2. Is Lord Denning's explanation of why "ethnic" was included in the statutory language convincing? Can you think of an alternative explanation?

3. In Lord Denning's reasons, a substantial amount of expert evidence (that is, evidence given by experts in the area under consideration) is presented. On what basis is this evidence accepted or rejected? Specifically, why does Lord Denning reject Dr Ballard's conclusion that Sikhs are an ethnic group?

4. All of the judges very reluctant to interfere with the "discretion" of the headmaster in running his school as he sees fit. Is that a reasonable approach for the judges to adopt? Could such an approach undermine the purpose of the Race Relations Act?

5. Lord Oliver mentions that Mr Mandla would not have sent his son to this school in any event because it conducted Christian religious education. Could you argue that such services are themselves contrary to the spirit of the Race Relations Act? Note here that Lord Denning stated that Jews definitely do constitute an "ethnic group" for the purposes of the legislation.

The case was then appealed to the House of Lords.

Mandla v Dowell Lee [1983] 1 All E.R. 1062, HL.

Lord Fraser of Tullybelton:

[Lord Fraser described the facts and the issue of statutory interpretation, before considering whether Sikhs constituted an ethnic group.]

". . . My Lords, I recognise that 'ethnic' conveys a flavour of race but it cannot, in my opinion, have been used in the 1976 Act in a strict racial or biological sense. For one thing it would be absurd to suppose that Parliament can have intended that membership of a particular racial group should depend on scientific proof that a person possessed the relevant distinctive biological characteristics (assuming that such characteristics exist). The practical difficulties of such proof would be prohibitive, and it is clear that Parliament must have used the word in some more popular sense. For another thing, the briefest glance at the evidence in this case is enough to show that, within the human race, there are very few, if any, distinctions which are scientifically recognised as racial.
. . .

I turn, therefore, to the third and wider meaning which is given in the *Supplement to the Oxford English Dictionary* vol I (A–G) (1972). It is as follows: 'pertaining to or having common racial, cultural, religious, or linguistic characteristics, esp. designating a racial or other group within a larger system . . .' Counsel for the appellants, while not accepting the third (1972) meaning as directly applicable for the present purpose, relied on it to this extent, that it introduces a reference to cultural and other characteristics, and is not limited to racial characteristics. The 1972 meaning is, in my opinion, too loose and vague to be accepted as it stands. It is capable of being read as implying that any one of the adjectives, 'racial, cultural, religious or linguistic' would be enough to constitute an ethnic group. That cannot be the sense in which 'ethnic' is used in the 1976 Act, as that Act is not concerned at all with discrimination on religious grounds. Similarly, it cannot have been used to mean simply any 'racial or other group'. If that were the meaning of 'ethnic', it would add nothing to the word group, and would lead to a result which would be unacceptably wide. But in seeking for the true meaning of 'ethnic' in the statute, we are not tied to the precise definition in any dictionary. The value of the 1972 definition is, in my view, that it shows that ethnic has come to be commonly used in a sense appreciably wider than the strictly racial or biological. That appears to me to be consistent with the ordinary experience of those who read newspapers at the present day. In my opinion, the word 'ethnic' still retains a racial flavour but it is used nowadays in an extended sense to include other characteristics which may be commonly thought of as being associated with common racial origin.

For a group to constitute an ethnic group in the sense of the 1976 Act, it must, in my opinion, regard itself, and be regarded by others, as a distinct community by virtue of certain characteristics. Some of these characteristics are essential; others are not essential but one or more of them will commonly be found and will help to distinguish the group from the surrounding community. The conditions which appear to me to be essential are these: (1) a long shared history, of which the group is conscious as distinguishing it from other groups, and the memory of which it keeps alive; (2) a cultural tradition of its own, including family and social customs and manners, often but not necessarily associated with religious observance. In addition to those two essential characteristics the following characteristics are, in my opinion, relevant: (3) either a common geographical origin, or descent from a small number of common ancestors; (4) a common language, not necessarily peculiar to the group; (5) a common literature peculiar to the group; (6) a common religion different from that of neighbouring groups or from the general community surrounding it; (7) being a minority or being an oppressed or a dominant group within a larger community, for example a conquered people (say, the inhabitants of England shortly after the Norman conquest) and their conquerors might both be ethnic groups. . . .

The result is, in my opinion, that Sikhs are a group defined by a reference to ethnic origins for the purpose of the 1976 Act, although they are not biologically distinguishable from the other people living in the Punjab. That is true whether one is considering the position before the partition of 1947, when the Sikhs lived mainly in that part of the Punjab which is now Pakistan, or after 1947, since when most of them have moved into India. It is, therefore, necessary to consider whether the respondent has indirectly discriminated against the appellants in the sense of s.1(1)(b) of the 1976 Act. That raises the two subsidiary questions. . . .

'Can comply'
It is obvious that Sikhs, like anyone else, 'can' refrain from wearing a turban, if 'can' is construed literally. But if the broad cultural/historic meaning of ethnic is the appropriate meaning of the word in the 1976 Act, then a literal reading of the word 'can' would deprive Sikhs and members of other groups defined by reference to their ethnic origins of much of the protection which Parliament evidently intended the 1976 Act to afford to them. They 'can' comply with almost any requirement or condition if they are willing to give up their distinctive customs and cultural rules. On the other hand, if ethnic means inherited and unalterable, as the Court of Appeal thought it did, then 'can' ought logically to be read literally. The word 'can' is used with many shades of meaning. In the context of s.1 (1)(b)(i) of the 1976 Act it must, in my opinion, have been intended by Parliament to be read not as meaning 'can physically', so as to indicate a theoretical possibility, but as meaning 'can in practice' or 'can consistently with the customs and cultural conditions of the racial group'. . . . Accordingly I am of opinion that the 'no turban' rule was not one with which the second appellant could, in the relevant sense, comply.

'Justifiable'
The word 'justifiable' occurs in s.1(1)(b)(ii). It raises a problem which is, in my opinion, more difficult than the problem of the word 'can'. But in the end I have reached a firm opinion that the respondent has not been able

to show that the 'no turban' rule was justifiable in the relevant sense. Regarded purely from the point of view of the respondent, it was no doubt perfectly justifiable. He explained that he had no intention of discriminating against Sikhs. . . . The reasons for having a school uniform were largely reasons of practical convenience, to minimise external differences between races and social classes, to discourage the 'competitive fashions' which he said tend to exist in a teenage community, and to present a Christian image of the school to outsiders, including prospective parents. The respondent explained the difficulty for a headmaster of explaining to a non-Sikh pupil why the rules about wearing correct school uniform were enforced against him if they were relaxed in favour of a Sikh. In my view these reasons could not, either individually or collectively, provide a sufficient justification for the respondent to apply a condition that is prima facie discriminatory under the 1976 Act.

An attempted justification of the 'no turban' rule, which requires more serious consideration, was that the respondent sought to run a Christian school, accepting pupils of all religions and races, and that he objected to the turban on the ground that it was an outward manifestation of a non-Christian faith. Indeed, he regarded it as amounting to a challenge to that faith. I have much sympathy with the respondent on this part of the case and I would have been glad to find that the rule was justifiable within the meaning of the statute, if I could have done so. But in my opinion that is impossible. The onus under para (b)(ii) is on the respondent to show that the condition which he seeks to apply is not indeed a necessary condition, but that it is in all circumstances justifiable 'irrespective of the colour, race, nationality or ethnic or national origins of the person to whom it is applied', that is to say that it is justifiable without regard to the ethnic origins of that person. But in this case the principal justification on which the respondent relies is that the turban is objectionable just because it is a manifestation of the second appellant's ethnic origins. That is not, in my view, a justification which is admissible under para (b)(ii). . . .

Final considerations

Before parting with the case I must refer to some observations by the Court of Appeal which suggest that the conduct of the Commission for Racial Equality in this case has been in some way unreasonable or oppressive. . . .

My Lords, I must say that I regard these strictures on the commission and its officials as entirely unjustified. The commission has had a difficult task, and no doubt its inquiries will be resented by some and are liable to be regarded as objectionable and inquisitive. But the respondent in this case, who conducted his appeal with restraint and skill, made no complaint of his treatment at the hands of the commission. He was specifically asked by some of my noble and learned friends to point out any part of the notes of his interview with the commission's official to which he objected, and he said there were none and that an objection of that sort formed no part of his case. The lady who conducted the interview on behalf of the commission gave evidence in the county court, and no suggestion was put to her in cross-examination that she had not conducted it properly. Opinions may legitimately differ as to the usefulness of the commission's activities, but its functions have been laid down by Parliament and, in my view, the actions of the commission itself in this case and of its official who interviewed the respondent on 3 November, 1978 were perfectly proper and in accordance with its statutory duty.

I would allow this appeal. The appellants have agreed to pay the costs of the respondent in this House and they do not seek to disturb the order for costs in the lower courts in favour of the present respondent made by the Court of Appeal."

[Lord Templeman delivered separate concurring reasons. Lord Edmund-Davies, Lord Roskill, and Lord Brandon of Oakbrook concurred in the reasons of Lord Fraser and Lord Templeman.]

Questions

1. Lord Fraser expressed his sympathy with the respondent's desire to run a "Christian" school. Are there other "outward manifestations" of non-Christian faiths which a school might be tempted to prohibit? Do you think it would be more "just" if symbols of Christianity were prohibited?

2. Note how Lord Fraser criticises the Court of Appeal for the way it describes the Commission for Racial Equality. How does he use the doctrine of the supremacy of Parliament to justify his criticism of the Court of Appeal?

Compare the following judgment which seeks to apply the reasoning in *Mandla v Dowell Lee* to what appear to be very similar facts:

Dawkins v Department of the Environment [1993] I.R.L.R. 284, CA.

Neill L.J.:

"This is an appeal by leave of the single Lord Justice by Mr Trevor Dawkins from the order of the Employment Appeal Tribunal dated 24 April 1991 allowing the appeal of Crown Suppliers (SA) Ltd from the decision of the Industrial Tribunal dated 28 March 1989. I shall call Mr Dawkins 'the appellant' and the Crown Suppliers (PSA) Ltd 'the PSA'. . . . The respondent to the appeal is now the Department of the Environment.

The facts
The PSA, which is part of the Home Civil Service, is responsible for *inter alia* providing transport for the government Interdepartmental Despatch Service (IDS). In June 1988 the PSA inserted an advertisement in the South London Press seeking experienced drivers for the IDS. The advertisement stipulated that the applicants should be aged between 25 and 45 with a clean driving licence. The appellant responded to the advertisement and attended at the PSA's premises for interview at 10 am on 28 June 1988.

Before the Industrial Tribunal there was a conflict of evidence as to the appearance of the appellant at the interview. It is sufficient to say that the appellant, who is a Rastafarian, attended wearing a hat and that underneath the hat he had long hair arranged in the form of dreadlocks. Miss Barbara Herbert, who conducted the interview with the appellant, explained to him that the SA expected their drivers to have short hair. The appellant indicated that he was not willing to cut his hair and the interview was then concluded amicably.

On 26 September 1988 the applicant applied to the Industrial Tribunal for a finding whether he had been discriminated against contrary to the Race Relations Act 1976. The appellant's complaint was heard on 16 and 17 January 1989 at London South. By the decision of the Industrial Tribunal which was sent to the parties on 28 March 1989 the tribunal found by a majority that the appellant's claim succeeded. The question of remedies was left over for a later occasion. By their majority decision the Industrial Tribunal held that the PSA had been guilty of both direct and indirect discrimination. They held that the appellant had been refused employment not because he was black but because of the opinion which Miss Herbert formed as to his unsuitability by reason of the length of his hair. The central question at issue before the Industrial Tribunal was whether or not Rastafarians constituted a racial group within the meaning of the 1976 Act. By a majority the Industrial Tribunal decided that Rastafarians did constitute such a group. In reaching this conclusion the Industrial Tribunal made a number of findings of fact which have not been challenged. The difference of opinion between the members of the Industrial Tribunal was as to the application of the law to these facts.

I should set out the findings of fact made by the Industrial Tribunal in paragraph 10 of their reasons. These findings were as follows:

'(i)   The Rastafarian movement as such began about 1930. We do not think it is possible to trace it back any further than this. It seems to us that it was in the decade between 1920 and 1930 that the ideas of Marcus Garvey began to crystallise, and that it cannot be said that the movement had any separate existence before 1930.

(ii)   That there is a distinct culture which although in some respects is vague and difficult to grasp seems to us nevertheless to exist. The fact that the Rastafarians do not, as most have, distinct centres of worship does not seem to us to be very material. We find that they do, as Dr Cashmore says, meet in groups in order to discuss matters of common interest as outlined in his evidence and that they do observe distinct customs such as a refusal to cut hair or to shave, and observe dietary laws and prohibitions on homosexuality and contraception. They also have, we find, a common language i.e. English and the Jamaican patois.

(iii)   They have a common geographical origin in that the majority of them come from Jamaica at least in origin, although by now a large number of Rastafarians in this country will have been born here.

(iv)   That there is some literature and some cultural tradition that is, that there is some poetry which is distinctive to the group and there is also reggae music. We feel that if a group shows a musical tradition then this must also be taken into account as well as a written or oral literary tradition.

(v)   That they do have a sense of being a minority and of being oppressed in that their distinctive appearance is likely to single them out for criticism by other members of the community thus causing them to have a feeling that they are a peculiar minority among other people.

(vi)   We also find that there has been continuity, albeit tenuous, from 1930. We think the answer here is that until about 1970 Rastafarians, at least in this country, were few and far between. This is probably why not many were noticed between the 1950s, when immigration from the West Indies to this country started, and 1970 when the movement seems to have been noticed. We think, however, that it can be shown that the movement has either here or in Jamaica or in other parts of the world been continuous since 1930.'

I shall have to return later to consider how the Industrial Tribunal applied the relevant law to these facts.

The Law

The complaint by the appellant was brought before the Industrial Tribunal in accordance with s.54(1) of the Race Relations Acts 1976 which provides that a complaint that another person has committed an act of discrimination against the complainant which is unlawful by virtue of art.II of the Act may be presented to an Industrial Tribunal. [Neill L.J. then explained the content and structure of the statutory regime]. . . .

In the present case the appellant claims that he was subjected to both direct and indirect racial discrimination in that he was refused employment by the PSA by reason of his membership of a particular racial group, namely the Rastafarians. It is contended on his behalf that Rastafarians constitute a group of persons who are defined by reference to their ethnic origins.

On behalf of the PSA it is accepted that the appellant was refused employment because he was a Rastafarian, but it is denied that Rastafarians constitute a group of persons defined by reference to their ethnic origins. It will be seen therefore that the crucial question to be decided by the Industrial Tribunal was whether or not Rastafarians were a group defined by reference to their ethnic origins. . . .

The decision of the Industrial Tribunal

In their full and careful reasons the Industrial Tribunal referred to the decisions in *Mandla* and in *King-Ansell*.[6] In addition they referred to the decision of the Court of Appeal in England in *Commission for Racial Equality v. Dutton* [1989] IRLR 8 (CA) where the question for decision was whether gypsies constituted an ethnic group within the meaning of the 1976 Act.

In paragraph 12 of their reasons the Industrial Tribunal considered whether Rastafarians satisfied the first of the 'essential' conditions set out in Lord Fraser's speech [i.e. whether the group can show a shared history]. . . .

The Industrial Tribunal were divided on the question whether a shared tradition of just under 60 years was long enough. Two members of the Tribunal were of the opinion that in the circumstances the test of a long shared history was satisfied because the test had to be examined not only in relation to its actual length but also by reference to its continuity and persistence. The third member disagreed on the basis that a far longer period of time than 60 years was required before it could be said that a group possessed a long shared history.

In paragraph 13 of the reasons the Industrial Tribunal considered the other conditions set out in Lord Fraser's speech. The majority considered that the condition of a cultural tradition was satisfied. In addition there was a unanimous finding that Rastafarians had a common geographical origin in that their ancestors came from Jamaica. The reasons continued:

'There is some sort of common literature, there is not a common religion, they do have a sense of being a minority or being an oppressed group because of their peculiar customs.'

---

6   *King-Ansell v Police* [1979] 2 N.Z.L.R. 531, a decision of the New Zealand Court of Appeal.

In the light of their findings the Industrial Tribunal decided by a majority of two to one that Rastafarians constituted a racial group within the definition in s.3(1) of the 1976 Act.

The PSA appealed.

The decision of The Employment Appeal Tribunal

The judgment of the Employment Appeal Tribunal was delivered by Tucker J. By a majority the appeal by the PSA was allowed. In their judgment the Employment Appeal Tribunal referred to the *Mandla* case and the *Dutton* case. . . . At [1991] ICR 583, 594 Tucker J. said:

> 'Applying those tests to Rastafarians, we ask whether they possess any of the characteristics of a race? We very much doubt whether the majority of Rastafarians can claim that they are of group descent, though some of them may be. Their geographical origin is Jamaica. We doubt whether they can be said to have a group history. . . . There is in our view insufficient to distinguish them from the rest of the Afro-Caribbean community so as to render them a separate group defined by reference to ethnic origins. They are a religious sect and no more.'

In any event returning to Lord Fraser's test, we are unable to agree with the majority of the Industrial Tribunal that Rastafarians have a long shared history. It cannot reasonably be said that a movement which goes back for only 60 years, i.e. within the living memory of many people, can claim to be long in existence. Its history, in the judgment of the majority, is insufficiently sustained. The fact that the movement has maintained itself and still exists is insufficient. We have no hesitation in disagreeing with the conclusion of the majority of the Tribunal on this point, because first we do not regard it as a finding of fact, and secondly, even if it were we would regard it as a finding which no reasonable Tribunal could make, and therefore perverse.

So far as Lord Fraser's second essential test is concerned, that of a cultural tradition of its own, our view is that Rastafarians are a group with very little structure, no apparent organisation and having customs and practices which have evolved in a somewhat haphazard way. Nevertheless, notwithstanding these reservations and placing them in the context of a formerly enslaved people striving for an identity, there may be a sufficient cultural tradition to satisfy the test, and we are not prepared to disagree with the finding of the Tribunal on this point.

These are the views of the majority of the members of the Tribunal. One member dissents from them. On the basis of a book *One Love Rastafari: History, Doctrine and Livity* by Jah Bones (not referred to in argument before us) he is of the view that Rastafarians have a sufficiently long shared history to fulfil the test. In addition he would hold that they are more than a religious sect. However, by a majority, we allow the appeal for the reasons which we have expressed.' . . .

Do the Rastafarians constitute a racial group?

. . . I am unable to accept that the Industrial Tribunal's decision by a majority that Rastafarians had a sufficiently long shared history to satisfy Lord Fraser's first condition was merely a finding of fact with which an appellate court cannot interfere. The finding that a group originated in 1930 was indeed a finding of fact, but a decision as to the length of a shared history, which is necessary for the purpose of satisfying a statutory test, is a very different matter. In any event it is important to remember that the relevant words in the statute are 'ethnic origins'.

. . .

It is clear that Rastafarians have certain identifiable characteristics. They have a strong cultural tradition which includes a distinctive form of music known as reggae music. They adopt a distinctive form of hairstyle by wearing dreadlocks. They have other shared characteristics of which both the Industrial Tribunal and the Employment Appeal Tribunal were satisfied. But the crucial question is whether they have established some separate identity by reference to their ethnic origins. In speaking about Rastafarians in this context I am referring to the core group, because I am satisfied that a core group can exist even though not all the adherents of the group could, if considered separately, satisfy any of the relevant tests.

It is at this stage that one has to take account of both the racial flavour of the word 'ethnic' and Lord Fraser's requirement of a long shared history. Lord Meston submitted that if one compared Rastafarians with the rest of the Afro-Caribbean community in this country, there was nothing to set them aside as a separate ethnic group. They are a separate group but not a separate group defined by reference to their ethnic origins. I see no answer to this submission.

Mr Whitmore quite rightly stressed that this case is concerned with identity. The question is: have the Rastafarians a separate ethnic identity? Do they stand apart by reason of their history from other Jamaicans?

In my judgment it is not enough for Rastafarians now to look back to a past when their ancestors, in common with other peoples in the Caribbean, were taken there from Africa. They were not a separate group then. The shared history of Rastafarians goes back only 60 years or so. One can understand and admire the deep affection which Rastafarians feel for Africa and their longing for it as their real home. But, as Mr Riza recognises, the court is concerned with the language of the statute. In the light of the guidance given by the House of Lords in *Mandla*, I am unable to say that they are a separate racial group.

I would dismiss the appeal.

Beldam L.J: I agree.

Sir John Megaw: I also agree.

Appeal dismissed with costs. Application for leave to appeal to the House of Lords refused."

Questions

1. After reading *Dawkins*, do you have a clear sense of when a "shared history" becomes a long one?

2. The majority of the Employment Appeal Tribunal described Rastafarian culture as "haphazard" and as lacking in structure and organisation. Are those relevant considerations? Could you argue that all cultural development is a haphazard process? Why is the degree of structure and organisation of culture relevant to a statute which deals with discrimination?

3. Note how the Employment Appeal Tribunal and the Court of Appeal refer to the fact–law distinction to overturn the Industrial Tribunal's finding that Rastafarians have a long shared history. Both the Employment Appeal Tribunal and the Court of Appeal held that this was a legal inference rather than a finding of fact. Is the distinction between fact and law any clearer in your mind after reading this case?

4. Remember that nowhere in the statute is there a definition of ethnicity which depends upon the existence of a long shared history. Reread Lord Fraser's judgment in *Mandla v Dowell Lee*. Is the existence of a long shared history a necessary requirement for the finding of an ethnic group in his analysis?

Although *Mandla* may be a case that considers the narrow issue of whether Sikhs constitute an "ethnic group", cases such as *Mandla* and *Dawkins* raise wider issues about the role of race in English law and legal history. For example, Herman has analysed the role that "the Jew" plays in English law, and the *Mandla* case is an important element of that analysis.

Didi Herman, "'An unfortunate coincidence': Jews and Jewishness in twentieth-century English judicial disourse" (2006) 33 *Journal of Law and Society* 277–301, at 277–278, 282, 283–284, 285–287:

"'The wandering Jew has no nation. He is a wanderer over the face of the earth.'

Lord Denning wrote these words in 1982, in a case that ostensibly had nothing to do with Jews at all. As Master of the Rolls at the Court of Appeal, Denning was writing one of the judgments in *Mandla* v. *Dowell Lee*, a Race Relations Act 1976 case about whether Sikhs constituted an 'ethnic group' for the purposes of the Act. He and his colleagues determined Sikhs did not; however, on appeal, the House of Lords overturned their decision in what became, and remains, the leading case on the meaning of 'ethnic group' under the Act. While Denning rejected the legitimacy of Sikhs as an ethnic group, albeit through affirming Jews as a (stateless) racial group, the House of Lords made little mention of Jews at all, despite relying heavily for their definition of 'ethnic group' on a New Zealand case about Jews. Subsequent cases relying on *Mandla* also failed to acknowledge the role played by 'the Jew' in the development of United Kingdom race relations law.

In this paper, I take this perhaps puzzling appearance (and disappearance) of 'the Jew' in *Mandla* as a springboard to being mapping the terrain of English judicial representations of 'the Jew'. I say *begin* mapping because very little work exists in this field. . . .

. . . Legal judgments, especially those that function as 'precedent', are authoritative statements of official state discourse. Judicial discourse has immediate, far-reaching, and often long-lasting material effects. More specifically in relation to the themes of this paper, judges are active creators of official *racial knowledge*. They are also *nation-builders*, engaging in strategies of *estrangement* and defining the boundaries of belonging. It is also important to recognize that, with few exceptions, English judges express and consolidate class power; their discourse on 'the Jew' is shaped by their elite class position and is thus different to working-class racial ideologies. Judicial racial discourse is thus about the intimate connection between cultural representation, class and state power, and resource allocation. . . .

An understanding of race as 'nation', and the role of these two in shaping the most fundamental aspects of personhood and character have a long pedigree in England. Long before (and indeed after) the 'race sciences' made their mark on knowledge, race was largely understood as heritage or *lineage*. Racial difference was familial, national, and environmental difference, albeit difference usually encoded in a racialized system of domination and subordination. In England, those persons originating from outside the British Isles, or even those indigenous to British territory deemed not descended from the 'Anglo-Saxon' race (for example, the Celts), were viewed as having a very different character from the English. Indeed, the process of nation-building was and remains partly a process of character-building.

> 'The construction of the nation space takes place alongside the production of national character as instances in which 'the nation' itself is fleshed out *as place and person*.'

The development and incorporation of the slavery enterprise into English 'normality', despite its earlier renunciation, is one of the most heinous examples of the production and consequences of these forms of racial belief in the modern period. However, in relation to Jews and Jewishness, understandings of race were also complicated by a much older Christian theology identifying Jews as the 'chosen people' of a sacred (if somewhat superseded) Christian text (the so-called 'Old Testament'). Jewishness implicated racial, religious, and national difference, although this was further complicated by the understanding of Jews, like Roma, as a 'nation' without a territory: '[Jews] were the ultimate incongruity: a *non-national nation*'. In *Mandla*, Denning puzzles over these incongruities . . .

Although, in 1982, Denning's use of a phrase like 'Jewish blood' was out of keeping with other representations of Jews at this time, and neither his colleagues at the Court of Appeal nor those at the House of Lords were prepared to use such language, an understanding of race as ancestry 'in the blood' was common place in English courts until the mid-twentieth century. As authority for his understanding, Denning notes a series of 1940s trust law cases that race Jews in this way, and also quotes with approval the definition of 'Jew' in the 1934 Concise Oxford Dictionary: 'a person of Hebrew race'.

. . . This line of cases shares a conception of 'the Jew' that is, literally 'Hebraic' in the biblical sense, and within which Denning's explicit invocation of 'the wandering Jew' seems wholly unremarkable (if anachronistic). While 'the Jew' is clearly racialized, the discourse of early twentieth-century race science is largely absent from these trust law cases about the transmission of wealth by propertied Jews. Instead, these twentieth-century judges seem to display an eighteenth-century understanding of race and nation as implicating bloodline and lineage, and to understand the 'ancient Israelite' as a kind of 'noble savage'. At times there is almost a certain sentimental reverence in which ancient Hebrews are held, of whom these wealthy testators are seen to be distant progeny. Inheritance, as expressed through the law of trusts, lends itself to this interpretation of Jewishness, as its subject-matter necessarily concerns propertied Jewish families reasonably well-settled in England. However, in cases in other legal spheres, race, nation, and character were usually deployed quite differently.

Rather than identifying Jews with the nation of ancient Israel, many judges were clearly perturbed by the 'eastern' immigrants arriving on British shores in the early part of the twentieth century. For these judges, Jewishness signified not the nobility of the ancient Israelites but the foreignness of the 'eastern character'. It was also in the first decades of the twentieth century that the figure of the 'Wandering Jew' became less associated with ancient Israelites and more with unwanted immigrants."

Questions

1. Can you find examples, drawn from the judgments in *Mandla* and *Dawkins*, in which, to use Herman's words, "judges are active creators of official racial knowledge"?

2. Do you agree with Herman's claim that "English judges express and consolidate class power"? Justify your answer.

Useful website addresses

UK Parliament, *http://www.parliament.uk* [Accessed May 12, 2010]
Bills presented to Parliament, *http://www.parliament.uk/bills/bills.cfm* [Accessed May 12, 2010]
Office of Public Sector Information, *http://www.opsi.gov.uk* [Accessed May 12, 2010]
Law Commission, *http://www.lawcom.gov.uk* [Accessed May 12, 2010]

6

STATUTORY INTERPRETATION: THE SEARCH FOR LEGISLATIVE INTENTION

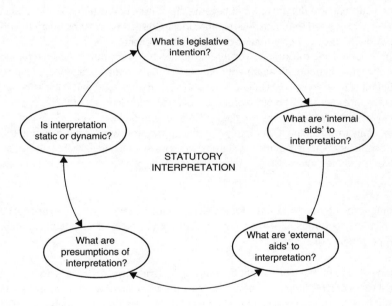

In this chapter, we continue our focus on statutory interpretation. We look primarily at the key issue of the role of the intention of the legislature in interpretation. By the end of this chapter, you should:

- appreciate the meaning of legislative intent and why it is relevant to statutory interpretation;

- recognise the role of "internal aids" to interpretation;

- be able to apply the rules on the admissibility of *Hansard* (the record of parliamentary debates) and appreciate the changing character of the rules;

- recognise the tension between legislative intent and the need for interpretation to reflect changing social conditions;

- recognise the role of the presumptions of interpretation and be able to apply them.

I. The Role of Intention and Purpose in Statutory Interpretation

Judges frequently justify statutory interpretations by claiming that they are advancing the "intention" of Parliament. This justification is closely connected to the idea of parliamentary supremacy: that judges simply apply the law which Parliament has enacted. However, the idea of legislative intention is a more difficult concept than you might think.

John Bell and Sir George Engle, *Cross on Statutory Interpretation*, 3rd edn (London: Butterworths, 1995), pp.24–27:

"The 'intention of Parliament' with regard to a particular statute cannot mean the intention of all those who were members of either House when the royal assent was given, for many of them might have been out of the country at all material times and never have heard of the statute. Equally plainly the phrase cannot mean the intention of the majority who voted for the statute as this will almost certainly have been constituted by different persons at the different stages of the passage of the Bill and, in any event, it would be rash to assume that all those who vote for it have the same intentions with regard to a particular piece of legislation. For example, it has been pointed out that, in a debate on what became the Statute of Westminster 1931, Winston Churchill and the Solicitor-General agreed that there was no obscurity in the provisions concerning the Irish Free State, although they took diametrically opposite views concerning their effect.

Someone bent on identifying the intention of specific human beings as that to which reference is made when people speak of the intention of Parliament might resort to the notion of agency. It could be said that the promoters of a Bill must have some consequences in mind as its general and particular effects, but promoters, whoever they may be, are initiators who place proposals before Parliament rather than act as its agents; and many Bills contain amendments which are not the work of the promoters. . . .

The court may justify the meaning it ultimately attaches to statutory words by suggesting that this is the meaning which, it believes, members of the legislature would have attached to them had the situation before the court been present to their minds. But, . . . the following words of a South African judge surely hold good for English law:

'Evidence that every member who voted for a measure put a certain construction upon it cannot affect the meaning which the court must place upon the statute, for it is the product, not of a number of individuals, but of an impersonal Parliament.'

This last quotation helps to make clear . . . that the question of legislative intention is not about the historical or hypothetical views of legislators, but rather concerns the meaning of words used in a particular context. The objective is not to reconstruct a psychological model of Parliament or the promoters of a Bill, or even of the drafter, and then to use it to determine what was meant by them when they used certain words, or what would have been provided had a particular eventuality been envisaged at the time of drafting or enactment. . . . Judges are concerned instead with using the conventions of ordinary language and of statutory interpretation to determine the meaning of words in their context. . . .

In the context of the interpretation of statutes there are three principal situations in which people in general and judges in particular speak of the intention of Parliament. In the first place, whenever the meaning of specific words is under consideration, the idea that a particular meaning is that which would or would not have been attached to a word or phrase by the average member of Parliament, sitting at the time when the statute was passed, may be expressed or refuted by some such statement as 'that is (or is not) what Parliament intended by those words'. Second, when the consequences of a particular construction are under consideration, the idea that a particular consequence might well have been in the mind of the average member of Parliament is often expressed by some such statement as 'that was likely (or unlikely) to have been the intention of Parliament'. Finally, although it is impossible to identify the individual members whose purpose it was, it is common to speak of the purpose, aim or object of a statute as the intention of

Parliament. The third situation is the most important if only because reflection upon it shows that those who feel uncomfortable about the use of the expression 'intention of Parliament' ought not to feel any more at ease if they abandon the phrase for some other one such as 'the intention of the statute', 'legislative purpose' or 'the object of the statute'. Only human beings can really have intentions, purposes or objects, but, in the situation under consideration, the intentions, purposes or objects are not those of identifiable human beings. The words are used by close analogy to the intentions of a single legislator. The analogy is more remote when the 'intention of Parliament' is used as a synonym for what the average member of Parliament of a particular epoch would have meant by certain words or expected as the consequences of a statutory provision."

In addition, although we have suggested that judges frequently turn to the "ordinary meaning" of statutory language in interpretation, this approach also is closely connected to the idea of legislative purpose.

John Bell and Sir George Engle, *Cross on Statutory Interpretation*, 3rd edn (London: Butterworths, 1995), p.32:

"'[T]he context of ordinary language' already involves a certain number of assumptions. Even in ordinary language, words have more than one meaning, *e.g.* a 'chair' can be something to sit on, the president of a meeting, or a job as a professor. The ordinary user of language selects the appropriate 'ordinary meaning' according to the context in which a communication takes place. Certain assumptions are made about the most likely use of the words in this context. Those assumptions relate, in part, to the purpose of the speaker or writer—if the word 'chair' is used by a university in an advertisement on the jobs page of a newspaper, it is unlikely to intend to refer to furniture. We still refer to this as an interpretation by reference to 'ordinary meaning' because the reader is able to rely on an immediate understanding of the purpose behind the use of the words without engaging in any further research. If this interpretation of the writer's words proves to be wrong, the reader can rightly complain that a warning should have been given that it was necessary to read the words in a different, less immediate context. Thus, an 'ordinary meaning' or 'grammatical meaning' does not imply that the judge attributes a meaning to the words of a statute independently of their context or of the purpose of the statute, but rather that he adopts a meaning which is appropriate in relation to the immediately obvious and unresearched context and purpose in and for which they are used. By enabling citizens (and their advisers) to rely on ordinary meanings unless notice is given to the contrary, the legislature contributes to legal certainty and predictability for citizens and to greater transparency in its own decisions, both of which are important values in a democratic society".

The judicial role in relation to the intention of the legislature sometimes has been explicitly considered by judges.

Duport Steels Ltd and others v Sirs and others [1980] 1 All E.R. 529, HL.

[The appeal concerned the interpretation of the Trade Union and Labour Relations Act 1974 and, in particular, whether the decision of a union in dispute with (the publicly owned) British Steel Corporation to extend a strike to the private steel sector was an action "in . . . furtherance of a trade dispute" and therefore not subject to a potential prosecution in tort. The House of Lords unanimously reversed the decision of the Court of Appeal (which included Lord Denning M.R.) which had found against the union.]

    Lord Scarman:

    ". . . [I]n the field of statute law the judge must be obedient to the will of Parliament as expressed in its enactments. In this field Parliament makes and unmakes the law, the judge's duty is to interpret and to apply the law, not to change it to meet the judge's idea of what justice requires. Interpretation does, of course, imply in the interpreter a power of choice where differing constructions are possible. But our law requires the judge to choose the construction which in his judgment best meets the legislative purpose of the enactment. If the result be unjust but inevitable, the judge may say so and invite Parliament to reconsider its provision. But he must not deny the statute. Unpalatable statute law may not be disregarded or rejected, merely because it is unpalatable. Only if a just result can be achieved without violating the legislative purpose of the statute may the judge select the construction which best suits his idea of what justice requires. Further, in our system the *stare decisis* rule applies as firmly to statute law as it does to the formulation of common law and equitable principles. And the keystone of *stare decisis* is loyalty throughout the system to the decisions of the Court of Appeal and this House. The Court of Appeal may not overrule a House of Lords decision; and only in the exceptional circumstances set out in the practice statement of 26 July 1966 will this House refuse to follow its own previous decisions.

Within these limits, which cannot be said in a free society possessing elective legislative institutions to be narrow or constrained, judges, as the remarkable judicial career of Lord Denning M.R. himself shows, have a genuine creative role. Greater judges are in their different ways judicial activists. But the Constitution's separation of powers, or more accurately functions, must be observed if judicial independence is not to be put at risk. For, if people and Parliament come to think that the judicial power is to be confined by nothing other than the judge's sense of what is right (or, as Selden put it, by the length of the Chancellor's foot), confidence in the judicial system will be replaced by fear of it becoming uncertain and arbitrary in its application. Society will then be ready for Parliament to cut the power of the judges. Their power to do justice will become more restricted by law than it need be, or is today."

II. Internal Aids to Finding Intention

To this point, our analysis of statutory interpretation has focused primarily upon the particular words which give rise to legal questions. But judges often find guidance to interpretation in *other* words within the context of the statute. For example, it is commonly stated that "an act should be read as a whole". Thus, in order to understand the meaning of a word or phrase, it may well be helpful to look at the broader context of the statute, which may shed light on the particular words in issue.

As well, there are a number of "rules" regarding the *admissibility* and *weight* of what are known as "internal aids" to the construction of statutes; that is, parts of a statute other than the enacted clauses themselves. These "rules" may seem quite arbitrary, but you should at least be aware that they exist.

Ian McLeod, *Legal Method*, 5th edn (Basingstoke: Palgrave Macmillan, 2005), pp.283–284, 285–287:

The anatomy of a statute
Preambles
"Where there is a preamble to a statute it will recite the reasons why the statute was passed. However, modern drafting practice in relation to Public Bills has almost entirely dispensed with the use of preambles, although they still appear in Private Bills, and therefore in Private Acts. It follows that their status for the purposes of interpretation is relatively insignificant in quantitative terms. Nevertheless, in those cases where preambles are encountered, their status is clear. According to Lord Normand in *Attorney-General v Prince Ernest Augustus of Hanover* [1957] 1 All ER 49, 'It is only when it conveys a clear and definite meaning in comparison with relatively obscure or indefinite enacting words that the preamble may legitimately prevail'. In practice, however, a preamble may prevail even over enacting words which are plain. . . .

Long titles
Long titles are much more important than preambles in practice, since all modern statutes have them. Moreover, as the leading cases show, they have much the same effect in practice. For example, in *R. v Galvin* [1987] 2 All ER 851, Lord Lane CJ, speaking of the Official Secrets Act 1911, and its predecessor of 1889, said:

'One can have regard to the title of a statute to help resolve an ambiguity in the body of it, but it is not, we consider, open to a court to use the title to restrict what is otherwise the plain meaning of the words of the statute simply because they seem to be unduly wide.'

In *Black-Clawson International Ltd v Papierwerke Waldhof-Aschaffenburg AG* [1975] 1 All ER 810, Lord Simon took the view that where a long title provides 'the plainest of all guides to the general objectives of a statute', there can be no justification for restricting its use to cases of ambiguity. . . .

Short titles

The short title is almost always found towards the end of the statute. The leading case is *Re Boaler* [1915] 1KB 21, where it was acknowledged that the short title is part of the Act, and as such the court can and should consider it. However, it is by definition a *short* title and therefore, as Scrutton LJ said, 'accuracy may be sacrificed to brevity'. Moreover, particular care should be taken when dealing with the short titles of old Acts. Before 1896 it was not the practice for Acts to have short titles, but the Short Titles Act of that year conferred short titles on many older Acts. However, all the short titles were not necessarily appropriate, so that, for example, the short title of the Criminal Procedure Act was given to a statute passed in 1865 which dealt with both criminal and civil procedure.

Headings and marginal notes

A glance at any substantial statute will reveal a collection of *headings* (also know as *cross-headings*) between groups of sections, and *marginal* notes (also known as *side-notes* or *shoulder notes*) in the margin. These are both inserted by the drafter and are never subject to debate by Parliament.

There is reasonably clear judicial consensus that marginal notes and headings are relevant to the process of interpretation, 'provided that we realize that they cannot have equal weight with the words of the Act'. (Lord Reid in *Director of Public Prosecutions v Schildkamp* [1969] 3 All ER 1640.)

More particularly, marginal notes may be used to identify the mischief at which the section is aimed, as Upjohn LJ explained in *Stephens v Cuckfield RDC* [1960] 2 QB 373:

> 'While the marginal note to a section cannot control the language used in the section, it is at least permissible to approach a consideration of its general purpose and the mischief at which it is aimed *with the note in mind*.' [Emphasis added.]

Schedules

Although some comments may be found which suggest there is some significance in the distinction between the main (or operative) part of an Act and a Schedule to an Act, in reality the distinction is purely a matter of form and not of substance, as Bennion explains:

> 'It is often convenient to incorporate part of the operative provisions of an Act in the form of a Schedule. The Schedule is often used to hive off provisions which are too long or detailed to be put in the body of the Act. This does not mean they are unimportant.' (*Statutory Interpretation*, 4th edn, 2002, p.574.)

Judicial authority to the same effect may be found in the judgment of Brett L.J. in *Attorney-General v Lamplough* (1878) 3 ExD 214:

> 'A schedule in an Act is a mere question of drafting, a mere question of words. The schedule is as much part of the statute, and is as much an enactment, as any other part.'

Transitional provisions

A statute which amends an existing statute may well contain provisions which regulate the transition from the old scheme to the new. These transitional provisions will be found towards the end of the statute, and their substance is not uncommonly contained in Schedules. For example, the provisions of the Magistrates' Courts Act 1980, which amended the procedure to be followed by a magistrates' court when committing a defendant for trial at the Crown Court, came into force on 6 July 1981. A Schedule to the Act contained transitional provisions relating to proceedings which had begun before 6 July.

Definition sections

Definition sections, which are commonly found towards the end of statutes but towards the beginning of statutory instruments, contain provisions of two types. First there are those which simply state that the defined terms shall 'mean' whatever the provision states them to mean. Secondly, there are those which state that the defined terms shall 'include' whatever the provision states them to include. In cases falling within the latter category the words will have not only their special statutory meaning but, according to Lord Selbourne L.C. in *Robinson v Baron-Eccles Local Board* (1883) 8 App Cas 798, they will also possess their 'ordinary, popular and natural sense whenever that would be applicable'. In other words, this category does not enact definitions in the strict sense of the term, since it is the nature of a definition to restrict, rather than simply to illustrate, the meaning of a word.

Commencement sections

Commencement sections are generally found towards the end of statutes. Section 4 of the Interpretation Act 1978, whose ancestry can be traced to the Acts of Parliament (Commencement) Act 1793, states that, where provision is made for an Act or part of an Act to come into force on a particular day, it comes into force at the beginning of that day; and that, where no such provision is made, an Act comes into force at the beginning of the day on which it receives the Royal Assent. The limited degree of retrospectivity inherent in this provision appears to cause no injustice in practice, and is in any event a marked improvement over the pre-1793 position, when Acts took effect from the beginning of the Parliamentary session in which they were passed. . . .

Section 4 of the 1978 Act is seldom relevant in practice, because statutes commonly state that they will come into force either on a particular future date, or on the expiry of a stated period after they receive the Royal Assent, or on whatever day may be appointed by the appropriate Secretary of State, who will usually be empowered to make a commencement order by way of a statutory instrument. Appointed days and commencement orders are frequently used when the successful implementation of an Act depends on things such as setting up administrative machinery, appointing staff, making delegated legislation, and so on."

III. External Aids to Finding Intention

If the task of judges in interpreting legislation is to seek out the intention of the legislature, then it would seem reasonable that they should turn to those materials produced by Parliament which might well describe what Parliament had in mind when it was enacting new law. Although a variety of documents are produced by Parliament which might provide some insight into its intention regarding a statutory word or phrase, the most obvious source undoubtedly is *Hansard*: the record of the debates in the two Houses of Parliament. It will perhaps come as a surprise to you that historically these debates were not admissible in courts, (i.e. counsel was not allowed to introduce them as evidence) in order to assist in determining the meaning of a statute. As Lord Simonds explained:

> "The part which is played in the judicial interpretation of a statute by reference to the circumstances of its passing is too well known to need re-statement. It is sufficient to say that the general proposition that it is the duty of the court to find out the intention of Parliament—and not only of Parliament but of Ministers also—cannot by any means be supported. The duty of the court is to interpret the words that the legislature has used. Those words may be ambiguous, but, even if they are, the power and duty of the court to travel outside them on a voyage of discovery are strictly limited."[1]

The relationship between what may have been intended by the legislature, and what was actually enacted, was described by the Earl of Halsbury L.C. As Lord Chancellor (a member of the govern-

---

[1]   *Magor and St Mellons Rural District Council v Newport Corporation* [1951] 2 All E.R. 839 at 841, HL.

ment), he had been responsible for legislation. Yet, as a member of the House of Lords, he had the task of interpreting it! In *Hilder v Dexter* [1902] A.C. 474, the Earl of Halsbury discussed this situation, and decided to remove himself from the case:

> "My Lords, I have more than once had occasion to say that in construing a statute I believe the worst person to construe it is the person who is responsible for its drafting. He is very much disposed to confuse what he intended to do with the effect of the language which in fact has been employed. At the time he drafted the statute, at all events, he may have been under the impression that he had given full effect to what was intended, but he may be mistaken in construing it afterwards just because what was in his mind was what was intended, though, perhaps, it was not done. For that reason I abstain from giving any judgment in this case myself; but at the same time I desire to say, having read the judgments proposed to be delivered by my noble and learned friends, that I entirely concur with every word of them. I believe that the construction at which they have arrived was the intention of the statute. I do not say my intention, but the intention of the Legislature. I was largely responsible for the language in which the enactment is conveyed, and for that reason, and for that reason only, I have not written a judgment myself, but I heartily concur in the judgment which my noble and learned friends have arrived at." (pp.477–478)

Note especially how the Earl of Halsbury differentiates between the intention of the individual responsible for the drafting of a piece of legislation, and the intention of the legislature as a whole. This distinction remains an important one, which we will explore in this chapter. The traditional approach to *Hansard* was substantially modified in 1992, when the House of Lords took the opportunity to change the rule in what became a "landmark" case.

Pepper (Inspector of Taxes) v Hart and related appeals [1993] 1 All E.R. 42, HL.

[The background to the case has been summarised by Bale]:

"*Pepper v Hart* was initially a run of the mill tax case involving the valuation of a fringe benefit. The taxpayers were nine teachers and the bursar of Malvern College who took advantage of a scheme which permitted staff members to have their children educated at the school for only 2% of the fees payable by the public. As higher-paid employees they were required to include in their income, as a benefit of employment, the cash equivalent of the benefit which s.63(1) of the Finance Act 1976 defined as 'an amount equal to the cost of benefit less so much (if any) of it as is made good by the employee to those providing the benefit.' The taxpayers contended that the cost of the benefit was the additional or marginal cost of educating an additional student in a school that had surplus capacity and, since this was less than the concessionary fees paid by them, the cash equivalent of the benefit was nil. The Revenue contended the cost of the benefit was the same for all pupils, namely, the average cost of educating each pupil. The taxpayers won before the special commissioner but the decision was reversed by Vinelott J., and that decision was affirmed by the Court of Appeal. The taxpayers then appealed to the House of Lords. After the first hearing before a panel of five Law Lords, three supported the assessment made by the Revenue and two would have held for the taxpayers. However, before the Lords rendered their decision, the debate in the House of Commons in 1976 concerning the Finance Bill came to their attention. The Financial Secretary in reply to a specific question about the tax treatment of concessionary fees for children of school staff stated that 'the benefit will be assessed on the cost to the employer, which would be very small indeed in this case.' *Hansard* clearly indicated that in determining the benefit to the employee the marginal cost and not the average cost was intended under the Finance Act 1976."[2]

Lord Mackay of Clashfern L.C., dissenting [Lord Mackay's discussion of the factual background to the case has been omitted]:

---

[2]   Gordon Bale, "Parliamentary debates and statutory interpretation: switching on the light or rummaging in the ashcans of the legislative process" (1995) 74 *Canadian Bar Review* 1 at 13.

". . . But much wider issues than the construction of the Finance Act 1976 have been raised in these appeals and for the first time this House has been asked to consider a detailed argument on the extent to which reference can properly be made before a court of law in the United Kingdom to proceedings in Parliament recorded in Hansard. . . .

The principal difficulty I have on this aspect of the case is that in Mr Lester's submission reference to parliamentary material as an aid to interpretation of a statutory provision should be allowed only with leave of the court and where the court is satisfied that such a reference is justifiable (a) to confirm the meaning of a provision as conveyed by the text, its object and purpose, (b) to determine a meaning where the provision is ambiguous or obscure or (c) to determine the meaning where the ordinary meaning is manifestly absurd or unreasonable.

I believe that practically every question of statutory construction that comes before the courts will involve an argument that the case falls under one or more of these three heads. It follows that the parties' legal advisers will require to study *Hansard* in practically every such case to see whether or not there is any help to be gained from it. I believe this is an objection of real substance. It is a practical objection, not one of principle. . . .

Your Lordships are well aware that the costs of litigation are a subject of general public concern and I personally would not wish to be a party to changing a well-established rule which could have a substantial effect in increasing these costs against the advice of the Law Commission and the Renton Committee unless and until a new inquiry demonstrated that that advice was no longer valid.

I do not for my part find the objections in principle to be strong and I would certainly be prepared to agree the rule should no longer be adhered to were it not for the practical consideration to which I have referred and which my noble and learned friend agrees to be of real substance. . . . If reference to parliamentary material is permitted as an aid to the construction of legislation which is ambiguous, or obscure or the literal meaning of which leads to an absurdity, I believe as I have said that in practically every case it will be incumbent on those preparing the argument to examine the whole proceedings on the Bill in question in both Houses of Parliament. Questions of construction may be involved on what is said in Parliament and I cannot see how if the rule is modified in this way the parties' legal advisers could properly come to court without having looked to see whether there was anything in the *Hansard* report on the Bill which could assist their case. If they found a passage which they thought had a bearing on the issue in this case, that passage would have to be construed in the light of the proceedings as a whole.

I fully appreciate, and feel the force of the narrowness of the distinctions which are taken between what is admissible and what is not admissible, but the exception presently proposed is so extensive that I do not feel able to support it in the present state of our knowledge of its practical results in this jurisdiction. For these reasons, I agree that these appeals should be allowed, although I cannot agree on the main issue for the discussion of which this further hearing was arranged."

Lord Browne-Wilkinson

[The discussion of the factual and legislative background has been omitted]:

Should the rule prohibiting reference to parliamentary privilege be relaxed?

"Under present law, there is a general rule that references to parliamentary material as an aid to statutory construction is not permissible (the exclusionary rule) (see *Davis v. Johnson* [1978] 1 All ER 1132, [1979] AC 264 and *Hadmor Productions Ltd v. Hamilton* [1981] 2 All ER 724, [1983] 1 AC 191). This rule did not always apply but was judge-made. Thus, in *Ash v. Abdy* (1678) 3 Swan 664, 36 ER 114 Lord Nottingham L.C. took judicial notice of his own experience when introducing the Bill in the House of Lords. The exclusionary rule was probably first stated by Willes J. in *Millar v. Taylor* (1769) 4 Burr 233 at 2332, 98 ER 21 at 217. However, *Re Mew and Throne* (1862) 31 L.J. Bcy 87 shows that even in the middle of the last century the rule was not absolute: in that case Lord Westbury L.C. in construing an Act had regard to its parliamentary history and drew an inference as to Parliament's intention in passing the legislation from the making of amendment striking out certain words.

The exclusionary rule was later extended so as to prohibit the court from looking even at reports made by commissioners on which legislation was based (see *Salkeld v. Johnson* (1848) 2 Exch 256 at 273, 154 ER 487 at 495). This rule has now been relaxed so as to permit reports of commissioners, including Law Commissioners, and white papers to be looked at for the purpose solely of ascertaining the mischief which the statute is intended to cure but not for the purpose of discovering the meaning of the words used by Parliament to effect such cure. . . . Indeed, in *Factortame Ltd v. Secretary of State for Transport* [1989] 2 All ER 692, [1990] 2 AC 85 your Lordships' House went further than this and had regard to a Law Commission report not only for the purpose of ascertaining the mischief but also for the purpose of drawing an inference as to parliamentary intention from the fact that Parliament had not expressly implemented one of the Law Commission's recommendations. . . .

[T]he reasons put forward for the present rule are, first, that it preserves the constitutional proprieties, leaving Parliament to legislate in words and the courts (not parliamentary speakers) to construe the meaning of the words finally enacted, second, the practical difficulty of the expense of researching parliamentary material which would arise if the material could be looked at, third, the need for the citizen to have access to a known defined text which regulates his legal rights and, fourth, the improbability of finding helpful guidance from *Hansard*.

The Law Commissions of England and Scotland in their joint report on *Interpretation of Statutes* and the Renton Committee on *Preparation of Legislation* both recognised that there was much to be said in principle for relaxing the rule but advised against a relaxation at present on the same practical grounds as are reflected in the authorities. However, both bodies recommended changes in the form of legislation which would, if implemented, have assisted the court in its search for the true parliamentary intention in using the statutory words. . . .

My Lords, I have come to the conclusion that, as a matter of law, there are sound reasons for making a limited modification to the existing rule (subject to strict safeguards) unless there are constitutional or practical reasons which outweigh them. In my judgment, subject to the questions of the privileges of the House of Commons, reference to parliamentary material should be permitted as an aid to the construction of legislation which is ambiguous or obscure or the literal meaning of which leads to an absurdity. Even in such cases references in court to parliamentary material should only be permitted where such material clearly discloses the mischief aimed at or the legislative intention lying behind the ambiguous or obscure words. In the case of statements made in Parliament, as at present advised I cannot foresee that any statement other than the statement of the minister or other promoter of the Bill is likely to meet these criteria.

I accept Mr Lester's submissions, but my main reason for reaching this conclusion is based on principle. Statute law consists of the words that Parliament has enacted. It is for the courts to construe those words and it is the court's duty in so doing to give effect to the intention of Parliament in using those words. It is an inescapable fact that, despite all the care taken in passing legislation, some statutory provisions when applied to the circumstances under consideration in any specific case are found to be ambiguous. One of the reasons for such ambiguity is that the members of the legislature in enacting the statutory provision may have been told what result those words are intended to achieve. Faced with a given set of words which are capable of conveying that meaning, it is not surprising if the words are accepted as having that meaning. Parliament never intends to enact any ambiguity. Contrast with that the position of the courts. The courts are faced simply with a set of words which are in fact capable of bearing two meanings. The courts are ignorant of the underlying parliamentary purpose. Unless something in other parts of the legislation discloses such purpose, the courts are forced to adopt one of the two possible meanings using highly technical rules of construction. In many, I suspect most, cases references to parliamentary materials will not throw any light on the matter. But in a few cases it may emerge that the very question was considered by Parliament in passing the legislation. Why in such a case should the courts blind themselves to a clear indication of what Parliament intended in using those words? The court cannot attach a meaning to words which they cannot bear, but if the words are capable of bearing more than one meaning why should not Parliament's true intention be enforced rather than thwarted?

A number of other factors support this view. As I have said, the courts can now look at white papers and official reports for the purpose of finding the 'mischief' sought to be corrected, although not at draft clauses or proposals for the remedying of such mischief. A ministerial statement made in Parliament is an equally authoritative source of such information; why should the courts be cut off from this source of information as to the mischief aimed at? In any event, the distinction between looking at reports to identify the mischief aimed at but not to find the intention of Parliament in enacting the legislation is highly artificial. Take the normal Law Commission report which analyses the problem and then annexes a draft Bill to remedy it. It is now permissible to look at the report to find the mischief and at the draft Bill to see that a provision in the draft was not included in the legislation enacted (see *Factortame v. Secretary of State for Transport* [1989] 2 All ER 692, [1990] 2 AC 85). There can be no logical distinction between that case and looking at the draft Bill to see that the statute as enacted reproduced, often in the same words, the provision in the Law Commission's draft. Given the purposive approach to construction now adopted by the courts in order to give effect to the true intentions of the legislature, the fine distinctions between looking for the mischief and looking for the intention in using words to provide the remedy are technical and inappropriate. Clear and unambiguous statements made by ministers in Parliament are as much the background to the enactment of legislation as white papers and parliamentary reports. . . .

It is said that parliamentary materials are not readily available to, and understandable by, the citizen and his lawyers, who should be entitled to rely on the words of Parliament alone to discover his position. It is undoubtedly true that *Hansard* and particularly records of committee debates are not widely held by libraries outside London and that the lack of satisfactory indexing of committee stages makes it difficult to trace the passage of a clause after it is redrafted or renumbered. But such practical difficulties can easily be overstated. It is possible to obtain parliamentary materials and it is possible to trace the history. The problem is one of expense and effort in doing so, not the availability of the material. In considering the right of the individual to know the law by simply looking at legislation, it is a fallacy to start from the position that all legislation is available in a readily understandable form in any event: the very large number of statutory instruments made every year are not available in an indexed form for well over a year after they have been passed. Yet, the practitioner manages to deal with the problem, albeit at considerable expense. Moreover, experience in New Zealand and Australia (where the strict rule has been relaxed for some years) has not shown that the non-availability of materials has raised these practical problems.

Next, it is said that lawyers and judges are not familiar with parliamentary procedures and will therefore have difficulty in giving proper weight to the parliamentary materials. Although, of course, lawyers do not have the same experience of these matters as members of the legislature, they are not wholly ignorant of them. If, as I think, significance should only be attached to the clear statements made by a minister or other promoter of the Bill, the difficulty of knowing what weight to attach to such statements is not overwhelming. In the present case, there were numerous statements of view by members in the course of the debate which plainly do not throw any light on the true construction of s.63. What is persuasive in this case is a consistent series of answers given by the minister, after opportunities for taking advice from his officials, all of which point the same way and which were not withdrawn or varied prior to the enactment of the Bill.

Then it is said that court time will be taken up by considering a mass of parliamentary material and long arguments about its significance, thereby increasing the expense of litigation. In my judgment, though the introduction of further admissible material will inevitably involve some increase in the use of time, this will not be significant as long as courts insist that parliamentary material should only be introduced in the limited cases I have mentioned and where such material contains a clear indication from the minister of the mischief aimed at, or the nature of the cure intended, by the legislation. Attempts to introduce material which does not satisfy those tests should be met by orders for costs made against those who have improperly introduced the material. Experience in the United States of America, where legislative history has for many years been much more generally admissible than I am now suggesting, shows how important it is to maintain strict control over the use of such material. That position is to be contrasted with what has happened in New Zealand and Australia (which have relaxed the rule to approximately the extent that I favour): there is no evidence of any complaints of this nature coming from those countries.

There is one further practical objection which, in my view, has real substance. If the rule is relaxed legal advisors faced with an ambiguous statutory provision may feel that they have to research the materials to see whether they yield the crock of gold, *i.e.* a clear indication of Parliament's intentions. In very many cases the crock of gold will not be discovered and the expenditure on the research wasted. This is a real objection to changing the rule. However, again it is easy to overestimate the cost of such research: if a reading of *Hansard* shows that there is nothing of significance said by the minister in relation to the clause in question, further research will become pointless.

In sum, I do not think that the practical difficulties arising from a limited relaxation of the rule are sufficient to outweigh the basic need for the courts to give effect to the words enacted by Parliament in the sense that they were intended by Parliament to bear. Courts are frequently criticised for their failure to do that. This failure is due not to cussedness but to ignorance of what Parliament intended by the obscure words of the legislation. The courts should not deny themselves the light which parliamentary materials may shed on the meaning of the words Parliament has used and thereby risk subjecting the individual to a law which Parliament never intended to enact.

Is there, then, any constitutional objection to a relaxation of the rule? The main constitutional ground urged by the Attorney General is that the use of such material will infringe s.1, Art.9 of the Bill of Rights as being a questioning in any court of freedom of speech and debates in Parliament. As I understand the submission, the Attorney General was not contending that the use of parliamentary material by the courts for the purposes of construction would constitute an 'impeachment' of freedom of speech since impeachment is limited to cases where a member of Parliament is sought to be made liable, either in criminal or civil proceedings, for what he has said in Parliament, *e.g.* by criminal prosecution, by action for libel or by seeking to prove malice on the basis of such words. The submission was that the use of *Hansard* for the purpose of construing an Act would constitute a 'questioning' of the freedom of speech or debate. The process, it is said, would involve an investigation of what the minister meant by the words he used and would inhibit the minister in what he says by attaching legislative effect to his words. This, it was submitted, constituted 'questioning' the freedom of speech or debate.

Article 9 is a provision of the highest constitutional importance and should not be narrowly construed. It ensures the ability of democratically elected members of Parliament to discuss what they will (freedom of debate) and to say what they will (freedom of speech). But, even given a generous approach to this construction, I find it impossible to attach the breadth of meaning to the word 'question' which the Attorney General urges. It must be remembered that art.9 prohibits questioning not only 'in any court' but also in any 'place out of Parliament'. If the Attorney General's submission is correct, any comment in the media or elsewhere on what is said in Parliament would constitute 'questioning' since all members of Parliament must speak and act taking into account what political commentators and others will say. Plainly art.9 cannot have effect so as to stifle the freedom of all to comment on what is said in Parliament, even though such comment may influence members in what they say.

In my judgment, the plain meaning of art.9, viewed against the historical background in which it was enacted, was to ensure that members of Parliament were not subjected to any penalty, civil or criminal, for what they said and were able, contrary to the previous assertions of the Stuart monarchy, to discuss what they, as opposed to the monarch, chose to have discussed. Relaxation of the rule will not involve the courts in criticising what is said in Parliament. The purpose of looking at *Hansard* will not be to construe the words used by the minister but to give effect to the words used so long as they are clear. Far from questioning the independence of Parliament and its debates, the courts would be giving effect to what is said and done there. . . .

According to my judgment the use of clear ministerial statements by the court as a guide to the construction of ambiguous legislation would not contravene art.9. No doubt all judges will be astute to ensure that counsel does not in any way impugn or criticise the minister's statement or his reasoning.

The Attorney General raised a further constitutional point, namely that for the court to use parliamentary material in construing legislation would be to confuse the respective roles of Parliament as the maker of law and the courts as the interpreter. I am not impressed by this argument. The law, as I have said, is to be found in the words in which Parliament has enacted. It is for the courts to interpret those words so as to give effect to that purpose. The question is whether, in addition to other aids to the construction of statutory words, the courts should have regard to a further source. Recourse is already had to white papers and official reports not because they determine the meaning of the statutory words but because they assist the court to make its own determination. I can see no constitutional impropriety in this.

Finally, on this aspect of the case, the Attorney General relied on considerations of comity: the relaxation of the rule would have a direct effect on the rights and privileges of Parliament. To the extent that such rights and privileges are to be found in the Bill of Rights, in my judgment they will not be infringed for the reasons which I have given. . . .

I therefore reach the conclusion . . . that the exclusionary rule should be relaxed so as to permit reference to parliamentary materials where: (a) legislation is ambiguous or obscure, or leads to an absurdity; (b) the material relied on consists of one or more statements by a minister or other promoter of the Bill together if necessary with such other parliamentary material as is necessary to understand such statements and their effect; (c) the statements relied on are clear. Further than this, I would not at present go."

[Lord Keith of Kinkel, Lord Bridge of Harwich, Lord Griffiths, Lord Ackner, Lord Oliver of Aylmerton all concurred in their reasons with Lord Browne-Wilkinson on the admissibility of *Hansard* in judicial proceedings. The appeal was allowed with costs.]

The reasons why the House of Lords decided to alter its historical approach to Parliamentary materials are varied.

Gordon Bale, "Parliamentary debates and statutory interpretation: switching on the light or rummaging in the ashcans of the legislative process" (1995) 74 *Canadian Bar Review* 1 at 17:

"A number of reasons combined to bring about the demise of the exclusionary rule. Perhaps the most important is the move toward a purposive approach to statutory interpretation that has gained momentum in Britain in the last four decades. Also the volume and complexity of modern statutes has required the judiciary to seek greater knowledge of the legislative context in order to construe them properly. There has been growing realization that the canons of interpretation are simply a grab bag of conflicting presumptions that offer little guidance to the proper interpretation of statutes. The powerful European influence exerted through greater contact with decisions of the European Court of Justice and the European Court of Human Rights has reinforced the advantage of a purposive approach to legislation in place of literal interpretation. Commonwealth countries, particularly Australia and New Zealand, have thrown out the traditional exclusionary rule. That this has been achieved without adverse consequences has exerted an influence in Britain. Another factor is that in spite of the rule judges frequently do look to the debates for guidance or to check that their interpretation accords with the purpose of the statute. Many counsel regarded this surreptitious peek at Hansard to be unfair to litigants because the exclusionary rule prevented them from making any submissions about the relevance and weight to accord the parliamentary record. Finally courts do not focus solely on the statute but look to extrinsic aids such as Reports of Royal Commissions, Law Commission Reports and White Papers at least to perceive the problem with which the statute was intended to cope. Admitting these extrinsic aids while excluding the sometimes more relevant parliamentary debates became logically indefensible. In view of the purposive approach to statutory interpretation the highly artificial distinction between looking for the mischief and not the intent appeared increasingly technical and inappropriate. Finally, counsel by wisely arguing for only limited modification of the exclusionary rule finessed the rule of law requirement that the statute book must remain a reliable guide to the citizen. Hansard will only be consulted when legislation is ambiguous, obscure or leads to an absurdity. The courts as interpreters will still be confined by the text but in the case of ambiguity they will not be confined *to* it. The appropriate separation of powers between parliament and the courts will be preserved."

The impact of the House of Lords decision in *Pepper v Hart* has been felt by practitioners, courts, and Parliament alike. The decision was not greeted with unqualified approval by any means, as the following extract suggests.

J.H. Baker, "Statutory interpretation and parliamentary intention" (1993) 52 C.L.J. 353 at 354:

"It is submitted that evidence of ministerial statements is not relevant evidence because, allowing that statutes should be interpreted according to the intention of Parliament, no individual member of Parliament is in a position to state what that intention is or to speak for the silent majority. Parliament acts as a corporate body and the only expression of its common intention is the text to which the Queen and both Houses have given their unqualified assent. What passes in one House is not formally known to the other, or to the sovereign. Even if it is thought that the intention of Parliament is the same thing as the common intention of the greatest number of its members, what one individual member says in debates cannot be cogent evidence of what every other member intends. His remarks may be based on a sound and impartial legal understanding of the issues, but they may not. They may persuade some, but they may not persuade others. There is no debate in which every member speaks, or even a majority of members, and so the prevailing view cannot be ascertained from the speeches. Nor does the fact that a Bill secured the necessary assents enhance the evidentiary value of previous statements. It is not uncommon to vote for motions even when one disagrees with some of the statements and arguments of the person proposing them, because one is satisfied with the wording and one is voting for the wording and its effect rather than for the sentiments expressed orally by its proposer. In other cases one may be persuaded to vote in favour by the different reasoning of a speaker following the first mover, though any consideration of such speeches is apparently excluded under the new rule. Certainly there is no procedure for members of Parliament to register assent to a Bill coupled with dissent from all or some of the reasons given by its promoters. Silence by members is therefore equivocal. . . .

It is remarkable that these well-known principles were not properly discussed in *Pepper v Hart*. The nearest we find to an implied response is the argument that the courts now take a purposive rather than a literal approach to construction. . . . The question is not whether the approach to interpretation is or should be purposive, which is not disputed, but how the purpose behind a document may properly and logically be established. In the case of statutes, it is axiomatic that the purpose to be sought is that of Parliament, and not that of the government. A minister speaks for the government, but not for Queen, Lords and Commons all at once. If the words of a minister are to be considered as evidence of parliamentary intention, should the minister be called as a witness so that he may be cross-examined? Apparently not. Again and again in the Lordships' speeches, the intention of the minister is equated with the intention of Parliament and is not regarded as a matter of evidence: the minister's words are to be read as a source of law, attached as it were to the Act. The exclusionary rule is consequently treated merely as a form of blindfold which for purely technical reasons serves to conceal the truth from the court. Yet what is in fact being concealed from the court is not the intention of Parliament, which can only be expressed in written form, but rather the policy of the government, which should be of no concern to the courts. It is, of course, a notorious fact that while a government remains in power it may whip in a majority of members of the House of Commons to vote in favour of its Bills. . . . It does not follow from *de facto* recognition of our party system, and is not a fact, that members belonging to the party in power may be whipped in to support the legal reasoning of a government minister, or the interpretation which he places on a particular Bill. The whip drives members' bodies into the lobby but is not used to correct their states of mind or to teach them law. It is surely an unwarranted assumption that a minister's interpretation of an ambiguous Bill indicates the intention even of the House of Commons, let alone of Parliament.

The government-centred approach of the House of Lords is, with respect, rather chilling. It is true that in the instant case it operated in favour of the taxpayer, but it must obviously work either way. In future, when an Act is unclear, the intention of Parliament is apparently to be equated with the policy of the government or with what a minister chose to say about that policy in the House of Commons. It took many centuries of constitutional struggle to eliminate the notion that the policy of the government should have the force of law; now, it seems, something very like it is slipping through the back door."

More recently, a critical analysis of the *Pepper v Hart* decision has been developed by Lord Steyn, one of the Law Lords.

Johan Steyn, *"Pepper v Hart*; a re-examination" (2001) *Oxford Journal of Legal Studies* 59 at 60–61, 63–69, 72:

"In our democracy the primary law-making function is entrusted to citizens assembled in two separate chambers of Parliament. The legislature enacts statutes in accordance with the law of Parliament for a European liberal democracy. Subject to general presumptions of constitutional importance, such as the rule of law and the principle of constitutionality, the critical thing is what the text of the law so enacted by Parliament provides. When controversy arises the contextual meaning of the enacted text is controlling. The intention of the majority of members of the legislature on the subject under discussion, assuming such a fact to be discoverable, does not have legal significance. Similarly, the views of the government, ministers, and whips—decisive as their decisions may be on the outcome of debates—do not have any relevance to the meaning of the legislation. Under our constitution Parliament enacts legislation, the courts interpret and apply the enacted laws and the executive acts in conformity with the law as interpreted by the courts. The executive is enormously powerful in getting its proposals enacted. But it has no law-making function and it has no authority to declare what the law is or will be if a Bill is enacted. . . .

My concern is with the effect and consequences of the central ruling in *Pepper v Hart*. Initially, my untutored view was that it must be right to let in *Hansard* material which can cast light on an ambiguous provision. And in 1996 I expressed that opinion in a public lecture. Recently, without expressing a view on the rival arguments of principle, I argued in a published essay that in the light of practical experience in the operation of *Pepper v Hart* it may have become an expensive luxury in our legal system. This was a view based on the meagre results yielded by the resort to *Hansard* set against the cost of producing such material. It has become the duty of lawyers to conduct such searches at pain of being judged to have been professionally negligent. . . .

Almost invariably such searches are fruitless. It remains my view that *Pepper v Hart* has substantially increased the cost of litigation to very little advantage. Many appellate judges share this view. . . .

It is sometimes meaningful and appropriate for a judge to refer to the intention of Parliament in recognition of its supreme law-making power. It is also perfectly sensible to say that legislation as duly promulgated reflects the will of Parliament. But it is quite a different matter to ascribe to a composite and artificial body such as a legislature a state of mind deduced from exchanges in debates. I am not saying that the law cannot ascribe to legal persons, such as companies and state agencies, an intention to commit particular acts. It can and often does. . . . But the argument that a legislature, operating through two chambers, each consisting of hundreds of members, may have an intention revealed by statements in debates raises distinctive problems. And until *Pepper v Hart* the common law, the law of Parliament, and our constitution knew no rule of attribution, or rule of recognition, treating statements of ministers as Acts of Parliament.

It is important to bear in mind precisely what is involved. The intention under consideration is one targeted on the meaning of language contained in a clause in a Bill and employed in a ministerial statement. A Bill is unique as a written document. First Parliamentary Counsel recently explained:

> '[a] Bill is not there to inform, to explain, to entertain or to perform any of the other usual functions of literature. A Bill's sole reason for existence is to change the law. The resulting Act is the law. A consequence of this unique function is that a Bill cannot set about communicating with the reader in the same way that other forms of writing do. It cannot use the same range of tools. In particular, it cannot repeat important points simply to emphasize their importance or safely explain itself by restating a proposition in different words. To do so would risk creating doubts and ambiguities that would fuel litigation. As a result, legislation speaks in a monotone and its language is compressed.'

Parliament can legislate only through the combined action of both Houses acting in accordance with the elaborate stages prescribed by the rules of Parliament. Although the legislative powers of Parliament are exercised by human beings, Parliament as an abstraction cannot have a state of mind like an individual. Parliament legislates by the use of general words. It would be strange use of language to say even of an individual legislator that he intended something in regard to the meaning of a Bill which was never present in his mind. To ascribe to all, or a plurality of legislators, an intention in respect of the meaning of a clause in a complex Bill and how it interacts with a ministerial explanation is difficult. The ministerial explanation in *Pepper v Hart* was made in the House of Commons only. What is said in one House in debates is not formally or in reality known to the members of the other House. How can it then be said that the minister's statement represents the intention of Parliament, i.e. both Houses? The Appellate Committee took the view that opposing views expressed by a person other than the promoter can safely be disregarded whenever a statement by a promoter is admitted. The statement of the promoter is treated as canonical. This is also an assumption which seems inherently implausible in respect of the ebb and flow of parliamentary debates. The relevant exchanges sometimes take place late at night in nearly empty chambers. Sometimes it is a party political debate with whips on. The questions are often difficult but political warfare sometimes leaves little time for reflection. These are not ideal conditions for the making of authoritative statements about the meaning of a clause in a Bill. In truth a minister speaks for the government and not for Parliament. The statements of a minister are no more than indications of what the government would like the law to be. In any event, it is not discoverable from the printed record whether individual members of the legislature, let alone a plurality in each chamber, understood and accepted a ministerial explanation of the suggested meaning of the words. For many the spectre of the ever watchful whips will be enough. They may agree on only one thing, namely, to vote yes. And they have no means of voting yes and registering at the same time disagreement with the explanation of the minister. Their silence is therefore equivocal. When one ponders such realities of parliamentary life the idea of determining from *Hansard* the true intention of Parliament on the meaning of a clause in a Bill, and an associated ministerial statement, looks more and more far fetched. In Black-Clawson Lord Reid, speaking with enormous parliamentary experience, said: 'We often say that we are looking for the intention of Parliament but that is not quite accurate. We are seeking the meaning of the words which Parliament used.'[3] It would have been a fiction for the House to say in *Pepper v Hart* that as a matter of historical fact the explanation of the Financial Secretary reflected the intention of Parliament. Such a fact cannot in the nature of things be deduced from *Hansard*. Arguably, the House may have had in mind in *Pepper v Hart* that an intention derivable from the Financial Secretary's statement ought to be imputed to Parliament. If that were the case, the reasoning would rest on a complete fiction. My view is that the only relevant intention of Parliament can be the intention of the composite and artificial body to enact the statute as printed. If there is substance in this part of my analysis, it tends to undermine the very core of the reasoning in *Pepper v Hart*.

It is now necessary to examine *Pepper v Hart* against a broader canvas. This requires consideration of the legal and practical consequences of the decision. I would argue that four propositions are sustainable. First, if the foundation requirements for the admission of a statement in *Hansard* are established it must be admitted. The court has no discretion. Secondly, the occasion to admit such a statement arises where, after exhausting normal methods of interpretation, there is an ambiguity, obscurity or absurdity in respect of the particular point of statutory interpretation and a promoting minister's statement is clear on the very question. In these circumstances it seems likely that a properly admitted statement will be a trump card or at the very least of considerable weight. Thirdly, in the real world of litigation it is impossible for a court to decline *in limine* to receive such a statement on the ground that the requirements of ambiguity, obscurity or absurdity are not satisfied. Such a refusal before all arguments have been deployed would be seen as a prejudgment of the case. This factor creates the opportunity for the full deployment of *Hansard* in a wide category of cases. Fourthly, it is in practice inevitable that the courts will from time to time allow such statements to determine whether there is ambiguity. Lord Browne-Wilkinson said: 'Having once looked at what was said in Parliament, it is difficult to put it out of mind'. This is underlined by the fact that, but for *Hansard*, the majority in *Pepper v Hart* would have decided in favour of the Revenue. In the real world it will be difficult to hold to a line that ambiguity, and so forth, must be determined only by reference to normal methods of interpretation. The third and fourth points are not critical to the rest of my argument but they underline the potential scope of *Pepper v Hart*.

---

[3] *Black-Clawson International Ltd v Papierwerke Waldhof-Aschaffenburg AG* [1975] A.C. 591 at 613–615.

There is a case for allowing a statute to be interpreted in favour of the taxpayer in accordance with a considered explanation given by a minister promoting the Bill. It is the argument that the executive ought not to get away with saying in a parliamentary debate that the proposed legislation means one thing in order to ensure the passing of the legislation and then to argue in court that the legislation bears the opposite meaning. That is what happened in *Pepper v Hart*. Lord Bridge of Harwich said that the Financial Secretary 'assured' the House that it was not intended to impose the relevant tax. He must have taken the view, as did other members of the majority, that the Revenue in imposing the tax were going back on an assurance to the House of Commons. That would have been an unfair result in a mature democracy. If such a consequence prevailed it might tend to undermine confidence in the legal system. Presented in this way the reasoning begins to look like an estoppel argument. An analogy springs to mind. English law adopts an objective approach to the construction of written contracts. The question is not what the parties subjectively intended. The task of the judge is to ascertain what in the context of the contract the language must reasonably be taken to mean. Evidence of what the parties intended is generally excluded. On the other hand, if one party has led the other to act in the belief that in their dealings the contract will have a certain meaning the first party will be estopped from raising a contrary contention. In this way English law tempers the rigidity of the objective theory and the relevant exclusionary rules. Whether one calls it an estoppel or not *Pepper v Hart* as decided on its facts can similarly be viewed as a tempering of the exclusionary rule in the interests of fairness. On this basis the impact of the decision could be confined to the admission against the executive of categorical assurances given by ministers to Parliament. This may be a defensible and principled justification of *Pepper v Hart*. And it does not involve a search for the phantom of a parliamentary intention.

But that is not how the reasoning of the House in *Pepper v Hart* was formulated. The House had before it a ministerial statement which it regarded as favouring the taxpayer. This framework dictated the shape of the arguments and the judgments. The converse case was not considered. What would the position have been if the statutory position had been truly ambiguous and the ministerial statement favoured the Revenue? *Ex hypothesi* the statement would have come from a minister promoting the Bill and would have been clear on the very question in issue. It would therefore have been a trump card. A judge who declined to give effect to it would, on the reasoning in *Pepper v Hart*, be thwarting the intention of Parliament. What then happens to the principle that if a taxation provision is reasonably capable of two alternative meanings, the courts will prefer the meaning more favourable to the subject? *Pepper v Hart* does not address this question. It also does not address the position where, in the face of an ambiguity, presumptions of general application with constitutional import, e.g. restrictively construing general words in a statute which appear wide enough to trench on the rule of law, would otherwise have been regarded as decisive. The criteria laid down for the admissibility of statements made by a minister are wide enough to cover any case where the statement supports the government view. Nevertheless, as I have explained, there may be a new but respectable argument that in the field of taxation and elsewhere, *Pepper v Hart* may only be used against the executive.

The basis on which the exclusionary rule was relaxed ignores constitutional arguments of substance. Lord Bridge described the rule as 'a technical rule of construction'. And implicitly that is how the majority approached the matter. Surely, it was much more. It was a rule of a constitutional importance which guaranteed that only Parliament, and not the executive, ultimately legislates; and that the courts are obliged to interpret and apply what Parliament has enacted, and nothing more or less. To give the executive, which promotes a Bill, the right to put its own gloss on the Bill is a substantial inroad on a constitutional principle, shifting legislative power from Parliament to the executive. Given that the ministerial explanation is *ex hypothesi* clear on the very point of construction, *Pepper v Hart* treats qualifying ministerial policy statements as canonical. It treats them as a source of law. It is in constitutional terms a retrograde step: it enables the executive to make law. It is to be noted that the objection is not to the idea of a judge looking at *Hansard*. For example, it may be unobjectionable for a judge to identify the mischief of a statute from *Hansard*. What is constitutionally unacceptable is to treat the intentions of the government as revealed in debates as reflecting the will of Parliament.

Let me look at some of the wider consequences of *Pepper v Hart*. *Prima facie* the statutes of our Parliament are regarded as 'always speaking' and not tied to the circumstances in which they were passed. A statute 'has a legal existence independently of the historical contingencies of its promulgation, and accordingly should be interpreted in the light of its place within the system of legal norms currently in force'.[4] This is a benign principle which allows for statutes to apply despite the inevitable changes in social conditions of society. It seems to me, it may be said that the position is crystallized as explained by the minister at the time. In the result the reference to *Hansard* settles an interpretation within the contemporary understanding of government and this introduces a new form of literalism. If that is so, a valuable capacity of our legal system to cope with changing conditions is lost. Another feature of our system which must be considered is the principle of legality. It does not permit general wording in statutes to erode basic rights and freedoms. There is too great a risk that the implications of general words may go unnoticed in the democratic process. If Parliament wishes to make inroads on basic rights it must squarely confront what it is doing. But what happens if the minister made a *Pepper v Hart* statement indicating an intention by general words to modify a basic right? Lord Lester of Herne Hill, the barrister who so ably and successfully argued *Pepper v Hart* in the House of Lords, has subsequently written that the courts will not 'permit ministers to interfere with basic rights and freedoms on the basis of what ministers say in Parliament'. But how can that be guaranteed if the legislation is ambiguous and there is a clear ministerial statement indicating that such an inroad on fundamental rights is intended? After all, under *Pepper v Hart* the court has no element of discretion. Another consequence of *Pepper v Hart* is on the drafting of statutes. That draftsmen will continue to draft with care and precision I do not doubt. But when political issues arise and ministers become involved *Pepper v Hart* offers an opportunity to call off a search for precision by making a statement. A likely effect of *Pepper v Hart* is to encourage imprecision in drafting in controversial measures.

A matter not considered in *Pepper v Hart* is the likely impact of the relaxation of the exclusionary rule on executive practice. It was always predictable that the behaviour of ministers would alter in response to the change announced in *Pepper v Hart*. After all, why should ministers not take advantage of the opportunity under *Pepper v Hart* to explain the effect of the legislation in the way in which the government would like to be understood? If this happens it must mark a constitutional shift of power from Parliament to ministers. . . .

I have challenged a judgment of Lord Browne-Wilkinson. His contribution to the development of English law as a judge, Vice-Chancellor, Law Lord and eventually Senior Law Lord has been immense. He is a great judge. But our allegiance must always be to the law. As lawyers our duty is to follow the evidence and arguments where they lead. I hope I have demonstrated that in *Pepper v Hart* issues of high principle were not examined and that a re-examination of that case is necessary. It is for you to judge whether I have succeeded in this task."

The years since the decision in *Pepper v Hart* have seen a good deal of uncertainty regarding how readily the courts should turn to *Hansard* to assist them in interpretation, and how much weight *Hansard* should be given if admissible. We can see this as a process by which the meaning of *Pepper v Hart* has taken time and subsequent case law to unfold and develop. An indication that the Law Lords wanted to *narrow* the interpretation of *Pepper v Hart* can be seen in the case of *Spath Holme*.

R. v Secretary of State for the Environment, Transport and the Regions and another, Ex p. Spath Holme Ltd **[2001] 1 All E.R. 195.**

Lord Bingham of Cornhill:

"My Lords, on 11 and 8 January 1999 the Secretary of State for Environment, Transport and the Regions and the Secretary of State for Wales (to whom I shall together refer as the ministers) made the Rent Acts (Maximum Fair Rent) Order 1999, SI 1999/6, which applied to England and Wales. They did so in the exercise of powers expressed to be conferred on them by s 31 of the Landlord and Tenant Act 1985 (the 1985 Act). Spath Holme Ltd, a landlord, sought to challenge the order, contending (among other things) that s 31 of the 1985 Act did not

---

[4] Sir Rupert Cross, *Statutory Interpretation* (3rd ed., 1995) 52; *Reg v Ireland* [1998] A.C. 147 at 158C–D; see als S.A. De Smith, Lord Woolf and J. Jowell, *Judicial Review of Administrative Action* (5th ed.) para 6–07.

give the ministers power to make it. Permission to apply for judicial review was refused by the single judge, but granted by the Court of Appeal which, at a further hearing ([2000] 1 All ER 884, [2000] 3 WLR 141), accepted Spath Holme's contention and quashed the order. The main question in this appeal to the House is whether the Court of Appeal was right to hold that s 31 of the 1985 Act gave the ministers no power to make the order. . .

During the last century England and Wales suffered from a persistent shortage of housing. The demand, in particular for private rented accommodation, was greater than the supply. This enabled some private landlords to exploit the scarcity of what they had to let by exacting exorbitant rents and letting on terms disadvantageous to the tenant. A series of statutes, beginning in 1915, sought to address this problem, by controlling the rents which could be charged and affording security of tenure to tenants. This control, beneficial though it was in many ways, tended by its very effectiveness to exacerbate the problem: the financial return to the landlord was at times so modest that there was very little incentive to let accommodation to private tenants, with the result that the supply of accommodation available for private letting tended to shrink. Thus statutes were passed with the object of giving landlords a return sufficient to induce them to make accommodation available.

The Rent Act 1965 was intended to revitalise the market in privately rented accommodation by introducing a new regime of what were called fair rents. These provisions were consolidated in the Rent Act 1968, extended in the Rent Act 1974 and consolidated in the Rent Act 1977, which remains in force. Section 70 of the Act governs the assessment of fair rents, which are to be open market rents adjusted to discount for scarcity and to disregard certain matters specified in s 70(3). While the statute does not in terms refer to open market rents, that has been held by the Court of Appeal to be the proper starting point in the process of assessing and registering a fair rent under the 1977 Act. . . .

In giving effect to this statutory regime, rent officers and rent assessment committees faced the practical difficulty that there was no open market in unregulated privately rented property with which comparison could be made. The years following 1965 were also years of very high inflation. The result was that rents set by rent officers and rent assessment committees did not keep up with inflation, to the benefit of tenants but to the obvious disadvantage of landlords. So the problem which Parliament had sought to address in 1965 once more became acute, and the market in privately rented accommodation declined. By the Housing Act 1988 it was again sought to stimulate a free market in such accommodation by providing for assured and assured shorthold tenancies, which (subject to a limited safeguard for some tenants) provided for rents to be negotiated and agreed between landlord and tenant. Regulated tenancies under the 1977 Act continued to exist, but no new regulated tenancies were to come into existence.

The 1988 Act had its desired effect of tempting private landlords back into the market. But it also had another effect, important for present purposes, of giving rise to rents negotiated between landlord and tenant in the market. Whereas rent officers and rent assessment committees had previously relied on other registered fair rents as the basis of comparison when setting fair rents, there was now available a range of comparators, drawn from the market, on which they could rely (subject to making the adjustments required by statute) instead of the less factual basis of previously registered fair rents. In most areas, rent officers and rent assessment committees took advantage of this new basis of comparison in undertaking their statutory task, but in some areas (notably London and the North West) they were reluctant to do so. In these areas the gap between registered fair rents and open market rents increased, to the point where the former were at a level about half the latter, even in the absence of scarcity. In the two judgments already mentioned the Court of Appeal clearly laid down the correct approach to the assessing of fair rents and at last even the rent officers and rent assessment committees who had previously been reluctant to do so gave effect to the basis of assessment prescribed by the 1977 Act. This had the unfortunate side effect that tenants whose rents had previously been registered at levels well below the adjusted open market level at which they should have been set suffered very sharp and unexpected increases in the rent payable.

The Minister for London and Construction made a statement on this subject in the House of Commons in January 1998 expressing the government's concern about the disproportionate increases which some regulated tenants had suffered, and a consultation paper was issued in May 1998 (*Limiting Fair Rent Increases: A Consultation Paper*. Department of the Environment, Transport and the Regions) outlining the options which had been identified and the action which the government provisionally favoured. The options were: (i) to do nothing and allow rent officers to continue to set fair rents in accordance with s 70 of the 1977 Act; (ii) to provide for a phasing of the rent increases over a period of two to three years; or (iii) to apply a maximum limit linked to the retail price index to increases in rents which had already been registered, but excluding lettings where a substantial increase in rent was attributable to repairs or improvements carried out by the landlord. The consultation paper made plain the government's provisional preference for the third of these options, which would be given effect by exercising the reserve power in s 31 of the 1985 Act.

Not surprisingly, tenants and tenants' associations supported the third option, while seeking a maximum percentage increase smaller than the government had proposed. Landlords and their associations favoured the first, or failing that, the second option. They opposed the third. This was understandable: since the cap was not to apply to rents registered for the first time, the third option if adopted would have the consequence that landlords who had previously been receiving a registered rent lower than it should have been if the rent had been assessed on the correct basis, and who had thereby been subsidising their tenants, were liable to suffer further loss through denial of the full increase to which adoption of the correct, adjusted market value, basis of assessment would have entitled them.

Following public consultation, the government adopted the third options, subject to a reduction in the maximum percentage increase as sought by tenants. The order was accordingly made by the ministers, 'in exercise of the powers conferred upon them' by s 31 of the 1985 Act. . . .

The main issue
At issue in this appeal is the scope of the order-making power conferred by s 31 of the 1985 Act: to what (if any) limits is that power subject? . . .

The 1985 Act did not itself repeal any earlier statutory provision. It was, however, one of three consolidating statutes passed in that year in the housing field, and the repeals, consequential amendments, transitional matters and savings in connection with each of the three were contained in a fourth Act, the Housing (Consequential Provisions) Act 1985, which provided for repeal of the whole of the Housing Rents and Subsidies Act 1975. While the propriety of referring to the provision consolidated in s 31 of the 1985 Act was in issue between the parties to this appeal, it was accepted that the provision which s 31 consolidated was s 11 of the 1975 Act. This section was preceded by a heading 'Rent—general power' and carried a sidenote 'Reserve power to limit rents'. . . .

This section, as its terms made plain, replaced the power previously conferred by s 11 of the Counter-Inflation Act 1973, which itself replaced the power conferred by s 2(4) of the Counter-Inflation (Temporary Provisions) Act 1972 (the 1972 Act). This context, as Mr Bonney submitted and the Court of Appeal accepted, showed that the power in s 11 of the 1975 Act, and therefore s 31 of the 1985 Act, was conferred, and conferred only, to enable the minister to restrict rents where such represented a significant cause of general inflation. This was the foundation of Mr Bonney's central argument that the order was ultra vires, since the minister in making it was not seeking to curb general inflation in the national economy.

It is a matter of historical record that in the early and mid-1970s excessive inflation in the national economy was a recognised major threat to the economic health and social cohesion of the nation. The 1972 and 1973 Acts to which I have referred were passed to counter that threat, and I think it plain from the terms of s 11 of the 1975 Act that it conferred a power to restrict rents where such represented a significant cause of general inflation. The more difficult, and for present purposes more crucial, question is whether that was the only purpose for which the s 11 power could be lawfully exercised. A number of considerations lead me to conclude that the power could in appropriate circumstances be used for other purposes as well. (1) Whereas the 1972 and 1973 Acts were expressly and exclusively directed to countering inflation, the 1975 Act was not. It repealed, in s 1, provisions of the Housing Finance Act 1972, which had changed the basis on which local authorities and new town corporations had determined their rents, and had led to their increasing such rents. It provided for the payment of subsidies to local authorities and new town corporations. It made provision for the phasing of increases of rent of certain registered regulated tenancies not covered by existing phasing provisions. It amended, in a way favourable to tenants, the basis on which fair rents were to be assessed. It reversed the decontrol of certain tenancies. It permitted increases in the rent of controlled tenancies to reflect the value of repairs effected by the landlord or any superior landlord. The 1975 Act accordingly contained a number of provisions, generally protective of tenants, no doubt reflecting at least a partial change of political priorities consequent upon a change of government. No reference was made to inflation or counter-inflation in the long title of the Act, nor in the body of the Act itself, save where reference was made to the short titles of previous Acts and the orders made under those Acts. (2) In marked contrast with the 1972 and 1973 Acts, the 1975 Act did not provide that the powers exercisable under it should cease to be exercisable after the expiration of a specified amount of time. If, when inflation was at its most threatening, Parliament thought it desirable to impose a strict time-limit on the exercise of ministerial powers, it is difficult to see any reason why, in 1975, that safeguard should have been thought unnecessary if inflation alone could justify exercise of the powers. (3) If Parliament had intended in 1975 to restrain the exercise of the s 11 power save for the purpose of countering inflation, I would expect the section to have been drafted, in the context of this Act, so as to make much more specific reference to that limitation. (4) Section 11 of the 1975 Act did not simply consolidate any earlier enactment.

I would not therefore hold, differing with respect from the Court of Appeal, that the scope of s 11 of the 1975 Act (and thus of s 31 of the 1985 Act) was or is limited in the way for which Mr Bonney contended. Section 11 of the 1975 Act conferred a reserve power, to be exercised by the minister if he reasonably judged it necessary or desirable to protect tenants from hardship caused by increased or excessive rents. To treat countering inflation as the sole mischief at which s 11 was directed is to fall into the fallacy identified by Lord Simon and Lord Diplock of treating a single identified mischief as the only mischief.

If, contrary to his main submission, the language and context of s 11 of the 1973 Act did not resolve the issue of interpretation in his favour, Mr Bonny submitted that it was appropriate, on the authority of *Pepper (Inspector of Taxes) v Hart* [1993] 1 All ER 42, [1993] AC 593, to refer to statements in Parliament which made plain that the scope of s 11 was intended to be limited in the way for which he contended. Mr Parker, for the ministers, submitted that reference should not be made to Hansard, but also that, if reference were made, it was clear that the scope of s 11 was not intended to be so limited. Thus the threshold question arises whether in this case, resort to Hansard should be permitted. . . .

I think it important that the conditions laid down by the House in *Pepper v Hart* should be strictly insisted upon. Otherwise, the cost and inconvenience feared by Lord Mackay ([1993] 1 All ER 42 at 48, [1993] AC 593 at 615), whose objections to relaxation of the exclusionary rule were based on considerations of practice not principle, will be realised. The worst of all worlds would be achieved if parties routinely combed through Hansard, and the courts dredged through conflicting statements of parliamentary intention (see [1993] 1 All ER 42 at 61, [1993] AC 593 at 631), only to conclude that the statutory provision called for no further elucidation or that no clear and unequivocal statement by a responsible minister could be derived from Hansard. I would further draw attention to the terms of *Practice Note (Procedure: Reference to Hansard)* [1995] 1 All ER 225, [1995] WLR 192 and *Practice Direction (House of Lords: Petitions for leave to appeal: Supporting documents)* [1993] 1 All ER 573, [1993] 1 WLR 303.

Since, for reasons I have already given, I do not regard the meaning or effect of s 11 of the 1975 Act as ambiguous or obscure or such as to give rise to absurdity, and the unease I felt on reading s 31 of the 1985 Act in isolation has been dispelled by considering s 11 in its social and factual context, I do not for my part find that the first threshold test for resorting to Hansard is met. In this, as in most cases, the statute should be treated as 'the formal and complete intimation to the citizen of a particular rule of the law which he is enjoined, sometimes under penalty, to obey and by which he is both expected and entitled to regulate his conduct' (*Pepper (Inspector of Taxes) v Hart* [1993] 1 All ER 42 at 52, [1993] AC 593 at 619 per Lord Oliver of Aylmerton). The present case illustrates the dangers of weakening the first threshold test. The House has been referred, as was the Court of Appeal, to a number of statements by several ministers with responsibility for the Bill. Understandably enough, they used different expressions, particularly when responding to points made in debate. Spath Holme have placed particular reliance on statements by ministers linking s 11 of the 1975 Act to inflation and the government's counter-inflation policy. The ministers had placed particular reliance on statements suggesting that the section could be used for other purposes as well. It is hard to judge the significance of these statements without reading the debates to discover what were the points to which ministers were responding. Reading the debates, one finds that the thrust of the Bill was modified and widened during its passage through Parliament. But nowhere did ministers give a categorical assurance that s 11 of the 1975 Act would not be invoked save to counter excessive inflation, and nowhere did ministers attempt to give a comprehensive legal definition of what s 11 meant. In my view, the third threshold test under *Pepper v Hart* is not satisfied in this case: there was no clear and unequivocal statement to the effect for which Spath Holme contended. . . .

Order

I would allow the ministers' appeal, quash the order made by the Court of Appeal and dismiss Spath Holme's application for judicial review. In accordance with the terms on which leave to appeal to the House was given, the ministers must pay Spath Holme's costs before the House and the order for costs made in the Court of Appeal will stand.

Lord Nicholls of Birkenhead:

My Lords, I have had the advantage of reading in draft the speech of my noble and learned friend Lord Bingham of Cornhill. In agreement with him I would allow this appeal. The one point on which I part company with him concerns the use of Hansard. On this matter there is a measure of disagreement between your Lordships.

I go back to first principles. The present appeal raises a point of statutory interpretation: what is the ambit of the power conferred on the minister by s 31(1) of the Landlord and Tenant Act 1985. No statutory power is of unlimited scope. The discretion given by Parliament is never absolute or unfettered. Powers are conferred by Parliament for a purpose, and they may be lawfully exercised only in furtherance of that purpose: 'the policy and objects of the Act', in the oft-quoted words of Lord Reid in *Padfield v Minister of Agriculture, Fisheries and Food* [1969] 1 All ER 694 at 699, [1968] AC 997 at 1030. The purpose for which a power is conferred, and hence its ambit, may be stated expressly in the statute. Or it may be implicit. Then the purpose has to be inferred from the language used, read in its statutory context and having regard to any aid to interpretation which assists in the particular case. In either event, whether the purpose is stated expressly or has to be inferred, the exercise is one of statutory interpretation.

Statutory interpretation is an exercise which requires the court to identify the meaning borne by the words in question in the particular context. The task of the court is often said to be to ascertain the intention of Parliament expressed in the language under consideration. This is correct and may be helpful, so long as it is remembered that the 'intention of Parliament' is an objective concept, not subjective. The phrase is a shorthand reference to the intention which the court reasonably imputes to Parliament in respect of the language used. It is not the subjective intention of the minister or other persons who promoted the legislation. Nor is it the subjective intention of the draftsman, or of individual members or even of a majority of individual members of either House. These individuals will often have widely varying intentions. Their understanding of the legislation and the words used may be impressively complete or woefully inadequate. Thus, when courts say that such-and-such a meaning 'cannot be what Parliament intended', they are saying only that the words under consideration cannot reasonably be taken as used by Parliament with that meaning. As Lord Reid said in *Black-Clawson International Ltd v Papierwerke Waldhof-Aschaffenburg AG* [1975] AC 591, 613: 'We often say that we are looking for the intention of Parliament, but that is not quite accurate. We are seeking the meaning of the words which Parliament used.'

In identifying the meaning of the words used, the courts employ accepted principles of interpretation as useful guides. For instance, an appropriate starting point is that language is to be taken to bear its ordinary meaning in the general context of the statute. Another, recently enacted, principle is that so far as possible legislation must be read in a way which is compatible with human rights and fundamental freedoms (see s 3 of the Human Rights Act 1998). The principles of interpretation include also certain presumptions. To take a familiar instance, the courts presume that a mental ingredient is an essential element in every statutory offence unless Parliament has indicated a contrary intention expressly or by necessary implication.

Additionally, the courts employ other recognised aids. They may be internal aids. Other provisions in the same statute may shed light on the meaning of the words under consideration. Or the aids may be external to the statute, such as its background setting and its legislative history. This extraneous material includes reports of Royal Commissions and advisory committees, reports of the Law Commission (with or without a draft Bill attached), and a statute's legislative antecedents.

Use of non-statutory materials as an aid to interpretation is not a new development. As long ago as 1584 the Barons of the Exchequer enunciated the so-called mischief rule. In interpreting statutes courts should take into account, among other matters, 'the mischief and defect for which the common law did not provide' (see *Heydon's Case* (1584) 3 Co Rep 7a, 7b). Nowadays the courts look at external aids for more than merely identifying the mischief the statute is intended to cure. In adopting a purposive approach to the interpretation of statutory language, courts seek to identify and give effect to the purpose of the legislation. To the extent that extraneous material assists in identifying the purpose of the legislation, it is a useful tool.

This is subject to an important caveat. External aids differ significantly from internal aids. Unlike internal aids, external aids are not found within the statute in which Parliament has expressed its intention in the words in question. This difference is of constitutional importance. Citizens, with the assistance of their advisers, are intended to be able to understand parliamentary enactments, so that they can regulate their conduct accordingly. They should be able to rely upon what they read in an Act of Parliament. This gives rise to a tension between the need for legal certainty, which is one of the fundamental elements of the rule of law, and the need to give effect to the intention of Parliament, from whatever source that (objectively assessed) intention can be gleaned. . . .

This constitutional consideration does not mean that when deciding whether statutory language is clear and unambiguous and not productive of absurdity, the courts are confined to looking solely at the language in question in its context within the statute. That would impose on the courts much too restrictive an approach. No legislation is enacted in a vacuum. Regard may also be had to extraneous material, such as the setting in which the legislation was enacted. This is a matter of everyday occurrence.

That said, courts should nevertheless approach the use of external aids with circumspection. Judges frequently turn to external aids for confirmation of views reached without their assistance. That is unobjectionable. But the constitutional implications point to a need for courts to be slow to permit external aids to displace meanings which are otherwise clear and unambiguous and not productive of absurdity. Sometimes external aids may properly operate in this way. In other cases, the requirements of legal certainty might be undermined to an unacceptable extent if the court were to adopt, as the intention to be imputed to Parliament in using the words in question, the meaning suggested by an external aid. Thus, when interpreting statutory language courts have to strike a balance between conflicting considerations. . . .

I turn to the present case. Read by itself, s 31(1) and (2) of the 1985 Act, coupled with its sidenote 'Reserve power to limit rents', suggests that the power thereby conferred is intended to be kept in reserve, available to be used by the minister in unforeseen circumstances when he reasonably considers this is necessary to promote fairness between landlords and tenants of dwellings. But, as so interpreted, the ambit of the power is extremely wide. Indeed, it is the very width of the power, as so interpreted, together with its derivation from the Counter-Inflation Act 1973, that raises questions. One is left in doubt whether, as contended by Spath Holme, there is some narrower interpretation which is to be preferred; for instance, that the power was conferred for use only for counter-inflationary purposes. The legislation is not clear. Thus it satisfies the first precondition for the use of parliamentary materials as an external aid. I have more difficulty over the third precondition (the statement relied upon must be clear). In considering whether a ministerial statement is clear and unequivocal, regard must be had to the circumstances in which it was made. Extempore answers given in the course of vigorous debate in the House or in committee cannot be expected to be as comprehensive and precise as more formal statements. Suffice to say, looking at them overall, the parliamentary statements relied upon in the present case do not contain a clear and unequivocal statement in favour of the interpretation contended for by Spath Holme. That being so, they are not useful as an external aid in support of that interpretation."

Lord Cooke of Thorndon:

"My Lords, having had the advantage of reading in draft the speech of my noble and learned friend Lord Bingham of Cornhill, I agree with his conclusion and largely with his reasons; but I wish to add something, mainly about Hansard. . . .

In the light of such statements it is difficult to agree with the Court of Appeal that it could not be clearer that the power was intended to be limited to counter-inflationary purposes. Neither in the legislative history nor in the parliamentary history can I find enough to justify reading down the power in the manner for which the landlords contend. The true interpretation, in my view, is the wide but not unlimited first alternative previously mentioned. The reserve power can legitimately be used to temper the effect of unexpected rent increases for tenants on fixed incomes, even though the rises result from a correct reinterpretation of the law rather than from general inflation. It is highly unlikely that the responsible Ministers would have meant to exclude such circumstances from the ambit of the power.

Reference to Hansard does not often help the courts with issues of statutory interpretation, but experience has shown that it does so occasionally. In this instance it is as helpful as the consultation paper of May 1998 . . .

As for the argument of expense, in some cases time may be more usefully spent in looking up Hansard than in compiling a dossier of general propositions and authorities on statutory interpretation or administrative law familiar to every judge.

It is necessary to distinguish two things often treated as if they were one. First there are cases in which the court can in the end derive real help from Hansard, even if it is not necessarily decisive help. I think that this case is an example. Hansard shows that the courts will not be thwarting a clear intention of the legislators by holding that the wider interpretation is correct. Secondly there is the question whether it is proper for counsel to cite Hansard. A practice of constant citation is unacceptable to the courts. Counsel must be expected to use their discretion. In this case I think that counsel for the landlords was fully justified in his citations. After all, they convinced the Court of Appeal. To shut out either party from relying on Hansard would have been, in my opinion, contrary to natural justice.

Accordingly I too would allow the appeal."

Lord Hope of Craighead:

". . . Then there is the question whether it is proper to examine the statements made by ministers during the passage of the 1975 Act through Parliament as reported in Hansard. Here again I think that it is, at best, highly doubtful whether in this case this exercise is legitimate. My own view is that it is not. It is important to appreciate the purpose for which your Lordships have been invited to undertake the exercise. It is not to construe words used in the legislation which are said to be ambiguous or obscure or which, having regard to their ordinary meaning, would lead to absurdity (see *Pepper (Inspector of Taxes) v Hart* [1993] All ER 42 at 69, [1993] AC 593 at 640 per Lord Browne-Wilkinson). Its purpose is to identify the reasons of policy for which the discretionary power to make orders restricting or preventing increases in rents was sought to be obtained from Parliament by the executive. It is not the language used by the draftsman that is in issue here, but what was in the mind of the minister.

In my opinion there are sound reasons of principle for rejecting the argument that statements made by ministers in Parliament may be used to identify the policy and objects of an enactment for the purpose of identifying the scope of a discretionary power which Parliament has conferred on the executive. As Lord Reid made clear in *Padfield's Case* ([1968] 1 All ER 694 at 699, [1968] AC 997 at 1030), the policy and objects of the Act must be determined by construing the Act. The underlying rule is that it is the intention of Parliament that defines the policy and objects of the Act, not the purpose or intention of the executive. The law-making function belongs to Parliament, not to the executive. . . .

As I have already sought to explain, the passages in Hansard to which your Lordships have been referred deal not with the meaning of words or possible interpretations of expressions that were or might be ambiguous but with statements made by ministers as to matters of policy. I consider that to permit resort to Hansard as a source for material of that kind to define the scope of a discretionary power conferred by Parliament would be to extend the decision in *Pepper v Hart* well beyond its proper limits. I respectfully agree with my noble and learned friend Lord Bingham, for all the reasons that he has given, that it is important that the conditions laid down by the House in that case should be strictly insisted upon. I also agree with him that, if a minister were to give a categorical assurance to Parliament that a discretionary power would not ever be used in a given set of circumstances, that statement would be admissible against the executive in order to control its exercise. But I also think that it is important to stress that as matter of principle the decision in *Pepper v Hart* should be confined to cases where the court is concerned with the meaning that is to be given to the words used in legislation by Parliament. It would be contrary to fundamental considerations of constitutional principle to allow it to be used to enable reliance to be placed on statements made in debate by ministers about matters of policy which have not been reproduced in the enactment. It is the words used by Parliament, not words used by ministers, that define the scope within which the powers conferred by the legislature may be exercised."

Lord Hutton:

". . . Because I am of opinion that the words of s 31 of the 1985 Act are clear and unambiguous I further consider that this case does not satisfy the first threshold test stated by Lord Browne-Wilkinson in *Pepper (Inspector of Taxes) v Hart* [1993] All ER 42 at 69, [1993] AC 593 at 640, with the agreement of the other members of the House, Lord Mackay of Clashfern LC dissenting, and that therefore it was inappropriate to refer to statements in Parliament in this case. I respectfully agree with my noble and learned friend Lord Bingham that the conditions laid down by the House in *Pepper v Hart* should be strictly adhered to; otherwise in many cases time will be taken up and costs will be incurred without assistance to the court in its task of construction by references by counsel to statements by Ministers and by the weighing of those statements by the court.

I think that where Lord Browne-Wilkinson referred to legislation which is 'ambiguous or obscure' he was referring to ambiguity or obscurity in the wording of a statutory provision, not to possible ambiguity as to the purpose for which Parliament gave a power."

Questions

1. Do you think the Law Lords in *Spath Holme* were "faithful" to the decision in *Pepper v Hart*?

2. Which of the judgments in *Spath Holme* did you find the most convincing? If you were deciding the case, do you think that you would have found reference to *Hansard* to be useful?

The Law Lords further refined the rule in *Pepper v Hart*, this time in the context of the Human Rights Act 1998, in *Wilson v First County Trust Ltd*. In reading what is a very significant case, be sure to note the facts and, in particular, how what looks like a straightforward case can lead to such complex legal issues of interpretation.

Wilson v First County Trust Ltd [2003] UKHL 40.

Lord Nicholls of Birkenhead:

"My Lords, in January 1999 Penelope Wilson borrowed £5,000 from a pawnbroker for a period of six months. The pawned property was her car, a BMW 318 Convertible. She did not repay the loan. The pawnbroker sought repayment, failing which the car would be sold. Mrs Wilson's response was to commence proceedings in the Kingston-upon-Thames County Court. She claimed the agreement was unenforceable because it did not contain all the prescribed terms. She sought an order for the return of her car. Alternatively she sought to reopen the agreement as grossly exorbitant. At the trial Mrs Wilson appeared in person. The pawnbroker was a two-man company, First County Trust Ltd. The company was represented in court by its finance director.

From these modest beginnings the County Court proceedings burgeoned into a case with wide-ranging implications. Neither Mrs Wilson nor First County Trust appeared before the House. But the Attorney General appeared on behalf of the Secretary of State for Trade and Industry. The Speaker of the House of Commons and the Clerk of the Parliaments intervened. They were represented by leading and junior counsel. The Finance and Leasing Association also intervened, as did four insurance companies which are among the largest providers of motor insurance in this country. And leading and junior counsel also appeared as amicus curiae.

The £250 fee: was it 'credit'?

When Mrs Wilson signed her agreement and pawn receipt she was charged a 'document fee' of £250. This was added to the amount of her loan. In the agreement the amount of the loan was stated as £5,250. The amount payable on redemption was £7,327, made up of £5,250 and interest of £1,827. The annual percentage rate of interest was stated to be 94.78%.

The agreement was a regulated agreement for the purposes of s 8 of the Consumer Credit Act 1974. A regulated agreement is not properly executed unless the document signed contains all the prescribed terms (s 61(1)(a)). One of the prescribed terms is the 'amount of the credit' (see reg 6 of and para 2 of Sch 6 to the Consumer Credit (Agreements) Regulations 1983, SI 1983/1553). The consequence of failure to state all the prescribed terms of the agreement is that the court is precluded, by s 127(3), from enforcing the agreement. In the absence of enforcement by the court the agreement is altogether unenforceable (s 65(1)).

On 24 September 1999 His Honour Judge Hull QC, in a carefully reasoned judgment, held that the fee of £250 was part of the amount of the credit. So the agreement was enforceable. He reopened the agreement as an extortionate credit bargain and reduced the amount of interest payable by one half. Mrs Wilson appealed to the Court of Appeal. Pending the hearing of her appeal she paid First County Trust £6,900 to redeem her car. That was in December 1999.

The appeal was heard in November 2000, shortly after the Human Rights Act 1998 came into force. The Court of Appeal, comprising Sir Andrew Morritt V-C, and Chadwick and Rix LJJ, allowed Mrs Wilson's appeal: see [2001] QB 407. Sir Andrew Morritt V-C recognised there was considerable force in First County Trust's submissions in support of the judge's view. But having analysed the statutory provisions, the court held that the £250 added to the loan to enable Mrs Wilson to pay the document fee was not 'credit' for the purposes of the Consumer Credit Act. So one of the prescribed terms was not correctly stated. In consequence the agreement was unenforceable. So also was the security. First County Trust was ordered to repay the amount of £6,900 Mrs Wilson had paid the company after Judge Hull's judgment together with interest amounting to £662. The overall result was that Mrs Wilson was entitled to keep the amount of her loan, pay no interest and recover her car.

The adjourned hearing

Sir Andrew Morritt V-C expressed concern at this outcome. He considered it might be arguable that s 127(3) of the 1974 Act infringes art 6(1) of the European Convention for the Protection of Human Rights and Fundamental Freedoms 1950 (as set out in Sch 1 to the 1998 Act) art 1 of the First Protocol to the Convention. The court adjourned the further hearing of the appeal for notice to be given to the Crown, pursuant to s 5 of the Human Rights Act, that the court was considering whether to make a declaration of incompatibility. The Secretary of State for Trade and Industry was then added as a party to the proceedings.

On 2 May 2001 the court gave judgment at the adjourned hearing (see [2001] EWCA Civ 633, [2001] 3 All ER 229, [2002] QB 74). The court held that the inflexible exclusion of a judicial remedy by s 127(3), preventing the court from doing what is just in the circumstances of the case, is disproportionate to the legitimate policy objective of ensuring that particular attention is paid to the inclusion of certain terms in the document signed by the borrower. It is not possible to read and give effect to s 113 or s 127(3) in a way compatible with First County Trust's convention rights. The court made a declaration, pursuant to s 4 of the 1998 Act, that s 127(3), in so far as it prevents the court from making an enforcement order under s 65 of the 1974 Act unless a document containing all the prescribed terms of the agreement has been signed by the debtor, is incompatible with the rights guaranteed to the creditor by art 6(1) of the Convention and art 1 of the First Protocol to the convention.

The Secretary of State appealed to your Lordships' House. First County Trust did not. The Secretary of State accepted that Mrs Wilson's agreement was not 'properly executed' within the meaning of s 61 of the 1974 Act. She accepted that, in consequence, no enforcement order could be made under s 65 and that the security over the car was unenforceable. The Secretary of State also accepted it is not possible to 'read down' the relevant provisions of the 1974 Act and thereby save them from any convention rights incompatibility otherwise existing. But she challenged the decision of the Court of Appeal on several grounds. Her primary submission was that the court has no jurisdiction to make a declaration of incompatibility in relation to events occurring before the 1998 Act came fully into force on 2 October 2000. Here, the agreement was made in January 1999 for a period of six months. Additionally, the parties' rights were determined before the 1998 Act came into force. The County Court decision was in September 1999. . . .

[I]nterpretation of the legislation in accordance with s 3 is an essential preliminary step to making a declaration of incompatibility. It is an essential preliminary step because the court cannot be satisfied the legislation is incompatible until effect has been given to the interpretative obligation set out in s 3. . . .

In the present case Parliament cannot have intended that application of s 3(1) should have the effect of altering parties' existing rights and obligations under the 1974 Act. For the purpose of identifying the rights of Mrs Wilson and First County Trust under their January 1999 agreement the 1974 Act is to be interpreted without reference to s 3(1).

It follows that, in this transitional type of case concerning the 1974 Act, no question can arise of the court making a declaration of incompatibility. For the reasons already considered, it is only when a court is called upon to interpret legislation in accordance with s 3(1) that the court may proceed, where appropriate, to make a declaration of incompatibility. The court can make a declaration of incompatibility only where s 3 is available as an interpretative tool. That is not this case. . . .

For these reasons the appeal by the Secretary of State must succeed. In this transitional type of case s 3(1) is inapplicable to the interpretation of the 1974 Act. Consequently, the court has no jurisdiction to make a declaration of incompatibility. The declaration made by the Court of Appeal should be set aside.

This conclusion makes it strictly unnecessary for the House to consider the further issues arising out of the judgment of the Court of Appeal. But it would not be satisfactory to leave these other issues unresolved. They have been fully argued by experienced counsel, the House has the benefit of the views of the Court of Appeal, and the issues are of importance to innumerable transactions being entered into every day. I turn, therefore, to consider what the position would be in this case had the 1998 Act applied.

. . . I now turn to consider whether a challenge to the compatibility of legislation with convention rights may be a further instance of the innocuous use by courts of statements made in Parliament.

The Human Rights Act 1998 requires the court to exercise a new role in respect of primary legislation. This new role is fundamentally different from interpreting and applying legislation. The courts are now required to evaluate the effect of primary legislation in terms of convention rights and, where appropriate, make a formal declaration of incompatibility. In carrying out this evaluation the court has to compare the effect of the legislation with the convention right. If the legislation impinges upon a convention right the court must then compare the policy objective of the legislation with the policy objective which under the convention may justify a prima facie infringement of the convention right. When making these two comparisons the court will look primarily at the legislation, but not exclusively so. Convention rights are concerned with practicalities. When identifying the practical effect of an impugned statutory provision the court may need to look outside the statute in order to see the complete picture, as already instanced in the present case regarding the possible availability of a restitutionary remedy. As to the objective of the statute, at one level this will be coincident with its effect. At this level, the object of s 127(3) is to prevent an enforcement order being made when the circumstances specified in that provision apply. But that is not the relevant level for convention purposes. What is relevant is the underlying social purpose sought to be achieved by the statutory provision. Frequently that purpose will be self-evident, but this will not always be so.

The legislation must not only have a legitimate policy objective. It must also satisfy a 'proportionality' test. The court must decide whether the means employed by the statute to achieve the policy objective is appropriate and not disproportionate in its adverse effect. This involves a 'value judgment' by the court, made by reference to the circumstances prevailing when the issue has to be decided. It is the current effect and impact of the legislation which matter, not the position when the legislation was enacted or came into force. (I interpose that in the present case no suggestion was made that there has been any relevant change of circumstances since the 1974 Act was enacted.)

When a court makes this value judgment the facts will often speak for themselves. But sometimes the court may need additional background information tending to show, for instance, the likely practical impact of the statutory measure and why the course adopted by the legislature is or is not appropriate. Moreover, as when interpreting a statute, so when identifying the policy objective of a statutory provision or assessing the 'proportionality' of a statutory provision, the court may need enlightenment on the nature and extent of the social problem (the 'mischief') at which the legislation is aimed. This may throw light on the rationale underlying the legislation.

This additional background material may be found in published documents, such as a government white paper. If relevant information is provided by a minister or, indeed, any other member of either House in the course of a debate on a Bill, the courts must also be able to take this into account. The courts, similarly, must be able to have regard to information contained in explanatory notes prepared by the relevant government department and published with a Bill. The courts would be failing in the due discharge of the new role assigned to them by Parliament if they were to exclude from consideration relevant background information whose only source was a ministerial statement in Parliament or an explanatory note prepared by his department while the Bill was proceeding through Parliament. By having regard to such material the court would not be 'questioning' proceedings in Parliament or intruding improperly into the legislative process or ascribing to Parliament the views expressed by a minister. The court would merely be placing itself in a better position to understand the legislation.

To that limited extent there may be occasion for the courts, when conducting the statutory 'compatibility' exercise, to have regard to matters stated in Parliament. It is a consequence flowing from the 1998 Act. The constitutionally unexceptionable nature of this consequence receives some confirmation from the view expressed in the unanimous report of the Parliamentary Joint Committee on Parliamentary Privilege (1999) (HL Paper 43-I, HC 214-I), p 28 (para 86)), that it is difficult to see how there could be any objection to the court taking account of something said in Parliament when there is no suggestion the statement was inspired by improper motives or was untrue or misleading and there is no question of legal liability.

I expect that occasions when resort to Hansard is necessary as part of the statutory 'compatibility' exercise will seldom arise. The present case is not such an occasion. Should such an occasion arise the courts must be careful not to treat the ministerial or other statement as indicative of the objective intention of Parliament. Nor should the courts give a ministerial statement, whether made inside or outside Parliament, determinative weight. It should not be supposed that members necessarily agreed with the minister's reasoning or his conclusions.

Beyond this use of Hansard as a source of background information, the content of parliamentary debates has no direct relevance to the issues the court is called upon to decide in compatibility cases and, hence, these debates are not a proper matter for investigation or consideration by the courts. In particular, it is a cardinal constitutional principle that the will of Parliament is expressed in the language used by it in its enactments. The proportionality of legislation is to be judged on that basis. The courts are to have due regard to the legislation as an expression of the will of Parliament. The proportionality of a statutory measure is not to be judged by the quality of the reasons advanced in support of it in the course of parliamentary debate, or by the subjective state of mind of individual ministers or other members. Different members may well have different reasons, not expressed in debates, for approving particular statutory provisions. They may have different perceptions of the desirability or likely effect of the legislation. Ministerial statements, especially if made ex tempore in response to questions, may sometimes lack clarity or be misdirected. Lack of cogent justification in the course of parliamentary debate is not a matter which 'counts against' the legislation on issues of proportionality. The court is called upon to evaluate the proportionality of the legislation, not the adequacy of the minister's exploration of the policy options or of his explanations to Parliament. . . ."

Lord Hope of Craighead:

"The boundaries between the respective powers and functions of the courts and of Parliament must, of course, be respected. It is no part of the court's function to determine whether sufficient reasons were given by Parliament for passing the enactment. On the other hand it has to perform the tasks which have been given to it by Parliament. Among those tasks is that to which s 4(1) refers. It has the task of determining, if the issue is raised, whether a provision of primary legislation is compatible with a convention right. It does not follow from recognition that there is an area of judgment within which the judiciary will defer to the elected body on democratic grounds that the court is absolutely disabled from forming its own view in these cases as to whether or not the legislation is compatible. That question is ultimately for the court not for Parliament, as Parliament itself has enacted. The harder that question is to answer, the more important it is that the court is equipped with the information that it needs to perform its task.

This, then, is the justification for resorting to Hansard in cases where the question at issue is not one of interpretation but whether the legislation is compatible. A cautious approach is needed, and particular care must be taken not to stray beyond the search for material that will simply inform the court into the forbidden territory of questioning the proceedings in Parliament. To suggest, as the Court of Appeal did ([2002] All ER 229 at [36]), that what was said in debate tends to confuse rather than illuminate would be to cross that boundary. It is for Parliament alone to decide what reasons, if any, need to be given for the legislation that it enacts. The quality or sufficiency of reasons given by the promoter of the legislation is a matter for Parliament to determine, not the court.

But proceedings in Parliament are replete with information from a whole variety of sources. It appears in a variety of forms also, all of which are made public. Ministers make statements, members ask questions or propose amendments based on information which they have obtained from their constituencies, answers are given to written questions, issues are explored by select committees by examining witnesses and explanatory notes are provided with Bills to assist members in their consideration of it. Resort to information of this kind may cast light on what Parliament's aim was when it passed the provision which is in question or it may not. If it does not this cannot, and must not, be a ground for criticism. But if it does, the court would be unduly inhibited if it were to be disabled from obtaining and using this information for the strictly limited purpose of considering whether legislation is compatible with convention rights. . . ."

Lord Hobhouse of Woodborough:

"The questions of justification and proportionality involve a sociological assessment—an assessment of what are the needs of society. This in part involves a legal examination of the content and legal effect of the relevant provision. But it also involves consideration of what is the mischief, social evil, danger etc which it is designed to deal with. Often these matters may already be within the knowledge of the court. But equally there will almost always be other evidentially valuable material which can be placed before the court which is relevant, such as reports that have been made, statistics that have been collected, and so on. Oral witnesses may have important evidence to give. To exclude such evidential material from the case merely because it is to be found in some statement made in Parliament is clearly wrong, particularly if ministerial statements made outside Parliament were already being relied on. This has nothing to do with investigating or questioning the will of Parliament. Parliament has spoken by passing the relevant Act. The evidence is admitted because it relates to making the required sociological assessment. It has long been the case that ministerial statements made in the House may be referred to when they are relevant to a question to be determined by a court. . . .

The Court of Appeal, having decided that they must consider s 4 and that art 1 was engaged, then entered upon a process of scrutinising what had been said in Parliament as reported in Hansard to see whether it disclosed any justification they were prepared to accept for the relevant provisions of the 1974 Act at the time they were enacted. This was an unacceptable approach and likely to give rise to abuse. It is not part of the duty of any member of Parliament to provide or state definitively in Parliament the justification for legislation which the legislature is content to pass. Still less was it the duty of anyone in 1974 to anticipate the passing of the 1998 Act 24 years later. I agree that that use of Hansard for that purpose has been rightly objected to. . . ."

Lord Schott of Foscote:

Use of Hansard

"On this issue I am in complete agreement with, and cannot usefully add anything to, what has been said by my noble and learned friend, Lord Nicholls of Birkenhead. . . .

Lord Rodger of Earlsferry:

I respectfully agree with Lord Nicholls of Birkenhead as to the disposal of all these grounds of appeal and, in particular, with what my noble and learned friend, Lord Hobhouse of Woodborough, has said on the use of Hansard."

Questions

1. Why do you think that this case prompted the intervention of the Speaker of the House of Commons and the Clerk of the Parliament? What issues of principle does it raise?

2. Do you think that the reasoning in *Wilson v First County Trust* is consistent with *Pepper v Hart*?

3. Are you surprised that a case involving a loan against a BMW 318 convertible has been the subject of a human rights case?

The *Wilson* case is a good example of the way in which an earlier case (*Pepper v Hart*) may be *narrowed* in its scope through judicial reasoning. Kavanagh explains the impact of *Wilson* on *Pepper v Hart*. Pay close attention to how she tries to read one case in light of the other.

Aileen Kavanagh, "*Pepper v Hart* and matters of constitutional principle" (2005) 121 L.Q.R. 98 at 114–115, 121–122:

"The reasoning in *Wilson* requires us to read *Pepper v Hart* in a narrow and qualified way. Although *Wilson* does not overrule *Pepper v Hart*,[5] it undercuts two aspects of the decision which were objectionable from a constitutional point of view. First, it casts considerable doubt on the plausibility of attributing the stated intention of individual Ministers to Parliament as a whole. Lord Nicholls noted that there were 'conceptual and constitutional difficulties in treating the intentions of the Government revealed in debates as reflecting the will of Parliament.'[6] As regards the question of whether ministerial statements could be attributed to Parliament as a whole, his Lordship noted that:

> 'different members may well have different reasons, not expressed in the debates, for approving particular statutory provisions. They may have different perceptions of the desirability or likely effect of the legislation. Ministerial statements, especially made *ex tempore* in response to questions, may sometimes lack clarity or be misdirected.'[7]

Thus the House of Lords will approach ministerial statements of intent with circumspection and be slow to assume that a ministerial statement, even of the promoting Minister, is supported by a majority in Parliament. They will scrutinise such a claim made by counsel to see whether their contention is well founded.

Secondly, the court in *Wilson* emphasised that ministerial statements should not be given the status of law.

---

[5] Counsel for the Secretary of State in *Wilson* did not challenge the authority of the *Pepper v Hart* decision, although they argued for a limited understanding of its import.

[6] At 59, citing Lord Steyn's Hart Lecture in support of this proposition.

[7] At 67.

Although Parliamentary debates may be used as background material, evidencing the context or purpose of an Act, statements by individual Ministers will not be deemed to determine or control statutory meaning.[8] This spirit of judicial caution reflects both the constitutional worry about attributing law-making power to ministerial silence or inaction, as well as the practical worry about the reliability of political debate in Parliament as a basis for determining statutory meaning. Any doubt about the status of such statements after *Pepper v Hart* has now been removed by *Wilson*. Thus, *Pepper v Hart* is tamed and muted, rather than eliminated altogether. Preserved is the discretion of the court to consult Parliamentary debates as background or contextual information, which may or may not cast light on what Parliament intended in enacting the statutory provision. But this material will only be invoked for the purpose of understanding the context and setting in which the legislation was enacted. Confining *Pepper v Hart* statements to this much less 'exalted role'[9] has the following important consequence. It is now open to the courts to adopt a statutory meaning which conflicts with a clear and unambiguous ministerial statement on the issue before the court. After all, if it were not possible for the courts to do this, then the statements would have the controlling or determinative force which the judges in *Wilson* were so keen to remove. So, even if the ministerial statement is expressed in a clear and unambiguous way as required by the rule in *Pepper v Hart*, the courts now have discretion to depart from it altogether in making their independent interpretive decision. . . .

A crucial difference between the decision in *Pepper v Hart* and that in *Wilson* concerns the way in which the House of Lords viewed the rule excluding judicial reference to *Hansard* as an aid to statutory construction. In *Pepper v Hart*, it was viewed as a 'technical rule of construction',[10] whereas in *Wilson* it raised 'a point of constitutional importance'.[11] Although there has been widespread agreement that the outcome of *Pepper v Hart* was correct, the reasoning relied on by the court to reach that result lost sight of the far-reaching constitutional implications of the decision, both as a matter of principle and practice. In *Wilson*, the House of Lords showed an acute awareness of these issues. The starting point for their assessment of the issue of judicial reliance on *Hansard* was 'to respect the roles of Parliament and the courts . . . the distinct roles of Parliament and the courts reflect on aspects of the separation of powers under this country's constitution.'[12] Moreover, the practical problems arising from *Pepper v Hart* were also addressed in *Wilson*. Lord Hobhouse gave a damning verdict on the practical impact of *Pepper v Hart* since it was decided in 1993:

> 'Judicial experience has taught me, particularly since I was appointed a member of this House, that the attempt by advocates to use Parliamentary material from *Hansard* as an aid to statutory construction has not proved helpful and the fears of those pessimists who saw it as simply a cause of additional expense in the conduct of litigation have been proved correct.'[13]

Wilson v First County Trust is a ringing endorsement of the traditional principle of interpretation that the court's duty is to give effect to the *enacted intention*, *i.e.* the intention of Parliament which is enacted in the statute which has the force of law. However, this does not entail a literal approach to statutory interpretation.[14] On the contrary,

---

[8] Confining ministerial statements to the lesser role of providing background to the enactment reflects the view expressed by Lord Wilberforce in *Black-Clawson* at 630: "It is not sound enough to ascertain, if that can be done, the objectives of any particular measure, and the background of the enactment; but to take the opinion, whether of a Minister or an official or a committee, as to the intended meaning in particular applications of a clause or phrase, would be a stunting of the law and not a healthy development."

[9] At 59.

[10] Lord Bridge, at 616.

[11] Lord Nicholls, at 54.

[12] Lord Nicholls, at 55.

[13] *Wilson v Secretary of State for Trade and Industry* [2003] 3 WLR 568 at 140. This verdict is also supported by Lord Hoffman in *Robinson* at 39–40.

[14] Lord Lester views the exclusionary rule as "part and parcel of . . . austere judicial literalism": "*Pepper v Hart* revisited" (1994) 15 Statute L. R. 10 at 13.

by giving effect to the *enacted intentions*, the courts thereby respect the integrity and burdens of the legislative process, by requiring legislators to accept responsibility for what they legislate, not what they meant or hoped to legislate. If the law is unclear or ambiguous, then it is the duty of the courts to resolve that issue, by making an independent assessment of what the statute means, relying on the canons and presumptions of statutory interpretation, the principle of legality and the rule of law, as well as any relevant contextual information at their disposal. As Lord Nicholls commented in relation to the provisions of the HRA: 'Skilfully drawn though these provisions are, they leave a great deal of open ground. There is room for doubt and for argument. It has been left to the courts to resolve these issues when they arise.'[15] By saying that it is the function of the courts to ascertain the will or intention of Parliament, we often neglect 'the important element of judicial construction; an element not confined to a mechanical analysis of today's words, but, if this task is to be properly done, related to such matters as intelligibility to the citizen, constitutional propriety, considerations of history, comity of nations, reasonable and non-retroactive effect and, no doubt, in some contexts, to social needs.'[16] This is not austere literalism. It is statutory interpretation carried out by an independent judiciary within the boundaries of constitutional principle."

Questions

1. To what extent has the application of *Pepper v Hart* by the courts been faithful to the original preconditions for the admissibility of *Hansard* imposed by the House of Lords?

2. "Both the principled and the practical objections to the admissibility of *Hansard* in courts are more compelling than any benefits that might be derived therefrom." Do you agree?

IV. Legislative Intention and Social Change

Up to this point, we have assumed that the courts, in interpreting legislation, focus upon finding the intention of the legislature. However, statutory language often must be interpreted over a long period. During that time, social conditions, attitudes and values may well have changed substantially. As a consequence, the interpretation which will seem reasonable and, indeed, necessary, to a majority of the population, may not have been that which would have been intended by those who voted for a statute in Parliament. To what extent, then, should courts adapt interpretation to meet the changing needs of a society? Should statutory interpretation be a *dynamic* or a *static* process? The issue has been confronted by courts on many occasions, some of them now legendary.

Henrietta Muir Edwards and others v Attorney-General for Canada [1930] A.C. 124, PC.

Lord Sankey L.C.:

"By s.24 of the British North America Act, 1867, it is provided that 'The Governor General shall from time to time, in the Queen's name, by instrument under the Great Seal of Canada, summon qualified persons to the Senate; and, subject to the provisions of this Act, every person so summoned shall become and be a member of the Senate and a senator.'

The question at issue in this appeal is whether the words 'qualified persons' in that section include a woman, and consequently whether women are eligible to be summoned to and become members of the Senate of Canada.

---

[15] *Parochial Church of the Parish of Aston Cantlow, Wilmcote in Billesley, Warwickshire v Wallbank* [2003] UKHL 37, [2003] 3 WLR 283 at 36.

[16] *Black-Clawson International Ltd v Papierwerke Waldhof-Aschaffenburg AG* [1975] A.C. 591 at 629–630, per Lord Wilberforce; see also F. Bennion, "*Hansard*–help or hindrance? A draftsman's view of *Pepper v Hart*" (1995) 15 Statute L.R. 149 at 162; R. Dworkin, *A Matter of Principle* (1985).

Of the appellants, Henrietta Muir Edwards is the Vice-President for the province of Alberta of the National Council of Women for Canada; Nellie L. McClung and Louise C. McKinney were for several years members of the Legislative Assembly of the said Province; Emily F. Murphy is a police magistrate in and for the said Province; and Irene Parlby is a member of the Legislative Assembly of the said Province and a member of the Executive Council thereof.

On August 29, 1927, the appellants petitioned the Governor General in Council to refer to the Supreme Court certain questions touching the powers of the Governor General to summon female persons to the Senate, and upon October 19, 1927, the Governor General in Council referred to the Supreme Court the aforesaid question. The case was heard before Anglin C.J., Duff, Mignault, Lamont, and Smith JJ., and upon April 24, 1928, the Court answered the question in the negative; the question being understood to be 'Are women eligible for appointment to the Senate of Canada.'

The Chief Justice, whose judgment was concurred in by Lamont and Smith JJ., and substantially by Mignault J., came to this conclusion upon broad lines mainly because of the common law disability of women to hold public office and from a consideration of various cases which had been decided under different statutes as to their right to vote for a member of Parliament.

Duff J., on the other hand, did not agree with this view. He came to the conclusion that women are not eligible for appointment to the Senate upon the narrower ground that upon a close examination of the British North America Act, 1867, the word 'persons' in s.24 is restricted to members of the male sex. The result therefore of the decision was that the Supreme Court was unanimously of the opinion that the word 'persons' did not include female persons, and that women are not eligible to be summoned to the Senate.

Their Lordships are of opinion that the word 'persons' in s.24 does include women, and that women are eligible to be summoned to and become members of the Senate of Canada.

In coming to a determination as to the meaning of a particular word in a particular Act of Parliament it is permissible to consider two points—namely: (i) The external evidence derived from extraneous circumstances such as previous legislation and decided cases. (ii) The internal evidence derived from the Act itself. As the learned counsel on both sides have made great researches and invited their Lordships to consider the legal position of women from the earliest times, in justice to their argument they propose to do so and accordingly turn to the first of the above points—namely: (i) The external evidence derived from extraneous circumstances. . . ."

[Lord Sankey then reviewed the historical position of women in relation to the holding of public office.]

"No doubt in any code where women were expressly excluded from public office the problem would present no difficulty, but where instead of such exclusion those entitled to be summoned to or placed in public office are described under the word 'person' different considerations arise.

The word is ambiguous, and in its original meaning would undoubtedly embrace members of either sex. On the other hand, supposing in an Act of Parliament several centuries ago it had been enacted that any person should be entitled to be elected to a particular office it would have been understood that the word only referred to males, but the cause of this was not because the word 'person' could not include females but because at common law a woman was incapable of serving a public office. The fact that no woman had served or has claimed to serve such an office is not of great weight when it is remembered that custom would have prevented the claim being made or the point being contested.

Customs are apt to develop into traditions which are stronger than law and remain unchallenged long after the reason for them has disappeared.

The appeal to history therefore in this particular matter is not conclusive. . . .

Their Lordships now turn to the second point—namely, (ii) the internal evidence derived from the Act itself.

. . .

The British North America Act planted in Canada a living tree capable of growth and expansion within its natural limits. The object of the Act was to grant a Constitution to Canada. 'Like all written constitutions it has been subject to development through usage and convention': *Canadian Constitutional Studies*, Sir Robert Borden (1922), p.55.

Their Lordships do not conceive it to be the duty of this Board—it is certainly not their desire—to cut down the provisions of the Act by a narrow and technical construction, but rather to give it a large and liberal interpretation so that the Dominion to a great extent, but within certain fixed limits, may be mistress in her own house, as the provinces to a great extent, but within certain fixed limits, are mistresses in theirs. 'The Privy Council, indeed, has laid down that Courts of law must treat the provisions of the British North America Act by the same methods of construction and exposition which they apply to other statutes. But there are statutes and statutes; and the strict construction deemed proper in the case, for example, of a penal or taxing statute or one passed to regulate the affairs of an English parish, would be often subversive of Parliament's real intent if applied to an Act passed to ensure the peace, order and good government of a British Colony': see *Clement's Canadian Constitution* (3rd ed., p.347). . . .

A heavy burden lies on an appellant who seeks to set aside a unanimous judgment of the Supreme Court, and this Board will only set aside such a decision after convincing argument and anxious consideration, but having regard: (1) To the object of the Act—namely, to provide a constitution for Canada, a responsible and developing State; (2) that the word 'person' is ambiguous, and may include members of either sex; (3) that there are sections in the Act above referred to which show that in some cases the word 'person' must include females; (4) that in some sections the words 'male persons' are expressly used when it is desired to confine the matter in issue to males; and (5) to the provisions of the Interpretation Act; their Lordships have come to the conclusion that the word 'persons' in s.24 includes members both of the male and female sex, and that, therefore, the question propounded by the Governor General should be answered in the affirmative, and that women are eligible to be summoned to and become members of the Senate of Canada, and they will humbly advise His Majesty accordingly."

Questions

1. The Judicial Committee of the Privy Council, composed primarily of the Law Lords, was the final court of appeal against decisions of colonial courts. Can you find out whether it still plays a role in deciding cases?

2. The "Persons Case", as it is widely known, is also famous for Lord Sankey's description of the British North America Act as a "living tree". What does this imply for the way in which courts approach the task of statutory interpretation? In this regard, what does Lord Sankey's comment that "there are statutes, and then there are statutes" actually mean?

The "Persons Case" is not solely of historical interest. Mossman argues that it exemplifies the way in which legal method itself is gendered.

Mary Jane Mossman, "Feminism and legal method: the difference it makes", in Martha Albertson Fineman and Nancy Sweet Thomadsen (eds), *At the Boundaries of Law* (New York: Routledge, 1991), pp.285–298:

"Just a few years before the nineteenth century drew to a close, Clara Brett Martin was admitted to the practice of law in Ontario, the first woman to become a lawyer in the British Commonwealth. Her petition for admission was initially denied by the Law Society on the basis that there were no precedents for the admission of women as lawyers. However, in 1892 a legislative amendment was passed permitting women to be admitted as solicitors; three years later, another legislative amendment similarly permitted women to be admitted as barristers. Clara Brett Martin herself was finally admitted in February 1897 as a barrister and solicitor.

Because of the admission arrangements in Ontario, it was the Law Society of Upper Canada, rather than a superior court, which reviewed the issue of Clara Brett Martin's entitlement to admission as a lawyer. By contrast, there was a court challenge in the Province of New Brunswick when Mabel Penury French sought admission as a lawyer there in 1905. When her application was presented to the court, the judges decided unanimously that there were no precedents for the admission of women, and denied her application. In the next year, however, after the enactment of a legislative amendment, French was admitted as a lawyer in New

Brunswick. The same pattern (judicial denial of the application followed by legislative amendment) occurred again some years later when she applied for admission by transfer in British Columbia, and in a number of other Canadian provinces when women applied for admission as lawyers.

In contrast to the cases where women sought to enter the legal profession and were denied admission by the courts, the celebrated Privy Council decision in the Persons case determined that Canadian women were eligible to participate in public life. . . .

The decisions in these cases offer an interesting historical picture of legal process in the cultural milieu of the early twentieth century. In the cases about the admission of women to the legal profession, judges accepted the idea that there was a difference between men and women, a difference which 'explained' and 'justified' the exclusion of women from the legal profession. Yet, the Privy Council's decision in the Persons case completely discounted any such difference in relation to the participation of women in public life.

The issue is why there were these differing approaches: was it the nature of the claims, the courts in which they were presented, or the dates of the decisions? More significantly, what can we learn from the reasoning in these cases about the nature of legal method, especially in the context of challenges to 'deeply-held beliefs, vested interests, and the status quo'? In other words, what do these cases suggest about the potential impact of feminism on legal method?

French's case in New Brunswick provides a good illustration of judicial decision making on the issue of women in law. Her case was presented to the court for direction as to the admissibility of women by the president of the Barristers' Society of New Brunswick (as *amicus curiae*), and the court decided that women were not eligible for admission. Indeed, Mr Justice Tuck emphatically declared that he had no sympathy for women who wanted to compete with men; as he said: 'Better let them attend to their own legitimate business'. . . .

The stated reasons in these cases were consistent with well-established principles of legal method. The principles can be analyzed in terms of three aspects: (1) the characterization of the issues; (2) the choice of legal precedents to decide the validity of the women's claims; and (3) the process of statutory interpretation, especially in determining the effect of statutes to alter common law principles. Both the principles themselves and their application to these specific claims are important for an understanding of the potential impact of feminism on legal method.

Characterizing the issue

In both *French* and the Persons case, the judges consistently characterized the issues as narrowly as possible, eschewing their 'political' or 'social' significance, and explaining that the court was interested only in the law. . . .

Equally clearly, the women claimants never intended to bring to the court a 'neutral' legal issue for determination; they petitioned the court to achieve their goals, goals which were unabashedly political. In the face of such claims, however, the court maintained a view of its process as one of neutral interpretation. More significantly, the court's power to define the 'real issues' carried with it an inherent absence of responsibility on the part of the (male) judges for any negative outcome. It was the law, rather than the (male) person interpreting it, which was responsible for the decision. The result of such a characterization process, therefore, is to reinforce the law's detachment and neutrality rather than its involvement and responsibility; and to extend these characteristics beyond law itself to judges and lawyers.

Yet, how can we accommodate this characterization of detachment and neutrality with the opinions expressed, especially in *French*, about the role of women? The ideas about gender-based difference expressed forcefully by Mr Justice Barker in that case appear very close to an expression about the 'desirability' of women as lawyers and not merely a dispassionate and neutral application of legal precedents. Thus, at least in *French*, there is inconsistency between the legal method declared by the judges to be appropriate, and the legal method actually adopted in making their decisions. In this context, the expressed idea of detachment and neutrality both masks and legitimates judicial views about women's 'proper' sphere.

Using precedents in the Common Law tradition

The existence of women's common law disability was regularly cited in both these cases as the reason for denying their claims to be admitted to the legal profession and to take part in public life. The judges used numerous precedents for their conclusion. . . . Obviously, the Privy Council was less concerned with the absence of precedent in their decision making than the judges in *French*. Is this approach simply an early example of a court of highest jurisdiction deciding not to be bound by precedent in appropriate cases, or is there some other explanation?

In terms of the legal method described by the judges, of course, there is no answer to this question. Neither the judgments in the Supreme Court of Canada, nor Lord Sankey's opinion in the Privy Council, expressly consider the reality of women's experience at that time at all, and they specifically do not consider the reality of experience for the actual women claimants in the Persons case. Thus, even if the judges' perspectives on women's place were different in the two courts, there is virtually nothing in the judgments expressly reflecting them. For this reason, it is impossible to demonstrate that Lord Sankey's differing perspective was the reason for the different outcome in the Privy Council. At the same time, it is hard to find any other convincing explanation.

What does, of course, seem clear is the existence of judicial choice in the application of precedents. In the process of choosing earlier cases and deciding that they are binding precedents, judges make choices about which aspects of earlier cases are 'relevant' and 'similar,' choices which are not neutral but normative. In suggesting that the earlier decisions (relied on by the Supreme Court of Canada as binding precedents) were not determinative, Lord Sankey was declaring that the earlier decisions should not be regarded as exactly the same as the situation before the court in the Persons case. In this way, Lord Sankey's decision demonstrates the availability of choice in the selection of facts, in the categorization of principles and in the determination of relevance. At the same time, his opinion completely obscures the process and standards which guided the choice he actually made. To the myth of 'neutrality,' therefore, Lord Sankey added the 'mystery' of choice.

Interpreting statutes and Parliament's intent

Even in the statutes which used gender-neutral language, however, there were problems of statutory interpretation in relation to these cases. The legislation reviewed in the Persons case, as well as that at issue in the admission of both Martin and French, used the word 'person' in describing the qualifications for being appointed to the Senate and called to the bar respectively. In the Persons case in the Supreme Court of Canada, Chief Justice Anglin expressed his surprise that such a monumental change in the position of women could be conferred by Parliament's use of such insignificant means; as he stated rhetorically: 'Such an extraordinary privilege is not conferred furtively'. Not surprisingly, he concluded that the women's claim must be dismissed because there was no evident express intent on the part of Parliament to effect the change advocated by them; the use of the word 'person' was not, by itself, sufficient. . . .

Once again, however, the opinion of the Privy Council is different. After reviewing at some length the legislative provisions of the B.N.A. Act, Lord Sankey stated conclusively:

> 'The word "person" . . . may include members of both sexes, and to those who ask why the word should include females, the obvious answer is why should it not. In these circumstances the burden is upon those who deny that the word includes women to make out their case.'[17]

Lord Sankey cited no precedent to support this presumption in favour of the most extensive meaning of the statutory language, even though it expressly contradicted the principles of statutory interpretation adopted by all the judges in the decision of the Supreme Court of Canada.

In the end, just as the Privy Council decision was puzzling in relation to the effect of legal precedents about women's common law disabilities, it is also difficult to reconcile Lord Sankey's conclusions about the interpretation of the statute to the principles and precedents accepted in the Supreme Court of Canada. Clearly, the Privy Council departed from the Supreme Court's approach to legal method in reaching its conclusion to admit the women's claim. What remains unclear are Lord Sankey's reasons for doing so.

---

[17]   This portion of the judgment has not been included in the excerpted case.

Feminism and legal method

In such a context, what conclusion is appropriate about feminism's potential for perspective transforming in the context of legal method?

The analysis of these cases illustrates the structure of inquiry identified as legal method. First of all, legal method defines its own boundaries: questions which are inside the defined boundaries can be addressed, but those outside the boundaries are not 'legal' issues, however important they may be for 'politics' or 'morals,' etc. Thus, the question of women becoming lawyers or Senators was simply a matter of interpreting the law; it did not require any consideration of utility or benefit to the women themselves or to society in general. The purpose and the result of the boundary-defining exercise is to confer 'neutrality' on the law and on its decision makers; in so doing, moreover, the process also relieves both the law and its decision makers of accountability for (unjust) decisions—('our whole duty is [only] to construe . . . the provisions of the [constitution]').

More serious is the potential for judicial attitudes to be expressed, and to be used in decision making (either explicitly or implicitly), when there is no 'objective' evidence to support them; because of the myth of neutrality which surrounds the process, such attitudes may acquire legitimacy in a way which strengthens and reinforces ideas in 'politics' and 'morals' which were supposed to be outside the law's boundary. After the decision in *French*, for example, women were different as a matter of law, and not just in the minds of people like Mr Justice Barker. Thus, the power to name the boundaries of the inquiry (and to change them, if necessary) makes legal method especially impervious to challenges from 'the outside.'

Second, legal method defines 'relevance' and accordingly excludes some ideas while admitting others. Some facts, such as inherent gender-based traits, were regarded as relevant in *French*, for example, while in both cases the actual conditions in which women lived their lives were not relevant at all. What was clearly relevant in both cases were earlier decisions about similar circumstances from which the judges could abstract principles of general application. That all of the earlier cases had been decided by men, who were interpreting legislation drafted when women had no voting rights, was completely irrelevant to the decision making in the cases analyzed; even though the cases represented direct and significant challenges to the continuation of gender-exclusive roles and the circumstances of the historical context may seem quite significant to women now. The irony of solemn judicial reliance on precedent in the context of significant efforts by women to change the course of legal history underlines the significant role of legal method in preserving the status quo.

Finally, the case analysis demonstrates the opportunity for choice in legal method: choice as to which precedents are relevant and which approach to statutory interpretation is preferred; and choice as to whether the ideas of the mainstream or those of the margins are appropriate. The existence of choice in legal method offered some possibility of positive outcomes in the women's rights cases, at the same time as legal method's definitions of boundaries and concept of relevance ensured that positive outcomes would seldom occur. Lord Sankey's opinion in the Privy Council is an example of choice in legal method, however, which is as remarkable for its common sense as it is for its distinctiveness in legal method. Yet because Lord Sankey obscured the reasons for his choice, he also preserved the power and mystery of legal method even as he endowed women with the right to be summoned to the Senate. Thus, the opportunity for choice of outcome, positive as it appears, will not automatically lead to legal results which successfully challenge 'vested interests' or the 'status quo,' especially in relation to the law itself.

The conclusion that legal method is structured in such a way which makes it impervious to a feminist perspective is a sobering one. Within the women's movement, it has concrete consequences for the design of strategies for achieving legal equality: it suggests, for example, the general futility of court action for achieving significant change in women's rights, even though such action may be useful to monitor interpretation by courts or to focus attention on legal problems. For a feminist who is also a lawyer, however, the effort of 'double-think' may be both taxing and ultimately frustrating; the needs of clients require her to become highly proficient at legal method at the same time as her feminist commitment drives her to challenge the validity of its underlying rationale.

This dilemma also exists for feminist scholars. Feminist legal scholars are expected to think and write using the approaches of legal method: defining the issues, analyzing relevant precedents, and recommending conclusions according to defined and accepted standards of legal method. A feminist scholar who chooses instead to ask different questions or to conceptualize the problem in different ways risks a reputation for incompetence in her legal method as well as lack of recognition for her scholarly (feminist) accomplishments. Too often, it seems almost impossible to be both a good lawyer and a good feminist scholar.

This dilemma is similarly acute for feminist law teachers and students. With the advent of large numbers of women law students and increased numbers of women on law faculties, many have concluded that there is now a feminist perspective in the law school. Such a conclusion ignores the power of legal method to resist structural change. For example, discussions about whether feminist law teachers should create separate courses with feminist approaches and content, or whether we should use such approaches and content in 'malestream' courses, or whether we should do both at once, etc clearly confirm the 'reality' of the existing categories of legal knowledge, and reinforce the idea of the feminist perspective as 'Other.' While the separate course approach marginalizes the feminist perspective, the process of 'tacking on' feminist approaches to malestream courses only serves to emphasize what is really important in contrast to what has been 'tacked on.' Even efforts to give equal time to the feminist perspective and to reveal the essential maleness of the 'neutral' approach may underline that what is male is what really has significance. On this basis, adding women's experience to the law school curriculum cannot transform our perspective of law unless it also transforms legal method.

Taking this conclusion seriously, as I think we must, leads to some significant conclusions for women who are feminists and who are lawyers, law teachers and law students. It is simply not enough just to introduce women's experience into the curriculum or to examine the feminist approach to legal issues, although both of these activities are important. Yet, especially because there is so much resistance in legal method itself to ideas which challenge the status quo, there is no solution for the feminist who is a law teacher except to confront the reality that gender and power are inextricably linked in the legal method we use in our work, our discourse, and our study. Honestly confronting the barriers of our conceptual framework may at least permit us to begin to ask more searching and important questions."

Questions

1. Why is the idea of precedent inherently conservative? If it is conservative, why is Lord Sankey's judgment so important?

2. Mossman mentions Clara Brett Martin, the first woman lawyer in the Commonwealth. Martin became a powerful symbol for equality in the legal profession but, after Mossman's article was published, it became apparent from Martin's private writings that she was vehemently anti-Semitic. It is worth remembering that historically the legal profession was closed not only to women, but also discriminated (and still does) on the basis of race, religion, ethnicity, class, sexuality, and other relations of power, which intersect in various ways. Do you think that Martin's accomplishments should be celebrated or not?

Another example of the contested relationship between legislative intention, precedent and social change can be found in the definitions of "spouse" and "family" in the law. These cases deal with the death of a "statutory tenant" in rent protected housing. Under the law, a member of the tenant's "family" living with him or her cannot be evicted.

Gammans v Ekins [1950] 2 K.B. 328, CA.

[The claimant, David Gammans, the owner of 177 Avery Lane, Gosport, a house within the Rent Restriction Acts, let it to a Mrs Smith who lived there until her death in 1949. The defendant, J.J. Ekins, had lived with her for a number of years, and had taken her name. In the neighbourhood they were thought to be man and wife. On the tenant's death the defendant refused to quit the premises claiming to be a member of the tenant's "family" within the meaning of s.12(1)(g) of the Increase of Rent and Mortgage Interest (Restrictions) Act 1920. The landlord in these proceedings claimed possession on the ground that the defendant was a trespasser.

The county court judge gave judgment for the defendant, finding him to be a member of the tenant's family. The landlord appealed.]

Asquith L.J. [after stating the facts]:

"It has been held that 'family' in s.12(1)(g) of the Act of 1920 should be given its popular meaning. Consanguinity is not a prerequisite of membership of the same family. On the authorities, not only are children members of their parents' family, but a husband is a member of his wife's, an adopted child a member of the adopter parents', and a husband, on unusual facts, has been held to be a member of the same family as his wife's niece. Mr Blundell, I think, was right in saying that the material decisions limit membership of the same 'family' to three relationships: first, that of children; secondly, those constituted by way of legitimate marriage, like that between a husband and wife; and thirdly, relationships whereby one person becomes in loco parentis to another. Beyond that point the law has not gone. I do not think that we should be justified in saying that the defendant was a member of the tenant's family. Either the relationship was platonic or it was not. The judge has not found which, and says that it makes no difference; but if their relations were platonic, I can see no principle on which it could be said that these two were members of the same family, which would not require the court to predicate the same of two old cronies of the same sex innocently sharing a flat.

If, on the other hand, the relationship involves sexual relations, it seems to me anomalous that a person can acquire a 'status of irremovability' by living or having lived in sin, even if the liaison has not been a mere casual encounter but protracted in time and conclusive in character.

But I would decide the case on a simpler view. To say of two people masquerading, as these two were, as husband and wife (there being no children to complicate the picture) that they were members of the same family, seems to be an abuse of the English language, and I would accordingly allow the appeal."

Jenkins L.J.:

"I agree. If the matter were free from authority, speaking for myself I would have little hesitation in holding that the defendant was not a member of the tenant's family within any ordinary accepted use of that expression or within the meaning of s.12(1)(g). There has, however, been a series of decisions, each of them addressed to the particular facts of the case before the court, which taken together have so extended the meaning of the word 'family' for the purposes of the sub-section as to make it possible to argue with a considerable degree of plausibility that there is no reason why the benefit of the sub-section should not be extended also to the defendant. But when the cases are examined, it will, I think, be found that none of them goes so far as we are invited to go in the present case. The defendant was not in my view a member of the tenant's family in any reasonable sense whatever. The parties, for reasons of convenience, had chosen to live together and the defendant, to avoid as he said gossip, had taken the tenant's name of Smith. The neighbours assumed that they were husband and wife and accepted them as such. I cannot regard this as giving the defendant the same claim to be considered a member of the tenant's family as if they had been lawfully man and wife. . . .

If the county court judge's decision were to stand, an alarming vista would, it seems to me, be opened up: if, for instance, brothers and sisters are members of the tenant's family, I see no reason why two friends should not set up house together, one changing his or her name to that of the other, and then give out that they were sisters or brother and sister as the case might be; in which case, provided that they were accepted as such in the neighbourhood, there would, by parity of reasoning, be no ground why, when one of them, being a statutory tenant of the house in which they both resided died, the other should not claim to be a member of the statutory tenant's family on account of the artificial relationship which they had chosen for their own purposes to adopt. I agree that the appeal should be allowed."

Evershed M.R.

[Evershed M.R. delivered concurring reasons and concluded with the comment]:

"It may not be a bad thing that by this decision it is shown that, in the Christian society in which we live, one, at any rate, of the privileges which may be derived from marriage is not equally enjoyed by those who are living together as man and wife but who are not married."

Questions

1. Why are all of the members of the Court of Appeal so troubled by the legal implications of a finding in favour of Ekins in this case? In their minds, what are the implications? Do those implications still seem unacceptable?

2. What is the *purpose* of the statutory provision in issue in this case? In light of that *purpose*, how would you define "family", *for the purposes of this statutory provision*?

Times change, and, sometimes, so does the interpretation of a statute, as the following judgment demonstrates.

Dyson Holdings Ltd v Fox [1975] 3 All E.R. 1031, CA.

Lord Denning M.R.:

"So far as we know, Jack Wright was a bachelor and Olive Agnes Fox was a spinster, who met 40 years ago and lived happily ever after. They lived together as man and wife. She took his name and was known as Mrs Wright. In 1940 they were bombed out and went to live at 3 Old Road, Lewisham. The rent book was in the name of Mr J Wright. They both went out to work and used their earnings to run the house. In every respect they were man and wife save that they had not gone through a ceremony of marriage.

After 21 years in the house, on 28 August 1961 Mr Jack Wright died. She remained on in the house and paid the rent, using the name Mrs Wright. The rent book remained in the name of 'J Wright' and the records of the landlord still showed the tenant as 'J Wright'.

I expect that the ownership changed hands from time to time, but in March 1973 the owners were a property company, Dyson Holdings Ltd. By this time Mrs Wright (as she was known) was herself getting on in years. She was 73. She wrote to the landlord asking for a statement of the weekly rent. She signed herself 'OA Wright'. This put the property company on enquiry. They asked their agents to call at the house. She told them that Mr Jack Wright died on 28 August 1961 and that she was his widow. The property company asked their agents to check up on the electoral roll. They did so. They found that she had given her name there as 'Olive Fox'. The property company inferred that she was not really his widow. If she had been his widow, she could, of course, have had protection under the Rent Acts. But, if she was not his widow, they thought they were entitled in law to get her out. So on 27 March 1973 they wrote to her:

> 'We are addressing you as Mrs O Wright although we understand from the Electoral Register that the person in occupation is Olive Fox and perhaps you would explain this in your reply. Until this matter is clarified, we are unable to accept any rent . . .'

So after all those years, the truth was out. She was not his widow. She was only a woman who had lived with him as his wife for 21 years. The property company refused to receive any rent from her and brought proceedings against her for possession on the ground that she was not protected by the Rent Act 1968. She had, they said, no tenancy and was a trespasser. They had accepted the rent from her, not knowing that the tenant had died. As soon as they discovered it, and that she was not his widow, they were entitled to possession. The judge accepted their argument. He held that he was bound by the decision of this court in *Gammans v. Ekins*. It was sad, he said, to have to turn this lady of 74 out; but felt he had no alternative. He ordered her out in 28 days. She appeals to this court.

Ever since 1920 the Rent Acts have protected a 'member of the tenant's family' in these words:

> '. . . the expression "tenant" includes a widow of a tenant . . . who was residing with him at the time of his death, or where a tenant . . . leaves no widow or is a woman, such member of the tenant's family so residing aforesaid as may be decided in default of agreement by the county court.'

So in the present case the lady is protected if she was a 'member of the tenant's family'; but not otherwise. Those words have often been considered by the courts. The cases collected are in Megarry on the Rent Acts. The word 'family' in the 1968 Act is not used in any technical sense, but in a popular sense. It is not used in the sense in which it would be used by a studious and unworldly lawyer, but in the sense in which it would be used by a man who is 'base, common and popular', to use Shakespeare's words . . . ."

[Lord Denning then considered *Gammans v Ekins*]:

"But is this court at liberty to reject the distinction? Are we bound by *Gammans v Ekins*? That case can be distinguished on narrow grounds, such as that the woman was the tenant and not the man, or that their relationship might perhaps have been platonic. But I dislike the device of distinguishing a case on narrow grounds. I prefer to say, as I have often said, that this court is not absolutely bound by a previous decision when it is seen that it can no longer be supported. At any rate, it is not so bound when, owing to the lapse of time, and the change in social conditions, the previous decision is not in accord with modern thinking. . . . I am glad to find that we are all of one mind on this, but in case there are some who are doubtful, I can put the case on a conventional ground.

It has been decided by the House of Lords that, when an Act uses an ordinary English word in its popular meaning as distinct from its legal meaning, it is for the tribunal of fact to decide whether or not that popular meaning covers the case in hand. The tribunal of fact must use its own understanding of the word and apply it to the facts which have been proved. A Court of Appeal should not interfere with its decision unless it was unreasonable in the sense that no tribunal acquainted with the ordinary use of language could reasonably reach that decision. That was the very ground of the decision of the House of Lords in *Brutus v. Cozens*.[18] In the light of that decision, it appears to me that *Gammans v. Ekins* was wrongly decided. In that case, the tribunal of fact—the county court judge—gave judgment for the man, finding him to be a 'member of the tenant's family'. The Court of Appeal recognised that the words were to be given their ordinary and popular meaning, but nevertheless they reversed the county court judge. I do not think they should have done. To my mind the decision of the county court judge in that case was a perfectly reasonable decision, as Evershed M.R. recognised. And, on the authority of *Brutus v. Cozens*, the Court of Appeal ought not to have interfered with it. They went wrong just as the Divisional Court did in *Brutus v. Cozens*.[19] Their decision cannot stand with that subsequent decision of the House of Lords. We are not, therefore, bound by it: see *Young v. Bristol Aeroplane*.[20]

I would, however, add a word of caution about *Brutus v. Cozens*. When an ordinary word comes to be applied to similar facts, in one case after another, it is very important that the various tribunals of fact should each apply it in the same way. For instance, if the question comes up: is an unmarried woman (living for many years as a man's wife) a member of his family? Each tribunal of fact should give the same answer. It would be intolerable if half of the judges gave one answer; and the other half another. . . .

So here in the present case, I think this court should give a definite ruling. We should rule that in this case this lady was a member of the tenant's family residing with him at the time of his death. As such, she was entitled to the protection of the Rent Acts. The property company were not entitled to turn her out. I would allow the appeal accordingly."

James L.J.

[James L.J. reviewed the decision in *Gammans v Ekins* and continued]:

"It is not so easy to decide whether in 1961 the ordinary man would have regarded the appellant as a member of Mr Wright's family. The changes of attitude which have taken place cannot be ascribed to any particular year. Had we to consider the position as at 1955 I would not be satisfied that the attitude reflected in the words of Asquith L.J. in *Gammans v. Ekins* had changed. I am confident that by 1970 the changes had taken

---

[18]   [1972] 2 All E.R. 1297, [1973] A.C. 854.
[19]   [1972] 2 All E.R. 1, [1972] 1 W.L.R. 484.
[20]   [1944] 2 All E.R. 293 at 298, [1944] K.B. 718 at 725.

place. There is no magic in the date 1961. I think that, having regard to the radical change which has by 1975 taken place, it would be a harsh and somewhat ossified approach to the present case to hold that in 1961 the appellant was not in the popular sense a member of the family.

I turn to the issue whether there is any rule of law which precludes the appellant being a member of the family for the purposes of the Rent Acts. If there is, it is to be found only in the decision of this court in *Gammans v. Ekins*. I confess that I have been troubled in the course of argument as to how far the decision of this court in that case is conclusive of the present appeal. The court in *Gammans v. Ekins* reversed the trial judge. They could not have done so unless the issue was a question of law. It is not a decision which can be explained on the basis of a question of fact. The cases which are said to be inconsistent with the decision are in my judgment not shown to be inconsistent. They are based on the added fact of birth of a child or children to the illicit union. . . . I cannot take the view that *Gammans v. Ekins* was wrongly decided. The decision is binding on this court, but it is binding only on the meaning to be given to 'family' at that time. The point decided was that applying the popular meaning of the word 'family' as it was used and understood in 1949 the evidence of relationship could not support a finding that the defendant was a member of the tenant's family. The decision is not authority for the proposition that at some later time a person in a similar position to Mr Ekins could not in law be a member of the tenant's family within the meaning of the increase of Rent and Mortgage Interest (Restrictions) Act 1920 and the Rent Act 1968. The word 'family' must be given its popular meaning at the time relevant to the decision in the particular case.

To hold that *Gammans v. Ekins* precludes the appellant from bringing herself within the Act would be to apply a precedent slavishly in circumstances to which it is not appropriate having regard to reality.

I would therefore allow this appeal."

Bridge L.J.

[Bridge L.J. considered *Gammans v Ekins* and continued]:

"Can we give effect to this change in social attitude and consequent change in the scope of a common English word without doing violence to the doctrine of judicial precedent and notwithstanding that in this case the appellant's status must be considered at the date of the original tenant's death in 1961? I have felt some hesitation on both these points, but in the end have concluded that it would be unduly legalistic to allow either consideration to defeat the appellant's claim. On the first point, if language can change its meaning to accord with changing social attitudes, then a decision on the meaning of a word in a statute before such a change should not continue to bind thereafter, at all events in a case where the courts have consistently affirmed that the word is to be understood in its ordinary accepted meaning. On the second point, where the modern meaning is plain, we should, I think, be prepared to apply it retrospectively to any date, unless plainly satisfied that at that date the modern meaning would have been unacceptable.

Accordingly I agree that this appeal should be allowed."

Appeal allowed. Leave to appeal to the House of Lords refused.

Questions

1. How do the members of the Court of Appeal in *Dyson Holdings v Fox* avoid the impact of the rules of precedent? Are the reasons convincing?

2. The law–fact distinction is used by Lord Denning to justify his departure from the precedent of *Gammans v Ekins*. How? Is the distinction clearer to you after reading his reasons?

Reading the case law on family members should make you think of other situations, some of which were raised by the judges themselves, that might come up in litigation. In the following case the surviving partner was successful when the case reached the House of Lords.

Fitzpatrick v Sterling Housing Association Ltd [1999] 4 All E.R. 705, HL.

Lord Slynn of Hadley:

"My Lords, throughout this century Parliament has provided statutory protection for residential tenants and for certain persons with what can be called derived rights from those tenants. . . .

The Rent Act 1977 consolidated the existing law, but s.76 of the Housing Act 1980 extended the rights to take over the tenancy to a surviving spouse of either sex and not just to the widow. The 1977 Act was amended by the Housing Act 1988. The result was that at the relevant time for the present case by Sch 1 to the 1977 Act as amended, an 'original tenant' was defined as the person 'who immediately before his death, was a protected tenant of the dwelling-house or the statutory tenant of it by virtue of his previous protected tenancy' (see para 1). Then it is provided in paras 2 and 3 that:

'2.—(1) The surviving spouse (if any) of the original tenant, if residing in the dwelling-house immediately before the death of the original tenant, shall after the death be the statutory tenant if and so long as he or she occupies the dwelling-house as his or her residence.

(2) For the purposes of this paragraph, a person who was living with the original tenant as his or her wife or husband shall be treated as the spouse of the original tenant.

(3) If, immediately after the death of the original tenant, there is, by virtue of sub-paragraph (2) above, more than one person who fulfils the conditions in sub-paragraph (1) above, such one of them as may be decided by agreement or, in default of agreement, by the county court shall be treated as the surviving spouse for the purposes of this paragraph.

3.—(1) Where paragraph 2 above does not apply, but a person who was a member of the original ten-ant's family was residing with him in the dwelling-house at the time of and for the period of 2 years immediately before his death then, after his death, that person or if there is more than one such person such one of them as may be decided by agreement, or in default of agreement by the county court, shall be entitled to an assured tenancy of the dwelling-house by succession.'

It is unnecessary for present purposes to set out the remainder of Sch 1. It is however to be noted that since the 1988 Act it is only the spouse (actual or deemed) who gets a statutory tenancy. Other family members get an assured tenancy which does not pass on to that person's successor whereas in the case of the spouse there may be further succession.

There are differences between this legislation and the Housing Acts dealing with public sector housing, but it does not seem to me necessary to set out those provisions here.

Mr John Thompson was the 'original tenant' of a flat known as 75A Ravenscourt Road, London W6 from 1972 until his death in his sixties on 9 November, 1994. That flat is part of a two-flat building of which the respondent is the registered freehold owner. Mr Martin Fitzpatrick, the appellant in these proceedings, lived with Mr Thompson in the flat from 1976 until the latter's death and has continued to live there since. It is agreed between the parties that the appellant and the deceased has been partners in a longstanding, close, loving and faithful, monogamous, homosexual relationship.

The appellant sought a declaration that he had succeeded to the tenancy under the Rent Act 1977, as amended. He claimed that he was 'a spouse' of the deceased in that he had been living with Mr Thompson 'as his wife or husband' or alternatively that he was a member of Mr Thompson's family.

Judge Colin Smith QC, in a sensitive and sympathetic judgment, found the relationship to have been of the description agreed by the parties to which I have referred. He related an accident in 1986 when Mr Thompson fell down the stairs and sustained a blood clot to the brain which led to his being in a coma for some months. When he came round he never spoke again. As the judge said:

'Eventually, after various unfortunate incidents at the hospital, the applicant took Mr Thompson home in April 1986 to care for him full time himself. The applicant took over the total care 24 hours a day for

Mr Thompson, feeding him and nursing him until his death in 1994. The applicant gave up his job and received benefit because he was unable to work, due to his full time care of Mr Thompson. Despite the loving and dedicated care of the applicant, Mr Thompson died in November 1994.'

The learned judge held, however, that the applicant could not succeed to the tenancy under either of the ways he put his claim. Waite and Roch LJJ ([1974] 4 All ER 991, [1998] Ch 304) agreed with him in the result, though expressing considerable sympathy and understanding of the position in which same-sex partners living together found themselves under the legislation as they, and in the case of Roch LJ with hesitation in respect of the second way of putting the claim, held it to be. They both considered that there were matters which Parliament ought to consider. Ward LJ, in a trenchant and detailed judgment, concluded that the appellant succeeded as a spouse of, but, if not, then as a member of the family of, the original tenant.

On this appeal to your Lordships' House the appellant put forward both grounds but he relies in the first place on para 2 of Sch 1 to the 1977 Act, as amended. 'Spouse', he says, is to be interpreted in the present climate as including two persons of the same sex intimately linked in a relationship which is not merely transient and which has all the indicia of a marriage save that the parties cannot have children. In the second place, he says that the intimacy of the relationship of two persons living together as he and Mr Thompson were is such that they should be regarded as constituting a family.

It has been suggested that for your Lordships to decide this appeal in favour of the appellant would be to usurp the function of Parliament. It is trite that that is something the courts must not do. When considering social issues in particular judges must not substitute their own views to fill gaps. They must consider whether the facts 'fall within the parliamentary intention' (see *Royal College of Nursing of the UK v Dept of Health and Social Security* [1981] 1All ER 545 at 565, [1981] AC 800 at 822 per Lord Wilberforce). Thus in the present context if, for example, it was explicit or clear that Parliament intended the word 'family' to have a narrow meaning for all time, it would be a court's duty to give effect to it whatever changes in social attitudes a court might think ought to be reflected in the legislation. Similarly, if it were explicit or clear that the word must be given a very wide meaning so as to cover relationships for which a court, conscious of the traditional views of society might disapprove, the court's duty would be to give effect to it. It is, however, for the court in the first place to interpret each phrase in its statutory context. To do so is not to usurp Parliament's function; not to do so would be to abdicate the judicial function. If Parliament takes the view that the result is not what is wanted it will change the legislation.

The question is, therefore, was the appellant the spouse of, or a member of the family of, Mr Thompson within the meaning of this Act? I stress 'within the meaning of this Act' since it is all that your Lordships are concerned with. In other statutes, in other contexts, the words may have a wider or a narrower meaning than here. I refer to the judgment of McHugh J in *Re Wakim, ex p McNally, Re Wakim, ex p Darvall, Re Brown, ex p Amann, Spinks v Prentice* (1999) 73 ALJR 839 at 850 in the High Court of Australia which recognises that changes in attitudes and perceptions may require a wider meaning to be given to a word such as 'marriage', at any rate in some contexts.

The first question then is whether the appellant was the 'spouse' of Mr Thompson within the meaning of para 2 of Sch 1 to the 1977 Act as amended. I recognise that if the non-gender specific noun 'spouse' stood alone the matter might be more debatable as Mr Blake QC contends, though the ordinary meaning is plainly 'husband' or 'wife'. In the context of this Act, however, 'spouse' means in my view legally a husband or wife. The 1988 amendment extended the meaning to include as a 'spouse' a person living with the original tenant 'as his or her wife or husband'. This was obviously intended to include persons not legally husband and wife who lived as such without being married. That *prima facie* means a man and a woman, and the man must show that the woman was living with him as 'his' wife; the woman that he was living with her as 'her' husband. I do not think that Parliament as recently as 1988 intended that these words should be read as meaning 'my same-sex partner', rather than specifically 'husband' or 'wife'. If that had been the intention, it would have been spelled out. The words cannot in my view be read as the appellant contends. I thus agree as to the result with the decision in *Harrogate BC v Simpson* (1984) 17 HLR 205. The appellant accordingly fails in the first way he puts his appeal. Whether that result is discriminatory against same-sex couples in the light of the fact that non-married different sex couples living together are to be treated as spouses, so as to allow one to succeed to the tenancy of the other may have to be considered when the Human Rights Act is in force. Whether the result is socially desirable in 1999 is a matter for Parliament.

Is it fatal to a claim to be a member of the family of the original tenant that the appellant cannot show that he was living with Mr Thompson as his husband or wife, the nearest family relationship he asserts? In my view it is not. If a person does not succeed on the first he may still succeed on the second category. Here the partner fails because the first category requires partners of different sexes. That he cannot satisfy. If he satisfies the definition of family he may still qualify.

I turn then to the second question which I, at any rate, have found a difficult one—difficult largely because of preconceptions of a family as being a married couple and, if they have children, their children; difficult also because of the result of some of the earlier cases when applying the law to the facts. It is, however, obvious that the word 'family' is used in a number of different senses, some wider, some narrower. 'Do you have any family?' usually means 'do you have children?' 'We're having a family gathering' may include often distant relatives and even close friends. The 'family of nations', 'the Christian family' are very wide. This is no new phenomenon. Roman law, as I understand it, included in the family all members of the social unit though other rights might be limited to spouses or heirs.

It is not an answer to the problem to assume (as I accept may be correct) that if in 1920 people had been asked whether one person was a member of another same-sex person's family, the answer would have been 'no'. That is not the right question. The first question is what were the characteristics of a family in the 1920 Act, and the second whether two same-sex partners can satisfy those characteristics so as today to fall within the word 'family'. An alternative question is whether the word 'family' in the 1920 Act has to be updated so as to be capable of including persons who today would be regarded as being of each other's family, whatever might have been said in 1920 . . .

If 'family' could only mean a legal relationship (of blood or by legal ceremony of marriage or by legal adoption) then the appellant would obviously fail. Over the years, however, the courts have held that this is not so. . . .

Given, on the basis of these earlier decisions that the word is to be applied flexibly, and does not cover only legally binding relationships, it is necessary to ask what are its characteristics in this legislation and, to answer that question, to ask further what was Parliament's purpose. It seems to me that the intention in 1920 was that not just the legal wife but also the other members of the family unit occupying the property on the death of the tenant with him should qualify for the succession. The former did not need to prove a qualifying period; as a member of the tenant's family a two-year residence had to be shown. If more than one person qualified, then, if no agreement can be reached between them, the court decided who should succeed.

The hallmarks of the relationship were essentially that there should be a degree of mutual interdependence, of the sharing of lives, of caring and love, of commitment and support. In respect of legal relationships these are presumed, though evidently they are not always present, as the family law and criminal courts know only too well. In de facto relationships these are capable, if proved, of creating membership of the tenant's family. If, as I consider, this was the purpose of the legislation, the question is then who in 1994 or today (I draw no distinction between them) are capable in law of being members of the tenant's family. It is not who would have been so considered in 1920. In considering this question it is necessary to have regard to changes of attitude. The point cannot have been better put than it was by Bingham MR in *R v Ministry of Defence, ex p Smith* [1996] 1 All ER 257 at 261–263, [1996] QB 517 at 552–554 when, although dealing with the validity of an administrative decision rather than the meaning of a few words in a statute, he said, after referring to changes of attitude in society towards same-sex relationships:

'I regard the progressive development and refinement of public and professional opinion at home and abroad, here very briefly described, as an important feature of this case. A belief which represented unquestioned orthodoxy in Year X may have become questionably by Year Y, and unsustainable by Year Z. Public and professional opinion are a continuum.'

If 'meaning' is substituted for 'opinion' the words are no less appropriate. In *Barclays Bank plc v O'Brien* [1993] 4 All ER 417 at 431, [1994] 1 AC 180 at 198 Lord Browne-Wilkinson (with whom other members of the House agreed) said that in relation to the equity arising from undue influence in a loan transaction:

> 'But in my judgment the same principles are applicable to all other cases where there is an emotional relationship between cohabitees. The "tenderness" shown by the law to married women is not based on the marriage ceremony but reflects the underlying risk of one cohabitee exploiting the emotional involvement and trust of the other. Now that unmarried cohabitation, whether heterosexual or homosexual, is widespread in our society, the law should recognise this.'

In particular, if the 1988 amendment had not been made ('as his or her wife or husband') I would have no hesitation in holding today when, it appears, one-third of younger people live together unmarried, that where there is a stable, loving and caring relationship which is not intended to be merely temporary and where the couple live together broadly as they would if they were married, that each can be a member of the other's family for the purpose of the 1977 Act.

If, as I think, in the light of all the authorities this is the proper interpretation of the 1920 Act I hold that as a matter of law a same-sex partner of a deceased tenant can establish the necessary familial link. They are capable of being, in Russell LJ's words in *Ross v Collins*, 'a broadly recognisable *de facto familial nexus*' (see [1964] 1 All ER 861, [1964] 1 WLR 425 at 432). It is then a question of fact as to whether he or she does establish the necessary link.

It is accordingly not necessary to consider the alternative question as to whether by 1999 the meaning of the word in the 1920 Act needs to be updated. I prefer to say that it is not the meaning which has changed but those who are capable of falling within the words have changed. . . .

It seems to be suggested that the result which I have so far indicated would be cataclysmic. In relation to this Act it is plainly not so. The onus on one person claiming that he or she was a member of the same-sex original tenant's family will involve that person establishing rather than merely asserting the necessary indicia of the relationship. A transient superficial relationship will not do even if it is intimate. Mere cohabitation by friends as a matter of convenience will not do. There is, in any event, a minimum residence qualification: the succession is limited to that of the original tenant. Far from being cataclysmic it is, as both the county court judge and the Court of Appeal appear to recognise, and as I consider, in accordance with contemporary notions of social justice. In other statutes, in other contexts, the same meaning may or may not be the right one. If a narrower meaning is required, so be it. It seems also to be suggested that such a result in this statute undermines the traditional (whether religious or social) concept of marriage and the family. It does nothing of the sort. It merely recognises that, for the purposes of this Act, two people of the same sex can be regarded as having established membership of a family, one of the most significant human relationships which both gives benefits and imposes obligations.

It is plain on the findings of the county court judge that in this case, on the view of the law which I have accepted, on the facts the appellant succeeds as a member of Mr Thompson's family living with him at his death.

On that ground I would allow the appeal."

Lord Nicholls of Birkenhead:

"My Lords, this appeal raises an important point on the interpretation of a provision in the Rent Acts. For many years certain residential tenants have enjoyed the benefits of fair rentals and protection from eviction conferred by successive Rent Acts. Ever since the earliest days of this legislation in 1920, these benefits have not been confined to the original tenant. Under the Increase of Rent and Mortgage Interest (Restrictions) Act 1920, s.12(1)(g), 'tenant' included the widow of a tenant in certain circumstances and, in other case, such 'member of the tenant's family' residing with him when he died as might be agreed or decided by the court. In addition to protecting the tenant personally, Parliament has always been concerned to protect the family unit of which the deceased tenant was a part. . . .

The question calling for decision in the present case is a question of statutory interpretation. It is whether the same-sex partner is capable of being a member of the other partner's family for the purposes of the Rent Act legislation. I am in no doubt that this question should be answered affirmatively. A man and woman living together in a stable and permanent sexual relationship are capable of being members of a family for this purpose. Once this is accepted, there can be no rational or other basis on which the like conclusion can be withheld from a similarly stable and permanent sexual relationship between two men or between two women. Where a relationship of this character exists, it cannot make sense to say that, although a heterosexual partner-ship can give rise to membership of a family for Rent Act purposes, a homosexual partnership cannot. Where sexual partners are involved, whether heterosexual or homosexual, there is scope for the intimate mutual love and affection and long-term commitment that typically characterise the relationship of husband and wife. This love and affection and commitment can exist in same-sex relationships as in heterosexual relationships. In sexual terms a homosexual relationship is different from a heterosexual relationship, but I am unable to see that the difference is material for present purposes. As already emphasised, the concept underlying member-ship of a family for present purposes is the sharing of lives together in a single family unit living in one house. . . .

This submission raises the question whether the word 'family' as used in the Rent Acts may change its meaning as ways of life and social attitudes change. Can the expression family legitimately be interpreted in 1999 as having a different and wider meaning than when it was first enacted in 1920? The principles applica-ble were stated cogently by Lord Wilberforce in *Royal College of Nursing of the UK v Dept of Health and Social Security* [1981] 1 All E.R. 545 at 564–565, [1981] AC 800 at 822. A statute must necessarily be interpreted having regard to the state of affairs existing when it was enacted. It is a fair presumption that Parliament's intention was directed at that state of affairs. When circumstances change, a court has to consider whether they fall within the parliamentary intention. They may do so if there can be detected a clear purpose in the legislation which can only be fulfilled if an extension is made. How liberally these principles may be applied must depend upon the nature of the enactment, and the strictness or otherwise of the words in which it was expressed.

In the present case Parliament used an ordinary word of flexible meaning and left it undefined. The under-lying legislative purpose was to provide a secure home for those who share their lives together with the origi-nal tenant in the manner which characterises a family unit. This purpose would be at risk of being stultified if the courts could not have regard to changes in the way people live together and changes in the perception of relationships. This approach is supported by the fact that successive Rent Acts have used the same undefined expression despite the far-reaching changes in ways of life and social attitudes meanwhile. It would be unat-tractive, to the extent of being unacceptable, to interpret the word 'family' in the 1977 Act without regard to these changes.

The change in attitudes towards unmarried couples cohabiting as husband and wife exemplifies this point. In *Gammans v Ekins* [1950] 2 KB 328 the court's decision was affected by its perception of the immorality of such a relationship. An immoral relationship did not come within the ambit of family in the Rent Acts. Asquith LJ said it would be anomalous that a person could acquire protection by living in sin even if the liaison was protracted in time and conclusive in character. Jenkins LJ described the relationship as no more than a liaison between two elderly people who chose to pose as husband and wife when they in fact were not. Evershed MR was more hesitant, but his conclusion was that it might be no bad thing to show that one of the privi-leges derivable from marriage was not equally enjoyed by those living together as man and wife but in fact unmarried.

In one respect of crucial importance there has been a change in social attitudes over the last half-century. I am not referring to the change in attitude toward sexual relationships between a man and woman outside marriage or toward homosexual relationships. There has been a widespread change in attitude toward such relationships, although differing and deeply felt views are held on these matters. These differing views are to be recognised and respected. The crucial change to which I am referring is related but different. It is that the morality of a lawful relationship is not now regarded as relevant when the court is deciding whether an individ-ual qualifies for protection under the Rent Acts. Parliament itself made this clear in 1988, when amending the Rent Acts in the 1988 Act. Paragraph 2(3) of Sch 1 envisages that more than one person may be living with the tenant as a surviving spouse under the extended definition. In so enacting the law, Parliament was not express-ing a view, either way, on the morality of such relationships. But by this provision Parliament made plain that, for purposes of Rent Act protection, what matters is the factual position. The same must be true of homosexual relationships.

It is for this reason that I do not accept the argument that the inclusion of a tenant's homosexual partner within the ranks of persons eligible to qualify as members of his family is a step which should be left to Parliament. It really goes without saying that in cases such as this the courts must always proceed with par-ticular caution and sensitivity. That is not to say the courts can never proceed at all. That is not what the Court of Appeal did in 1975 when deciding the *Dyson Holdings* case. Nor should this course commend itself to your Lordships in the present case.

In this regard, at the risk of repetition, it is necessary to stress the limited nature of the decision in this case. The courts have already decided that the undefined expression 'family' is to be given a wide meaning in the context of the Rent Acts. The courts have already decided that family included relationships other than those based on consanguinity or affinity. To include same-sex partners is to do no more than apply to them the same rationale as that underlying the inclusion of different sex partners. The decision goes no further than this. The decision leaves untouched questions such as whether persons of the same sex should be able to marry, and whether a stable homosexual relationship is within the scope of the right to respect for family life in art.8 of the Convention for the Protection of Human Rights and Fundamental Freedoms (Rome, 5 November 1950; TS 71 (1953); Cmd 8969).

I would allow this appeal. It is not disputed that if a same-sex partner can qualify as a member of the ten-ant's family, the appellant does in fact qualify. He and the original tenant, until the latter's death, lived together for many years in a stable homosexual relationship. The judge found they enjoyed a very close, loving and monogamous homosexual relationship. In my view the appellant falls within para 3."

Lord Clyde:

". . . The problem in the present case is to determine what, short of blood or marriage, may evidence the common bond in a partnership of two adult persons which may entitle the one to be in the common judgment of society a member of the other's family. It seems to me that essentially the bond must be one of love and affection, not of a casual or transitory nature, but in a relationship which is permanent or at least intended to be so. As a result of that personal attachment to each other, other characteristics will follow, such as a readi-ness to support each other emotionally and financially, to care for and look after the other in times of need, and to provide a companionship in which mutual interests and activities can be shared and enjoyed together. It would be difficult to establish such a bond unless the couple were living together in the same house. It would also be difficult to establish it without an active sexual relationship between them or at least the potentiality of such a relationship. If they have or are caring for children whom they regard as their own, that would make the family designation immediately obvious, but the existence of children is not a necessary element. Each case will require to depend eventually upon its own facts.

The concept of the family has undergone significant development during recent years, both in the United Kingdom and overseas. Whether that is a matter for concern or congratulation is of no relevance to the present case, but it is properly part of the judicial function to endeavour to reflect an understanding of such changes in the reality of social life. Social groupings have come to take a number of different forms. The form of the single parent family has been long recognised. A more open acceptance of differences in sexuality allows a greater recognition of the possibility of domestic groupings of partners of the same sex. The formal bond of marriage is now far from being a significant criterion for the existence of a family unit. While it remains as a particular for-malisation of the relationship between heterosexual couples, family units may now be recognised to exist both where the principle members are in a heterosexual relationship and where they are in a homosexual or lesbian relationship. . . .

It was suggested that if the present appeal was allowed there would be great uncertainty in the ascer-tainment of successors to statutory tenancies. I am not persuaded that such fears are justified. There may at present be need on occasion to explore the facts of particular cases to discover whether a person was living with the original tenant 'as his or her wife or husband'. In relation to the word 'family', it is difficult to devise a construction which will obviate inquiry unless a very restrictive view of the scope of a family is taken. Once it is accepted, as it has been in the cases, that the application extends beyond the scope of strictly legal relationships, some inquiry may well be involved into the facts which are alleged to be sufficient to constitute the necessary nexus. It does not seem to me that the recognition that a person living together with another in a homosexual relationship may qualify as a member of the other's family is likely to lead to any significant uncertainties in the application of the statutory provision.

Ward LJ expressed an anxiety that he might be exceeding the limits of the judicial function in reaching his decision. Judicial activism certainly has to be tempered by due restraint, and the drawing of the boundary of the judicial task is often delicate and sometimes controversial. I do not consider that the boundary is being passed in the present case. What we are concerned with is the application of a word recognised as being loose and flexible. Parliament has in other contexts provided definitions of the kind of relationships which it intends should be affected by particular provisions. For example, under s.113 of the Housing Act 1985 a person was a 'member of another's family' if he was the spouse of that person, or if he and that person lived together as husband and wife, or if he was that person's parent, grandparent, child, grandchild, brother, sister, uncle, aunt, nephew or niece. In marked distinction to that kind of approach Parliament has in relation to protected tenancies under the Rent Act 1977 left the word 'family' to be applied by the courts without the guidance of statutory definition. The court in the *Dyson Holdings* case accordingly applied the word as was appropriate to the social circumstances prevailing at that period, innovating on its earlier application. If, as I believe, the word is now appropriate to cover a homosexual partnership of the kind which existed in the present case, it seems to me consistent with the intention of Parliament that it should be applied.

I would allow the appeal."

Lord Hutton (dissenting): . . .

The second issue: para 3(1) of Sch 1

"The secondary submission advance on behalf of Mr Fitzpatrick was that if the wording of para 2(2) excluded the relationship of a couple of the same sex, the consideration that the relationship is akin to marriage nevertheless qualifies it as being familial in character so that, within the meaning of para 3(1), Mr Fitzpatrick was a member of Mr Thompson's family. In considering this submission it is relevant at the outset to have regard to the scheme of Sch 1 to the 1977 Act. Whilst in earlier provisions in the Rent Acts legislation a distinction was not drawn between a widower of the tenant and a member of the tenant's family, so that under the Increase of Rent and Mortgage Interest (Restrictions) Act 1920 it was held that a widower was a member of the tenant's family (*see Salter v Lask, Lask v Cohen* [1925] 1KB 584), it is apparent that Sch 1 to the 1977 Act deals separately with the surviving spouse of the tenant and a person living with the tenant as his or her wife or husband on the one hand and with a member of the tenant's family on the other hand. If Mr Fitzpatrick were entitled to claim the protection given by Sch 1 it would appear appropriate that he should obtain protection under para 2 and not under para 3, because the essence of his claim is that the relationship which he shared with Mr Thompson was the same relationship as that shared between a husband and wife or a couple living together as husband and wife, save that the relationship was homosexual and not heterosexual. Therefore, if (as I would hold) Parliament did not intend that a homosexual partner should obtain protection under para 2, it would appear to be a somewhat strained and artificial construction to hold that Mr Fitzpatrick is entitled to obtain protection under para 3.

In *Harrogate BC v Simpson* (1984) 17 HLR 205 at 210 Watkins LJ stated:

> 'Mrs Davies, who appears for the [claimants], contends that, if Parliament had wished homosexual relationships to be brought into the realm of the lawfully recognised state of a living together of man and wife for the purpose of the relevant legislation, it would plainly have so stated in that legislation, and it has not done so. I am bound to say that I entirely agree with that.'

If it was the intention of Parliament that a homosexual partner should have the same protection under the Rent Acts as a heterosexual partner I think that in 1988 Parliament would have used express words in para 2(2) of Sch 1 to place a homosexual partner in the same position as an unmarried heterosexual partner rather than leave it to the courts to extend the meaning of the phrase 'a member of the original tenant's family' in para 3(1) to include a homosexual relationship. Instead in para 2(2) Parliament used terminology similar to that recently held by the Court of Appeal in *Simpson's* case to be confined to a heterosexual relationship. . . .

I fully recognise the strength of the argument, eloquently stated at the conclusion of Waite LJ's judgment that Parliament should change the law to give protection to the homosexual partner of a deceased tenant and also to other persons who lived with and gave devoted care to deceased tenants. But in my opinion such changes can only be made by Parliament and accordingly I would dismiss the appeal.

Lord Hobhouse of Woodborough (dissenting):

. . . The statutory provisions upon which Mr Fitzpatrick relies form part of a scheme for the transfer of protected tenancies following the death of the original tenant which Parliament has substantially revised from time to time. Since legislation of this type was first introduced in 1915, the provisions have gone through a number of versions and most of the decided cases have inevitably dealt with those earlier versions. In my judgment, the current wording must be construed having regard to the revised scheme of which it now forms part. Parliament has from time to time considered and decided to what extent the rights of succession should be increased or varied, most recently in 1988, and has amended the Act. The Act is social legislation. There are competing social policies and choices that are relevant to the decision what statutory rights of succession should be granted. The situation is complex. There are conflicting interests; indeed the subject matter of these provisions is private law property rights. Inevitably, boundaries have to be drawn which may on occasions give rise to hard cases.

I mention this aspect not only because it is important but also because it is possible to have sympathy for those in the position of Mr Fitzpatrick. A social argument can be made on their behalf for sympathetic treatment. They are at least as meritorious as some of those who clearly come within the scheme. But likewise they are not less meritorious than some of those who clearly fall outside the scheme—devoted and caring friends who have lived for a long time with the tenant in the premises but have never engaged in sexual relations with the tenant. Similarly, some may argue that, in view of changing social attitudes to homosexual relationships, the time has come as a matter of policy to equate such relationships with heterosexual ones. But such matters are for Parliament, not the courts. It is an improper usurpation of the legislative function, for a court to adopt social policies which have not yet been incorporated in the relevant legislation.

In the present case, the courts have been urged to extend by a process of liberal interpretation the concept of family to cover homosexual relationships and relationships of close long-lasting friendship. It is submitted that the usage of the word 'family' may vary from time to time and that it has no constant meaning; that accordingly it should now in 1999 be given an up-to-date meaning; that spouse includes a homosexual relationship 'akin' to marriage; that immigration law has recently been revised to take account of such relationships. This type of argument and its proper limits were considered in the speech of Lord Wilberforce in *Royal College of Nursing of the UK v Dept of Health and Social Security* [1981] 1 All E.R. 545 at 564–565, [1981] AC 800 at 822, to which we were referred by Mr Blake QC who appeared for Mr Fitzpatrick on this appeal. Lord Wilberforce said:

'In interpreting an Act of Parliament it is proper, and indeed necessary, to have regard to the state of affairs existing, and known by Parliament to be existing, at the time. It is a fair presumption that Parliament's policy or intention is directed to that state of affairs . . . when a new state of affairs, or a fresh set of facts bearing on policy, comes into existence, the courts have to consider whether they fall within the parliamentary intention. They may be held to do so if they fall within the same genus of facts as those to which the expressed policy has been formulated. They may also be held to do so if there can be detected a clear purpose in the legislation which can only be fulfilled if the extension is made . . . In any event there is one course which the courts cannot take under the law of this country: they cannot fill gaps; they cannot by asking the question, "What would Parliament have done in this current case, not being one in contemplation, if the facts had been before it?", attempt themselves to supply the answer, if the answer is not to be found in the terms of the Act itself.'

Applying this to the present case, the relevant Act was passed in 1977 and has been amended since. On any view it is difficult to see what fresh set of facts has since come into existence. Homosexual relationships have been known about and existed throughout any relevant period of time and homosexual couples have shared accommodation. Not much has changed; the highest that it can be put is that the public attitude to such rela-tionships has changed. This has nothing to do with any social policy concerning statutory tenancies by succes-sion. If, contrary to what I have just said, it does have relevance, it is a matter for Parliament to consider, not for the courts to ask themselves: 'What would Parliament do now?' But even then one has to take into account that this legislative scheme was amended as recently as 1988. . . .

The word 'family' is as has often been said not a term of art but describes a unit which has the familial char-acteristics. One such characteristic is the existence of blood relationships. Thus, in *Hawes v Evenden* [1953] 2 All ER 737, [1953] 1 WLR 1169, a group which consisted of the tenant, his mistress of some 12 years and their two children was easily recognised as being a family (cf *Gammans v Ekins* [1950] 2 All ER 140, [1950] 2 KB 328). In *Brock v Wollans* [1949] 1 All ER 715, [1949] 2 KB 388 a woman, who had at the age of five in 1912 been informally adopted by the tenant and brought up as his daughter and who returned later in her life (after her husband had died) to live with the tenant, was held to be a member of his family, even though not a blood relation. It was his de facto adoption of her whilst a child that made her a part of his family.

The limits upon the ambit of the word family were most forcefully expressed in *Gammans v Ekins* [1950] 2 All ER 140, [1950] 2 KB 328. A childless couple were living together as man and wife but they had not married. The woman was not part of the man's family. Asquith LJ, using language which would scarcely be acceptable today, unequivocally rejected the idea that mere friendship or a sexual relationship between two people of the same or a different sex could amount to a family. He and other members of the Court of Appeal affirmed that the concept of family must involve blood or affinity. The only exception was relationships whereby one person becomes *in loco parentis* to another, *e.g. Brock v Wollans*.

Returning to the speech of Lord Diplock in the *Carega Properties* case, he left open the questions raised by *Dyson Holdings Ltd v Fox* [1979] 2 All ER 1084 at 1085, [1979] 1 WLR 928 at 930. As I have already observed, the legislature has, by the amendments which it has chosen to make to the 1977 Act, already addressed the impli-cations of that decision. Lord Diplock's *ratio decidendi* follows on a reference to *Gammans v Ekins* and *Ross v Collins*. Lord Diplock chose to adopt as his own what was said by Russell LJ in the second of these cases:

'Granted that "family" is not limited to cases of strict legal familial nexus, I cannot agree that it extends to a case such as this. It still requires, it seems to me, at least a broadly recognisable de facto familial nexus. This may be capable of being found and recognised as such by the ordinary man—where the link would be strictly familial had there been a marriage or where the link is through adoption of a minor, de jure or de facto, or where the link is "step", or where the link is "in-law" or by marriage. But two strangers cannot, it seems to me, ever establish artificially for the purposes of this section a familial nexus by acting as broth-ers or as sisters, even if they call each other such and consider their relationship to be tantamount to that. Nor, in my view, can an adult man and woman who establish a platonic relationship establish a familial nexus by acting as a devoted brother and sister or father and daughter would act, even if they address each other as such and even if they refer to each other as such, and regard their association as tantamount to such. Nor, in my view, would they indeed be recognised as familial links by the ordinary man.' (See [1979] 2 All ER 1084 at 1087, [1979] 1 WLR 928 at 931.)

This ratio decidendi is binding upon your Lordships. It is consistent with the arguments of Mr Fitzpatrick. Living together as homosexual lovers is not a familial relationship. It is a different relationship: for present purposes, as counsel said, no better and no worse—no less or more meritorious, just different. At one stage of his submis-sions, Mr Blake expressly disavowed any reliance upon the existence of sexual relations between Mr Fitzpatrick and Mr Thompson. But Mr Blake would have been wrong to abandon, if this was what he was doing, this plank of his case. Absent a sexual relationship, the relationship would have been no more than one of caring friendship which on any view does not suffice. He has to be able to say that the existence of a (formerly active) homosexual relationship makes all the difference. Stripped of that feature he cannot, on the English authorities, succeed.

It is understandable why Mr Blake shrank from putting his client's case in that way. It would expose the degree of the extension of the previous authorities for which he has to contend and points up the lack of support for his argument in the drafting of paras 2 and 3 of Sch 1. If Parliament had wished to take this further radical step, extending the rights of succession to protected tenancies, it would have given some hint of its intention in the amendments which it made after 1977. It has manifested no such intention. *The Dyson Holdings* decision has been recognised by the legislature in its amendment of para 2. The argument of Mr Blake would seem to treat as family two persons of the opposite sex living together in the same flat or house who have or have had a long term stable sexual relationship but do not choose to be known as man and wife. Regardless of the reason for their choice, para 2(2) makes it essential that each should be living as the wife or husband of the other. If your Lordships are being asked to say that nevertheless the survivor should still qualify as family under para 3 on the strength of the decision in the *Dyson Holdings* case, the invitation should in my judgment be rejected. The amendment to para 2 has laid down the relevant criterion which the relationship must satisfy. By a parity of reasoning, the *Dyson Holdings* case does not now provide Mr Fitzpatrick with a route down which he can pass asserting an equivalence between homosexual and heterosexual relationships.

The word 'family', as I have previously observed, is not a term of art. It is a word which is used to refer to a scheme of relationships having certain characteristics. All those characteristics may not be present in every case; this is the nature of descriptive words. But in any case there must be sufficient of the relevant characteristics to justify the application of the descriptive term. In deciding a legal question it is necessary to decide on which side of the line the individual case falls. This exercise is not one of choosing what social policy to support. It involves looking at the language of the statute construed in its legislative context and having regard to the previous decisions of the courts. The decided authorities have told us what the relevant characteristics are. The legislative context has been made clear by the history of the amendments made. The fundamental difficulty for Mr Fitzpatrick is that he is seeking to establish a legal right against the owners of the property, the [claimants] in the action, based upon the advocacy of a social policy which may one day be adopted by the legislature but which has not yet been incorporated in legislation and which anticipated the essential policy and drafting decisions which would have to be taken by the legislature."

Questions

1. If you were counsel arguing that your client had the requisite "familial link" in a tenancy case, how would you seek to convince the court? What factors seem to be most important and why?

2. Identify passages from the judgments in *Fitzpatrick* in which the majority attempt to answer the "floodgates" argument.

3. Evaluate the judgments of the Law Lords in terms of the degree to which they exemplify "judicial activism" or "judicial conservatism". Provide evidence from the judgments to support your assessment.

4. Of what relevance is the fact that—as Lord Hobhouse writes—"the subject matter of these provisions is private law property rights"? What are the "competing social policies" to which he refers? Which policy does he prioritise in this case?

Finally, we turn to the question of exclusion of same-sex partners from the definition of "spouse" for the purposes of succession to a statutory tenancy. The issue in the following case concerns whether that exclusion is contrary to the Human Rights Act 1998. The *Mendoza* case is also important more generally with respect to principles of statutory interpretation and the Human Rights Act and we will consider it further in Ch.7. However, at this point it is useful for how the *Fitzpatrick* reasoning is extended further, with greater protection for the surviving partner.

Ghaidan v Mendoza [2004] UKHL 30.

Lord Nicholls of Birkenhead:

"My Lords, on the death of a protected tenant of a dwelling-house his or her surviving spouse, if then living in the house, becomes a statutory tenant by succession. But marriage is not essential for this purpose. A person who was living with the original tenant 'as his or her wife or husband' is treated as the spouse of the original tenant: see para 2(2) of Sch 1 to the 1977 Act. In *Fitzpatrick v Sterling Housing Association Ltd* [2001] 1 AC 27 your Lordships' House decided this provision did not include persons in a same-sex relationship. The question raised by this appeal is whether this reading of para 2 can survive the coming into force of the 1998 Act. In *Fitzpatrick's* case the original tenant had died in 1994.

In the present case the original tenant died after the 1998 Act came into force on 2 October 2000. In April 1983 Mr Hugh Wallwyn-James was granted an oral residential tenancy of the basement flat at 17 Cresswell Gardens, London SW5. Until his death on 5 January 2001 he lived there in a stable and monogamous homosexual relationship with the defendant Mr Juan Godin-Mendoza. Mr Godin-Mendoza is still living there. After the death of Mr Wallwyn-James the landlord, Mr Ahmad Ghaidan, brought proceedings in the West London County Court claiming possession of the flat. Judge Cowell held that on the death of Hugh Wallwyn-James Mr Godin-Mendoza did not succeed to the tenancy of the flat as the surviving spouse of Hugh Wallwyn-James within the meaning of para 2 of Sch 1 to the 1977 Act, but that he did become entitled to an assured tenancy of the flat by succession as a member of the original tenant's 'family' under para 3(1) of that Sch.

Mr Godin-Mendoza appealed, and the Court of Appeal, comprising Kennedy, Buxton and Keene LJJ, allowed the appeal ([2002] EWCA Civ 1533, [2003] Ch 380). The court held he was entitled to succeed to a tenancy of the flat as a statutory tenant under para 2. From that decision Mr Ghaidan, the landlord, appealed to your Lordships' House.

I must first set out the relevant statutory provisions and then explain how the 1998 Act comes to be relevant in this case. Paras 2 and 3 of Sch 1 to the 1977 Act provide:

'2(1) The surviving spouse (if any) of the original tenant, if residing in the dwelling-house immediately before the death of the original tenant, shall after the death be the statutory tenant if and so long as he or she occupies the dwelling-house as his or her residence.

(2) For the purposes of this para, a person who was living with the original tenant as his or her wife or husband shall be treated as the spouse of the original tenant.

3(1) Where para 2 above does not apply, but a person who was a member of the original tenant's family was residing with him in the dwelling-house at the time of and for the period of 2 years immediately before his death then, after his death, that person or if there is more than one such person such one of them as may be decided by agreement, or in default of agreement by the county court, shall be entitled to an assured tenancy of the dwelling-house by succession.'

On an ordinary reading of this language para 2(2) draws a distinction between the position of a heterosexual couple living together in a house as husband and wife and a homosexual couple living together in a house. The survivor of a heterosexual couple may become a statutory tenant by succession, the survivor of a homosexual couple cannot. That was decided in *Fitzpatrick's* case. The survivor of a homosexual couple may, in competition with other members of the original tenant's 'family', become entitled to an assured tenancy under para 3. But even if he does, as in the present case, this is less advantageous. Notably, so far as the present case is concerned, the rent payable under an assured tenancy is the contractual or market rent, which may be more than the fair rent payable under a statutory tenancy, and an assured tenant may be evicted for non-payment of rent without the court needing to be satisfied, as is essential in the case of a statutory tenancy, that it is reasonable to make a possession order. In these and some other respects the succession rights granted by the statute to the survivor of a homosexual couple in respect of the house where he or she is living are less favourable than the succession rights granted to the survivor of a heterosexual couple.

Mr Godin-Mendoza's claim is that this difference in treatment infringes art 14 of the European Convention for the Protection of Human Rights and Fundamental Freedoms (as set out in Sch 1 to the 1998 Act) read in conjunction with art 8. Article 8 does not require the state to provide security of tenure for members of a deceased tenant's family. Art 8 does not in terms give a right to be provided with a home: *Chapman v UK* (2001) 10 BHRC 48 at 72 (para 99). It does not 'guarantee the right to have one's housing problem solved by the authorities': *Marzari v Italy* (1999) 28 EHRR CD 175 at 179. But if the state makes legislative provision it must not be discriminatory. The provision must not draw a distinction on grounds such as sex or sexual orientation without good reason. Unless justified, a distinction founded on such grounds infringes the convention right embodied in art 14, as read with art 8. Mr Godin-Mendoza submits that the distinction drawn by para 2 of Sch 1 to the 1977 Act is drawn on the grounds of sexual orientation and that this difference in treatment lacks justification.

That is the first step in Mr Godin-Mendoza's claim. That step would not, of itself, improve Mr Godin-Mendoza's status in his flat. The second step in his claim is to pray in aid the court's duty under s 3 of the 1998 Act to read and give effect to legislation in a way which is compliant with the convention rights. Here, it is said, s 3 requires the court to read para 2 so that it embraces couples living together in a close and stable homosexual relationship as much as couples living together in a close and stable heterosexual relationship. So read, para 2 covers Mr Godin-Mendoza's position. Hence he is entitled to a declaration that on the death of Mr Wallwyn-James he succeeded to a statutory tenancy.

Discrimination

The first of the two steps in Mr Godin-Mendoza's argument requires him to make good the proposition that, as interpreted in *Fitzpatrick's* case, para 2 of Sch 1 to the 1977 Act infringes his convention right under art 14 read in conjunction with art 8. Article 8 guarantees, among other matters, the right to respect for a person's home. Article 14 guarantees that the rights set out in the convention shall be secured 'without discrimination' on any grounds such as those stated in the non-exhaustive list in that art. . . .

In the present case para 2 of Sch 1 to the 1977 Act draws a dividing line between married couples and cohabiting heterosexual couples on the one hand and other members of the original tenant's family on the other hand. What is the rationale for this distinction? The rationale seems to be that, for the purposes of security of tenure, the survivor of such couples should be regarded as having a special claim to be treated in much the same way as the original tenant. The two of them made their home together in the house in question, and their security of tenure in the house should not depend upon which of them dies first.

The history of the Rent Act legislation is consistent with this appraisal. A widow, living with her husband, was accorded a privileged succession position in 1920. In 1980 a widower was accorded the like protection. In 1988 para 2(2) was added, by which the survivor of a cohabiting heterosexual couple was treated in the same way as a spouse of the original tenant.

Miss Carss-Frisk QC submitted there is a relevant distinction between heterosexual partnerships and same-sex partnerships. The aim of the legislation is to provide protection for the traditional family. Same-sex partnerships cannot be equated with family in the traditional sense. Same-sex partners are unable to have children with each other, and there is a reduced likelihood of children being a part of such a household.

My difficulty with this submission is that there is no reason for believing these factual differences between heterosexual and homosexual couples have any bearing on why succession rights have been conferred on heterosexual couples but not homosexual couples. Protection of the traditional family unit may well be an important and legitimate aim in certain contexts. In certain contexts this may be a cogent reason justifying differential treatment: see *Karner v Austria* (2003) 14 BHRC 674 at 682 (para 40). But it is important to identify the element of the 'traditional family' which para 2, as it now stands, is seeking to protect. Marriage is not now a prerequisite to protection under para 2. The line drawn by Parliament is no longer drawn by reference to the status of marriage. Nor is parenthood, or the presence of children in the home, a precondition of security of tenure for the survivor of the original tenant. Nor is procreative potential a prerequisite. The survivor is protected even if, by reasons of age or otherwise, there was never any prospect of either member of the couple having a natural child.

What remains, and it is all that remains, as the essential feature under para 2 is the cohabitation of a heterosexual couple. Security of tenure for the survivor of such a couple in the house where they live is, doubtless, an important and legitimate social aim. Such a couple share their lives and make their home together. Parliament may readily take the view that the survivor of them has a special claim to security of tenure even though they are unmarried. But the reason underlying this social policy, whereby the survivor of a cohabiting heterosexual couple has particular protection, is equally applicable to the survivor of a homosexual couple. A homosexual couple, as much as a heterosexual couple, share each other's life and make their home together. They have an equivalent relationship. There is no rational or fair ground for distinguishing the one couple from the other in this context . . .

This being so, one looks in vain to find justification for the difference in treatment of homosexual and heterosexual couples. Such a difference in treatment can be justified only if it pursues a legitimate aim and there is a reasonable relationship of proportionality between the means employed and the aim sought to be realised. Here, the difference in treatment falls at the first hurdle: the absence of a legitimate aim. None has been suggested by the First Secretary of State, and none is apparent. . . .

In the present case the only suggested ground for according different treatment to the survivor of same sex couples and opposite sex couples cannot withstand scrutiny. Rather, the present state of the law as set out in para 2 of Sch 1 to the 1977 Act may properly be described as continuing adherence to the traditional regard for the position of surviving spouses, adapted in 1988 to take account of the widespread contemporary trend for men and women to cohabit outside marriage but not adapted to recognise the comparable position of cohabiting same-sex couples. I appreciate that the primary object of introducing the regime of assured tenancies and assured shorthold tenancies in 1988 was to increase the number of properties available for renting in the private sector. But this policy objective of the Housing Act 1988 can afford no justification for amending para 2 so as to include cohabiting heterosexual partners but not cohabiting homosexual partners. This policy objective of the Act provides no reason for, on the one hand, extending to unmarried cohabiting heterosexual partners the right to succeed to a statutory tenancy but, on the other hand, withholding that right from cohabiting homosexual partners. Paragraph 2 fails to attach sufficient importance to the Convention rights of cohabiting homosexual couples. . . .

24. In my view, therefore, Mr Godin-Mendoza makes good the first step in his argument: para 2 of Sch 1 to the 1977 Act, construed without reference to s 3 of the 1998 Act, violates his convention right under art 14 taken together with art 8.

Section 3 of the 1998 Act

I turn next to the question whether s 3 of the 1998 Act requires the court to depart from the interpretation of para 2 enunciated in *Fitzpatrick's* case.

Section 3 is a key section in the 1998 Act. It is one of the primary means by which convention rights are brought into the law of this country. Parliament has decreed that all legislation, existing and future, shall be interpreted in a particular way. All legislation must be read and given effect to in a way which is compatible with the Convention rights 'so far as it is possible to do so'. This is the intention of Parliament, expressed in s 3, and the courts must give effect to this intention.

Unfortunately, in making this provision for the interpretation of legislation, s 3 itself is not free from ambiguity. Section 3 is open to more than one interpretation. The difficulty lies in the word 'possible'. Section 3(1), read in conjunction with s 3(2) and s 4, makes one matter clear: Parliament expressly envisaged that not all legislation would be capable of being made convention-compliant by application of s 3. Sometimes it would be possible, sometimes not. What is not clear is the test to be applied in separating the sheep from the goats. What is the standard, or the criterion, by which 'possibility' is to be judged? A comprehensive answer to this question is proving elusive. The courts, including your Lordships' House, are still cautiously feeling their way forward as experience in the application of s 3 gradually accumulates. . . .

In some cases difficult problems may arise. No difficulty arises in the present case. Para 2 of Sch 1 to the 1977 Act is unambiguous. But the social policy underlying the 1988 extension of security of tenure under para 2 to the survivor of couples living together as husband and wife is equally applicable to the survivor of homosexual couples living together in a close and stable relationship. In this circumstance I see no reason to doubt that application of s 3 to para 2 has the effect that para 2 should be read and given effect to as though the survivor of such a homosexual couple were the surviving spouse of the original tenant. Reading para 2 in this way would have the result that cohabiting heterosexual couples and cohabiting heterosexual couples would be treated alike for the purposes of succession as a statutory tenant. This would eliminate the discriminatory effect of para 2 and would do so consistently with the social policy underlying para 2. The precise form of words read in for this purpose is of no significance. It is their substantive effect which matters.

For these reasons I agree with the decision of the Court of Appeal. I would dismiss this appeal."

Lord Steyn:

"My Lords, in my view the Court of Appeal came to the correct conclusion. I agree with the conclusions and reasons of my noble and learned friends Lord Nicholls of Birkenhead, Lord Rodger of Earlsferry and Baroness Hale of Richmond. In the light of those opinions, I will not comment on the case generally. . . ."

Lord Millett:

". . . I agree with all my noble and learned friends, whose speeches I have had the advantage of reading in draft, that such discriminatory treatment of homosexual couples is incompatible with their rights under the European Convention for the Protection of Human Rights and Fundamental Freedoms 1950 (as set out in Sch 1 to the Human Rights Act 1998) and cannot be justified by any identifiable legitimate aim. I am, moreover, satisfied by the powerful and convincing speech of my noble and learned friend Baroness Hale of Richmond that for the reasons she gives such treatment is not only incompatible with the convention but is unacceptable in a modern democratic society at the beginning of the 21st century. This is not to say that it was always, or even until fairly recently, unacceptable; but times change, and with them society's perceptions change also (a commonplace usually dignified by being rendered in Latin).

It follows that, unless the court can apply s 3 of the 1998 Act to extend the reach of para 2(2) to the survivor of a couple of the same sex, it must consider making a declaration of incompatibility under s 4. The making of such a declaration is in the court's discretion (s 4 provides only that the court 'may' make one); and it may be a matter for debate whether it would be appropriate to do so at a time when not merely has the Government announced its intention to bring forward corrective legislation in due course (as in *Bellinger v Bellinger* [2003] UKHL 21, [2003] 2 All ER 593, [2003] 2 AC 467) but Parliament is currently engaged in enacting remedial legislation. It is, however, unnecessary to enter upon this question, for there is a clear majority in favour of the view that s 3 can be applied to interpret para 2(2) in a way which renders legislative intervention unnecessary.

I have the misfortune to be unable to agree with this conclusion. I have given long and anxious consideration to the question whether, in the interests of unanimity, I should suppress my dissent, but I have come to the conclusion that I should not. The question is of great constitutional importance, for it goes to the relationship between the legislature and the judiciary, and hence ultimately to the supremacy of Parliament. Sections 3 and 4 of the 1998 Act were carefully crafted to preserve the existing constitutional doctrine, and any application of the ambit of s 3 beyond its proper scope subverts it. This is not to say that the doctrine of Parliamentary supremacy is sacrosanct, but only that any change in a fundamental constitutional principle should be the consequence of deliberate legislative action and not judicial activism, however well meaning. . . .

It is obvious that, if para 2(2) of Sch 1 to the Rent Act 1977 as amended had referred expressly to 'a person of the opposite sex' who was living with the original tenant as his or her husband or wife, it would not be possible to bring the paragraph into conformity with the convention by resort to s 3. The question is whether the words 'of the opposite sex' are implicit; for if they are, then same result must follow. Reading the paragraph as referring to persons whether of the same or opposite sex would equally contradict the legislative intent in either case. I agree that the operation of s 3 does not depend critically upon the form of words found in the statute; the court is not engaged in a parlour game. But it does depend upon identifying the essential features of the legislative scheme; and these must be gathered in part at least from the words that Parliament has chosen to use. Drawing the line between the express and the implicit would be to engage in precisely that form of semantic lottery to which the majority rightly object.

In the present case both the language of para 2(2) and its legislative history show that the essential feature of the relationship which Parliament had in contemplation was an open relationship between persons of the opposite sex. I take the language first. Para 2(1) provides that 'the surviving spouse' of the deceased tenant shall succeed to the statutory tenancy. The word 'spouse' means a party to a lawful marriage. It may refer indifferently to a lawfully wedded husband or a lawfully wedded wife, and to this extent is not gender specific. But it is gender specific in relation to the other party to the relationship. Marriage is the lawful union of a man and a woman. It is a legal relationship between persons of the opposite sex. A man's spouse must be a woman; a woman's spouse must be a man. This is of the very essence of the relationship, which need not be loving, sexual, stable, faithful, long-lasting, or contented. Although it may be brought to an end as a legal relationship only by death or an order of the court, its demise as a factual relationship will usually have ended long before that.

Another basic feature of marriage is that it is an openly acknowledged relationship. From the earliest times marriage has involved a public commitment by the parties to each other. Whether attended by elaborate ceremonial or relatively informal, and whether religious or secular, its essence consists of a public acknowledgment of mutual commitment. Even primitive societies demand this, because the relationship does not concern only the immediate parties to it. The law may enable them to dispense with formalities, but not with public commitment. In some Polynesian societies, it is said, young men and women marry by the simple process of taking a meal together in public.

Paragraph 2(2) provides that a person who was living with the original tenant 'as his or her wife or husband' shall be treated as 'the spouse of the original tenant'. Mathematically there are four possibilities: 'his wife', 'her wife', 'her husband' and 'his husband'. But two of these are nonsense. A man cannot have a husband; and a woman cannot have a wife. In order to be treated as the spouse of the original tenant, a person must have been living openly with the tenant as his wife or her husband. In any given case, of course, only one person can qualify. If the tenant was a man, that person must have been his wife or have lived with him as his wife; if a woman, he must have been her husband or lived with her as such. The para is gender-specific.

It seems clear that Parliament contemplated an open relationship, whether legal (para 2(1)) or de facto (para 2(2)), the essential feature of which is that, unlike other relationships, it subsists and can subsist only between persons of the opposite sex. A loving relationship between persons of the same sex may share many of the features of a de facto marriage. It may, as Baroness Hale describes it, be 'marriage-like'; but it is not even de facto a marriage, because it lacks the defining feature of marriage.

In my opinion the words 'of the opposite sex' are unmistakably implicit. Although not expressed in terms, they are manifest on the face of the statute. The parties are not required merely to live together but to do so *as husband and wife*. They are not merely given the same rights as married persons but are treated as if they were married persons. If the draftsman had inserted the words 'being of the opposite sex' expressly he would have produced a comical tautology. If he had inserted the words 'whether of the same or opposite sex' he would have produced a self-contradictory nonsense. Persons cannot be or be treated as married to each other or live together as husband and wife unless they are of the opposite sex. It is noticeable that, now that Parliament is introducing remedial legislation, it has not sought to do anything as silly as to treat same sex relationships as marriages, whether legal or de facto. It pays them the respect to which they are entitled by treating them as conceptually different but entitled to equality of treatment. . . .

The present case is concerned with the second change: the introduction of para 2(2). This was compelled by changes in society. Couples are increasingly living together openly as man and wife without actually marrying. It is possible that this will become the norm rather than the exception. To extend the privileges of marriage to those who choose not to marry was formerly highly controversial; it was thought by many to undermine the status of marriage. It is less controversial today. By 1988 Parliament considered that it was sufficiently acceptable to enact it in legislation.

By enacting para 2(2), therefore, Parliament was responding to changes in society. The timing of such a response is, under our constitutional arrangements, peculiarly a matter for the legislature and not the judiciary. Parliament's policy, however, had not changed. The survivor, whether a spouse or merely treated as a spouse, should still have the right to succeed to the statutory tenancy by virtue of his or her status. The difference was that he or she no longer had to prove that the relationship was recognised by law; it was sufficient that it existed in fact. The claimant no longer had to produce a marriage certificate; it was sufficient that he or she and the deceased tenant had lived openly together as husband and wife. This probably was seen as entrenching on the landlord's rights, for it must have been far from clear in 1988 that the 'common law wife' or husband was a member of the other party's family. But landlords do not ask to see their tenants' marriage certificates; and the encroachment, if any, was easily justifiable.

The expression 'living together as man and wife' or 'as husband and wife' is in general use and well under-stood. It does not mean living together as lovers whether of the same or the opposite sex. It connotes persons who have openly set up home together as man and wife. While other factors may be significant where the question arises between the parties themselves, in a context such as the present it must depend largely if not exclu-sively on outward appearances. It cannot depend on the relationship being a happy, or long-lasting, or stable one. This would be contrary to the Parliament's long-standing policy: the survivor must succeed by virtue of his or her status. He or she is to be treated as having been the spouse of the original tenant because that is what, to all intents and purposes and to all outward appearances, the claimant was. This is, of course, not to say that they must hold themselves out as husband and wife: couples who live together as husband and wife rarely do so. It means only that they must appear to the outside world as if they were husband and wife.

There is, indeed, a paradox at the heart of modern society. For centuries the civil and canon law, the common law of Europe as it has been called, did not require any form of religious or secular ceremony to constitute a marriage. Persons who openly set up home together and lived together as man and wife were presumed to be married; and if they had consummated the marriage they *were* married; marriage was by habit and repute. The combined effect of the Council of Trent and the Marriage Acts put an end to all that. But there is nothing new in treating men and women who live openly together as husband and wife as if they were married; it is a reversion to an older tradition.

By 1988 Parliament, therefore, had successively widened the scope of para 2(1). First applying only to the tenant's widow, it was extended first to his or her surviving spouse and later to a person who had lived with the tenant as his or her spouse though without actually contracting a legally binding marriage. The common feature of all these relationships is that they are open relationships between persons of the opposite sex. Persons who set up home together may be husband and wife or live together as husband and wife; they may be lovers; or brother and sister; or friends; or fellow students; or share a common economic interest; or one may be economi-cally dependent on the other. But Parliament did not extend the right to persons who set up home together; but only to those who did so *as husband and wife*.

Couples of the same sex can no more live together as husband and wife than they can live together as brother and sister. To extend the para to persons who set up home as lovers would have been a major cat-egory extension. It would have been highly controversial in 1988 and was not then required by the convention. The practice of ontracting states was far from uniform; and Parliament was entitled to take the view that any further extension of para (2) could wait for another day. One step at a time is a defensible legislative policy which the courts should respect. Housing Acts come before Parliament with some frequency; and Parliament was entitled to take the view that the question could be revisited without any great delay. It is just as important for legislatures not to proceed faster than society can accept as it is for judges; and under our constitutional arrangements the pace of change is for Parliament.

In my opinion all these questions are essentially questions of social policy which should be left to Parliament. For the reasons I have endeavoured to state it is in my view not open to the courts to foreclose them by adopting an interpretation of the existing legislation which it not only does not bear but which is manifestly inconsistent with it.

I would allow the appeal.

Lord Rodger of Earlsferry:

"My Lords, I have had the advantage of considering the speeches of my noble and learned friends, Lord Nicholls of Birkenhead, Lord Steyn and Baroness Hale of Richmond, in draft. I agree with them and would accordingly dismiss the appeal. . . ."

Baroness Hale of Richmond:

"My Lords, it is not so very long ago in this country that people might be refused access to a so-called 'public' bar because of their sex or the colour of their skin; that a woman might automatically be paid three quarters of what a man was paid for doing exactly the same job; that a landlady offering rooms to let might lawfully put a 'no blacks' notice in her window. We now realise that this was wrong. It was wrong because the sex or colour of the person was simply irrelevant to the choice which was being made: to whether he or she would be a fit and proper person to have a drink with others in a bar, to how well she might do the job, to how good a tenant or lodger he might be. It was wrong because it depended on stereotypical assumptions about what a woman or a black person might be like, assumptions which had nothing to do with the qualities of the individual involved: even if there were any reason to believe that more women than men made bad customers this was no justification for discriminating against all women. It was wrong because it was based on an irrelevant characteristic which the woman or the black did not choose and could do nothing about.

When this country legislated to ban both race and sex discrimination, there were some who thought such matters trivial, but of course they were not trivial to the people concerned. Still less trivial are the rights and freedoms set out in the European Convention for the Protection of Human Rights and Fundamental Freedoms 1950 (as set out in Sch 1 to the Human Rights Act 1998). The state's duty under art 14, to secure that those rights and freedoms are enjoyed without discrimination based on such suspect grounds, is fundamental to the scheme of the convention as a whole. It would be a poor human rights instrument indeed if it obliged the state to respect the homes or private lives of one group of people but not the homes or private lives of another.

Such a guarantee of equal treatment is also essential to democracy. Democracy is founded on the principle that each individual has equal value. Treating some as automatically having less value than others not only causes pain and distress to that person but also violates his or her dignity as a human being. The essence of the convention, as has often been said, is respect for human dignity and human freedom: see *Pretty v United Kingdom* (2002) 12 BHRC 149 at 184 (para 65). Second, such treatment is damaging to society as a whole. Wrongly to assume that some people have talent and others do not is a huge waste of human resources. It also damages social cohesion, creating not only an under-class, but an under-class with a rational grievance. Third, it is the reverse of the rational behaviour we now expect of government and the state. Power must not be exercised arbitrarily. If distinctions are to be drawn, particularly upon a group basis, it is an important discipline to look for a rational basis for those distinctions. Finally, it is a purpose of all human rights instruments to secure the protection of the essential rights of members of minority groups, even when they are unpopular with the majority. Democracy values everyone equally even if the majority does not. . . .

We are not here concerned with a difference in treatment between married and unmarried couples. The European Court of Human Rights accepts that the protection of the 'traditional family' is in principle a legitimate aim: see *Karner v Austria* (2003) 14 BHRC 674, at 682 (para 40). The traditional family is constituted by marriage. The convention itself, in art 12, singles out the married family for special protection by guaranteeing to everyone the right to marry and found a family. Had para 2 of Sch 1 to the Rent Act 1977 stopped at protecting the surviving spouse, it might have been easier to say that a homosexual couple were not in an analogous situation. But it did not. It extended the protection to survivors of a relationship which was not marriage but was sufficiently like marriage to qualify for the same protection. It has therefore to be asked whether opposite and same-sex survivors are in an analogous situation for this purpose.

There are several modern statutes which extend a particular benefit or a particular burden, granted to or imposed upon the parties to a marriage, to people who are or were living together 'as husband and wife': see *e.g.* s 62(1) of the Family Law Act 1996 and s 137(1) of the Social Security Contributions and Benefits Act 1992. Working out whether a particular couple are or were in such a relationship is not always easy. It is a matter of judgement in which several factors are taken into account. Holding themselves out as married is one of these, and if a heterosexual couple do so, it is likely that they will be held to be living together as such. But it is not a pre-requisite in the other private and public law contexts and I see no reason why it should be in this one. What matters most is the essential quality of the relationship, its marriage-like intimacy, stability, and social and financial interdependence. Homosexual relationships can have exactly the same qualities of intimacy, stability and inter-dependence that heterosexual relationships do.

It has not been suggested to us that the nature of the sexual intimacies each enjoys is a relevant difference. Nor can the possibility of holding oneself out as a legally married couple be a relevant difference here. Homosexuals cannot hold themselves out as legally married, but they can if they wish present themselves to the world as if they were married. Many now go through ceremonies of commitment which have the same social and emotional purpose as wedding ceremonies—to declare the strength and permanence of their commitment to one another, their families and friends. If the Civil Partnership Bill now before Parliament becomes law, an equivalent status will be available to them.

The relevant difference which has been urged upon us is that a heterosexual couple may have children together whereas a homosexual couple cannot. But this too cannot be a relevant difference in determining whether a relationship can be considered marriage-like for the purpose of the 1977 Act. First, the capacity to bear or beget children has never been a pre-requisite of a valid marriage in English law. Henry VIII would not otherwise have had the problems he did. Even the capacity to consummate the marriage only matters if one of the parties thinks it matters: if they are both content the marriage is valid. A marriage, let alone a relationship analogous to marriage, can exist without either the presence or the possibility of children from that relationship. Secondly, however, the presence of children is a relevant factor in deciding whether a relationship is marriage-like but if the couple are bringing up children together, it is unlikely to matter whether or not they are the biological children of both parties. Both married and unmarried couples, both homosexual and heterosexual, may bring up children together. One or both may have children from another relationship: this is not at all uncommon in lesbian relationships and the court may grant them a shared residence order so that they may share parental responsibility. A lesbian couple may have children by donor insemination who are brought up as the children of them both: it is not uncommon for each of them to bear a child in this way. A gay or lesbian couple may foster other people's children. When the relevant sections of the Adoption and Children Act 2002 are brought into force, they will be able to adopt: this means that they will indeed have a child together in the eyes of the law. Thirdly, however, there is absolutely no reason to think that the protection given by the 1977 Act to the surviving partner's home was given for the sake of the couple's children. Statutes usually make it plain if they wish to protect minor children. These days, the succession is likely to take place after any children have grown up and left home. Children, whether adult or minor, who are still living in the home may succeed as members of the family under para 3 of the Sch 1. It is the longstanding social and economic interdependence, which may or may not be the product of having brought up children together, that qualifies for the protection of the Act. In the days when the tenant was likely to be a man with a dependent wife, it was understandable that preference was given to the widow over anyone else in the family. But in 1980 that preference was extended to widowers, whether or not they were dependent upon the deceased wife. In 1988 it was extended to the survivor of unmarried marriage-like relationships, again irrespective of sex or financial dependence.

Homosexual couples can have exactly the same sort of interdependent couple relationship as heterosexuals can. Sexual 'orientation' defines the sort of person with whom one wishes to have sexual relations. It requires another person to express itself. Some people, whether heterosexual or homosexual, may be satisfied with casual or transient relationships. But most human beings eventually want more than that. They want love. And with love they often want not only the warmth but also the sense of belonging to one another which is the essence of being a couple. And many couples also come to want the stability and permanence which go with sharing a home and a life together, with or without the children who for many people go to make a family. In this, people of homosexual orientation are no different from people of heterosexual orientation.

It follows that a homosexual couple whose relationship is marriage-like in the same ways that an unmarried heterosexual couple's relationship is marriage-like are indeed in an analogous situation. Any difference in treatment is based upon their sexual orientation. It requires an objective justification if it is to comply with art 14. Whatever the scope for a 'discretionary area of judgment' in these cases may be, there has to be a legitimate aim before a difference in treatment can be justified. But what could be the legitimate aim of singling out heterosexual couples for more favourable treatment than homosexual couples? It cannot be the protection of the traditional family. The traditional family is not protected by granting it a benefit which is denied to people who cannot or will not become a traditional family. What is really meant by the 'protection' of the traditional family is the encouragement of people to form traditional families and the discouragement of people from forming others. There are many reasons why it might be legitimate to encourage people to marry and to discourage them from living together without marrying. These reasons might have justified the Act in stopping short at marriage. Once it went beyond marriage to unmarried relationships, the aim would have to be encouraging one sort of unmarried relationship and discouraging another. The Act does distinguish between unmarried but marriage-like relationships and more transient liaisons. It is easy to see how that might pursue a legitimate aim and easier still to see how it might justify singling out the survivor for preferential succession rights. But, as Buxton LJ ([2002] 4 All ER 1162 at [21]), pointed out, it is difficult to see how heterosexuals will be encouraged to form and maintain such marriage-like relationships by the knowledge that the equivalent benefit is being denied to homosexuals. The distinction between heterosexual and homosexual couples might be aimed at discouraging homosexual relationships generally. But that cannot now be regarded as a legitimate aim. It is inconsistent with the right to respect for private life accorded to 'everyone', including homosexuals, by art 8 since *Dudgeon v UK* (1981) 4 EHRR 149. If it is not legitimate to discourage homosexual relationships, it cannot be legitimate to discourage stable, committed, marriage-like homosexual relationships of the sort which qualify the survivor to succeed to the home. Society wants its intimate relationships, particularly but not only if there are children involved, to be stable, responsible and secure. It is the transient, irresponsible and insecure relationships which cause us so much concern.

I have used the term 'marriage-like' to describe the sort of relationship which meets the statutory test of living together 'as husband and wife'. Once upon a time it might have been difficult to apply those words to a same-sex relationship because both in law and in reality the roles of the husband and wife were so different and those differences were defined by their genders. That is no longer the case. The law now differentiates between husband and wife in only a very few and unimportant respects. Husbands and wives decide for themselves who will go out to work and who will do the homework and child care. Mostly each does some of each. The roles are interchangeable. There is thus no difficulty in applying the term 'marriage-like' to same-sex relationships. With the greatest respect to my noble and learned friend, Lord Millett, I also see no difficulty in applying the term 'as husband and wife' to persons of the same sex living together in such a relationship. As Mr Sales, for the Secretary of State, said in argument, this is not even a marginal case. It is well within the bounds of what is possible under s 3(1) of the Human Rights Act 1998. If it is possible so to interpret the term in order to make it compliant with convention rights, it is our duty under s 3(1) so to do.

Hence I agree that this appeal should be dismissed for the reasons given by my noble and learned friend, Lord Nicholls of Birkenhead. I also agree with the opinions of my noble and learned friends, Lord Steyn and Lord Rodger of Earlsferry, on the scope and application of s 3 of the 1998 Act."

Questions

1. Why does Lord Millett conclude that two people "cannot be or be treated as married to each other or live together as husband and wife unless they are of the opposite sex"? Is the opposing proposition necessarily "self-contradictory nonsense" and "silly", as Lord Millett describes?

2. Does Lord Millett make a convincing argument that this case raises the important issue of the supremacy of Parliament? Do you think the Law Lords should have left this issue to Parliament to correct through the Civil Partnership Act?

3. How does Baroness Hale attempt to demonstrate that this case raises issues of fundamental human rights? What analogies does she draw to support her reasoning? Does she ignore the "competing social policies" that Lord Hobhouse found to be important in *Fitzpatrick*?

4. Why is Lord Millett concerned that the speeches of the majority of the Law Lords may leave unclear whether qualification for the tenancy "is dependent on status and not merit"? What does he mean by this paragraph?

V. Interpretive Policies and Presumptions

Throughout the history of statutory interpretation, numerous presumptions—both linguistic and policy-based—have grown up in the law. It is important that you are familiar with them so that you can recognise whether they are relevant to a particular case.

Peter Goodrich, *Reading the Law* (Oxford: Blackwell, 1986), pp.57–59:

"Special rules prescribing how certain commonly used combinations of words are to be interpreted have arisen. For example, the *ejusdem generis* rule deals with the combination of specific and general terms. It requires that where three or more specific examples are followed by a general word, then the parameters of the general category are to be determined by the common characteristics of the specific words (*Palmer v Snow* [1900] 1 QB 725, at 727). The *noscitur a sociis* rule prescribes that words are to take their meaning from their context (*Muir v Keay* [1875] LR 10 QB 594). A further category of aids to interpretation are general principles by which the task of interpretation is to be assisted. Many of the principles are general guides describing the attributes of the activity of legislation. For example in *Morris v Beardmore* [1980] 2 All ER 753, the court had to consider the legislative provisions relating to the taking of specimens of breath by the police. The dispute related to the power of the police to enter private premises to effect a breathalyser test. In interpreting the statutory provision, Lord Scarman made the following reference to a general principle:

> 'When for the detection, prevention or prosecution of crime Parliament confers on a constable a power or right which curtails the rights of others it is to be expected that Parliament intended the curtailment to extend no further than its express authorisation. A constable, who in purported execution of his duty has infringed rights which Parliament has not expressly curtailed, will not, therefore, be able to show that he has acted in execution of his duty, unless (and this will be rare) it can be shown by necessary implication that Parliament must have intended to authorise such infringement (763 b–c).'

The narrow construction of penal provisions is another example of a similar principle, as seen in *R. v. Cuthbertson* [1980] 2 All ER 41 where Lord Diplock applied a restrictive principle to the interpretation of the Misuse of Drugs Act 1971, s.23 in the following fashion: 'the fact that the section is a penal provision is in itself a reason for hesitating before ascribing to phrases used in it a meaning broader than they would normally bear' (404). The above selection of secondary techniques is not exhaustive; it is merely a selection to draw attention to various categories of method and technique.

A final matter which demands consideration again focuses upon the relationship between the judiciary and the legislature. As has already been noted, the act of interpretation through the ascription of meaning to the text may be viewed as a law-making function. Whilst reference has been made to strategies available to the courts which purport to deny the law-making nature of interpretation, such strategies are not completely successful; even in explicit practice, successive readings purporting to follow a literal interpretation, for example, may not be in total agreement as to the meaning of the text. In the event of such an outcome a question arises as to the status of the respective interpretations. Suggestions that one judicial interpretation may or must be privileged can be read to imply that the interpretation is a source of law superior to the actual words of the statutory text, which directly challenges the position of the text as the supreme source of law. In *Ogden Industries v. Lucas* [1970] AC 113, Lord Upjohn considered the matter and concluded:

> 'It is quite clear that judicial statements as to the construction and intention of an Act must never be allowed to supplant or supersede its proper construction and *courts must beware of falling into the error of treating the law to be laid down by the judge in construing the Act rather than found in the Act itself*. No doubt a decision on particular words binds inferior courts on the construction of those words on similar facts but beyond that the observations of the judges on the construction of statutes may be of the greatest help and guidance but are entitled to no more than respect and cannot absolve the court from its duty in exercising an independent judgment [emphasis added by Goodrich].'

His observations provide a striking illustration of the narrow political line formally espoused by the judiciary, one which in the last instance predictably asserts the superiority of the legal text over its interpreters and wittingly or unwittingly denies that the ritual claim to 'literal obedience' to the statutory text may mask any number of strategies of interpretation."

The presumptions of interpretation can be illustrated through examples.

Gregory v Fearn [1953] 1 W.L.R. 974, CA.

"Appeal from Judge Caporn sitting at Nottingham County Court.

The [claimant], A. R. Gregory, acting in the course of his normal business as an estate agent, on April 2, 1952, which was a Sunday, signed a contract of agency for the sale of a house, whereby the vendor, the defendant, George Fearn, agreed to pay to the [claimant] £100 when the property was sold, the property to be deemed to have been sold 'and the commission payable on the receipt of a deposit or a purchase agreement being entered into by a purchaser.' Subsequently, the estate agent brought proceedings to recover the commission, alleging that he had introduced a purchaser, one Owen, who had entered into a purchase agreement, but had subsequently refused to complete because he found that he would not be able to use the premises for business purposes. Owen alleged that the [claimant] had misrepresented to him that it could be so used.

Judge Caporn held that as the contract appointing the [claimant] agent for the vendor had been made on a Sunday and involved the doing by the [claimant] of his ordinary business as an estate agent, it offended against section 1 of the Sunday Observance Act, 1677, and, consequently, that the [claimant] could not rely on it. He further decided, on other grounds which are not material to this report, that the [claimant] would not have been able to establish his claim to the commission even if the contract had been valid.

The [claimant] appealed.

Evershed M.R., after referring to the facts: Judge Caporn concluded against the [claimant] on the ground among others, that the agreement fell within the prohibition of section 1 of the Sunday Observance Act, 1677, as having involved the doing on the Lord's Day of business or work by a tradesman, that is, an estate agent, in his ordinary calling.

On the view which I take, it is not strictly necessary to decide that point. But it seems to me, as at presently advised, that Mr Heald is right when he says that an estate agent is not a 'tradesman' within the contemplation of that section, even if the execution by him of a contract of this kind was the doing of business or work in his ordinary calling. At first sight, Mr Heald's argument appeared to be difficult, because the formula in section 1 of the Act of 1677 is 'no tradesman, artificer, workman, labourer, or other person whatsoever'; and assuming that an estate agent is not a tradesman, he would be, prima facie, within the formula 'other person whatsoever.' It has, however, long been established that those words 'other person whatsoever' are to be construed *ejusdem generis* with those which precede it: so that, for the defendant to succeed on this point, it must be shown that an estate agent is a tradesman or something sufficiently like a tradesman to be covered by the ejusdem generis rule. . . ."

[Evershed M.R. dismissed the appeal. Birkett L.J. and Romer L.J. concurred].

McBoyle v United States 293 U.S. 25 (1930).

Mr Justice Holmes

[Mr Justice Holmes delivered the opinion of the US Supreme Court:]

"The petitioner was convicted of transporting from Ottawa, Illinois, to Guymon, Oklahoma, an airplane that he knew to have been stolen, and was sentenced to serve three years' imprisonment and to pay a fine of $2,000. The judgment was affirmed by the Circuit Court of Appeals for the Tenth Circuit 43 F (2d) 273. A writ of certiorari was granted by this Court on the question whether the National Motor Vehicle Theft Act applies to aircraft. . . . That Act provides:

> 'Sec 2. That when used in this Act: (a) The term "motor vehicle" shall include an automobile, automobile truck, automobile wagon, motor cycle, or any other self-propelled vehicle not designed for running on rails; . . . Sec 3. That whoever shall transport or cause to be transported in interstate or foreign commerce a motor vehicle, knowing the same to have been stolen, shall be punished by a fine of not more than $5,000, or by imprisonment of not more than five years, or both.'

Section 2 defines the motor vehicles of which the transportation in interstate commerce is punished in section 3. The question is the meaning of the word 'vehicle' in the phrase 'any other self-propelled vehicle not designed for running on rails.' No doubt etymologically it is possible to use the word to signify a conveyance working on land, water or air, and sometimes legislation extends the use in that direction. . . . But in everyday speech 'vehicle' calls up the picture of a thing moving on land. . . . For after including automobile truck, automobile wagon and motor cycle, the words 'any other self-propelled vehicle not designed for running on rails' still indicate that a vehicle in the popular sense, that is a vehicle running on land, is the theme. It is a vehicle that runs, not something, not commonly called a vehicle, that flies. Airplanes were well known in 1919, when this statute was passed; but it is admitted that they were not mentioned in the reports or in the debates in Congress. It is impossible to read words that so carefully enumerate the different forms of motor vehicles and have no reference of any kind to aircraft, as including airplanes under a term that usage more and more precisely confines to a different class. . . .

Although it is not likely that a criminal will carefully consider the text of the law before he murders or steals, it is reasonable that a fair warning should be given to the world in language that the common world will understand, of what the law intends to do if a certain line is passed. To make the warning fair, so far as possible the line should be clear. When a rule of conduct is laid down in words that evoke in the common mind only the picture of vehicles moving on land, the statute should not be extended to aircraft, simply because it may seem to us that a similar policy applies, or upon the speculation that, if the legislature had thought of it, very likely broader words would have been used.

Judgment reversed."

Questions

1. Do you think that the presumptions of interpretation dictate the results of cases? As a judge, would you find them to be useful?

2. To what extent do you think the presumptions of interpretation are a matter of "common sense"? Do you think it makes sense that an aeroplane was found not to be a vehicle for the purposes of the statute? Why?

7

STATUTORY INTERPRETATION: THE IMPACT OF THE LAW OF THE EUROPEAN UNION AND EUROPEAN HUMAN RIGHTS LAW

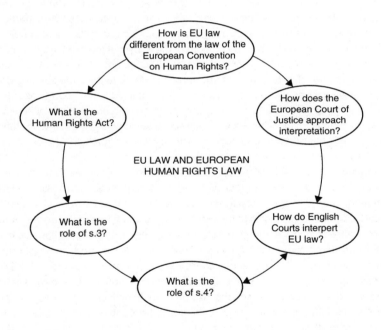

In this chapter, we look at the impact of the law of the European Union and the European Convention on Human Rights on statutory interpretation. By the end of this chapter, you should:

- appreciate how approaches to the interpretation of European law differ from the common law tradition;

- recognise the issues of interpretation raised by the Human Rights Act for our courts;

- be able to analyse critically the human rights jurisprudence of our courts;

- be able to argue in favour of your preferred approach to interpretation under the Human Rights Act;

- appreciate and be able to evaluate the ways in which the Human Rights Act can give rise to critical and sceptical reactions to rights.

I. Statutory Interpretation in the European Court of Justice

We looked at the constitutional implications of membership in the European Union in Ch.4. Now, we examine the implications of membership for statutory interpretation. We begin with the European Court of Justice which, along with the Court of First Instance, is the judicial arm of the EU.

Paul Craig and Gráinne de Búrca, *EU Law: Text, Cases and Materials*, 3rd edn (Oxford: Clarendon Press, 2003), pp.98–99:

"In the years of so-called institutional malaise or stagnation, the Court arguably played a 'political' role through law, attempting to render the Treaty effective when its provisions had not been implemented as required by the Community, and to render secondary legislation effective when it had not been properly implemented by the Member States. It took an active part in the creation of the internal market through the litigation which came before it, by requiring the 'negative' removal of national barriers to trade, at a time when progress towards completing the Single Market through positive legislative harmonization was hindered by institutional inaction.

The Court has achieved the hobby-horse status which it occupies amongst European lawyers as much on account of its reasoning and methodology as on account of the impact of its decisions. Its approach to interpretation is generally described as purposive or teleological, although not in the sense of seeking the purpose or aim of the authors of the text. The fact that *the travaux préparatoires* to the original Treaties were never published meant these were never used as a source, and this is reflected in the Court's case law. In the case of secondary legislation, although the discussions at Council and Commission meetings are not published, declarations and extracts from the minutes have occasionally been relied on as aids to interpretation before the Court. Occasionally the ECJ has referred to such material for assistance, but in most cases it has denied its relevance if it does not appear in the text of the legislation itself.

Rather than adopting a narrower historical–purposive approach, the Court tends to examine the whole context in which a particular provision is situated, and gives the interpretation most likely to further what the Court considers that provision in its context sought to achieve. Often this is far from a literal interpretation of the Treaty or of legislation in question, even to the extent of flying in the face of the express language. This aspect of the Court's methodology has attracted considerable criticism, although it has also had robust defenders from amongst the academic community, from its former personnel, and from amongst practitioners.

Probably the most famous of the Court's earlier critics was Hjalte Rasmussen, whose 1986 critique of the Court's policy-making was one of the earliest sustained attacks on what the author viewed as its illegitimate practices. His thesis was that the Court has sought 'inspiration in guidelines which are essentially political in nature and hence, not judicially applicable. This is the root of judicial activism which may be a usurpation of power'.[1] He did not criticize all 'activism', but rather that which he believed to have lost popular legitimacy. In discussing Judge Pescatore's celebrated comment about the judges of the early ECJ having '*une certaine ideé de l'Europe*' of their own, Rasmussen's book, using terms which, although written more than fifteen years ago, could equally well be used today, referred to 'society's declining taste for a precipitated process of integration'.

There were mixed reactions to Rasmussen's strongly argued and polemical work from an academic community which had largely been supportive of the Court's strategy. Mauro Cappelletti in particular argued that Rasmussen's critique lacked a historical dimension, that any constitutional court should have the courage to enforce its 'higher law' against temporary pressures, and that the ECJ's vision 'far from being arbitrary, is fully

---

[1]   H. Rasmussen, *On Law and Policy in the European Court of Justice* (Nijhoff, 1986), 62.

legitimate, for it is rooted in the text, most particularly in the Preamble and the first articles of the EEC Treaty'. Some years ago a high-profile and more political attack on the methodology of the ECJ was made by Sir Patrick Neill, in his 'case study in judicial activism', in which he argued that the Court was a dangerous institution, skewed by its own policy considerations and driven by an elite mission.

In defence of the Court's 'constitutional' role, however, Advocate General Jacobs has argued that it plays an essential role in preserving the balance between the Community and the Member States, and in developing constitutional principles of judicial review."

A good example of a broad, contextual approach to interpretation can be found in the ECJ's interpretation of the "free movement" provisions of the EC Treaty. The relevant Treaty provision is art.39(3) (formerly 48(3)), which provides that the freedom of movement of workers shall entail the right "(a) to accept offers of employment actually made; (b) to move freely within the territory of the Member States for this purpose . . .". The question was whether this included the right of a citizen of the EC (as it then was) to look for work in another Member State.

R. v Immigration Appeal Tribunal, Ex p. Antonissen **[1991] E.C.R. I–745, ECJ.**

European Court of Justice:

"1.   By an order of 14 June 1989, which was received at the Court on 21 September 1989, the High Court of Justice, Queen's Bench Division, referred to the Court for a preliminary ruling under Article 177 of the EEC Treaty two questions on the interpretation of the provisions of Community law governing the free movement of workers as regards the scope of the right of residence of nationals of Member States seeking employment in another Member State.

2.   The questions arose in proceedings between Mr Gustaff Desiderius Antonissen, a Belgian national, and the Secretary of State for Home Affairs, who on 27 November 1987 decided to deport him from the United Kingdom.

3.   Mr Antonissen arrived in the United Kingdom in October 1984. He had not yet found work there when, on 3 March 1987, he was sentenced by the Liverpool Crown Court to two terms of imprisonment for unlawful possession of cocaine and possession of that drug with intent to supply. He was released on parole on 21 December 1987.

4.   The decision to order Mr Antonissen's deportation was based on section 3(5)(b) of the Immigration Act 1971 ('the 1971 Act'), which authorizes the Secretary of State to deport foreign nationals if he considers that it would be 'conducive to the public good'.

5.   Mr Antonissen lodged an appeal against the Secretary of State's decision with the Immigration Appeal Tribunal. Before the Tribunal Mr Antonissen argued that since he was a Community national he must qualify for the protection afforded by Council Directive 64/221/EEC of 25 February 1964 on the coordination of special measures concerning the movement and residence of foreign nationals which are justified on grounds of public policy, public security or public health. The Tribunal took the view that, since he had been seeking employment in the United Kingdom for more than six months, he could no longer be treated as a Community worker and claim that the directive should apply in his case. The Tribunal based this part of its decision on paragraph 143 of the Statement of Changes in Immigration Rules (HC169), adopted pursuant to the 1971 Act, under which a national of a Member State may be deported if, after six months from admission to the United Kingdom, he has not yet found employment or is not carrying on any other occupation.

6.   His appeal being dismissed, Mr Antonissen made an application for judicial review to the High Court of Justice, Queen's Bench Division, which stayed the proceedings and referred the following questions to the Court of Justice for a preliminary ruling:

'1 For the purpose of determining whether a national of a Member State is to be treated as a
"worker" within the meaning of Article 48 [now 39] of the EEC Treaty when seeking employment
in the territory of another Member State so as to be immune from deportation save in accordance
with Council Directive 64/221 of 25 February 1964, may the legislature of the second Member State
provide that such a national may be required to leave the territory of that State (subject to appeal) if
after six months from admission to that territory he has failed to enter employment?
2 In answering the foregoing question what weight if any is to be attached by a court or tribunal of
a Member State to the declaration contained in the minutes of the meeting of the Council when the
Council adopted Directive 68/36?'

7.   Reference is made to the Report for the Hearing for a fuller account of the facts of the case before the
      national court, the applicable legislation and the written observations submitted to the Court, which are
      mentioned or discussed hereinafter only in so far as is necessary for the reasoning of the Court.

8.   By means of the questions submitted to the Court for a preliminary ruling the national court essentially
      seeks to establish whether it is contrary to the provisions of Community law governing the free move-
      ment of workers for the legislation of a Member State to provide that a national of another Member
      State who entered the first State in order to seek employment may be required to leave the territory of
      that State (subject to appeal) if he has not found employment there after six months.

9.   In that connection it has been argued that, according to the strict wording of Article 48 of the Treaty,
      Community nationals are given the right to move freely within the territory of the Member States for the
      purpose only of accepting offers of employment actually made (Article 48 [now 39] (3)(a) and (b)) whilst
      the right to stay in the territory of a Member State is stated to be for the purpose of employment (Article
      48 [now 39] (3)(c)).

10.   Such an interpretation would exclude the right of a national of a Member State to move freely and to stay
      in the territory of the other Member States in order to seek employment there, and cannot be upheld.

11.   Indeed, as the Court has consistently held, freedom of movement for workers forms one of the founda-
      tions of the Community and, consequently, the provisions laying down that freedom must be given a
      broad interpretation.

12.   Moreover, a strict interpretation of Article 48 [now 39] (3) would jeopardize the actual chances that a
      national of a Member State who is seeking employment will find it in another Member State, and would,
      as a result, make the provision ineffective.

13.   It follows that Article 48 [now 39] (3) must be interpreted as enumerating, in a non-exhaustive way,
      certain rights benefiting nationals of Member States in the context of the free movement of workers and
      that that freedom also entails the right for nationals of Member States to move freely within the terri-
      tory of the other Member States and to stay there for the purposes of seeking employment.

14.   Moreover, this interpretation of the Treaty corresponds to that of the Community legislature, as appears
      from the provisions adopted in order to implement the principle of free movement, in particular Articles
      1 and 5 of Regulation No 1612/68/EEC of the Council of 15 October 1968 on freedom of movement for
      workers within the Community, which presuppose that Community nationals are entitled to move in
      order to look for employment, and hence to stay, in another Member State.

15.   It must therefore be ascertained whether the right, under Article 48 [now 39] and the provisions of
      Regulation No 1612/68, to stay in a Member State for the purposes of seeking employment can be sub-
      jected to a temporal limitation.

16.   In that regard, it must be pointed out in the first place that the effectiveness of Article 48 [now 39] is
      secured in so far as Community legislation or, in its absence, the legislation of a Member State gives

persons concerned a reasonable time in which to apprise themselves, in the territory of the Member State concerned, of offers of employment corresponding to their occupational qualifications and to take, where appropriate, the necessary steps in order to be engaged.

17.   The national court referred to the declaration recorded in the Council minutes at the time of the adoption of the aforesaid Regulation No 1612/68 and of Council Directive 68/36/EEC (of the same date) on the abolition of restrictions on movement and residence within the Community for workers of Member States and their families. That declaration read as follows:

'Nationals of a Member State as referred to in Article 1 [of the directive] who move to another Member State in order to seek work there shall be allowed a minimum period of three months for the purpose; in the event of their not having found employment by the end of that period, their residence on the territory of this second State may be brought to an end.

However, if the above mentioned persons should be taken charge of by national assistance (social welfare) in the second State during the aforesaid period they may be invited to leave the territory of this second State.'

18.   However, such a declaration cannot be used for the purpose of interpreting a provision of secondary legislation where, as in this case, no reference is made to the content of the declaration in the wording of the provision in question. The declaration therefore has no legal significance. . . .

21.   In the absence of a Community provision prescribing the period during which Community nationals seeking employment in a Member State may stay there, a period of six months, such as that laid down in the national legislation at issue in the main proceedings, does not appear in principle to be insufficient to enable the persons concerned to apprise themselves, in the host Member State, of offers of employment corresponding to their occupational qualifications and to take, where appropriate, the necessary steps in order to be engaged and, therefore, does not jeopardize the effectiveness of the principle of free movement. However, if after the expiry of that period the person concerned provides evidence that he is continuing to seek employment and that he has genuine chances of being engaged, he cannot be required to leave the territory of the host Member State.

22.   It must therefore be stated in reply to the questions submitted by the national court that it is not contrary to the provisions of Community law governing the free movement of workers for the legislation of a Member State to provide that a national of another Member State who entered the first State in order to seek employment may be required to leave the territory of that State (subject to appeal) if he has not found employment there after six months, unless the person concerned provides evidence that he is continuing to seek employment and that he has genuine chances of being engaged."

As you can recognise, the style of the judgment in *Antonissen* is very different from a common law case. As well, the method of interpretation is far from the literal approach characteristic of common law. This method has been criticised, as the following extract demonstrates.

Trevor C. Hartley, "Five forms of uncertainty in European Community law" (1996) 55 C.L.J. 265 at 278:

"As is well known, the European Court adopts a different method of interpretation from that usually followed by English courts. Where a provision is clear and unambiguous, English courts will usually follow the plain meaning of the words used; the European Court, on the other hand, gives much greater emphasis to ensuring that the objective of the measure is attained. In order to do so, it will sometimes depart from the plain meaning.

The objection to this from a constitutional point of view is that it involves the Court taking on a legislative role and revising the work of the legislator. From a more general point of view, it raises the question how the objective of a measure is to be determined. The Treaties express the will of the Member States; most EC legislation is adopted by the Council, which is made up of the representatives of the Member States. In either case, therefore, the objective of a provision must depend on the intention of the Member States. As was said previously, however, the Member States often have no common intention, and are united only in their agreement to adopt a certain form of words. In such a case, an objective cannot be ascribed to the measure beyond that implied by the words themselves.

This question has been discussed recently in another article, in which examples were given of cases in the constitutional sphere in which it was thought that the European Court had departed from the plain meaning of the words used. Here, a different example will be chosen, the *Antonissen* case. The provision in question in that case, Article 48 [now 39] (3) EC, is clear and unambiguous in so far as it concerns persons migrating to find work: it does not cover them. The Court, however, refused to accept that this was the correct interpretation. It gave three reasons: first, that such an interpretation would exclude the right of a Community migrant to move freely to another Member State to seek employment; secondly, that the Court had previously held that provisions—such as Article 48 [now 39]—that lay down the right of free movement of workers must be given a broad interpretation, since such freedom constitutes one of the foundations of the Community; and finally, that a 'strict' interpretation of Article 48 [now 39] (3) 'would jeopardise the actual chances that a national of a Member State who is seeking employment will find it in another Member State, and would, as a result, make the provision ineffective.'

The argument may be set out as follows: first, it is assumed—reasonably enough—that the objective of Article 48 [now 39] is to allow nationals of one Member State to obtain employment in another; secondly, it is assumed—again reasonably—that this will be more difficult if workers cannot travel to another Member State to look for employment on the spot: from these two assumptions the conclusion is drawn that the plain meaning of the words must be ignored so as to ensure that workers have this right.

The objection to this is that it fails to recognise the possibility that, though the authors of the Treaty may have wished to make it easier for Community nationals to work in another Member State, this might not have been the only consideration they had in mind. Law-making almost always involves balancing conflicting interests and objectives. The words of a provision express the way the balance is struck by the legislator. To assume that there is only one objective, or that one objective must be pursued irrespective of all other considerations, is both irresponsible and naïve.

In the case of Article 48 [now 39] EC, another objective that the Member States presumably had in mind was to avoid an influx of unemployed migrants who might be unable to support themselves. The wording of Article 48 [now 39] (3) reflects the balance struck by the Member States when they signed the Treaty in 1957. No doubt the situation changed as the years passed, and by 1968 the Member States were willing to take a further step. They could have done this by granting a right of entry in the legislation they adopted that year. They did not do this. Instead, they made the 'secret' declaration. The purpose of this was apparently to ensure that the right was granted under national law, rather than under Community law, thus allowing the Member States to decide its precise extent. This may have represented a compromise between those Member States that wanted to give further rights to migrant workers and those that were concerned about the economic and social consequences.

Where the text of a provision is itself unclear, the European Court's method of interpretation may not lead to any greater uncertainty; in some cases, indeed, it may be a good solution. Where the words of the provision are clear, however, it produces uncertainty, since it is never possible to predict with accuracy what the Court will regard as the objectives of the provision, what it will consider necessary to ensure their attainment and how far it will be willing to go in departing from the words of the provision in order to achieve those objectives."

Another unique characteristic of European legislation is the fact that there are many official languages of the EU. As Millett argues:

"Because all . . . language versions are authentic, the literal meaning of a Community legislative text in one language cannot be relied on as a conclusive guide to its meaning. It has to be compared with the other language versions, and in the practice of the Court of Justice—usually also checked against another criterion of interpretation, such as the purpose of the provision in question. Thus the multilingual nature of Community legislation necessarily reduces the importance of the literal method of interpretation, which contrasts with the predominant place it enjoys in the interpretation of British domestic legislation."[2]

It is also important that "every provision of Community law must be placed in its context and interpreted in the light of the provisions of Community law as a whole, regard being had to the objectives thereof and to its state of evolution at the date on which the provision in question is to be applied."[3] Finally, "although the Treaties contain the fundamental provisions on which the Community's legal order is based, when it comes to Regulations, Directives and Decisions, the Community know no doctrine of legislative supremacy. For example, the Court may quash Community legislation which contravenes the general principles of Community law."[4]

II. THE IMPACT OF EUROPEAN COMMUNITY LAW ON INTERPRETATION IN DOMESTIC COURTS

As we have already seen, the principle of the supremacy of Parliament has been modified by the courts in light of Britain's membership in the European Community and European Union. In Ch.4, we looked at the decision of the European Court of Justice and House of Lords in *Factortame No.2* [1991] 1 All E.R. 70, in which it was held to be the duty of national courts to override rules of national law which were in conflict with directly enforceable rules of European Community law. Our focus in this section is on a distinct, but related, issue: the approaches which domestic courts take to the interpretation of European legislation. As we discussed in the previous section, the European Court of Justice, in keeping with its continental European roots, takes a rather different approach to statutory interpretation than is typical of a common law court. Thus, we can ask, to what extent should (and do) common law courts adopt such an approach to statutory interpretation when dealing with EC legislation? Although national courts sometimes will refer questions concerning the interpretation of EC law to the ECJ pursuant to art.234 (formerly 177) of the EC Treaty, in some cases they will interpret legislation themselves in light of European law. An early, and at that time unorthodox approach, was advocated many years ago by Lord Denning:

> "Seeing these differences, what are the English courts to do when they are faced with a problem of interpretation? They must follow the European pattern. No longer must they examine the words in meticulous detail. No longer must they argue about the precise grammatical sense. They must look to the purpose or intent. To quote the words of the European Court in the *Da Costa*[5] case: they must limit themselves to deducing from 'the wording and the spirit of the treaty the meaning of the Community rules . . .'. They must not confine themselves to the English text. They must consider, if need be, all the authentic texts, of which there are now eight. They must divine the spirit of the treaty and gain inspiration from it. If they find a gap, they must fill it as best they can. They must do what the framers of the instrument would have done if they had thought about it. So we must do the same. Those are the principles, as I understand it, on which the European Court acts."[6]

For Lord Denning, Britain's entry into the European Community provided a handy justification for a liberal, "gap-filling" approach to statutory interpretation; one which was more in keeping with his long-preferred method.

Some years later, Lord Diplock pointed to both similarities and differences between the approach of the European Court of Justice and English courts:

---

[2] Timothy Millett, "Rules of interpretation of EEC legislation" (1989) 10 *Statute Law Review* 163.

[3] *CILFIT v Ministry of Health* [1982] E.C.R. 3415.

[4] Ian McLeod, *Legal Method* (5th ed., Palgrave Macmillan, Basingstoke, 2005) p.327.

[5] [1963] C.M.L.R. 224 at 237.

[6] *H.P. Bulmer Ltd and another v J. Bollinger SA and others* [1974] 2 All E.R.1226 at 1237–1238, CA.

"The European court, in contrast to English courts, applies teleological rather than historical methods to the interpretation of the Treaties and other Community legislation. It seeks to give effect to what it conceives to be the spirit rather than the letter of the Treaties; sometimes, indeed, to an English judge, it may seem to the exclusion of the letter. It views the Communities as living and expanding organisms and the interpretation of the provisions of the Treaties as changing to match their growth. For these reasons the European Court does not apply the doctrine of precedent to its own decisions as rigidly as does an English court. Nevertheless, as any browsing in the Common Market Law Reports will show, the European Court too seeks to maintain consistency in its decisions in the interest of legal certainty. Consequently in the opinions of the Advocates General and the judgments of the court itself, citations of previous judgments in the court are as frequent as citations of previous authority in judgments of English courts. Thus, when there is a *cursus curiae*, a series of decisions to the same effect, or what is described in the court's own rules. . . as 'an established body of case law' an English court if the case before it is one to which an established body of case law plainly applies, may properly take the view that no real question of interpretation is involved that makes reference under article 177 [now 234] necessary in order to give judgment."[7]

In *Henn and Darby*, Lord Diplock also warned of the "danger of an English court applying English canons of statutory construction to the interpretation of the Treaty or, for that matter, of Regulations or Directives".[8]

The issue is made more complex when domestic legislation is enacted in order to fulfil obligations under European Community law. In this situation, courts here may be faced with the task of interpreting law made in this country in order to comply with European law. How should our courts interpret in that situation? The following case represents a judicial response.

Litster and others v Forth Dry Dock and Engineering Co Ltd and another [1989] 1 All E.R. 1134, HL.

Lord Oliver of Aylmerton:

"My Lords, this appeal raises, not for the first time, the broad question of the approach to be adopted by courts in the United Kingdom to domestic legislation enacted in order to give effect to this country's obligations under the EEC Treaty. The legislation with which the appeal is concerned is a statutory instrument made on 14 December 1981 pursuant to para 2(2) of Sch 2 to the European Communities Act 1972 and entitled the Transfer of Undertakings (Protection of Employment) Regulations 1981, SI 1981/1794. The regulations were made by the Secretary of State, and this is common ground, in order to give effect to EC Council Directive 77/187 adopted by the Council of the European Communities on 14 February 1977 to provide for the approximation of the laws of the member states relating to the safeguarding of employees' rights in the event of transfer of undertakings, businesses or parts of businesses. The question which arises is whether it has achieved this object.

The approach to the construction of primary and subordinate legislation enacted to give effect to the United Kingdom's obligations under the EEC Treaty have been the subject matter of recent authority in this House (see *Pickstone v Freemans plc* [1988] 2 All ER 803, [1989] AC 66) and is not in doubt. If the legislation can reasonably be construed so as to conform with those obligations, obligations which are to be ascertained not only from the wording of the relevant directive but from the interpretation placed on it by the Court of Justice of the European Communities, such a purposive construction will be applied even though, perhaps, it may involve some departure from the strict and literal application of the words which the legislature has elected to use.

---

[7] *Henn and Darby v Director of Public Prosecutions* [1981] A.C. 850 at 905, HL.
[8] *Henn and Darby v Director of Public Prosecutions* [1981] A.C. 850 at 904, HL.

It will, I think, be convenient to consider the terms of the directive and the regulations before outlining the circumstances in which the instant appeal arises. The broad scope of the directive appears from the following two recitals:

'Whereas economic trends are bringing in their wake, at both national and Community level, changes in the structure of undertakings, through transfers of undertakings, businesses or parts of businesses to other employers as a result of legal transfers or mergers; Whereas it is necessary to provide for the protection of employees in the event of a change of employer, in particular, to ensure that their rights are safeguarded . . .'

By art.1 it is provided that the directive shall apply to the transfer of an undertaking, business or part of a business to another employer. Article 2 contains definitions, the relevant ones for present purposes being:

'(a) "transferor" means any natural or legal person who, by reason of a transfer within the meaning of Article 1(1), ceases to be the employer in respect of the undertaking, business or part of the business; (b) "transferee" means any natural or legal person who, by reason of a transfer within the meaning of Article 1(1), becomes the employer in respect of the undertaking, business or part of the business . . .'

Section II is headed '*Safeguarding of employees' rights*' and contains three articles of which the relevant ones for present purposes are arts 3 and 4. Article 3 provides (so far as material):

'1. The transferor's rights and obligations arising from a contract of employment or from an employment relationship existing on the date of a transfer within the meaning of Article 1(1) shall, by reason of such transfer, be transferred to the transferee. . .' . . .

Article 4 is, so far as material, in the following terms:

'1. The transfer of an undertaking, business or part of a business shall not in itself constitute grounds for dismissal by the transferor or the transferee. This provision shall not stand in the way of dismissals that may take place for economic, technical or organisational reasons entailing changes in the workforce . . .
    2. If the contract of employment or the employment relationship is terminated because the transfer within the meaning of Article 1(1) involves a substantial change in working conditions to the detriment of the employee, the employer shall be regarded as having been responsible for termination of the contract of employment or of the employment relationship.' . . .

Turning now to the 1981 regulations, which came into operation in 1982 and which represent the British government's perception at that time of its obligations under the directive, these provide for relevant purposes as follows: . . .

'5(1) A relevant transfer shall not operate so as to terminate the contract of employment of any person employed by the transferor in the undertaking or part transferred but any such contract which would otherwise have been terminated by the transfer shall have effect after the transfer as if originally made between the person so employed and the transferee.
    (2) Without prejudice to paragraph (1) above, on the completion of a relevant transfer—(a) all the transferor's rights, powers, duties and liabilities under or in connection with any such contract, shall be transferred by virtue of this Regulation to the transferee; and (b) anything done before the transfer is completed by or in relation to the transferor in respect of that contract or a person employed in that undertaking or part shall be deemed to have been done by or in relation to the transferee.
    (3) Any reference in paragraph (1) or (2) above to a person employed in an undertaking or part of one

transferred by a relevant transfer is a reference to a person so employed immediately before the transfer, including, where the transfer is effected by a series of two or more transactions, a person so employed immediately before any of those transactions . . .

8(1) Where either before or after a relevant transfer, any employee of the transferor or transferee is dismissed, that employee shall be treated for the purposes of art.V of the 1978 Act and Articles 2 to 41 of the 1976 Order (unfair dismissal) as unfairly dismissed if the transfer or a reason connected with it is the reason or the principal reason for his dismissal. . . .'

It will be seen that, as is to be expected, the scope and purpose of both the directive and the regulations are the same, that is to ensure that on any transfer of an undertaking or part of an undertaking, the employment of the existing workers in the undertaking is preserved or, if their employment terminates solely by reason of the transfer, that their rights arising out of that determination are effectively safeguarded. It may, I think, be assumed that those who drafted both the directive and the regulations were sufficiently acquainted with the realities of life to appreciate that a frequent, indeed, possibly the most frequent, occasion on which a business or part of a business is transferred is when the original employer is insolvent, so that an employee whose employment is terminated on the transfer will have no effective remedy for unfair dismissal unless it is capable of being exerted against the transferee. It can hardly have been contemplated that, where the only reason for the determination of the employment is the transfer of the undertaking or the relevant part of it, the parties to the transfer would be at liberty to avoid the manifest purpose of the directive by the simple expedient of wrongfully dismissing the workforce a few minutes before the completion of the transfer. The European Court has expressed, in the clearest terms, the opinion that so transparent a device would not avoid the operation of the directive, and if the effect of the regulations is that under the law of the United Kingdom it has that effect, then your Lordships are compelled to conclude that the regulations are gravely defective and the government of the United Kingdom has failed to comply with its mandatory obligations under the directive. If your Lordships are in fact compelled to that conclusion, so be it; but it is not, I venture to think, a conclusion which any of your Lordships would willingly embrace in the absence of the most compulsive content rendering any other conclusion impossible.

My Lords, the circumstances in which the question has arisen for decision in the instant case are these. The first respondents, Forth Dry Dock and Engineering Co Ltd, carried on a business of ship repairers at the Edinburgh dry dock, premises which they held under a lease from the Forth Ports Authority. At the material time, the 12 appellants were tradesmen employed in that business. They were part of a permanent workforce of skilled shipworkers of various trades who had been continuously employed by the first respondents since 1981 or 1982. In the year 1983 the group of companies of which the first respondents formed part was in financial difficulties and the receiver of the various companies in the group (including the first respondents) was appointed by the debenture holder, Lloyd's Bank, on September 28, 1983. The workforce was then told by the receiver's representative, a Mr Page, that the intention was to sell the business as a going concern and that their jobs would be safe. That belief may have been genuinely entertained at the time, but it was falsified in the event.

On 23 November 1983 the second respondents, Forth Estuary Engineering Ltd (Forth Estuary) was incorporated. A few days before the transfer of the first respondents' assets, which took place on 6 February 1984, the capital of Forth Estuary was increased from £1,000 to £20,000: 85% of the issued capital became vested in a Mr Brooshooft, who had been a financial adviser to the first respondents' company, and 10% in a Mr Hughes, who had been a director of and had managed the business of the first respondents. On 6 February 1984 an agreement was entered into between the first respondents, the receivers and Forth Estuary under which (a) all the first respondents' business assets, consisting of plant, machinery, equipment, furniture and office equipment specified in a schedule, were acquired by Forth Estuary at a price of £33,500 payable on execution of the agreement, (b) the first respondents undertook to cease business at close of business on that day (at which time the sale and purchase was to be carried into effect) and (c) the first respondents undertook forthwith to relinquish their rights under the lease of the dry dock which they held from the ports authority. Before this, it is not clear exactly when, Forth Estuary had obtained from the Forth Ports Authority a new lease of the property previously let to the first respondents (with the exception of one shed). It is interesting to note that under cl

14 of this agreement, its construction, validity and performance were to be governed by English law and the courts of England were given exclusive jurisdiction. As a matter of English law, therefore, the ownership of the assets transferred passed in equity to Forth Estuary on the execution of the agreement and those assets were, assuming, as we must assume, that the consideration was then paid as provided by the agreement, then held by the transferor as a bare trustee for the transferee. Up to this point the appellants had continued to be employed by the first respondents. It had, however, clearly been determined by the receivers, and, one infers, by Forth Estuary, that that situation was not to be permitted to continue and it is difficult, if not impossible, to resist the inference that the reason why it was not to be permitted to continue was that both parties were well aware of the provisions of the regulations to which I have already referred. It can hardly have been merely a fortunate coincidence that officers from the redundancy payments section of the Department of Employment were already at the dock on that afternoon when Mr Hughes and Mr Page arrived at approximately 3 pm having come straight from the office of Messrs Brodies, where the agreement had been signed. They addressed the workforce and told them that the business was to close down at 4.30 pm that day and that they were dismissed 'with immediate effect'. Each of the appellants was given a letter from the receivers under the first respondents' letterhead which was dated 6 February 1984 and was, so far as material, in the following terms:

> 'We would advise you that no further funds can be made available to pay your wages with effect from the close of business today and accordingly we have to inform you that your employment with the company is terminated with immediate effect. No payments will be made in respect of your accrued holiday pay, or the failure to give you your statutory period of notice. Under the Insolvency provisions of the Employment Protection Act, any claim you may have for the above will, subject to certain limitations, be paid to you by the Department of Employment out of the Redundancy Fund . . . Your wages up to the date of dismissal will be paid in the normal way and you will be issued with a P45 from the company's head office.'

One of the less creditable aspects of the matter is that one of the appellants, Mr Walker, who was the union shop steward, asked specifically whether the business was being taken over by Forth Estuary, and was told by Mr Hughes that he knew nothing about a new company taking over, while Mr Page said that he knew nothing about a company called Forth Estuary Engineering. This indicates a calculated disregard for the obligations imposed by reg 10 of the 1981 regulations. Within 48 hours of their dismissal, the appellants learned, at the local job centre, that Forth Estuary was recruiting labour and a group of them went to fill in application forms for employment. None was successful and indeed only three former employees of the first respondents were taken on. Work which was in progress on the vessels on 6 February was subsequently continued and completed by Forth Estuary, which very soon had a workforce of similar size to that of the first respondents, embracing the same trade but recruited at lower rates of pay elsewhere than from the existing employees. . . .

Two questions then arise. First, was the time which elapsed between the dismissals and the transfer of so short a duration that, on the true construction of reg 5, the appellants were 'employed immediately before' the transfer, as required by para (3) of that regulation? Second, if the answer to that question is in the negative, what difference (if any) does it make that the reason, or the principal reason, for the dismissals was, as it clearly was, the imminent occurrence of the transfer so that the dismissals were, by reg 8(1), deemed to be unfair dismissals? . . .

Regulation 8(1) does not follow literally the wording of Art.4(1). It provides only that if the reason for the dismissal of the employee is the transfer of the business, he has to be treated 'for the purposes of art.V of the 1978 Act' as unfairly dismissed so as to confer on him the remedies provided by ss.69–79 of the Act (including, where it is considered appropriate, an order for reinstatement or re-engagement). If this provision fell to be construed by reference to the ordinary rules of construction applicable to a purely domestic statute and without reference to treaty obligations, it would, I think, be quite impermissible to regard it as having the same prohibitory effect as that attributed by the European Court to art.4 of the directive. But it has always to be borne in mind that the purpose of the directive and of the regulations was and is to 'safeguard' the rights of employees on a transfer and that there is a mandatory obligation to provide remedies which are effective and not merely symbolic to which the regulations were intended to give effect. The remedies provided by the 1978 Act in the case of an insolvent transferor are largely illusory unless they can be exerted against the transferee as the directive contemplates and I do not find it conceivable that, in framing regulations intending to give effect to the directive, the Secretary of State could have envisaged that its purpose should be capable of being avoided by the transparent device to which resort was had in the instant case. . . . Having regard to the manifest purpose of the regulations, I do not, for my part, feel inhibited from making such an implication in the instant case. The provision in reg 8(1) that a dismissal by reason of transfer is to be treated as an unfair dismissal, is merely a different way of saying that the transfer is not to 'constitute a ground for dismissal' as contemplated by art.4 of the directive and there is no good reason for denying to it the same effect as that attributed to that article. In effect this involves reading reg 5(3) as if there were inserted after the words 'immediately before the transfer' the words 'or would have been so employed if he had not been unfairly dismissed in the circumstances described in reg 8(1)'. For my part, I would make such an implication which is entirely consistent with the general scheme of the regulations and which is necessary if they are effectively to fulfil the purpose for which they were made of giving effect to the provisions of the directive. . . .

In the instant case it is quite clear that the reason for the dismissal of the appellants was the transfer of the business which had just been agreed and was going to take place almost at once. The effect of reg 5, construed as I have suggested that it should be, is that their employment continued with Forth Estuary. I would therefore allow the appeal. . . ."

[Lord Keith of Kinkel, Lord Brandon of Oakbrook, Lord Templeman, and Lord Jauncey of Tullichettle also allowed the appeal].

III. THE INTERPRETATION OF EUROPEAN HUMAN RIGHTS LAW

We have already looked at the impact of the European Convention on Human Rights on the principle of the supremacy of Parliament through the role of the European Court of Human Rights in Strasbourg. Courts in this country also operate under the presumption that Parliament intends to comply with *international* law. This is another principle of statutory interpretation. As a consequence, courts have been prepared to examine international treaties, which the UK Government has signed, as an aid in the interpretation of *ambiguous* legislation.[9]

This has been important with respect to the European Convention on Human Rights. Prior to incorporation into English law, the Convention has only been of assistance to domestic courts as an aid in interpreting ambiguous legislation.[10] With the coming into force of the Human Rights Act 1998, the role of the European Convention on Human Rights in the interpretation of domestic law has changed dramatically.

At the time of its enactment, there was much speculation as to the possible impact of the Human Rights Act 1998 on statutory interpretation.

Geoffrey Marshall, "Interpreting interpretation in the Human Rights Bill" [1998] P.L. 167 at 167:

The meaning of "possible" in Clause 3
"In the first place it is not clear how the phrase 'so far as it is possible to do so' is to be understood. In some sense or other anything is possible if those who apply rules of interpretation are willing to stretch, change or apply them differently. Is Clause 3 intended to change the existing rules of interpretation whenever a

---

[9] See *James Buchanan & Co Ltd v Babco Forwarding & Shipping (UK) Ltd* [1978] A.C. 141, HL; *Fothergill v Monarch Airlines Ltd* [1981] A.C. 251, HL.

[10] See e.g. *Brind v Secretary of State for the Home Department* [1991] 1 All E.R. 720, HL; *Derbyshire County Council v Times Newspapers and others* [1992] 3 Al E.R. 65, A.C.; *R v Secretary of State for the Home Department and another* Ex p. *Norney and others* (1995) 7 Admin. L.R. 861, HC.

question of Convention rights is an issue? The Government White Paper 'Rights Brought Home' implies that some change is intended. It says that the Bill 'goes far beyond the present rule which authorises the courts to take the Convention into account in resolving any ambiguity in a legislative provision'. What the authors of the White Paper mean by going beyond the present rule is uncertain. At the Committee stage of the Bill in the House of Lords, Lord Cooke of Thorndon suggested that what is prescribed by Clause 3 differs from the present rules in that 'it enjoins a search for possible meanings as distinct from the true meaning which has been the traditional approach'. But the disjunction between the meaning now to be sought and the true meaning is an odd one, particularly as Lord Cooke went on to say that the new kind of interpretation now enjoined 'is not a strained interpretation but one that is *fairly* possible'. Does that mean that the courts should be encouraged to disregard the true (or most obvious or likely) meaning in some degree, but not to strain or distort it too grossly? Another possibility as to the meaning of 'possible' is of course that it means that if, when the normal rules of construction are applied, it is possible fairly to say that a legislative provision has a particular meaning and if that meaning is compatible with the Convention it should be so interpreted and if not, not. But if that is what it means, Clause 3 is redundant. On the other hand, if Clause 3 is not redundant, then we do not know what it means.

Legislative ambiguity and convention rights

In introducing the Bill the Lord Chancellor explained the purpose of Clause 3 by saying that 'If it is possible to interpret a statute in two ways—one compatible with the Convention and one not—the courts will always choose the interpretation which is compatible'. But leaving aside the difficulty of knowing what it means to say that there is a possibility of such an interpretation what are we to understand by an interpretation that is 'compatible with Convention rights'? Is this the same as an ambiguity that is resolved by reference to Convention rights or (in the language of the White Paper) interpreting legislation 'so as to uphold Convention rights'? In what kinds of cases will Convention rights be relevant to the resolving of ambiguity in a statutory provision?

Issues of construction that arise in the application of the language of statutes generally raise a question as to whether particular persons or circumstances fall within the general terms of the statutes. *Harris v DPP*[11] is a not untypical example. That involved the interpretation of section 139 of the Criminal Justice Act 1988. The guilt of the accused, who was charged with possession of a prohibited article, namely a sharply pointed blade, depended on the meaning of 'folding pocket knife' since such knives were excluded from the operation of the statute. It was held that a small bladed knife whose blade could only be folded by operating a locking button was a fixed blade knife, not a folding pocket knife. Here the statute could be said to be capable of being interpreted in two ways. But is this the kind of case in which the existence of the Human Rights Bill and its putatively new rule of interpretation is relevant? Can it be said that since the Convention protects the right to liberty of the person and the right to fair trials, it becomes relevant in every criminal proceeding on the grounds that criminal conviction involves a loss of liberty and that guilt has to be established in accordance with the provisions of the Convention? If so, which of the two interpretations of 'folding pocket knife' is more compatible with the Convention? Is either? There is already said to be a presumption enjoining in some degree strict construction of penal statutes so as to give the benefit of the doubt to an accused where there is genuine uncertainty as to the proper application of statutory language. The principle seems to have been somewhat submerged in recent times when public policy and purposive interpretation have appeared to suggest that the courts will only apply the presumption 'if there are no considerations indicating the desirability of a wider interpretation', and public policy together with the intention of Parliament may often suggest a wider interpretation.

But is it to be supposed that Clause 3 of the Human Rights Bill creates a new or extended version of that presumption, so that the courts are to lean towards the construction that will lead to acquittal whenever any possible construction of statutory language might lead to that result? It would be odd to suppose that

---

11 [1993] W.L.R. 82.

the Convention could prescribe such a conclusion whenever anyone alleged its relevance, or that Clause 3 is intended to change the approach to such questions of construction throughout the criminal law. . . .

'Reading or giving effect'

Although Clause 3 is headed 'Interpretation of legislation' what it says is that primary and subordinate legislation should be 'read and given effect' in a way which is compatible with the Convention. 'Read and given effect' may be intended to be read as meaning 'interpreted', but it would seem that it must involve not merely the resolution of ambiguity in statutory provisions but also the question whether a provision of primary or secondary legislation can be treated as being compatible or incompatible with rights guaranteed in the Convention. This seems not so much a question of interpretation or construction of language but of assessment or characterisation or proper description of the relevant legislative provision when placed alongside the relevant right or rights in the Convention. It is only as a result of such assessment or reading of the statutory provision that the court can be in a position to make—when necessary—the determination of incompatibility which should lead to parliamentary remedial action under Clause 10 of the Bill. If a litigant establishes that the statutory provision in question is incompatible with, or infringes the Convention, his right under the Convention is upheld (though the legislation remains valid under the provisions of Clause 3(b)) and his only remedy is a declaration of incompatibility until remedial action is taken. If the court finds that the legislation is compatible with the Convention the litigant fails to establish that he is entitled to protection under the Convention over and above that provided by the United Kingdom legislation.

At this point a startling paradox suggests itself about the wording of Clause 3. What it commands is the opposite of what might be assumed from a reading of the White Paper and the parliamentary statements made in introducing Clause 3. The White Paper says that the courts will be required to uphold the Convention rights unless it is impossible to do so. So a hopeful litigant under the Human Rights Bill might assume that the courts would lean towards holding that the Convention right in issue should prevail over the legislative provision under attack, which it can only do if the legislation is inconsistent or incompatible with the Convention right. But what Clause 3 urges the court to do, wherever possible, is to find that the legislation is *compatible* with the Convention rights. If it is so compatible, the Convention has no bite on the legislation and the litigant seeking protection under the Convention not provided for by the legislation loses his case. The more faithfully the courts follow the injunction to read legislation as being compatible with the Convention the less effect the Convention will have. If it were to have the advertised effect of allowing the Convention more easily to trump legislation that threatens rights, Clause 3 should presumably have provided that, whenever the possibility arises, primary and secondary legislation should be treated as *incompatible* with the Convention rights unless such a finding is ruled out because the legislation is clearly compatible. But then the only remedy would be a declaration of incompatibility until (and if) remedial action is taken under Clause 10.

Many speakers in the debate on the Human Rights Bill praised its drafting as ingenious and subtle. Perhaps, as with the failure of Clauses 3 and 4 to implement the White Paper's commitment to incorporate the Convention rights in United Kingdom law, the so-called interpretation provision in Clause 3 is a further example of ingenuity gone wrong. What interpretation the courts will place on Clause 3 is impossible to know."

In the years since the Human Rights Act was enacted, the courts have applied the legislation in a number of different contexts. In the following extract, Lady Justice Arden, a member of the Court of Appeal, explains the patterns of interpretation that have emerged.

Rt. Hon. Lady Justice Arden DBE, "The interpretation of UK domestic legislation in the light of European Convention on Human Rights jurisprudence" (2004) 25 *Statute Law Review* 165 at 170–179:

"All the cases which I shall consider have been decided by the House of Lords, rather than in the lower courts. It will be seen that there has been a steep learning curve for the courts in relation to section 3(1).

The first case is *R v A(No. 2)*.[12] In this case, the appeal was by a defendant to a criminal charge of rape and concerned the question of whether certain evidence concerning the sexual behaviour of the complainant would be admissible at trial. The defendant wanted to adduce evidence of the complainant's sexual behaviour in the three weeks prior to the alleged rape. However, section 41 of the Youth Justice and Criminal Evidence Act 1999 prohibits the admission of evidence as to the complainant's sexual behaviour unless certain conditions are fulfilled. The conditions permit the admission of evidence of sexual behaviour on the issue of consent if the prior sexual behaviour was so similar to sexual behaviour of the complainant that the similarity cannot be explained as a coincidence. But further conditions are attached to this exception, including a condition that the behaviour should have taken place as part of the event or at or about the same time as the alleged rape.[13] The House of Lords held that the accused's Convention right to a fair trial might be violated if relevant evidence of the kind sought to be addressed by the appellant was excluded. The question then arose whether section 41 could be construed so as to prevent any violation of the defendant's rights. On this, their Lordships expressed different views. First, Lord Steyn made some general observations about section 3:

> '44. On the other hand, the interpretative obligation of section 3 of the 1998 Act is a strong one. It applies even if there is no ambiguity in the language in the sense of the language being capable of two different meanings. It is an emphatic adjuration by the legislature: *R v Director of Public Prosecutions*, ex parte *Kebilene* [2000] 2 AC 326, per Lord Cooke of Thornden, at p. 373F; and my judgment at 266B . . . In accordance with the will of Parliament as reflected in section 3 it will sometimes be necessary to adopt an interpretation which linguistically may appear strained. The techniques to be used will not only involve the reading down of expressed language in a statute but also the implication of provisions. A declaration of incompatibility is a measure of last resort. It must be avoided unless it is plainly impossible to do so. If a *clear* limitation on Convention rights is stated in terms, such an impossibility will arise: *Secretary of State for the Home Department*, ex parte *Simms* [2000] 2 AC 115, 132A–B per Lord Hoffmann. There is, however, no limitation of such a nature in the present case.
>
> 45. In my view, section 3 requires the court to subordinate the niceties of the language of section 41(3)(c) and in particular the touchstone of coincidence, to broader considerations of relevance judged by logical and common sense criteria of time and circumstances. After all, it is realistic to proceed on the basis that the legislature would not, if alerted to the problem, have wished to deny the right to an accused to put forward a full and complete defence by advancing truly probative material. It is therefore possible under section 3 to read section 41, and in particular section 41(3)(c) as subject to the implied provision that evidence or questioning which is required to ensure a fair trial under article 6 of the Convention should not be treated as inadmissible. The result of such reading would be that sometimes logically relevant sexual experiences between a complainant and an accused may be admitted under section 41(3)(c) . . .'

Lord Hope of Craighead took a different view. He considered that the question whether section 41 was incompatible with the Convention could not be finally determined at the pre-trial stage. Accordingly, he considered it was neither necessary nor appropriate to resort to the interpretive obligation in section 3 of the Human Rights Act 1998. Lord Hope added:

> '108. I should like to add, however, that I would find it very difficult to accept that it was permissible under section 3 of the Human Rights Act 1998 to read into section 41(3)(c) a provision to the effect that evidence or questioning which was required to ensure a fair trial under article 6 of the Convention should not be treated as admissible. The rule of construction which section 3 lays down is quite unlike any previous rule of statutory interpretation. There is no need to identify any ambiguity or absurdity.

---

12 [2002] 1 AC 45.
13 Section 41(3)(c).

Compatibility with Convention rights is the sole guiding principle. This is the paramount object which the rule seeks to achieve. But the rule is only a rule of interpretation. It does not entitle the judges to act as legislators . . .

109. In the present case it seems to me that the entire structure of section 41 contradicts the idea that it is possible to read into it a new provision which would enable the courts to give leave whenever it was of the opinion that this was required to ensure a fair trial. The whole point of this section, as was made clear during the debates in Parliament, was to address the mischief which was thought to have arisen due to the width of the discretion which had previously been given to the trial judge. A deliberate decision was taken not to follow the examples which were to be found elsewhere, such as in section 275 of the Criminal Procedure (Scotland) Act 1995, of provisions which give an overriding discretion to the trial judge to allow the evidence or questioning where it would be contrary to the interests of justice to exclude it. Section 41(2) forbids the exercise of such discretion unless the court is satisfied as to the matters which that section identifies. It seems to me that it would not be possible, without contradicting the plain intention of Parliament, to read in a provision which would enable the court to exercise a wider discretion than that permitted by section 41(2).

I would not have the same difficulty with a solution which read down the provisions of sections (3) or (5), as the case may be, in order to render them compatible with the Convention right but if that were to be done it would be necessary to identify precisely (a) the words used by the legislature which would otherwise be incompatible with the Convention right and (b) how those words were to be construed, according to the rule which section 3 lays down to make them compatible. That, it seems to me, is what the rule of construction requires. The court's task is to read and give effect to the legislation which it is asked to construe . . .'

The other members of the House in substance agreed with Lord Steyn's approach. Lord Slynn held:

'It seems to me that your Lordships cannot say that it is not possible to read section 41(3)(c) together with article 6 of the Convention rights in a way which will result inj a fair hearing. In my view, section 41(3)(c) is to be read as permitting the admission of evidence or questioning which relates to a relevant issue in the case and which the trial judge considers is necessary to make the trial a fair one.'[14]

Lord Clyde held:

'If a case occurred where the evidence of the complainant's sexual behaviour was relevant and important for the defence to make good a case of consent, then it seems to me that the language would have to be strained to avoid the injustice to the accused of excluding them from a full and proper presentation of the defence.'[15]

Lord Hutton held:

'. . . pursuant to the obligation imposed by section 3(1) that section 41 be read and given effect in a way which is compatible with article 6, I consider that section 41(3)(c) should be read as including evidence of such previous behaviour by the complainant because the defendant claims that her sexual behaviour on previous occasions was similar, and the similarity was not a coincidence because there was a causal connection which was her affection for, and feelings of attraction towards, the defendant.'[16]

---

[14] Para. 13.
[15] Para 136.
[16] Para. 163.

The next case is *R v. Lambert*.[17] There were a number of issues in this case including an issue as to retrospectivity of the Human Rights Act 1998. I propose to refer to the case only in so far as it is relevant to section 3 of the Human Rights Act 1998. As to the facts, the appellant was found in possession of a package which contained controlled drugs and he was charged with an offence of possessing controlled drugs contrary to section 5(3) of the Misuse of Drugs Act 1971. He was convicted. His defence was that he did not know or suspect that the package contained controlled drugs. Section 28(2) of the 1971 Act provides that subject to section 28(3):

> '. . . it shall be a defence for the accused to prove that he neither knew of, nor suspected, nor had reason to suspect the existence of some fact alleged by the prosecution which it was necessary for the prosecution to prove if he is to be convicted of the offence charged.'

Section 28(3) provides that the accused is not to be acquitted simply because he does not know that the substance was not the particular controlled drug but that he should be acquitted 'if he proves that he neither believed nor suspected nor had reason to suspect that the substance or product in question was a controlled drug.' At trial, the appellant failed to make out his defence under section 28 and was convicted. One of the grounds of his appeal against his conviction was that section 28 was in violation of article 6 of the Convention since by reversing the onus of proof it violated the presumption of innocence. All the members of the House of Lords, excluding Lord Hutton who did not find it necessary to deal with the point, but including Lord Steyn who dissented in the result, held that, in accordance with section 3(1) of the 1998 Act, section 28 could be read as merely imposing an evidential burden. As the judge had given the correct direction, the conviction stood. Lord Clyde indeed considered that it required not straining of the language of section 28 to construe the references to proof as intending an evidential burden and not a persuasive one. Accordingly, in his judgment, the construction was well with the word 'possible' for the purposes of section 3.

The application of section 3 was dealt with in most detail by Lord Hope. First, he repeated the point that he had made in *R v. A (No. 2)* that section 3 did not enable the courts to legislate but merely to interpret legislation. Secondly, he held that it was necessary to identify the word or phrase which, if given its ordinary meaning, was incompatible with Convention rights and to say how the word or phrase was to be construed if it was to be made compatible. He held that the justification for this approach was to be found in the nature of section 3:

> 'Its primary characteristic, for present purposes, is its ability to achieve certainty by the use of clear and precise language. It provides a set of rules by which, according to the ordinary meaning of the words used, the conduct of affairs may be regulated. So far as possible judges should seek to achieve the same attention to detail in their use of language to express the effect of applying section 3(1) as the Parliamentary draftsman would have done if he had been amending the statute. It ought to be possible for any words that need to be substituted to be fitted into the statute as if they had been inserted there by amendment. If this cannot be done without doing such violence to the statute as to make it unintelligible or unworkable the use of this technique will not be possible. It will then be necessary to leave it to Parliament to amend the statute and to resort instead to the making of a declaration of incompatibility.'[18]

Lord Hope then discussed the techniques that could be used under section 3:

> '81. As to the techniques that may be used, it is clear that the courts are not bound by previous authority as to what the statute means. It has been suggested that a strained or non-literal construction may be adopted, that words may be read in by way of addition to those used by the legislator and that the words may be "read down" to give them a narrower construction than their ordinary meaning would bear: *Clayton & Tomlinson*,

---

[17] [2002] 2 AC 545.
[18] Para. 157.

> *The Law of Human Rights* (2000), vol. 1, p.168, para. 4.28. It may be enough simply to say what the effect of the provision is without altering the ordinary meaning of the words used: see *Brown v. Stott* 2000 JC 328, 355B–C, per Lord Justice General Rodger. In other cases, as in *Vasquez v. The Queen* [1994] 1 WLR 1304, the words used will require to be expressed in different language in order to explain how they are to be read in a way that is compatible. The exercise is one of translation into compatible language from language that is incompatible. In other cases, as in *R v. A (No.2)* [2002] 1 AC 45, it may be necessary for words to be read in to explain the meaning that must be given to the provision if it is to be compatible. But the interpretation of a statute by reading words to give effect to the presumed intention must always be distinguished carefully from amendment. Amendment is a legislative act. It is an exercise that must be reserved to Parliament.'

Lord Hope went on to hold that the words 'to prove' in section 28(2) should be read as 'to give sufficient evidence' and that the same meaning should be given to the words 'if he proves' in section 28(3).[19]

R v. A (No. 2) and *R v. Lambert* represent the high water mark of the application of the interpretative obligation. There have been at least three other cases in which use of the interpretative obligation in section 3 has been rejected and declarations of incompatibility have been made. In the first, *Re S (Minors) (Care Order: Implementation of Care Plan)*,[20] the issue was whether the court could by using section 3 of the Human Rights Act 1998 interpret the Children Act 1989 as enabling the judge to establish milestones in a care plan and impose obligations on the Local Authority to act if those milestones were not met. This was called a 'starring' system.

The House of Lords held, in essence, that it was a cardinal principle of the Children Act 1989, that the courts were not empowered to intervene in the way local authorities discharged their parental responsibilities under final care orders and that the starring system introduced by the Court of Appeal was inconsistent with that cardinal principle and went beyond the boundary of interpretation. The principal speech was give by Lord Nicholls, with whom all the other members of the House agreed. This speech contains some important observations on the effect of Section 3 of the 1998 Act. Lord Nicholls starts by making the point that section 3 is 'forthright, uncompromising language', but continues:

> '38. But the reach of this tool is not unlimited. Section 3 is concerned with interpretation. This is apparent from the opening words of section 3(a): "so far as it is possible to do so" . . .
>
> 39. In applying section 3 courts must be ever mindful of this outer limit. The Human Rights Act reserves the amendment of primary legislation to Parliament. By this means the Act seeks to preserve Parliamentary sovereignty. The Act maintains the constitutional boundary. Interpretation of statutes is a matter for the courts; the enactment of statutes, and the amendment of statutes, are matters for Parliament.'

Lord Nicholls continued by saying that the area of real difficulty was in identifying the limits of interpretation in a particular case. He observed that the problem was more acute today than in the past because courts are more liberal in their interpretation of all manner of documents. Lord Nicholls continued:

> 'For present purposes it is sufficient to say that a meaning which departs substantially from a fundamental feature of an Act of Parliament is likely to have crossed the boundary between interpretation and amendment. This is especially so where the departure has important practical repercussions which the court is not equipped to evaluate. In such a case the overall contextual setting may leave no scope for rendering the statutory provision Convention compliant by the legitimate use of the process of interpretation. The boundary line may be crossed even though limitation on Convention rights is not stated in express terms. Lord Styen's observations in *R v. A (No. 2)* [2002] 1 AC 45, 68D–E, para. 44 are not to be read as meaning

---

[19]   Para. 94.
[20]   [2002] AC 291.

that a clear limitation on Convention rights in terms is the only circumstance in which an interpretation incompatible with Convention rights may arise.'[21]

Lord Nicholls went on to say, effectively in agreement with Lord Hope, that when applying section 3:

'. . . it is important the court should identify clearly the particular statutory provision or provisions whose interpretation leads to that result. Apart from all else, this should assist in ensuring the court does not inadvertently stray outside its interpretative jurisdiction.'[22]

It is not, therefore, surprising that in two further cases the House of Lords has also made declarations of incompatibility. The first was *R (Anderson) v. Secretary of State for the Home Department*[23] where the issue was whether the statutory provision which enabled the Secretary of State to fix the tariff period to be served by mandatory life sentence prisoners was inconsistent with article 6 of the Convention. The House of Lords held that it was, and went on to make a declaration of incompatibility. The House rejected the submission that the statutory provision could be interpreted in such a way as to be compatible with the Convention under section 3(1) of the 1998 Act. Memorably, Lord Bingham held:

'To read section 29 as precluding participation by the Home Secretary, if it were possible to do so, would not be judicial interpretation but judicial vandalism: it would give the section an effect quite different from that which Parliament intended and would go well beyond any interpretative process sanctioned by section 3 of the 1998 Act. (*In Re S (Minors) Care Order: Implementation of Care Plan*) [2002] 2 AC 291, 313–314, para. 41).'[24]

Lord Steyn added:

'It would not be interpretation but interpolation inconsistent with the plain legislative intent to entrust the decision to the Home Secretary, who was intended to be free to follow or reject judicial advice. Section 3(1) is not available where the suggested interpretation is contrary to expressed statutory words or is by implication necessarily contradicted by the statute: *In Re S (Minors) Care Order: Implementation of Care Plan*) [2002] 2 AC 291, 313–314, para. 41, per Lord Nicholls of Birkenhead.'[25]

The third case *Bellinger v. Bellinger*.[26] In this case, the petitioner, who was registered male at birth, had undergone gender reassignment and subsequently went through the ceremony of marriage with a man. She sought a declaration that her marriage was valid. Section 11(c) of the Matrimonial Causes Act 1973 provides that 'a marriage . . . shall be void on the following grounds only, that is to say . . . that the parties are not respectively male and female . . .'. The House of Lords held that this provision referred to a person's biological gender at birth and thus that the appellant was not entitled to a declaration that her marriage to a male was valid and subsisting. The House of Lords further held that, since there was no provision for the recognition of gender reassignment for the purposes of marriage, section 11(c) was a continuing obstacle to the petitioner entering into a valid marriage with a man and that section 11(c) of the 1973 Act was therefore incompatible with her right to respect for her private and family life and her right to marry pursuant to articles 8 and 12 respectively of the Convention. Accordingly the House of

---

[21] Para. 40.

[22] Para. 41.

[23] [2003] 1 AC 837.

[24] Para. 30.

[25] Para 59.

[26] [2003] 2 AC 467.

Lords made a declaration of incompatibility. Only Lord Hope and Lord Hobhouse specifically referred to section 3. Lord Hope contented himself by saying that he did not consider that the House of Lords could solve the problem judicially by means of the interpretative obligation in section 3(1) of the 1998 Act.[27] Lord Hobhouse came to the same conclusion. He said: 'This would, in my view, not be an exercise in interpretation however robust. It would be a legislative amendment making a legislative choice as to what precise amendment was appropriate.'[28]

Conclusions

I will now endeavour to draw the threads together.

First, as the recent decisions of the House of Lords make it clear, section 3(1) only creates an interpretative duty, and does not impose a duty on the courts to rewrite the law. Section 3(1) requires the courts to read and give effect to legislation. It does not provide that 'nothing in any enactment can violate a Convention right and that it should be given effect accordingly'. The duty is only one of interpretation, and there may come a stage where interpretation in a manner compatible with Convention rights is impossible, as the last three cases to which I have referred show.

Second, it has never been open to doubt that section 3(1) is not a judicial override. Usually bills of rights enable courts to strike down legislation, as happens in the United States. But that is not the position in the United Kingdom. The reason is the reason that I gave at the outset, namely that the Human Rights Act 1998 also preserves Parliamentary sovereignty. Another way of putting this point is that the United Kingdom does not have a proper bill of rights. But that is what Parliament has decided should happen.

Third, although the task is one of interpretation, it is not the traditional task of interpretation. New rules and canons of interpretation apply to it. In particular, the doctrine of precedent does not apply in the same way. If a statute was interpreted before the commencement of the Human Rights Act 1998, that interpretation will not be binding on a court after the commencement of the Act if it is shown to result in violation of a Convention right. Where the position is that the courts have construed legislation on a previous occasion in accordance with the Convention but Convention jurisprudence has since then itself moved on in accordance with the evolutive approach adopted by the Strasbourg court, it is an open question whether the doctrine of precedent applies so that only a higher court may depart from a previously Convention compliant interpretation.

Fourth, *Re S (Minors) (Care Order: Implementation of Care Plan)*,[29] makes it clear that Lord Hope's view has prevailed that, when a court is applying section 3, the court must identify the word or phrase which given its ordinary meaning is incompatible with the Convention and say how the word or phrase is to be construed if it is to be made compatible. To this extent, the process of statutory interpretation is the same as in any other case.

Fifth, there are, however, features of interpretation under section 3 which are inconsistent with statutory interpretation in other circumstances. As Lord Hope's discussion on various techniques shows, it may be necessary to write in words or give them a different meaning in order to ensure compatibility. Further, there is no need to identify any ambiguity or absurdity before applying section 3. The only touchstone is incompatibility. Moreover, section 3 applies even if the statute was passed before the Human Rights Act 1998. The courts are not, therefore, seeking the intention of Parliament when it enacted the statute in question. It is seeking to apply the will of Parliament as subsequently expressed.

There are all sorts of consequences of this new approach. One of the reasons given for requiring the identification of the precise wording of the enactment to be construed is that this is likely to achieve greater certainty. However, there is still a very large area of uncertainty. If a statute is incompatible with human rights, there may be a number of ways in which it could be construed in order to make it compatible. For example, in *R v. A (No. 2)* the majority applied section 3(1) by reading section 41 as subject to an implied provision that evidence or

---

[27] Para. 69.

[28] Para. 78.

[29] [2002] 2 AC 291.

questioning required to ensure a fair trial under article 6 of the Convention should not be treated as inadmissible. This is a very open ended type of construction since it does not resolve the problem of what evidence or questioning would violate article 6. Moreover, there is bound in any case to be a number of ways in which the court can resolve a question of incompatibility. For instance, in *R v. Lambert*,[30] the court could have held that section 28 required the prosecution to prove the negative in all circumstances. The fact that there is a spectrum of ways of construing a provision which is incompatible in order to make it compatible introduces considerable uncertainty into the statute book. This is obviously undesirable because it means that more and more questions of construction have to be litigated in the courts.

The interpretative duty may also shatter long-held beliefs about statutory interpretation. One of the sacred cows of statutory interpretation is that a word must have the same meaning every time it is used. This is a great anchor for draftsman and judge alike. But if an expression in a particular section has to be given a special meaning for Convention reasons, it does not necessarily follow that it should have the same meaning in the rest of the Act.

Before the decisions in *Re S (Minors) (Care Order: Implementation of Care Plan)*, *Anderson* and *Bellinger*, it seemed to me that the proper approach to section 3(1) was very unclear. But the House of Lords has now provided considerable guidance. However, it is still true to say that the courts are feeling their way towards a set of rules and canons of construction that will apply where section 3(1) is in point. It is perhaps not surprising that those rules and canons of construction have not been developed already. They are bound to take many years to develop. Nevertheless, the process is one of interpretation and the courts' traditional role in that respect has not been radically altered."

Questions

1. Do you think that the Law Lords *interpreted* the law in *R. v A*, or did they *rewrite* the law? Defend your answer.

2. What does Lady Justice Arden mean when she concludes that, with respect to the Human Rights Act, "new rules and canons of interpretation apply"? What are they?

3. Do you think that the Law Lords reached the right results in the cases discussed by Lady Justice Arden? Do you disagree with any of them?

4. Do you agree that the "House of Lords has now provided considerable guidance" in the interpretation of s.3 of the Human Rights Act? Explain.

In *R. v A*, one of the cases discussed by Lady Justice Arden, the Law Lords considered legislation which foreclosed the use of "sexual history evidence" as between a defendant and the complainant. In this case, the Law Lords used s.3 of the Human Rights Act in order to provide trial judges with the *discretion* to allow such evidence where necessary to ensure a fair trial. This decision is very controversial, as Firth explains below.

Georgina Firth, "The rape trial and sexual history evidence—*R v A* and the (un)worthy complainant" (2006) 57 *Northern Ireland Legal Quarterly* 442 at 451–453, 454–456, 461–463:

"*R v A* was a case concerned with the wording of section 41 of the Youth Justice and Criminal Evidence Act 1999 and the blanket prohibition on the use of sexual history evidence as between the defendant and the complainant. The Lords were able to consider the circumstances under which such evidence could be admitted, despite the explicitly exclusionary nature of the legislation involved, because of the introduction of the Human Rights

---

[30] [2002] 2 AC 545.

Act 1998 into English Law. In brief, the facts of the case were that the defendant, A, had been charged with rape. His defences were that the complainant had consented or alternatively that he honestly believed that she had consented. The basis for this belief in consent was that he asserted that he and the complainant had been having a consensual sexual relationship for three weeks prior to the alleged rape. She denied this.

In the course of lengthy judgments, the Lords held that, subject to the importance of seeking to protect the complainant from indignity and humiliating questions, the test of admissibility was whether the evidence and questioning relating to it was nevertheless 'so relevant to the issue of consent that to exclude it would endanger the fairness of the trial.' The decision as to relevance was to be a matter for the trial judge based on the individual facts of each case.

The judgment therefore appears, on the face of it, to be an attempt to balance the rights of the defendant to a fair trial under article 6 against the interests of the complainant. However, as I will now explore, the narratives and discourses operating throughout the judgments are likely to have the effect of subverting the intention and policy behind the enactment of section 41, of turning the provision completely on its head by inserting a condition of relevance subject to judicial control and re-introducing the possibility of sexual history evidence being routinely admitted in trials that do not conform to the ideal of 'real rape.' This clearly has important implications for women who have had a sexual relationship with their alleged rapist in the past.

There was a marked shift in their Lordship's judgments from an acceptance of general notions of the unfairness of admitting sexual history evidence to an attempt, through a particularistic approach, to justify the admission of sexual history evidence as between the complainant and the defendant. The Law Lords re-introduced the traditional distinction between sex with the defendant and sex with other men in order to enable them to justify a difference in treatment between the admissibility of such evidence by a logical process of syllogistic reasoning. For example, Lord Steyn supported the 'commonsensical' nature of his argument by drawing an analogy between evidence of sexual history between the two parties to the incident in question and a murder suspect who has previously vowed to kill the victim. This, he argued, is logically relevant to the issue of intent in the same way that evidence of previous sexual history may be relevant to consent. The Lords thus purported to show that it was a matter of 'common sense' that the inadmissibility of sexual history evidence generally had never been intended to encompass evidence relating to a sexual relationship between a complainant and the assailant.

Further, they posited that the test for the admissibility of such evidence must be relevance and the determination of relevance is best left to the discretion of the judges. This raises several questions, not least as to what meaning the Lords were placing on the term relevance in this context. As Redmayne suggests relevance can be a complex issue, encompassing 'common sense' intuitions and notions of probative force, *i.e.* ability to assist in proving one of the issues in the case. Their Lordships appeared to be arguing that sexual history evidence with the defendant is relevant because it is probative to the issue of consent and they were eager to focus on this and distance themselves from any accusation that they were undermining the legislation by attacking the credibility of a complainant through the admission of such evidence. However, I would suggest that throughout the judgments there is a continual slippage between the discrete issues of consent and credibility. Clearly underlying the use of the terms 'relevance' and 'common sense' in at least some of the judgments, is the intuition or assumption that if the complainant has slept with the accused before, then she is more likely to consent to sleep with him again than she would be if he were a stranger. However, is this assumption a legitimate one to draw? . . .

In general, the Lordships' judgments develop their commonsensical proposition by setting up a sliding scale of 'connection' between one extreme, an isolated incident of sex some time in the past and at the other, a continuous period of co-habitation during which 'two young people had lived together and had sex as part of a happy relationship'. Lord Slynn noted that he suspects that the '*ordinary man or woman on the street would find* (the exclusion of such evidence) *very strange*' thus inferring that their Lordships' understanding of common sense was drawn from and encompassed societal and cultural notions of what is right and appropriate. The inclusion of the 'ordinary woman' in this context could be said to smack of tokenism given the general thrust of the judgments but it is clearly a rhetorical device to suggest that the Lords are enlightened; that they do not subscribe to purely male concepts of common sense but that they appreciate the concerns of women about the issue of rape and its enforcement.

Lords Steyn and Hope focused on the difference between (real) rape, where there is extreme violence and little difficulty in proving the fact of the rape, and the acquaintance situation, where consent is in issue and proof is more 'sensitive and difficult'. In stressing the difficulties of proof in dating or acquaintance situations, Lords Steyn and Hope both implicitly placed judges in a position of authority as the most likely persons to be able to find the 'truth' of an allegation and yet reflected the difficulty that the law has in distinguishing between rape and normal masterful seduction. They utilised this 'difficulty', situated as one of proof rather than of ideology, to infer that a woman's sexual reputation, at least as far as the specific defendant is concerned, may be relevant in the jury's determination of her consent. In drawing this implicit inference, they thus reinforced the very myths and stereotypes about the 'woman scorned' that they purport to have disregarded in this 'modern' age.

Lord Clyde, however, went slightly further and in doing so interestingly revealed that, on the level of imagination, it is beyond the law's understanding that there may be many reasons why a woman, having had consensual sex with a man on one occasion, would be less likely to agree to sexual intercourse with him on a future occasion, that acquaintance rape can be 'real' rape. He notes at paragraph [114] that section 2 of the 1976 Act dealt only with *rape* and not the complainant's *sexual experience* with the defendant. In distinguishing rape as involving 'other men' and (normal) sexual experience as involving this defendant, Lord Clyde thus, perhaps unwittingly, revealed the inherent sexism inscribed into the language of the criminal law. Clearly, in order to reach his conclusion, Lord Clyde must have started from the historical premise that 'unchaste' women were more likely to consent to sexual intercourse and to lie about it when they did. For Lord Clyde, it seems that in an acquaintance situation, all sex is normal *i.e.* consensual sex and once a woman has shown a propensity to have sex with a particular man, her right to withdraw her consent is severely circumscribed.

Clearly, in seeking to justify their 'commonsensical' intuitions as to relevance, the Lords struggled to differentiate between a general propensity to consent to sex and a specific propensity to consent to sex with this defendant. In order to avoid appearing to subscribe to the myth that unchaste women are more likely to consent to sex, some of their Lordships and in particular Lord Hutton attempted to justify the inclusion of sexual history evidence with the defendant by stating that it was not relevant simply because of the bare fact of the relationship (in comparison with Lord Steyn) but because it has some different quality, *i.e.* that it is evidence to show a particular mindset or to show affection. But what does this mean? What is behind this if not the inference that a complainant has a propensity to consent with a particular defendant because she has consented before? . . .

The reasoning in the decision is decidedly suspect. Despite the Lords' repeated assertions that the sexual conduct of complainants was relevant neither to their credibility nor in general terms to the likelihood of their consent, a number of situations in which the Lords regarded sexual history evidence as potentially relevant relied in part upon outdated and illegitimate notions concerning credibility and consent. It was the acceptance of such evidence as relevant that resulted in the conclusion that sexual history evidence could, in some circumstances, still be admissible. Further, by characterising the balance to be struck as one between the State and the accused, rather than one between the interests of rape complainants and their assailants, the Lords failed to pay much more than lip service to the appalling difficulties faced by the victims of rape.

As noted above, the Lords appeared to reject the traditional view that a woman's sexual history was relevant to her credibility and to the likelihood of her having consented to the sexual intercourse at issue. However, by permitting the introduction of sexual history evidence on the grounds of a relationship between the complainant and the accused, the Lords are continuing to allow juries to judge women on the basis of their sexual behaviour. . . .

R v A demonstrates that in the area of defendant's rights, the Human Rights Act will be of great significance. The rights enshrined in the ECHR tend to provide defendants with remedies against undue process violations such as undue delay or the admission and exclusion of certain types of evidence. They may also impact on the substance of criminal law in situations where criminal offences are drawn in discriminatory terms or fail to accord with fundamental principles. However, it is clear from my analysis of the judgments in '*A*', that the downside of incorporation of fundamental rights is that they may undermine or restrict the protection afforded to complainants where this conflicts with the rights of the defendant."

Questions

1. Do you think Firth is correct that the judgments in *R. v A* "are likely to have the effect of subverting the intention and policy" behind the enactment of legislation?

2. When do you think sexual history evidence is "relevant"? Do you agree with Lord Steyn that it is a matter of "common sense"?

3. Do you think that the balance to be struck in *R. v A* is between the state and the accused, or is it between rape complainants and their assailants? Who does the Human Rights Act protect in this case?

A summary of developments in statutory interpretation is provided in the following two excerpts.

Francesca Klug, "The long road to human rights compliance" (2006) 57 *Northern Ireland Legal Quarterly* 186 at 195–198:

"The new rule of statutory interpretation in section 3 of the HRA—that primary and subordinate legislation must 'so far as it is possible to do so' be 'read and given effect in a way which is compatible with the Convention rights'—is a significant departure from the past. Prior to the HRA, statutory review outside the context of EU law, was virtually non-existent. Where a compatible interpretation is not 'possible', higher courts can make a 'declaration of incompatibility' under section 4(2) HRA. In similar circumstances, subordinate legislation can be set aside, unless 'primary legislation prevents removal of the incompatibility'.

According to Lord Irvine, the Lord Chancellor, section 3 was intended to go:

> 'far beyond the [then] present rule. It will not be necessary to find an ambiguity. On the contrary, the courts will be required to interpret legislation so as to uphold the Convention rights unless the legislation itself is so clearly incompatible with the Convention that it is impossible to do so.'

This was intended as a 'strong form' of incorporation.

Following a series of bold but controversial early decisions, it soon became apparent that the HRA's scheme has the capacity to alter law and practice to give substantive protection to individual rights. The courts have applied section 3 to 'read down' over-broad legislation, re-interpret provisions to provide new safeguards, or give a statutory provision a meaning it would not ordinarily bear. It also became clear that the courts are most likely to apply section 3 forthrightly to re-interpret legislation where their own powers are at issue, and are least likely to do so where questions of resource allocation or decisions outside their traditional expertise are at stake.

Compared to the early days of HRA jurisprudence, a reasonably consistent consensus has now emerged on the judicial interpretation of HRA section 3 and its interrelationship with section 4. On the one hand, although it is clear that 'section 3 itself is not free from ambiguity',[31] there is now broad agreement that what Lord Steyn calls an 'excessive concentration on the linguistic features of the [statute to be interpreted]' should be substituted in favour of a 'purposive' approach concentrating on 'the importance of the fundamental right involved'.[32] As Lord Nicholls has pointed out, once it is accepted that section 3 was intended to supersede the pre-HRA legislative ambiguity principle of re-interpretation, Parliament cannot intend the courts to 'depend critically upon the particular form of words adopted by the parliamentary draftsman' in the legislation in question without making the application of section 3 'something of a semantic lottery'.[33]

---

[31]   *Ghaidan v Ghodin-Mendoza* [2004] 2 AC 557 at 27.
[32]   *Ghaidan v Ghodin-Mendoza* [2004] 2 AC 557 at 41.
[33]   *Ghaidan v Ghodin-Mendoza* [2004] 2 AC 557 at 31.

On the other hand, Lord Steyn has rowed back from his earlier implication in *R v A*[34] that there is a presumption that Convention rights should override the provisions of other statutes unless there are *express* words to the contrary.[35] In *Anderson* he accepted that re-interpretation 'is not available where the suggested interpretation . . . *is by implication necessarily contradicted by the statute'*.[36]

The search to nail down the characteristics indicating such a 'contradiction' has also borne fruit. Lord Rodger argued in *Ghaidan* that section 3 'does not allow the court to change the substance of a provision completely, to change a provision from one where Parliament says that x is to happen into one saying x is not to happen'.[37] In Lord Nicholl's terms '[t]he meaning imported by application of section 3 must be compatible with the *underlying thrust* of the legislation being construed'.[38]

Applying this construction, the phrase in the 1977 Rent Act 'as his or her wife or husband'[39] was re-interpreted to mean '*as if they were* his wife or husband' in *Ghaidan*.[40] This was viewed as in line with the *thrust* of the statute which had already been amended to include cohabiting, as well as married couples but discriminated against gay and lesbian partners. However to read section 29 of the Crime (Sentences) Act 1997 in *Anderson* as precluding the Home Secretary from participating in setting the minimum period served by a mandatory life prisoner, was not deemed 'possible' when the provision was drafted for that precise purpose. Such an application of section 3, according to Lord Bingham would 'not be judicial interpretation but judicial vandalism . . .'[41]

The fact that a re-interpretation was not 'possible' did not mean the courts could do nothing, however, as they would have under the *ancien regime*. Instead, they made a Declaration under HRA section 4 that section 29 of the 1997 Act was incompatible with ECHR Article 6. The government responded by repealing section 29 to remove the role of the Home Secretary in setting minimum terms of imprisonment.

Declarations of Incompatibility (DoIs) have not been the paper tiger that many critics feared. They [have] been more frequent than predicted and in virtually all cases have led to changes in the law or in practice. The higher courts have issued 17 DoIs in five years, of which 11 are still standing. The most notable example was, of course, the House of Lords' declaration in December 2004 that section 23 of the Anti-terrorism, Crime and Security Act 2001 was incompatible with ECHR Articles 5 and 14. The government did not seek to renew the offending provision and the 10 remaining prisoners, who were subject to indefinite detention when Part 4 of the Act expired, were released, although they now remain subject to 'control orders' or detention pending deportation."

Alec Samuels, "Human Rights Act 1998 Section 3: A New Dimension to Statutory Interpretation?" (2008) 29 *Statute Law Review* 130 at 130–131; 137–138:

"Is this a new dimension to statutory interpretation? A distortion of the traditional approach to statutory interpretation? Or a recognition of what has been a trend anyway? Or what has been going on anyway? Or the fulfilment of international obligations? Is the section proving easy or difficult to apply? What effect is it having upon the understanding of the statutory law? Is there a new element of uncertainty in prediction? A leading statement of principle comes from Lord Bingham in *Sheldrake*,[42] deriving from *Ghaidan*, as follows: (i) The interpretative obligation under section 3 is very strong and far reaching and may require the judge to depart

---

[34] *R v A (no. 2)* [2001] 3 All ER 1.

[35] *R v A (no. 2)* [2001] 3 All ER 1 at 44.

[36] *R (Anderson) v Secretary of State for the Home Department* [2003] 1 AC 837, para. 59 (Klug's emphasis).

[37] *Ghaidan v Ghodin-Mendoza* [2004] 2 AC 557 at 110.

[38] *Ghaidan v Ghodin-Mendoza* [2004] 2 AC 557, para. 33 (Klug's emphasis).

[39] Para. 2, Sch 1 Rent Act 1977.

[40] *Ghaidan v Ghodin-Mendoza* [2004] 2 AC 557 at 51.

[41] *R (Anderson) v Secretary of State for the Home Department* [2003] 1 AC 837 at 30.

[42] *Sheldrake v DPP* (2004) UKHL 43; (2005) 1 AC 264, para 28.

from the legislative intention of Parliament. (ii) Convention-compliant interpretation under section 3 is the primary remedial measure, and a declaration of incompatibility is exceptional. (iii) Parliament envisaged that a need for a declaration of incompatibility would rarely arise. (iv) There is a limit beyond which a Convention-compliant interpretation is not possible. This may be because the interpretation would be incompatible with the underlying thrust of the legislation, would not go with the grain of it, would call for legislative deliberation, would change the substance of a statutory provision completely, would remove its pith and substance, or would violate a cardinal principle of the legislation. Section 3 is of general application; it does neither depend upon ambiguity or absurdity in the statute to be construed nor depend upon particular words; it does not call for excessive concentration upon linguistic features. There is a strong rebuttable presumption that an inconsistent or seemingly inconsistent statute can be rendered Convention-compliant, provided that there is no violence to the language and no 'judicial vandalism'. Section 3 is an interpretive section not an amending section, even though the interpretation may turn out to be abnormal. The section is the primary means of ensuring compatibility. If compliance cannot be achieved, then a declaration of incompatibility may be made, and Parliament can act if it wishes. In most cases, reliance upon section 3 is unnecessary because the statute is clear and compatibility is clear. . . .

It might seem strange that having found a statute to be incompatible with the Convention the judge can 'merely' declare it to be incompatible rather than strike it down. However, it seems that the judges are content with the declaratory power, as they do not wish to interfere with the sovereign Parliament and they are confident that the executive and legislature will act on the declaration and remedy the statutory defect, or the aggrieved citizen will go to the ECHR in Strasbourg and obtain judgment and compel the government to fulfil its international legal obligations under the Convention.

To distil or elicit any working principles or rules or guidance from the cases is not easy. The judge must adopt a strong, robust, radical approach. He must take a broad approach not a narrow legalistic approach. The interpretation of the language of the statute may be stretched, even stretched to the limit. The risk of incompatibility must always be borne in mind. The judge must strive to give effect to Convention rights and to the Strasbourg jurisprudence. Parliament must be presumed to have wished and intended to comply with and not to breach the Convention. In practice, it is extremely difficult to persuade the judge that a statute is incompatible with the Convention. Traditional English law and continental law, reflecting their respective cultures, have developed very differently in the past. Society has changed since the C19 and C20, and the judge may read old statutes in a contemporary manner and take account of changing social and economic trends, for example in attitudes to human rights and sexual orientation and social security. The judge must search for a legitimate, justified, reasonable, and proportionate interpretation."

Questions

1. Why do you think courts seem unwilling to interpret s.3 of the Human Rights Act broadly "where questions of resource allocation" are raised?

2. What does Klug mean when she states that Declarations of Incompatibility "have not been the paper tiger that many critics feared"? Have they, in fact, been ineffective?

3. What does it mean to say that "the interpretation of the language of the statute may be stretched, even stretched to the limit"? Can such an approach be constitutionally justified?

We have already considered the *Ghaidan v Mendoza* case in Ch.6. In the following extract from the decision of the Law Lords, we focus on the approach to s.3 of the Human Rights Act.

Ghaidan v Mendoza [2004] UKHL 30.

Lord Nicholls of Birkenhead:

Section 3 of the Human Rights Act 1998

"25. I turn next to the question whether section 3 of the Human Rights Act 1998 requires the court to depart from the interpretation of paragraph 2 enunciated in *Fitzpatrick's* case.

26. Section 3 is a key section in the Human Rights Act 1998. It is one of the primary means by which Convention rights are brought into the law of this country. Parliament has decreed that all legislation, existing and future, shall be interpreted in a particular way. All legislation must be read and given effect to in a way which is compatible with the convention rights 'so far as it is possible to do so'. This is the intention of Parliament, expressed in s 3, and the courts must give effect to this intention.

27. Unfortunately, in making this provision for the interpretation of legislation, s 3 itself is not free from ambiguity. Section 3 is open to more than one interpretation. The difficulty lies in the word 'possible'. Section 3(1), read in conjunction with s 3(2) and s 4, makes one matter clear: Parliament expressly envisaged that not all legislation would be capable of being made convention-compliant by application of s 3. Sometimes it would be possible, sometimes not. What is not clear is the test to be applied in separating the sheep from the goats. What is the standard, or the criterion, by which 'possibility' is to be judged? A comprehensive answer to this question is proving elusive. The courts, including your Lordships' House, are still cautiously feeling their way forward as experience in the application of s 3 gradually accumulates.

28. One tenable interpretation of the word 'possible' would be that s 3 is confined to requiring courts to resolve ambiguities. Where the words under consideration fairly admit of more than one meaning the convention-compliant meaning is to prevail. Words should be given the meaning which best accords with the Convention rights.

29. This interpretation of s 3 would give the section a comparatively narrow scope. This is not the view which has prevailed. It is now generally accepted that the application of s 3 does not depend upon the presence of ambiguity in the legislation being interpreted. Even if, construed according to the ordinary principles of interpretation, the meaning of the legislation admits of no doubt, s 3 may nonetheless require the legislation to be given a different meaning. The decision of your Lordships' House in *R v A* [2001] UKHL 25, [2001] 3 All ER 1, [2002] 1 AC 45 is an instance of this. The House read words into s 41 of the Youth Justice and Criminal Evidence Act 1999 so as to make that section compliant with an accused's right to a fair trial under art 6. The House did so even though the statutory language was not ambiguous.

30. From this it follows that the interpretative obligation decreed by s 3 is of an unusual and far-reaching character. Section 3 may require a court to depart from the unambiguous meaning the legislation would otherwise bear. In the ordinary course the interpretation of legislation involves seeking the intention reasonably to be attributed to Parliament in using the language in question. Section 3 may require the court to depart from this legislative intention, that is, depart from the intention of the Parliament which enacted the legislation. The question of difficulty is how far, and in what circumstances, s 3 requires a court to depart from the intention of the enacting Parliament. The answer to this question depends upon the intention reasonably to be attributed to Parliament in enacting s 3.

31. On this the first point to be considered is how far, when enacting s 3, Parliament intended that the actual language of a statute, as distinct from the concept expressed in that language, should be determinative. Since s 3 relates to the 'interpretation' of legislation, it is natural to focus attention initially on the language used in the legislative provision being considered. But once it is accepted that s 3 may

require legislation to bear a meaning which departs from the unambiguous meaning the legislation would otherwise bear, it becomes impossible to suppose Parliament intended that the operation of s 3 should depend critically upon the particular form of words adopted by the parliamentary draftsman in the statutory provision under consideration. That would make the application of s 3 something of a semantic lottery. If the draftsman chose to express the concept being enacted in one form of words, s 3 would be available to achieve convention-compliance. If he chose a different form of words, s 3 would be impotent.

32. From this the conclusion which seems inescapable is that the mere fact the language under consideration is inconsistent with a convention-compliant meaning does not of itself make a convention-compliant interpretation under s 3 impossible. Section 3 enables language to be interpreted restrictively or expansively. But s 3 goes further than this. It is also apt to require a court to read in words which change the meaning of the enacted legislation, so as to make it convention-compliant. In other words, the intention of Parliament in enacting s 3 was that, to an extent bounded only by what is 'possible', a court can modify the meaning, and hence the effect, of primary and secondary legislation.

33. Parliament, however, cannot have intended that in the discharge of this extended interpretative function the courts should adopt a meaning inconsistent with a fundamental feature of legislation. That would be to cross the constitutional boundary s 3 seeks to demarcate and preserve. Parliament has retained the right to enact legislation in terms which are not convention-compliant. The meaning imported by application of s 3 must be compatible with the underlying thrust of the legislation being construed. Words implied must, in the phrase of my noble and learned friend Lord Rodger of Earlsferry, 'go with the grain of the legislation'. Nor can Parliament have intended that s 3 should require courts to make decisions for which they are not equipped. There may be several ways of making a provision convention-compliant, and the choice may involve issues calling for legislative deliberation. . . .

35. In some cases difficult problems may arise. No difficulty arises in the present case. Paragraph 2 of Sch 1 to the Rent Act 1977 is unambiguous. But the social policy underlying the 1988 extension of security of tenure under para 2 to the survivor of couples living together as husband and wife is equally applicable to the survivor of homosexual couples living together in a close and stable relationship. In this circumstance I see no reason to doubt that application of s 3 to para 2 has the effect that para 2 should be read and given effect to as though the survivor of such a homosexual couple were the surviving spouse of the original tenant. Reading para 2 in this way would have the result that cohabiting heterosexual couples and cohabiting heterosexual couples would be treated alike for the purposes of succession as a statutory tenant. This would eliminate the discriminatory effect of para 2 and would do so consistently with the social policy underlying para 2. The precise form of words read in for this purpose is of no significance. It is their substantive effect which matters.

36. For these reasons I agree with the decision of the Court of Appeal. I would dismiss this appeal. . . ."

Lord Millett (dissenting):

"68. In my view s 3 does not entitle the court to supply words which are inconsistent with a fundamental feature of the legislative scheme; nor to repeal, delete, or contradict the language of the offending statute. As Lord Nicholls said in *Rojas v Berllaque (A-Gl for Gibraltar intervening)* [2003] UKPC 76 at [24], [2004] 1 LRC 296 at [24], [2004] 1 WLR 201: 'There may of course be cases where an offending law does not lend itself to a sensible interpretation which would conform to the relevant Constitution.' This is more likely to be the case in the United Kingdom where the court's role is exclusively interpretative than in those territories (which include Gibraltar) where it is quasi-legislative.

69. I doubt that the principles which I have endeavoured to state would be disputed; disagreement is likely to lie in their application in a particular case. So it may be helpful if I give some examples of the way in which I see s 3 as operating.

70.   In the course of his helpful argument counsel for the Secretary of State, who did not resist the application of s 3, acknowledged that it could not be used to read 'black' as meaning 'white'. That must be correct. Words cannot *mean* their opposite; 'black' cannot *mean* 'not black'. But they may *include* their opposite. In some contexts it may be possible to read 'black' as meaning 'black or white'; in other contexts it may be impossible to do so. It all depends on whether 'blackness' is the essential feature of the statutory scheme; and while the court may look behind the words of the statute they cannot be disregarded or given no weight, for they are the medium by which Parliament expresses its intention.

71.   Again, 'red, blue or green' cannot be read as meaning 'red, blue, green or yellow'; the specification of three only of the four primary colours indicates a deliberate omission of the fourth (unless, of course, this can be shown to be an error). Section 3 cannot be used to supply the missing colour, for this would be not to interpret the statutory language but to contradict it.

72.   The limits on the application of s 3 may thus be in part at least linguistic, as in the examples I have given, but they may also be derived from a consideration of the legislative history of the offending statute. Thus, while it may be possible to read 'cats' as meaning 'cats or dogs' (on the footing that the essential concept is that of domestic pets generally rather than felines particularly), it would obviously not be possible to read 'Siamese cats' as meaning 'Siamese cats or dogs'. The particularity of the expression 'Siamese cats' would preclude its extension to other species of cat, let alone dogs. But suppose the statute merely said 'cats', and that this was the result of successive amendments to the statute as originally enacted. If this had said 'Siamese cats', and had twice been amended, first to read 'Siamese or Persian cats' and then to read simply 'cats', it would not, in my opinion, be possible to read the word 'cats' as including 'dogs'; the legislative history would demonstrate that, while Parliament had successively widened the scope of the statute, it had consistently legislated in relation to felines, and had left its possible extension to other domestic pets for future consideration. Reading the word 'cats' as meaning 'cats or dogs' in these circumstances would be to usurp the function of Parliament. . . .

77.   It is obvious that, if para 2(2) of Sch 1 to the Rent Act 1977 as amended had referred expressly to 'a person of the opposite sex' who was living with the original tenant as his or her husband or wife, it would not be possible to bring the paragraph into conformity with the Convention by resort to s 3. The question is whether the words 'of the opposite sex' are implicit; for if they are, then the same result must follow. Reading the paragraph as referring to persons whether of the same or opposite sex would equally contradict the legislative intent in either case. I agree that the operation of s 3 does not depend critically upon the form of words found in the statute; the court is not engaged in a parlour game. But it does depend upon identifying the essential features of the legislative scheme; and these must be gathered in part at least from the words that Parliament has chosen to use. Drawing the line between the express and the implicit would be to engage in precisely that form of semantic lottery to which the majority rightly object. . . .

94.   By 1988 Parliament, therefore, had successively widened the scope of para 2(1). First applying only to the tenant's widow, it was extended first to his or her surviving spouse and later to a person who had lived with the tenant as his or her spouse though without actually contracting a legally binding marriage. The common feature of all these relationships is that they are open relationships between persons of the opposite sex. Persons who set up home together may be husband and wife or live together as husband and wife; they may be lovers; or brother and sister; or friends; or fellow students; or share a common economic interest; or one may be economically dependent on the other. But Parliament did not extend the right to persons who set up home together; but only to those who did so *as husband and wife*.

95.   Couples of the same sex can no more live together as husband and wife than they can live together as brother and sister. To extend the paragraph to persons who set up home as lovers would have been a

major category extension. It would have been highly controversial in 1988 and was not then required by the convention. The practice of contracting states was far from uniform; and Parliament was entitled to take the view that any further extension of para (2) could wait for another day. One step at a time is a defensible legislative policy which the courts should respect. Housing Acts come before Parliament with some frequency; and Parliament was entitled to take the view that the question could be revisited without any great delay. It is just as important for legislatures not to proceed faster than society can accept as it is for judges; and under our constitutional arrangements the pace of change is for Parliament."

[Lord Steyn, Lord Rodger of Earlsferry and Baroness Hale of Richmond delivered separate reasons concurring with Lord Nicholls of Birkenhead.]

Questions

1. Do you agree with Lord Nicholls that s.3 requires the courts "to read in words which change the meaning of the enacted legislation"? What criticism could be made of this approach to interpretation?

2. Do you agree with Lord Millett that the "essential feature" of this legislation was that it was restricted to opposite-sex couples? Justify your answer.

3. Does Lord Millet make a compelling point that "it is just as important for legislatures not to proceed faster than society can accept as it is for judges"?

4. If you were a member of the panel of Law Lords in *Ghaidan v Mendoza*, would you agree with Lord Nicholls or Lord Millett? Explain your decision.

Although the cases described above suggest the *significance* of the Human Rights Act 1998 for statutory interpretation by judges, it should also be appreciated that the courts may sometimes be reluctant to accept arguments that Convention rights have been breached. A good example of *deference* to Parliament by the Court of Appeal with respect to rights arguments can be seen in the following case, in which the Court was required to interpret the Housing Act 1988. This case raises the important issue of what constitutes a "public" authority under the Act, as well as the substantive rights which were alleged to have been breached.

Poplar Housing Regeneration Community Association Ltd v Donoghue [2001] 4 All E.R. 604, CA.

Lord Woolf C.J.:

The background
"This is an appeal from an order of District Judge Naqvi dated 5 December 2000. The judge gave permission to appeal and directed that the appeal should be heard by the Court of Appeal pursuant to CPR 52.14 on the ground that the appeal raises important points of principle and practice.

    The proceedings started in the Bow County Court as a straightforward claim for possession of 31 Nairn Street London E14 0LQ, of which the defendant was the tenant and which is owned by the claimant housing association, Poplar Housing and Regeneration Community Association Ltd (Poplar). On the day of the hearing, 5 December, 2000, the proceedings were in the ordinary housing list. It had not been appreciated that the defendant wished to raise the issue that to make an order for possession would contravene her rights to respect for her private and family life and respect for her home contrary to art.8 of Sch 1 to the Human Rights Act 1998. Fortunately, notwithstanding the novel nature of the contention, District Judge Naqvi was in a position to consider the arguments which were advanced before him and give judgment straight away. We have a copy of the judgment and we commend the judge on the manner in which he dealt with the case.

The approach of the judge

As he points out in his judgment, although this was not how the case was initially presented, the tenancy was an assured shorthold tenancy subject to s.21 of the Housing Act 1988. Section 21 deals with the recovery of possession on the expiry or termination of assured shorthold tenancies. Under the section, the court's discretion not to make an order for possession is strictly limited.

Section 21(1) applies to orders for possession of dwelling houses after the coming to an end of an assured shorthold tenancy for a fixed term. The defendant did not have a fixed term tenancy. She had a periodic tenancy. Periodic tenancies are dealt with by s.21(4). Section 21(4) provides:

> 'Without prejudice to any such right as is referred to in subsection (1) above, a court *shall* make an order for possession of a dwelling-house let on an assured shorthold tenancy which is a periodic tenancy if the court is satisfied—(a) that the landlord, or, in the case of joint landlords, at least one of them has given to the tenant a notice in writing stating that, after a date specified in the notice, being the last day of a period of the tenancy and not earlier than two months after the date the notice was given, possession of the dwelling-house is required by virtue of this section; and (b) that the date specified in the notice under paragraph (a) above is not earlier than the earliest day on which, apart from section 5(1) above, the tenancy could be brought to an end by a notice to quit given by the landlord on the same date as the notice under paragraph (a) above.' (My emphasis.)

It will be observed that s.21(4) appears to be mandatory in its terms. The court has to make an order for possession if there is a tenancy to which the subsection applies and the appropriate notice has been given. There is no requirement for the court to be satisfied that it is *reasonable* to make an order.

The first point taken on behalf of the defendant before the judge was that the notice which had been given did not comply with s.5 of the Protection from Eviction Act 1977. The judge held that s.5 only applied to purely common law notices to quit and not to statutory notices under s.21(4) of the 1988 Act. No appeal has been pursued in respect of that holding.

The judge then turned his attention to the Human Rights Act argument. It was contended that to make an order for possession would contravene arts 6 and 8 of the European Convention for the Protection of Human Rights and Fundamental Freedoms (Rome, 4 November 1950; TS 71 (1953); Cmd 8969) (as set out in Sch 1 to the 1998 Act) and would involve interpreting s.21(4) in a manner which is not compatible with the 1998 Act. The judge rejected these contentions as well. He said:

> 'If I were to read s.21(4) of the 1988 Act in the way in which I am being enjoined to do, this would, in effect, enable people who were intentionally homeless, and that is a finding that has been already made by the local authority, which has been reviewed and has not been challenged, the final decision having been made a year ago in November 1999, to jump the housing queue, that would impede the human rights of others and that is the proviso to Art.8(2) that I have got in mind, "the protection of the rights and freedoms of others".'

He did, however, postpone the date on which the order came into force for 42 days. This was the maximum extension which he was entitled to give. This was because of the defendant's exceptional personal circumstances. In addition, as already stated, the judge gave permission to the defendant to appeal directly to the Court of Appeal.

It is the defendant's contention that the judge should have adjourned the hearing so as to enable her to place before the court the substantial evidence, which is now before this court, in support of her appeal. The evidence is directed to the issues of whether the housing association is a public body or performing a public function and whether any breach of art.9 could be justified on the grounds set out in art.8(2).

In our judgment, where it is possible for a judge to give a decision summarily, as the judge did here, in a case where there will almost certainly be an appeal, there can be substantial advantages in adopting this approach. It can avoid expense and delay being incurred both at first instance and in the Court of Appeal.

The facts

The defendant moved into 31 Nairn Street in March 1998. She then had three children aged three, four and five. At the time of the possession proceedings she was expecting her fourth. The tenancy was granted by the London Borough of Tower Hamlets (Tower Hamlets) pursuant to its duties as the local housing authority under s.188 of the Housing Act 1996. The tenancy was a weekly non-secure tenancy under para 4 of Sch 1 to the Housing Act 1985. This was recorded in the written agreement dated 25 February 1998. The property was later transferred to Poplar. Poplar was created as a housing association by Tower Hamlets in order to transfer to it a substantial proportion of the council's housing stock.

The defendant had been provided with housing by Tower Hamlets pending a decision as to whether she was intentionally homeless. On 16 September 1999, Tower Hamlets decided she was intentionally homeless and notified the defendant to this effect (s 184 of the 1996 Act). The reason given was that the defendant had left an assured shorthold tenancy to live with her sister. A review of this decision was conducted by Tower Hamlets at the request of the defendant on 29 November 1999. The decision was confirmed. Previously the defendant would have been able, if she wished, to challenge the decision on an application for judicial review. However, by November 1999, the procedure for challenging the decision was by way of appeal to the county court. The defendant did not appeal.

In January or February 2000, Tower Hamlets issued proceedings for possession against the defendant. The authority then discovered that it was not the landlord and proceedings were withdrawn. On 26 June 2000, Tower Hamlets wrote to the defendant informing her that she was a tenant of Poplar and was subject to an assured shorthold tenancy. On 27 June, a notice was served by Poplar under s.21(4) of the 1988 Act. On 19 October 2000, the present proceedings were commenced. . . .

The issues to which this appeal gives rise

If it were not for contentions based on the 1998 Act, there would be no possible basis for interfering with the judge's decision. There is no ambiguity in the terms of s.21(4) of the 1988 Act. Poplar could not obtain possession without an order of a court but the court was required to make the order if the defendant had a tenancy which was subject to s.21(4) and the proper notice was served (which in this case are now not in dispute).

On this appeal, as in the court below, the contentions of the defendant depend upon art.8, coupled with art.6, of the convention set out in Sch 1 to the 1998 Act. Article 8 is in the following terms:

'Right to respect for private and family life

    1. Everyone has the right to respect for his private and family life, his home and his correspondence.

    2. There shall be no interference by a public authority with the exercise of this right except such as is in accordance with the law and is necessary in a democratic society in the interests of national security, public safety or the economic well-being of the country, for the prevention of disorder or crime, for the protection of health or morals, or for the protection of the rights and freedoms of others.'

In considering art.1, it is helpful in this context to have in mind art.1 of the First Protocol of the convention set out in Pt II of Sch 1 to the 1998 Act. Article 1 provides: 'Every natural or legal person is entitled to the peaceful enjoyment of his possessions. No one shall be deprived of his possessions except in the public interest and subject to the conditions provided for by law . . .

Article 6 entitles the defendant to a fair trial of her right to remain in her home. There is no question of that right being infringed. If we hold that she is entitled to rely on art.8, it may be necessary for the case to be remitted to the county court to determine whether it is reasonable to make an order of possession. As to art.8, it appears to us that the following issues require consideration. (1) Did the judge adopt an appropriate procedure to determine the art.8 issue? (The procedural issue.) (2) Is Poplar a public body or was it performing functions of a public nature? (The public body issue.) (3) Did making an order for possession contravene art.8? (The art.8 issue.) (4) If it did, is a declaration of incompatibility the appropriate remedy? (The remedy issue.)

The procedural issue

As already indicated, the defendant complains that the judge dealt with the art.8 issues in far too summary a manner. Poplar, on the other hand, contends, though not with much enthusiasm, that this was the only appropriate way for the judge to deal with the issue. It would have been wrong of the judge to grant an adjournment so that the defendant could place before the court the evidence that she contended was required since this would have contravened the clear terms of s.21(4) of the 1988 Act. Even if art.8 was contravened, the correct remedy would be to grant a declaration of incompatibility, which would be available on an appeal. It was not for the judge to interpret s.21(4) in a way which gave him discretion to decide whether or not to make an order for possession.

In general terms, we have already indicated our approval of the approach of the judge. This does not mean that we consider that the judge was not required to deal with the art.8 issue once it was raised before him. In our judgment, the judge was required to deal with the defendant's contention, notwithstanding the language of s.21(4). Section 7 of the 1998 Act provides, so far as relevant:

> '(1) A person who claims that a public authority has acted (or proposes to act) in a way which is made unlawful by section 6(1) may . . . (b) rely on the Convention right or rights concerned in any legal proceedings, but only if he is (or would be) a victim of the unlawful act.'

If the defendant is right in her contentions as to the manner in which art.8 applies to her tenancy, then she is a 'victim'. Furthermore, if she is right, Poplar is a public authority. She is therefore entitled to rely on art.8 'in any legal proceedings'. The judge clearly accepted that this was the situation and that is why he set out his views as to why art.8 did not apply to her tenancy. If the defendant is right, the question of incompatibility will have to be considered, but unless 21(4) is found to be incompatible, the case will have to be remitted so that a judge can, in the light of her circumstances, decide how he should exercise the discretion he would then have. The issue is there confined to whether the judge was entitled to decide the matter on the limited material that was then available without granting and adjournment.

For reasons we have partly explained, we consider that the judge was entitled to dispose of the case as he did. He sensibly cut through the issues by accepting for the purpose of his decision that Poplar was at least performing a public function in terminating the defendant's tenancy and seeking possession and that art.8(1) therefore applied. He focused on art.8(2) and decided s.21(4) did not offend art.8 on the ground that the purpose s.21(4) serves is within art.8(2). A district judge is familiar with housing issues and is perfectly entitled to apply his practical experience and common sense to an issue of this sort. It is not necessary at his level to hold a state trial into successive governments' housing policies in order to balance the public and private issues to which art.8 gives rise. A great deal of expense and delay was avoided in a case which he was aware would be likely to come before this court in any event. (There is no power to make a declaration of incompatibility in the county court.)

Mr Luba QC, on behalf of the defendant, advanced an argument based on the fact that the court is itself a public authority (s 6(3)(a) of the 1998 Act). However, if there is no contravention of art.8 on which the defendant is entitled to rely, this argument does not avail the defendant.

If courts of first instance are encouraged to deal with Human Rights Act issues summarily, we appreciate, and the present appeal makes clear, that the Court of Appeal will have to be flexible in relation to its own procedures. The outcome of this appeal to a substantial extent depends upon the legislative framework. However, that legislation has to be interpreted against the factual background of how the legislation works on the ground. When it became apparent that this court was going to decide for itself the principal issues involved rather than remit the appeal, if successful, to the court below, the parties wished to place additional evidence before the court. This was done, with our agreement, after the completion of the oral argument. It inevitably meant that the preparation of this judgment was somewhat delayed.

We are very grateful to the parties for the manner in which they have marshalled the evidence and for the further written argument which they have provided. We have considered whether we needed to hear further oral argument but have come to the conclusion that this is not necessary. The evidence, together with the written arguments, makes the positions of the parties clear. We need no further assistance in order to give our decision as to the outcome of this appeal.

The legislative framework

In order to determine the remaining issues, it is critical to have in mind the manner in which the legislative framework, which sets out the duties which are owed to tenants in the position of the defendant, and under which a registered social landlord (RSL) such as Poplar operates, has evolved.

The law affecting tenants of domestic accommodation has suffered from a failure to conduct a satisfactory review and consolidation of the legislation. This is despite a continuous process of amendment as the various governments of the day struggled to address the expense and chronic lack of accommodation for the less well-off members of society. The Law Commission has now been given the responsibility of remedying this situation. Until this happens, in order to understand the present legislative position, it is helpful to keep the historic position in mind.

At one time, the private sector was heavily controlled in order to mitigate the hardship caused to tenants by a shortage of housing. Rents were carefully controlled and tenants were given a substantial measure of statutory protection against eviction. So far as the private sector has been concerned, generally the policy has been to reduce this control. The change of policy reflected the belief of governments that excessive control resulted in a deterioration in the quality and quantity of housing available in the private sector. This, it is said, has a variety of undesirable economic consequences for the public in general and the poorer members of society in particular.

The statutory responsibility of providing for those who do not have homes was and is that of local government, acting through housing authorities. In particular, boroughs such as Tower Hamlets are subject to a range of statutory duties to provide social housing. For this purpose, as Mr Gahagan points out in his written evidence on behalf of the Department, until the 1990s, local government authorities were not only responsible for the availability of local housing, but in addition acted as social landlords with their own housing stock. However, over the last decade, a number of local housing authorities have transferred their stock of housing to RSLs. This policy is considered to have been successful and is being expanded.

Part IV of the 1996 Act governs the allocation of housing accommodation by local housing authorities. A housing authority can select someone to be a secure tenant, or an introductory tenant, or nominate someone to be an assured tenant of RSL stock. Before the housing authorities can allocate accommodation, the person to whom the accommodation is to be allocated must fulfil the qualifying requirements. For this purpose, housing authorities establish and maintain a register of qualifying persons (s 162 of the 1996 Act). Applicants have a right of review of decisions by authorities not to place them on a register or to remove them from a register. Housing authorities must also publish a scheme for determining priorities and procedures. The policy behind the 1996 Act, according to Mr Gahagan, was to create a 'single route' through the housing register into social housing and remove a perceived fast track into such housing for households accepted as statutorily homeless. . . .

Mr Gahagan in his statement makes it clear that in many areas, particularly in London and the South East, demand for social housing far outweighs supply and therefore allocation must be made according to the degree of housing need and how long the applicants have been waiting. He also states:

'47. The purpose of the homelessness legislation is to provide a safety net for people who have become homeless through no fault of their own and would be vulnerable if they were not provided with temporary accommodation until a more settled housing solution becomes available. If people accepted as unintentionally homeless and in priority need were provided with accommodation with security of tenure, this would displace applicants with greater claim to scarce social housing. This would not be in the interests of public policy since it would amount to a fast track into a secure social tenancy for people accepted as statutorily homeless and would create a perverse incentive for people to apply for homelessness assistance. 48. The provision of temporary accommodation can be expensive for authorities, particularly in areas of high demand where they do not have sufficient accommodation of their own and must make arrangements with other landlords. A guiding principle underlying the legislation is that authorities are not obliged to secure accommodation, other than very briefly if the applicant has priority need, for people who have made themselves homeless intentionally. Such applicants are expected to make their own arrangements to find accommodation for themselves. 49. The interim duty to accommodate those applicants who appear to be homeless and have a priority need, pending completion of inquiries and a decision as to whether a substantive duty is owed, is a very important aspect of the safety net. It is essential to the public policy interest, however, that authorities can bring such interim accommodation to an end where they are satisfied that the applicant does not qualify for further assistance.'

The role of housing associations in providing accommodation has equally been affected by government policy.

Housing associations were very much the 'legal embodiment of the voluntary housing movement' as Mr Brockway, another witness on behalf of the Department, stated. Originally, many were small local charities, though others were large entities endowed by wealthy employers or philanthropists. The legal definition of a housing association is contained in s.1(1) of the Housing Associations Act 1985. This section makes it clear that a housing association may be a charity, an industrial and provident society, or a company which does not trade for profit and which has among its objects the provision of housing accommodation. Some are fully mutual co-operative organisations. Throughout the twentieth century many housing associations were funded by grants or loans usually through local authorities. In 1964, the Housing Corporation (the Corporation) was created and thereafter most of the public funding was channelled through the Corporation. The Corporation was granted supervisory powers by the Housing Act 1974. There are now 4,000 housing associations, of which approximately 2,200 are registered with the Corporation as RSLs. Since 1988, RSLs have been required to borrow funds in the private markets to supplement public funding. To date, some £20bn has been raised outside the public sector borrowing requirement. The other major development has been the growth in the transfer of housing stock from local authorities to RSLs. Both under the previous and the present government, some 500,000 dwellings have been transferred in this way. Today, there are 1.5 million dwellings in the ownership of RSLs.

Under Pt I of the 1996 Act, the Corporation is given two basic roles. These are to provide funding to RSLs and to regulate them. The funding is payable by way of grant under s.18 of the 1996 Act. Regulation covers the area of governance, finance and housing management. If performance fails, the Corporation can exercise a number of powers; it can withdraw funding, make appointments to the governing body of the RSL and remove employees or governing body members (Sch 1 of the Act).

Section 170 of the 1996 Act importantly provides:

'Where a local housing authority so request, a registered social landlord shall co-operate to such an extent as is reasonable in the circumstances in offering accommodation to people with priority on the authority's housing register.'

Section 213 of the 1996 Act also requires 'other bodies' to co-operate with housing authorities to assist in the discharge of their functions, subject to the request for co-operation being reasonable in the circumstances. 'Other bodies' includes RSLs: s.213(2)(a). Mr Brockway states that in most local authority areas, the housing authority will have nomination agreements with RSLs. These agreements enable the authority to nominate tenants, to whom the RSLs should grant tenancies, from the housing registers.

Many local authorities have transferred some or all of their housing stock to one or more RSL. This has happened so far as Poplar is concerned. Poplar was created for the purpose of taking over part of the housing stock of the borough of Tower Hamlets. It was a condition of Tower Hamlets receiving funding that this should happen. The funding came from the government under a scheme (the Estates Renewal Challenge Fund) designed to bring about the repair and improvement of old housing stock, the improvement of security for occupants of estates, to tackle anti-social behaviour and crime and to develop community initiatives. The transfer of the council stock to Poplar was only possible where there was a majority vote by tenants in favour of the transfer of the particular housing stock involved. No payment was involved for the transfer. The properties transferred were regarded as having a negative value because of their state of repair. Mr Brockway makes it clear that the government's policy was that the RSLs should be private sector bodies. The way they were funded was dependent on this. Mr Brockway states that as a matter of policy the Corporation has always asked RSLs to grant the most secure form of tenure available to its tenants. This will usually be achieved by granting periodic tenancies of which possession can only be achieved on discretionary grounds. Such tenancies are accepted by Mr Luba as providing the necessary protection which he submits is necessary to comply with art.9 of the convention. The Corporation requires that if a tenant has an assured tenancy, then an order for possession can only be sought if it is reasonable to seek the order.

However, guidance has been given by the Corporation to RSLs to grant assured shorthold tenancies where special circumstances exist. Those circumstances include where the provision of accommodation is to be temporary, as was the position in the case of the defendant.

Mr Christopher Holmes, the director of Shelter, has provided evidence for the defendant. Based on his experience, he states that in practical terms, particularly where large-scale voluntary transfers have occurred, housing associations provide the means whereby accommodation is made available to homeless persons. This can include interim accommodation under s.188 of the 1996 Act while the priority of an applicant is being determined and where, as in the case of the defendant, the applicant has been found to be homeless intentionally. Mr Holmes goes on to point out:

'To enable the statutory duties imposed on local authorities to be discharged appropriately, close co-operation with housing associations continues beyond the point where accommodation is made available. When duties come to an end and accommodation is to be recovered, notification will pass from the authority to the association and possession will be recovered in due course. In effect, the association acts as a conduit for the authority's decision on whether a duty arises or has come to an end.'

He adds:

'Although there is no doubt that housing associations have their own constitutions and mechanisms for governance, in the practical day-to-day management of both long-term and short-term provision for the homeless, they are inextricably linked to the statutory framework imposing duties on local authorities and associations alike.'

He further adds:

'The complex nature of housing associations, run as they are, by unpaid persons and with their own constitutions, is apparent. And yet the associations are free to decide key issues regarding investment of funds and the nature of refurbishment and development works. Although tied in with local authorities in terms of allocations and homelessness, this does not, of itself, alter the fundamentally private nature of associations. There are many bodies which are required to act in accordance with public powers, duties and functions but which remain essentially private bodies. Railtrack is an example.'

Later, having referred to Mr Brockway's approach that any RSL taking over the stock of a housing authority will be a private sector body, Mr Holmes adds: 'This is, of course, the case but the day-to-day management of that stock may in my view be properly categorised as a public function in the circumstances I have described in this statement.'

He also refers to the fact that RSLs are subject to the scheme introduced by s.51 of the 1996 Act for the investigation of complaints by the independent housing ombudsman. Mr Holmes does not accept that the use of assured shorthold tenancies by RSLs is necessary. His complaints include the fact that:

'More and more tenants are losing their homes on mandatory grounds. The government's own homelessness statistics show that, between 1992 and 1999, there was an increase of nearly 63% in the number of households accepted as homeless and in priority need following the recovery of possession of premises let on an assured shorthold tenancy. The loss of a shorthold is now the third most common reason for homelessness given by persons accepted as homeless by local authorities. In some areas of high housing demand it is the most common reason.'

He supports his view by referring to cases which illustrate the disadvantage of assured shorthold tenancies.

Public bodies and public functions

The importance of whether Poplar was at the material times a public body or performing public functions is this: the 1998 Act will only apply to Poplar if it is deemed to be a public body or performing public functions. Section 6(1) of the 1998 Act makes it unlawful for a public authority to act in a way which is incompatible with a convention right. Section 6(3) states that a 'public authority' includes 'any person certain of whose functions are functions of a public nature'. Section 6(5) provides: 'In relation to a particular act, a person is not a public authority by virtue only of subsection (3)(b) if the nature of the act is private.'

The defendant relies on the witness statements of Mr David Cowan, a lecturer of law at the University of Bristol (specialising in housing law and policy) and of Professor Alder of the University of Newcastle in support of her contention that Poplar is a public authority within s.6. Both Mr Cowan and Professor Alder acknowledge that the questions raised are ones of importance and of some debate in academic circles. However, Mr Cowan says it is 'tolerably clear that RSLs do fall within the definition of public authority under s.6(1)' as they are performing public functions.

Mr Cowan says:

'The obligation to provide interim accommodation under Pt VII (homelessness) of the Housing Act 1996 pending inquiries is owed by the local authority to the homeless applicant. That is clearly a public function. The accommodation can be provided by an RSL (see s.206(1)(b)). An RSL which provides that accommodation is thus fulfilling a public function. Where, as here, the accommodation provided to the homeless household in satisfaction of the duty was originally owed by the local authority, but subsequently transferred to the RLS *whilst the duty was ongoing*, then the public nature of a function is made all the clearer. The decision to seek possession of the property once the relevant inquiries and a decision on the homelessness application have been made, are all part and parcel of that function. It is therefore clear that this case does not fall within the exemption of activities covered by s.6(5).'

We agree with Mr Luba's submissions that the definition of who is a public authority, and what is a public function, for the purposes of s.6 of the 1998 Act, should be given a generous interpretation. However, we would suggest that the position is not as simple as Mr Cowan suggests. The fact that a body performs an activity which otherwise a public body would be under a duty to perform cannot mean that such performance is necessarily a public function. A public body in order to perform its public duties can use the services of a private body. Section 6 should not be applied so that if a private body provides such services, the nature of the functions are inevitably public. If this were to be the position, then when a small hotel provides bed and breakfast accommodation as a temporary measure, at the request of the housing authority that is under a duty to provide that accommodation, the small hotel would be performing public functions and required to comply with the 1998 Act. This in not what the 1998 Act intended. The consequence would be the same where a hospital uses a private company to carry out specialist services, such as analysing blood samples. The position under the 1998 Act is necessarily more complex. Section 6(3) means that hybrid bodies, who have functions of a public and private nature are public authorities, but not in relation to acts of a private nature. The renting out of accommodation can certainly be of a private nature. The fact that through the act of renting by a private body a public authority may be fulfilling its public duty, does not automatically change into a public act what would otherwise be a private act. . . .

The purpose of s.6(3)(b) is to deal with hybrid bodies which have both public and private functions. It is not to make a body, which does not have responsibilities to the public, a public body merely because it performs acts on behalf of a public body which would constitute public functions were such acts to be performed by the public body itself. An act can remain of a private nature even though it is performed because another body is under a public duty to ensure that that act is performed. . . .

The approach of Professor Alder differs from that of Mr Cowan. He states that there is no single factor that determines whether a function is a public function. He adds:

> 'The meaning of "public function" is not necessarily the same in the different contexts where the matter arises . . . Analogies, particularly in respect to the test for determining which bodies are susceptible to judicial review in the Administrative Court may be helpful, given that one purpose of judicial review is to ensure that public bodies are subject to high standards of conduct the same being true of the [convention]. There is also an analogy with the test that is being developed in European Community law for determining whether a body is a public body, namely "a body, whatever its legal form, which has been made responsible, pursuant to a measure adopted by the state, for providing a public service under the control of the state and which has for that purpose special powers beyond those which result from the normal rules applicable in relations between individuals . . ." (*Foster v British Gas plc* Case C-188/89 [1990] 3 All ER 897 at 922, [1991] 1 QB 405 at 427, [1990] ECR I-3313 at 3348–3349 (par 20)).'

In coming to his conclusion that in this case the activities of Poplar are within s.6, the professor relies upon the charitable status of Poplar; the fact that Poplar is subject to the control of the Corporation; the sanctions which the Corporation can apply; the provision of public funding to Poplar; the standards which Poplar is required to adopt in the exercise of its powers; the control which the Corporation can exert over the exercise of Poplar's powers; and local authority involvement.

Both the Department and Poplar dispute that Poplar is a public authority. Mr Philip Sales helpfully adopts the distinction correctly identified by Clayton and Tomlinson *The Law of Human Rights* (2000) vol 1, p 189 (para 5.08) between *standard public* authorities, *functional* public authorities and courts and tribunals. Mr Sales submits, and we, like Professor Alder and Mr Holmes, would agree that housing associations as a class are not standard public authorities. If they are to be a public authority this must be because a particular function performed by an individual RSL is a public as opposed to a private act. The RSL would then be a functional, or hybrid, public authority.

In support of his contention, Mr Sales draws attention to the following features of housing associations. (a) They vary vastly in size. (b) Their structure is that of an ordinary private law entity. (c) As to regulation by the Corporation he points to the fact that many financial institutions are regulated by the Bank of England but this does not make them public bodies. Furthermore, the Corporation gives each RSL freedom to decide how it achieves what is expected of it. (d) Members of the RSL are not appointed by, or answerable to, the government but are private individuals who volunteer their services. Even in the rare cases where the Corporation makes appointments, the appointee owes his duty to the RSL. (e) In *R v Servite Houses, ex p Goldsmith* [2001] BLGR 55 Moses J decided a housing association was not subject to judicial review. (f) Although an RSL is funded in part out of public funds, the major source of its income is its rental income. In any event, this is not by any means conclusive (see *Peabody Housing Association Ltd v Green* (1979) 38 P&CR 644 at 660, 662).

In coming to our conclusion as to whether Poplar is a public authority within the 1998 Act meaning of that term, we regard it of particular importance in this case that (i) while s.6 of the 1998 Act requires a generous interpretation of who is a public authority, it is clearly inspired by the approach developed by the courts in identifying the bodies and activities subject to judicial review. The emphasis on public functions reflects the approach adopted in judicial review by the courts and text books since the decision of the Court of Appeal (the judgment of Lloyd LJ) in *R v Panel on Take-overs and Mergers, ex p Datafin plc (Norton Opax plc intervening)* [1987] 1 All ER 564, [1987] QB 815. (ii) Tower Hamlets, in transferring its housing stock to Poplar, does not transfer its primary public duties to Poplar. Poplar is no more than the means by which it seeks to perform those duties. (iii) The act of providing accommodation to rent is not, without more, a public function for the purposes of s.6 of the 1998 Act. Furthermore, that is true irrespective of the section of society for whom the accommodation is provided. (iv) The fact that a body is a charity or is conducted not for profit means that it is likely to be motivated in performing its activities by what it perceives to be the public interest. However, this does not point to the body being a public authority. In addition, even if such a body performs functions that would be considered to be of a public nature if performed by a public body, nevertheless, such acts may remain of a private nature for the purpose of s.6(3)(b) and (5). (v) What can make an act, which would otherwise be private, public, is a feature or a combination of features which impose a public character or stamp on the act. Statutory authority for what is done can at least help to mark that act as being public; so can the extent of control over the function exercised by another body which is a public authority. The more closely the acts that could be of a private nature are enmeshed in the activities of a public body, the more likely they are to be public. However, the fact that the acts are supervised by a public regulatory body does not necessarily indicate that they are of a public nature. This is analogous to the position in judicial review, where a regulatory body may be deemed public but the activities of the body which is regulated may be categorised private. (vi) The closeness of the relationship which exists between Tower Hamlets and Poplar. Poplar was created by Tower Hamlets to take a transfer of local authority housing stock; five of its board members are also members of Tower Hamlets; Poplar is subject to the guidance of Tower Hamlets as to the manner in which it acts towards the defendants. (vii) The defendant, at the time of the transfer, was a sitting tenant of Poplar and it was intended that she would be treated no better and no worse than if she remained a tenant of Tower Hamlets. While she remained a tenant, Poplar therefore stood in relation to her in very much the position previously occupied by Tower Hamlets.

While these are the most important factors in coming to our conclusion, it is desirable to step back and look at the situation as a whole. As is the position on applications for judicial review, there is no clear demarcation line which can be drawn between public and private bodies and functions. In a borderline case, such as this, the decision is very much one of fact and degree. Taking into account all the circumstances, we have come to the conclusion that while activities of housing associations need not involve the performance of public functions, in this case, in providing accommodation for the defendant and then seeking possession, the role of Poplar is so closely assimilated to that of Tower Hamlets that it was performing public and not private functions. Poplar therefore is a functional public authority, at least to that extent. We emphasise that this does not mean that all Poplar's functions are public. We do not even decide that the position would be the same if the defendant was a secure tenant. The activities of housing associations can be ambiguous. For example, their activities in raising private or public finance could be very different from those under consideration here. The raising of finance by Poplar could well be a private function.

The art 8 issue

To evict the defendant from her home would impact on her family life. The effect of art.8(2) of the convention is therefore critical. The starting point is the fact that after the order for possession was obtained, Tower Hamlets continued to owe a limited duty to provide the defendant with assistance as a person who was found to be intentionally homeless. This was so even though Poplar's responsibility came to an end. If the defendant had not fallen into one of the special categories, she would have been provided with greater security of occupation.

Mr Holmes recognises that the defendant could not expect security of tenure, but he submits that there should be a residual discretion to protect the defendant's basic human rights. He also submits that this would not in practice give rise to undesirable consequences, to which the witnesses for the Department refer, but this is very much a matter of judgment.

There is certainly room for conflicting views as to the social desirability of an RSL being able to grant assured shorthold tenancies which are subject to s.21(4) of the 1988 Act. Mr Holmes considers the present policy mistaken. However, in considering whether Poplar can rely on art.8(2), the court has to pay considerable attention to the fact that Parliament intended when enacting s.21(4) to give preference to the needs of those dependent on social housing as a whole over those in the position of the defendant. The economic and other implications of any policy in this area are extremely complex and far-reaching. This is an area where, in our judgment, the courts must treat the decisions of Parliament as to what is in the public interest with particular deference. The limited role given to the court under s.21(4) is a legislative policy decision. The correctness of this decision is more appropriate for Parliament than the courts and the 1998 Act does not require the courts to disregard the decisions of Parliament in relation to situations of this sort when deciding whether there has been a breach of the convention.

The defendant's lack of security is due to her low priority under the legislation because she was found to be intentionally homeless. She was and must be taken to be aware that she was never more than a tenant as a temporary measure. In the case of someone in her position, even if she is a mother of young children, it is perfectly understandable that Parliament should have provided a procedure which ensured possession could be obtained expeditiously and that Poplar should have availed itself of the procedure.

Tenants in the position of the defendant have remedies other than under s.21(4) which are relevant when considering art.8. There are provisions for appeal against the decision that a person is intentionally homeless. There is a regulatory role of the corporation and there is the ombudsman. There is also the fact that RSLs are subject to considerable guidance as to how they use their powers.

We are satisfied, that notwithstanding its mandatory terms, s.21(4) of the 1988 Act does not conflict with the defendant's right to family life. Section 21(4) is certainly necessary in a democratic society in so far as there must be a procedure for recovering possession of property at the end of a tenancy. The question is whether the restricted power of the court is legitimate and proportionate. This is the area of policy where the court should defer to the decision of Parliament. We have come to the conclusion that there was not contravention of art.8 or of art.6.

The incompatibility issue

As we have decided that there is no contravention of arts 6 and 8, strictly, there is no need for us to speculate as to whether, if there had been a contravention, this would have created a situation of incompatibility. We note that if we decided that there was a contravention of art.8, the Department would prefer us not to interpret s.21(4) 'constructively' but instead to grant a declaration of incompatibility. However, so far, the sections of the 1998 Act dealing with interpretation and incompatibility have been subject to limited guidance and for that reason we hope it will be helpful if we set out our views even though they are strictly obiter.

The relevant sections of the 1998 Act are ss.3 and 4. They are in the following terms:

> '3. *Interpretation of legislation*—(1) So far as it is possible to do so, primary legislation and subordinate legislation must be read and given effect in a way which is compatible with the Convention rights.
>
>> (2) This section—(a) applies to primary legislation and subordinate legislation whenever enacted; (b) does not affect the validity, continuing operation or enforcement of any incompatible primary legislation; and (c) does not affect the validity, continuing operation or enforcement of any incompatible subordinate legislation if (disregarding any possibility of revocation) primary legislation is compatible with a Convention right.
>
> 4. *Declaration of incompatibility*—(1) Subsection (2) applies in any proceedings in which a court determines whether a provision of primary legislation is compatible with a Convention right.
>
>> (2) If the court is satisfied that the provision is incompatible with a Convention right, it may make a declaration of incompatibility.
>>
>> (3) Subsection (4) applies in any proceedings in which a court determines whether a provision of subordinate legislation, made in the exercise of a power conferred by primary legislation, is compatible with a Convention right.
>>
>> (4) If the court is satisfied—(a) that the provision is incompatible with a Convention right, and (b) that (disregarding any possibility of revocation) the primary legislation concerned prevents removal of the incompatibility, it may make a declaration of that incompatibility.

(5) In this section "court" means—(a) the House of Lords; (b) the Judicial Committee of the Privy Council; (c) the Courts-Martial Appeal Court; (d) in Scotland the High Court of Justiciary sitting otherwise than as a trial court or the Court of Session; (e) in England and Wales or Northern Ireland, the High Court or the Court of Appeal.

(6) A declaration under this section ("a declaration of incompatibility")—(a) does not affect the validity, continuing operation or enforcement of the provision in respect of which it is given; and (b) is not binding on the parties to the proceedings in which it is made.'

It is difficult to overestimate the importance of s.3. It applies to legislation passed both before and after the 1998 Act came into force. Subject to the section not requiring the court to go beyond that which is possible, it is mandatory in its terms. In the case of legislation predating the 1998 Act where the legislation would otherwise conflict with the convention, s.3 requires the court to now interpret legislation in a manner which it would not have done before the 1998 Act came into force. When the court interprets legislation usually its primary task is to identify the intention of Parliament. Now, when s.3 applies, the courts have to adjust their traditional role in relation to interpretation so as to give effect to the direction contained in s.3. It is as though legislation which predates the 1998 Act and conflicts with the convention has to be treated as being subsequently amended to incorporate the language of s.3. However, the following points, which are prob-ably self-evident, should be noted: (a) unless the legislation would otherwise be in breach of the convention s.3 can be ignored (so courts should always first ascertain whether, absent s.3, there would be any breach of the convention); (b) if the court has to rely on s.3 it should limit the extent of the modified meaning to that which is necessary to achieve compatibility; (c) s.3 does not entitle the court to *legislate* (its task is still one of *interpretation*, but interpretation in accordance with the direction contained in s.3); (d) the views of the parties and of the Crown as to whether a 'constructive' interpretation should be adopted cannot modify the task of the court (if s.3 applies the court is required to adopt the s.3 approach to interpretation); and (e) where despite the strong language of s.3, it is not possible to achieve a result which is compatible with the convention, the court is not required to grant a declaration and presumably in exercising its discretion as to whether to grant a declaration or not it will be influenced by the usual considerations which apply to the grant of declarations.

The most difficult task which courts face is distinguishing between legislation and interpretation. Here prac-tical experience of seeking to apply s.3 will provide the best guide. However, if it is necessary in order to obtain compliance to radically alter the effect of the legislation this will be an indication that more than interpretation is involved.

In this case Mr Luba contends that all that is required is to insert the words 'if it is reasonable to do so' into the opening words of s.21(4). The amendment may appear modest but its effect would be very wide indeed. It would significantly reduce the ability of landlords to recover possession and would defeat Parliament's original objective of providing certainty. It would involve legislating.

Finally, we are prepared to grant the parties declarations if this will assist them to seek permission to appeal. Despite this, the parties should not assume permission to appeal will be granted. The decision whether to grant permission or to leave the decision to grant permission to the Lords, should not be affected by the fact that the appeal involves the 1998 Act. The House of Lords should normally be allowed to select for itself the appeals which it wishes to hear. The appeal is dismissed.

Appeal dismissed. Permission to appeal refused."

Questions

1. Summarise the facts of the case, explaining particularly why Poplar Housing served a notice to quit on Donoghue.

2. Lord Woolf states that there are four issues in this case: (i) the procedural issue; (ii) the public body issue; (iii) the art.8 issue; (iv) the remedy issue. For each issue, state in the form of a question

precisely what the Court of Appeal was called upon to answer. In other words, frame each issue as a question which states the underlying substantive legal issue.

3. Give the Court of Appeal's answer to each of the questions you have just posed. Try to limit your answer to one sentence for each issue.

4. With respect to the public body issue, why will this be of such importance, not only in this case, but in Human Rights Act case law more generally? What section of the Human Rights Act is relevant to this issue? What factors motivated the Court to reach the conclusion it did on this issue?

5. How widely do *you* think art.8 should be interpreted? Why?

6. Explain the basis on which the defendant argued that her art.8 European Convention rights were infringed by the actions of Poplar Housing.

7. With respect to the incompatibility issue, Lord Woolf distinguishes between the functions of *legislating* and *interpreting*. What point is Lord Woolf trying to make? Why does Lord Woolf suggest that a finding in favour of Donoghue would have crossed the line between interpretation and legislation? Do you think that distinction can be maintained in the "Human Rights Act era"?

Finally, we include a more sceptical voice on the desirability of the Human Rights Act 1998 and the implications it has, not only for statutory interpretation, but more widely for society.

Adam Tomkins, "Introduction: on being sceptical about human rights", in K.D. Ewing and Adam Tomkins (eds), *Sceptical Essays on Human Rights* (Oxford: Oxford University Press, 2001), pp.110:

"Human rights have played a central role in the rhetoric (if not the reality) of international relations—from the United Nations down—ever since the mid-twentieth century. But over the past two decades human rights have additionally come to enjoy an ever more dominant position in national constitutional or public law. This has been as true for Canada and New Zealand as it has been for Poland and Hungary. One of the last countries in the common law world, and one of the last countries in Europe, to allow its domestic legal system to embrace human rights is the United Kingdom. At the turn of the millennium, however, human rights are beginning to be paraded as a central pillar of even the UK's rapidly changing legal order. After years of argument, Parliament in 1998 at last enacted legislation to 'bring rights home' as the government rather jingoistically put it. The Human Rights Act 1998, which came fully into force in October 2000, gives effect to a unique form of 'domestic incorporation' of (most of) the substantive provisions of the European Convention on Human Rights, a treaty which the UK had been bound by (but only as a matter of international law—and not therefore within the UK's own domestic legal system) since the Convention first came into force, in 1953. The Human Rights Act is, loosely, the UK's Bill of Rights, the UK's approximate equivalent of the Canadian Charter on Fundamental Freedoms (1982), of the New Zealand Bill of Rights Act (1990), and of the constitutional texts of countless emergent democracies from the Baltic States of north-east Europe to the turbulent but thrilling polity of the new South Africa. Human rights law is a global phenomenon to which, it seems, the UK is no longer immune. . . .

The Human Rights Act 1998 was one of the most widely celebrated statutes to have been passed by Parliament in many years. Nowhere were the celebrations more pronounced or more intense than among communities of lawyers. The celebration has taken many forms: from the self-congratulatory back-slapping of Tony Blair's Lord Chancellor to the publication of an enormous pile of both academic and practitioner-oriented literature which seeks to explain, to expound and to expand lawyers' understandings of the manifold changes which this legislation is assumed to necessitate. . . . In the clamour for liberal self-congratulation, and in the rush to explain how the UK has at last brought rights home, there has been little space for dissent, for critique, or even for doubt. . . ."

[Tomkins goes on to consider the broad sets of reasons to be sceptical of human rights.]

"A good number of different reasons can be identified, for example, in support of the proposition that we should be sceptical of rights (our first category of scepticism). First, rights-talk is inherently antagonistic, and encourages litigation. Secondly, human rights law imagines a paradigm in which there are two parties (the individual rights-holder and the public authority), a model which squeezes out any room for the *res publica*, for the public interest, along with any third party interests which, in the absence of their being 'victims', find it incredibly difficult to get into or otherwise be heard in court. Thirdly, human rights law reduces the relationship between the citizen and the state to one of regulation and quasi-contract—a bill of rights is a list of the clauses in the contract of good governance. The state will be allowed to tax you, to coerce you, to imprison you, to impose restrictions and constraints on you, and you will tolerate (and indeed support and protect—even be prepared to die for) the political, regulatory, military, and economic coercive power of the state on condition that the state respects your rights. Not only does this result in the state being portrayed in unambiguously negative terms, seemingly denying the good that the state is in a unique position to provide in terms of housing the homeless, healing the sick, educating both young and old, and providing welfare for the disadvantaged, and so on, but it also imagines that the individual wants nothing more than to be left alone, that freedom from government, rather than participation in government, is the goal. It also apparently—and dangerously—imagines that any political grievance can be successfully remedied by filing a lawsuit.

Fourthly, human rights law is insufficiently sensitive to the hegemonic power of its own discourse. Rights are an incredibly powerful rhetorical tool, and they get everywhere, strangling other devices, stymieing alternative developments. . . . Similarly, but more broadly, locating the task of enforcing rights in the courts can lead to the suffocating of alternative avenues for dispute resolution. What fate awaits ministerial responsibility, or the Parliamentary Commissioner for Administration (the ombudsman) after the Human Rights Act?

That there is life beyond the courtroom, but that institutions such as Parliament, ombudsmen, and others are likely to find it more difficult to make their scrutineering voices fully heard in the new post Human Rights Act legal order, connects with the second category of scepticism . . .: scepticism about judges. Why should it be the unrepresentative, overwhelmingly white male upper-middle-class judiciary of the UK's creaking courts who enjoy the emancipation that will come to them with the Human Rights Act? There are two questions here: why give power to *these* people, and why *not* give it to others? Even if the reasons for being sceptical about rights can be overcome, and we decide that we do properly want rights-talk to play a greater role in our polity, why give the job of talking that talk to the judges? After all, what have they done to show either that they deserve, or that they are the appropriate body to enjoy, this newfound role of constitutional referee. By inflating the power and responsibility of the judiciary, the influence and contribution which could be offered from other less well-dressed, but perhaps better-suited, institutions has been sidelined and overlooked . . .

As to the third and final category of scepticism, namely scepticism about the specific content of, and omissions from, the ECHR and the HRA, this really speaks for itself, and little needs to be added here. Clearly the rights protected under the terms of the ECHR are partial in two senses. They are incomplete, in that there are many, many other social or political goods which we might want to be protected, or at least respected, in our polity but which do not find their way into the Act. But they are also partial in the more profound, and more disturbing, sense in that they represent a particular political—and party-political—vision of what it is that society should privilege and prioritize. In the ECHR, and thereby in the HRA, for example, we find the paradigmatic right of liberal political theory (freedom of expression) but not the core of republican philosophy or deliberative democracy (freedom of information, open government, and guarantees of full participation). Property is protected for those who possess it, but the homeless have no right to be housed. Religious freedom is protected, but not the right to an adequate standard of health care. And so on, and on. Social and economic rights are nowhere to be seen in the new liberal order: only a select few rights have been 'brought home' in the Not-Very-Many-Human-Rights Act of 1998."

Questions

1. What are the various grounds on which Tomkins is sceptical of the Human Rights Act 1998? To what extent are you persuaded by his arguments?

2. To what extent can the cases discussed in this chapter be explained and analysed in terms of Tomkins's analysis?

8

JUDGE-MADE LAW: AN INTRODUCTION TO COMMON LAW REASONING

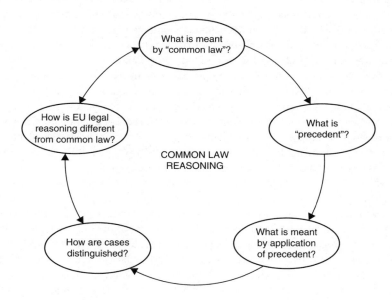

In this chapter our attention turns to "judge-made law". This refers to the common law, which is often described as the foundation of our legal system. By the end of this chapter, you should:

- appreciate the key concepts and methods for analysing legal judgments;

- recognise how and why these methods have developed in an English context;

- understand the techniques lawyers use to determine the parts of a judgment which are of most use to them;

- be able to reflect on the ways in which these legal methods can limit the sorts of issues considered in the courts.

I. Key Concepts and Terminology

It can be confusing for new law students to listen to discussion about the common law because it actually has a number of meanings and is used in different contexts. The abstract from Downes maps out the three different uses of the phrase. It also draws our attention to the rather piecemeal fashion in which the concepts emerged. In this chapter we will be focusing on the second category of common law that he discusses.

T.A. Downes, *Textbook on Contract*, 5th edn (London: Blackstone Press, 1997), pp.2–4:

Three meanings of "Common Law"

Historical: common law and equity

"After the Norman conquest of England local laws gave way to a general law of the country, which became known as the common law. The king's courts became the most important forum for the resolution of disputes between citizens. An action could only be brought in these courts by obtaining (purchasing) a writ. Over time the forms of such writs became fixed, and only Parliament could approve a new type of writ designed to meet a claim which could not be accommodated within the existing writs and forms of action. This rigidity in the legal system was often the cause of hardship to individual litigants, and the practice grew of petitioning the king for justice in the individual case. The petitions were dealt with by the chancellor, who in this period was a man of the church and who was regarded as the 'conscience' of the king. In due course a formal procedure for such petitions evolved, culminating in a Court of Chancery, presided over by the Lord Chancellor, applying a system of rules known as 'equity' rather than the common law of the ordinary courts.

Although the Court of Chancery was effective in remedying injustices, the existence of parallel jurisdictions brought problems and injustices of its own. Chancery developed procedures separate from, but at least as complex as, those of the common law courts. A litigant had to be sure of the classification of the rule he sought to have applied, in order to commence his action in the right court. The equity of the Chancery Court became a set of rules almost as precise as those of the common law. In the case of conflict between the two systems, the rules of equity prevailed. Parliament sought to put an end to these divisions with the Judicature Acts 1873–1875, which established a unified system of courts which were charged with applying both the common law and equity.

To the non-lawyer 'equity' is probably synonymous with the idea of natural justice. Although that was the origin of the Chancery jurisdiction, it has long since disappeared from the rules of equity. The rules of equity are just as capable today as those of the common law of producing resolutions of disputes which may be viewed as just or unjust. Indeed, since the two types of rules are now applied by the same courts, there is little significance left in the distinction. Nevertheless, in two respects it has left a legacy which still has an impact on today's courts. In the first place, while common law rules are available to [claimants] as of right, equitable remedies are discretionary in the sense that they are subject to some general conditions of availability. For example, there is no absolute right to specific performance of a contract. Secondly, the existence of parallel systems of rules, the one based on formal procedures, the other based originally on the idea of substantial justice, has allowed some judges to invoke the tension between the two systems as a source of judicial creativity in developing the law to meet new situations. For example, Lord Denning has used this device in relation to the enforceability of promises and in relation to contracts affected by mistake.

Common law and statute

In another sense, the common law is the law applied by the courts developed through the system of precedent without reference to legislation passed by Parliament. Although statute has become the most prolific source of law in this country, this has only relatively recently been the case. Centuries ago, much of the law was applied by the courts independently of any statutory source. The constitutional fiction was that the judges merely declared what the law was, as though it was already there and merely had to be discovered. Today it is accepted that the courts created the law, although there is no reason to suppose they often acted arbitrarily in so doing. No doubt they acted in response to the values and needs of society, as they perceived them, in making law. This process created the body of the common law, which in this sense includes the law made by all the courts, including those of Chancery.

Common law as a 'family' of legal systems
A wider meaning still of 'common law' is a description of a group of related legal systems. The English legal system was exported around the world wherever British influence dominated. The legal systems of the USA, and of the 'old' Commonwealth countries, are all based on the English common law. In much the same way, the legal systems of continental European countries were exported around the world. They are usually described as the civil law systems, of which the most influential has been that of France, because by producing the Code Civil Napoleon gave to France the first modern European legal system, which was copied elsewhere."

Questions

1. Imagine that you have been asked to give a five-minute presentation to your class on the concept of common law. Sketch out in rough how you would approach the task.

2. Reflect for a minute on the law you have studied so far in your law programme. How much of it has been common law?

3. Can you think of any advantages or disadvantages when judges play such an important role in the development of legal principles?

We will consider many of the points which Downes raises throughout this chapter. For our purposes, he provides a good introduction to many of the terms which we will be using when looking at ideas around common law reasoning in more depth. Central to that method of reasoning are the ideas of "case law" and "precedent". Appreciating the idea of judicial precedent is essential if you are to understand the impact that a particular judgement has on subsequent cases in which the same issue is raised. When you write essays and answer problem questions, one of the key skills you will need to develop is the ability to identify precedents which support the argument you are making and those which could be used by opponents to undermine your case.

Rupert Cross and J.W. Harris, *Precedent in English Law*, 4th edn (Oxford: Clarendon Press, 1991), pp.3–5:

"'[R]ules of precedent' . . . are designed to give effect to the far more fundamental rule that English law is to a large extent based on case-law. 'Case-law' consists of the rules and principles stated and acted upon by judges in giving decisions. In a system based on case-law, a judge in a subsequent case *must* have regard to these matters; they are not, as in some other legal systems, merely material which he *may* take into consideration in coming to his decision. . . .

Some branches of our law are almost entirely the product of the decisions of the judges whose reasoned judgments have been reported in various types of law report for close on 700 years. Other branches of our law are based on statutes, but, in many instances, case-law has played an important part in the interpretation of those statutes. As the sovereignty of Parliament is more complete in England than practically anywhere else in the world, it might be thought that the rigidity of the doctrine of precedent in this country is of no particular importance because any unsatisfactory results of case-law can be swept away by legislation, but the promotion of a statute on matters of this nature is often slow and difficult. There are many instances in which the recommendations of Royal Commissions and Law Revision Committees, designed to ameliorate the situation produced by case-law have been ignored, apparently for no other reason than pressure on parliamentary time."

In the same publication, Cross and Harris suggest that the number of instances in which this happens will be reduced. This is because there are now a number of law-reforming agencies, such as the Law Commission, the Office for Criminal Justice Reform and the Criminal Law Revision Committee. Of these, the Law Commission is the most important and its reports can be of considerable use to law students. To date, it has been responsible for more than 2,000 obsolete acts being repealed, and two-thirds of new legislation recommended by the commission is implemented. Set up by statute in 1965, it is charged with the task of reviewing the law with a view to systematic development and reform, including, in particular, codification. Recent work includes a review of the law relating to insurance contracts, unfair terms in contracts, remedies against public authorities and the law of murder. Its ninth programme of reform commenced in April 2005 and its tenth programme starts in 2007. In its July 2002 White Paper, *Justice for All*, the Government stated its intention to codify the criminal law and plans to follow this up with the codification of criminal evidence. As a result, the Law Commission has published a number of consultation documents on criminal offences and has expressed the view that the law would be more accessible to citizens and easier for the courts to understand if combined in a set of statutory codes. The implications for the judiciary are quite significant as the role for case law would undoubtedly be diminished as a result.

Understanding the relationship between statutes and common law is a vital element in appreciating common law reasoning and the interface between these two sources of law. It is particularly important to understand that when making or developing the law the judiciary exercises its power with considerable caution. The result is that radical shifts are unusual. In the following classic extract Llewellyn teases out this point in more detail.

K.N. Llewellyn, *The Bramble Bush* (New York: Oceana Publications, 1996), pp.87–88:

"Now the essential differences between statutes and the law of case decisions are these. A judge makes his rule in and around a specific case, and looking backward. The case shapes the rule; the judge's feet are firmly on the particular instance; his rule is commonly good sense, and very narrow. And any innovation is confined regularly within rather narrow limits—partly by the practice of trying hard to square the new decision with old law; it is hard to keep daring innovations even verbally consistent with old rules. And partly innovation is confined through conscious policy: case law rules (though new) are applied as *if* they had always been the law; this derives from our convention that 'judges only declare and do not make the law'. Knowing that the effect of their ruling will be retroactive, and unable to foresee how many men's calculations a new ruling may upset, the judges move very cautiously into new ground. Then, when a case has been decided, it enters into the sea of common law—available to any court within the Anglo-American world, and peculiarly, within this country. Finally, and important here, case law is flexible around the edges; the rules are commonly somewhat uncertain in their wording, and not too easy to make definite. Else why your study?

But statutes are made relatively in the large, to cover wider sweeps, and looking forward. They apply only to events and transactions occurring *after* they have come into force; that element of caution disappears. They are, moreover, recognized machinery for readjustment of the law. They represent not single disputes, but whole classes of disputes. They are political, not judicial in their nature, represent readjustments along the lines of balance of power, decide not single cases by a tiny shift of a rule, but the rearrangement of a great mass of clashing interests. Statute-making, too, is confined within what in relation to society at large is a straightened margin of free movement; but in comparison to courts the legislature is a horse without a halter."

Questions

1. What reasons can you think of for judicial restraint in making and developing the law?

2. What does this tell us about the constitutional relationship between the judiciary and legislature?

Whilst it is important to understand the different functions of case law and legislation and the reasons for caution when laying down new judicial precedent, this should not cause you to underestimate its importance. The English legal system would grind to a halt very quickly if we had to rely on the legislature to respond to new problems and issues brought before the courts. In spite of the ever-increasing amount of statute law, much of our law is still common law and certain law can only be found in case law. So, for instance, there is no statute which prescribes that a person should pay their debts, perform a contract, or pay damages for trespass, libel or slander. Statutes complement the common law and are given meaning by judicial interpretation of their contents. However, as Geldart reminds us, where statute and common law both seek to regulate a particular type of behaviour, priority is given to the wording in a statute.

William Geldart, *Introduction to English Law*, 11th edn (Oxford: Oxford University Press, 1995), p.3:

"Where Statute Law and Common Law come into competition, it is the former that prevails. Our law sets no limits to the power of Parliament. As the constitutionalist A.V. Dicey wrote a century ago, 'The sovereignty of Parliament is (from a legal point of view) the dominant characteristic of our political institutions.' No court or judge can refuse to enforce an Act of Parliament, though in the exercise of its duty to interpret an Act a court may sometimes alter considerably the effect that the legislators had intended the Act to have. No development of the Common Law can repeal an Act of Parliament, but large parts of the Common Law have from time to time been abolished by Act of Parliament, and their place has been taken by statutory rules."

In the extract which follows, Cownie, Bradney and Burton remind us that precedent is not only of use in filling in the gaps left by Parliament or in the process of adjudication. They argue that it can also have an impact on those thinking of pursuing a case to court.

Fiona Cownie, Anthony Bradney and Mandy Burton, *English Legal System in Context*, 4th edn (Oxford: Oxford University Press, 2007), pp.86–88:

"Law is not just a mechanism for settling disputes. It is also a way of avoiding disputes; of telling people how they might order their lives so that disputes can be avoided. If people are to do this they must know what the law is; they must know how judges will settle a dispute should a matter come to court. Law must be predictable. Lawyers must be able to tell their clients how to run their affairs. Judges must be able to announce what the law will be to the world at large. One must be able to know what the law is before going to court, for this would be expensive both financially and socially. Moreover, the law must be removed from the judges. Judges must be there not to decide cases on their own initiative. They must be there to apply a known set of rules to the facts before them. The job of the judge must be stripped of any subjective or personal element. Law must be a system of rules not of men. It has been argued that a system of precedent can be of assistance in allowing all these things to be done.

A previous Lord Chancellor, Lord MacKay, has described the advantages of precedent in this way:

> '. . . a scheme of precedent is clearly capable of providing important benefits. It assists litigants to assess the nature and scope of legal obligations and, to the extent that it enables them to predict the likely outcome of disputes, it restricts the scope of litigation. By allowing the vast bulk of disputes to be settled in the shadow of the law, a system of precedent prevents the legal apparatus from becoming clogged by a myriad of single instances. It reflects a basic principle of the administration of justice that like cases should be treated alike and therefore generates a range of expectations from different participants in the legal process. Rules of law based on a system of precedent are therefore likely to exhibit characteristics of certainty, consistency and uniformity.'

Precedent, on this argument, provides certainty, consistency and thus a measure of clarity. People know not only what the law is but also what it will be. In principle, the ordinary person, the ordinary lawyer, the humblest judge is in just as good a position as the judge in the highest court to look back and see what the law was and, thus, see what the law will be. However, in providing this consistency, precedent also carries a disadvantage.

Precedent carries with it the unlikely message that those that came before us knew as much as we do now;

that those in the past are good judges of what we should do in the present. One past Lord Chancellor, in a book of political philosophy, has caricatured the lawyer's idea of precedent thus:

'Failing all else, their last resort will be: "This was good enough for our ancestors and who are we to question their wisdom?" Then they'll settle back in their chairs, with an air of having said the last word on the subject—as if it would be a major disaster for anyone to be caught being wiser than his ancestors!'

Precedent is conservative. It favours the status quo. Precedent slows down the pace of change within the legal system. In a world where things are constantly in flux, where things are always changing and where the pace of change seems to ever increase, the very advantages of precedent can thus be a disadvantage. By making the law predictable, precedent also makes it predictable that law will be suitable for old social conditions but not for those that presently obtain. Law is certain but also certainly out-dated. Law is consistent but also consistently wrong.

For traditional theorists the solution to these problems are clear. The legislature exists to change legal rules. Parliament has the political legitimacy to amend the rules of the game. The judiciary, being unelected professionals who merely have a particular technical competence, are simply there to apply those rules which the legislature have made, or by implication, approved.

There are several problems with this account of the judge's role. One difficulty is its political naiveté. The parliamentary timetable is a crowded matter. There is not the time to debate all the legislation that the government would like to put forward in order to fulfil its own programme. There is still less time for measures which may be of great moment or importance within a narrow area of law but which are of no pressing weight for the population taken as a whole. There is almost no time at all for ideas for legislation which are not favoured by the government. A second problem for this traditional account of precedent is that most people, including most judges, now accept that judges do indeed make law."

Questions

1. How would you define the idea of precedent? What functions does it perform?

2. Explain the relationship between common law and statutory law. To what extent are they symbiotic?

3. What is meant by the claim that the common law is "unwritten"? In what way is the claim misleading?

4. In Ch.10 we will return to a discussion of the mystique of legal language in our consideration of the role of the legal profession. For present purposes it would be interesting for you to reflect on the number of new words and phrases you have learnt as a law student which would not be understood by those who had not studied law.

II. Finding Precedents in the Common Law

So far you have learnt that case law consists of the rules and principles stated by judges in giving decisions. In common law systems a judge in a subsequent case *must* have regard to that decision if it was given by a court above it in the hierarchy. Moreover, appellate courts, other than the House of Lords, are bound by their previous decisions. But how does one go about finding judicial precedents in the English legal system? The most succinct answer to this question is that precedents can be found in the reports of cases brought to court, especially those of the superior courts. However, Geldart reminds us that this is a fairly recent development.

William Geldart, *Introduction to English Law*, 11th edn (Oxford: Oxford University Press, 1995) pp.4–6:

"How do we know the law? Here there is a great difference between Statute and Common Law. A statute is drawn up in a definite form of words, and these words have been approved by Parliament and have received the Royal assent. . . .

On the other hand we have no authoritative text of the Common Law. There is no one form of words in which it has as a whole been expressed at any time. Therefore in a sense one may speak of the Common Law as unwritten law in contrast with Statute Law, which is written law. Nevertheless the sources from which we derive our knowledge of the Common Law are in writing or print. First among these come the reported decisions of the judges of the English courts. Ever since the reign of Edward I there have been lawyers who have made it their business to report the discussions in court and the judgments given in cases which seemed of legal interest. The earliest of these reports are the Year-Books. They are reports of cases made by anonymous reporters from the time of Edward I to that of Henry VIII. These are followed by reports produced by lawyers reporting under their own names. They were at first published (like textbooks) only as and when the author, or the representatives of a deceased author, saw fit to do so. It was not until the end of the eighteenth century that reports began to be regularly published contemporaneously with the decisions of the cases reported. At the beginning these reports seem to have served mainly the purpose of instruction and information. The fact that a judge had stated that such and such was the law was evidence, but not more than evidence, that such was the law. He might have been mistaken; another judge might perhaps decide differently. But in course of time we find a change in the attitude of judges and lawyers towards reported decisions. The citation of decided cases becomes more frequent; greater and greater weight is attached to them as authorities. From the sixteenth century onwards we may say that decided cases are regarded as a definite authority, which, at least in the absence of special reasons to the contrary, must be followed for the future. For the last [45] years, at any rate, the decisions of judges of the higher courts have had a binding force for all similar cases which may arise in the future."

This historical development of the common law, and the rules of precedent in particular, have also been traced by Goodrich who introduces us to the important concept of ratio decidendi.

Peter Goodrich, *Reading the Law* (Oxford: Blackwell, 1986), pp.70–72:

"The rapid development and stabilization of a system of common law during the thirteenth century was accompanied by the emergence of an early professional legal class, based at Westminster and skilled in oral pleading. Paradoxically the notions of oral pleading (narrators) and of an unwritten law were short-lived and the history of the common law is by and large a history of the recording and documentation of custom in a professional and extremely obscure language, that of law French, and hidden in technical and often verbose reports, initially of pleadings (plea rolls) and later of arguments and judgments (*Year Books*). In many senses it would be inaccurate to regard the common law as ever having been wholly unwritten in its character; it is simply unwritten in the technical sense of not being 'written law' (*ius scriptum*) or legislation. From a very early date, and certainly from the ninth century, the basic rules of general custom—of royally approved practices—were collected and recorded, most famously by King Alfred who compiled a dome-book or *liber judicialis* for use throughout the kingdom of Wessex. The book was lost but is known to have been a resource for information and knowledge of common law until the mid-fifteenth century and is said by Blackstone to have 'contained, we may probably suppose, the principal maxims of the common law, the penalties for the misdemeanours and the forms of judicial proceedings'. The substantive significance of the dome-book as a record of law and procedures is limited, however, by the subsequent Danish and Norman invasions and the separation of local and general customs. . . .

The plea rolls were written records of pleadings made at Westminster which frequently did not include the judgment in the case while the *Year Books*, which started reporting cases from 1292, report the oral arguments before the courts in law French and are, in terms of the legal knowledge they presuppose, extremely demanding upon the reader. The law administered as the common law from Westminster was already inaccessible, esoteric and extremely technical, an 'occult science' which needed to be extracted with great difficulty and skill from the lengthy and arcane books of the law. These reports of arguments and judgments were neither official nor necessarily accurate. As Plucknett describes them:

'The whole business of pleading orally . . . was an immensely skilful and recondite game, conducted with great virtuosity by the leaders of the bar, and keenly relished by all others who were sufficiently learned to understand what it was all about. After such a display, it was an anti-climax to think of a decision. Time after time the Year Books will give pages of subtle fencing until we get the words: "and so to judgment". What the judgment was, nobody knew and nobody cared; what interested the reader was not the substantive law involved in a case, but the technique of conducting the pleadings. . . .'

The Year Books were eventually superseded by the ad hoc development of law-reporting from the early sixteenth century, when named private reporters would recall and publish more or less detailed and more or less accurate accounts of cases; Plowden, Dyer and Coke were among the most significant of the early reporters. The quality and content of the reports produced by the named reporters between 1550 and 1790 varied greatly and while frequent reference was made to earlier decisions, the reporting was frequently 'casual and careless' and on occasions 'grossly inadequate'. Again we would observe that such a haphazard written record of the common law hardly indicates any great certainty, predictability or widespread knowledge of law and procedure. Nor could one view the system of common-law judgment as a coherent and complete system of legal rules or as, in its modern sense, a legal order. It is only in the late eighteenth and early nineteenth centuries, with the renewed influence of Roman-law doctrines and classifications, with the shift from law French to the vernacular and with the emergence of professional and later official law reports that it becomes possible even to contemplate referring to the common law as a coherent system of rules or as an order of precedent. . . .

The modern and purportedly highly distinctive conception of a common-law system of binding precedent, of *stare rationibus decidendi*, meaning to follow the reasoning of previous decisions (*stare decisis*), dates back to the early years of the nineteenth century, if not before. In broad terms, the conception of binding precedent refers to the following of the rules (*rationes decidendi*) laid down in previous decisions and its logical form and entailment are classically set out by Justice Parke in *Mirehouse v. Rennell* [1833] 1 Cl and F 527, 546, in the following terms:

> 'Our common law system consists in the applying to new combinations of circumstances those rules which we derive from legal principles and judicial precedents; and for the sake of attaining uniformity, consistency and certainty, we must apply those rules, where they are not plainly unreasonable and inconvenient, to all cases which arise; and we are not at liberty to reject them, and to abandon all analogy to them, in those to which they have not yet been judicially applied. . . . It appears to me to be of great importance to keep this principle of decision steadily in view, not merely for the determination of a particular case, but for the interests of law as a science.'

In short, legal decisions are to be arrived at, where the dispute is governed by the unwritten or common law, by reference, either directly or by analogy, to the rules set down in previously decided cases. Such pre-existent rules or principles (reasonings) are to be followed, according to Justice Parke, even where the deciding judge does not view them to be necessarily the best means to deciding the disputed issue: predictability and consistency of legal decision-making are accorded greater value than particular justice.

This early view of precedent was developed during the nineteenth century into what is traditionally regarded as one of the strictest and most extreme systems of precedent known in the history of western legal systems. While the rest of Europe entered the age of codifications and the emergent nation-states placed their faith in publicly available written codes of national law, the English developed and refined an antiquated system of highly technical and highly particular legal decisions into the modern common law. The motives behind the development belong firmly in the European political and economic context of the nineteenth century. For the common-law system, the nineteenth century was also an age of statute law, of partial codifications and of consolidating Acts, the great upsurge coming in the 1830s and continuing unabated to the present day. Parallel to this development of what were seen as systematizing, simplifying and democratizing statute laws was the development of the common law as national law, it being the peculiar view of English lawyers that common law represented a unique and jealously guarded national legal achievement. It was, however, only with the aid of principles drawn from the academics and the civil law, that the common law could be developed into a coherent and largely self-sufficient system of legal decision-making. In 1861, in *Beamish v Beamish* [1861] 9

H.L. Cases 274, the House of Lords decided that precedent decisions of the House were to be binding in future cases, even upon the House itself. Only Parliament could alter the decisions of the House of Lords, a view reiterated in *London Street Tramways Co. Ltd v London County Council* [1898] A.C. 375, 38, by Lord Halsbury in a succinct statement that 'a decision of the House on a question of law is conclusive', a view which remained the law until 1966 when the House of Lords issued a Practice Statement declaring that, in a limited number of circumstances, the House would no longer be bound to follow its earlier decisions. The lower courts, the Court of Appeal in particular (see *Davis v Johnson* [1979] A.C. 264), however, remain bound by their own earlier decisions and the system of precedent in general is still doctrinally stated to be one of binding or strict precedent. The strongest legal argument is one which cites the *ratio decidendi* of a relevant precedent case; the issue of the forms which a precedent may take and the manner of its discovery and application are still the central methodological issues within the common law, although, paradoxically, 'theorists have not been able to agree upon an answer to the question, what is a *ratio*? Nor is there agreement as to the test to be used to identify a *ratio*, once the basic meaning of the term has been defined'."

III. THE PROCESS OF COMMON LAW REASONING: "THINKING LIKE A LAWYER"

The process of learning to think like a lawyer is a difficult one which you will only begin to understand in your first year of study. As Goodrich's analysis of the common law demonstrated, the history of the common law has been a rather haphazard process, in which general rules emerged from remedies granted in particular disputes. This process of moving from specific disputes to the development of general rules, (i.e. precedents), which are then applicable to a wide range of cases, is central to common law reasoning. It is a method of reasoning known as inductive (moving from the specific to the general), and is a facet of legal method in which you will have to become well versed.

In the following extract from his series of lectures to new law students, Llewellyn advises students of the key tasks they need to perform when they come to read a case with a lawyer's eyes and determine how useful it will be to them. He starts with a fundamental concept when he makes reference to the ratio decidendi, or reason for deciding a case.

K.N. Llewellyn, *The Bramble Bush* (New York: Oceana Publications, 1996), pp.84–86:

"1) (a) There is first the question of what the court *actually decided* in a given case . . . And the question of what express *ratio decidendi* it announced. These are facts of observation. They are the starting point of all discussion. Until you have them there is no use doing any arguing about anything.

1) (b) There is the question of *what the rule of the case is*, as derived from its comparison with a number of other cases. This is not so simple, but the technical procedures for determining it are clear. Skilled observers should rather regularly be able to agree on two points: (i) the reasonably safe maximum rule the case can be used for; (ii) the reasonably certain minimum rule the case must be admitted to contain.

2) As against both of these, there is the question of the manner, attitude and accuracy of the court's *interpretation* or transformation of the raw evidence. Here judgment factors enter, and you and I may not agree about it. But at least we can keep the level of discussion separate from the levels just above. There we *presuppose* facts as they *result* from this interpretation we are here discussing; and we look to the rule laid down upon the facts already transformed.

3) There is the question of what the *probable* precedent value of the case is, in a given court or in general. Here, too, judgment factors enter very largely, and objective agreement is not to be expected; for we must draw into our thinking the results of our work on the second level, and must draw further things as well. Yet here, too, as to the *level* of discourse all can agree: it is a question of predicting what some court will in fact do. You can phrase this, if you will, in terms of Ought: what some court will understand this case to tell it to do. . . .

4)   There is the question of *estimating what consequences the case* (and its effects on other cases) will have to laymen: the relation between the *ways* of the court and the *ways* of those affected by the court. This I take again to be purely on the level of description or prediction, but to be a very complicated matter, and one which involves even more information from outside the cases than does problem 3. The consequences may turn, for instance, on the persons concerned making quite inaccurate prediction of how later cases will eventuate—on their quite misinterpreting the case, on their readjusting their own ways not to their actual environment, but to an *imaginary* environment of court ways.

5)   (a) There is the question of *evaluating* the court's action in the case—of concluding how desirable it is. And this is of course the most complicated of all, because it includes all the foregoing, and various premises also as to what values are to be taken as the baseline and the goal. What is utterly vital to see at least is that you cannot begin on this *until you have settled* the matters in the first and second problems, and grappled with those in the third and fourth. And, finally, that this matter of evaluation, while it presupposes the others, in no way touches the *level* on which they are discussed.

5)   (b) There is the evaluation of the court's decision or ratio from the angle of *doctrine*. Here some premise or concept is *assumed*, as authoritatively given, and the court's action is tested for whether it is or is not dogmatically *correct*, when compared with the premise. Less dogmatically minded thinkers use the same technique, on the same *logical* level, to see not whether the case is 'correct', but whether it *squares* with a given hypothesis (either of doctrine or of prediction)—*i.e.*, to test its consistency with some formulation of a 'rule' derived inductively from other cases. It should be clear that this touches neither 3, nor 4, nor (really) 5a."

Vandevelde explores these points in much more detail and suggests specific techniques which might be of value to students learning their trade. In particular, he focuses on how one goes about gleaning what rule is applied or developed in a specific case. His arguments reveal that different lawyers may come to different conclusions about a case depending on how they interpret or categorise different types of behaviour. In this sense, there is never a definitive answer to questions about what constitutes the ratio, or rule, established in a judgment.

Kenneth J. Vandevelde, *Thinking Like a Lawyer* (Boulder: Westview Press, 1996), pp.49–55:

"The lawyer synthesizes the new rule by a method similar to the logical process of induction. Induction is a method of reasoning that, in essence, proceeds from the particular to the general.

For example, after tasting several raisins and finding that each of them is sweet, one may reason by induction that all raisins taste sweet. Induction produces a conclusion that is probable, though not certain. No matter how many raisins one eats, the possibility always exists that the next one may taste different from the others.

Nevertheless, courts formulate rules of law by a process that is inductive in form. If a number of cases have been decided in which a particular right or duty was found to exist, then the court may conclude that the same right or duty exists in all similar cases. By studying several particular instances, the court formulates a general rule.

For example, assume that various courts decide a number of cases imposing a duty on landowners to warn guests about various conditions on the land, such as a concealed pit, quicksand, or an unstable slope. As the number of cases grows, it becomes possible to think of these cases as collectively establishing a rule that requires the landowner to warn guests about hazards. In this situation, a rule is formulated by a process of induction. The rule, however, is broader than any of the specific cases on which it was based. The whole thus becomes greater than the sum of the parts.

By creating a rule broader than any one prior case, the court creates a rule broad enough to apply to the novel case. The novel case, accordingly, can be decided by application of the newly synthesized rule.

As noted above, induction does not compel a particular conclusion but can only suggest that the conclusion is probable. In the same way, the court is not compelled to accept the new, broader rule. Just as tasting a few raisins does not force one to conclude that all raisins taste the same, the prior decisions in cases involving certain specific hazards do not require the court to decide that other hazards are subject to the same rule. The court may correctly note that the holdings in the prior cases did not reach beyond quicksand, a concealed pit, and an unstable slope and may decide not to extend the holdings beyond those situations. . . .

The problem of indeterminacy

The premise for using inductive reasoning is that several similar items have been identified about which a generalization can safely be made. Yet, the lawyer will find that the process of formulating a generalization is not a mechanical one. Rather, it is a process that requires the exercise of judgment and that can lead to more than one result.

The lawyer must make at least two decisions in synthesizing the rule. First, the lawyer must decide which facts to include in the factual predicate, thus determining how to characterize the prior cases. Each of the prior cases may be subject to multiple characterizations, depending upon which facts of those cases the lawyer chooses to emphasize. In deciding how to characterize the cases included in the rule, the lawyer in effect is choosing the elements of the rule.

For example, the lawyer may characterize the cases involving the quicksand, the concealed pit, and the unstable slope as cases involving abnormal conditions, provided that each condition was abnormal for that area. Or, the lawyer may characterize them as cases involving hazards, because each condition was dangerous. Alternatively, the lawyer may characterize them as cases involving concealed hazards, on the theory that none of the hazards was obvious to the casual observer. Or, the cases may be characterized as involving natural hazards, if they were not the result of human activity. Finally, the lawyer may choose to emphasize the especially dangerous nature of the hazards and characterize the cases as involving life-threatening hazards.

All of these characterizations may be equally accurate. No one characterization is the 'correct' one that must be chosen to the exclusion of the others. The process of characterizing the facts is indeterminate. The lawyer can reach a particular characterization only by the exercise of judgment.

A second decision the lawyer must make is to set the level of generality at which the new rule should be formulated. This means deciding whether the prior cases are to be described in broad, general terms or in narrow, specific terms.

In the case of the concealed pit, the unstable slope, and the quicksand, for example, the lawyer must decide at what level of generality to characterize the conditions on the land that give rise to a duty to warn. At one extreme, they could be characterized as hazards. In that case, the lawyer could conclude that the various cases identified by research establish a general rule that the landowner has a duty to warn guests about all hazards on the land.

At the other extreme, the lawyer could characterize the conditions as falling within the three narrow categories of quicksand, concealed pits, and unstable slopes. Each of these categories might be characterized even more narrowly so that, under the lawyer's characterization of the rule, a landowner has a duty to warn only of concealed pits of a certain depth, unstable slopes of a specified angle, and quicksand pools of a particular size.

Between these extremes is a range of possible rules of differing levels of generality. The term 'life-threatening hazards,' for example, is more specific than the term 'hazards.'

Each of these levels of generality may yield a rule that is equally accurate. No particular level of generality is correct to the exclusion of the others. The choice of the level of generality at which to state the rule is indeterminate. The lawyer's selection of a particular level of generality must therefore be based on the exercise of judgment. Different lawyers generalizing about the same group of cases will produce rules at different levels of generality.

The judgments concerning which facts to include in the factual predicate and the level of generality at which to state a rule are interrelated. The more general the rule, the fewer the facts that need to be specified. For example, if the rule is formulated as applying to all hazards, then whether the hazards are natural or life-threatening is irrelevant and would not be specified in the rule. Put another way, stating the rule at a high level of generality allows the lawyer to be agnostic about which of various specifics to include in the factual predicate.

The corollary, of course, is that if the lawyer decides to include numerous detailed facts in the factual predicate, then, necessarily, the rule cannot be stated at a high level of generality.

Addressing indeterminacy through policy judgments

The lawyer may attempt to solve the indeterminacy involved in synthesizing a rule by referring to the policies underlying the cases. In this situation, the lawyer uses the underlying policies as a guide in selecting the facts to include in the factual predicate of the rule and in choosing the level of generality at which to state the rule. As will be seen, however, use of the underlying policies does not entirely solve the problem of indeterminacy.

The first decision the lawyer must make is to select the facts to include in the factual predicate of the rule. As an initial matter, some of the prior cases may have specified that certain facts were dispositive. For example, the case involving the pit may have specified that a duty to warn was imposed because the pit was a concealed hazard; that is, the case made clear that the holding imposing a duty was based on the presence of two facts—the fact that the condition was hazardous and the fact that it was concealed.

To the extent that the prior cases leave unclear which facts were dispositive, the lawyer selects for inclusion in the newly synthesized rule those facts in the prior cases that were relevant to accomplishing the underlying policies. For instance, if the policy was solely the protection of personal safety, then the fact that the conditions were natural probably should not matter, since a condition may be hazardous whether it is natural or not. Nor perhaps should it matter that the conditions were concealed, since even an obvious hazard can threaten safety. If the policy, however, was to encourage people to be responsible for their own safety, then the fact that the condition was concealed becomes more relevant. In such situations, the court may wish to deny recovery to guests who put themselves at risk by encountering an obvious hazard.

A second decision the lawyer must make is to select the level of generality at which to state the elements in the newly synthesized rule. As a practical matter, the lawyer must state the elements in terms general enough to include the facts of any prior case from which the rule is being synthesized. Thus, if the lawyer wishes to include the quicksand, the slope, and the pit cases, then a term at least as general as 'hazard' may have to be used. Any narrower term could arguably exclude some of the cases.

The lawyer must also state the elements in terms at least general enough to include the novel case to which the rule will be applied. For example, assume that the lawyer concluded that, in the prior cases, the quicksand, the pit, and the slope were all in some way concealed, and thus the term 'concealed hazard' would include all prior cases. The lawyer's client, however, was injured by a hazard that was not really concealed, although the client unfortunately did not notice it. If the lawyer characterizes the facts of the prior cases as involving concealed hazards, the very case for which a rule is being formulated will be excluded. Accordingly, the lawyer characterizes the facts of the prior cases in still more general terms—perhaps as 'hazards'—in order to include the case under consideration.

The lawyer, however, also has the choice of synthesizing a rule in terms broader than is absolutely necessary in order to include the prior cases and the current case. Assume for a moment that the term 'concealed hazard,' in fact, would embrace all of the cases, then so would the more general term 'hazards' and the even more general term 'potentially dangerous conditions.' The lawyer must decide whether to use one of these more general characterizations or to be only as general as is absolutely necessary to include the current case.

In choosing the level of generality, the lawyer must avoid overreaching. In other words, the lawyer cannot formulate the rule in terms so broad that it includes new cases that make the policy judgments underlying the prior cases inapplicable. If the rule is too broad, application of the rule can yield undesirable results.

For example, assume that in the quicksand, pit, and slope cases the courts were attempting to strike a balance between, on the one hand, compensating injury and, on the other hand, encouraging safety by refusing to compensate the careless. In each case, the court held that because the hazard was concealed, the victim could not have avoided injury by exercising care. Thus, the policy of encouraging safety did not preclude imposing liability on the landowner.

The lawyer who characterizes these cases as imposing liability for all 'hazards' may well be overreaching, because the policy judgments in the prior cases would not apply to any case in which the hazard was obvious. In the case of an obvious hazard, the victim might well have avoided injury by exercising care, and thus the policy judgment made in the prior cases does not apply. In cases in which the hazard is obvious, the policy of encouraging safety could require leaving the careless [claimant] uncompensated by not imposing liability on the landowner.

Thus, the lawyer must state the newly synthesized rule at a level of generality sufficient to include the prior cases and the client's case. At the same time, the rule must not be stated at a level of generality high enough to encompass new cases in which the policies underlying the prior cases would require a different result.

Between these extremes, however, the lawyer may well have some degree of choice. Thus, reference to the underlying policies may not eliminate all of the indeterminacy in synthesizing a new rule.

Using rule synthesis as an advocate

The discussion in the previous section implicitly assumed to some extent that the lawyer, in synthesizing a new rule, was acting as a dispassionate observer, looking for the 'true' nature of the rule that would explain the prior cases as well as govern the new case.

Yet, the lawyer engaged in the synthesis of a new rule is very often acting as an advocate, with the purpose of either constructing a new rule that will compel the result the client seeks or opposing the creation of the new rule. Let us consider the tactical moves that a lawyer in either situation may make in support of a client's position.

Supporting the new rule

First, the lawyer attempting to create the rule probably wants to generalize from as many cases as possible. Recall that the lawyer would probably argue that the rule being advocated is not a new rule at all but rather a well-established rule perhaps not previously articulated in explicit terms. The more cases that have recognized the rule, the more the rule looks like a well-established rule of law that the court must apply and the less the courts feel that it has ventured onto new terrain.

Second, the lawyer obviously wants to include in the factual predicate of the rule only those facts that clearly have counterparts in the current case. At times, that may be difficult because the court in a prior case may have stated explicitly that a particular fact—say, the fact that the hazard was concealed—was dispositive. If the fact was dispositive in the prior case from which the new rule is to be synthesized, then the fact generally has to be included in the new rule as well.

There is at least one argument the lawyer can make for excluding the dispositive fact from the new rule, and this is to contend that the dispositive fact was a sufficient, but not a necessary, condition for the result reached in the prior case. Thus, the fact need not be an element of the rule. This argument is bolstered considerably if the dispositive fact was absent from some prior cases. Even if it was present in all of them, the lawyer can argue that it was only a sufficient fact. This is done by demonstrating that the policies underlying the rule do not dictate that it be present. The lawyer might argue, for example, that the only policy mentioned by the court in the prior case was protecting persons against avoidable injury and that policy would have required imposition of a duty to warn whether the hazard was concealed or not. The lawyer is arguing, in effect, that the fact of concealment was not truly necessary to the result and any statements about the necessity of the fact should be considered dictum. Further, because the policy underlying the rule does not require that the hazard be concealed, the prior court's dictum to the effect that a concealed condition was a necessary fact should not be followed.

Third, the lawyer probably wants to formulate the rule in the most general terms possible, without over-reaching. A more general rule embraces more prior cases because the broad language used obscures the minor differences among the cases, thus allowing more cases to fall within the rule. As explained above, the more cases that seem to have embraced the rule, the more willing the court will be to apply it in the novel case. At the same time, the broader the rule, the more likely it is to encompass the lawyer's case.

Opposing the new rule

A lawyer opposing recognition of the new rule may also employ a set of standard tactical moves. First, the lawyer attempts to restrict the number of cases on which the generalized rule may be based. This is done by confining the prior cases to their facts. That is, the lawyer points out that the quicksand case addressed only quicksand; the concealed pit case, only concealed pits; the unstable slope case, only unstable slopes. Therefore, anything beyond quicksand, concealed pits, and unstable slopes is mere dictum that need not be followed. Ultimately, the argument is that no general rule exists; there are only several specific rules, none of which applies here. This argument, in essence, is an appeal to the reluctance of courts to make new law.

Second, the lawyer tries to identify dispositive facts in the prior cases that are not present in the novel situation, searching through the prior cases for as many details as can be found and arguing that all of these details were necessary to (not merely sufficient for) the decisions and thus belong in the factual predicate of any newly synthesized rule. Thus, for example, the lawyer may argue that the quicksand, pit, and slope are all concealed, life-threatening natural hazards and thus the rule should be limited to concealed, life-threatening natural hazards. Obviously, the strategy is to formulate a rule that excludes the current case.

Third, the lawyer tries to formulate the rule as narrowly as possible, again with the hope that it will exclude the current case. One way to do this is to characterize the facts narrowly—a concealed pit would be called a concealed pit, not a hazard or an abnormal condition. For this argument to be effective, the lawyer must be prepared to explain why the policy judgments that underlie the rule do not apply in the same way when the rule is formulated in more general terms; that is, the lawyer must explain why a rule formulated in more general terms would overreach."

Questions

1. Define inductive reasoning and explain its relevance to common law analysis.

2. What does Vandevelde mean by his use of the term *dispositive*? How would you go about determining which facts are dispositive in a case?

3. What does it mean to develop a synthesised rule? Think of a leading case you have read recently and consider how the judges moved from the specific facts of a case to consideration of a general rule.

Vandevelde's description of common law advocacy provides a good introduction to how lawyers deal with precedent in a common law system. From his explanation, it is clear that the process involves fitting the precedents together in such a way as to form a general rule, that can then be applied to a new factual situation. It should also be clear to you that there is no one way in which the cases can fit together. After all, a new factual situation is a legal dispute with parties and legal representatives on both sides trying to make the precedents fit together to reach the outcome they desire. Thus, when dealing with common law problem cases, it is imperative that you realise that there is no one "right answer". Instead, there are good answers, which engage with the cases creatively, while not trying to construct rules from them which the facts of those cases cannot realistically support.

One of the things lawyers have to learn to do is to identify which parts of a judgment are important. Vandevelde mentions in the passage above that a lawyer may characterise a statement in a precedent as merely "dictum"; and, therefore, as not "binding" on a future court. There is a crucial distinction in common law reasoning between the ratio decidendi of a precedent, and those parts of a judgment which are merely obiter dicta. It is important to appreciate that it is only the former which is binding in the English system of precedent. Understanding common law reasoning requires an appreciation of the often difficult distinction between the ratio and obiter. In the extract which follows, Cross and Harris suggest other ways of identifying the most important parts of judgments.

R. Cross and J.W. Harris, *Precedent in English Law*, 4th edn (Oxford: Clarendon Press, 1991), pp.39–43:

"It is not everything said by a judge when giving judgment that constitutes a precedent. In the first place, this status is reserved for his pronouncements on the law, and no disputed point of law is involved in the vast majority of cases that are tried in any year. The dispute is solely concerned with the facts. For example, the issue may be whether a particular motorist was driving carelessly by failing to keep a proper look-out or travelling at an excessive speed. No one doubts that a motorist owes a legal duty to drive carefully and, very frequently, the only question is whether he was in breach of that duty when he caused damage to a pedestrian or another motorist. Cases in which the only issues are questions of fact are usually not reported in any series of law reports, but it is not always easy to distinguish law from fact and the reasons which led a judge of first instance or an appellate court to come to a factual conclusion are sometimes reported at length. For example, an employer is under a legal duty to provide his employees with a reasonably safe system of working. The question whether that duty has been broken is essentially one of fact, but the law reports contain a number of cases in which judges have expressed their views concerning the precautions which an employer should have taken in particular instances. When an injury would not have occurred if a workman had been wearing protective clothing it has been said that his employer ought to have insisted that such clothing should have been worn instead of merely rendering it available for those who desired to wear it, but the House of Lords has insisted that observations of this nature are not general propositions of law necessarily applicable to future cases and the decisions based upon them do not constitute a precedent. There is no point in endeavouring to ascertain the *ratio decidendi* of such cases.

The second reason why it is not everything said by a judge in the course of his judgment that constitutes a precedent is that, among the propositions of law enunciated by him, only those which he appears to consider necessary for his decision are said to form part of the *ratio decidendi* and thus to amount to more than an *obiter dictum*. If the judge in a later case is bound by the precedent according to the English doctrine of *stare decisis*, he must apply the earlier *ratio decidendi* however much he disapproved of it, unless, to use the words of Lord Reid, he considers that the two cases are 'reasonably distinguishable'. Dicta in earlier cases are, of course, frequently followed or applied, but dicta are never of more than persuasive authority. There is no question of any judge being bound to follow them. Even when the *ratio decidendi* of a previous case is merely a persuasive authority, it must be followed in later cases unless the judge has good reason to disapprove of it. It constitutes a precedent, and the difference between a persuasive precedent and an *obiter dictum* is only slightly less significant than that between binding and persuasive precedents. If, for example, a High Court judge of first instance comes to the conclusion that a proposition of law contained in a previous opinion of another High Court judge of first instance is ratio, he will be a great deal more reluctant to differ from it than would be the case if he was satisfied that it was merely a *dictum*, although a judge of first instance is not bound to follow the decision of another judge of first instance.

The distinction between *ratio decidendi* and *obiter dictum* is an old one. As long ago as 1673 Vaughan C.J. said:

> 'An opinion given in court, if not necessary to the judgment given of record, but that it might have been as well given if no such, or a contrary had been broach'd, is no judicial opinion; but a mere gratis dictum. . . .'

There are undoubtedly good grounds for the importance attached to the distinction between *ratio decidendi* and *obiter dictum*. In this context an obiter dictum means a statement by the way, and the probabilities are that such a statement has received less serious consideration than that devoted to a proposition of law put forward as a reason for the decision. It is not even every proposition of this nature that forms part of the *ratio decidendi*. To quote Devlin J., as he then was:

> 'It is well established that if a judge gives two reasons for his decision, both are binding. It is not permissible to pick out one as being supposedly the better reason and ignore the other one; nor does it matter for this purpose which comes first and which comes second. But the practice of making judicial observations *obiter* is also well established. A judge may often give additional reasons for his decisions without wishing to make them part of the *ratio decidendi*; he may not be sufficiently convinced of their cogency as to want them to have the full authority of a precedent, and yet may wish to state them so that those who later may have the duty of investigating the same point will start with some guidance. This is a matter which

the judge himself is alone capable of deciding, and any judge who comes after him must ascertain which course has been adopted from the language used and not by consulting his own preferences.'

One thing which a judge cannot do is to prevent his decision on a point of law from constituting a precedent.

The above remarks of Lord Devlin represent orthodox judicial theory, and, at first sight, the power they concede to those who decide a case may seem somewhat surprising. If a judge has this amount of freedom to determine which of his observations is *ratio decidendi* and which *obiter dictum*, is there not a grave danger that he will exercise an undue influence on the future development of the law? He only has to state twenty propositions and say that he bases his decision on each of them to have created twenty new legal rules. It is true that the majority of the judges of former times would have denied that they possessed any power to make new law, but we are primarily concerned with the contemporary situation in which the declaratory theory of judicial decision no longer holds sway. It is also true that the last thing any modern English judge would wish to do is to fetter his successors by laying down a multitude of superfluous rules. But just now we are concerned with legal theory. The answer to the question raised is that there are several considerations which may be said to redress the balance in favour of the judges who come afterwards. No doubt the *ratio decidendi* of a previous case has to be gathered from the language of the judge who decided that case, but it is trite learning that the interpreter has nearly as much to say as the speaker so far as the meaning of words is concerned. Of even greater significance is the existence of certain rules of judicial practice concerning the construction to be placed by a future judge upon past decisions. By stressing the necessity of having regard to the facts of the previous case and the language of prior or subsequent judgments, these rules greatly curtail the influence that can be exercised on legal development by means of the reasons which a particular judge sees fit to give for his decisions."

One of the primary ways in which judges can exercise a high degree of control over the meaning of a precedent is through the use of analogical reasoning. That is, judges can extend the scope of a precedent to cover new situations by drawing *analogies* between the facts of the case at hand, and the precedent. Alternatively, the judge may *distinguish* the immediate case from the precedent on the basis that there is a *material* difference between them; which means the precedent will not be applied to the facts at issue. The "art" of applying and distinguishing case law is one of the most important skills for the student of the common law to develop and, indeed, for any legal advocate.

In the extract below, Vandevelde reviews the various options open to advocates and students in their treatment of previous cases. He describes processes which may appear complex at this stage of your studies but will become much easier to understand and appreciate the more cases you read.

Kenneth J. Vandevelde, *Thinking Like a Lawyer* (Boulder: Westview Press, 1996), pp.91–98:

Arguments for following the precedent

"As an initial matter, the lawyer arguing that a prior case should be followed in a later case emphasizes the numerous factual similarities between the two cases. Strictly speaking, the only relevant facts are those whose existence would further or impede one of the underlying policies. The advocate arguing that a prior case should be followed, however, rarely limits the argument to those facts. Rather, the advocate includes in the recitation of similarities virtually any fact that is not a trivial coincidence.

Second, the advocate argues that the inevitable dissimilarities are irrelevant, the basic contention being that none of the facts that make the cases different is relevant to furthering or impeding any of the underlying policies. Obviously, for example, the fact that the parties' names differ is irrelevant to any legitimate policy. To the extent possible, the advocate makes a parallel argument with respect to any dissimilarity between the cases.

This argument may be difficult to make where the court in the prior case has stated explicitly that a particular fact, not present in the current case, is dispositive. The best argument for following the case in that situation is to point out that in light of the policies underlying the prior case, the prior case would have been decided the same way even without the so-called dispositive fact. The lawyer is arguing, in effect, that the fact was not truly necessary to the result. Since it was not actually necessary to the result, any discussion of that fact should be considered dictum and need not be followed. It may be difficult to prevail in this argument because it requires the court to disregard how another court characterized its own decision.

A third technique for arguing that a precedent should be followed is to state the factual predicate of the precedent at a higher level of generality. For example, if the prior case held that the presence of a concealed pit on the land gives rise to a duty on the part of the landowner to warn a guest, but the current case involves a guest who fell down a slope, the lawyer for the injured guest may characterize the prior case as involving a 'hazard' rather than a concealed pit. As the language becomes more general, it will tend to encompass the facts of the current situation. . . .

A fourth technique is to characterize the prior case, not in terms of its facts but in terms of the underlying policy judgments, which the lawyer argues should be followed. For example, the lawyer seeking to impose on a landowner a duty to warn customers about concealed hazards on the land may rely on cases holding that a manufacturer has a duty to warn consumers of product defects. The lawyer would then argue that the prior cases adopted a policy of protecting the unwary against physical injury and that such policy should prevail in the current case as well. This technique may require manipulating the level of generality at which the policy underlying the precedent is stated. The product defect cases, for example, may have described the underlying policy as protecting the stream of commerce against unsafe instrumentalities. By restating the policy more generally as protecting the unwary, the lawyer makes the policy seem applicable to the subsequent case. That is, the impression is created that the result the lawyer seeks in the later case would further the policies articulated in the earlier case.

Arguments for distinguishing the precedent
The arguments for distinguishing a prior case mirror those for following it. First, the lawyer emphasizes every possible difference between the two cases, being especially alert to facts that the court in the prior case regarded as dispositive. Even if the facts were only sufficient for the holding and not necessary, the lawyer notes that the dispositive facts are not present in this case. If the later case differs concerning some such dispositive fact, then it is likely the court will distinguish the two cases. Assuming that the cases do not differ concerning any fact explicitly considered dispositive in the earlier case, the lawyer attempting to distinguish the precedent may nevertheless point to differences in other facts in an effort to make the cases appear as different as possible.

Second, the lawyer attempts to dismiss similarities between the cases as irrelevant. If possible, the lawyer argues that particular facts in the precedent that are similar to those in the later case were not explicitly found to be dispositive and are therefore irrelevant coincidences. If the facts were held to be dispositive, the lawyer can attempt to argue that the facts were not relevant to accomplishing the underlying policy, although this can obviously be a difficult argument to make.

Third, the lawyer attempting to distinguish the cases characterizes the precedent in the narrowest possible terms. The lawyer states the facts and the legal consequence with great specificity, noting that any broader reading would constitute dictum, which the court need not follow. By stating the facts at very specific levels, the lawyer produces new dissimilarities. Thus, a pit is not merely a pit, but a concealed, life-threatening, 20-foot-deep pit.

Fourth, the lawyer may contend that the policy judgments underlying the prior case do not apply to the current case. This argument may follow any of several different approaches.

One approach is to argue that the policies that prevailed in the prior case require a different result in this case than was reached in the prior case. For example, assume that the prior case held that the government has the power to prohibit the use of offensive language on a television broadcast because the danger that a youngster might be injured by hearing the language outweighed the broadcaster's right to use it. In a later case, a television station broadcasts a documentary that realistically portrays the lives of young drug users in an effort to persuade juveniles that drug use could ruin their lives. To make the documentary more realistic and thus more credible, the station broadcasts film of drug users engaged in conversation with the police, their families, and each other—conversation involving the use of the same offensive language. The lawyer might argue that, in this case, the policy of protecting children actually would be *furthered* by permitting the offensive language to be broadcast. Thus, to further the policy that prevailed in the prior case the court should distinguish the prior case and void, rather than uphold, the ban on offensive language. . . .

Finally, the lawyer can argue that if the precedent is applied to this case, *stare decisis* would require that it also be applied to other cases in which it would produce a clearly undesirable result. This, again, is the parade of horribles or the slippery slope argument. The lawyer demonstrates that this case is indistinguishable from other hypothetical cases in which application of the precedent would lead to undesirable results. As with legal reasoning in the deductive form, this argument is distinguished by not requiring a demonstration that following the precedent would lead to a bad result in this case, only that it would entail application of the precedent to other cases in which it would produce an undesirable result. . . .

The problem of competing analogies

The prior discussion has assumed that the lawyer was attempting to determine whether one precedent should be followed or distinguished in deciding a current dispute. The precedent must be followed if it is like the current case.

Often, however, the lawyer encounters a situation where there are two or more precedents, each of which is like the current case in some respects. The problem is that the two precedents reached opposite results and thus both cannot be followed. In other words, the lawyer must choose between competing analogies. . . .

The lawyer nevertheless chooses between the competing analogies using the same techniques that are used to decide whether to follow or distinguish a single precedent. The correct analogy is the one that seems most like the current case, taking into account all similarities and dissimilarities."

This passage makes clear that lawyers can have considerable impact on the development of common law and that the application of precedent is far from being a mechanical act. On the contrary, the tactical devices employed by lawyers in their attempts to ensure that the outcome of the case is most favourable to their client can lead to shifts in the values which underpin the treatment of particular cases. The potential for this to occur will be made clear in the case study on negligence that we visit in the next chapter. The tension between creativity and conservatism is summarised by Lord Denning in his typically flamboyant style.

Lord Denning, *The Discipline of Law* (London: Butterworths, 1979), p.285:

"To a student of jurisprudence this doctrine of precedent exercises a particular fascination. He is hypnotised by it. To a practising lawyer it is *Mr. Facing-both-ways*. He is attracted or repelled by it according as to whether it is for him or against him. He can argue either way, as you please. To a Judge it comes, if he chooses, as a way of escape. He does not have to think for himself or to decide for himself. It has already been decided by the previous authority. But not so for most Judges. Whilst ready to applaud the doctrine of precedent when it leads to a just and fair result, they become restless under it when they are compelled by it to do what is unjust or unfair. This restlessness leads them to various expedients to get round a previous authority. But never to depart from it altogether—except for an absolution recently granted by the House of Lords to themselves, though not vouchsafed by them to others."

Question

Consider the following problem. Construct arguments for the claimant and defendant, and then consider how, as a judge, you would decide the case and prepare reasons. You should draw upon the material on precedent which we have examined thus far as a guide for discerning the ratio decidendi of your precedent, and how to apply or distinguish it.

Edmund M.A. Kwaw, *The Guide to Legal Analysis, Legal Methodology and Legal Writing* (Toronto: Edmond Montgomery, 1992), p.198:

"You are a judge in a case in which Jason, a truck driver, and Louis, a pedestrian, are suing a day nursery. You learn from the evidence that as Jason was driving, he saw a little girl dart through the gate of the day nursery onto the road. He swerved to avoid hitting her. In doing so, he knocked down Louis, who happened to be walking on the sidewalk at that moment, and his truck also struck a lamp post. Jason suffered shock and Louis sustained bruises and a fractured leg. You learn from the evidence that the gate of the day nursery should not have been opened without a teacher or other adult being present. No one can explain how the gate got open. The only precedent is the (hypothetical) case that follows.

Samson v Dunlop

Dunlop was a local farmer who had a flock of sheep. He was assisted in his work by three sheep dogs, Wolfie, Blackie, and Spotty. The three dogs were regarded as the best sheep dogs in the county. One day something peculiar happened. Instead of rounding up the sheep as they were supposed to, the three dogs began attacking the sheep. There was a stampede and the fence that kept the sheep in was broken. As the sheep rushed out, Samson the letter carrier, who happened to be riding along on his bicycle, swerved to avoid colliding with the sheep. Samson lost control of the bicycle and smashed into a tree. In an action brought by Samson against Dunlop, the court held that farmers who were in control of livestock owed a legal duty to ensure that the livestock did not injure other people."

IV. The Implications of Membership in the European Union on Common Law Reasoning

As we have seen in previous chapters, membership of the European Union (EU) legal order is now a central element of our legal system. Consequently, an understanding of how precedent works within a common law system must be supplemented by an understanding of the systems and methods of legal reasoning employed elsewhere in the EU. Significantly, the EU emerged from the *civilian* rather than the *common law* tradition, in which precedent does not hold the same power. Moreover, membership of the EU means that English courts are also subject to the jurisdiction of the European Court of Justice (ECJ). Here, our interest is in how the concept of precedent must be modified to take European law into account. We have already considered the basic structure of that legal order in Ch 4. We begin here with the status of cases decided by the ECJ when they are considered by domestic courts.

Colin Manchester and David Salter, *Exploring the Law: The dynamics of precedent and statutory interpretation*, 3rd edn (London: Sweet and Maxwell, 2006), pp.135–39:

"Although ss. 2 and 3 [of the European Communities Act 1972] leave a number of matters unclear, the ECJ has nevertheless provided some indication of its views, where a case has been referred to it under Art. 234 (ex 177), of how its ruling in that case should be regarded on return of the case to the court which referred it. The ECJ stated in Case 29/68 *Milchkontor v Haupzollamt Saarbrucken* [1969] ECR 165 (*Milchkontor*) that a ruling given by it is binding on the court receiving it. To this extent, the notion of one court binding another court is introduced into the EC legal order. This is not, however, a departure from the principle of *res judicata*, i.e. that the decision in a case is generally final and binding only as between the parties to that case, since the ruling given by the ECJ on an Art. 234 (ex 177) reference is confined to the particular case in question. This ruling consists of an interpretation or exposition of EU law, formulated in the abstract as a proposition of law rather than one which is dependent upon the material facts of the case, although the proposition will be formulated by reference to those facts. Although binding only on the parties to the case, the ruling is, however, one which the ECJ (presumably) expects English courts in future to follow, although it would (presumably) be a matter for the English courts to determine in what way that should be achieved. Not only might the ECJ expect English courts to follow rulings under Art. 234 (ex 177) following references from English courts, but it may also expect any of its other decisions (including rulings under Art. 234 (ex 177) following references from courts in other Member States) to be followed. However, it is clear that, as a matter of EU law, it would be open to an English court in any future case to refer the case before it to the ECJ under Art. 234 (ex 177) for a ruling on EC law, notwithstanding the existence of a previous ruling or any other ECJ decision on the particular point.

On receipt of a ruling under Art. 234 (ex 177) from the ECJ, it will be for the English court to apply the ruling to the facts of the case before it. When a ruling is so applied, it may, from a traditional English perspective, become part of the *ratio* of that case and thus become part of a proposition of law based on the material facts of that case. As such, the ruling, as part of the *ratio* of the case, would therefore (presumably) be capable of forming a binding precedent, in the English sense, for application in future cases, although, of course, it would be open to a subsequent court to limit the scope of such *ratio* (and thus ruling) by distinguishing it on the ground that the case before it had materially different facts.

Whilst a ruling by the ECJ returned to an English court may become part of the *ratio* of a case in the manner indicated above, it is less clear how any ruling returned to a national court of another Member State or any other decision of the ECJ may do so. In any event, to the extent that any ECJ ruling or decision has become part of the *ratio* of a case, the binding nature of the *ratio* may be called into question . . .

It is clear from the above that ECJ cases may have a number of implications for the English doctrine of precedent. The extent of such implications, as will be seen below, may vary depending upon whether a court, when considering a point of EU law, decides to refer the case to the ECJ under Art. 234 (ex 177) or decides itself to interpret that point.

(i) Implications of a decision to refer to the ECJ under Art. 234 (ex 177)

When cases have been referred to the ECJ and rulings on points of EU law have been received by the courts which referred the cases, those courts invariably seem to have accepted the rulings as binding on them (in accordance with the ECJ's stated view in *Milchkontor*). On receipt of such rulings, it is necessary for English courts to decide how the interpretations or expositions of EU law contained therein should be applied to the facts of the case. This may involve a consideration of the impact of the ruling on the provision in question in the English legislation and, as seen, different approaches have been adopted on this matter. In some cases, courts have regarded rulings as setting out a proposition of EU law which should be applied in preference to a provision in English legislation deemed to be inconsistent with that proposition (Priority Approach), an approach adopted, for instance, by the Court of Appeal in *Macarthys*, in which Lord Denning M.R. stated (at [1981] 1 All ER 111, 120):

> 'We have now been provided with the decision of that court [the ECJ]. It is important now to declare, and it must be made plain, that the provisions of article 119 of the EEC Treaty [as interpreted by the ECJ on an Article 177 reference from the present case] take priority over anything in our English statute on equal pay which is inconsistent with art.119.'

In other cases, courts have regarded the rulings as an aid to interpretation of a provision in English legislation. Thus courts have, on some occasions, used the ruling as an aid to resolving an ambiguity (Ambiguity Interpretation Approach) and, on other occasions, to interpret a provision in English legislation (not regarded as containing any ambiguity) in whatever manner is necessary to secure compliance with EU law (General Interpretation Approach). An instance of a court using a ruling as an aid to interpretation can be seen in *Garland*, where the House of Lords used a ruling to resolve an ambiguity in section 6(4) of the Sex Discrimination Act 1975 and where Lord Diplock stated (at [1982] 2 All ER 402, 416) that it was necessary to obtain a ruling from the ECJ 'so as to provide the House with material necessary to aid it in construing s.6(4) of the Sex Discrimination Act 1975.'

On occasions, courts receiving rulings have also expressed views (*obiter*) as to the status that such rulings will have in future cases. Thus, when the Court of Appeal in *Macarthys* received a ruling from the ECJ that Art. 119 (now 141) of the EC Treaty required equal pay for men and women even where they were not employed at the same time, Lord Denning M.R. stated (at [1981] 1 All ER 111, 120): 'That interpretation must now be given by all the courts in England. It will apply in this case and in any such case hereafter.' Similarly, Lord Diplock in the House of Lords in *Garland*, reflecting on the decision in that case to make a reference to the ECJ under Article 177 (now 234), stated (at [1982] 2 All ER 402, 415) that 'it was desirable to obtain a ruling of the European Court that would be binding on all courts in England, including this House.'

Such statements indicate that rulings containing an interpretation or exposition of EU law will be of general application, i.e. not limited in scope to future cases in which the *ratio* of the particular case in question might be considered applicable in view of the materially similar facts, and will apply irrespective of the position in the court hierarchy of either the court receiving the ruling or of any later court applying it. By regarding rulings returned to English courts as being generally binding in this way (subject to exercise of the right to refer under Art. 234 (ex 177)), the above statements appear to regard these rulings in much the same way as any other decisions of the ECJ (including rulings under Art.234 (ex 177) following references from courts in other Member States), a matter which is considered immediately below.

(ii) Implications of a decision by an English court to interpret EC law

. . . English courts may have regard to ECJ cases. These cases may include previous rulings under Art. 234 (ex 177) following references from English courts or from courts in other Member States, as well as any other decisions of the ECJ. English courts appear to regard ECJ cases in each instance as being binding generally. As a consequence, interpretations of EU law contained in such ECJ cases may be binding on an English court in a particular case, irrespective of the presence or absence of similar material facts between the ECJ case(s) and the case in question and irrespective of the position of the English court in the court hierarchy.

Instances of where English courts have had regard to ECJ case law when interpreting EU law have included the decision of the Court of Appeal in *Pickstone* and the decision of the House of Lords in *Henn*. The Court of Appeal in *Pickstone* was concerned with interpreting two points of EC law, determining the scope of the principle of equal pay based on Art. 119 (now 141) and determining whether that principle had direct effect as regards work of equal value. On the first point, two of the three members of the Court of Appeal, Nicholls and Purchas L.JJ., found guidance on the interpretation of Art. 119 (now 141) in different decisions of the ECJ, notwithstanding material differences in the facts of those cases from the case in question. Nicholls L.J. referred to the case of *Macarthys*, an earlier ECJ case in which a ruling had been given under Art. 177 (now 234) following a reference from the English Court of Appeal, whilst Purchas L.J., found guidance on the interpretation of Art. 119 (now 141) in *Defrenne*, an earlier case in which a ruling had been given under Art. 177 (now 234) following a reference from a Belgian court. On the second point, Nicholls and Purchas L.JJ., referred to two ECJ decisions, Case 96/80 *Jenkins v Kingsgate (Clothing Productions) Ltd* [1981] 1 ECR 911 and *Worringham*, in which rulings had been given under Art. 177 (now 234) following references from English courts. These cases provided interpretations on the direct effect[iveness] of the principle of equal pay based on Art. 119 (now 141) and were considered to have application in preference to an earlier Court of Appeal decision on direct effect[iveness], *O'Brien v Sim-Chem Ltd*. [1980] 2 All E.R. 307. In *Henn*, the House of Lords had regard to a 'well-established body of case law of the European court' (per Lord Diplock at [1981] AC 850, 905), that provided guidance on the interpretation of Art. 30 (now 28) of the EC Treaty, under which quantitative restrictions on importation of goods as between Member States were prohibited, when determining the scope of that article."

V. Big Issues Relating to Common Law Reasoning

In this final section, we look at the broader, more theoretical implications of the common law system of precedent. Central to that inquiry is the issue, already hinted at above, of the extent to which we can say that judges are "makers" of law; rather than simply engaged in the task of "declaring" a common law that is already "there". Although it may seem obvious to us, at the start of the twenty-first century, that judges are lawmakers, this viewpoint at one time would have been considered very radical. The common law was assumed to be already "there", and had always been there, just waiting to be declared by judges in the interpretation of cases. Cotterrell describes this as a "paradox" of the common law.

Roger Cotterrell, *The Politics of Jurisprudence*, 2nd edn (Oxford: Oxford University Press, 2003), pp.26–29:

"A paradox seems to lie at the heart of classical common law thought. Common law as the embodiment of ancient wisdom is revealed by judges, not created by them. It is, therefore, always already existent. Yet obviously it develops with the accumulation, reinterpretation and restatement of precedents and the adjustment of legal doctrine to new circumstances reflected in the never-ending succession of cases brought before courts. How is the evolution of law explained in this conception? And why is it not possible to assert openly that judges *make* law, even if only within strict limits which would fix them as clearly subordinate to recognised legislators, such as (in the context of English history) a parliament or the monarch?

The formal answer to this last question is that law embodies an ancient wisdom which may, according to some conceptions of common law, be considered timeless or, according to others, be seen as continually evolving through collective experience. On either view judges can only reflect this wisdom and not change it. In some classical common law thought the claim of timelessness is taken to fantastic lengths. Influential seventeenth century lawyers, such as Sir Edward Coke, 'argued on the flimsiest of evidence that the common laws, including their most detailed procedural provisions, dated from the earliest times': even Magna Carta was treated as declaring ancient law, confirming and making enforceable rights which had long existed. Coke claimed that in all its major parts the law and constitution had remained unchanged since the Saxon era and even before. These strange views were always controversial but the reason for asserting them at times when the authority of common law was seriously challenged (as in the early seventeenth century) is not hard to see. This authority was traditional in nature. Rooting it in a distant or even mythical past emphasised that it was certainly not derived from the present power of any monarch or other political authority.

The authority or legitimacy of common law as a legal order entitled to the highest respect was seen as residing not in the political system but in the community. If a judge *made* law this could only be as an exercise of political power. Deliberate lawmaking would be a political act. But according to common law theory, judges' authority is not as political decision-makers (certainly not as delegate of the king or parliament) but as representatives of the community. Hence they have authority only to *state* the community's law, not to impose law upon the community as if they were political rulers or the servants of such rulers. And the community is to be understood here as something uniting past and present, extending back through innumerable past generations as well as encompassing the present one.

Clearly, if the term 'community' were to be defined rigorously in this context it would be necessary to ask who exactly is in this community and what is its nature. It would also be necessary to consider the compatibility of this communitarian conception of law with the fact that the judges referred to here are judges of the *royal* courts, the instruments of a centralised justice promoted by kings. But these issues are typically absent from classical common law thought. So, for Coke, the common law is simply 'the most ancient and best inheritance that the subjects of this realm have'.

The usual way of conceptualising this apparently unchanging inheritance in classical common law thought is as *custom*. As Brian Simpson remarks, it is odd nowadays to think of law in this way because lawyers are used to treating this law as set in place by the judges. But this is another example of the tendency to impose alien modern theoretical conceptions on common law. Just as common law is not strictly to be thought of, in the classical conception, as rules, neither is it decisions. To term it 'a residue of immutable custom' is more accurate, but does not confront the fact that common law thought embraces complex notions explaining and justifying past practices (not just stating them as custom) and providing guidance for future conduct. Equally common law thought allows the development of new doctrines and ideas, so has a dynamism which custom may lack. Because of these characteristics Simpson prefers the term common law customary law, rather than custom. But this does not solve the theoretical problem of its development. Customary law still has the character of custom, looking to the past rather than guiding the future. It states established practice rather than of developing legal doctrine to meet changing times.

The problem is not that custom is changeless: there is no reason why it cannot be considered to change over time, so law as an expression of custom can also change. The problem is that common law thought itself cannot really address this change or explain it as a *legal* process. The mechanisms of change are in society (or the community). Law changes solely through the mysterious processes by which custom changes. To explain or even recognise explicitly processes of legal change, classical common law thought would need some kind of sociological insight. But the common lawyers were hardly sociologists. Common law thought predated any modern social science and, in any event, its practical case-by-case view of legal development would have found little room for any explicit general theory of social or cultural change. So classical common law thought emphasised continuity (which it could interpret legally in terms of precedents and principles), rather than change (for which it could find no specifically legal criteria of evaluation).

Historically, the conundrum of law as changeless yet always changing was avoided by devices made possible by cultural conditions. Common law was considered to be unwritten. Blackstone, following Hale, distinguished 'the common law, or *lex non scripta* of this kingdom' from the written law of Acts of Parliament. Even though this unwritten law was eventually reported in written form, the fact that the law itself was still considered unwritten presumably allowed individual innovation to be forgotten, subsumed in the image of a changeless collective legal knowledge. As the anthropologist Jack Goody has noted about societies lacking writing, it is not that the creative element is absent in them or that 'a mysterious collective authorship, closely in touch with the collective consciousness, does what individuals do in literate cultures. It is rather that the individual signature is always getting rubbed out in the process of generative transmission'. Certainly common law's unwritten character was seen as one of its strengths, making possible 'a flexible system which had developed along with the English people itself'.

In the early ages of common law the lack of writing allowed a convenient amnesia. Blackstone wrote in the eighteenth century that 'in our law the goodness of a custom depends upon its having been used time out of mind; or, in the solemnity of our legal phrase, time whereof the memory of man runneth not to the contrary. This it is that gives its weight and authority'. The traditional authority of common law required that its customs be shrouded in antiquity. But in the Middle Ages two or three lifetimes would be enough to make a principle of common law immemorial; 'in ten or twenty years a custom was of long standing; in forty years it was "age-old"'. Later the flexibility of memory was less satisfactory. When, in the seventeenth century, lawyers such as Coke found it necessary to assert with the greatest possible force the traditional authority of common law against the king, the 'idea of the immemorial . . . took on an absolute colouring . . . It ceased to be a convenient fiction and was heatedly asserted as literal historical truth'.

It can easily be seen, therefore, that common law thought eventually backed itself into a corner. First, the idea that the law was unwritten gradually became a mere fiction as the common law was recorded—preserved, explained and digested in written form in public records, law reports and 'the authoritative writings of the venerable sages of the law'. Secondly, the purely traditional authority of the law eventually demanded an utterly unrealistic claim of unbroken continuity from ancient times. And, finally, the declaratory theory of common law judging had to be maintained in the face of abundant evidence of conscious judicial innovation in legal doctrine.

Three responses to this situation were possible. One was to declare that common law possessed no authority by which it could develop further. Legal innovation could only come through Acts of Parliament or other legislative acts. Thus, as one judge put the matter, 'It is in my opinion impossible for us now to create any new doctrine of common law'.

A second response was to embrace openly the idea that judges sometimes make law, discard all fictions and go on to ask serious questions as to *how* and under what conditions they should make it. But this pragmatic approach also involved discarding all the standard assumptions underpinning the authority and legitimacy of common law. Traditional authority would need to be replaced with something else—perhaps the charismatic authority of individual wise judges, a conception of delegated political power or, as in the United States, the authority of a specific constitutional document providing the ultimate foundation of legal and judicial systems. In any event such a new foundation of judicial authority, if it could be found, would be something different from that presupposed in classical common law thought.

A third solution was to discard the notion of common law as custom and the formal idea of an unchanging ancient law, and to emphasise instead the complex conception of the judge as spokesperson for the community—neither individual creator of law nor mere restator of ancient truths, but representative of an evolving collective consciousness."

Questions

1. Why do you think that commentators such as Edward Coke found it necessary to argue that common law is the embodiment of ancient wisdom?

2. Although modern observers of the use of precedent are much more likely to acknowledge that judges play an active role in creating law, there may be dangers in taking this argument to its logical conclusion. Think of as many reasons as you can as to why this might be the case.

The issue of whether judges merely "declare" the law which is already "there", and the degree to which precedent operates as an effective constraint upon judicial decision making, have long been the subject of vigorous debate. Beginning in the 1930s, "American legal realism" drew into question these established "truths". One of the members of this school, Jerome Frank, was particularly sceptical of the constraints which the common law mode of thought claimed to impose upon judges. It has been argued that most lawyers today are realists in one form or another, but Frank was particularly radical in his claim that there was a great divergence between what judges say in their decisions, (i.e. what they claim is the basis for their decisions, such as precedent), and what *really* is operating on judges in the process of decision making (which Frank viewed as an emotional response to the particular facts of the case). Thus, for legal realists, the gap between the rhetoric of common law judging, and its reality, was potentially vast.

Jerome Frank, *Law and the Modern Mind* (Gloucester, Massachussetts: Peter Smith, 1970), pp.159–162:

"Lawyers and judges purport to make large use of precedents; that is, they purport to rely on the conduct of judges in past cases as a means of procuring analogies for action in new cases. But since what was actually decided in the earlier cases is seldom revealed, it is impossible, in a real sense, to rely on these precedents. What the courts in fact do is to manipulate the language of former decisions. They could approximate a system of real precedents only if the judges, in rendering those former decisions, had reported with fidelity the precise steps by which they arrived at their decisions. The paradox of the situation is that, granting there is value in a system of precedents, our present use of illusory precedents makes the employment of real precedents impossible.

The decision of a judge after trying a case is the product of a unique experience. 'Of the many things which have been said of the mystery of the judicial process,' writes Yntema, 'the most salient is that *decision is reached after an emotive experience in which principles and logic play a secondary part*. The function of juristic logic and the principles which it employs seem to be like that of language, to describe the event which has already transpired. These considerations must reveal to us the impotence of general principle to control decision. Vague because of their generality, they mean nothing save what they suggested in the organized experience of one who thinks them, and, because of their vagueness, they only remotely compel the organization of that experience. The important problem . . . is not the formulation of the rule but the ascertainment of the cases to which, and the extent to which, it applies. And this, even if we are seeking uniformity in the administration of justice, will lead us again to the circumstances of the concrete case . . . The reason why the general principle cannot control is because it does not inform . . . It should be obvious that when we have observed a recurrent phenomenon in the decisions of the courts, we may appropriately express the classification in a rule. But the rule will be only a mnemonic device, a useful but hollow diagram of what has been. It will be intelligible only if we *relive again the experience of the classifier'*.

The rules a judge announces when publishing his decision are, therefore, intelligible only if one can relive the judge's unique experience while he was trying the case—which, of course, cannot be done. One cannot even approximate that experience as long as opinions take the form of abstract rules applied to facts formally described. Even if it were desirable that, despite its uniqueness, the judge's decision should be followed, as an analogy, by other judges while trying other cases, this is impossible when the manner in which the judge reached his judgment in the earlier case is most inaccurately reported, as it now is. You are not really applying his decision as a precedent in another case unless you can say, in effect, that, having relived his experience in the earlier case, you believe that he would have thought his decision applicable to the facts of the latter case. And as opinions are now written, it is impossible to guess what the judge did experience in trying a case. The facts of all but the simplest controversies are complicated and unlike those of any other controversy; in the absence of a highly detailed account by the judge of how he reacted to the evidence, no other person is capable of reproducing his actual reactions. The rules announced in his opinions are therefore often insufficient to tell the reader why the judge reached his decision.

Dickinson admits that the 'personal bent of the judge' to some extent affects his decisions. But this 'personal bent,' he insists, is a factor only in the selection of new rules for unprovided cases. However, *in a profound sense the unique circumstances of almost any case make it an 'unprovided case' where no well-established rule 'authoritatively' compels a given result*. The uniqueness of the facts and of the judge's reaction thereto is often concealed because the judge so states the facts that they appear to call for the application of a settled rule. But that concealment does not mean that the judge's personal bent has been inoperative or that his emotive experience is simple and reducible."

Questions

1. Although Frank's views may accord with many "common sense" assumptions about human nature, why would they be threatening to common law judges, and those who place great "faith" in the common law?

2. Having read some of his ideas, why do you think Frank was described as a "realist"?

3. If you subscribe to Frank's views, what does that suggest about the sort of skills that are important for legal advocacy? In other words, in order to achieve a "good" result for your client, is an intricate knowledge of the relevant precedents of prime importance, or are other skills at least as crucial? What might those skills be?

Frank's scepticism, which was directed to the traditional understanding of precedent, seems less radical today. In part, this is because many writers and commentators on the law recognise quite openly that the process of deciding whether cases are analogous or distinguishable is itself laden with political and social values, and is not a "neutral", formalistic process.

Fiona Cownie, Anthony Bradney and Mandy Burton, *English Legal System in Context*, 4th edn (Oxford: Oxford University Press, 2007), pp.103–104:

"We can see an alternative to the traditional approach to precedent if we return to one of the essential features of any theory of precedent; the desire to treat similar cases in the same fashion and thus bring both certainty and consistency to the law. Here the basic question is how do we decide that two cases are or are not alike? Traditional theories approach this question on the basis that it is simply a matter of close reasoning to see what are and what are not the significant and trivial aspects of the two cases in issue. However, we have seen that, in law, as in other disciplines, what makes something trivial or significant does not depend solely on linguistic features. Nothing is essentially significant or essentially trivial. Meaning is socially defined by the small community of English lawyers. Thinking like a lawyer means not arguing more rigorously than others but, literally, thinking in the way that a lawyer would. . . . Prediction is achieved not just because the same rules are followed but because of an ability to empathise with those whose thought processes are being considered. One seeks to use words and judgments in the way other English lawyers would use them.

Several writers have argued that in considering how this social effect of language occurs we need to consider the influence of what they have called the legal canon in legal reasoning. . . . A canon is an accepted body of literature which it is said one should know if one is to be knowledgeable about a particular area. But a canon is more than simply a certain set of books (or in the case of a legal system, judgments). The works that constitute the canon are chosen for their alleged value. This value is moral or political. Works in the canon say something about the spirit of the system. However, since the canon reflects values in the system the selection of what is and what is not in the canon is in itself a value-laden act. The canon reflects and reinforces the politics of those who constitute the community for whom it operates. In the context of law this means that the influence of the canon on legal argument is itself not a value-free act. Arguments which are not reflective of the values of the canon will find it harder to find a purchase within the system.

The notion of the canon provides a framework within which the more traditional accounts of ratio and obiter can work. It allows us to understand how legal arguments can be acceptable even if they are not logical. The idea of a canon helps to explain how, on the one hand, there can be irresolvable problems in traditional accounts of precedent and yet, on the other hand, there can still be a reasonable degree of consistency and certainty in English legal reasoning. Social pressures supplement the principles of English legal reasoning to produce comparatively predictable outcomes to legal arguments. This explanation, though, has consequences for our understanding of the nature of legal reasoning. If reasoning is in part social, in part about values, who does the reasoning matters. The social background of judges and lawyers will affect how they respond to, and help construct, the atmosphere which in turn creates the canon."

Cownie, Bradney and Burton make an important point that one of the tasks of a legal method course must be to teach students how "to use words and judgments in the way other English lawyers would use them". It remains important for the lawyer to be able to speak within that "traditional" legal discourse—since that is what is expected of them. In that sense, law remains a conservative enterprise, in that one must use a language expected of you. It remains difficult to alter and broaden the scope of legal reasoning, so as to encompass broader perspectives. However, that is not to say that legal method and discourse forecloses innovation. Instead, it suggests that for the critical or radical lawyer, the task becomes particularly challenging. He or she must be able to converse in traditional legal discourse *at least as well* as his or her adversaries, but at the same time, must try to expand its scope and achieve outcomes more in keeping with what "social justice" demands.

The job is not helped for the lawyer by the traditional differentiation between "law" (supposedly neutral, apolitical, and value-free) and "policy" (which is assumed to be something other than law). As Sugarman argues, the categories of common law thought, which have been entrenched through traditional legal education, have served to create this law/policy dichotomy, which conveniently serves to disguise the politics of law.

David Sugarman, "'A hatred of disorder': legal science, liberalism and imperialism" in Peter Fitzpatrick (ed) *Dangerous Supplements* (London: Pluto Press, 1991), pp.34–35:

"The 'black letter' tradition continues to overshadow the way we teach, write and think about law. Its categories and assumptions are still the standard diet of most first-year law students and they continue to organise law textbooks and casebooks. Stated baldly it assumes that although law may appear to be irrational, chaotic and particularistic, if one digs deep enough and knows what one is looking for, then it will soon become evident that the law is an internally coherent and unified body of rules. This coherence and unity stems from the fact that law is grounded in, and logically derived from, a handful of general principles, and that whole subject areas such as contract and torts are distinguished by some common principles or elements which fix the boundaries of the subject. The exposition and systematisation of these general principles and the techniques required to find and to apply both them and the rules that they underpin, are largely what legal education and scholarship are all about.

The claim that law is unified and coherent is also sustained by a battery of dualisms: common law/statute law, law/politics, law/state, law/morality, legal/empirical, technique/ substance, form/substance, means/ends, private law/public law, law/history, law/theory, which make it more tenable to regard law as 'pure' and 'scientific'.

Despite the variety of producers and consumers of legal discourse, it is what the judges say and the sup-posed needs of the legal profession as narrowly defined, that have had the greatest magnetic pull over the nature and form of legal education and scholarship. Other aspects that are equally important to understanding law, such as legislation, the operation of law in practice, as well as the history, theory, morality and politics of law, are ignored or marginalised.

The 'black letter' tradition is also the bearer of an important political message. The message is that the law (primarily through case law) and the legal profession (centrally, the judiciary) play a major role in protect-ing individual freedom; and that the rules of contract, torts and constitutional law, for example, confer the maximum freedom on individuals to act as they wish without interference from other individuals or the state. Policing the boundaries within, and between, legal subject areas constitutes a major foundation of the rule of law. In this way, the form as well as the content of the law become synonymous with our very definitions of indi-vidual freedom and liberty, and thereby acquire an additional patina of reverence and universality. The world, as pictured within the conceptual categories of legal thought, is basically sound. It is more or less the best that is realisable. In so far as a better world is possible, it would not fundamentally differ from the present.

Like any closed model of rationality, the 'black letter' tradition is shot through with contradictions, omis-sions and absurdities, which generations of judges and jurists have sought to repress. For instance, the notion of law as resting upon an objective body of principle founders when we consider that the quest for underlying principles must involve a selection from the sum of principles available and, therefore, has a strong evalua-tive element. Principles are thus inseparable from interpretation and theory which, in turn, are determined by values. Thus, the schizophrenia of the first-year law student: when is it that s/he is supposed to talk about 'law', and when is it that s/he can talk about 'policy'? We are heirs of this schizophrenia."

Because the common law is founded upon a set of legal categories and principles, it becomes nec-essary for people to "translate" social disputes and problems into those legal categories; to "fit" the issue into an existing category, no matter how inappropriate it might seem. This is a process of *abstraction*, and it is central to common law reasoning. However, one of the key problems with such a form of reasoning is that "common sense" is frequently lost sight of as analogies are drawn between factual situations and legal disputes which seem to bear little resemblance to each other, as Mansell, Meteyard, and Thomson illustrate through three cases.

Wade Mansell, Belinda Meteyard, and Alan Thomson, *A Critical Introduction to Law* 3rd edn (London: Cavendish, 2004), pp.50–52:

"*Ashford v. Thornton* is very much a case which marks the transition, albeit a late one, from the explicit avoid-ance of issues to a format which decides hard cases by reference not to social facts but to structured legal cat-egories and technicalities. The case of *Ashford v Thornton* held in 1818, that under some circumstances trial by battle was still available to an accused. The Chief Justice Lord Ellenborough ruled, in words which take us back very explicitly to rule magic, as follows:

'The general law of the land is in favour of the wager of battles, and it is our duty to pronounce the law as it is, and not as we may wish it to be. Whatever prejudices therefore may justly exist against this mode of trial, still as it is the law of the land, the Court must pronounce judgment for it.'

Incidentally, but as a matter of interest, many of the legal authorities considered on reaching that decision had lived in Normandy prior to the Norman Conquest of 1066.

Ashford v Thornton also provides us with an (admittedly extreme) example of the translation process used by law to put questions into a resolvable form. The application against Abraham Thornton at the behest of William Ashford, the deceased woman's brother was put in the following terms:

> 'For that he the said Abraham Thornton not having the fear of God before his eyes, but being moved and seduced by the instigation of the devil, on the 27th day of May, in the 57th year of the reign of our Sovereign Lord George the Third by the Grace of God, &c with force of arms at the parish of Sutton-Coldfield in the county of Warwick, in and upon the said Mary Ashford spinster, in the peace of God and our said lord the King, then and there being feloniously, wilfully, and of his malice aforethought, did make an assault, and that the said did take the said Mary Ashford into both his hands, and did then and there feloniously, wilfully, violently, and of his malice aforethought, case, throw, and push the said Mary Ashford into a certain pit of water, wherein there was a great quantity of water, situation in the parish of Sutton-Coldfield aforesaid in the county aforesaid, by means of which said casting, throwing, and pushing of the said Mary Ashford into the pit of water aforesaid by the said A Thornton in form aforesaid, she, the said M Ashford in the pit of water aforesaid with the water aforesaid, was then and there choaked, suffocated, and drowned, of which said choking, suffocating, and drowning she, the said M Ashford, then and there instantly died. And so the said A Thornton, her the said Mary Ashford in manner and form aforesaid feloniously and wilfully, and of his malice aforethought, did kill and murder against the peace of our said lord the King his Crown and dignity.' (*Ashford v Thornton* (1818) 106 ER 149).

While we would not now expect to see charges framed in such a way this *reductio ad absurdum* does make manifest the legal method of translating social events into legal format.

The second English case which we can use to illustrate both the sidestepping of the issues and the way law justifies decisions by referring to pre-existing rules is the case of *Thompson v London and Midland Railway* [1930] 1 KB 41, which, although aged, seems almost contemporaneous to lawyers.

The facts of that case as heard by the court were that the tragic Mrs Thompson had wished to travel for a day's outing from Manchester to Darwin on the London and Midland Railway. Mrs Thompson could neither read nor write and she requested her niece to purchase her rail ticket for her. When the niece bought the ticket, she might have seen on the front of the ticket the words: 'excursion. For conditions see back.' Had Mrs Thompson's niece then turned the ticket over she would have seen a notice to the effect that the ticket was issued subject to the conditions in the rail company's timetables. The timetables were on sale at the ticket office, and one of the conditions attaching to the issue of excursion tickets according to the timetable was that all liability for injury to excursion passengers, however caused, was excluded.

Without being aware of these conditions, Mrs Thompson set off for Darwin. Unfortunately, when the train arrived at Darwin and its arrival was announced to passengers, Mrs Thompson stepped out only to discover that there was no platform outside her door, as the train in which she was a passenger was longer in length than the Darwin station platform. Mrs Thompson was injured in the fall and sought compensation from the railway company. The *legal* issue of the case did not concern itself with Mrs Thompson's injuries except extraordinarily indirectly. Mrs Thompson must have been amazed to discover what the question of her compensation turned upon, namely: 'Was the clause excluding liability for injury to be found in the timetable which was available at the ticket office, a part of the contract of carriage entered into by Mrs Thompson via her niece as agent and the railway company?'.

The court held that Mrs Thompson was unable to recover. They did so by referring to previous cases and the rules that they had laid down. The questions they asked were not concerned with what seemed the most socially relevant facts—the injury to Mrs Thompson and her need for compensation—but rather to the rules and circumstances under which it would be held that a party to a contract had had 'constructive' notice of the existence of a clause which purported to limit liability. Having said that, it must be conceded that, to many law students, the legal question will seem the obvious one. So commonsensical has contract become that many on hearing the facts of Mrs Thompson's case will want to know immediately the terms which governed the transaction. . . .

For a more modern and equally striking example of the 'translation' process at work, readers may wish to turn to the decision of the European Court of Justice in *SPUC v Grogan* [1991] 3 CMLR 689. The case arose out of a decision of the Irish Supreme Court to grant an injunction to restrain a student organisation from publishing and distributing guides to abortion clinics in the UK. It appeared to raise fundamental questions relating to the protection of human rights and to necessitate a balancing of the 'right to life' contained in the Irish Constitution on the one hand, and freedom of expression protected by Community law on the other. Translated into a form susceptible to adjudication by a reluctant European Court, however, the case was deemed to hinge rather upon the meaning of 'services' within the European Community Treaty and the capacity of the Irish restriction upon the provision of information to interfere with the cross-border supply of services in the Community's internal market. Ultimately, the decision of the Court was predicated upon the fact that the students responsible for the distribution of the information were not financially rewarded for their activities and hence not economically tied to the clinics in the UK whose services they were advertising. For the European Court, 'buying' an abortion was seen in the same light as the purchase of an insurance policy."

Questions

1. Compare the "common sense" and "legal" construction of the issues in the three cases.

2. To what extent do you think that "translation" of the issues into legal discourse distorted what was really going on?

Useful website addresses

You might find it useful to look at the Law Commission website (*http://www.lawcom.gov.uk* [Accessed May 12, 2010]) which contains details of its publications and the areas of law that it currently has under review. In addition to explaining its own programmes of reform the "Law Under Review" section contains summarised official law reform projects by other government bodies.

Office for Criminal Justice Reform, *http://www.cjsonline.gov.uk* [Accessed May 12, 2010]

Department of Business, Innovation and Skills, "Better Regulation", *http://www.berr. gov.uk/bre* [Accessed on May 12, 2010]

Supreme Court and House of Lords judgments, *http://www.parliament.uk/business/judicial_work. cfm* [Accessed on May 12, 2010]

HM Court Service (judgments going back to 1996), *http://www.hmcourts-service. gov.uk/cms/judg-ments.htm* [Accessed on May 12, 2010]

9

JUDGE-MADE LAW: A CASE STUDY ON THE LAW OF NEGLIGENCE

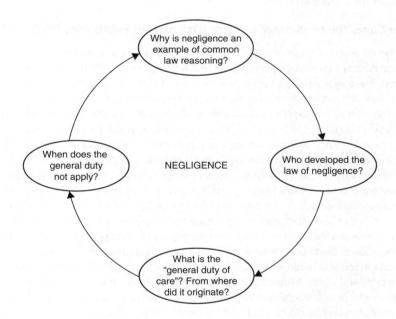

In this chapter we apply the material on case law which we examined in Ch.8 to the development of a particular area of law: the general duty of care in tort. By the end of this chapter, you should:

- be able to identify how common law reasoning differs from civilian methods;
- be aware of the difficulties associated with the identification of the ratio decidendi;
- understand how new doctrines emerge and the various ways in which they are open to interpretation;
- appreciate the social and political context in which the modern doctrine of negligence arose.

The material in this chapter is designed to help you to get a better "feel" for the central common law concepts of precedent, ratio decidendi, obiter dictum, as well as the application and distinguishing of cases. It is also designed to give you practice reading common law judgments, and we conclude this chapter with an exercise to test your ability to work with precedents and to engage in common law analysis.

We have chosen the law of negligence as our case study for several reasons. First and foremost, we believe that it provides a particularly good illustration of the way in which new areas of the common law develop, and how the development of one area is linked to the limitations of another field of the common law, in this case contract. Second, the historical development of the law of negligence vividly demonstrates the importance of the personal contribution of individual judges to the development of the common law. Third, the case law underscores the difficulty of discerning the ratio decidendi of a case given the dynamic character of common law reasoning. Finally, negligence demonstrates a relationship between "law" and "morality", which we have touched upon in earlier chapters and would like you to reflect on again here.

We begin with an explanation by Peter Cane of how the common law approach to judicial reasoning differs radically from the civilian method. Understanding the different styles will be of importance to you in your studies as you will be required to read and understand common law judgments as well as those of the European Court.

Peter Cane, *The Anatomy of Tort Law* (Oxford: Hart Publishing, 1997), pp.2–3:

"If you look at a typical text on the law of tort in any common law jurisdiction (that is, where the applicable law is, or is derived from or based on English law), you will find the law discussed and expounded in terms of a number of 'torts'. These include the tort of negligence, the tort of nuisance, the tort of conversion, the tort of defamation, and so on. Indeed, one author has constructed an 'alphabetical list of known torts' containing more than 70 entries. This approach to expounding tort law I shall call the 'common law approach'. This approach is in notable contrast to that adopted in civil law jurisdictions (that is, where the law is derived from or based on Roman law). France provides, perhaps, the most extreme example of the civil law approach: there, much of the law of delict (or 'tort') is derived from a few very general provisions in the *Code Civil*, such as Article 1382: 'Every act whatever . . . which causes damage to another obliges him by whose fault the damage occurred to repair it'. This provision has two notable features: first, it is very general, and secondly, it bases liability directly on a principle of personal responsibility for damage caused by faulty conduct. The common law approach, by contrast, has at least two important characteristics relevant to the present discussion. First, and putting the point very crudely, whereas a French lawyer might see the process of deciding particular legal disputes as involving the application of broad general principles to particular facts, the common lawyer is more likely to think of that process in terms of determining whether a particular fact situation fits into a framework of rules and quite narrow principles which define the elements of 'tort'. Secondly, the common lawyer tends to view the elements of particular torts as technical requirements of the law rather than as applications of ethical principles of personal responsibility concerned with what people ought or ought not to do, such as that people ought not to cause damage deliberately. The common lawyer's understanding of the law of tort consists largely of knowledge about the technical definitions of legal terms and concepts and about fact situations which have, in the past, been held to give rise to tort liability. The typical common lawyer would not (in a professional capacity, at least) think of the law of tort as a set of ethical principles of personal responsibility, principles about how people ought and ought not to behave in their dealings with others."

The emergence of a doctrine of negligence, now one of the most important in the legal landscape, came about slowly. This is typical of the English legal system in which the development of judge-made doctrine is incremental. One of your chief tasks as a student of law will be to trace how doctrines emerge and change over a series of cases. In the case of negligence, it arose because of the failure of existing law to deal with certain scenarios in which one person was harmed through no fault of his or her own and the person who inflicted the harm did not intend to cause harm. These situations did not involve maliciousness or wickedness as might be required by the criminal offences of fraud or assault. Neither did they involve situations in which the parties were bound by a contract in which they had volunteered to become involved with each other. In the present context, it is particularly important to understand the relationships between contract and the tort of negligence. For many years, the notion of privity of contract meant that people who had not taken part in making a contract had no legal right to sue if the bargain was not fulfilled. Prior to the emergence of the tort of negligence it was widely held that the voluntary entering into a relationship with another party by means of contract should be the only form of civil liability or bond recognised by law. But what happened if someone purchased a bar of chocolate from a shopkeeper which contained glass? Responsibility for the glass did not lie with the shopkeeper but with the manufacturer. But the customer did not have a contract with the manufacturer, only the shopkeeper. This approach also meant that the wife of a tenant could not sue the landlord if she hurt her leg when she slipped through a rotten floorboard. It was the husband who had the contract with the landlord in the form of a lease. The law of negligence evolved as a reaction to such problems. The development of that principle can best be understood through an examination of a series of cases. Our story begins in the late nineteenth century with a very important case.

Heaven v Pender (1883) 11 QBD 503, CA.

Brett M.R.:

"In this case the [claimant] was a workman in the employ of Gray, a ship painter. Gray entered into a contract with a shipowner whose ship was in the defendant's dock to paint the outside of his ship. The defendant, the dock owner, supplied, under a contract with the shipowner, an ordinary stage to be slung in the ordinary way outside the ship for the purpose of painting her. It must have been known to the defendant's servants, if they had considered the matter at all, that the stage would be put to immediate use, that it would not be used by the shipowner, but that it would be used by such a person as the [claimant], a working ship painter. The ropes by which the stage was slung, and which were supplied as a part of the instrument by the defendant, had been scorched and were unfit for use and were supplied without reasonably careful attention to their condition. When the [claimant] began to use the stage the ropes broke, the stage fell, and the [claimant] was injured. The Divisional Court held that the [claimant] could not recover against the defendant. The [claimant] appealed. The action is in form and substance an action for negligence. That the stage was, through want of attention of the defendant's servants, supplied in a state unsafe for use, is not denied. But want of attention amounting to a want of ordinary care is not a good cause of action, although injury ensue from such want, unless the person charged with such want of ordinary care had a duty to the person complaining to use ordinary care in respect of the matter called in question. Actionable negligence consists in the neglect of the use of ordinary care or skill towards a person to whom the defendant owes the duty of observing ordinary care and skill, by which neglect the [claimant], without contributory negligence on his part, has suffered injury to his person or property. The question in this case is whether the defendant owed such a duty to the [claimant].

    If a person contracts with another to use ordinary care or skill towards him or his property the obligation need not be considered in the light of a duty; it is an obligation of contract. It is undoubted, however, that there may be the obligation of such a duty from one person to another although there is no contract between them with regard to such duty. Two drivers meeting have no contract with each other, but under certain circumstances they have a reciprocal duty towards each other. So two ships navigating the sea. So a railway company which has contracted with one person to carry another has no contract with the person carried but has a duty towards that person. So the owner or occupier of house or land who permits a person or persons to come to his house or land has no contract with such person or persons, but has a duty towards him or them. It should be observed that the existence of a contract between two persons does not prevent the existence of the suggested duty between them also being raised by law independently of the contract, by the facts with regard to which the contract is made and to which it applies an exactly similar but a contract duty. We have not in this case to consider the circumstances in which an implied contract may arise to use ordinary care and skill to avoid danger to the safety of person or property. We have not in this case to consider the question of a fraudulent misrepresentation express or implied, which is a well recognised head of law. The questions which we have to solve in this case are—what is the proper definition of the relation between two persons other than the relation established by contract, or fraud, which imposes on the one of them a duty towards the other to observe, with regard to the person or property of such other, such ordinary care or skill as may be necessary to prevent injury to his person or property; and whether the present case falls within such definitions. When two drivers or two ships are approaching each other, such a relation arises between them when they are approaching each other in such a manner that, unless they use ordinary care and skill to avoid it, there will be a danger of an injurious collision between them. This relation is established in such circumstances between them, not only if it be proved that they actually know and think of this danger, but whether such proof be made or not. It is established, as it seems to me, because any one of ordinary sense who did think would at once recognise that if he did not use ordinary care and skill under such circumstances there would be such danger. And every one ought by the universally recognised rules of right and wrong, to think so much with regard to the safety of others who may be jeopardised by his conduct; and if, being in such circumstances, he does not think, and in consequence neglects, or if he neglects to use ordinary care or skill, and injury ensue, the law, which takes cognisance of and enforces the rules of right and wrong, will force him to give an indemnity for the injury. In the case of a railway company carrying a passenger with whom it has not entered into the contract of carriage the law implies the duty, because it must be obvious that unless ordinary care and skill be used the personal safety of the passenger must be endangered. With regard to the condition in which an owner or occupier leaves his house or property other phraseology has been used, which it is necessary to consider. If a man opens his shop or warehouse to customers it is said that he invites them to enter, and that this invitation raises the relation between them which imposes on the inviter the duty of using reasonable care so to keep his house or warehouse that it may not endanger the person or property of the person invited. This is in a sense an accurate phrase, and as applied to the circumstances a sufficiently accurate phrase. Yet it is not accurate if the word 'invitation' be used in its ordinary sense. By opening a shop you do not really invite, you do not ask A. B. to come in to buy; you intimate to him that if it pleases him to come in he will find things which you are willing to sell. So, in the case of shop, warehouse, road, or premises, the phrase has been used that if you permit a person to enter them you impose on yourself a duty not to lay a trap for him. This, again, is in a sense a true statement of the duty arising from the relation constituted by the permission to enter. It is not a statement of what causes the relation which raises the duty. What causes the relation is the permission to enter and the entry. But it is not a strictly accurate statement of the duty. To lay a trap means in ordinary language to do something with an invitation. Yet it is clear that the duty extends to a danger the result of negligence without intention. And with regard to both these phrases, though each covers the circumstances to which it is particularly applied, yet it does not cover the other set of circumstances from which an exactly similar legal liability is inferred. It follows, as it seems to me, that there must be some larger proposition which involves and covers both sets of circumstances. The logic of inductive reasoning requires that where two major propositions lead to exactly similar minor premisses there must be a more remote and larger premiss which embraces both of the major propositions. That, in the present consideration, is, as it seems to me, the same proposition which will cover the similar legal liability inferred in the cases of collision and carriage. The proposition which these recognised cases suggest, and which is, therefore, to be deduced from them, is that whenever one person is by circumstances placed in such a position with regard to another that every one of ordinary sense who did think would at once recognise that if he did not use ordinary care and skill in his own conduct with regard to those circumstances he would cause danger of injury to the person or property of the other, a duty arises to use ordinary care and skill to avoid such danger. Without displacing the other propositions to which allusion has been made as applicable to the particular circumstances in respect of which they have been enunciated, this proposition includes, I think, all the recognised cases of liability. It is the only proposition which covers them all. It may, therefore, safely be affirmed to be a true proposition, unless some obvious case can be stated in which the liability must be admitted to exist, and which yet is not within this proposition. There is no such case. Let us apply this proposition to the case of one person supplying goods or machinery, or instruments or utensils, or the like, for the purpose of their being used by another person, but with whom there is no contract as to the supply. The proposition will stand thus: whenever one person supplies goods, or machinery, or the like, for the purpose of their being used by another person under such circumstances that every one of ordinary sense would, if he thought, recognise at once that unless he used ordinary care and skill with regard to the condition of the thing supplied or the mode of supplying it, there will be danger of injury to the person or property of him for whose use the thing is supplied, and who is to use it, a duty arises to use ordinary care and skill as to the condition or manner of supplying such thing. And for a neglect of such ordinary care or skill whereby injury happens a legal liability arises to be enforced by an action for negligence. This includes the case of goods, &c., supplied to be used immediately by a particular person or persons or one of a class of persons, where it would be obvious to the person supplying, if he thought, that the goods would in all probability be used at once by such persons before a reasonable opportunity for discovering any defect which might exist, and where the thing supplied would be of such a nature that a neglect of ordinary care or skill as to its condition or the manner of supplying it would probably cause danger to the person or property of the person for whose use it was supplied, and who was about to use it. It would exclude a case in which the goods are supplied under circumstances in which it would be a chance by whom they would be used or whether they would be used or not, or whether they would be used before there would probably be means of observing any defect, or where the goods would be of such a nature that a want of care or skill as to their condition or the manner of supplying them would not probably produce danger of injury to person or property. The cases of vendor and purchaser and lender and hirer under contract need not be considered, as the liability arises under the contract, and nor merely as a duty imposed by law, though it may not be useless to observe that it seems difficult to import the implied obligation into the contract except in cases in which if there were no contract between the parties the law would according to the rule above stated imply the duty. . . .

I cannot conceive that if the facts were proved which would make out the proposition I have enunciated, the law can be that there would be no liability. Unless that be true, the proposition must be true. If it be the rule the present case is clearly within it. This case is also, I agree, within that which seems to me to be a minor proposition—namely, the proposition which has been often acted upon, that there was in a sense, an invitation of the [claimant] by the defendant, to use the stage. The appeal must, in my opinion, be allowed, and judgment must be entered for the [claimant]."

Cotton L.J.:

"Bowen, L.J., concurs in the judgment I am about to read. In this case the defendant was the owner of a dock for the repair of ships, and provided for use in the dock the stages necessary to enable the outside of the ship to be painted while in the dock, and the stages which were to be used only in the dock were appliances provided by the dock owner as appurtenant to the dock and its use. After the stage was handed over to the shipowner it no longer remained under the control of the dock owner. But when ships were received into the dock for repair and provided with stages for the work on the ships which was to be executed there, all those who came to the vessels for the purpose of painting and otherwise repairing them were there for business in which the dock owner was interested, and they, in my opinion, must be considered as invited by the dock owner to use the dock and all appliances provided by the dock owner as incident to the use of the dock. To these persons, in my opinion, the dock owner was under an obligation to take reasonable care that at the time the appliances provided for immediate use in the dock were provided by him they were in a fit state to be used—that is, in such a state as not to expose those who might use them for the repair of the ship to any danger or risk not necessarily incident to the service in which they are employed. . . . I think that the same duty must exist as to things supplied by the dock owner for immediate use in the dock, of which the control is not retained by the dock owner, to the extent of using reasonable care as to the state of the articles when delivered by him to the ship under repair for immediate use in relation to the repairs. For any neglect of those having control of the ship and the appliances he would not be liable, and to establish his liability it must be proved that the defect which caused the accident existed at the time when the article was supplied by the dock owner. . . .

This decides this appeal in favour of the [claimant], and I am unwilling to concur with the Master of the Rolls in laying down unnecessarily the larger principle which he entertains, inasmuch as there are many cases in which the principle was impliedly negatived. . . .

In declining to concur in laying down the principle enunciated by the Master of the Rolls, I in no way intimate any doubt as to the principle that anyone who leaves a dangerous instrument, as a gun, in such a way as to cause danger, or who without due warning supplies to others for use an instrument or thing which to his knowledge, from its construction or otherwise, is in such a condition as to cause danger, not necessarily incident to the use of such an instrument or thing, is liable for injury caused to others by reason of his negligent act.

For the reasons stated I agree that the [claimant] is entitled to judgment, though I do not entirely concur with the reasoning of the Master of the Rolls."

Questions

1. How would you determine which of the facts are material in *Heaven v Pender*?

2. How does the judgment of Brett M.R. differ from that of Cotton L.J.? What rule for determining liability is formulated by Brett M.R.? By contrast, on what basis does Cotton L.J. find the defendants liable? Which is the broader rule (that is, of wider application)?

3. What is the ratio decidendi of *Heaven v Pender*?

The contrasting approaches in *Heaven v Pender* underscore a tension at the heart of the historical development of the law of negligence. As Howarth has explained:

> "The English legal system has never quite decided whether it is a general principle system or a specific interest or circumstance system. In the nineteenth century, the English judges leant heavily towards the specific interest or circumstance view, although discontent with that approach produced a few notable counterblasts, most famously that of Brett M.R. in *Heaven v Pender*. The view appeared to be that to allow legal liability to extend beyond the bounds of contract, that is beyond the bounds of what people had subjected themselves to voluntarily, would be to impose an intolerable burden of state interference upon them. In consequence, the presumption had to be against liability, a presumption displaced only by established rules of custom and practice."
> (David Howarth, *Textbook on Tort*, London: Butterworths, 1995, pp.162–163)

The reluctance to develop a general duty-imposing principle outside of the realm of contract, apparent in the judgment of Cotton L.J., is also exemplified by the decision of the House of Lords a few years later in *Derry v Peek* (1889) 14 App.Cas. 337, HL. In *Derry v Peek*, the material facts were as follows. The promoters of a company were sued for a false statement written in a document designed to invite the public to purchase shares in a company. The statement, although false, was made honestly but the promoters may have been careless in determining whether it was true or not. If Brett M.R.'s test had been widely accepted and applied to these facts, might the promoters have been liable for damages? In fact, in *Derry v Peek* the promoters were found not to be liable in damages. Lord Herschell explained (at 376):

> "I have arrived with some reluctance at the conclusion to which I have felt myself compelled, for I think those who put before the public a prospectus to induce them to embark their money in a commercial enterprise ought to be vigilant to see that it contains such representations only as are in strict accordance with fact, and I should be very unwilling to give any countenance to the contrary idea. I think there is much to be said for the view that this moral duty ought to some extent to be converted into a legal obligation, and that the want of reasonable care to see that statements, made under such circumstances, are true, should be made an actionable wrong. But this is not a matter fit for discussion on the present occasion. If it is to be done the legislature must intervene and expressly give a right of action in respect of such a departure from duty."

This passage demonstrates a judicial mindset, which you will encounter frequently in your legal studies, whereby a judge refuses to take a course of action, but encourages the legislature to embark on it instead. Why do you think Lord Herschell felt unable to create (or "find") a duty of care whereby the promoters of the company could be held responsible for their statements of encouragement to investors? In fact, the legislature did intervene with the Directors' Liability Act 1890.

In the years following *Heaven v Pender*, Brett M.R. became Lord Esher. He figures prominently in another famous negligence case, *Le Lievre and Dennes v Gould*. The case concerned the liability of a surveyor to a mortgagee for statements made as to the progress of a building. There was no contractual relationship between the parties (a vitally important point in all of these cases). The Court of Appeal found no liability, and Lord Esher goes on at some length to interpret the earlier decision of the Court of Appeal in *Heaven v Pender*. The passage usefully demonstrates the way in which the ratio of a common law case comes to be determined definitively in light of the way in which courts subsequently interpret it.

Le Lievre and Dennes v Gould [1893] 1 Q.B. 491, CA.

Lord Esher M.R.:

". . . No doubt the defendant did give untrue certificates; it was negligent on his part to do so, and it may even be called gross negligence. But can the [claimants] rely upon negligence in the absence of fraud? The question of liability for negligence cannot arise at all until it is established that the man who has been negligent owed some duty to the person who seeks to make him liable for his negligence. What duty is there when there is no relation between the parties by contract? A man is entitled to be as negligent as he pleases towards the whole world if he owes no duty to them. The case of *Heaven v Pender* has no bearing upon the present question. That case established that, under certain circumstances, one man may owe a duty to another, even though there is no contract between them. If one man is near to another, or is near to the property of another, a duty lies upon him not to do that which may cause a personal injury to that other, or may injure his property. For instance, if a man is driving along a road, it is his duty not to do that which may injure another person whom he meets on the road, or to his horse or his carriage. In the same way it is the duty of a man not to do that which will injure the house of another to which he is near. If a man is driving on Salisbury Plain, and no other person is near him, he is at liberty to drive as fast and as recklessly as he pleases. But if he sees another carriage coming near to him, immediately a duty arises not to drive in such a way as is likely to cause an injury to that other carriage. So, too, if a man is driving along a street in a town, a similar duty not to drive carelessly arises out of contiguity or neighbourhood. That is the effect of the decision in *Heaven v Pender*, but it has no application to the present case. . . . A charge of fraud is such a terrible thing to bring against a man that it cannot be maintained in any Court unless it is shewn that he had a wicked mind. That is the effect of *Derry v Peek*. What is meant by a wicked mind? If a man tells a wilful falsehood, with the intention that it shall be acted upon by the person to whom he tells it, his mind is plainly wicked, and he must be said to be acting fraudulently. Again, a man must also be said to have a fraudulent mind if he recklessly makes a statement intending it to be acted upon, and not caring whether it be true or false. I do not hesitate to say that a man who thus acts must have a wicked mind. But negligence, however great, does not of itself constitute fraud. The official referee who tried this case and heard the evidence came to the conclusion that the defendant, though he had acted negligently, had not wilfully made any false statement, or been guilty of any fraud. All that he had done was to give untrue certificates negligently. Such negligence, in the absence of contract with the [claimants], can give no right of action at law or in equity. All the grounds urged on behalf of the [claimants] fail, and the appeal must be dismissed."

Questions

1. How does Lord Esher reformulate *Heaven v Pender* in light of the judgment of the House of Lords in *Derry v Peek*?

2. How does Lord Esher distinguish the case of *Heaven v Pender*?

3. How would you frame the *ratio* of Lord Esher's judgment in *Le Lievre v Gould*?

The distinction between negligence and fraud is an important one. Fraud is a state of mind which is not easy to prove in court. Negligence, also a state of mind, implies carelessness, as opposed to "wickedness", and therefore is easier to establish.

You may well have noticed an important feature of both *Derry v Peek* and *Le Lievre v Gould*. Unlike *Heaven v Pender*, the facts of these cases do not involve claimants who have been physically injured, nor has the property of the claimants been physically damaged. As a consequence, we say that these claimants have suffered "economic loss" rather than "physical damage". This is a vitally important distinction in the law of torts, one which you no doubt will spend a great deal of time grappling with in your tort law courses! For our purpose, the important point is that the judiciary has been very reluctant to allow recovery for "pure" economic loss in its various forms, for a number of reasons. The cases of *Derry v Peek* and *Le Lievre v Gould* provide early examples of that unwillingness. The cases demonstrate the power of judges to restrict or to encourage the development of a doctrine.

I. The Development of a General Duty of Care

So far we have seen that the judiciary was reluctant to recognise a general duty of care in the absence of contract but the idea finally appeared to be accepted in what is widely viewed as the most famous and important negligence case in the common law world. It is a Scottish case and, as a consequence, some of the procedural terminology appears "foreign" to English lawyers. However, its importance in the development of a general duty of care in negligence transcends its Scottish roots and for that reason we present a large section of the text from the case.

M'Alister (or Donoghue) (Pauper) v Stevenson [1932] A.C. 562, HL.

[By an action brought in the Court of Session the appellant, who was a shop assistant, sought to recover damages from the respondent, who was a manufacturer of aerated waters, for injuries she suffered as a result of consuming part of the contents of a bottle of ginger-beer which had been manufactured by the respondent, and which contained the decomposed remains of a snail. The appellant by her condescendence averred that the bottle of ginger-beer was purchased for the appellant by a friend in a café at Paisley, which was occupied by one Minchella; that the bottle was made of dark opaque glass and that the appellant had no reason to suspect that it contained anything but pure ginger-beer; that the said Minchella poured some of the ginger-beer out into a tumbler, and that the appellant drank some of the contents of the tumbler; that her friend was then proceeding to pour the remainder of the contents of the bottle into the tumbler when a snail, which was in a state of decomposition, floated out of the bottle; that as a result of the nauseating sight of the snail in such circumstances, and in consequence of the impurities in the ginger-beer which she had already consumed, the appellant suffered from shock and severe gastro-enteritis. The appellant further averred that the ginger-beer was manufactured by the respondent to be sold as a drink to the public (including the appellant); that it was bottled by the respondent and labelled by him with a label bearing his name; and that the bottles were thereafter sealed with a metal cap by the respondent. She further averred that it was the duty of the respondent to provide a system of working his business which would not allow snails to get into his ginger-beer bottles, and that it was also his duty to provide an efficient system of inspection of the bottles before the ginger-beer was filled into them, and that he had failed in both these duties and had so caused the accident.

The respondent objected that these averments were irrelevant and insufficient to support the conclusions of the summons.

The Lord Ordinary held that the averments disclosed a good cause of action and allowed a proof.

The Second Division by a majority (the Lord Justice-Clerk, Lord Ormidale, and Lord Anderson; Lord Hunter (dissenting) recalled the interlocutor of the Lord Ordinary and dismissed the action].

Lord Buckmaster (DISSENTING):

"... In my view, therefore, the authorities are against the appellant's contention and apart from authority it is difficult to see how any common law proposition can be formulated to support her claim.

The principle contended for must be this—that the manufacturer, or, indeed, the repairer, of any article, apart entirely from contract, owes a duty to any person by whom the article is lawfully used to see that it has been carefully constructed. All rights in contract must be excluded from consideration of this principle, for such rights undoubtedly exist in successive steps from the original manufacturer down to the ultimate purchaser, embraced in the general rule that an article is warranted as reasonably fit for the purpose for which it is sold. Nor can the doctrine be confined to cases where inspection is difficult or impossible to introduce. This conception is simply to misapply to tort doctrines applicable to sale and purchase.

The principle of tort lies completely outside the region where such considerations apply, and the duty, if it exists, must extend to every person who, in lawful circumstances, uses the article made. There can be no special duty attaching to the manufacture of food, apart from those implied by contract or imposed by statute. If such a duty exists it seems to me it must cover the construction of every article, and I cannot see any reason why it should not apply to the construction of a house. If one step, why not 50? Yet if a house be, as it sometimes is, negligently built, and in consequence of that negligence the ceiling falls and injures the occupier or anyone else, no action against the builder exists according to English law, although I believe such a right did exist according to the laws of Babylon. Were such a principle known and recognised, it seems to me impossible, having regard to the numerous cases that must have arisen to persons injured by its disregard, that with the exception of *George v Skivington* [(1869) L.R. 5 Exch.1] no case directly involving the principle has ever succeeded in the courts, and were it well known and accepted much of the discussion of the earlier cases would have been waste of time. . . ."

Lord Atkin:

"My Lords, the sole question for determination in this case is legal: Do the averments made by the pursuer in her pleading, if true, disclose a cause of action? I need not restate the particular facts. The question is whether the manufacturer of an article of drink sold by him to a distributor, in circumstances which prevent the distributor or the ultimate purchaser or consumer from discovering by inspection any defect, is under any legal duty to the ultimate purchaser or consumer to take reasonable care that the article is free from defect likely to cause injury to health. I do not think a more important problem has occupied your Lordships in your judicial capacity: important both because of its bearing on public health and because of the practical test which it applies to the system under which it arises. The case has to be determined in accordance with Scots law; but it has been a matter of agreement between the experienced counsel who argued this case, and it appears to be the basis of the judgments of the learned judges of the Court of Session, that for the purposes of determining this problem the laws of Scotland and of England are the same. I speak with little authority on this point, but my own research, such as it is, satisfies me that the principles of the law of Scotland on such a question as the present are identical with those of English law; and I discuss the issue on that footing. The law of both countries appears to be that in order to support an action for damages for negligence the complainant has to show that he has been injured by the breach of a duty owed to him in the circumstances by the defendant to take reasonable care to avoid such injury. In the present case we are not concerned with the breach of the duty; if a duty exists, that would be a question of fact which is sufficiently averred and for present purposes must be assumed. We are solely concerned with the question whether, as a matter of law in the circumstances alleged, the defender owed any duty to the pursuer to take care.

It is remarkable how difficult it is to find in the English authorities statements of general application defining the relations between parties that give rise to the duty. The Courts are concerned with the particular relations which come before them in actual litigation, and it is sufficient to say whether the duty exists in those circumstances. The result is that the Courts have been engaged upon an elaborate classification of duties as they exist in respect of property, whether real or personal, with further divisions as to ownership, occupation or control, and distinctions based on the particular relations of the one side or the other, whether manufacturer, salesman or landlord, customer, tenant, stranger, and so on. In this way it can be ascertained at any time whether the law recognizes a duty, but only where the case can be referred to some particular species which has been examined and classified. And yet the duty which is common to all the cases where liability is established must logically be based upon some element common to the cases where it is found to exist. To seek a complete logical definition of the general principle is probably to go beyond the function of the judge, for the more general the definition the more likely it is to omit essentials or to introduce non-essentials. The attempt was made by Brett M.R. in *Heaven v Pender*, in a definition to which I will later refer. As framed, it was demonstrably too wide, although it appears to me, if properly limited, to be capable of affording a valuable practical guide.

At present I content myself with pointing out that in English law there must be, and is, some general conception of relations giving rise to a duty of care, of which the particular cases found in the books are but instances. The liability for negligence, whether you style it such or treat it as in other systems as a species of 'culpa,' is no doubt based upon a general public sentiment of moral wrongdoing for which the offender must pay. But acts or omissions which any moral code would censure cannot in a practical world be treated so as to give a right to every person injured by them to demand relief. In this way rules of law arise which limit the range of complainants and the extent of their remedy. The rule that you are to love your neighbour becomes in law, you must not injure your neighbour; and the lawyer's question, Who is my neighbour? Receives a restricted reply. You must take reasonable care to avoid acts or omissions which you can reasonably foresee would be likely to injure your neighbour. Who, then, in law is my neighbour? The answer seems to be—persons who are so closely and directly affected by my act that I ought reasonably to have them in contemplation as being so affected when I am directing my mind to the acts or omissions which are called in question. This appears to me to be the doctrine of *Heaven v Pender*, as laid down by Lord Esher (then Brett M.R.) when it is limited by the notion of proximity introduced by Lord Esher himself and A.L. Smith L.J. in *Le Lievre v Gould*. Lord Esher says: 'That case established that, under certain circumstances, one man may owe a duty to another, even though there is no contract between them. If one man is near to another, or is near to the property of another, a duty lies upon him not to do that which may cause a personal injury to that other, or may injure his property.' So A.L. Smith L.J.: 'The decision of *Heaven v Pender* was founded upon the principle, that a duty to take due care did arise when the person or property of one was in such proximity to the person or property of another that, if due care was not taken, damage might be done by the one to the other.' I think that this sufficiently states the truth if proximity be not confined to mere physical proximity, but be used, as I think it was intended, to extend to such close and direct relations that the act complained of directly affects a person whom the person alleged to be bound to take care would know would be directly affected by his careless act. That this is the sense in which nearness or 'proximity' was intended by Lord Esher is obvious from his own illustration in *Heaven v Pender* of the application of his doctrine to the sale of goods. 'This' (i.e. the rule he has just formulated) 'includes the case of goods, etc., supplied to be used immediately by a particular person or persons, or one of a class of persons, where it would be obvious to the person supplying, if he thought, that the goods would in all probability be used at once by such persons before a reasonable opportunity for discovering any defect which might exist, and where the thing supplied would be of such a nature that a neglect of ordinary care or skill as to its condition or the manner of supplying it would probably cause danger to the person or property of the person for whose use it was supplied, and who was about to use it. It would exclude a case in which the goods are supplied under circumstances in which it would be a chance by whom they would be used or whether they would be used or not, or whether they would be used before there would probably be means of observing any defect, or where the goods would be of such a nature that a want of care or skill as to their condition or the manner of supplying them would not probably produce danger of injury to person or property.' I draw particular attention to the fact that Lord Esher emphasizes the necessity of goods having to be 'used immediately' and 'used at once before a reasonable opportunity of inspection.' This is obviously to exclude the possibility of goods having their condition altered by lapse of time, and to call attention to the proximate relationship, which may be too remote where inspection even of the person using, certainly of an intermediate person, may reasonably be interposed. With this necessary qualification of proximate relationship as explained in *Le Lievre v Gould*, I think the judgment of Lord Esher expresses the law of England; without the qualification, I think the majority of the Court in *Heaven v Pender* were justified in thinking the principle was expressed in too general terms. There will no doubt arise cases where it will be difficult to determine whether the contemplated relationship is so close that the duty arises. But in the class of case now before the Court I cannot conceive any difficulty to arise. A manufacturer puts up an article of food in a container which he knows will be opened by the actual consumer. There can be no inspection by any purchaser and no reasonable preliminary inspection by the consumer. Negligently, in the course of preparation, he allows the contents to be mixed with poison. It is said that the law of England and Scotland is that the poisoned consumer has no remedy against the negligent manufacturer. If this were the result of the authorities, I should consider the result a grave defect in the law, and so contrary to principle that I should hesitate long before following any decision to that effect which had not the authority of this House. I would point out that, in the assumed state of the authorities, not only would the consumer have no remedy against the manufacturer, he would have none against any one else, for in the circumstances alleged there would be no evidence of negligence against any one other than the manufacturer; and, except in the case of a consumer who was also a purchaser, no contract and no warranty of fitness, and in the case of the purchase of a specific article under its patent or trade name, which might well be the case in the purchase of some articles of food or drink, no warranty protecting even the purchaser-consumer. There are other instances than of articles of food and drink where goods are sold intended to be used immediately by the consumer, such as many forms of goods sold for cleaning purposes, where the same liability must exist. The doctrine supported by the decision below would not only deny a remedy to the consumer who was injured by consuming bottled beer or chocolates poisoned by the negligence of the manufacturer, but also to the user of what should be a harmless proprietary medicine, an ointment, a soap, a cleaning fluid or cleaning powder. I confine myself to articles of common household use, where every one, including the manufacturer, knows that the articles will be used by other persons than the actual ultimate purchaser—namely, by members of his family and his servants, and in some cases his guests. I do not think so ill of our jurisprudence as to suppose that its principles are so remote from the ordinary needs of civilized society and the ordinary claims it makes upon its members as to deny a legal remedy where there is so obviously a social wrong. . . .

If your Lordships accept the view that the appellant's pleading discloses a relevant cause of action, you will be affirming the proposition that by Scots and English law alike a manufacturer of products which he sells in such a form as to show that he intends them to reach the ultimate consumer in the form in which they left him, with no reasonable possibility of intermediate examination, and with the knowledge that the absence of reasonable care in the preparation or putting up of the products will result in injury to the consumer's life or property, owes a duty to the consumer to take that reasonable care.

It is a proposition that I venture to say no one in Scotland or England who was not a lawyer would for one moment doubt. It will be an advantage to make it clear that the law in this matter, as in most others, is in accordance with sound common sense. I think that this appeal should be allowed."

Lord Thankerton:

". . . We are not dealing here with a case of what is called an article *per se* dangerous or one which was known by the defender to be dangerous, in which cases a special duty of protection or adequate warning is placed upon the person who uses or distributes it. The present case is that of a manufacturer and a consumer, with whom he has no contractual relation, of an article which the manufacturer did not know to be dangerous, and, unless the consumer can establish a special relationship with the manufacturer, it is clear, in my opinion, that neither the law of Scotland nor the law of England will hold that the manufacturer has any duty towards the consumer to exercise diligence. In such a case the remedy of the consumer, if any, will lie against the intervening party from whom he has procured the article. . . .

The special circumstances, from which the appellant claims that such a relationship of duty should be inferred, may, I think, be stated thus, namely, that the respondent, in placing his manufactured article of drink upon the market, has intentionally so excluded interference with, or examination of, the article by any intermediate handler of the goods between himself and the consumer that he has, of his own accord, brought himself into direct relationship with the consumer, with the result that the consumer is entitled to rely upon the exercise of diligence by the manufacturer to secure that the article shall not be harmful to the consumer. If that contention be sound, the consumer, on her showing that the article has reached her intact, and that she has been injured by the harmful nature of the article owing to the failure of the manufacturer to take reasonable care in its preparation before its enclosure in the sealed vessel, will be entitled to reparation from the manufacturer.

In my opinion, the existence of a legal duty in such circumstances is in conformity with the principles of both the law of Scotland and the law of England. The English cases demonstrate how impossible it is finally to catalogue, amid the ever-varying types of human relationships, those relationships in which a duty to exercise care arises apart from contract, and each of these cases relates to its own set of circumstances, out of which it was claimed that the duty had arisen. In none of these cases were the circumstances identical with the present case as regards that which I regard as the essential element in this case, namely, the manufacturer's own action in bringing himself into direct relationship with the party injured."

[Lord Thankerton would allow the appeal.]

Lord Macmillan:

". . . The law takes no cognizance of carelessness in the abstract. It concerns itself with carelessness only where there is a duty to take care and where failure in that duty has caused damage. In such circumstances carelessness assumes the legal quality of negligence and entails the consequences in law of negligence. What then are the circumstances which give rise to this duty to take care? In the daily contacts of social and business life human beings are thrown into or place themselves in an infinite variety of relationships with their fellows, and the law can refer only to the standards of the reasonable man in order to determine whether any particular relationship gives rise to a duty to take care as between those who stand in that relationship to each other. The grounds of action may be as various and manifold as human errancy, and the conception of legal responsibility may develop in adaptation to altering social conditions and standards. The criterion of judgment must adjust and adapt itself to the changing circumstances of life. The categories of negligence are never closed. The cardinal principle of liability is that the party complained of should owe to the party complaining a duty to take care and that the party complaining should be able to prove that he has suffered damage in consequence of a breach of that duty. Where there is room for diversity of view is in determining what circumstances will establish such a relationship between the parties as to give rise on the one side to a duty to take care and on the other side to a right to have care taken.

To descend from these generalities to the circumstances of the present case I do not think that any reasonable man or any twelve reasonable men would hesitate to hold that if the appellant establishes her allegations the respondent has exhibited carelessness in the conduct of his business. For a manufacturer of aerated water to store his empty bottles in a place where snails can get access to them and to fill his bottles without taking any adequate precautions by inspection or otherwise to ensure that they contain no deleterious foreign matter may reasonably be characterised as carelessness without applying too exacting a standard. But, as I have pointed out, it is not enough to prove the respondent to be careless in his process of manufacture. The question is: Does he owe a duty to take care, and to whom does he owe that duty? I have no hesitation in affirming that a person who for gain engages in the business of manufacturing articles of food and drink intended for consumption by members of the public in the form in which he issues them is under a duty to take care in the manufacture of these articles. That duty, in my opinion, he owes to those whom he intends to consume his products. He manufactures his commodities for human consumption; he intends and contemplates that they shall be consumed. By reason of that very fact he places himself in a relationship with all the potential consumers of his commodities, and that relationship, which he assumes and desires for his own ends, imposes upon him a duty to take care to avoid injuring them. He owes them a duty not to convert by his own carelessness an article which he issues to them as wholesome and innocent into an article which is dangerous to life and health.

It is sometimes said that liability can arise only where a reasonable man would have foreseen and could have avoided the consequences of his act or omission. In the present case the respondent, when he manufactured his ginger-beer, had directly in contemplation that it would be consumed by members of the public. Can it be said that he could not be expected as a reasonable man to foresee that if he conducted his process of manufacture carelessly he might injure those whom he expected and desired to consume his ginger-beer? The possibility of injury so arising seems to me in no sense so remote as to excuse him from foreseeing it. Suppose that a baker through carelessness allows a large quantity of arsenic to be mixed with a batch of his bread, with the result that those who subsequently eat it are poisoned, could he be heard to say that he owed no duty to the consumers of his bread to take care that it was free from poison, and that, as he did not know that any poison had got into it, his only liability was for breach of warranty under his contract of sale to those who actually bought the poisoned bread from him? Observe that I have said 'through carelessness' and thus excluded the cases of a pure accident such as may happen where every care is taken. I cannot believe, and I do not believe, that neither in the law of England nor in the law of Scotland is there redress for such a case. The state of facts I have figured might well give rise to a criminal charge, and the civil consequences of such carelessness can scarcely be less wide than its criminal consequences. Yet the principle of the decision appealed from is that the manufacturer of food products intended by him for human consumption does not owe to the consumers whom he has in view any duty of care, not even the duty to take care that he does not poison them.

. . . It must always be a question of circumstances whether the carelessness amounts to negligence and whether the injury is not too remote from the carelessness. I can readily conceive that where a manufacturer has parted with his product and it has passed into other hands it may well be exposed to vicissitudes which may render it defective or noxious and for which the manufacturer could not in any view be held to be to blame. It may be a good general rule to regard responsibility as ceasing when control ceases. So, also, where between the manufacturer and the user there is interposed a party who has the means and opportunity of examining the manufacturer's product before he reissues it to the actual user. But where, as in the present case, the article of consumption is so prepared as to be intended to reach the consumer in the condition in which it leaves the manufacturer and the manufacturer takes steps to ensure this by sealing or otherwise closing the container, so that the contents cannot be tampered with, I regard his control as remaining effective until the article reaches the consumer and the container is opened by him. The intervention of any exterior agency is intended to be excluded, and was in fact in the present case excluded. It is doubtful whether in such a case there is any redress against the retailer."

[Lord Macmillan would allow the appeal.]

[Lord Tomlin (dissenting) delivered reasons for dismissing the appeal.]

Note that the factual question—whether *in fact* there was a snail in the ginger beer—was never considered, as the case did not go to trial. The judgment deals with the prior question whether, even if the facts are true, there is any cause of action. Thus, the Law Lords, for the purposes of argument on this point, assumed the facts as alleged by the claimant to be true. Had the case then gone to trial, those factual allegations would have had to be proven.

Questions

1. What are the material facts of *Donoghue v Stevenson*? What is the legal issue at stake?

2. The majority consisted of three Law Lords. How would you state the ratio decidendi of the case? Are there a variety of ways in which it can be stated? List a series of different possible ratios, in order of their breadth of scope. Do Lords Atkin, Macmillan and Thankerton seem to be in agreement as to what their ruling in this case stands for?

3. Does Lord Atkin's formulation of the duty of care in negligence differ from Lord Esher's formulation in *Le Lievre v Gould*? If so, how?

4. The judgments in *Donoghue v Stevenson* again exemplify the point that the history of negligence in this country is a story of tension between the imposition of a general duty of care, and a number of discrete duties applicable to different situations. Try to find specific references to this tension in the various judgments in *Donoghue v Stevenson*.

Although you were asked to state the ratio decidendi of *Donoghue v Stevenson*, you should not be concerned if you found no easy answer to the question! In fact, it was pointed out by Heuston, on the 25th anniversary of the decision, that the determination of the ratio of *Donoghue v Stevenson* is a far from straightforward task.

R.F.V. Heuston, *"Donoghue v Stevenson* in retrospect" (1957) 20 M.L.R. 1 at 5:

The ratio decidendi of the case

"The ascertainment of the *ratio decidendi* of any decision given by an appellate court in the course of which several judgments have been delivered is notoriously a difficult task. One problem may be disposed of at once. It was agreed between counsel and stated by the judges in all the courts that the relevant principles of Scots and English law were identical. Now it has always been assumed that in such a case a decision of the House of Lords on an appeal from the Court of Session is binding on all courts in the English hierarchy. Those who adhere to a mechanical test for distinguishing *ratio decidendi* from *obiter dictum* would no doubt be obliged to deny this, for in a Scots appeal the only issue in the case is Scots law, and any statement as to the meaning or effect of English law must necessarily be *obiter*. It seems safer to say that the principles stated in *Donoghue v Stevenson* have been universally recognised to be authoritative in England as well as in Scotland, and to turn to the more difficult task of discovering what those principles are. Lord Wright has appropriately referred to the decision to illustrate the proposition that 'Notwithstanding all the apparatus of authority, the judge has nearly always some degree of choice. . . . The higher the court, the less is the decisive weight of authority and the freer the choice.' On the assumption that it is possible to draw from a given decision as many general propositions as there are possible combinations of distinguishable facts, Professor Stone has observed that the decision could be restricted to mean that there is a duty not to sell opaque bottles of beverage containing dead snails to Scots widows, or expanded to mean that there is a duty not to distribute defective objects of any kind whatsoever which cause damage of any kind to any person into whose hands the object may come.

Now as between the parties themselves there can be no doubt that the case decided that if the pursuer could prove that which she averred she would have a good cause of action. So the case decided at least some-thing to do with the duty owed by a supplier of chattels. There are some authorities who would deny that the case decided any more. This appears to have been the view taken by the experienced reporter who framed the 'somewhat conservatively worded headnote,' and in several later cases we find clear statements that the *ratio decidendi* is so confined. Nevertheless there has been a persistent belief that the case is authority for something more. Lord Normand has put this most clearly. 'The argument for the defender was that there were certain rela-tionships, such as physical proximity or contract, which alone give rise to duties in the law of quasi-delict or tort, and that the relationship between the pursuer and defender was not one of them.' The decision was that the categories of negligence are not closed and that duties of care are owed, not only to physical neighbours, but to anyone who is 'my neighbour' in the wider sense, as stated by Lord Atkin, 'of a person . . . "so closely and directly affected by my act that I ought reasonably to have (him) in contemplation as being so affected when I am direct-ing my mind to the acts or omissions which are called in question."' This is the neighbour principle so familiar to us all. Our inquiry at the moment is limited to discovering how far this principle can fairly be said to form a, or part of the, *ratio decidendi* of the judgment of (i) Lord Atkin himself, (ii) the majority of the House of Lords.

(i) A fair reading of the whole judgment in its context, not concentrating on this or that passage to the exclu-sion of others, makes it plain that Lord Atkin intended to show (a) that the liability of a supplier of chattels is not limited to cases in which the parties are in physical proximity to each other: a duty of care may exist even in the absence of spatial or temporal 'proximity' if there is a probability of harm inherent in the relationship of the parties, and the facts of the case before him provided a model for such a relationship; (b) that 'there must be, and is, some general conception of relations giving rise to a duty of care, of which the particular cases found in the books are but instances.' He then states the 'neighbour principle' in the term which we have already cited, and concludes that this 'appears to me to be the doctrine of *Heaven v Pender* as laid down by Lord Esher when it is limited by the notion of proximity introduced by Lord Esher himself and A.L. Smith L.J. in *Le Lievre v Gould*.' It is impracticable to draw a clear line anywhere between the two parts of the judgment. The reasoning is everywhere dovetailed and interlocked. The neighbour principle is part of the *ratio decidendi* of Lord Atkin's judgment, for it is a step in the argument, a vital link in the chain of reasoning which led to the formulation of the principle about manufacturers' liability. The significance to be attached to the neighbour principle will be discussed in detail later: it is enough to say here that it has been accepted by many as showing that *Donoghue v*

Stevenson provides a general criterion of liability—at least in the tort of negligence, and possibly throughout the whole field of tort. So that when Dean Wright tells us that 'Whether that decision will be expanded into a broad revolutionary principle or confined to a narrow category is one of the most important decisions that modern courts must make' it seems clear that he is not referring only to the part of the decision which deals with manufacturers' liability. Even those who, like Mr Landon, say that 'all that *Donoghue v Stevenson* has done is to add a new category of negligence to our law' have been obliged to meet the argument that at least one law lord attempted to state the principle upon which such an addition had been made.

(ii) Whatever the status of the 'neighbour principle' in Lord Atkin's own judgment, it hardly seems possible to say that it forms part of the *ratio decidendi* of the decision, for the two other members of the majority seem to have been careful to avoid expressing their concurrence with it. Lord Thankerton said that he agreed with Lord Atkin's speech, but it is the proper inference from the context of this remark that his agreement was confined to that part of the speech which analyses the English cases on manufacturers' liability. In any case, he expressly said that it was impossible to catalogue finally the circumstances in which a duty of care might arise. Lord Macmillan recognised that new duties might be created—'the categories of negligence are never closed'—but maintained a cautious silence about the principle or principles upon which this might be done.

Two further points may be made. First, it is preferable to refer to this particular part of the judgment as enshrining a 'principle' and not a 'rule.' The former word connotes a degree of flexibility and adaptability which the latter does not. 'A principle is the broad reason which lies at the base of a rule of law: it has not exhausted itself in giving birth to that particular rule but is still fertile.' If, as is generally believed, Lord Atkin's judgment forms a guide for the future as well as an appraisal of the past, it is best to describe it in a way which will enable us to use its potentialities to the utmost. Secondly, there seems to be little profit in an attempt to discover the sources of the ideas expounded in the neighbour principle. Lord Atkin himself expressly refers to Lord Esher and indirectly to the lawyer's question to Jesus which inspired the story of the Good Samaritan. . . .

The conclusion is that there are four propositions for which the case commonly is (or can be) cited as authority: (1) that negligence is a distinct tort; (2) that the absence of privity of contract between [claimant] and defendant does not preclude liability in tort; (3) that manufacturers of products owe a duty of care to the ultimate consumer or user; and (4) that the criterion of the existence of a duty in the law of negligence (or perhaps in any part of the law of tort) is whether the defendant ought reasonably to have foreseen that his acts or omissions would be likely to result in damage to the [claimant]. Of these, only the second and third, and possibly the first, can truly be said to form part of the *ratio decidendi* of the decision. The fourth proposition, although perhaps the most commonly cited and in many ways the most significant, cannot properly be regarded a part of the *ratio decidendi* of the decision. No amount of posthumous citation can of itself transfer with retrospective effect a proposition from the status of *obiter dictum* to that of *ratio decidendi*; no doubt it will serve to magnify greatly the interest and importance of the case, but that is another matter."

Given the variety of propositions for which the case of *Donoghue v Stevenson* might stand, it should seem increasingly clear to you that the ratio of a case is a fairly flexible concept. The idea that there is necessarily a single, clear, and uncontentious ratio to any given case thus becomes unsustainable, as MacCormick illustrates using the example of *Donoghue v Stevenson*.

Neil MacCormick, *Legal Reasoning and Legal Theory* (Oxford: Clarendon Press, 1978), pp.84–86:

"[T]here is a possibility that some precedents contain relatively clear rulings on fairly sharply defined points of law, and that others contain implicit rulings of similar, but perhaps less, relative clarity. Yet others because of judicial disagreement or simply confusion contain none. It is only a dogmatic fiction that the third class has anything which could reasonably be called a *ratio* at all, and the truth is that in relation to that type of case even the most rigid doctrine of binding precedent cannot in practice obligate the judge in a later case to do more than find some 'explanatory' proposition which is consistent with the actual decision of the precedent case and also relevant to the instant case; all the better if his 'explanatory' proposition squares in some degree with some at least of what was said in the confused or conflicting opinion or opinions given in the precedent.

It should be remarked also that even where an express ruling is given encapsulating the kind of 'proposition' wherewith Lord Atkin concluded his speech in *Donoghue*, the doctrine of precedent even in its English form leaves the subsequent court with a significant 'explanative' discretion: it is at best the proposition, not the particular words in which it was couched, that is binding. Therefore the later Court is free to re-express the proposition, together with further conditions or qualifications which may be deemed appropriate to novel types of circumstance as revealed by the later case. That the norms of the system leave its operators with that discretion gives interpreters of the system a problem which has sometimes been mistakenly supposed to be more than a problem of words: in *Donoghue v Stevenson* a certain 'proposition' was laid down about the manufacturer's duty to consumers of his products; in *Haseldine v Daw* ([1941] 2 KB 343; [1941] 3 All E.R. 156) for example, the negligent repair of a defective lift was brought within the doctrine and the repairers held liable to those injured in its collapse (observe that the dissents of Lords Tomlin and Buckmaster had dealt with the case of repairers, though none of the affirming majority did); is the 'ratio' of *Donoghue v Stevenson* the explicit ruling as given by the judges in *Donoghue* itself, or that ruling as re-expressed and extended in *Haseldine*?

The only observation I wish to make is that answering that question does not add to our knowledge of the real world at all. All that it does is to stipulate a particular usage for the technical term *ratio*, which is in fact somewhat ambiguous in its ordinary use, precisely because it is variably used in practice. Sometimes it is used as referring to the proposition as actually laid down in the original decision of a case, sometimes to that proposition as explained reinterpreted qualified or whatever in later cases.

There is not the least probability of any stipulation by me determining usage, so I offer none; I only observe that among judges and practitioners the predominant operational usage of the term *ratio* seems to be as referring to express statements of propositions of law made by judges in their justifying opinion in recorded cases, and (if my opinion matters) that seems to be the least confusing usage available for the term."

MacCormick makes the important point that often the ratio of a case can only be determined in light of what judges subsequently make of it. That is particularly apt in the case of *Donoghue v Stevenson*. The central question of whether the majority of the Lords sought to establish a general duty of care in negligence can only be answered by examining how other courts then applied their reasoning. Four years after *Donoghue v Stevenson*, an indication of its potential to be used more broadly than in cases involving common household goods or food and beverage was apparent in a judgment of the Judicial Committee of the Privy Council. In reading the excerpt below, think about how the material facts may be similar to those in *Donoghue v Stevenson*, despite their superficial difference.

Grant v Australian Knitting Mills Ltd [1936] A.C. 85, PC.

Lord Wright:

"The appellant is a fully qualified medical man practising at Adelaide in South Australia. He brought his action against the respondents, claiming damages on the ground that he had contracted dermatitis by reason of the improper condition of underwear purchased by him from the respondents, John Martin & Co., Ld, and manufactured by the respondents, the Australian Knitting Mills, Ld. The case was tried by Sir George Murray, Chief Justice of South Australia, who, after a trial lasting for twenty days, gave judgment for the appellant against both respondents for 245l and costs. On appeal the High Court of Australia set aside that judgment by a majority. Evatt J. dissented, and agreed in the result with the Chief Justice though he differed in regard to the Sale of Goods Act, 1895. Of the majority, the reasoning of Dixon J., with whom McTiernan J. concurred, was in effect that the evidence was not sufficient to make it safe to find for the appellant. Starke J., who accepted substantially all the detailed findings of the Chief Justice, differed from him on his general conclusions of liability based on these findings.

The appellant's claim was that the disease was caused by the presence, in the cuffs or ankle ends of the underpants which he purchased and wore, of an irritating chemical, namely, free sulphite, the presence of which was due to negligence in manufacture, and also involved on the part of the respondents, John Martin & Co., Ltd, a breach of the relevant implied conditions under the Sale of Goods Act.

The underwear, consisting of two pairs of underpants and two singlets, was bought by the appellant at the shop of the respondents, John Martin & Co., Ld, who dealt in such goods, and who will be hereafter referred to as 'the retailers,' on June 3, 1931. The retailers had in ordinary course at some previous date purchased them with other stock from the respondents, the Australian Knitting Mills, Ld, who will be referred to as the manufacturers; the garments were of that class of the manufacturers' make known as Golden Fleece. The appellant put on one suit on the morning of Sunday, June 28, 1931; by the evening of that day he felt itching on the ankles but no objective symptoms appeared until the next day, when a redness appeared on each ankle in front of an area of about two and a half inches by one and a half inches. The appellant treated himself with calamine lotion, but the irritation was such that he scratched the places till he bled. On Sunday, July 5, he changed his underwear and put on the other set which he had purchased from the retailers; the first set was washed and when the appellant changed his garments again on the following Sunday he put on the washed set and sent the others to the wash; he changed again on July 12. Though his skin trouble was getting worse, he did not attribute it to the underwear, but on July 13 he consulted a dermatologist, Dr Upton, who advised him to discard the underwear, which he did, returning the garments to the retailers with the intimation that they had given him dermatitis; by that time one set had been washed twice and the other set once. The appellant's condition got worse and worse; he was confined to bed from July 21 for seventeen weeks; the rash became generalized and very acute. In November he became convalescent and went to New Zealand to recuperate. He returned in the following February, and felt sufficiently recovered to resume his practice, but soon had a relapse, and by March his condition was so serious that he went in April into hospital, where he remained until July. Meantime, in April, 1932, he commenced this action, which was tried in and after November of that year. Dr Upton was his medical attendant throughout and explained in detail at the trial the course of the illness and the treatment he adopted. Dr de Crespigny also attended the appellant from and after July 22, 1931, and gave evidence at the trial. The illness was most severe, involving acute suffering, and at times Dr Upton feared that his patient might die.

It is impossible here to examine in detail the minute and conflicting evidence of fact and of expert opinion given at the trial: all that evidence was meticulously discussed at the hearing of the appeal before the Board. It is only possible to state briefly the conclusions at which the Lordships, after careful consideration, have arrived.

[Lord Wright reviewed the evidence and concluded that the Chief Justice's findings of fact at trial should be upheld]. . . .

That conclusion means that the disease contracted, and the damage suffered by the appellant, were caused by the defective condition of the garments which the retailers sold to him, and which the manufacturers made and put forth for retail and indiscriminate sale. The Chief Justice gave judgments against both respondents, against the retailers on the contract of sale, and against the manufacturers in tort, on the basis of the decision in the House of Lords in *Donoghue v Stevenson*. The liability of each respondent depends on a different cause of action, though it is for the same damage. It is not claimed that the appellant should recover his damage twice over; no objection is raised on the part of the respondents to the form of the judgment, which was against both respondents for a single amount.

So far as concerns the retailers, Mr Greene conceded that if it were held that the garments contained improper chemicals and caused the disease, the retailers were liable for breach of implied warranty, or rather condition, under s.14 of the South Australia Sale of Goods Act, 1895, which is identical with s.14 of the English Sale of Goods Act, 1893. . . .

The retailers, accordingly, in their Lordships' judgment are liable in contract: so far as they are concerned, no question of negligence is relevant to the liability in contract. But when the position of the manufacturers is considered, different questions arise: there is no privity of contract between the appellant and the manufacturers: between them the liability, if any, must be in tort, and the gist of the cause of action is negligence. The facts set out in the foregoing show, in their Lordships' judgment, negligence in manufacture. According to the evidence, the method of manufacture was correct: the danger of excess sulphites being left was recognized and was guarded against: the process was intended to be fool proof. If excess sulphites were left in the garment, that could only be because some one was at fault. The appellant is not required to lay his finger on the exact person in all the chain who was responsible, or to specify what he did wrong. Negligence is found as a matter of inference from the existence of the defects taken in connection with all the known circumstances: even if the manufacturers could by apt evidence have rebutted that inference they have not done so.

[Lord Wright went on to consider the relevance of *Donoghue v Stevenson*]. . . .

It is clear that the decision treats negligence, where there is a duty to take care, as a specific tort in itself, and not simply as an element in some more complex relationship or in some specialized breach of duty, and still less as having any dependence on contract. All that is necessary as a step to establish the tort of action-able negligence is to define the precise relationship from which the duty to take care is to be deduced. It is, however, essential in English law that the duty should be established: the mere fact that a man is injured by another's act gives in itself no cause of action: if the act is deliberate, the party injured will have no claim in law even though the injury is intentional, so long as the other party is merely exercising a legal right: if the act involves lack of due care, again no case of actionable negligence will arise unless the duty to be careful exists. In *Donoghue*'s case the duty was deduced simply from the facts relied on—namely, that the injured party was one of a class for whose use, in the contemplation and intention of the makers, the article was issued to the world, and the article was used by that party in the state in which it was prepared and issued without it being changed in any way and without there being any warning of, or means of detecting, the hidden danger: there was, it is true, no personal intercourse between the maker and the user; but though the duty is personal, because it is *inter partes*, it needs no interchange of words, spoken or written, or signs of offer or assent; it is thus different in character from any contractual relationship; no question of consideration between the parties is relevant: for these reasons the use of the word 'privity' in this connection is apt to mislead, because of the suggestion of some overt relationship like that in contract, and the word 'proximity' is open to the same objection; if the term 'proximity' is to be applied at all, it can only be in the sense that the want of care and the injury are in essence directly and intimately connected; though there may be intervening transactions of sale and purchase, and intervening handling between these two events, the events are themselves unaf-fected by what happened between them: 'proximity' can only properly be used to exclude any element of remoteness, or of some interfering complication between the want of care and the injury, and like 'privity' may mislead by introducing alien ideas. Equally also may the word 'control' embarrass, though it is conveniently used in the opinions in *Donoghue*'s case to emphasize the essential factor that the consumer must use the article exactly as it left the maker, that is in all material features, and use it as it was intended to be used. In that sense the maker may be said to control the thing until it is used. But that again is an artificial use, because, in the natural sense of the word, the makers parted with all control when they sold the article and divested themselves of possession and property. An argument used in the present case based on the word 'control' will be noticed later.

It is obvious that the principles thus laid down involve a duty based on the simple facts detailed above, a duty quite unaffected by any contracts dealing with the thing, for instance, of sale by maker to retailer, and again by retailer to consumer or to the consumer's friend.

It may be said that the duty is difficult to define, because when the act of negligence in manufacture occurs there was no specific person towards whom the duty could be said to exist: the thing might never be used: it might be destroyed by accident, or it might be scrapped, or in many ways fail to come into use in the normal way: in other words the duty cannot at the time of manufacture be other than potential or contingent, and only can become vested by the fact of actual use by a particular person. But the same theoretical difficulty has been disregarded in cases like *Heaven v Pender*, or in the case of things dangerous *per se* or known to be dangerous . . . . In *Donoghue*'s case the thing was dangerous in fact, though the danger was hidden, and the thing was dangerous only because of want of care in making it; as Lord Atkin points out in *Donoghue's case*, the distinction between things inherently dangerous and things only dangerous because of negligent manufacture cannot be regarded as significant for the purpose of the questions here involved.

One further point may be noted. The principle of *Donoghue*'s case can only be applied where the defect is hidden and unknown to the consumer, otherwise the directness of cause and effect is absent: the man who consumes or uses a thing which he knows to be noxious cannot complain in respect of whatever mischief follows, because it follows from his own conscious volition in choosing to incur the risk or certainty of mischance.

If the foregoing are the essential features of *Donoghue*'s case, they are also to be found, in their Lordships' judgment, in the present case. The presence of the deleterious chemical in the pants, due to negligence in manufacture, was a hidden and latent defect, just as much as were the remains of the snail in the opaque bottle: it could not be detected by any examination that could reasonably be made. Nothing happened between the making of the garments and their being worn to change their condition. The garments were made by the manufacturers for the purpose of being worn exactly as they were worn in fact by the appellant: it was not contemplated that they should be first washed. It is immaterial that the appellant had a claim in contract against the retailers, because that is a quite independent cause of action, based on different considerations, even though the damage may be the same. Equally irrelevant is any question of liability between the retailers and the manufacturers on the contract of sale between them. The tort liability is independent of any question of contract.

It was argued, but not perhaps very strongly, that *Donoghue*'s case was a case of food or drink to be consumed internally, whereas the pants here were to be worn externally. No distinction, however, can be logically drawn for this purpose between a noxious thing taken internally and a noxious thing applied externally: the garments were made to be worn next the skin: indeed Lord Atkin specifically puts as examples of what is covered by the principle he is enunciating things operating externally, such as 'an ointment, a soap, a cleaning fluid or cleaning powder.'

Mr Greene, however, sought to distinguish *Donoghue*'s case from the present on the ground that in the former the makers of the ginger-beer had retained 'control' over it in the sense that they had placed it in stoppered and sealed bottles, so that it would not be tampered with until it was opened to be drunk, whereas the garments in question were merely put into paper packets, each containing six sets, which in ordinary course would be taken down by the shopkeeper and opened, and the contents handled and disposed of separately, so that they would be exposed to the air. He contended that though there was no reason to think that the garments when sold to the appellant were in any other condition, least of all as regards sulphur contents, than when sold to the retailers by the manufacturers, still the mere possibility and not the fact of their condition having been changed was sufficient to distinguish *Donoghue*'s case: there was no 'control' because nothing was done by the manufacturers to exclude the possibility of any tampering while the goods were on their way to the user. Their Lordships do not accept that contention. The decision in *Donoghue*'s case did not depend on the bottle being stoppered and sealed: the essential point in this regard was that the article should reach the consumer or user subject to the same defect as it had when it left the manufacturer. That this was true of the garment is in their Lordships' opinion beyond question. At most there might in other cases be a greater difficulty of proof of the fact.

Mr Greene further contended on behalf of the manufacturers that if the decision in *Donoghue*'s case were extended even a hair's-breadth, no line could be drawn, and a manufacturer's liability would be extended indefinitely. He put as an illustration the case of a foundry which had cast a rudder to be fitted on a liner: he assumed that it was fitted and the steamer sailed the seas for some years: but the rudder had a latent defect due to faulty and negligent casting, and one day it broke, with the result that the vessel was wrecked, with great loss of life and damage to property. He argued that if *Donoghue*'s case were extended beyond its precise facts, the maker of the rudder would be held liable for damages of an indefinite amount, after an indefinite time, and to claimants indeterminate until the event. But it is clear that such a state of things would involve many considerations far removed from the simple facts of this case. So many contingencies must have intervened between the lack of care on the part of the makers and the casualty that it may be that the law would apply, as it does in proper cases, not always according to strict logic, the rule that cause and effect must not be too remote: in any case the element of directness would obviously be lacking. . . .

In their Lordships' opinion it is enough for them to decide this case on its actual facts. No doubt many difficult problems will arise before the precise limits of the principle are defined: many qualifying conditions and many complications of fact may in the future come before the Courts for decision. It is enough now to say that their Lordships hold the present case to come within the principle of *Donoghue*'s case, and they think that the judgment of the Chief Justice was right in the result and should be restored as against both respondents, and that the appeal should be allowed, with costs here and in the Courts below, and that the appellant's petition for leave to adduce further evidence should be dismissed, without costs."

Questions

1. The case of *Grant v Australian Knitting Mills* usefully illustrates how the breadth of *Donoghue v Stevenson* was a live issue at that time. In what ways did counsel for Australian Knitting Mills try to convince the Law Lords that the ratio decidendi should be read narrowly, so that the facts of *Grant* could be distinguished from *Donoghue v Stevenson*?

2. What responses to those arguments were made by Lord Wright? How did he respond to the argument made by counsel that if this case was decided in favour of the appellant, the "floodgate" of claims will be opened?

3. To what extent does it appear, on reading *Grant v Australian Knitting Mills*, that a general principle of liability was emerging within English law?

The tension between a general principle of liability and specific duties giving rise to liability continued. For example, in *Deyong v Shenburn* [1946] 1 K.B. 227, CA, a case which concerned stolen garments and a pantomime dame, Du Parcq L.J. held:

> "There are well-known words of Lord Atkin in *Donoghue v Stevenson* as to the duty towards one's neighbour. It has been pointed out (and this only shows the difficulty of stating a general proposition which is not too wide) that unless one somewhat narrows the term of the proposition as it has been stated, one would be including in it something which the law does not support. It is not true to say that wherever a man finds himself in such a position that unless he does a certain act another person may suffer, or that if he does something another person will suffer, then it is his duty in the one case to be careful to do the act and in the other case to be careful not to do the act. Any such proposition is much too wide. There has to be a breach of a duty which the law recognizes, and to ascertain what the law recognizes regard must be had to the decisions of the courts. There has never been a decision that a master must, merely because of the relationship which exists between master and servant, take reasonable care for the safety of his servant's belongings in the sense that he must take steps to ensure, so far as he can, that no wicked person shall have an opportunity of stealing the servant's goods. That is the duty contended for here, and there is not a shred of authority to suggest that any such duty exists or ever has existed (p.233)."

You will recall that in the cases of *Derry v Peek* and *Le Lievre v Gould*, the courts were not prepared to find a duty of care in the case of economic loss, as opposed to physical damage to person and property. In the wake of *Donoghue v Stevenson*, the question remained of interest: does *Donoghue v Stevenson* apply only to physical injury to person or property, or does its logic extend to economic loss? After all, economic loss is a form of injury to property. This issue became tied up with the distinction between negligent words and negligent acts, and whether one could be held liable for negligent words. That distinction, as you will discover in your tort law course, is a rather confused one, and has not been a particularly helpful distinction in analysing these issues. In any event, the extent to which *Donoghue v Stevenson* could be read as establishing a general principle applicable to economic loss—which would allow courts to revisit the issue raised in cases such as *Derry v Peek* and *Le Lievre v Gould*—came before the Court of Appeal in *Candler v Crane*.

Candler v Crane, Christmas & Co [1951] 2 K.B. 164, CA.

[The claimant was considering the possibility of his investing 2,000*l* in a limited liability company, but, before deciding to do so, desired to see the accounts of the company. The managing director of the company accordingly instructed the defendants, the accountants of the company, who were getting out the accounts, to press on and complete them, informing a clerk of the accountants, who had been requested by them to prepare the accounts, that they were required to be shown to the claimant who to his knowledge was a potential investor in the company. The clerk accordingly prepared the accounts and at the request of the managing director showed them to and discussed them with the claimant who took a copy of them and submitted them to his own accountant for advice. As a result the claimant invested his money in the company. The accounts were carelessly prepared, contained numerous false statements and gave a wholly misleading picture of the state of the company, which was wound up within a year, the claimant losing the whole of his investment. In an action brought by the claimant against the defendants, Lloyd-Jacob J. found that the clerk was not guilty of fraud, but had been "extremely careless in the preparation of the accounts", and that the resulting damage to the claimant was plain. He held that the clerk had acted within the course of his employment, but dismissed the action on the ground that the defendants owed no duty of care to the claimant. The claimant appealed.]

Denning L.J.

[Denning L.J. was asked to read his judgment first]:

"... This case raises a point of law of much importance; because Mr Lawson on behalf of the [claimant] submitted that, although there was no contract between the [claimant] and the accountants, nevertheless the relationship between them was so close and direct that the accountants did owe a duty of care to him within the principles stated in *Donoghue v Stevenson*; whereas Mr Foster on behalf of the accountants submitted that the duty owed by the accountants was purely a contractual duty owed by them to the company, and therefore they were not liable for negligence to a person to whom they were under no contractual duty. ... The only defences raised by the accountants at the hearing of the appeal were: (1) that Fraser was not acting in the course of his employment; and (2) that, even if he were, they owed no duty of care to the [claimant] [Lord Denning then considered the first issue, and found that Fraser was acting in the course of his employment]. ...

Now I come to the great question in the case: did the accountants owe a duty of care to the [claimant]? If the matter were free from authority, I should have said that they clearly did owe a duty of care to him. They were professional accountants who prepared and put before him these accounts, knowing that he was going to be guided by them in making an investment in the company. On the faith of those accounts he did make the investment, whereas if the accounts had been carefully prepared, he would not have made the investment at all. The result is that he has lost his money. In the circumstances, had he not every right to rely on the accounts being prepared with proper care; and is he not entitled to redress from the accountants on whom he relied? I say that he is, and I would apply to this case the words of Knight Bruce, L.J. in an analogous case ninety years ago: 'A country whose administration of justice did not afford redress in a case of the present description would not be in a state of civilization'.

Turning now to authority, I can point to many general statements of principle which cover the case made by some of the great names in the law ... [b]ut it is said that effect cannot be given to these statements of principle, because there is an actual decision of this court in 1893 which is to the contrary, namely *Le Lievre v Gould*.

Before I consider the decision in *Le Lievre v Gould* itself, I wish to say that, in my opinion, at the time it was decided current legal thought was infected by two cardinal errors. The first error was one which appears time and time again in nineteenth century thought, namely, that no one who is not a party to a contract can sue on it or on anything arising out of it. This error has had unfortunate consequences both in the law of contract and in the law of tort. So far as contract is concerned, I have said something about it in *Smith v River Douglas Catchment Board*. So far as tort is concerned, it led the lawyers of that day to suppose that, if one of the parties to a contract was negligent in carrying it out, no third person who was injured by that negligence could sue for damages on account of it ..., except in the case of things dangerous in themselves, like guns. This error lies at the root of the reasoning of Bowen, L.J., in *Le Lievre v Gould*, when he said that the law of England 'does not consider that what a man writes on paper is like a gun or other dangerous instrument', meaning thereby that, unless it was a thing which was dangerous in itself, no action lay. This error was exploded by the great case of *Donoghue v Stevenson*, which decided that the presence of a contract did not defeat an action for negligence by a third person, provided that the circumstances disclosed a duty by the contracting party to him.

The second error was an error as to the effect of *Derry v Peek*, an error which persisted for thirty-five years at least after the decision, namely, that no action ever lies for a negligent statement even though it is intended to be acted on by the [claimant] and is in fact acted on by him to his loss. . . .

Let me now be constructive and suggest the circumstances in which I say that a duty to use care in statement does exist apart from a contract in that behalf. First, what persons are under such duty? My answer is those persons such as accountants, surveyors, valuers and analysts, whose profession and occupation it is to examine books, accounts, and other things, and to make reports on which other people—other than their clients—rely in the ordinary course of business. Their duty is not merely a duty to use care in their reports. They have also a duty to use care in their work which results in their reports. Herein lies the difference between these professional men and other persons who have been held to be under no duty to use care in their statements, such as promoters who issue a prospectus: *Derry v Peek* (now altered by statute), and trustees who answer inquiries about trust funds: *Low v Bouverie*. Those parties do not bring, and are not expected to bring, any professional knowledge or skill into the preparation of their statements: they can only be made responsible by the law affecting persons generally, such as contract, estoppel, innocent misrepresentation or fraud. But it is very different with persons who engage in a calling which requires special knowledge and skill. From very early times it has been held that they owe a duty of care to those who are closely and directly affected by their work. . . .

Secondly, to whom do these professional people owe this duty? I will take accountants, but the same reasoning applies to the others. They owe the duty, of course, to their employer or client; and also I think to any third person to whom they themselves show the accounts, or to whom they know their employer is going to show the accounts, so as to induce him to invest money or take some other action on them. But I do not think the duty can be extended still further so as to include strangers of whom they have heard nothing and to whom their employer without their knowledge may choose to show their accounts. Once the accountants have handed their accounts to their employer they are not, as a rule, responsible for what he does with them without their knowledge or consent. . . .

Thirdly, to what transactions does the duty of care extend? It extends, I think, only to those transactions for which the accountants knew their accounts were required. For instance, in the present case it extends to the original investment of 2,000*l* which the [claimant] made in reliance on the accounts, because the accountants knew that the accounts were required for his guidance in making that investment; but it does not extend to the subsequent 200*l* which he made after he had been two months with the company. This distinction, that the duty only extends to the very transaction in mind at the time, is implicit in the decided cases. . . .

My conclusion is that a duty to use care in statement is recognized in English law, and that its recognition does not create any dangerous precedent when it is remembered that it is limited in respect of the persons by whom and to whom it is owed and the transactions to which it applies.

One final word: I think that the law would fail to serve the best interests of the community if it should hold that accountants and auditors owe a duty to no one but their client. Its influence would be most marked in cases where their client is a company or firm controlled by one man. It would encourage accountants to accept the information which the one man gives them, without verifying it; and to prepare and present the accounts rather as a lawyer prepares and presents a case, putting the best appearance on the accounts they can, without expressing their personal opinion of them. This is, to my way of thinking, an entirely wrong approach. There is a great difference between the lawyer and the accountant. The lawyer is never called on to express his personal belief in the truth of his client's case; whereas the accountant, who certifies the accounts of his client, is always called on to express his personal opinion as to whether the accounts exhibit a true and correct view of his client's affairs; and he is required to do this, not so much for the satisfaction of his own client, but more for the guidance of shareholders, investors, revenue authorities, and others who may have to rely on the accounts in serious matters of business. If we should decide this case in favour of the accountants there will be no reason why accountants should ever verify the word of the one man in a one-man company, because there will be no one to complain about it. The one man who gives them wrong information will not complain if they do not verify it. He wants their backing for the misleading information he gives them, and he can only get it if they accept his word without verification. It is just what he wants so as to gain his own ends. And the persons who are misled cannot complain because the accountants owe no duty to them. If such be the law, I think it is to be regretted, for it means that the accountants' certificate, which should be a safeguard, becomes a snare for those who rely on it. I do not myself think that it is the law. In my opinion accountants owe a duty of care not only to their own clients, but also to all those whom they know will rely on their accounts in the transactions for which those accounts are prepared.

I would therefore be in favour of allowing the appeal and entering judgment for the [claimant] for damages in the sum of 2,000*l*."

Asquith, L.J.:

"On two points I entirely agree with the judgment delivered by Denning, L.J. I agree that the cause of action based on an alleged breach of duty occurring after the [claimant] became a shareholder cannot be made out if only because the damage relied on preceded the breach. I also agree, for the reasons he has given, that Fraser was clearly acting within the scope of his employment by the defendant firm in showing the draft accounts and giving certain other information to the [claimant].

But I have the misfortune to differ from my brother on the more important point raised in this case.

[Asquith, L.J. then considered the case law, culminating with *Donoghue v Stevenson*]. . . .

Apart, however, from any limitation which should be read into Lord Atkin's language by reference to the facts of the case before him—the '*subjecta materies*'—it seems to me incredible that if he thought his formula was inconsistent with *Gould*'s case he would not have said so. This case, now nearly sixty years old, had at that time stood for nearly forty years. He must have considered it closely. Yet his only reference to it is as annexing a valid and essential qualification to Lord Esher's formula in *Heaven v Pender*. Not a word of disapproval of the decision on its merits. The inference seems to me to be that Lord Atkin continued to accept the distinction between liability in tort for careless (but non-fraudulent) misstatements and liability in tort for some other forms of carelessness, and that his formula defining 'who is my neighbour' must be read subject to his acceptance of this overriding distinction. . . .

In what has gone before it has been assumed that the two Law Lords who agreed with Lord Atkin's opinion or result accepted the broad formula about 'my duty to my neighbour' which he laid down, as well as in the narrow proposition limited to the liability of the negligent manufacturer of a chattel which reaches the consumer, without an opportunity of intermediate examination, and injures him. This assumption seems to me more than questionable. Lord Thankerton, though he says that he entirely agreed with Lord Atkin's discussion of the authorities, is clearly considering the authorities in their application to the narrow ambit of a manufacturer's liability, chattels and physical injury. His judgment does not travel outside these limits. Nor do I read Lord Macmillan's judgment as indorsing the wider proposition. There is a passage in which he lays down certain general propositions. It would have been easy for him to have adopted Lord Atkin's formula in terms if he had thought so broad a proposition justified. But when he says in an oft-quoted phrase, 'the categories of negligence are never closed' he is not, in my view, accepting an acid test of liability valid in all circumstances—he does not mention the word 'neighbour'; he is merely saying that in accordance with changing social needs and standards new classes of persons legally bound or entitled to the exercise of care may from time to time emerge—in this case by the addition of a careless manufacturer or circulator of a chattel—as parties bound, *vis-à-vis* consumers, or users, as parties entitled. In other words, what Lord Macmillan envisaged was the addition of another slab to the existing edifice, not a systematic reconstruction of the edifice on a single logical plan.

For these reasons I am of the opinion that *Donoghue*'s case neither reverses nor qualifies the principle laid down in *Gould*'s case. . . .

In the present state of our law, different rules still seem to apply to the negligent misstatement on the one hand and to the negligent circulation or repair of chattels on the other; and *Donoghue*'s case does not seem to me to have abolished these differences. I am not concerned with defending the existing state of the law or contending that it is strictly logical—it clearly is not. I am merely recording what I think it is.

If this relegates me to the company of 'timorous souls', I must face that consequence with such fortitude as I can command. I am of opinion that the appeal should be dismissed."

Cohen L.J.

[Cohen L.J. delivered a judgment in substantial agreement with Asquith L.J. He reasoned the decision in *Le Lievre v Gould* was binding upon him]:

"The principle of that decision seems to me directly in point in the present case. It is binding on us unless it can be said to be inconsistent with some other decision of this court or of the House of Lords. I am unable to find any such decision. Mr Lawson asked us to say that it is inconsistent with the principle laid down by Lord Atkin in *Donoghue v Stevenson*. It is to be observed that in *Donoghue v Stevenson* Lord Atkin himself cited with approval some passages from the judgments of Lord Esher, M.R. and A.L. Smith, L.J. in *Le Lievre v Gould*, and I am unable to believe that if he had thought the *ratio decidendi* in that case was wrong he would have cited those passage without making it clear that he was not approving the decision. I think, therefore, that although the relevant passages in Lord Atkin's speech are couched in such general terms that they might possibly cover the case of negligent misstatement, that question was not present to Lord Atkin's mind or intended to be covered by his statement. . . .

I would only add that despite the observations of my brother Denning, I do not think the conclusion I have reached will encourage accountants to fall short of the high standard of conduct which the Institutes to which they belong have laid down for their members.

In the result this appeal will be dismissed."

The judgment in *Candler v Crane, Christmas & Co* is of particular interest because of the way in which it demonstrates how judges engage in the process of applying and distinguishing precedents which are binding, and which may not be easy to reconcile. In this case, the impact of *Le Lievre v Gould* was at issue, in light of the subsequent decision of the House of Lords in *Donoghue v Stevenson*.

Questions

1. How does the interpretation placed on the decisions by Denning L.J. differ from that of Asquith and Cohen L.JJ.? Which did you find more convincing and why?

2. Denning L.J. justifies his approach through an appeal to "policy". What policy arguments are deployed by him? How does Cohen L.J. seek to respond to them?

3. The judgment of Asquith L.J. might be described as an example of judicial conservatism in the development of the common law. Which portion of his judgment explicitly adopts a conservative approach to the role of a Court of Appeal judge in the development of the common law? Did you find this approach satisfying? Give reasons for your response.

4. To what extent do the judgments suggest that different judges see themselves as having different roles to play in the development of doctrine?

Given the hierarchy of courts in the United Kingdom, and the nature of a system of binding precedent, it was ultimately up to the House of Lords to consider the impact of *Derry v Peek* and *Le Lievre v Gould* in light of *Donoghue v Stevenson*. The question of the extent of a duty of care owed in the making of negligent misstatements was finally resolved by the House of Lords in 1963.

Hedley Byrne & Co Ltd v Heller & Partners Ltd [1964] A.C. 465, HL.

Lord Reid:

"My Lords, this case raises the important question whether and in what circumstances a person can recover damages for loss suffered by reason of his having relied on an innocent but negligent misrepresentation. I cannot do better than adopt the following statement of the case from the judgment of McNair J.: 'This case raised certain interesting questions of law as to the liability of bankers giving references as to the credit-worthiness of their customers. The [claimants] are a firm of advertising agents. The defendants are merchant bankers. In outline, the [claimants'] case against the defendants is that, having placed on behalf of a client, Easipower Ltd, on credit terms substantial orders for advertising time on television programmes and for adver-tising space in certain newspapers on terms under which they, the [claimants], became personally liable to the television and newspaper companies, they caused inquiries to be made through their own bank of the defend-ants as to the credit-worthiness of Easipower Ltd who were customers of the defendants and were given by the defendants satisfactory references. These references turned out not to be justified, and the [claimants] claim that in reliance on the references, which they had no reason to question, they refrained from cancelling the orders so as to relieve themselves of their current liabilities. . . . [His Lordship stated the facts and continued:] The appellants now seek to recover this loss from the respondents as damages on the ground that these replies were given negligently and in breach of the respondents' duty to exercise care in giving them. In the judgment McNair J. said: 'On the assumption stated above as to the existence of the duty, I have no hesitation in holding (1) that Mr Heller was guilty of negligence in giving such a reference without making plain—as he did not—that it was intended to be a very guarded reference, and (2) that properly understood according to its ordinary and natural meaning the reference was not justified by facts known to Mr Heller.

Before your Lordships the respondents were anxious to contest this finding, but your Lordships found it unnecessary to hear argument on this matter, being of opinion that the appeal must fail even if Mr Heller was negligent. Accordingly I cannot and do not express any opinion on the question whether Mr Heller was in fact negligent. But I should make it plain that the appellants' complaint is not that Mr Heller gave his reply without adequate knowledge of the position, nor that he intended to create a false impression, but that what he said was in fact calculated to create a false impression and that he ought to have realised that. And the same applies to the respondents' letter of November 11.

McNair J. gave judgment for the respondents on the ground that they owed no duty of care to the appel-lants. He said: 'I am accordingly driven to the conclusion by authority binding upon me that no such action lies in the absence of contract or fiduciary relationship. On the facts before me there is clearly no contract, nor can I find a fiduciary relationship. It was urged on behalf of the [claimant] that the fact that Easipower Ltd were heavily indebted to the defendants and that the defendants might benefit from the advertising campaign financed by the [claimants], were facts from which a special duty to exercise care might be inferred. In my judg-ment, however, these facts, though clearly relevant on the question of honesty if this had been in issue, are not sufficient to establish any special relationship involving a duty of care even if it was open to me to extend the sphere of special relationship beyond that of contract and fiduciary relationship.'

The judgment was affirmed by the Court of Appeal both because they were bound by authority and because they were not satisfied that it would be reasonable to impose upon a banker the obligations suggested. . . .

The appellants' first argument was based on *Donoghue v Stevenson*. That is a very important decision, but I do not think that it has any direct bearing on this case. That decision may encourage us to develop existing lines of authority, but it cannot entitle us to disregard them. Apart altogether from authority, I would think that the law must treat negligent words differently from negligent acts. The law ought so far as possible to reflect the standards of the reasonable man, and that is what *Donoghue v Stevenson* sets out to do. The most obvious difference between negligent words and negligent acts is this. Quite careful people often express definite opin-ions on social or informal occasions even when they see that others are likely to be influenced by them; and they often do that without taking that care which they would take if asked for their opinion professionally or in a business connection. The appellant agrees that there can be no duty of care on such occasions, and we were referred to American and South African authorities where that is recognised, although their law appears to have gone much further than ours has yet done. But it is at least unusual casually to put into circulation negligently made articles which are dangerous. A man might give a friend a negligently-prepared bottle of home-made wine and his friend's guests might drink it with dire results. But it is by no means clear that those guests would have no action against the negligent manufacturer.

Another obvious difference is that a negligently made article will only cause one accident, and so it is not very difficult to find the necessary degree of proximity or neighbourhood between the negligent manufacturer and the person injured. But words can be broadcast with or without the consent or the foresight of the speaker or writer. It would be one thing to say that the speaker owes a duty to a limited class, but it would be going very far to say that he owes a duty to every ultimate 'consumer' who acts on those words to his detriment. It would be no use to say that a speaker or writer owes a duty but can disclaim responsibility if he wants to. He, like the manufacturer, could make it part of a contract that he is not to be liable for his negligence: but that contract would not protect him in a question with a third party, at least if the third party was unaware of it.

So it seems to me that there is good sense behind our present law that in general an innocent but negligent misrepresentation gives no cause of action. There must be something more than the mere misstatement. I therefore turn to the authorities to see what more is required. The most natural requirement would be that expressly or by implication from the circumstances the speaker or writer has undertaken some responsibility, and that appears to me not to conflict with any authority which is binding on this House. . . .

A reasonable man, knowing that he was being trusted or that his skill and judgment were being relied on, would, I think, have three courses open to him. He could keep silent or decline to give the information or advice sought: or he could give an answer with a clear qualification that he accepted no responsibility for it or that it was given without that reflection or inquiry which a careful answer would require: or he could simply answer without any such qualification. If he chooses to adopt the last course he must, I think, be held to have accepted some responsibility for his answer being given carefully, or to have accepted a relationship with the inquirer which requires him to exercise such care as the circumstances require.

If that is right, then it must follow that *Candler v Crane, Christmas & Co.* was wrongly decided. . . . This seems to me to be a typical case of agreeing to assume a responsibility: they knew why the [claimant] wanted to see the accounts and why their employers, the company, wanted them to be shown to him, and agreed to show them to him without even a suggestion that he should not rely on them.

The majority of the Court of Appeal held that they were bound by *Le Lievre v Gould* and that *Donoghue v Stevenson* had no application. In so holding I think that they were right. The Court of Appeal have bound themselves to follow all *rationes decidendi* of previous Court of Appeal decisions, and, in face of that rule, it would have been very difficult to say that the ratio of *Le Lievre v Gould* did not cover *Candler's* case. Denning L.J., who dissented, distinguished *Le Lievre v Gould* on its facts, but, as I understand the rule which the Court of Appeal have adopted, that is not sufficient if the *ratio* applies; and this is not an appropriate occasion to consider whether the Court of Appeal's rule is a good one. So the question which we now have to consider is whether the ratio of *Le Lievre v Gould* can be supported. . . . [Lord Reid went on to conclude that the *ratio* in *Le Lievre v Gould* was 'wrong'.]

Now I must try to apply these principles to the present case. What the appellants complain of is not negligence in the ordinary sense of carelessness, but rather misjudgement, in that Mr Heller, while honestly seeking to give a fair assessment, in fact made a statement which gave false and misleading impression of his customer's credit. It appears that bankers now commonly give references with regard to their customers as part of their business. I do not know how far their customers generally permit them to disclose their affairs, but, even with permission, it cannot always be easy for a banker to reconcile his duty to his customer with his desire to give a fairly balanced reply to an inquiry. And inquirers can hardly expect a full and objective statement of opinion or accurate factual information such as skilled men would be expected to give in reply to other kinds of inquiry. So it seems to me to be unusually difficult to determine just what duty beyond a duty to be honest a banker would be held to have undertaken if he gave a reply without an adequate disclaimer of responsibility or other warning. . . . [H]ere the appellants' bank, who were their agents in making the inquiry, began by saying that 'they wanted to know in confidence and without responsibility on our part,' that is, on the part of the respondents. So I cannot see how the appellants can now be entitled to disregard that and maintain that the respondents did incur a responsibility to them. . . .

I am therefore of opinion that it is clear that the respondents never undertook any duty to exercise care in giving their replies. The appellants cannot succeed unless there was such a duty and therefore in my judgment this appeal must be dismissed."

[Lord Morris of Borth-y-Gest, Lord Hodson, Lord Devlin and Lord Pearce agreed that the appeal should be dismissed.]

Questions

1. It is important to realise that while *Hedley Byrne* is significant for its recognition of the possibility that a negligent misstatement can give rise to a duty of care, on the facts of this case liability had been excluded by contract. If you were giving legal advice to a bank, the day after *Hedley Byrne* was decided, what would you advise them to do in order to protect themselves from such actions?

2. Note the comments about stare decisis delivered by Lord Reid. How convinced is Lord Reid by Denning L.J.'s attempt in *Candler v Crane, Christmas & Co* to distinguish *Le Lievre v Gould*? Given that Lord Reid disagreed with the approach taken by the majority in *Candler v Crane, Christmas & Co* and with the decision in *Le Lievre v Gould*, why do you think he was not more positive about Denning L.J.'s dissent in *Candler v Crane, Christmas & Co*?

The reasoning of the House of Lords in *Hedley Byrne* was part of a move towards the general principle of liability which, it might be argued, began with Lord Atkin's judgment in *Donoghue v Stevenson*. The tension between the specific duty versus general duty approaches continued throughout the twentieth century.

David Howarth, *Textbook on Tort* (London: Butterworths, 1995), pp.164–165:

"[I]n the 1960s and 1970s, the general principle view came to the fore. In *Hedley Byrne v Heller* [1964] AC 465, *Home Office v Dorset Yacht* [1970] AC 1004 and ultimately in *Anns v Merton London Borough Council* [1978] AC 728 the House of Lords came to the conclusion that there ought to be a presumption in favour of liability for harm caused by carelessness. The Anns 'two-stage' test, as formulated by Lord Wilberforce, was simply that there ought to be liability for harm caused by fault (stage 1) unless there were good reasons why not (stage 2). Anns inspired judges such as Lord Scarman to say in *McLoughlin v O'Brian* [1983] 1 AC 410 that principle required the application of *Donoghue* 'untrammelled by spatial, physical or temporal limits'.

But a reaction set in after *Anns* and *McLoughlin*, led by Lord Keith of Kinkel. . . . Lord Keith's favourite text in cases such as *Yuen Kun Yeu v A-G (Hong Kong)* [1988] AC 175 and *Murphy v Brentwood District Council* [1991] 1 AC 398 and Lord Bridge's favourite text in *Caparo v Dickman* [1990] 2 AC 605 and *Curran v Northern Ireland Co-ownership Housing Association* [1987] AC 718 was a passage from the judgment of the Australian judge Brennan J. in *Sutherland Shire Council v Heyman* (1985) 6 ALR 1. Brennan J. had said that:

'It is preferable, in my view, that the law should develop novel categories incrementally and by analogy with established categories, rather than by a massive extension of a prima facie duty of care restrained only by indefinable "considerations which ought to negative, or to reduce or limit the scope of the duty or the class of person to whom it is owed."'

Ultimately, Lord Bridge went the whole way back to the pre-*Donoghue* circumstances and interests approach and declared in *Caparo* that:

> 'I think the law has now moved in the direction of attaching greater significance to the more traditional categorisation of distinct and recognisable situations as guides to the existence, scope and the limits of the varied duties of care which the law imposes.'

It seems, however, that just as *Anns* and *McLoughlin v O'Brian* marked the high point of the last upswing of the general principles approach, *Caparo* may mark the high point of the swing in the opposite direction. Cases such as *Spring v Guardian Assurance* [1994] 3 All E.R. 129 and *Henderson v Merrett Syndicates Ltd* [1994] 3 All E.R. 506 seem to point to the construction of general principles of liability that cut across the traditional categories of tort and contract and if they do not point to the return to the *Anns* approach or, even more, to a French approach, at least there is again a consciousness that it is possible to construct principles and rules that go beyond mere analogies with the existing case law."

The significance of the decision of the House of Lords in *Donoghue v Stevenson*, and particularly the judgment of Lord Atkin, cannot be underestimated. Both the rhetorical style and the reasoning provide a model of the analytical power of common law reasoning. Lord Atkin's biographer also notes, however, that the importance of the decision in the development of the law of negligence was recognised far more quickly in the Commonwealth than it was at home.

Geoffrey Lewis, *Lord Atkin* (Oxford: Hart Publishing, 1999), pp.63, 65–67:

"The decision worked a legal revolution. According to the style of the modern appellate judgment, the majority did not content themselves with a conclusion wide enough only to decide the dispute. They surveyed the entire field and found the state of the law wanting. In order that the debris of the old cases should not stand in the way of development which was consonant with both common sense and social needs, a framework had to be worked out within which the law of negligence could grow, unconstrained by illogical or nice distinctions. To achieve this, the reactionaries had first to be beaten out of their entrenchments. When seven years later Lord Atkin was presented for an Honorary doctorate at Liverpool University, his eulogium described him as 'what is very rare in England, a legal scientist, a judge who is not content merely to settle present disputes, but seeks to expand and develop those underlying principles which are to be applied to other disputes'; and went on to contrast him with those judges 'who lack his imaginative courage'.

> 'They are content to be guided and seek for authority as an easy substitute for independent action. They take refuge in precedent as in a protective shell: like the mollusc, they attain safety at the price of flexibility and mobility, and practitioners and students alike search their judgments in vain for those general ideas which are the life of the law.'

Courage of that order was necessary, and judgment too, for however obvious the good sense of the decision now seems, it was less evident then than the dangers of the limitless field which had been opened up.

Yet the revolution was not destructive. That was why Atkin particularly, but his fellow judges of the majority also, took such pains in analysing and explaining the old cases. They were not tempted to smash the clay and start again. The growth was organic and was later described by Lord Devlin in these words:

'What *Donoghue v Stevenson* did may be described as the widening of an old category or as the creation of a new and similar one. The general conception can be used to produce other categories in the same way. An existing category grows as instances of its application multiply until the time comes when the cell divides.'

It is a feature of English law that most of its best modern jurisprudence is to be found in the great opinions and judgments in the Law Reports and not in academic writings. The most thoughtful attempts to analyse the methods and effects of the decision of the majority in *Donoghue v Stevenson* are to be found in two later decisions of the House of Lords in the same field which were themselves milestones. *Hedley Byrne* in 1963 and the Dorset Yacht Case in 1970. Here it was said for the first time with authoritative clarity that Lord Atkin's 'general conception' of neighbourhood is not a universal rule of law to be applied literally as if it were a statute, but is a guide to the circumstances in which a duty of care may be held to exist. The most lasting value of the case will be to show 'how the law can be developed to solve particular problems'. . . .

Considering that Lord Atkin thought and said that no more important problem had occupied the Law Lords, their decision on *Donoghue v Stevenson* received only a modest welcome in the professional journals of the day. Sir Frederick Pollock contributed a short article to the *Law Quarterly Review* entitled 'The Snail in the Bottle, and Thereafter' in which he praised 'the Scots Lords of Appeal for overriding the scruples of English colleagues who could not emancipate themselves from the pressure of a supposed current of authority in English Courts'. Professor Winfield wrote: 'it cannot be doubted that the decision meets the needs of the community', and the opinion of the *Solicitors' Journal* was that it would 'govern millions of small transactions every day in the whole of the United Kingdom'. But no writer appreciated the significance of the general conception of foreseeability which Atkin had propounded. Where it was discussed it was generally misunderstood. Within a few weeks of the House of Lords' decision, the Court of Appeal presided over by Lord Justice Scrutton had to decide a case in which it was argued that *Donoghue v Stevenson* had changed the law. The jib of a crane had fallen and killed a skilled erector who had noticed that some cogwheels did not fit well, but had not appreciated the extent of the danger and had started to work the crane. His widow's claim against the manufacturer had been withdrawn from the jury by Mr Justice McCardie, and the Court of Appeal refused to disturb the decision. Scrutton adopted a minatory tone: 'English judges' he said, 'have been slow in stating principles going beyond the facts they are considering. They find themselves in a difficulty if they state too wide propositions and find that they do not suit the actual facts.' In his view Lord Atkin had stated his general proposition too widely, and the real ground of the decision was no more than the definition of 'a manufacturer's liability to the ultimate consumer when there is no reasonable possibility of intermediate examination of the product'.

Fears about the implications of Atkin's general conception continued to trouble some. As late as 1941, the writer of a note in the *Law Quarterly Review* seized on a phrase of Atkin's in a recent case that 'Every person, whether discharging a public duty or not, is under a common law obligation to some persons in some circumstances to conduct himself with reasonable care so as not to injure those who are likely to be affected by his want of care', and supposed that in so saying Atkin had repented and accepted that 'the criterion of "neighbourly duty", was not a universal one'. The qualification would, the writer thought, 'bring tranquillity to many minds that, for the past nine years, have been sorely harassed in the attempt to reconcile the decision in that case with the normal trend of the development of our law'.

The reception which was accorded to the decision in the Commonwealth showed more understanding than at home. A full and thoughtful article in the *Canadian Bar Review*, although written from Oxford, said that 'Lord Atkin's judgment is at once stamped as perhaps the most impressive and certainly the most authoritative effort ever made to generalise the English law of negligence', and described the neighbour principle as 'a guide to judges where before there was none'.

And Mr Justice Evatt, with whom Atkin seems to have corresponded regularly, wrote from the High Court of Australia in March 1933:

'. . . The Snail Case has been the subject of the keenest interest and debate at the Bar and in the Sydney and Melbourne Law Schools: on all sides there is profound satisfaction that, in substance, your judgment and the opinion of Justice Cardozo of the U.S.A. coincide, and that the common law is again shown to be capable of meeting modern conditions of industrialisation, and of striking through forms of legal separateness to reality. There is an article in the *Canadian Bar Review* which expresses the Australian view as well as that of Canada. . . .'

The revolution brought about by *Donoghue v Stevenson* was so quiet that it passed completely unnoticed by the general public who were so closely affected by it: and its true nature was perhaps not fully understood even by the profession until Lord Devlin's speech in 1963 in the *Hedley Byrne* Case. The general conception of neighbourly duty was not a proposition which had been stated too widely. It was a statement which called the law of negligence into existence as a separate civil wrong, and enabled that branch of the law to develop on common sense lines so as to become the most important and far-reaching of all civil wrongs. In the fifty years which have passed since the decision it has renewed itself again and again, and has demonstrated its usefulness in all manner of circumstances. There is no sign that its power of adaptability is waning, nor is there any reason why it should. This power is due more than anything else to the moral spirit which animated Lord Atkin's speech, an object lesson, as Lord Wright said, of liberal thought in the handling of principles which has influenced the common law in all its branches.

Atkin and his colleagues found a tangled mass of old decisions but no decision of the House directly in point. The step which they took to bring order to the chaos was one which was impelled by the ordinary needs of British society and the assumptions which it made about right and wrong. They were doing something which every legal system requires of its law makers, parliamentary or judicial, that of constantly relating the law to the tacitly accepted moral principles of their own society.

In retrospect the decision now seems so clearly right and just that it makes one marvel at the state of the law before 1932; but the increasing certainty which time brings that an important decision is right is the highest tribute that can be accorded to the judgment of those who made it."

II. THE POLITICS OF COMMON LAW REASONING

You will learn more about the tensions in the development of the general duty of care in your tort law courses. For our purposes, one of the important points is that all of these developments have occurred through judicial reasoning, rather than legislative intervention. The development of a general duty of care—as well as attempts by courts to avoid its implications and to return to a series of specific duties to which analogies must be drawn in order to found a duty—is a prime example of how common law reasoning is an ongoing process engaged in by judges. After reading the cases on the development of negligence discussed above, it would be difficult to say that judges were merely "declaring" a common law which was already "there". The conclusion, rather, seems clearly to be that judges have been engaged in the "making" of law. The politics of the common law is an obvious issue to consider once we have reached the conclusion that judges are engaged in a process of law "making". You might want to consider at this point the different visions that judges have of their role and power which are demonstrated in the judgments we have been considering.

Edmund M.A. Kwaw, *The Guide to Legal Analysis, Legal Methodology and Legal Writing* (Toronto: Edmond Montgomery, 1992), pp.89–90:

Criticism of traditional Common Law analysis

"Traditional common law legal analysis has been criticized, especially by scholars of the critical legal studies school. These scholars argue that common law legal analysis paints an incomplete and unrealistic picture of the process of adjudication. According to their criticism, the principles of common law legal analysis—the doctrines of precedent, *stare decisis*, and *ratio decidendi*—are based on the misconception that there is a separate and distinct form of legal reasoning and analysis, which ultimately leads to the correct decision. The reality, the critics argue, is that, first, the above principles are so vague that they do not always lead to a logical conclusion or rationale in difficult cases, and some precedents are followed while others are not. Second, the nature of common law legal analysis is such that there are many different interpretations, distinctions, and justifications, which bestow on judges a significant amount of discretion. The principles of common law legal analysis therefore serve only to mask the values, ideology, preferences, and priorities of judges, which ultimately have an effect on the outcome of a case. . . .

The critics argue that the crucial questions always left unanswered are how do judges decide which precedent to follow and what approach do judges adopt in determining the significance of an ambiguous precedent? The answers, it is contended, lie in the values and priorities of different judges; these are the result of a mix of political, social, institutional, and experiential factors. This is clearly shown in the development of the law with regard to negligent misstatements discussed above.

In 1889, the English House of Lords decided in *Derry v Peek* that unless fraud was established, a [claimant] could not bring an action for a statement that was made negligently but in good faith. In 1914, however, this precedent was not followed in *Nocton v Ashburton*. The court said that the decision in *Derry v Peek* had not precluded actions for statements where there existed a fiduciary relationship between the parties. Why the court had not taken into account the relationship between those who issued and prepared the company prospectus and the [claimant] in *Derry*, was not explained. This was followed in 1951 in *Candler v Crane, Christmas & Co*, which also involved the preparation of company accounts. The House of Lords held that no fiduciary relationship existed. Subsequently, however, in *Hedley Byrne & Co Ltd v Heller & Partners Ltd* decided in 1964, the law lords held that *Nocton* did not refer only to fiduciary relationships, but to all special relationships where one party trusted another to do something on his or her behalf. The court offered no explanation for not finding such a special relationship in *Candler*. All that the House of Lords said was that *Candler* had been wrongly decided.

In all these cases the House of Lords never provided any explanation of how it determined if it was bound by a precedent. There was no indication that the majority in the House were not, in reality, deciding the various cases on the basis of what they wished the law to be. Thus, although it was not stated in the discussion of all the precedents, the above cases could not have been decided without some ultimate reference to the values and choices of the judges concerned.

What the above suggests is that the doctrines of precedent and *stare decisis* cannot lead to a specific result or rationale in certain cases. Neither do these doctrines ensure continuity, predictability, rationality, or objectivity. Instead of determining the principles and outcomes of cases, they seem to support such outcomes."

Questions

1. Do you agree with Kwaw's assessment of common law reasoning? Defend your position.

2. Is it inevitable that judges must bring their own politics to the process of judicial decision making? Can it be avoided? If so, how?

Kwaw's focus is on how stare decisis in the common law system masks the underlying political and social choices which are made by judges. A further aspect of the development of the duty of care in negligence has also been subject to critique. If you review the judgments which have been excerpted in this chapter, you will notice that judges have frequently referred to the standard of the "reasonable man" as the basis for determining whether a duty of care was breached. Within judicial reasoning, this "reasonable man" standard is assumed, somehow, to operate objectively, neutrally, apolitically, and uncontroversially. Of course, if you think about it, there is no one, universal "reasonable man" standard. The determination of reasonableness inevitably involves social, cultural and political choices, and the standard of reasonableness will vary depending upon one's views and politics. Yet, common law reasoning tends to mask such choices within the language of reasonableness. Feminist tort theory in particular has usefully interrogated the gendering of the "reasonable man".

Joanne Conaghan, "Feminist perspectives on the law of tort" in Paddy Ireland and Per Laleng (eds) *The Critical Lawyers' Handbook 2* (London: Pluto Press, 1997), pp.127–128:

"The feminist critique of negligence's 'reasonable man' raises issues of form as well as substance. In other words, it is not just the content of the standard being applied which is under scrutiny, it is also the application of a single and allegedly objective, universal standard to human behaviour at all. What feminist legal theory reveals (in the company of critical legal theory in general) is that law is neither politically nor morally neutral but is value-laden: it is an expression of particular values and assumptions about the distribution of resources in society (and individual access to them) which has blatantly political consequences. Thus judges when assessing reasonable behaviour, whether they are articulating their own subjective opinions or whether they are engaged in a genuine attempt to give expression to what they believe are prevailing social standards of proper behaviour, are making, in effect, policy-based decisions, that is, decisions which appeal to particular values and moral preferences governing individual relationships with each other and with the state. These are values about which reasonable people may well disagree.

Thus the conventional understanding of the reasonable man as an objective measure of human behaviour is a legal fiction: he is in fact merely a particular expression of appropriate human behaviour inevitably reflecting the values and assumptions, experience and understanding of those responsible for his birth and subsequent upbringing. For this reason it is not enough to simply replace the 'reasonable man' standard with an appeal to the 'reasonable person' as is the practice in some of the more 'politically correct' textbooks. The reasonable person is no more objective than the reasonable man. Indeed the claim to objectivity is itself contentiously male: objectivity, it is alleged, is the method by which men's point of view is privileged and women's silenced."

III. CASE LAW EXERCISE

Your client, Kirit, is a regular patron of a pub. One evening he consumed five pints of lager there, all of which were served to him by Barbara, the proprietor. Kirit normally only drinks lemonade, but was upset because of an argument he had had earlier with his wife, Carol. He became extremely intoxicated and then began to abuse other patrons in the pub. He was promptly asked to leave the establishment by Barbara. It was obvious to everyone at that point that Kirit was very unsteady on his feet. Because of her long acquaintance with Kirit, Barbara was aware that the location of Kirit's house required him to cross a very busy road after leaving the pub. In fact, the road has a reputation in the neighbourhood for being dangerous for pedestrians, even when they are sober. Upon leaving the pub, Kirit stumbled down the street, into the busy road, was hit by a passing motorist and badly injured. He now wishes to sue Barbara in negligence. The only relevant authorities in this case are *Barrett v Ministry of Defence* [1995] 3 All E.R. 87, CA; and *Crocker v Sundance Northwest Resorts* [1988] 1 S.C.R. 1186, a decision of the Supreme Court of Canada. The relevant portions of *Barrett* are set out below, and *Crocker* is sufficiently discussed, for our purposes, within the judgment in *Barrett*. Read the judgment as excerpted, and answer questions which follow it.

Barrett v Ministry of Defence [1995] 3 All E.R. 87, CA.

Beldam L.J.:

"In these proceedings Mrs Dawn Barrett, widow of Terence Barrett, claims damages for herself and her son Liam under the Fatal Accidents Act 1976 and for the benefit of the estate of her deceased husband under the Law Reform (Miscellaneous Provisions) Act 1934. She blames the appellant, the Ministry of Defence, for the death of her husband who was serving in the Royal Navy. On May 12, 1993 Judge Phelan, sitting as a deputy judge of the High Court, gave judgment for the [claimant] for £160,651.16. . . . The appellant in this appeal challenges one of the two grounds on which the judge found it to have been in breach of duty to the deceased. . . .

At the time of his death Terence Barrett, the deceased, was thirty years of age and a naval airman serving at a shore based establishment of the Royal Navy at Barduffos in northern Norway. The naval base is somewhat isolated and the shore facilities are uninviting. It was used for a series of training exercises known as 'Exercise Clockwork'. On January 6, 1988 detachments of marine commandos, together with No 845 Helicopter Squadron from Royal Naval Air Station, Yeovilton arrived to take part in one of these training exercises. The deceased was attached to the squadron.

Because the recreational facilities ashore were limited, the appellant had installed several video rooms, computer equipment, a gymnasium, a sauna and other recreational and educational facilities. Within the base there were three bars: the ward room, the senior rates' bar and the junior rates' bar, at which duty free drink could be obtained. Drinking in these bars when off duty was one of the main recreations of personnel attached to the base. In January 1988 the senior naval officer at Barduffos was Lt Cdr Lomax. The evidence was to show that his attitude to the enforcement of the Queen's Regulations for the Royal Navy 1967 (BR 31) and of standing orders, in particular to excessive drinking and drunkenness, was unusually lax. As a consequence of the death of the deceased he was charged with and pleaded guilty to a breach of Art.181 of the Queen's Regulations, which provides: 'It is the particular duty of all officers, Fleet Chief Petty Officers, Chief Petty Officers and leading ratings actively to discourage drunkenness, over-indulgence in alcohol and drug abuse by naval personnel both on board and ashore. . . .' His plea of guilty acknowledged that he had negligently performed the duty of actively discouraging drunkenness and over-indulgence in alcohol. . . .

The facts leading up to the death of the deceased were not in dispute. He died in his bunk between 2 am and 2.30 am on the morning of Saturday, January 23, 1988. Friday, January 22 was the deceased's thirtieth birthday. He had recently learned that after some ten years' service he was to be promoted leading hand and so had additional reason to celebrate. Friday evening was customarily an evening for heavy drinking. On this Friday a Hawaiian party event had been organised in the senior rates' bar. A number of the senior rates attending the party decided they would compete to see who could drink the most. Very substantial quantities of duty free spirits were consumed.

The deceased went to the junior rates' bar at about 9.15 pm to begin his celebrations. Having placed money behind the bar to treat his mess mates, the judge found he himself consumed there three cans of cider and two double Bacardis. At about 10.30 pm he was invited to the senior rates' bar where he was bought six Bacardis, each of which was a double measure. By about 11 pm he had consumed a minimum of four ciders and nine double Bacardis. It was not, however, suggested that the barmen in charge of either bar had served him personally with this number of drinks. Most of the drinks were bought for him. At about 11.30 pm he returned to the junior rates' bar to get fuel for his cigarette lighter and then went back to the senior rates' bar where, shortly afterwards, he became unconscious. He was carried back to the junior rates' bar where he was placed on a chair in the lobby. He was seen there by Lt Cdr Parker who had just returned from sledging. The deceased was then in a collapsed state and insensible. Petty Officer Wells, the duty senior rate whose office was nearby, organised a stretcher and the deceased was taken to his cabin where he was placed in his bunk in the recovery position. He was in a coma but tossing and turning. He was visited on about three occasions by the duty ratings. When his cabin mate went to turn in at about 2.30 am, he found that the deceased had vomited, had inhaled his vomit and was apparently asphyxiated. Attempts were made to revive him but without success. A board of inquiry was held and a ship's inquiry and many statements were taken from witnesses. Based on these statements and the evidence which he had heard, the judge found that at this isolated base cases of drunkenness, especially at the weekends, were commonplace and that disciplinary action that might lead to punishment was not taken.

The judge also found there was a much more relaxed attitude to drinking tolerated at this base than there would be in the United Kingdom. Drunkenness was common at the weekends when the men were off duty and especially on Friday nights. The judge summarised the situation disclosed by the evidence as 'a perfectly deplorable situation'.

The appellant does not challenge this assessment of the discipline at Barduffos. Of the deceased the judge found that he was quite a heavy drinker and this was widely known. There was little inducement for anyone to go ashore for recreation for alcohol prices were remarkably high in Norway and astonishingly low in the base. A good range of recreational facilities existed but boredom was inevitable and foreseeable. He was under the appellant's codes of discipline and it controlled all facilities. Disciplinary codes existed which, if implemented, would have greatly reduced drunkenness. He said that the deceased was a heavy drinker introduced to a potentially dangerous situation. In these circumstances the judge held that it was foreseeable in this particular environment that the deceased would succumb to heavy intoxication. Although it was only in exceptional circumstances that a defendant could be fixed with a duty to take positive steps to protect a person of full age and capacity from his own weakness, he considered in the exceptional circumstances that arose in this case it was just and reasonable to impose a duty to take care on the appellant. He also held that the appellant was in breach of that duty because it failed to enforce the standards it itself set in matters of discipline. . . .

The appellant does not challenge the judge's findings that it was in breach of duty to take care of the deceased once he had collapsed and it had assumed responsibility for him.

The appellant's principal ground of appeal is that the judge was wrong to hold that it was under any duty to take care to see that the deceased, a mature man thirty years of age, did not consume so much alcohol that he became unconscious. If the deceased himself was to be treated as a responsible adult, he alone was to blame for his collapse. . . .

The purpose of Queen's Regulations and standing orders is to preserve good order and discipline in the service and to ensure that personnel remain fit for duty and while on duty obey commands and off duty do not misbehave bringing the service into disrepute. All regulations which encourage self-discipline, if obeyed, will incidentally encourage service personnel to take greater pride in their own behaviour but in no sense are the regulations and orders intended to lay down standards or to give advice in the exercise of reasonable care for the safety of the men when off duty drinking in the bars.

The judge placed reliance on the fact that it was foreseeable that if the regulations and standing orders were not properly enforced in this particular environment the deceased would succumb to heavy intoxication. He also said it was just and reasonable to impose a duty in these circumstances. . . .

In the present case the judge posed the question whether there was a duty at law to take reasonable steps to prevent the deceased becoming unconscious through alcohol abuse. He said his conclusion that there was such a duty was founded on the fact that: 'It was foreseeable in the environment in which the defendant grossly failed to enforce their regulations and standing orders that the deceased would succumb to heavy intoxication.' And in these circumstances that it was just and reasonable to impose a duty.

The respondent argued for the extension of a duty to take care for the safety of the deceased from analogous categories of relationship in which an obligation to use reasonable care already existed. For example, employer and employee, pupil and schoolmaster, and occupier and visitor. It was said that the appellant's control over the environment in which the deceased was serving and the provision of duty free liquor, coupled with the failure to enforce disciplinary rules and orders were sufficient factors to render it fair, just and reasonable to extend the duty to take reasonable care found in the analogous circumstances. The characteristic which distinguishes those relationships is reliance expressed or implied in the relationship which the party to whom the duty is owed is entitled to place on the other party to make provision for his safety. I can see no reason why it should not be fair, just and reasonable for the law to leave a responsible adult to assume responsibility for his own actions in consuming alcoholic drink. No one is better placed to judge the amount that he can safely consume or to exercise control in his own interest as well as in the interest of others. To dilute self-responsibility and to blame one adult for another's lack of self-control is neither just nor reasonable and in the development of the law of negligence an increment too far. . . .

The respondent placed reliance on *Crocker v Sundance Northwest Resorts Ltd* [1988] 1 SCR 1186, a decision of the Supreme Court of Canada. . . . In [Crocker] . . . the defendant was held liable to an intoxicated [claimant] for permitting him to take part in a dangerous ski hill race which caused him to be injured. The defendant had taken the positive step of providing him with the equipment needed for the race knowing that he was in no fit state to take part. The [claimant] had consumed alcohol in the defendant's bars. Liability was based not on permitting him to drink in the bars but in permitting him to take part in the race. . . . [T]he court founded the imposition of a duty on factors additional to the mere provision of alcohol and the failure strictly to enforce provisions against drunkenness.

In the present case I would reverse the judge's finding that the appellant was under a duty to take reasonable care to prevent the deceased from abusing alcohol to the extent he did. Until he collapsed I would hold that the deceased was in law alone responsible for his condition. Thereafter, when the appellant assumed responsibility for him, it accepts that the measures taken fell short of the standard reasonably to be expected. It did not summon medical assistance and its supervision of him was inadequate. . . .

The deceased involved the appellant in a situation in which it had to assume responsibility for his care and I would not regard it as just and equitable in such circumstances to be unduly critical of the appellant's fault. I consider a greater share of blame should rest upon the deceased than on the appellant and I would reduce the amount of the damages recoverable by the respondent by two-thirds holding the appellant one third to blame. . . ."

Saville L.J.: "I agree."

Neill L.J.: "I also agree."

Questions

1. What were the material facts of *Barrett*?

2. What was the ratio decidendi of *Barrett*?

3. In Barrett, the trial judge found the appellant in breach of a duty to the deceased on two grounds. Which ground was conceded by the appellant to be a breach of its duty?

4. How would you describe the political ideology which underpins the judgment in Barrett? Individualist? Welfarist? Why?

5. Construct a brief argument on the law in favour of your client Kirit, which you could use in civil proceedings lodged against Barbara.

Essay question

"The descriptive question that lawyers debate is whether in fact courts resolve issues primarily by the application of rules or by the application of policies. The orthodox view is that judges apply rules through the logical processes of deduction and analogy, turning to policies only in the occasional hard case. The competing theory is that judges in reality intuit the best result, that is, the result that is most satisfactory to them as a matter of policy, and only then do they turn to the rules to explain and justify the result they have reached on other grounds. In this view, the judge may even have the sensation of following the rules, but the interpretation of those rules as the judge applies them is guided by prior intuition about the most desirable resolution. In this way, the rules can seem to produce the correct result." (Kenneth J. Vandevelde, *Thinking Like a Lawyer* (Boulder: Westview Press, 1996), p.66).

Comment on the above quotation, using the cases discussed in this chapter as the basis for your answer. Describe the "values and assumptions" which have informed the development of a general duty of care in negligence.

10

THE LEGAL PROFESSIONS

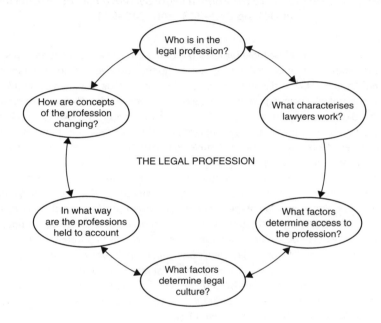

The aim of this chapter is to encourage you to reflect on how legal education prepares lawyers for life as a practitioner and affects their behaviour. We consider what sociologists call the "socialisation process" whereby novices are introduced to, and internalise, the norms of the professional group to which they aspire to join. By the end of this chapter, you should:

- recognise the key characteristics of the legal profession;

- appreciate how the characteristics of the profession have changed over time;

- understand how recent changes to the professions are likely to effect their structure and functions;

- be able to reflect on the problem of lack of diversity amongst the judiciary and the impact this is likely to have on judicial reasoning.

I. LAW AS PROFESSION

When compared to many other jurisdictions, the legal profession in England is unusual because it has two distinct types of lawyers, solicitors and barristers. The distinctions between the two are becoming less important but have traditionally led to strict demarcations in terms of the work that each is expected, or allowed, to do. The number of practising solicitors totalled 112,589 at 31 December, 2009, having risen by an annual average of four per cent since 1979. In addition there were 12,136 barristers in private practice at December 2008. Approximately 3,000 more lawyers work "in house" for a wide variety of companies, government departments and agencies. Traditionally, the organisation of the practising legal profession in England and Wales differed from that in many other countries in that there remains an important distinction between solicitors who usually come together to form partnerships and barristers in private practice who remain self employed but work in chambers. We start with an overview of the characteristics of modern legal practice and a discussion of the ways in which the organisation and regulation of the profession is changing.

Martin Partington, *An Introduction to the English Legal System* (Oxford: Oxford University Press, 2006), pp.242–243, 246, 248–251:

Independence
One of the key attributes claimed for the legal profession is that it should be independent. This is, constitutionally, an extremely important claim. It involves lawyers asserting their right to give advice independently of the views of the government of the day, and being protected if they do so. It also involves a professional obligation to take on cases which may be widely regarded as disagreeable or distasteful. The proposition that a person is innocent until proved guilty depends on lawyers being willing to develop and advance arguments on behalf of their clients no matter how unpleasant those clients may be. The 'cab-rank' principle which applies to the Bar, whereby barristers are professionally obliged to take on whatever case comes to them next, is perhaps the clearest example of the operation of this principle.

The assertion of independence also implies that the professions should be left free to regulate themselves in accordance with their own rules of professional conduct, and without interferences from government. As will be seen, there has been significant erosion of the freedom from government intervention in the legal profession over recent years. The abolition of restrictive practices, the changes to legal aid, and modes of dealing with complaints about the quality of work can be noted as examples of increased government intervention. Each example of government involvement may be justified, particularly in contexts where the legal profession has not been willing to reform itself in ways which the public interest may seem to demand. However, the question where the boundaries should be drawn in the involvement of government in the legal profession is one that needs constant attention, if the role of the legal profession in assisting the individual, often against agencies of the state or other powerful bodies, is not to be compromised.

There have been two principal issues which have led the government increasingly to intervene in the way the legal professions operate. First, over the last thirty or more years, there has been a steady attack on the restrictive practices that the legal profession asserted for itself.

Secondly, there has been increased emphasis on the importance of professional lawyers responding to complaints made about the quality of the services they provide. Although the legal professions have sought to address these issues, government has not been convinced that they are addressing them with sufficient efficiency. This has led government to intervene increasingly in this context as well. . . .

Trends in legal practice
As a consequence of these and other developments, in the same way that the institutional framework of the legal system has undergone profound change in recent years, so too has the legal profession itself. A number of trends affecting the profession are noted here.

The blurring of the distinction between solicitors and barristers
First, although the line between 'solicitor' and 'barrister' can still be drawn as a matter of professional identity, the practical implications of the distinction are far fewer today than they were twenty years ago. Many of the services which used to be the exclusive preserve of one branch of the profession are now open to all.

There has been a concern that there should be no unnecessary restrictions on the tasks which people may perform within the legal system. The most important change in this context has been the adoption by statute of the principle that the highest judicial offices should be open to solicitors just as much as to barristers (who formerly had a monopoly on in relation to these appointments).

Fusion? The obvious question that these developments pose is whether the time has not come when the two branches of the legal profession should fuse into a single profession, as happens in most other countries in the world. Should the long-standing distinction between solicitors and barristers continue to be defended? This is an issue that has been debated on many occasions, though surprisingly not seriously in the last few years, despite the developments which have occurred and which are sketched out above. The arguments asserted by the Bar for its independence, in delivering both advocacy and other forms of legal advice, are actually very powerful, more powerful than some of the advocates for fusion allow. But in other countries with fused professions, the independence of the advocate is still strongly asserted. Other ways could be found to protect professional independence without the retention of a divided profession. It seems inconceivable that at some point in the not too distant future this issue should not again become the subject of public debate.

Growth and globalization

A second trend to be noted is the growth in the size of law firms and the increasingly global scope of their practices. These have resulted from the context within which lawyers practise, which cannot be divorced from other changes in the economy based at large. The last twenty years have seen a major shift from an economy based on manufacturing to one based on services. Increased globalization of the world economy has led to a growth in the need for lawyers able to advise corporations about all the national contexts within which they are required to operate. Globalization in the provision of legal services has accompanied the globalization of the economy. British lawyers have responded in a variety of ways:

- Many of the large law firms in the City of London have gone through substantial programmes of merger and expansion;

- Significant groupings of leading firms in provincial commercial centres—e.g. Leeds, Birmingham, Bristol—have also developed, either through mergers and takeovers or the creation of 'networks' of legal practices.

- Many of these firms have established presences in other key centres of economic activity, in Europe, the Middle East, the Far East and the Americas.

- Mergers of English law firms with firms in other countries in Europe and the United States have resulted in the creation of new forms of international partnership.

- There has been a significant increase in the presence of overseas law firms, in particular US law firms, in London, which has added to the competitive pressures on British-based firms.

- There have been moves towards the creation of professional groupings that cut across traditional disciplinary boundaries—in particular, lawyers and accountants. The issue of the establishment of multidisciplinary partnerships, discussed in the Clementi report, is now clearly on the policy agendas of the professional bodies.

There is every likelihood of further developments of these kinds in the years ahead.

Specialization and niche practices

A third trend to be noted has been the increasing development of specialist/niche practices. In part this is a response to the trend towards 'mega-lawyering' noted in the previous section. Increasingly, small firms of solicitors and sets of barristers' chambers have come to specialize in particular areas—family law, criminal law, employment law, housing law, to give some examples. These developments have been supported in part by the legal professional bodies themselves. For example, the Law Society has established a number of specialist panels which practitioners may join, including the Children's Panel, the Mental Health Panel and the [Clinical] Negligence Panel.

In addition, members of the profession themselves have taken the lead in establishing an increasing number of specialist groups, many of which cross over traditional solicitor/ barrister boundaries. There are now well over forty such groups. They act in a variety of ways:

- They may be able to act collaboratively (within the competitive market) to promote the specialist services that they offer (thereby seeking to exclude non-specialists from their work).

- Some, such as the Solicitors' Family Law Association, have promoted new modes of legal practice, designed to provide a different form of lawyering for their clients—in the context of family law, a less confrontational approach designed to assist those whose relationships have broken down.

- Others, such as the [Intellectual Property] Lawyers' Association, have developed specialist programmes of advanced legal education and training designed to give their members specialist expertise and, thus, it is hoped, a competitive edge in the market.

- The specialist lawyer groups have also developed a very important influence in government. They are able to offer advice on how particular areas of legal practice may be affected by proposed policy changes, in ways in which the general professional bodies such as the Law Society of Bar Council, may be unable to achieve.

Legal services to the poor
A fourth noteworthy trend in the shape of the legal profession has been a complete transformation in the operation of the legal aid scheme. . . . Here the principal point to note is that, whereas ten years ago in effect any firm of solicitors who wished to do legal aid work could do so, now only those firms with a contract to provide services from the Legal Services Commission are able to undertake publicly funded legal aid work. Many practitioners who used to do modest amounts of legal aid work as part of a portfolio of general legal services have been affected by these changes.

High street practice
A consequence of these last two developments is that the generalist 'high street practices', found in smaller towns, suburban areas and other locations, which have in the past provided a general service to private clients, have come under increasing commercial pressure and face considerable uncertainty. The ability to make a living from a mixed practice of some criminal work, some property transactions (such as conveyancing or probate), a little bit of family and divorce work, and some personal injuries work, which even ten years ago was quite common, is now increasingly difficult. Many of the remaining sole practitioners and small firms fall into this category. The future of the 'generalist' high street practice is under considerable threat, unless those who remain in this sector of the legal services market are prepared to rethink their commercial strategies."

Significant changes to the organisation and regulation of legal services have been introduced in recent years. The rationale for change has been that lawyers have enjoyed a monopoly over many legal services and have placed insufficient weight on consumer needs and interests. The momentum for reform can be traced to the publication of a report by the Office of Fair Trading called *Competition in Professions* in March 2001 which recommended that unjustified restriction on competition should be removed. The government responded with a consultation paper and report into competition and regulation in the legal services market which concluded that the existing framework for legal services was out of date, inflexible, over-complex and lacked accountability or transparency. The Clementi Report was commissioned by the government to review the situation and reported in 2004.

Review of the Regulatory Framework for Legal Services in England and Wales (The Clementi Report) Volume one, 2004, paras 14–16, *www.legal-services-review.org.uk/content/report/chapter-f.htm*:

"The private client, as distinct from the large corporate client, is unlikely to appreciate the differences in training, competencies and regulation between different categories of what they perceive to be 'lawyers'. This is not surprising given that the purchase of legal services by such consumers is infrequent and that the consumer's prime concern is usually about outcomes—e.g. a successful conveyancing transaction—rather than the means of its delivery. Nonetheless, customers generally are interested in low prices and an efficient service, and where the nature of the services is better understood, as in the conveyancing market, customers do 'shop around'. Providers react to competitive pressures by quoting competitively for the work.

Recent research provides some background to the concerns which consumers have about how traditional legal firms operate. Research carried out by MORI shows that lawyers are not universally seen as customer focussed, approachable or easy to comprehend. Other work shows that inertia, through a feeling that 'nothing can be done', combined with a lack of knowledge about how civil law could help, act as barriers to people purchasing legal services. The Law Society's submission to the Consultation Paper comments, based on research they have carried out, that whilst cost was important 'Consumers were, in fact, more concerned about the perceived unapproachability of solicitors and their apparent attitudes to their customers'.

A survey carried out for the Consumers' Association shows a perceived lack of client care by lawyers. The main reasons for dissatisfaction were, in descending order: excessive delays, not carrying out services with reasonable skill, making mistakes, failing to return phone calls or to reply to letters and unprofessional behaviour. While the Consumers' Association themselves point out that their survey is not taken from a representative sample of the population (or lawyers' clients), it does provide a useful snapshot of some important concerns consumers have. It is of note that these concerns relate as much to the quality of business service that is provided, as to the quality of the legal advice itself."

The Clementi Report resulted in the publication of a White Paper in 2005 and to the passing of The Legal Services Act 2007 which has been described as introducing "seismic" shifts to the professions. The Act was responsible for introducing three changes into the management and regulation of legal services. Firstly, it established The Legal Services Board which came into to being on January 1, 2009 and has been fully operational since January 1, 2010. The overriding mandate of the Board is to ensure that regulation of the professions is carried out in the public interest; and that the interests of consumers are placed at the heart of the system. Independent of both Government and the legal profession, the Board sits at the apex of a new regulatory regime and is responsible for *overseeing* the work of ten separate regulators governing professional standards which include the Solicitors Regulation Authority, the Bar Standards Board, the Institute of Legal Executives, the Council for Licensed conveyancers and the Chartered Institute of Patent Attorneys. The Act also created the Office for Legal Complaints a new consumer-focused organisation established to develop and administer an independent ombudsman scheme to deal with complaints by consumers regarding poor service from a legal practitioner. The service to the consumer will be free but the complainant will normally be expected to exhaust the possibility of resolution through use of the providers in-house complaints systems before approaching the Office for Legal Complaints. Finally, the Act set out arrangements to facilitate the setting up of "legal disciplinary partnerships" allowing barristers, solicitors, legal executives and other professionals such as surveyors to work together in firms. New provisions in relation to "alternative business structures" will also allow law firms to be partly owned by non-lawyers leading some commentators to suggest that the Legal Services Act makes the UK the most liberal legal services market in the world.

Questions

1. Can you think of any advantages to clients in different types of professions being able to form partnerships together?

2. Is it time for the two branches of the legal profession to fuse so that the roles of adviser and advocate are combined as happens in most other jurisdictions? Can you think of arguments to support the proposition that they should not merge?

3. Do you think that lawyers should have a professional obligation to take on cases where they dis-
    approve of the conduct of their client? How does the cab-rank rule allow the profession to claim
    independence? Give reasons for your answer.

4. Is there a danger of solicitors and barristers being de-professionalised as they are subjected to
    closer scrutiny closed and allowed to enter into partnerships with others?

Solicitors and barristers are commonly described as members of the legal profession but what does
it mean to be a member of a profession? What is it that makes lawyers different from other workers?
Do they share some of the characteristics of other groups that are labelled as professionals, such
as doctors or teachers? The subject is one on which there has been much debate. In the following
extract Phil Harris reviews some of the key arguments which have been put forward in attempts to
distinguish the work undertaken by lawyers from other types of employment.

Phil Harris, *An Introduction to Law*, 6th edn (London: Butterworths, 2002), pp.439–440:

"Lawyers have traditionally held themselves out as 'professionals', which, sociologically, carries the implication
that, as professionals, lawyers occupy key positions within society, respected by lay people as having possession
of specialised knowledge and the claimed ability to solve clients' problems. The sociological analyses of professions suggest that professional people are identifiable by reason of their possession of five traits, or characteristics: (i) command of a systematic body of theoretical and specialised knowledge; (ii) professional authority; (iii)
the approval and support of the community; (iv) a rigorous code of ethics regulating their activities; and (v) a
professional 'culture'. A somewhat similar set of characteristics was listed in the Benson Commission report in
1979, and it has been commented that this approach:

> 'ensured that, among other things, self-regulation would continue and that the "altruistic" nature of the
> lawyer/client relationship would preclude the introduction of the market. The client would continue to
> be grateful to the lawyer for a service based on trust, confidentiality, and independence rather than upon
> competition and economic choice. The term "money" was not to be discussed with or by the client, as the
> crucial terms were "service" and "justice"—and on justice no price can be placed.'

. . . It is the body of professional knowledge, and the claim to be able to use it to deal with clients' disputes and
problems, that maintains and enhances the lawyer's professional authority. Lawyers present themselves to
clients, and indeed to the community, as having an *authoritative voice* on all legal matters, and this arguably
structures to a great extent the relationship between lawyer and client. Some have argued that the professional–client relationship is one based on *power*: the professional has what the client wants or needs: he or she
defines the manner in which the service is to be given and, equally importantly, defines the very *nature* of the client's problem. Typically, the client cannot argue that the professional's opinion or advice is wrong, inaccurate or
inappropriate, for it is usually acknowledged by the client that the professional knows best what is in the client's
interests.

   Abel, drawing up sociological analyses of professions, has produced a substantial analysis of the legal
profession in the United Kingdom, and the ways in which it has attempted to respond to both criticism and
structural changes in the market for legal services. He notes that:

> 'Producers of a service who succeed in constructing a marketable commodity only become an occu-
> pation. In order to become a profession they must seek social closure. This project has two dimen-
> sions: market control and collective social mobility . . . All occupations are compelled by the market to
> compete . . .
>   The professional project is directed not only toward controlling the market but also toward enhanc-

ing professional status . . . the lengthy training professionals must complete perhaps may be better understood not as the acquisition of technical skills but as a sacrifice necessary to justify future privilege: only this can make sense of the relative poverty endured by students . . . the tedium of study, the indignities of apprenticeship, the anxiety inflicted by examinations and the lengthy postponement of adulthood.'

. . . All lawyers undergo extensive periods of education, both through formal academic learning and through practical training in legal work. In the case of solicitors, this practical training takes the form of a two-year period, after obtaining a law degree and completing the one-year, full-time Legal Practice Course, in a training contract with a firm of practitioners. For intending barristers, the period of training is rather more complicated and less financially secure, but possibly more intensive because of the immersion of the novice in the traditions and practices of the Bar. Apart from undertaking various examinations in law, the prospective barrister must also join one of the four Inns of Court, where the life of the barrister is learned. The various rules and institutions of the Bar serve to socialise the novice into the established ways of that branch of the profession, where customs, tradition and etiquette play so great a part. Barristers' professional, and often much of their social, life involves an exclusive and somewhat socially isolated experience, where the company in which they move comprises, very often, other barristers and judges who are members of the same Inn."

Others have also commented on the close link between professionalisation and the education process. In his discussion of the role of legal skills within the law school curriculum Andrew Boon develops these arguments:

Andrew Boon, "History is past politics: a critique of the legal skills movement in England and Wales" (1998) 25 *Journal of Law and Society* 151–56:

"The starting point is to recognize the importance of the functional and symbolic role that education played in the English legal profession's claim for respectability and status. At the earliest opportunity both branches of the profession established apprenticeship as the main route into the profession. It is significant to the argument developed in this essay that [trainee contracts] were a moral rather than a cognitive training. The decline of professionalism in law was brought about by prospective entrants forsaking the five-year articled clerkship in favour of the law degree. The personal relationships of solicitors had been the cement of the profession, and the means by which it continuously reproduced itself as a club of white, middle-class males. More importantly, articles of clerkship guaranteed the commitment and values of entrants to the profession. They offered 'a period of hardship, drudgery and semi-servitude' which '. . . instilled respect for one's elders, for their experience, for their manners, conventions and ethics and for their sense of corporate honour' and offered 'cast-iron guarantees about the attitudes demeanour and commitment of those who were to enter the profession.' Wider access to educational opportunities, and a rapidly changing practice environment, precipitated a search for new means of ensuring professional inclusiveness and the reproduction of professional values. . . .

The declining fortunes of the profession was a catalyst of the move to a vocational education built about skills. Until the 1970s the legal profession assumed that there was nothing to fear from the state. It acted as if there was a tacit agreement which secured its privileges in return for a commitment to act in the public interest. From the end of the decade, however, the notion that lawyers' perception of the public interest was at best misconceived, or at worst partial and self-interested, gained ground. Sociologists came to see professions as a means of concentrating and exercising power, and their ethical commitments as elements of an ideological weaponry which operated to justify privilege. The benefits offered by professions to clients as consumers, and the wider society, were called into question. The profession's record in relation to conveyancing and criminal legal aid were particularly important for they implied that lawyers systematically exploited two of its main constituencies; the middle classes on the one hand and the state on the other.

The undermining of the profession's public image prepared the ground for the political onslaught on the profession's jurisdiction by the Thatcher governments of the 1980s. In the environment of uncertainty created, competition and levels of competence were causes of deep concern. Until that time professional knowledge had always been inextricably linked with professional power. Professions were seen to exercise market control through the construction of a 'professional commodity' spanning the technical and ideological spheres. The commodity was built on the notion of technical skill and inherent uncertainty such that professional education was preparation for the exercise of discretion. With the failure of the five-year articles, the last association with an educational tradition which had helped to secure professional power, was university style education. Universities were also, however, experiencing change. Their use of transmission modes of teaching assumed that learners were an intellectually and socially homogeneous group, an assumption which was manifestly less true as access widened from the late 1960s. The professional bodies colluded with a hidden agenda of traditional legal education, the belief that, by keeping the arts of practice 'secret' until admission, it was possible to maintain the fine balance between technicality and indeterminacy and, thereby, to maintain professional mystique. The rationalization of technical skills not only signalled the failure of this approach, it threatened two fundamental assumptions. First, the idea that professional expertise was found and transmitted only within the body of the profession, and, second, the idea that a rigid distinction between academic and professional programmes was inevitable."

Questions

1. In the Administration of Justice Act 1985, the Thatcher government abolished the statutory protection enjoyed by solicitors in their monopoly of conveyancing. This allowed licensed conveyancers, who were not required to have a law degree, to oversee the transfer of real estate. This provoked outrage amongst solicitors. Why do you think they were so concerned? Did this reform undermine any of the claims to professionalism and social closure identified by Harris?

2. What threats to the work of barristers and solicitors are posed by the Legal Services Act 2007?

In order to gain a clearer understanding of how lawyers acquire the specialist knowledge they do and why certain types of knowledge are privileged over others it is necessary to look at the role of the law school in the socialisation process.

Fiona Cownie, Anthony Bradney and Mandy Burton, *English Legal System in Context*, 4th edn (Oxford: Oxford University Press, 2007), pp.129–130, 132–134:

"University law schools are not simply one of the bureaucratic divisions of a university. Law schools, like departments of other disciplines in universities, are examples of specific cultures which are separated both from the outside world and from other cultures within the university.

'The tribes of academe . . . define their own identities and defend their own patches of intellectual ground by employing a variety of devices geared to the exclusion of illegal immigrants. Some . . . are manifest in physical form ("the building occupied by the English department", in Clark's words); others emerge in the particularities of membership and constitution (Waugh's "complex of tribes, each with its own chief and elders and witch-doctors and braves"). Alongside these structural features of disciplinary communities, exercising an even more powerful integrating force, are their more explicitly cultural elements: their traditions, customs and practices, transmitted knowledge, beliefs, morals and rules of conduct, as well as their symbolic forms of communication and meanings they share.'

It is this culture which helps define the values of university law schools. Identifying the culture of the university law school is difficult. 'Our law schools, despite sharing a common culture, are probably too diverse to lend themselves to reliable generalisation.' Individual variations in practice can appear to be more important than common themes. University law schools are found in old and new universities. They may be faculties on their own or departments within a faculty of social sciences. The largest faculties number in excess of 1,000 students while the smallest may be no more than several hundred. Staff sizes vary in similar proportions. However, despite all these important variations there are, nevertheless, some dominant ideas which prevail in most law schools and which constitute the culture of the university law school. . . .

In an early, very influential, article Kennedy argued that '[l]aw schools are intensely political places despite the fact that the modern law school seems intellectually unpretentious, barren of theoretical ambition or practical vision of what social life might be'.

Kennedy's argument pointed to a number of features which he thought were important in the ideological impact of the university law school. First, the law school was hierarchical, with the nature of the relationship between lecturer and student being determined by the lecturer. Second, the study of law involved the study of a new language. Third, law was put forward as a matter of rules. Fourth, in applying these rules one's emotions or sympathies were deemed to be irrelevant. Finally, the law school provided no overt theory in its teaching which could act as a source for critique:

> 'Teachers convince students that legal reasoning exists, and is different from policy analysis, by bully-ing them into accepting as valid in particular cases arguments about legal correctness that are circular, question-begging, incoherent, or so vague as to be meaningless. Sometimes these are just arguments from authority, with the validity of the authoritative premise put outside discussion by professorial fiat. Sometimes they are policy arguments (e.g. security of transaction, business certainty) that are treated in a particular situation as though they were rules that everyone accepts but that will be ignored in the next case when they would suggest that the decision was wrong. Sometimes they are exercises in formal logic that wouldn't stand up for a minute in a discussion between equals (e.g. the small print in a form contract represents the "will of the parties".)'

Using these methods, black-letter law presents itself, through the cases, statutes and textbooks, as a form of objective knowledge; there is a legally correct outcome to a particular dispute which, with proper training, the student will discern. A failure to see the objectively right answer by the student is characterised by the lecturer (and frequently the student) as a failure to learn the language of law or a failure in knowing the correct rules or an inability to disentangle one's emotional or political sympathies from one's intellectual understanding of the law. However, in Kennedy's view, in fact all there is in law is a distinctive argumentative technique. This tech-nique does not determine any particular outcome; does not produce a closure which will require a predestined answer. Legal technique is simply a form of argument that literally will sound right to another lawyer.

One of the results of the black-letter approach to law teaching is that there appears to be a strict separation of the question of what law is and what law should be. In learning the former, questions about the latter do not need to be raised. Outcomes of cases do not need justifying from either an ethical or a political standpoint. They simply are the law. Thus, in the British context, Fitzpatrick has argued that '[t]he deep complicities between professional and academic conceptions of law produced an English jurisprudence that . . . protected law from significant engagement with political and social issues'. Indeed, it has been argued that raising questions about the social impact of particular legal rules is not appropriate within a law school. 'The desired result, at the end of legal training, is a competent lawyer who can analyse and apply legal doctrine in an intelligent and disinterested fashion.' Law is seen as a value-free tool.

Kennedy's argument directly opposes this traditional approach. In his view the outcomes to cases are deter-mined not by the content of the rules themselves or by the nature of legal argument but by the policy biases, conscious and unconscious, of those who deal with them: '[E]verything taught [in the university law school], except the formal rules themselves and the argumentative techniques for manipulating them, is policy and nothing more'. The constant repetition of particular policy outcomes in individual cases reinforces a message that such outcomes are natural, inevitable and right. Students are learning an '[i]ndividualism [that] provides a justification for the fundamental legal institutions of criminal law, property, tort and contract'. The fact that these policy outcomes are not explicitly examined or set into any kind of social context further reinforces this message about their naturalness. On this view, by 'learning the law' students are also learning a set of political and ethical values that are oriented towards the status quo."

The issue of lawyers preserving the status quo is taken up by Cotterell in his consideration of the effects of lawyers on the law. However, it can be seen from the following extract that he is more positive about the prospects of legal creativity than Kennedy.

Roger Cotterrell, *The Sociology of Law: An introduction*, 2nd edn (London: Butterworths, 1992), pp.201–202, 192–193:

"One writer has suggested that the general conservatism that almost all commentators see as a dominant characteristic of lawyers derives from three sources related specifically to legal practice. First, lawyers are preoccupied with application of a *continuing* set of rules and principles—a stable, monolithic doctrinal structure of order. Secondly, there is the lawyer's 'more immediate and selfish interest in preserving his intellectual capital—the knowledge of the system in which he was trained' and, thirdly, 'there is the tendency of lawyers, and especially of the leading and most able lawyers, to be closely identified in interest with the establishment of the time—the men in power or the men who have prospered'. De Tocqueville wrote of lawyers as 'attached to public order beyond every other consideration', as having 'nothing to gain by innovation'. Morris Finer, himself an eminent British lawyer, remarked that the '*status quo* is part of [the lawyer's] mental capital. Every legal reform robs him of an asset he has worked hard to acquire'.

To write of conservatism in this context may be, however, to use too crude and unenlightening a concept. Throughout modern history there have been 'rebel' or 'radical' lawyers. Lawyers, after all, are not merely concerned with order, but with a particular kind of order: that which can be embodied in the legal doctrine that provides the basis of their professional claim to special expertise. The lawyer's professional commitment to the integrity of doctrine may easily be extended to a professional rejection and condemnation of those forms of order (for example, government by arbitrary terror or unfettered administrative discretion) that are not seen as encompassed by rational, systematic legal doctrine.

Furthermore, certain characteristics of legal doctrine which are adopted as the basis of lawyer's values may assume such importance in elaborated and extended forms that they become the basis of radical legal practice. Thus the concept of the rule of law (with its derivative principles of equal protection under the law and due process of law or natural justice in trial or quasi-judicial proceedings), together with the individualistic orientation of Western law, sometimes become the foundation of forceful advocacy of human rights or civil rights and demands for new forms of representation to bring the claims of the poor and of disadvantaged minorities before the law.

Finally, if lawyers in general have a strong interest in the protection of their 'mental capital', they are also sufficiently close to legal doctrine to recognise its contingent character, its *lacunae* and ambiguities, and to put into perspective (and so identify means of reforming) what appear to others as its awesome complexities. . . .

Maureen Cain, adopting Marx's term, argues that the lawyer is a 'conceptive ideologist': a translator rather than a controller; not dominating the client but translating the client's objectives into the terms of legal discourse and devising the means of achieving them within the framework of law. If this role can be attributed to the solicitors Cain studied and whom she sees as serving middle-class clients it fits more obviously elite lawyers serving powerful business organisations. Their role is to innovate and find ways within the legal system to protect their clients' interests. Today this is clearly a role that takes account of the uncertainties or leeways of legal doctrine—the complex interactions of rule and discretion. . . . Thus the elite legal adviser's role is far from being merely to 'state the law'. The expertise required is one that can use creatively both the certainties and uncertainties of law in strategies that are to the client's advantage. In general, insofar as the business world requires lawyers it needs strategists and troubleshooters, not jurists; experts who can obtain maximum freedom and maximum benefits for the enterprise from government and who can use the threat but rarely the reality of litigation creatively as a precision tool for furtherance of corporate interest. This situation reflects both the increasing significance of legal expertise in a climate of extensive government regulation of business and differences between businessmen's and lawyers' typical views of business transactions."

II. ACCESS TO THE LEGAL PROFESSION

The issue of membership of, and access to, the legal professions has become a central theme of studies of the legal professions. This is because one of the ways in which the conservatism of lawyers discussed above is explained is by reference to the narrow sections of society from which the profession is drawn. It has been argued that there is a significantly better gender balance amongst those entering the legal profession now than there was 25 years ago. Statistics illustrate that more women than men now enter law school and become solicitors than did so 25 years ago. But this progress seems slow when one considers that women were first admitted to the profession almost 90 years ago. Phil Harris has considered the record of the professions in relation to gender and ethnicity and has also drawn attention to the ongoing significance of class.

Phil Harris, *An Introduction to Law*, 6th edn (London: Butterworths, 2002), pp.449–453:

"In so far as educational background is an indicator of social class, a survey carried out by the Law Society's Research and Policy Planning Unit in 1989 of a sample of about 1,000 solicitors showed that over one-third had attended a fee-paying independent (or public) school; 11% had attended direct-grant grammar schools; 34% had been to state grammar schools, and only 14% had attended secondary modern or comprehensive schools. The survey report states however that the proportion of solicitors who have attended independent or public school has been declining over the years. There is now clearly a need for new surveys to provide updated information to see how far this trend has progressed.

The peculiarities of recruitment into the legal profession, coupled with its unique position within the social structure, still tend to favour the middle- and upper-middle class aspirant lawyer. The sheer cost of legal education, particularly postgraduate training, is, for many potential recruits, probably prohibitive, and these expenses must be found during the period of training, when novices are not allowed to take on cases for themselves and earn their own fees. Since 1990 the Bar has operated a scheme whereby barristers' chambers pay their pupils during their pupillage year; initially the amount payable was £6,000 per year (though some barristers' chambers paid pupils rather more than that) and has now been increased to £10,000. Even after qualification, however, a high income is not immediately guaranteed, partly because barristers must build up their reputation before cases begin to arrive regularly, and partly because fees earned for the first few cases may well take months to be paid. In many cases, too, pupil barristers will start their careers with substantial debt incurred as a result of the cost of the initial stages of legal education and training.

For an intending solicitor, the two years spent as a trainee are usually fairly lean financially, as they, too, will in all probability have built up substantial debts and are by no means well-paid—in 2000 the minimum starting salary for trainee solicitors was £13,600 in London and £12,000 elsewhere. Such considerations suggest that an intending lawyer, whichever branch of the profession he or she chooses, would do well to come from a background which is financially secure, and preferably have some form of independent income with which to supplement the leaner times of training and early experience. Not surprisingly, surveys have shown that many lawyers *do* come from middle- and upper-middle-class backgrounds: for example, studies of judges, who are traditionally recruited from the ranks of barrister, clearly show a predominance of public school and Oxford or Cambridge university educational backgrounds.

Not only is the legal profession predominantly middle- and upper-middle class; it is also a profession long dominated by *white male* practitioners. The significantly lower proportion of black and other ethnic minority lawyers to white, and the lower numbers of women in the profession (especially the Bar) has attracted considerable criticism over the years. With regard to solicitors, it was not until 1985 that a Race Relations Committee was established by the Law Society to monitor entry by members of black and other ethnic minority communities. In 1986 only 1% of solicitors with practising certificates came from such backgrounds, though this figure had risen to 6% by 1999–2000, and in the same year the Law Society reported that 19% of admissions to the Roll were from ethnic minority backgrounds. There is, however, evidence of discrimination against black students upon graduation, and of difficulties due to ethnic background in the working environment even when jobs can be obtained. And Law Society statistics relating to the year 1999–2000 indicate that over half of solicitors from ethnic minority groups holding practising certificates were employed not in private practice but by other employing organisations.

The picture with respect to barristers is little better. Although the Bar has long attracted—and indeed encouraged—students from overseas, the expectation was that, once qualified, they would return to practise in their home countries. . . .

There is little doubt that the Bar's record on this issue is unimpressive. There remains evidence that black barristers experience discrimination and racism both in obtaining places in chambers and in obtaining work. In order to do something to remedy the situation, the Bar announced in 1991 a 5% target for the employment of black barristers and solicitors entering practice: in 2000, the Bar's published statistics indicated that just under 9% of barristers came from non-white backgrounds, as did (in July 2001) 18% of registered pupils.

The number of women practising lawyers is rather higher for both branches of the profession but, even here, there is no reason to believe that equality has been achieved. Despite a lamentable history within the solicitors' branch that included a ban on women until 1919 (a change forced on the profession by legislation passed in that year), the proportion of women becoming solicitors has risen dramatically in recent years and in 1999–2000 was 53% of the total admitted to the Roll, with women also accounting for 36% of all solicitors with practising certificates in that year. But this does not mean that there is equality in terms of career progression, although the situation is slowly improving: Law Society figures for 1999–2000 show that of solicitors with 10–19 years' experience in private practice, 84% of men were partners (or sole practitioners) compared with 58% of women. Probably more depressing is a research finding that almost a third of women solicitors have experienced sexual discrimination at work, and one in five have experienced harassment. A survey of 631 members of the Association of Women Solicitors reported in 2001 that 32% said they had experienced sex discrimination at work, compared with 2% and 4% respectively who claimed to have suffered discrimination on grounds of race or disability.

The history of the Bar is similar to that of the Law Society. Abel, reviewing the various surveys carried out over the past 30 years or so, identifies a number of barriers operating to discriminate against women at the Bar: discrimination in obtaining pupillages and tenancies; scholarships awarded by the Inns of Court which are available only to men; the exclusion of women from meetings; the refusal of banks to grant overdraft facilities to women barristers starting out in their careers; the obstacles posed by the profession's unconscious acceptance of the traditional division of labour in childrearing which forced many women to leave the profession for family reasons; and so on. The Benson Commission found that overall, women barristers earn substantially less that their male counterparts. Although the number of women becoming barristers has risen dramatically (women now account for about 30% of all barristers, as compared with about 13% in 1985) there are very few female heads of chambers, and in 1998 women comprised only 7% of QCs."

In their longitudinal study of over 3,000 law students from a range of universities, Boon, Duff and Shiner have charted the nature of the "disadvantages" suffered by many prospective entrants to the legal profession. Their six-year survey charted the progress of a one-year cohort from the second year of their law degree to the point when most of the cohort had been qualified for two years. Their analysis suggests that a small proportion of students from minority or disadvantaged backgrounds make it to a point where they are assessed on their abilities rather than their social background.

Andrew Boon, Liz Duff and Michael Shiner, "Career paths and choices in a highly differentiated profession: the position of newly qualified solicitors" (2001) 64 M.L.R. 567–569, 591:

"In the early stages of training and qualification sex is not a significant factor, but segmentation on grounds of ethnicity and class begins immediately. Advantage and disadvantage are therefore systemic factors in selection for the profession. Work placements play a key role in selection for traineeship, particularly in City firms and large provincial firms, thus prejudicing those who are unable to work for free during vacations. Lack of finance also prevents many potential applicants from accepting places on the Legal Practice Course (the LPC), the solicitors' vocational course, or the Bar Vocational Course (the BVC), the Bar's equivalent. Sponsorship during the Legal Practice Course was offered by wealthy firms, mainly those in the City, to applicants who took the CPE, studied at Oxbridge and/or the College of Law. Multivariate analysis suggests that membership of an ethnic minority group or a family where neither parent had a degree or a professional qualification, significantly reduces the chances of receiving an offer of a training contract and of receiving an early offer. What is the impact of these factors on professional demographics once aspiring solicitors have qualified?

The sixth survey found those surviving the attrition of initial selection in a strong position. Those completing the training contract were virtually guaranteed suitable employment and 62 per cent of solicitors qualified for more than two years remained with the firm or organisation in which they had trained. Perhaps surprisingly, given earlier findings, ethnicity was not a significant factor here. Indeed, there was no real evidence of disadvantage, or inequality in the allocations of jobs, or in the initial and medium-term rates of retention of solicitors among those completing their training. Some differences did emerge, however. Graduates from the College of Law were more likely to be retained by the firm with which they trained than students studying the Legal Practice Course at new universities. . . .

The Entry to the Legal Profession project charts the fortunes of a cohort of students as they spread across a range of legal organisations and embark on increasingly specialised legal careers. Just as the profession is increasingly segmented, the selection process is also. Although it distributes entrants according to crude measures of academic achievement, such as the educational establishment attended, it actually allocates individuals to firms according to characteristics such as class and ethnicity. The relative position of women, granted access to training on almost equal terms, is already beginning to deteriorate. The focus of discussion regarding access to the profession has therefore shifted from exclusion to differentiation and subordination."

It is likely that the factors identified by Boon and colleagues will have a knock-on effect on entry to the judiciary. Women continue to be poorly represented amongst the judiciary, although the Department for Constitutional Affairs (DCA), the Judicial Appointments Commission and the Directorate of Judicial Offices published a diversity strategy in May 2006 to try and combat the problem of under-representation. Government statistics show that as of April 2009 just one of the 12 Justices of the Supreme Court is a woman, and that women made up just 8 per cent of Lord Justices of Appeal, 14 per cent of High Court Judges, 14 per cent of circuit judges and 13 per cent of Recorders. The number of women sitting as District Judges increased from 19 per cent in 2003 to 42 per cent in 2007 but has since fallen to 33 per cent. Ethnic minorities have not fared so well. There are no members of ethnic minority groups in the Supreme Court or Court of Appeal. They make up 4 per cent of judges in the High Court, 2 per cent on circuit, 6 per cent of all recorders and 4 per cent of all district judges.

Research conducted for the DCA and published in 2006 explored why women and ethnic minorities were under-represented in the judiciary.

Department for Constitutional Affairs, *Judicial Diversity: Findings of a Consultation with Barristers, Solicitors and Judges: Final Report*, p.5

"Although the DCA was praised for having started to make some changes to improve judicial diversity, there remained amongst many [lawyers] a general lack of belief that the system would ever change in a significant way. In many respects it was seen to be so deeply rooted in the entire legal system that it was considered futile to concentrate just on the judiciary when the problems were linked intrinsically with the law as a whole. Some felt that members of the senior judiciary were wedded to the current system and were extremely resistant to change. . . .

There was a prevalent concern about 'fitting in' to the judiciary and a strong belief that the judiciary only welcomed those in its own image (i.e. white males from the 'right' social background). Whilst some white males felt that this was an issue for them, the perceived requirement to fit in is exacerbated for women and those from minority ethnic groups. Many talk of having to mould themselves to a certain stereotype to ensure success in the law; others that they would not consider the judiciary because they assume that they either would not be deemed to be a suitable candidate or that they would not want to work in such a culture."

More recently still a 2010 report of the Ministry of Justice's Advisory panel on Judicial Diversity asserted that whilst change must be implemented as a comprehensive package of reform, the existing tripartite judicial diversity strategy between the Lord Chancellor, the Lord Chief Justice and the Chairman of the Judicial Appointments Commission needed refocusing and extending to include the leaders of the legal profession. It was recommended that this "Judicial Diversity Taskforce" should oversee an agreed action plan for change as a result of this Panel's findings and publish an annual report that demonstrates where progress has been made and where it has not. The report recognized that there was no quick fix to moving towards a more diverse judiciary but that what was lacking to date was a coherent and comprehensive strategy to promote diversity. It stressed that initiatives should not just be addressed to recruiting the best talent into the profession but also to retaining it. Recommendations included ensuring that lawyers from all backgrounds recognize early on in their career that becoming a judge could be a possibility for them; encouraging the legal professions to make more effort to promote diversity at all levels; an open selection processes that promote diversity and recognized potential at both entry and, progression points; the evolution of the Judicial Studies Board (JSB) into a Judicial College which could provide training on developing judicial skills and terms and new, more flexible, terms and conditions of employment that fully support diversity.

Question

Discrimination in the profession is clearly a matter for concern amongst professional bodies. Imagine you have just been appointed as a policy officer at the Ministry of Justice. How would you set about tackling the problems outlined above?

III. THE POLITICS OF THE JUDICIARY

Major concerns have also been raised about the extent to which the role of the judiciary, in particular the judges in the higher courts, can be seen to overlap with political decision making. Debate in this field has been spearheaded by John Griffith whose seminal book on the politics of the judiciary suggested that the social and political background of the judiciary makes a particular, and conservative, style of decision-making more likely. In the extract below, Phil Harris expands on the particular contribution to this debate made by John Griffith.

Phil Harris, *An Introduction to Law*, 6th edn (London: Butterworths, 2002), pp.430–434:

"Griffith has catalogued and discussed the extent to which the role of the judiciary (in particular the judges of the higher courts) can be seen to overlap into the sphere of political decision-making. In particular, Griffith discusses the broad areas of industrial relations, personal rights and freedoms, property rights and squatters, judicial control on ministerial discretion, the uses of conspiracy, and cases involving students and trade union members. He argues that 'judges are part of the machinery of authority within the State and as such cannot avoid the making of political decisions'; and that the senior judges in particular have, by reason of their legal education and their working life as practising barristers, 'acquired a strikingly homogeneous collection of attitudes, beliefs, and principles, which to them represents the public interest'. For Griffith, the idea of an impartial and neutral judiciary, especially in cases involving a political element, is mythical:

'. . . judges in the United Kingdom cannot be politically neutral because they are placed in positions where they are required to make political choices which are sometimes presented to them, and often presented by them, as determinations of where the public interest lies; . . . that interpretation of what is in the public interest and therefore politically desirable is determined by the kind of people they are and the position they hold in our society; . . . this position is part of established authority and so is necessarily conservative and illiberal.'

When first published, Griffith's book met with considerable criticism, particularly, as one might expect, from members and ex-members of the judiciary. Lord Devlin, once a judge in the House of Lords, responded to some of Griffith's assertions and arguments. To a large extent, Devlin's reply may be summarised as a resounding 'so what?' To begin with, he explains, there is no denying the homogeneity of political and other outlooks on the part of the judges, but then the same is true of most other institutions in our society, or at least, those of them which 'like the law are not of a nature to attract the crusading or rebellious spirit'.

Further, argues Devlin, the question posed by Griffith, which is 'do the judges allow their devotion to law and order to distort their application of the law when they apply it to those who do not think as they do?' is beset by the twin difficulties of lack of unanimity among the senior judges whom Griffith, according to Devlin, seeks to present as 'a small group of senior judges who are policy makers': 'The law lords are sometimes divided: more frequently they quarrel with the Court of Appeal.' And the constraints imposed by the length of Griffith's book do not, argues Devlin, allow any rigorous analysis of the cases under discussion. Devlin accepts that Griffith's perspective may be seen as the view from the left, and explains that criticisms of the judiciary might also be made by those taking a different ideological stance: 'Professor Griffith cites cases on the use of police powers which he finds to be "alarming"; someone right of centre could probably produce a list of cases which would alarm him by their tenderness towards crime.' In short, Devlin is inclined to the view that too much is made by Griffith of the 'politics of the judiciary', for 'their politics are hardly more significant than those of the army, the navy and the airforce; they are as predictable as those of any institution where maturity is in command'.

. . . [Harris goes on to note one key factor which limits the 'politics' of judicial decision making.] [A]n important constraining factor is the necessity, noted by Weber, Frank and others, for judicial decisions to be presented not as the outcome of subjective, arbitrary or capricious reasoning by the judge, but as the result of the application of objective criteria. This is the difference between the statement 'in my opinion, you are guilty' and the statement 'according to the law, you are guilty'. The former statement we would regard as somewhat suspect, as being unfair or biased. The issue of public credibility and confidence in the judiciary is once again relevant here: we would not place much faith in a legal system which allowed judges to decide cases according to their whim or their personal views about the parties to a dispute. We expect judges to decide cases in accordance with existing law, without personal views or prejudices colouring their judgment."

The politics of the judiciary frequently becomes more explicit and recognisable when judges are asked to consider the "public interest" in cases. In these situations, ideological assumptions about society often come to the surface. Moreover, judicial decision making in this context often appears to assume that there is a shared system of values throughout society, that judges are equipped to identify them, and that they can be maintained through the power of law.

Phil Harris, *An Introduction to Law*, 6th edn (London: Butterworths, 2002), pp.495–497:

"[T]he judicial protection of moral standards extends beyond the range of criminal law. Such concerns are the basis of much judicial comment and decisions in family law, and in the law of contract we find cases such as that of *Pearce v Brooks* in 1866, where the judges refused to accept the legality of an agreement between the plaintiffs and the defendant whereby the former had hired out a carriage to the latter, to be used for the purposes of prostitution. In *Glynn v Keele University* in 1971, a student who was excluded from residence on the campus for nude sunbathing failed in his attempt to challenge this disciplinary action. Although the court accepted that, in denying him a chance to put his side of the case, the university official had acted in breach of natural justice, the court none the less felt that the offence was such as to 'merit a severe penalty according to any standards current even today'. And in 1971, in *Ward v Bradford Corpn*, the Court of Appeal denied a remedy to a student teacher who had broken the rules of her hall of residence by permitting her boy-friend to remain in her room overnight for a period of about two months. She had been expelled by the college and, despite irregularities in the manner in which the disciplinary procedure had been carried out, Lord Denning stated firmly his belief that her behaviour was not suitable for a trainee teacher: 'she would never make a teacher. No parent would knowingly entrust their child to her care.'

In such matters of morality, the tension between judicial conservatism and an increased social tolerance of moral behaviour which is not to everyone's taste, is manifest. It is worth asking the question whether, in today's climate in which sexual and other moral matters are relatively freely discussed and practices once regarded as beyond the pale are fairly openly indulged in, the attitude of the judges may in some cases be too far removed from the 'real social world', so to speak, to protect the interests of all involved. Having said this, however, one outstanding case in which the judges showed themselves well aware of modern public attitudes towards sexual morality was *R. v R.* in 1991—the case which overturned the common law rule that a husband could not be criminally liable for committing rape upon his wife. In the Court of Appeal, Lord Lane stated that the old common-law rule had become 'anachronistic and offensive and we consider that it is our duty having reached that conclusion to act upon it'—a view with which the House of Lords unanimously agreed.

Other notable areas where the courts have referred, in the various cases before them, to the 'public interest', or equivalent terms, include the law of property, where the judges have consistently upheld the protection of traditional rights to private property as against, for example, private tenants (through restrictive interpretation of rent legislation) and squatters; the law relating to conspiracy where, until the Criminal Law Act 1977 clarified and somewhat restricted the range of the offence, the judges had been quite prepared to uphold convictions for the offence, even though the activity allegedly planned by the conspirators had not been carried out; and the law relating to public order and industrial disputes.

The problems underlying these assumptions and views on the part of the judiciary revolve around the difficulty of identifying exactly what constitutes the 'public interest' in a given area—even if such a monolithic entity exists at all. By what criteria do the judges, who wield considerable power in such cases, discover which particular body of attitudes or standards in our society constitute *the* public interest? Perhaps Lord Devlin, once again, expressed the view of most judges:

> 'English law has evolved and regularly uses a standard which does not depend on the counting of heads. It is that of the reasonable man. . . . It is the viewpoint of the man in the street. . . . He might also be called the right-minded man. For my purpose I should like to call him the man in the jury-box, for the moral judgment of society must be something about which any twelve men or women drawn at random might after discussion be expected to be unanimous.'

But how likely is such a consensus? Society is by no means homogeneous: it is composed of many groups and individuals differing in terms of sex, age, ethnic and cultural background, social class and political power. Would it be possible to obtain a unanimous judgment from any group of randomly selected people on the issues of industrial relations, prostitution or any of the other areas where the assumptions held by the judges, particularly in the appellate courts, have come to the fore? Surely *any* interest group might convincingly register a belief that *their* policies, beliefs or attitudes were an accurate reflection of a 'public morality' or a 'public interest'? Unless we are, literally, to embark upon a national referendum on all such matters, there would seem to be no clear way of ascertaining what the majority of people believe to be right or acceptable behaviour, with any degree of accuracy.

Furthermore, Lord Devlin and other judges using similar terminology commit a serious analytical error in using phrases such as 'society believes this' or 'society has decided that'. Such loose phrases obscure the fact of pluralistic interests and differential access to policy-making channels within the social structure. What is, therefore, presented as being in the 'public interest' may in fact serve limited, sectional interests. As Coulson and Riddell put it:

> '. . . to say that a decision is in the national interest usually means to identify the interests of one group of the population as the National Interest, while conveniently forgetting the interests of those members of

the nation who are not benefited by the decision. By the appeal to nationalism, sectional decisions may appear more palatable to people they don't benefit.' "

Questions

1. Do you think that the judiciary are capable of being neutral? Give reasons for your answer.

2. What do you think is meant by the term "political judgments"? Can you think of any cases you have read where the judgment could be classified as political? Explain why.

It has been argued that the ideological underpinnings of judicial decision making are particularly apparent in the way in which the judiciary talk about "common sense" in their judgments. Graycar argues that an underlying gendered perspective is at work in these judicial pronouncements.

Regina Graycar, "The gender of judgments: an introduction" in Margaret Thornton (ed) *Public and Private: Feminist legal debates* (Melbourne: Oxford University Press, 1995), pp.266–272:

"I have suggested that the role of judging is gendered and implicitly male, and I think this follows inexorably from a history of social, political and legal practices, and beliefs now deeply entrenched in the substantive body of law with which judges work. Given the fact that women were not even permitted to practise law until well into this century, there is no question that the substantive legal doctrines we use on a day-to-day basis were developed by men, with their problems and concerns in mind, and reflecting their perspectives on the world. Despite the relatively recent entry of women into the profession, and their increasing numbers . . . legal doctrines and legal reasoning appear to have remained almost completely impervious to perspectives other than those of the (dominant) White, middle-class male. . . .

   If law was developed by men in accordance with their needs and experiences and has neither dealt well with women, nor reflected their lives or experiences, then perhaps everything would change if there were some more women in there. But I am not very confident that, simply by adding some women to the bench and stirring, we will automatically change the male-centredness of law and legal reasoning. For a number of reasons—such as the ways in which legal education has been conducted to date and the ways in which certain forms of utterance are privileged by law in the construction of what is authoritative, and by corollary, what (or who) lacks credibility—I am somewhat sceptical of the view that simply as a result of women being there, everything will be different. We may just be adding more women to the bench—nothing more, nothing less. After all, the 'institution' of law remains and its '[i]nstitutional design is a way of allocating authority across different sets of actors', while ensuring that the 'legal texts always operate from a particular strategy of framing facts'. But if we could further our understanding of what judges know, how they know it, how this shapes the construction of reality in judgments—that is, how judges 'orient' their narratives—and how this is all affected by gender, then maybe things *could* change. While there are any number of barriers to women's stories being heard in courts and, even if heard, being given credibility and authority, judges' speech is quintessentially authoritative. Judges are speakers whose verdicts count, both generally, in that they have considerable social status and, most particularly for these purposes, in their power to construct realities in the domain of law."

Rackley explores this issue in terms of the appointment of the first female Law Lord.

Erika Rackley, "Difference in the House of Lords" (2006) 15 *Social & Legal Studies* 163 at 163, 167–168:

"On Monday 12 January 2004, Brenda Hale became the first female law lord, ending over 600 years of male exclusivity among the members of the House of Lords' appellate committee. As expected, her appointment was widely reported in the British press. The combination of her pioneering achievement, her candid exposure of the inherent sexism in her profession, and her willingness to acknowledge the importance of talking about 'clothes, cooking and childcare' was seen by some, including Hale herself, as making her 'just a bit different' from her male colleagues. Her perceived difference fuelled first impressions of her as a judge with a 'touch of humanity' and secured her place alongside the likes of *Sex and the City* actor Cynthia Nixon, BBC *Fame Academy* winner Alex Parks, Swedish foreign minister Anna Lidah, Canadian–Iranian photo-journalist Zahra Kazemi and film icon Katherine Hepburn in the Guardian's list of 'Women We Loved in 2003'. Others, however, saw Hale's elevation to the House of Lords as 'epitomis[ing] the moral vacuum within our judiciary and wider establishment'. In particular, her trailblazing appointment reignited the *Daily Mail's* vicious and highly personal campaign against an apparently 'ferocious feminist' intent on destroying the institution of marriage and other family values. As the 'pro' and 'anti' Hale camps battled it out in the press, early indications were that Brenda Hale had the potential to be 'trouble with a capital H'.

However, as time has passed, the warnings of an imminent adjudicative apocalypse seem somewhat misplaced. Brenda Hale appears to have successfully carved out a role as 'one of our more thoughtful' law lords. In fact, she has been anything but trouble. Her subversive tendencies appear—at least for the time being—to be in check, her potential difference contained. In fact, as the novelty of a lady amid the lords begins to wear off, one might legitimately begin to wonder what all the fuss was about: what is so special about having a lady in the House? Put another way, can difference make a difference to the House of Lords? . . .

Unsurprisingly perhaps, she also believes 'the case for increasing diversity on the Bench, not only in gender and ethnicity, is not just a fashionable and self-interested prejudice. It is overwhelming'. Her motivation is transformative rather than simply curative. A more diverse judiciary, she suggests, will not only meet the demands of democratic legitimacy and equal opportunities—increasing public confidence through a shrewd use of human resources which addresses the disadvantages of the current judiciary—but may also, through the incorporation of a variety of perspectives, make a difference to the judgments made: 'I would like to think that a wider experience of the world is helpful: knowing a little about bearing and bringing up children must make some difference . . . [although] there have been some wonderful family judges who have never changed a nappy or cooked a fish finger in their lives'.

Nevertheless, although Hale believes women lawyers and judges have 'moved on' from an understandable reluctance to 'acknowledge or claim the right to be different', her relationship with 'difference' remains somewhat prickly:

> We should not expect women judges to 'make a difference' in the sense that they are likely to make different decisions from men . . . We are all lawyers first and men or women second . . . But if it were as simple as that, why should having more women on the bench be expected to increase public confidence in its decision? Window dressing is important, as every retailer knows, but isn't it necessary also to improve the products on sale? The difference is more subtle.

Indeed, in her article 'Equality and the Judiciary: Why Should We Want More Women Judges?', Hale suggests that her academic career, her reforming inclinations and her 'tendency to go native' are 'at least as influential' in relation to on her 'small offerings on the bench' as her gender. Her support for a more diverse judiciary is not grounded in the somewhat controversial belief that women judges speak in a 'different voice' or that men and women necessarily 'judge' differently—'the great majority of judgments I have written or spoke could just as easily have been written or spoken by a man'. Rather, it lies in an understanding that the perspectives and experiences of women judges *as women* necessarily inform their judgments and that 'the experience of leading those lives should be just as much part of the background and experience which shapes the law as the experience of leading men's lives has been for centuries'. In short, Hale recognises that who the judge *is* matters both in terms of 'the kind of story ultimately told, and for the way that story reaches the law and the law reaches that story'. This is deeply subversive. It explodes a paradox underlying current discourses on adjudication where on the one hand women judges are viewed as desirable in order to broaden the ranges of perspectives on the bench, thus making the judiciary more representative, while on the other judges are supposed to be without perspective, thus suggesting there is little need for a representative judiciary. As traditional understandings of the judge and judging—a fairy tale of one 'almost superhuman in wisdom, in propriety, in decorum and in humanity' able to apply the law in a neutral and detached way—lie in ruin, Hale challenges us to reconsider our adjudicative expectations; to confront our Herculean demons in order to let go of the superhero and embrace the ((wo)man) judge. As difference—found in the distinctiveness of perspective and experience—becomes not an end in itself but rather a route to engendering diverse perspectives on adjudication, justice and law, it throws a spotlight onto previously unimagined adjudicative alternatives and new ways forward. Put another way, there is more to difference than simply window dressing; its strategic subtlety not only masks its irritant potential but also the extent to which difference can 'make a difference'."

We have considered the different ways in which judicial "common sense" reflects, not sense which is "common" to everyone, but a particular perspective on the world, grounded frequently in assumptions about gender, race, sexuality, class, and other relations of power. The question whether a more diverse judiciary, composed of more women and members of ethnic minorities could make a "difference" to the outcome of judicial decision making is questioned by Graycar. Whether her concerns prove to be valid remains to be seen. It seems appropriate since we teach law and you are studying it to return again to the part that legal education plays in the creation and maintenance of discriminatory practice.

Jill Abramczyk, "The tyranny of the majority: liberalism in legal education" (1992) 5 *Canadian Journal of Women and the Law* 442 at 451:

"One of the results of the primacy of liberal objectivity is that one dominant but narrow perspective becomes the most (or only) acceptable approach in the law school classroom, and in legal discourse in general. To the extent that this perspective encodes a particular view of the world, and a particular vision of the way in which the world should be ordered, liberalism can be both 'dominant' and a vehicle for entrenching systemic domination. Ignorance of the experience of others, and disrespect for those who are 'different' from the dominant culture, is thereby legitimized. Those who are different become 'outsiders', the oddities at whom we laugh or shake our heads. Any structural forces are systematically ignored.

Legal reasoning is taught 'as though enduring principles of social organization [are] imbedded in the logic of the doctrines themselves,' rather than as though the doctrines have political and ethical meanings. That law students study rules, which do not take into account backgrounds, socialization, or political beliefs, illustrates that legal reasoning treats people and conflicts as atomistically as liberalism does. When the gender, class, race, age, and gender orientation of the people involved are excluded systematically from discussion, the underlying principles of doctrines and their political and ethical meanings are disregarded. . . . [I]t encourages students to accept at face value what they are told is 'reality' without being encouraged or taught to question it, or to analyze it from any number of critical/analytical perspectives. . . .

Liberal theory directs that the application of 'legal reasoning' leads to 'sound law', which conforms to 'legal conventions concerning interpretation, precedent, rights and so forth, rather than by conformity to political goodness'. Legal reasoning 'says it can take us from legal premises (precedents, notions of rights) to determine answers without resort to political or ethical choice.' The law student is taught that legal reasoning leads us to the 'correct' legal result, and indeed, that there is *one* correct legal result.

This result, and the reasoning produced, is presented as being logical, objective, and neutral. Events are presented 'as they are', in full confidence that the presentation is free from any particular perspective or ideology. But it bears repeating that (legal) reasoning necessarily reflects the perspectives of its participants, and that those perspectives are not neutral. As has been noted, 'most professors, just as most legislators, and judges, and lawyers are white and male and middle-class and heterosexual.' "

A major element in the construction of the "ideal lawyer" through legal education is indoctrination in the form of traditional visions of what constitutes legal method. Williams has illustrated this method of reasoning through the telling of a story, which highlights the pitfalls of "thinking like a lawyer".

Patricia J. Williams, *The Alchemy of Race and Rights* (Cambridge, MA: Harvard University Press, 1991), pp.12–13:

"Walking down Fifth Avenue in New York not long ago, I came up behind a couple and their young son. The child, about four or five years old, had evidently been complaining about big dogs. The mother was saying, 'But why are you afraid of big dogs?' 'Because they're big,' he responded with eminent good sense. 'But what's the difference between a big dog and a little dog?' the father persisted. 'They're *big*,' said the child. 'But there's really no difference,' said the mother, pointing to a large slathering wolfhound with narrow eyes and the calculated amble of a gangster, and then to a beribboned Pekinese the size of a roller skate, who was flouncing along just ahead of us all, in that little fox-trotty step that keep Pekinese from ever being taken seriously. 'See?' said the father. 'If you look really closely you'll see there's no difference at all. They're all just dogs.'

And I thought: 'Talk about your iron-clad canon. Talk about a static, unyielding, totally uncompromising point of reference. These people must be lawyers. Where else do people learn so well the idiocies of High Objectivity? How else do people learn to capitulate so uncritically to a norm that refuses to allow for difference? How else do grown-ups sink so deeply into the authoritarianism of their own world view that they can universalize their relative bigness so completely that they obliterate the subject positioning of their child's relative smallness? (To say nothing of the position of the slathering wolfhound, from whose own narrow perspective I dare say the little boy must have looked exactly like a lamb chop.)'"

You may want to keep Williams's story in mind as you proceed through your study of legal method. It provides a useful reminder of the dangers of uncritically accepting legal reasoning as a means of discovering the "truth" of things, erasing individual perspectives and differences in social positioning in the process.

Questions

1. How do you react to the criticisms of legal reasoning and of "thinking like a lawyer"?

2. Define "legal method" (you may want to revise your answer when you reach the end of the book and in three years' time).

Useful website addresses

Judicial Studies Board, *http://www.jsboard.co.uk* [Accessed May 13, 2010]

Law Society of England and Wales, *http://www.lawsociety.org.uk* [Accessed May 13, 2010] see in particular "Promoting equality and diversity"

Bar Council, *http://www.barcouncil.org.uk* [Accessed May 13, 2010] see in particular the Equality and Diversity Code to the Bar

Judiciary of England and Wales, *http://www.judiciary.gov.uk* [Accessed May 13, 2010]

Judicial Appointments and Conduct Ombudsman, *http://www.judicialombudsman.gov.uk* [Accessed May 13, 2010]

Judicial Appointments Commission, *http://www.judicialappointments.gov.uk* [Accessed May 13, 2010]

Ministry of Justice, *http://www.justice.gov.uk* [Accessed May 13, 2010]

Judicial appointments, *http://www.dca.gov.uk/judicial/appointments/ jappinfr.htm* [Accessed May 13, 2010]

Statistics on judicial appointments, *http://www.dca.gov.uk/judicial/judapp.htm* [Accessed May 13, 2010]

Solicitors Regulation Authority, *http://www.sra.org.uk* [Accessed May 13, 2010]

Bar Standards Board, *http://www.barstandardsboard.org.uk* [Accessed May 13, 2010]
Legal Services Board, *http://www.legalservicesboard.org* [Accessed May 13, 2010]
Office for Legal Complaints, *http://www.officeforlegalcomplaints.org.uk* [Accessed May 13, 2010]
Feminist Judgements Project, *http://www.kent.ac.uk/law/fjp* [Accessed May 13, 2010]
Equal Justices Initiative, *http://www.law.qmul.ac.uk/eji/index.html* [Accessed May 13, 2010]

11

DISPUTE RESOLUTION: THE COURTS AND ADJUDICATION

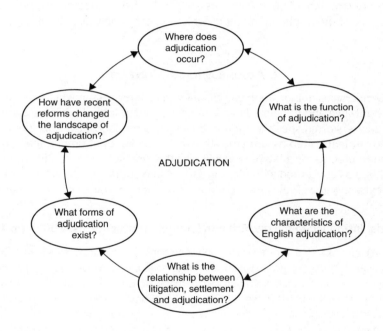

We turn our attention, in this chapter and the next, to the *processes* used to resolve disputes in the English legal system. We do not attempt to present a comprehensive explanation of the detailed rules of civil or criminal procedure. Instead, we focus on the values and assumptions which underpin the various forms of dispute resolution which are provided or sanctioned by the state. By the end of this chapter, you should:

- understand the constitutional function of courts in England and Wales;
- be able to identify features which characterise the courts and adjudication;
- know how to distinguish between adversarial and inquisitorial processes;
- appreciate the significance of plea bargaining and out-of-court settlement;
- be conversant with debates about the relative values of formalism and informalism;
- be aware of adjudicatory forums other than the courts.

Twenty years ago the inclusion of chapters on the principles of adjudication and alternatives to it would have been unthinkable in a book of this kind. For many years law students and legal academics focused their attention almost exclusively on litigation in the higher courts without paying heed to theories of adjudication or the significance of dispute resolution outside of the courts. Times have changed. Not only has the government become increasingly interested in reforming the litigation system and diverting cases away from the courts, but calls have also been made for methods of dispute resolution which are less costly, speedier, less adversarial, more sensitive to non-legal issues in disputes and better able to repair relationships. As a result academics and practitioners now need to know about a range of dispute resolution techniques. The Woolf Reports published in 1995 and 1996 heralded a radically different approach to the resolution of disputes within the English legal system. Attitudes towards the handling of criminal cases has also changed in the wake of a series of high-profile cases involving unsafe convictions and an emerging interest in restorative justice. The education of law students would now be seriously lacking if they graduated without an understanding of the variety of dispute resolution methods which are commonly used by litigants and their lawyers.

I. Adjudication in Context

Within liberal democracies adjudication can be defined as a process in which a neutral third party imposes an authoritative and principled decision on the disputants which is supported by reasoned opinion. Lawyers often speak as though they have a monopoly over dispute resolution and adjudication and students often assume that they will spend a lot of time managing litigation. In fact, if you go on to practise as a lawyer you will find that you spend relatively little time in court and that you will be as concerned with planning to avoid disputes as you will with their resolution. In the opening extract below, Phil Harris reminds us of the importance of looking at disputes in a broader context.

Phil Harris, *Introduction to Law*, 6th edn (London: Butterworths, 2002), pp.155–156:

"Every social group contains within it the elements and conditions in which disputes will arise. Even the smallest social group will experience disputes between its members, and, as we would expect, the larger and more complex a social group becomes, the more varied and, perhaps, frequent will be the disputes which crop up within it. Hardly a day goes by in people's everyday lives without some problem occurring, some argument arising, or some resentment or frustration being felt by one person or group over the activities of another. Family rows, arguments with friends, confrontations at work and so on are familiar to most people, as are the various solutions which we use to deal with those disputes.

The simplest disputes are dealt with by various informal, often quite good-natured means. Within family units, there may be an invocation of an established family custom or rule, or the calling-in of a third party to mediate in the dispute. Rarely would family squabbles result in the initiation of any kind of formal proceedings to settle the matter. Similarly, the social and economic world outside such small units as friends or family rests upon various types of relationships between, for example, business enterprises, employers and employees, traders and consumers, and citizens and government agencies. When considering the frequency with which something goes wrong with the smooth running of these relationships, and a dispute arises, it is important to appreciate that the informal resolution of the problem, through concessions or compromise is by far the most usual way of settling the matter.

This mode of settling disputes through concession or compromise is especially important where the parties to the dispute are in some long-standing or permanent relationship with each other. In domestic situations, feuding neighbours will rarely resort to litigation to solve their disputes, partly because theirs is a continuing relationship, as is the relationship between employer and employee, or landlord and tenant. In the sphere of commercial agreements and business contracts, research by Macaulay, among others, has suggested that people in business rarely invoke the law as a means of resolving business disputes over their contractual agreements, mainly because this is seen as having the effect of perpetuating the conflict and polarising the disputants, instead of resolving the particular problem without damaging the continuing business relationships of the parties. . . .

Although the vast majority of disputes are settled by informal means, there will, at least in more complex and technologically developed societies, be various official, formal institutions and agencies whose purpose is the resolution of disputes. The clearest examples in our own society of such agencies are, of course, the courts of law and tribunals, one of whose most important functions is the authoritative settlement of disputes through the application of legal rules."

It is important to stress from the outset that *methods* of dispute resolution should not be seen as synonymous with particular forums or places. Adjudication, mediation and negotiation each occur in a variety of different settings. Moreover, the notion of adjudication should not be seen as interchangeable with state-funded systems for the resolution of disputes. Rather, adjudication is a process which is used in private forums as well as public. Possibly the best example is commercial arbitration. This point is taken up by Cownie, Bradney and Burton who encourage us to place our study of disputes in this broader context.

Fiona Cownie, Anthony Bradney and Mandy Burton, *English Legal System in Context*, 4th edn (Oxford: Oxford University Press, 2007), p.6–8:

There are many examples of private mechanisms and institutions which mirror the state's attempts to prevent or resolve disputes. All of these mechanisms and institutions are largely ignored in texts on 'the English legal system'.

Separating dispute-resolution mechanisms, which owe their authority to the state from voluntary mechanisms and writing only about the former, significantly reduces the amount of dispute resolution which is being discussed. Statistically, many disputes are in fact resolved by non-state agencies. The form that such dispute resolution takes varies. Someone mediating between quarrelling friends is a form of dispute resolution; so are arbitration procedures established by retail associations to deal with customer disputes; so are dispute resolution procedures within a Quaker Meeting; so are disciplinary procedures in universities; so are many other things. The essential difference between all of these non-state structures and the state courts is that if parties to a dispute follow the findings of such non-state agency they usually do so of their own volition. Parties choose whether or not they will use these agencies. Both parties must accept their jurisdiction. In the case of state courts the state itself can compel the presence of one of the parties to an action. Parties are obliged to take part in proceedings whether they want to or not.

Non-state dispute resolution agencies must operate within the shadow of the law. They may use state law by, for example, making their decisions the subject of a binding contract. Thus, for example, in the United Kingdom the Jewish Beth Din, a court established under Jewish religious law (though open to both Jews and non-Jews), requires those who wish to use it to accept the provisions of the Arbitration Act 1996."

Having placed the idea of adjudication in context, we go on in the next section to look at the way in which adjudication has been conceived of in England and Wales. We focus in particular on the constitutional and social functions of adjudication and the trial.

II. THE CONSTITUTIONAL FUNCTION OF ADJUDICATION AND THE TRIAL

The provision of state-sanctioned systems for the redress of citizen grievances is one of the core rights enshrined in the Magna Carta and this obligation has traditionally been satisfied by the adjudication of disputes in public courts. The constitutional significance of the trial in Anglo-American contexts is explored by Robert Burns in his work on the "received view" of the trial.

Robert P. Burns, *A Theory of the Trial* (Princeton and Oxford: Princeton University Press, 1999), pp.11–15:

The Rule of Law

The Received View understands the trial as a necessary institutional device for actualizing the Rule of Law in situations where there are disputes of fact. The trial allows punishments to be imposed or civil wrongs to be righted only after a careful factual analysis of what actually occurred, *specifically structured for the application of an established legal rule to the exclusion of other possible norms*. Simply put, the trial is designed, so this under-standing goes, to guarantee that the trier of fact will 'follow the law.' Defenders of the Rule of Law argue its importance from four somewhat independent bases. The first basis is one of substantive legitimacy. In natural law theories, the law embodies the principles of natural justice in a manner both deeper and more refined than the probable institutions of any specific judge or jury. In theories that trace the legitimacy of law to a version of popular sovereignty, including most positivist theories, the Rule of Law ensures that democratic judgment, constitutionally structured and channelled, will be brought to bear on individual cases.

The second basis for the Rule of Law focuses more on the dangers of the abuse of power by individual government actors. Law's inevitable generality and relatively fixed meanings limit what a 'magistrate' may do and prevent him from inflicting 'arbitrary' inquiries. The Rule of Law requires that '[n]o organ of the State may render an individual decision which would not conform to a general rule previously stated.' It 'means that gov-ernment in all its action is bound by rules fixed and announced beforehand—rules which make it possible to foresee with fair certainty how the authority will use its coercive powers in given circumstances and to plan one's individual affairs on the basis of this knowledge.'

A corollary to the law as limitation on the power of officialdom is its role in protecting the liberty of the citizen, the third basis of the Rule of Law. The Rule of Law is 'closely related to liberty' in that it allows the citizen, through his voluntary choices, to control the time and place the coercive engines of government may be brought to bear on him.

Finally, the Rule of Law 'implies the precept that similar cases be treated similarly.' Consistency itself will prevent a wilful official from injuring Citizen A, whom he dislikes, if the rule he thereby establishes will injure Citizen B, whom he favors. Consistency, or the 'principle of regularity,' however, is not merely a policing device to constrain government action. It rests on substantive grounds as well—the principle of equal respect for persons, a basic norm of morality as well as of legality.

The Trial in Service to the Rule of Law

The Rule of Law requires a process for making factual determinations. As Rawls puts it:

> 'If laws are directives addressed to rational persons for their guidance, courts must be concerned to apply and to enforce these rules in an appropriate way. A conscientious effort must be made to determine whether and infraction has taken place and to impose the correct penalty. Thus, a legal system must make provisions for conducting orderly trials and hearings; it must contain rules of evidence that guarantee rational procedures of inquiry. While there are variations in these procedures, the Rule of Law requires some form of due process: that is, a process reasonably designed to ascertain the truth, in ways consist-ent with the other ends of the legal system, as to whether a violation has taken place and under what circumstances.'

Factual accuracy is clearly important to those who defend the Rule of Law on substantive grounds. The higher or more refined notions of justice embedded in the law all, as applied, take the form of hypothetical imperatives. For example, *if* the buyer has made an offer for real estate accompanied by a valuable consideration that has been accepted and is not against public policy, *then* the sale shall be specifically enforced. The condition to be fulfilled for the application of the law is factual, and substantive justice will be achieved if the facts are found accurately. Indeed, especially in systems of common law adjudication, the authoritative forms exist as a never completely determined tension among announced facts, results and rationales. When the 'next case' arises, it is a matter of argument as to which facts were crucial to the result in the earlier case, and the first court's own recital of its rationale may prove to be 'dictum' and not itself authoritative. Facts are more closely drawn up into the rule than are the court's explanations of its decisions. For the individual case to be justly decided, facts must be accurately determined and available in a form that will allow the preferred norms to be 'applied.'

For those who understand the Rule of Law as a limitation on arbitrary government action, accuracy in fact-finding is also important: officials who can manipulate the facts to bring them under any rule that allows them to pursue their plans will be wholly unconstrained by legal norms. Nor will citizens who wish to enjoy their liberty without coercive interference be safe if officials are simply *unable* to determine reliably whether a citizen has stayed within the lines protected by the law. Finally, factual accuracy is crucial if similar cases are to be treated similarly. Without it, legal results will be distributed randomly and without regard to similarities and differences among real-world situations.

Without the right kinds of procedural devices to determine particular cases, the notion that the Rule of Law actually prevails must become illusory or ideological. Lawyers in the English-speaking world have been too practical, and too committed to the Rule of Law, to allow that to happen, at least without a fight. Of course, one need only glance at human history to understand that 'government of laws, not of men' is an utopian ideal. Yet much of the genius of the Anglo-American tradition has been poured into the construction of institutions that actually attempt the incarnation of utopian ideals."

In his interim report on the civil justice system Lord Woolf reinforced the continuing need for the state to fulfil these goals through the English litigation system.

Lord Woolf, *Access to Justice: Interim report, www.lcd.gov* (June 1995):

The importance of civil justice
"A system of civil justice is essential to the maintenance of a civilised society. The law itself provides the basic structure within which commerce and industry operate. It safeguards the rights of individuals, regulates their dealings with others and enforces the duties of government. The administration of civil justice plays a role of crucial importance in maintaining this structure as Sir Jack Jacob, the doyen of civil proceduralists, observed in 'The Reform of Procedural Law':

> 'It manifests the political will of the State that civil remedies be provided for civil rights and claims and that civil wrongs, whether they consist of infringements of private rights in the enjoyment of life, liberty, property or otherwise, be made good, so far as practicable, by compensation and satisfaction, or restrained, if necessary, by appropriate relief. It responds to the social need to give full and effective value to the substantive rights of members of society which would otherwise be diminished or denuded of worth or even reality.'

Effective access to the enforcement of rights and the delivery of remedies depends on an accessible and effective system of litigation. Lord Diplock drew attention to the constitutional role of our system of justice and the constitutional right which individuals have to obtain access to it in *Bremer v South India Shipping Corporation Ltd* (1981) A.C. 909, 917, when he said:

> 'Every civilised system of government requires that the state should make available to all its citizens a means for the just and peaceful settlement of disputes between them as to their respective legal rights. The means provided are courts of justice to which *every citizen has a constitutional right of access* in the role of [claimant] to obtain the remedy to which he claims to be entitled in consequence of an alleged breach of his legal or equitable rights by some other citizen, the defendant.'

To which statement I would add that he is also entitled to access today in order to seek a remedy for the adverse effects of a breach of public duty."

Questions

1. Do you agree that it is important for law students to have an understanding of dispute resolution which takes place outside of the courts? Give reasons for your answer.

2. Can you think of any reasons why disputants might prefer to have their dispute resolved in a private forum? Can you think of any disadvantages of legal disputes being resolved outside of the courts?

3. What is the relationship between the trial and the rule of law?

4. What is adjudication? How many different systems other than the courts can you identify which make use of this type of dispute resolution?

III. KEY CHARACTERISTICS OF THE TRIAL

A number of features of adjudication in common law jurisdictions distinguish them from trials which evolved in civil legal systems. The most important of these is that they are conducted according to adversarial principles.

A. Adversarial and inquisitorial systems

The following extract from Farrar and Dugdale explains the distinction between the adversarial approach and trials organised around inquisitorial principles.

John D. Farrar and Anthony M. Dugdale, *Introduction to Legal Method*, 3rd edn (London: Sweet and Maxwell, 1990), pp.62–73:

"It might seem obvious that to solve a dispute you must first discover the true facts, but we should remember that this has not always been the case in our legal system and neither is it entirely the case today. For much of the Middle Ages our courts did not find the facts at all, rather they presided over an ordeal. If the disputant survived the ordeal, e.g. his hand had not festered after being burnt by a hot iron, then God had intervened in his favour and that proved his allegations. This method of resolving disputes is often referred to as that of 'Proof' as opposed to 'Trial'. It worked because it was acceptable to the parties. Today it would seem irrational and hence unacceptable but we still accept other methods which do not involve finding the facts, e.g. mediation of industrial disputes. To understand why this is so we should perhaps remember one further point; there is often no absolute, irrefutable way of determining what facts are true. Truth is as elusive in this as in other contexts. Consequently the question is not how we should find the truth but rather what are the acceptable means of dealing with a dispute as to the facts. In this chapter we shall examine the two main approaches taken by adjudicators, the adversarial and inquisitorial methods, and then after comparing the merits of these methods, examine briefly the other approaches adopted in our society.

The adversarial method

The adversarial method is one which gives the parties and their lawyers a great deal of control over the way in which facts are collected and presented. Each party to the dispute will collect its own evidence in the form of witnesses, expert opinions, etc, and will present that evidence to the court in the way most favourable to its own version of the facts and adverse to that of the other party. The role of the judge is limited to that of an umpire, ensuring that the evidence is presented in accordance with certain ground rules such as the rule that a lawyer must not ask his own party's witnesses questions which 'lead' them to a particular answer, e.g., 'You did see X, didn't you?' The judge must not intervene to question a witness himself save to clarify an ambiguity in the witness's answers. When all the evidence has been presented he must decide which version of the facts he prefers. He may very well feel that some important evidence is missing, that the lawyers have failed to ask the right questions or call all the relevant witnesses but there is nothing he can do about that. He must make up his mind on the basis of the evidence presented by the two adversaries.

The inquisitorial method

The characteristic of this method lies in the fact that the adjudicating body has considerable control over the way in which the evidence is collected and presented. Just as there are varieties of adversarial method, there are also varieties of inquisitorial method. We can illustrate two such by reference to the system for determining disputes about Industrial Injury Benefit. A person is entitled to benefit if he satisfies a number of conditions including (1) that he is an employee rather than being self-employed and (2) that his injury was caused by an accident at work. Disputes as to the first issue are determined by a government minister, the Secretary of State. In practice this usually means that a civil service lawyer will conduct an inquiry and report to the minister who will then make his decision. If the decision goes against the claimant he can appeal to the ordinary courts and have the decision overturned if it was supported by no evidence. Subject to this check, the process is a good illustration of purely inquisitorial method, with the decision maker or his investigator in absolute control of the collection of evidence. Disputes as to the second issue are resolved by a tribunal. At first sight the proceedings before the tribunal may appear adversarial in nature; the claimant will present his case and then the social security officer will present the administration's view of the facts. But appearance deceives; the officer is regarded more as an investigator providing information for the tribunal than as an adversary of the claimant; similarly the claimant's role is to provide information and answer questions. The tribunal controls the proceedings: indeed, it may appoint its own expert assessor. The method is modified inquisitorial: the tribunal does not investigate itself but adopts an inquisitorial attitude whilst relying on the information and investigation of others."

Distinctions between adversarial and inquisitorial systems can be harder to understand in practice. In part, this is because few legal systems are organised exclusively around one model or because they change over time. This point is brought out in the following extract by McEwan.

Jenny McEwan, "Ritual, fairness and truth: the adversarial and inquisitorial models of criminal trial", in Antony Duff, Lindsay Farmer, Sandra Marshall and Victor Tadros (eds) *The Trial on Trial Vol 1: Truth and due process* (Oxford: Hart Publishing, 2004), pp.51–53:

"The current debate on the reforms in the Criminal Justice Act demonstrates the continued willingness of legal traditionalists to fight tooth and nail in defence of the adversarial features of the criminal trial in England and Wales. The common law tradition has many influential adherents who believe that the adversarial trial is the embodiment of procedural justice. The Philips commission of 1981 noted some of the shortcomings of adversarial procedures, but concluded that even if it were desirable to change over to a fully-fledged inquisitorial system, the effect would be so fundamental 'upon institutions that had taken centuries to build that it would be impossible on political and practical grounds.' Nevertheless, legislative reforms chip away at the purity of the adversarial model across Britain. Indeed, many jurisdictions find themselves with cause to reconsider the wisdom of retaining the harsher features of their adversarial inheritance; reforms in the pursuit of efficiency and reduced cost, the admission of reliable and relevant evidence and the humane treatment of witnesses are being considered and implemented all over the world. Yet, at about the same time, the criminal justice systems of continental Europe, never pure exemplars of the inquisitorial paradigm, have shown some impatience with certain elements of their own structures. Some have introduced more adversarial elements, so that now, anything resembling a truly inquisitorial system is impossible to find. Germany abolished the examining magistrate in 1975, and Italy in 1988. Could it be the case that civil and common law jurisdictions are evolving simultaneously from their opposite ends of the spectrum to harmonise naturally into a uniform, 'mixed' system? Such a development would certainly be convenient in terms of inter-state cooperation in the detection and policing of international crime, but there may be practical difficulties. Against establishing a more inquisitorial procedure in common law jurisdictions, it has been argued that putting the burden of inquiry upon the judge is reasonable where the source of the law is a code plus academic commentaries. But Anglo-American law is more complicated, and it makes sense to impose the burdens of effort and expense upon the parties.

If it were possible to start afresh, with a blank sheet of paper on which one could design the perfect adjudicative system for the administration of criminal justice, what would be the rational choice? The Chinese were effectively in that position recently. They consulted widely, considered the advantages and shortcomings of the kinds of criminal trial conducted in various modern states, and eventually opted for a system with many adversarial features. The reasons for this decision may have been political and historical rather than philosophical; whether or not in a perfect society one system could be said to be superior to other is not a question this paper can address."

Dugdale and Farrar distinguish between the adversarial and inquisitorial methods of resolving disputes but the answer to the question of *why* the adversarial system has become so important in an English context is left unaddressed. In the following extract, Mulcahy attempts to explain the attractions of an adversarial system.

Linda Mulcahy, "Feminist fever? Cultures of adversarialism in the aftermath of the Woolf reforms" (2005) 58 *Current Legal Problems* 215, at 218–220:

The Concept of Adversarialism

"Adversarialism has traditionally been perceived as the cornerstone of procedures which built on the early English system of law, with no parallel outside common law jurisdictions. Despite this common assertion, legal historians have suggested that it is actually a relatively youthful organizing concept for civil procedure. Evidentiary rules which reflected this approach only began to crystallize in the late-eighteenth and nineteenth centuries when the judiciary began to abdicate its inquisitorial discretion. Landsman has argued that, in the early eighteenth century, the court functioned as an inquiring body in which judicial questioning, direction and control were seen as fundamental attributes of the system whilst the role of opposing counsel was marginal. It is, in his view, only since the beginning of the nineteenth century that the courtroom contest became strikingly more adversarial and advocates and their cross-examination of witnesses was placed at centre stage. Miller has gone so far as to suggest that 'an historian at some future date may look back and declare that the so-called English adversarial system was—to whatever extent it existed—a mere blip in the 900 year history of the common law system'.

The adoption of an adversarial model of litigation has a number of practical implications, many of which have been challenged by recent reforms. Most notably, it is clear that the parties and their advisers are able to retain control over the gathering of information, the sifting and selection of evidence and the forms of inquiry to be used when interrogating the other side's evidence. It follows that witnesses are perceived to 'belong' to those who select, call and pay them. This is evident in the way that witnesses who could be of use to one side but are in danger of giving evidence that would be of benefit to the other side are termed 'hostile'. Indeed the Court of Appeal found in *Abbey National v Key Surveyors* that, on occasion, the experts could become more adversarial than the parties themselves. . . .

The Rise of the Adversarial Ideal

So how is it that adversarialism came to have such a hold on English litigation? It is clear that advocate-led legal proceedings are a relatively recent development in the history of English procedure and that judges were afforded a much more interventionist role in earlier centuries. The pivotal role of counsel took much longer to develop in the criminal sphere than the civil sphere. Defence counsel were virtually unknown in the sixteenth century because of the fear that they would slow proceedings down. It was assumed that the parties knew their case better than anyone else and could rely on a paternalistic judiciary for legal advice. The practice of having barristers in court became more usual towards the end of the eighteenth century, but was still not common, and counsel in criminal cases were not formally allowed to sum up on behalf of the accused until 1836.

Various explanations have been advanced for the development of the advocate-led adversarial system in common law countries. The first of these relates to the reluctance of the lay judiciary to get involved in the intricacies of the case being argued. There has been a long-standing and widespread use of lay adjudicators in English courts in the form of the jury and magistrates. Indeed, Anglo-American theories of court procedure have glorified novice amateurs as fact-finders. But in parallel with this rhetoric there has also been a concern that lay adjudicators have difficulties dealing with technical or complex issues. Over time judges sought refuge from getting too deeply involved in the finer details of fact by allowing the parties to make their own case. As a result it became the job of the parties to bring out the facts by way of spasmodic argument in the courtroom. As Damaska has argued: 'It is therefore no wonder that the oldest and most widely accepted justification for distinctive Anglo-American evidence rules is the need to compensate for the alleged intellectual and emotional frailties of amateurs cast in the role of occasional judges.' This devolution of responsibility for the technical aspects of cases gradually evolved into a procedure dominated by advocates and their cross-examinations.

A second explanation of the growth of the trend towards adversarial procedures in the eighteenth and nineteenth centuries is that the shift reflects loyalty to a particular vision of the relationship between the citizen and the state. It is no coincidence that increasing reliance on adversarial methods occurred in the same year as increasing adherence to the principles of utilitarianism and the glorification of the autonomous individual. It was in the classic period of *laissez-faire* ideology that the adversarial genre of proceeding obtained quasi-constitutional backing from the assumption that civil justice cases were best seen as a dispute between two competent and autonomous individuals, each of whom had their own selfish motivations for presenting the most persuasive case. According to this scheme, the role of the state was that of a mere umpire and its responsibility was limited to providing dispute resolution mechanisms in order to retain peace and harmony in society and to enforce the rights of individuals. Viewed in this way, we can see the growth of adversarialism as the classic liberal impulse to keep the state, in the guise of the judiciary, at arms' length from the parties.

The third explanation depends on a feminist analysis of legal procedure. This is a theory of adversarialism which is less often mooted in legal journals and deserving of more attention as a result. Put simply, feminists have seen the orientation towards adversarialism as a masculine one. Indeed, it has been persuasively argued that it is masculine moral philosophy which has shaped not just our litigation system but also a much broader trend towards suppression of the feminist voice within contemporary legal culture. Nowhere is this more apparent than in the courtroom where the hostile egotism of possessive individualism has been clearly marked. Brown has, for instance, characterized adversarialism as requiring 'high octane' masculine values such as performance, control, security of transaction and standardization for its survival. These values are in complete opposition to feminine approaches to dispute resolution."

Questions

1. Can you think of cases which are better suited to the adversarial or to the inquisitorial system? Give reasons for your answers.

2. Why do you suppose that common law systems have tended to adopt adversarial forms of adjudication while legal systems based on civil codes have veered towards the inquisitorial?

B. Trial by jury

The system of trial by jury has historically been seen as one of the great strengths of the English legal system.

Trial by jury became an important part of common law procedure in the early thirteenth century when the judges questioned panels of local representatives who were already present in court and were expected to have some local knowledge of the case or the litigants. By the end of the fourteenth century jurors were being treated as a group of judges rather than as witnesses.

Lord Griffiths, "The History and Future of the Jury" (1987) 18 *Cambrian Law Review* 5, at 6–8:

"The historical origin of the jury can be traced to the Norman Conquest in 1066 and the word jury, of course, comes from the Norman French—je jure, I swear. In its beginnings the jury had no concern with any trial process but was a device created by the Normans to bring the aid of the spiritual or supernatural to the administrative arm of government. In those far-off days the best way to guarantee that a man would tell the truth was to force him to swear an oath before he gave the information you required. Sadly, I fear, no longer true to-day. The first jurors were those compelled to give information on oath for the King's purposes such as the compiling of the Domesday book.

It was not until a hundred years later that Henry II, perhaps the greatest of all legal administrators, first introduced the jury into the criminal process. By the Assize of Clarendon in 1166 a local jury was required to present to the King's itinerant justices those suspected of committing crimes in their locality. But the jury took no part in the trial itself which was settled by battle or by ordeal.

It was Henry II who also introduced the jury into the civil process. By the Grand Assize it was ordered that in a dispute to the title of land a litigant, rather than have the issue determined by battle, might obtain a writ in the Royal Courts to summon a jury. These were knights of the neighbourhood who had to take an oath and say which of the disputants was entitled to the land. The first to have 12 oaths in his favour won the day—and herein probably lies the origin of the number of the jury as 12 and perhaps the seeds of the old unanimity rule.

The next step forward came as a result of Pope Innocent III issuing an edict in 1215 forbidding trial by ordeal. Trial by battle had never been popular with the English, perhaps they were smaller than the Normans; and so deprived of the opportunity of settling guilt by ordeal the judges looked for some alternative. They turned to the jury. Would the accused 'put himself upon his country'—would he accepted the verdict of his countrymen. Now as those countrymen were the sale same men that had presented the accused for trial, and as they would be required to return a verdict based on their own knowledge of guilt and without hearing evidence, this method of trial was more popular with the judges than the accused. If the accused refused to 'put himself upon his country' he remained in gaol. But the judges' commission included that of 'general gaol delivery' and so various inducements were employed to persuade the accused to change his mind. Many brave men died under these inducements described as 'peine forte et dure' rather than accept the inevitable jury verdict in which case they died as felons and their lands were escheated and lost to their families.

Gradually over the centuries the jury moved from deciding issues on their own knowledge to trying cases upon the evidence. But it was not until about the beginning of the sixteenth century that significant assistance was provided by evidence and some two centuries later that it became established that a jury should return a verdict according to the evidence rather than of its own knowledge.

Throughout this period of its development the judges exerted a strict degree of control over the jury. If they disagreed with the verdict of the jury they did not hesitate to show their displeasure. . . .

There were other unattractive features of jury service in those days. Until the Juries Act of 1870 the rule was that the jury should be kept without meat, drink, fire or candle until they reach a verdict. . . .

And it is recorded by Blackstone in his Commentaries that a judge need not wait for a verdict beyond the next assize, but could take the jury with him in the next town in a cart. It was known as carting the jury and is, I suppose, the origin of the expression 'I'm being carted off to do so and so.' Poor jury—I often wonder how they got back.

Now I should like to turn to the radical changes in the composition of the jury that have been introduced during the span of my own legal experience.

Lord Devlin delivering the Hamlyn Lecture in 1956 said of the English jury that it was 'Male, middle aged, middle minded, and middle class.' This flowed from the provisions of the Juries Act 1825 which required as a qualification for jury service that a person should be a property owner or a householder—so all citizens who were not property owners or householders were excluded from jury service which included the great majority of young people and women.

Our male, middle of the road jury was required to return a unanimous verdict, and Lord Devlin ventured the opinion that 'it is very unlikely that in England there will in the foreseeable future be any alteration in the property qualification' and so far as the requirement of unanimity is concerned his advice was 'that it would not be wise to tamper with it until the need for alteration was shewn to be overwhelming.'

So much for the length of the most omniscient judicial foresight. How quickly things changed. In 1967 the majority verdict was introduced—it was not a bare majority as they have in Scotland, but a majority of at least 10 to 2. As with all reforms of the jury it was bitterly opposed at the time; but that it was a sensible and necessary reform I have no doubt. The spur that prompted it was the post-war emergence of organised crime on a scale we had not previously encountered, and with it the suspicion that one member of a jury was frequently being suborned either by bribery or intimidation. Such matters are always very difficult to prove but there seemed to be no other reasonable explanation for so many hung juries, particularly at the Old Bailey; one had after all only to corrupt or terrorise one member of the jury to prevent a conviction—it is very much more difficult to achieve if three members of the jury have to be turned and the risk of being detected in the process is much greater. Despite the opposition at the time to the introduction of the majority verdict it is, I believe, now generally accepted as constituting a satisfactory and safe verdict. I certainly think that it is."

In his seminal work on the history of the trial, Langbein continues the history of trial by jury by explaining how the rise of the adversarial trial impacted on the role and function of the jury.

John H. Langbein, *The Origins of the Adversary Criminal Trial* (Oxford: Oxford University Press, 2003), pp.318–321:

"The purpose of the lawyer-free . . . trial that had emerged in the sixteenth century was to provide an opportunity for the accused to respond in person to the charges and the evidence against him . . . lawyerization changed the theory of criminal trials in a quite unforeseen way. Across the eighteenth century the adversary dynamic altered the very purpose of the trial, by making the trial into an opportunity for defense counsel to test the prosecution case.

This change in the function of trial was reflected in counsel's growing effectiveness in diminishing or controlling what other participants in the trial said or did. Thus, in lawyer-dominated trials the prosecutor and the other witnesses on both sides ceased to speak in their own narratives; solicitors prepared them to testify, and counsel's so-called direct examination guided them through their lawyer-prepared testimony. Witness testimony was ever more hewn to fit lawyers' scripts. The criminal accused, if he spoke at all, was subordinated to his lawyers in like fashion. This adversary dynamic also affected the role of trial jurors.

Muting the jury
In the age of the [lawyer free trial], jurors had often joined in the conversation, to ask questions or to make observations. For example, in the trial of a woman charged in 1733 with stealing money from the victim's trousers in a bawdy house, a juror is recorded asking him: 'Were your Breeches up or down when you lost the Money?' (answer: down). At the trial of a defendant accused of receiving stolen property, a juror questioned him about his defense: 'Had not you one of the Warnings [that is, handbills] that were given out on this Occasion? For it is common to send them to Watchmakers as well as to Goldsmiths.' Jurors not only questioned witnesses, they sometimes asked for further witnesses to be summoned, and they also volunteered information about persons, places, and commercial practices.

By the last quarter of the eighteenth century, as the initiative in adducing fact passed to counsel, it became less common for jurors at the Old Bailey to remark directly on the facts or to question witnesses. When a juror's observation entailed a statement of fact about a person or an event, it amounted to unsworn testimony, in tension with the growing emphasis upon the cross-examination of testimony. At a murder trial in 1755 one of the jurors announced: 'I know something of the prisoner; may I be sworn now and tell it before my brother jurymen go out?' (The judge had him sworn and he testified to an incident of drunken behavior by the defendant.) Blackstone, writing in 1768, said the practice 'now universally obtains, that if a juror knows any thing of the matter in issue, he may be sworn as a witness, and give his evidence publicly in court.'

Toward the end of the century we see counsel's attitude hardening against questioning by jurors. During a trial in 1784 Garrow was cross-examining the prosecutor about the characteristics of the allegedly stolen property. When one of the jurors asked a question of a similar sort, Garrow protested:

> MR. GARROW. My Lord, if Gentlemen of the Jury, without seen the drift of my question, are to prevent an answer by asking others, and so to decide for themselves, I despair of doing anything for the prisoner.
> COURT. They may ask questions.
> MR GARROW. Certainly, my Lord, and as to the truth of this witness's evidence that must be considered by the Jury alone; but I submit it is perfectly novel for any body except the Court to break into my examination till I have done with the witness.
> COURT. Then go on.

Garrow's objection, although expressed as a point of sequence (counsel examines first), had a deeper import. Questions deferred often lose their context or immediacy, become inapt, and go unasked. Garrow's deeper meaning in this exchange was that lawyerization had clipped the jurors' wings. Adversary criminal trials did not leave room for jurors to participate in framing the inquiry, for the same reason it pressured the judge to stand down from such work. The system of adversary presentation of proofs was antithetical to nonadversary initiatives in adducing the facts, whether from judge or from jurors. The lawyer-conducted trial was no longer centered on the questions that, however clumsily, had been at the center of a contested altercation trial, namely, what really happened, and what did the accused really do. Adversary procedure refocused the trial on a different question—whether defense counsel had succeeded in raising sufficient doubt about the strength of the prosecution case. Defense counsel did not want other participants cluttering that inquiry with other questions, especially with questions about the truth. The age of the . . . trial as an open discussion among the participants was past."

Over time, even further constraints have been placed on the jury. Today juries weigh the evidence and testimony to determine questions of fact, while judges usually rule on questions of law. Criminal juries now decide less than 1 per cent of all criminal cases in England and Wales although they do try the defendants charged with the most serious criminal offences. Juries are unheard of in civil trials save for those involving libel and slander. In 2007 the government tried to further limit the use of juries in complex fraud trials in the Fraud (Trials without jury) Bill but this was blocked by the House of Lords because of the jury's contribution to the preservation of the liberty of the individual and to the legitimacy of Government. Despite regular threats on the part of successive governments to further limit the scope of juries important claims continue to be made about the significance of the constitutional function of the jury. The subject has sufficient contemporary significance for Lord Falconer to have published a consultation paper in 2005 which aimed to discover what more could be done by government to help jurors perform their role. Since April 2004 changes to the Criminal Justice Act have also been introduced to compel previously exempt people such as judges and lords to fulfil their duty to serve on juries. In the following extract, Cownie, Bradney and Burton explain some of the reasons for the ongoing popularity of the jury.

Fiona Cownie, Anthony Bradney and Mandy Burton, *The English Legal System in Context*, 4th edn (Oxford: Oxford University Press, 2007), pp.326–327:

"The role of juries within 'the English legal system' has been much debated over the last two centuries. The topic provokes 'comments which are frequently little short of hysterical'. On the one hand, Lord Devlin, a former Lord of Appeal in Ordinary, has described it as 'the lamp that shows freedom lives'. On the other hand it has been the subject of severe criticism by police, academics and politicians.

The essence of the jury trial in England and Wales is the idea that 12 people are drawn at random and, without training, asked to assess the factual circumstances that surround a particular case. Their verdict of 'not guilty' or 'guilty', given if necessary on a majority basis of 10 to two, is their view of the facts. The judge takes responsibility for the law, so that if the prosecution allege a series of factual hypotheses which, in the view of the judge, are not sufficient to constitute legal proof of the crime concerned even if they are true, the judge will direct the jury to find the defendant not guilty. At the moment, the prosecution have no power to appeal against a judge directed acquittal.

Although the jury can usefully be compared with lay magistrates and tribunal wing-people, in that they are all non-lawyers who nevertheless make legally binding decisions within 'the English legal system', jurors stand out as being unique even within this group. Jurors have no qualification in terms of knowledge or skill which distinguishes them from others within England and Wales. Moreover they are not merely untrained: since they sit as jurors for only a short time they do not even acquire that knowledge that comes with experience.

Various merits have been ascribed to the institution. It has been said that it prevents the application of unpopular laws and that it allows truth to be established against a background of community values and senti-ment. At the same time, it has also been said that the idea of the jury, with its emphasis on the importance of the views of the untrained amateur, 'which affirms that all grades of capacity above drivelling idiocy are alike fitted for the exalted office of sifting truth from error, may excite the derision of future times'. Juries have also been accused of being too quick to acquit. It has also been said that their decisions are sometimes based on a-rational as well as irrational considerations. Sifting these various views requires a clear view of the purpose of the jury. One cannot simply enquire into what the jury does and then decide whether or not it is performing at a satisfactory level. One must first establish what role or roles the jury *should* have.

Bankowski has argued that the role of the jury runs counter to the normal consensual processes found in the criminal court. . . . The jury, on his argument, is not there to find the truth but, rather, is there to vali-date truth. The jury can provide an alternative to the legal construction of truth which is based upon the doctrinal rules and the lawyerly culture which we have described elsewhere in this book. This view supports the opinion that juries have a democratic role to play, but does so at the expense of ascribing to the jury any superior ability to assess the facts in the case. The jury is there to represent community values, even some-times whey they run counter to the dictates of the law. Juries are there to decide what behaviour is permissi-ble, and when they find behaviour permissible, to find a defendant not guilty. On this view, for lawyers to say that a particular jury's decision was wrong is to miss the point of the jury. It is precisely the fact that [juries] may make decisions which lawyers, using legal criteria, consider to be wrong which gives the jury its place in the legal system. . . . The twin difficulties with this view are, first, that it ascribes to the jury an ability to represent a single community and, second, that it leaves at risk the person who stands outside the commu-nity. A randomly selected jury might find it difficult to represent any single community and might find this task even more problematic in the context of a pluralistic multi-cultural society. There might be some merit in an argument opposing community values to legalistic values bit it is less obvious that there is merit in opposing the values of 12 individuals drawn together in a random manner to those which come from a com-munity of lawyers used to thinking about the application of law. A jury which refuses to convict even though a person is legally guilty might seem defensible if it refuses on the basis of a community morality of fairness but less easy to defend is the jury who adjudges the defendant's actions guilty because they live outside the self-same community morality although they and other objective observers would say that they act within the law."

The results of a study of public attitudes towards the jury published by the Ministry of Justice in 2009 confirm that trials by jury attract high confidence ratings from the public and that the jury promotes civic engagement.

Questions

1. What do you consider to be the advantages of trial by jury?

2. How important do you think it is in the twenty-first century for defendants to be judged by their "peers"?

IV. BARGAINING IN THE SHADOW OF THE LAW

Despite the focus on courts so for in this chapter most cases which enter the litigation system are either abandoned or settled prior to adjudication. Negotiated settlements are agreements in which the claimant in civil cases undertakes not to pursue their case any further in exchange for payment or another remedy. In the majority of cases, this agreement will be expressed in a written contract which is enforceable in the courts. Negotiated settlement can occur at any time, but traditionally has tended to take place shortly after key events, such as the exchange of expert evidence, or shortly before the parties are due to attend a hearing. Plea bargaining is the equivalent process in the criminal justice system. This is the name given to agreements between prosecutors and defence lawyers that the defendant plead guilty to some charges on the basis that the prosecutors drop the remainder.

The obvious advantages of negotiated settlement and plea bargaining are that they constitute a quicker more predictable end to the dispute, save court time, reduce costs and allow greater flexibility. In a civil context it can also eliminate the risk of having to pay the costs of your opponent should you proceed to a court or tribunal and lose your case.

Whilst negotiation can be distinguished from adjudication, it is a mistake to view adjudicated and negotiated outcomes as separate phenomena. Negotiated settlements and plea bargaining often occur in conjunction with an assessment on the part of both sides of the strength of their case were they to have it adjudicated. This means that, among other things, the parties will have to assess whether they have legal precedents in their favour. It is in this way that adjudicated cases and reported judgements are said to bestow a bargaining "endowment" on the parties. In fact, the relationship between litigation and negotiation is such that the American academic Galanter has relabelled the process of agreeing settlement "litigotiation". In the following extract, Genn considers the civil practice in a UK context.

Hazel Genn, "Access to just settlements: the case of medical negligence" in A.A.S. Zuckerman and Ross Cranston (eds) *Reform of Civil Procedure: Essays on "Access to Justice"* (Oxford: Clarendon Press, 1995), pp.396–397:

"The vast majority of civil claims are settled without trial and in personal injury and medical negligence cases settlement is clearly the norm. One study found that 97% of successful personal injury cases settled out of court. In the recent Law Commission study of damages payments in personal injury (including medical negligence) cases it was found that 94% of plaintiffs receiving between £5,000 and £20,000 in damages had settled their claims out of court, and among those who received over £20,000, some 91% had settled their claims out of court.

Settlement is so pervasive that it has been argued that in civil litigation those cases that result in contested hearings are to be considered as deviant. Therefore, when we talk about refining litigation procedures we are considering the procedures by which the parties move toward settlement rather than trial. The conduct of negotiations and the path to settlement are largely dictated by court procedures. There is no separate settlement procedure. Settlement is achieved by preparing for trial—going through the ritualistic procedures determined appropriate for adversarial contest in open court. Parties who want peace and want it on good terms have no alternative, within the context of adversarial court procedures, but to prepare for war. 'There are not two distinct processes, negotiation and litigation; there is a single process of disputing in the vicinity of official tribunals that we might call litigotiation, that is, the strategic pursuit of a settlement through mobilizing the court process.' Once the parties are committed to litigation, there are no procedures that might facilitate creative outcomes or that might minimise conflict. Negotiation within the litigation context is 'fundamentally different from the negotiations that might occur over the purchase of a house or in the context of developing a political agreement'. Indeed, if one were to devise a system in which disputes could be rapidly negotiated to a compromise leaving both parties reasonably content with the outcome, one would be highly unlikely to start with anything resembling the rules of court."

A number of commentators have drawn attention to the problems of negotiated settlement. In a much cited article on the topic, Fiss outlines the dangers of disputes being settled away from the courts.

Owen M. Fiss, "Against settlement" (1984) 93 *Yale Law Journal* 1073, at 1085–1087:

Justice rather than peace

"The dispute-resolution story makes settlement appear as a perfect substitute for judgment, as we just saw, by trivializing the remedial dimensions of a lawsuit, and also by reducing the social function of the lawsuit to one of resolving private disputes. In that story, settlement appears to achieve exactly the same purpose as judgment—peace between the parties—but at considerably less expense to society. The two quarrelling neighbors turn to a court in order to resolve their dispute, and society makes courts available because it wants to aid in the achievement of their private ends or to secure the peace.

In my view, however, the purpose of adjudication should be understood in broader terms. Adjudication uses public resources, and employs not strangers chosen by the parties but public officials chosen by a process in which the public participates. These officials, like members of the legislative and executive branches, possess a power that has been defined and conferred by public law, not by private agreement. Their job is not to maximize the ends of private parties, nor simply to secure the peace, but to explicate and give force to the values embodied in authoritative texts such as and Constitution and statutes: to interpret those values and to bring reality into accord with them. This duty is not discharged when the parties settle.

In our political system, courts are reactive institutions. They do not search out interpretive occasions, but instead wait for other to investigate and present the law and facts. A settlement will thereby deprive a court of the occasion, and perhaps even the ability, to render an interpretation. A court cannot proceed (or not proceed very far) in the face of a settlement. To be against settlement is not to urge that parties be 'forced' to litigate, since that would interfere with their autonomy and distort the adjudicative process; the parties will be inclined to make the court believe that their bargain is justice. To be against settlement is only to suggest that when the parties settle, society gets less than what appears, and for a price it does not know it is paying. Parties might settle while leaving justice undone. The settlement of a school suit might secure the peace, but not racial equality. Although the parties are prepared to live under the terms they bargained for, and although such peaceful coexistence may be a necessary precondition of justice, and itself a state of affairs to be valued, it is not justice itself. To settle for something means to accept less than some ideal.

I recognize that judges often announce settlements not with a sense of frustration or disappointment, as my account of adjudication might suggest, but with a sigh of relief. But this sigh should be seen for precisely what it is: It is not recognition that a job is done, nor an acknowledgment that a job need not be done because justice has been secured. It is instead based on another sentiment altogether, namely, that another case has been 'moved along,' which is true whether or not justice has been done or even needs to be done. Or the sigh might be based on the fact that the agony of judgment has been avoided.

There is, of course, sometimes a value to avoidance, not just to the judge, who is thereby relieved of the need to make or enforce a hard decision, but also to society, which sometimes thrives by masking its basic contradictions. But will settlement result in avoidance when it is most appropriate? Other familiar avoidance devices, such as certiorari, as least promise a devotion to public ends, but settlement is controlled by the litigants, and is subject to their private motivations and all the vagaries of the bargaining process. There are also dangers to avoidance, and these may well outweigh any imagined benefits. Partisans of ADR—Chief Justice Burgher, or even President Bok—may begin with a certain satisfaction with the status quo. But when one sees injustices that cry out for correction—as Congress did when it endorsed the concept of the private attorney general and as the Court of another era did when it sought to enhance access to the courts—the value of avoidance diminishes and the agony of judgment becomes necessary. Someone has to confront the betrayal of our deepest ideals and be prepared to turn the world upside down to bring those ideals to fruition."

Concern about outcomes negotiated as a result of plea bargaining have also been expressed.

S.H. Bailey, Jane Ching, M.J. Gunn and David Ormerod, *Smith, Bailey and Gunn on the Modern English Legal System*, 4th edn (London: Sweet and Maxwell, 2002), pp.1140–1142:

"The importance attached to the accused's freedom to enter the plea desired is reflected in the 'plea bargaining' cases where it was suspected that unfair pressure had been placed on the accused. 'Plea bargaining . . . describes the practice whereby the accused enters a plea of guilty in return for which he will be given some consideration that results in sentence concession.' There are a number of ways in which this problem arises.

The first method can be accurately described as charge bargaining: a plea arrangement made between prosecution and defence counsel whereby a plea of guilty to a lesser charge on the indictment is accepted in return for the prosecution not proceeding with the more serious charge(s). The second method by which the sentence concession is obtained is a plea of guilty to the offence charged. A guilty plea attracts a lighter sentence. The amount of discount can be substantial. In some cases the discount will operate not only to reduce the severity of a particular form of sentence but also to alter the type of sentence from, for example, custodial to non-custodial. The prosecution are not obliged to accept a plea of guilty to a lesser alternative offence. If the prosecution do reject such a plea, the prosecution can call evidence of it in the trial.

The value of a guilty plea in the criminal process is that it reduces the time and money spent on achieving convictions, it obviates the need for a trial and the inherent difficulties of proof, it spares the witnesses an experience which can be both unpleasant and distressing, and it is alleged to demonstrate an attitude of contrition and remorse on the part of the accused. The advantages to the prosecution of offering concessions or inducements to persuade the accused to plead guilty are the certainty and economy thereby secured. These advantages must be balanced against the need to ensure that offenders are convicted of offences only when they are actually guilty and which properly represent the seriousness of their behaviour. The danger of the accused pleading guilty under pressure to obtain the maximum sentencing discount or failing to make a free informed decision about his plea should not be underestimated.

The dangers associated with sentence discount which increase the possibility of innocent people pleading guilty are well established:

> '[The sentencing discount], by encouraging defendants to convict themselves through a guilty plea, [reduces the effect of the due process] and the principle that the burden of proof rests on the prosecution. The prosecution of cases involving no more than vague allegations and other potential misuses of state prosecutorial power may be left unchecked. Moreover, the high guilty plea rate to which the sentence discount contributes means that there is little incentive for the prosecuting authorities to ensure that only properly prepared cases are brought to trial . . . A further problem is that the discount principle penalises those who stand on their right to put the prosecution to proof.'

The *Criminal Statistics for England and Wales* 2000 reveal that 76 per cent of those who pleaded not guilty were given immediate custody on conviction whereas only 64 per cent of those pleading guilty were, on conviction given immediate custody. In addition, the average sentence length for a not guilty plea resulting in conviction was 39 months compared with 24 months following the guilty plea.

For a truly guilty defendant and the prosecution, a plea bargain represents a mutually beneficial compromise. A guilty plea is obtained and so is a sentence concession. However, these concessions also operate (intentionally) as inducements and create enormous pressure on the accused who is at his/her most vulnerable in facing this most difficult of decisions in the criminal process. There are significant problems both with charge-bargaining and with the sentence discount.

The Attorney-General has issued guidelines regarding the acceptance of pleas by the prosecution. These draw attention to the overriding principle that justice must be conducted in public except in exceptional circumstances. When prosecutors accept pleas or reduce charges they should be prepared to explain their reasons in open court. Full records should be kept of discussions in chambers.

Although the early research of McCabe and Purves suggested that the guilty pleas obtained were justified in the light of the evidence and the benefit to the criminal justice system, subsequent research has largely demonstrated that defendants' changes of plea, especially when late, are contrary to the actual wishes of the accused, being based upon the advice of the lawyers, resulting in the supposed imprisonment of innocent people. Having noted the inability of the judiciary to control this problem, Sanders and Young conclude that charge bargaining has the 'potential to undermine adversarial due process and to increase the risk that innocent persons will plead guilty'. They point out that in 1993 the Royal Commission on Criminal Justice merely stated that it could 'see no objection to such discussions, but the earlier they take place the better: consultation between counsel before the trial would often avoid the need for the case to be listed as a contested trial'. The concern of the Commission was with the wastage of resources of the 'cracked trial', that is the trial which was believed to be contested, but at which the accused pleads guilty."

Questions

1. Summarise the benefits and disadvantages of out-of-court settlement in the civil justice system and plea bargaining in the criminal system. Are the problems you have identified of equal magnitude?

2. What factors do you think the parties take into account when deciding to negotiate in this way? To what extent do you think they pay heed to the bargaining endowment of the law?

V. Tribunals

So far in this chapter we have been talking almost exclusively about court-based adjudication and settlement which occurs in its shadow. In this section we will turn to tribunals, an alternative form of adjudication funded by the state. When adjudication in the courts is compared with adjudication in tribunals, we discover that the courts deal with only a small minority of cases adjudicated by state employees.

The distinctions made between the courts and tribunals tend to rest on the degree of formality employed. Court-based adjudication is the most formalised and ritualised of dispute resolution methods, especially when cases reach the higher courts. Considerable emphasis is placed on predetermined and highly structured rules of evidence which determine what can be said by whom and in what circumstances. Courtrooms can be imposing and the sense of authority is reinforced by the fact that most judges, barristers and court staff wear special robes and wigs. The question of how "court-like" tribunals should be continues to be an important theme in reviews of the justice system. As you read the material which follows, you might reflect on the suggestion that the virtues of tribunals are lost when they start to replicate the ordinary courts.

The origin of the modern day system of tribunals is often traced back to 1957 when the Government set up the Franks Committee. This resulted in the Report of the Committee on Administrative Tribunals, which was followed in 1958 by the Tribunals and Inquiries Act. The Franks Committee famously stated that tribunals should be characterised by openness, fairness, and impartiality. In recent years these principles have been reframed by the Administrative Justice and Tribunals council as openness and transparency; fairness and proportionality; impartiality and independence; and equality of access to justice.

We start our consideration of the function of tribunals by looking in more depth at the differences between adjudication in courts of law and administrative tribunals. We begin with two seminal works on the similarities and differences between the two which suggest that the distinction between the process of adjudication in courts and tribunals is that tribunals are much more flexible and informal. Tribunals also tend to have three decision-makers including a lawyer as chair in contrast to many courts in the English legal system which have just one. They are also less likely to be bound by precedent and to have specialist adjudicators who have a familiarity with the context in which the dispute they are adjudicating arose. The following extract explains that the type of cases considered by tribunals are also distinctive, as is their approach to dispute resolution.

Harry Street, *Justice in the Welfare State*, 2nd edn (London: Stevens & Sons, 1975), pp.2–9:

The Welfare State

"We have the main clue once we see that this trend [towards administrative tribunals] started when Lloyd George pioneered his National Health Insurance Act of 1911. It is the extension of the Welfare State which leads to matters being taken away from the courts. When the State provides benefits for citizens it has to devise machinery for ascertaining who has a good claim. When the State imposes controls there has to be a procedure which ensures that the citizen's freedom is not interfered with in an arbitrary manner. The 1911 Act set up special tribunals to handle contested claims for unemployment benefit. These tribunals worked exceptionally well, so much so that the sceptical became convinced that the judges were not the only ones who could do justice in disputes between the government and the public. These unemployment tribunals became the pattern for many others.

We usually call all these bodies administrative tribunals. The name is a good one. It distinguishes them from the ordinary courts. It also reminds us that it is a question of policy to be resolved by the Administration what arrangements are appropriate for deciding a particular set of claims. For instance, the Government decides to introduce a State scheme of unemployment benefits. It works out how the money is to be raised and prescribes the qualification for benefit, and the manner of making payments. It has to meet the situation where a citizen claims benefit and a government official does not accept this claim. It is purely an administrative matter how the Act is going to handle those contested issues. That matter will be resolved, not by laying it down that because there is a dispute it is a judicial question for a judge, but by asking what, in the circumstances, is the most efficient manner of performing this administrative task.

Links with government

We can readily see how decisions like that are closely linked with the Administration. Plainly the Administration is going to be responsible for the routine day to day payment of benefits. It will be less than say one case in ten thousand where there is an unresolved doubt about a claim to benefit. The Administration will be inclined to regard that one in ten thousand cases as just another administrative problem—calling for a special solution, yes—but it would be natural for it to think of recourse to some institution connected with the responsible department, rather than for it to say: 'This is a judicial issue, which must obviously be decided by one of Her Majesty's judges.' What I have just said about benefits is also true of granting a licence to do something or other, or of other ways in which the State now regulates our activities.

What is needed above all else is a cheap and speedy settlement of disputes. For these cases we do not want a Rolls–Royce system of justice. Some would say that there is too much of the Rolls and not enough of the Mini even in much of our trials in the law courts. . . .

The quest for speed, cheapness and efficiency

There are many other explanations for this movement away from the ordinary courts. Ministers and their top civil servant advisers have in this century frequently come to doubt whether the courts are the appropriate body to decide many of these new cases. They see rightly that many of these disputes are not merely about private rights: the public good on the one hand and the interest of the particular citizen on the other must be weighed in the balance. They look at many decisions in the courts, even at the level of the House of Lords, and find them wanting in that they appear to disregard the social element of a problem. For example, the courts have chosen to hold that there is no law against letting a tumble-down house; even though the landlord knew of the defects, he is held by them not to be liable to anybody injured on the premises because of their defective condition. Again, the courts held that traders who were determined to obtain a monopoly were free to combine together in order to drive a rival trader out of business. Administrators asked themselves whether judges who arrived at such decisions could be relied on to show a proper regard for the public interest, which would often be paramount or decisive in cases referred to them.

There was also a lack of confidence in the way in which courts interpreted Acts of Parliament. This was important because the new kinds of decisions were almost always ones where the meaning of a section of an Act had to be found. . . . Politicians feared that the courts might frustrate the social purposes of their Acts if they approached cases in this constricted literal fashion. A more serious charge has been levelled at the judges; that they brought to statutory interpretation nineteenth-century notions of the inviolability of property; that they would lean over backwards to find that a statute had not taken away an individual's property rights, even if expropriation for public purposes on payment of compensation was the cardinal aim of the Act. Of course it does not matter whether these suspicions and attitudes of our politicians and civil servants were well-founded; I am looking for the reasons why they diverted topics away from the judges. I am not saying that all their reasons were valid.

Whatever his other faults, the politician or civil servant is sometimes prepared to admit that he might have been wrong, and to change his mind. Flexibility is seen as a key attribute in a decision-maker. Yet the courts have long had a different approach: that once a decision has been reached in a case, it should be a binding precedent for other judges to follow in similar future cases. If the new class of cases had been tried by the courts, principles would have become rigid; courts would have to do for evermore what their predecessors had done, even though they were convinced that the earlier decisions were wrong. It was thought that this judicial inflexibility was inappropriate for many of the new kinds of decision.

The ordinary judge has to be a jack of all trades. This week he may try a murderer, and next week he may hear successively running-down claims, industrial accidents, claims by a deceived house buyer for recovery of his purchase price, and actions for breach of contract to deliver goods. Many of the new State schemes are extraordinarily complex; mastery of the laws can be obtained only by intense specialisation. Governments therefore thought it wise to set up tribunals specially to handle cases under any one particular item of social legislation; they felt that judges who were general practitioners could not be expected to have the necessary expertise and ready familiarity with these detailed new provisions. Sometimes it was considered that the neces-sary consistency of decision could be attained only if all cases were decided by the same person. Rent tribunals are an obvious example. Nobody would pretend that the reasonable rent of a furnished house or flat can be determined with mathematical precision. Public confidence would be lost if, say, comparable flats in the same block were given markedly different rent ceilings—we know how magistrates are criticised for having different ideas about fines for road traffic offences such as speeding. Continuity and consistency of decision should ensue if the same personnel make decisions in a given area.

There is another less obvious but equally important reason for the development of administrative tribunals. The High Court judge and the lawyer who practises before him have an instinctive yearning for certainty; they like their law to be cut and dried, to have it settled once and for all so that lawyers and their clients know exactly where they stand. There is a lot to be said for this view. We are all entitled to know, for instance (or to have our solicitor tell us), whether what we propose to do is a crime. If we buy a house, we do not want to be told that in the present state of the law it is uncertain whether we shall acquire a good title to it. But the administra-tors maintain that they cannot run the modern State like that. They talk of the formulation of standards. They see a stage between a fixed rule and anarchy. They find it impossible to legislate in advance for every specific instance. For them decision-making is not then some mechanical process; one cannot use a slot machine or even a computer in order to obtain the answer. In their statutes they use words like 'fair', 'adequate' and 'reasonable,' intending that these standards shall be applied to particular cases in the light of experience. They doubt whether judges will find it congenial to work in this way. They also observe that when judges have in the past had to handle such concepts they have been prone to crystallise what should have been merely instances of the standard into rigid legal rules from which they would depart only with reluctance. For instance, courts which had to decide whether a motorist was driving with reasonable care would be tempted to say, once it had been held that a motorist was liable for not being able to pull up within the range of his lights, that a new rule of law had emerged for all circumstances—that it was always careless not to be able to pull up within the limits of one's vision.

Whitehall did not want this to happen to their administrative standards. They see them as flexible. Take some examples from modern administrative schemes. Are premises educationally suitable? Is a building of special architectural interest? Has a man capacity for work? Is employment available in a district? We see that not only must these standards be developed in the light of experience; technical experts must assist in applying them. The working out of these from case to case is not for lawyers and judges alone; the educationist, the architect, the town planner, the valuer, the industrialist and the trade union official have to participate in this task. Neither politicians nor the judges themselves regarded the courts as ideally equipped for duties of this kind.

The judging process in many of these areas demands an adaptability which judges are not accustomed to display. A local valuation court is not content to sit back and listen to what the house owner and rating officer tell them about the rateable value of the house; its members go and see for themselves. A social security tribunal dealing with a claim for industrial injuries can interrupt the hearing for half an hour to go and visit the scene of the accident. Judges do not do this kind of thing (at least publicly); those who decide these new kinds of dispute must.

A related point is the traditional passiveness of courts—they act only when someone takes the initiative in bringing matters before them. If supervision is to be effective, then sometimes representatives of the administrative agency must unearth wrongdoers and bring them before the agency for a hearing. This approach is commonplace in America in such matters, for example, as monopolies, restrictive practices and false advertising, and there are signs that we may follow in some spheres of administrative control.

Unless a litigant engages a lawyer he is never at ease in court. The judge is aloof, the procedure is formal, there is an atmosphere of uncomfortable dignity. A man likes to be able to have his say in his own way, unrestrained by the niceties of the rule against hearsay evidence and the rest. He often does not want to be reprimanded every time—and it will be often—that he fails to distinguish between cross-examining a witness and making a point in his own favour. Administrative tribunals are sufficiently informal to permit these liberties; courts never are."

In this account of tribunals, Street clearly sees tribunals as superior to courts in many ways, including their ability to protect the public interest. By way of contrast, Abel-Smith and Stevens do not see such a clear distinction between the two.

Brian Abel-Smith and Robert Stevens, *In Search of Justice: Society and the Legal System* (London: Penguin, 1968), pp.224–228:

The difference between courts and tribunals

"A foreign non-lawyer who was unaware of the prestige of the British judiciary and of traditional concepts such as the separation of powers, which have come to be associated with courts rather than tribunals, might well ask what the difference really is between a court and a tribunal. What does it matter if some particular adversary procedures have come to be called courts while others are described as tribunals? Both are normally established under statutes. Both interpret laws made by or under statute as well as their own case law, although the latter may be more flexible under administrative tribunals. Both are normally chaired by persons appointed by the Lord Chancellor, although in the case of most courts there are no other members of the bench.

We would argue that such differences as there are between them are not in any sense fundamental but at most differences in degree. Tribunals tend to include a much wider range of skills on the bench; and the most significant hallmark of policy-oriented tribunals is specialization. The most cursory examination of the courts shows that the decision-makers consist of lawyers or laymen or both. Trusted laymen (JPs) staff the majority of magistrates' courts. They also sit with legally qualified chairmen at county quarter sessions. . . .

Tribunals, on the other hand, normally use as decision-takers and not just as witnesses, persons with specialized experience (employers or trade unionists) and persons with professional skills other than legal skills. Thus doctors sit on tribunals which assess the degree of disability in National Insurance claims. Those with expertise in housing problems and land prices sit on Rent Assessment Committees and on the Lands Tribunal. Employers and trade unionists sit on social security tribunals because their knowledge of labour practices is considered valuable. Tribunals are developed ad hoc, and their composition is decided to suit the precise function each is intended to serve. Specialization is therefore one of the most obvious aspects of tribunals, and it is the main distinguishing feature between the ordinary courts and the policy-oriented type of tribunal . . . Specialization is also a mark of the 'court-substitute' type of tribunal, such as the Rent Tribunals, the Rent Assessment Committees, Industrial Tribunals and the various social security tribunals. But again it is a question of degree rather than basic difference—the Companies Court and the Commercial Court are specialized lists within the court structure.

With respect to the court-substitute type of tribunals we would argue that the chief features which distinguish them from the regular courts are their cheapness, their speed and efficiency, their privacy and their informality. Civil courts, with the exception of Magistrates' courts in certain types of case, charge fees. Tribunals do not. Thus, Rent Tribunals, National Insurance Tribunals and the like emphasize lack of expense. Those appearing before such tribunals can be represented by persons other than lawyers, and this also helps to keep costs down—particularly where parties are represented by trade unionists. Persons must have the permission of the court to be represented by a non-lawyer in a county court or a magistrate's court, and there is no precedent for such representation before the High Court. At the same time, and even bearing in mind the dangers of excessive legalism, we think it dangerous that any form of legal aid is unknown before most tribunals. . . .

Tribunals are as informal as is consistent with an orderly conduct of their affairs. The attempt is usually made to create an atmosphere in which people who appear in person will not feel ill at ease or nervous. While the magistrates' courts, particularly in juvenile cases, go some way in the same direction, the physical layout of courts, the robes and modes of address are forbidding even for persons with considerable poise and self-confidence in any other setting. Moreover, as we have seen, the attitude of some judges and occasionally their remarks can be such as to humiliate litigants. But this difference must not be overestimated. In particular, the increase in legal chairmen and legal representation since 1958 has often eradicated this difference.

Another articulated difference between courts and tribunals as a whole lies in the more restricted rights of appeal found in many of the latter (although the Franks Report, which led to the Tribunal and Enquiries Act, 1958, was in many senses a victory for the lawyers and so led to a wider right of appeal from tribunals). . . .

Some lawyers would argue that there was a further fundamental difference between the two streams. Courts are said to be administering rules of law while tribunals are thought to be administering both law and policy. We would maintain that no such clear line can or should be drawn. Indeed it was the evolution of this myth which helped establish the tribunal system by convincing the judges of the ordinary courts that they were concerned with legal but not with policy questions. But continued insistence on this unsatisfactory distinction makes it increasingly difficult to entrust new matters to the courts or to merge courts and tribunals. Properly understood, tribunals are a more modern form of court. In some cases they may have more discretion than the courts, and this is particularly true of the policy-oriented tribunals. But certainly they have no more discretion than the Chancery Division has in handling trusts, wards or companies. Conversely the court-substitute tribunals are often as precedent-conscious as, and may even exercise a much narrower discretion than, the ordinary courts.

But we would reaffirm our position that there is no fundamental difference between courts and tribunals. We would argue, therefore, that every effort should be made to merge the two. A well-structured court system, with reform and flexible procedures based on the county court or Civil Tribunal, with specialized 'lists', might then offer a general adjudicatory system, with a spectrum of judges specialized in the many fields in which a potential litigant might be interested."

Such was the popularity of tribunals that in the wake of the Franks Report tribunals evolved rapidly in a piecemeal and haphazard way which led to considerable variation in approach and practice. The result was that by the twenty first century there existed over 60 different jurisdictions handling over half a million cases a year run by different parts of government and covering subjects as diverse as social security, employment, asylum, tax, land registration and mental health. The Leggatt Review of tribunals published in March 2001 found that the methods employed were often old fashioned and that the procedure could be daunting for users.

Sir Andrew Leggatt, One System, One Service: Report of the review of tribunals, (*www.tribunals-review.org.uk*, 2001), Overview paras 3–8:

Independence

"The Franks Committee said that tribunals should be independent, accessible, prompt, expert, informal, and cheap. The most important of these qualities is independence. Even in cases where the protection of the Human Rights Act is not available on technical grounds, users are in any event entitled at common law to a fair hearing by an independent and impartial tribunal. Yet nowadays when a department of state may provide the adminis-trative support for a tribunal, may pay the fees and expenses of tribunal members, may appoint some of them, may provide IT support (often in the form of access to departmental systems), and may promote legislation pre-scribing the procedure which it is to follow, the tribunal neither appears to be independent, nor is it independent in fact. Responsibility for tribunals and their administration should not lie with those whose policies or decisions it is the tribunals' duty to consider. Otherwise for users, as has been said, 'Every appeal is an away game.'

A Tribunals Service

There is only one way to achieve independence and coherence: to have all the tribunals supported by a Tribunals Service, that is, a common administrative service. It would raise their status, while preserving their distinctness from the courts. In the medium term it would yield considerable economies of scale, particularly in relation to the provision of premises for all tribunals, common basic training, and the use of IT. It would also bring greater administrative efficiency, a single point of contact for users, improved geographical distribution of tribunal centres, common standards, an enhanced corporate image, greater prospects of job satisfaction, a better relationship between members and administrative staff, and improved career patterns for both on account of the size and coherence of the Tribunals Service. It should be committed by Charter to provide a high quality, unified service, to operate independently, to deal openly and honestly with users of tribunals, to seek to maintain public confidence, and to report annually on its performance.

Administrative support

The independence of tribunals would best be safeguarded by having their administrative support provided by the Lord Chancellor's Department. The Lord Chancellor's policy responsibilities do not give rise to tribunal cases. He has extensive experience of managing courts, and already appoints most tribunal members. He is also responsible for the administration of the Judicial Studies Board, through which the training of judges is supervised, and the training of tribunal members should be furthered. As a Minister he is answerable to Parliament, and so to the public, for the proper functioning of our system of justice. He is uniquely well placed to protect the independence of those who sit in tribunals as well as of the judiciary, through a Tribunals Service and a Tribunals System analogous with, but separate from, the Court Service and the courts.

Helping users

It should never be forgotten that tribunals exist for users, and not the other way round. No matter how good tri-bunals may be, they do not fulfil their function unless they are accessible by the people who want to use them, and unless the users receive the help they need to prepare and present their cases. Working where possible with user groups, tribunals should do all they can to render themselves understandable, unthreatening, and useful to users, who should be able to obtain all the information they need about venues, timetables, and sources of professional advice. Some of the main needs relating to access identified by responses to the Consultation Paper are for original decision-makers to produce reasoned decisions in plain English or Welsh, and to give a proper explanation of the appeal process.

Legal representation

Tribunals are intended to provide a simple, accessible system of justice where users can represent themselves. So it is discouraging to note the growing perception that they cannot. Every effort should be made to reduce the number of cases in which legal representation is needed. Logically that can only be done by seeking to ensure (a) that decision-makers give comprehensible decisions, (b) that the Tribunals Service provides users with all requisite information, (c) that voluntary and other advice groups are funded so that they can offer legal advice, and (d) that the tribunal chairmen are trained to afford such assistance as they legitimately can by ensuring that the proceedings are intelligible and by enabling users to present their cases. But however good the support, there will always be a residual category of complex cases in which legal representation is imperative. Voluntary and community bodies should be funded so that they can provide it. Only as a last resort should it be provided by legal aid.

A Tribunals System

Combining the administration of different tribunals will provide the basis for a relationship between them. But that association cannot properly be called a Tribunals System until true coherence has been established by bringing within one organisation without discrimination all those tribunals which are concerned with disputes between citizen and state (in the guise of either central or local government) and those which are concerned with disputes between parties. Only so will tribunals acquire a collective standing to match that of the Court System and a collective power to fulfil the needs of users in the way that was originally intended."

The Leggatt Report's call for a more unified tribunals structure supported by an independent Tribunals Service was largely accepted in the White paper *Transforming Public Services: Complaints, Redress and Tribunals* followed published in 2004 and led to The Tribunals, Courts and Enforcement Act 2007. Under this new scheme tribunals remain a distinctive part of the justice system, separate from the courts and with a special responsibility to provide speedy, expert and accessible justice in specialist areas of the law.

Most pre-Leggatt tribunals have now been combined into the "First–tier Tribunal", a generic tribunal established by the Tribunals, Courts and Enforcement Act 2007. This is divided into six "chambers" each of which cover a specialist area such as pensions, tax and social entitlement. An "Upper Tribunal" has been also been created to deal with appeals from, and enforcement of, decisions of the First-tier Tribunal. Those who sit on tribunal panels in the First-tier and Upper Tribunal are now judges, with new members being appointed through the independent Judicial Appointments Commission. This shift in thinking about the status to be accorded tribunals is highly significant and will no doubt do much to raise the profile of administrative tribunals in the eyes of the public.

One important implication of the legislation is that tribunal judges now enjoy the same guarantees of independence as their colleagues who sit in courts. The office of Senior President of Tribunals has also been established as an autonomous position. The office is a novel, and entirely new constitutional entity with UK wide responsibilities. Unlike the functions of the Lord Chief Justice which are confined to England and Wales, the Senior President's responsibilities may extend to all or part of the United Kingdom, depending on the statutory extent of the each jurisdiction. The post holder is not formally subject to the authority of either the Lord Chancellor or the chief justices although they must cooperate on matters of training, welfare and guidance. However, the first Senior President has indicated that he expects to take his lead from the chief justices, as heads of the judiciary in their respective parts of the UK, on matters of common interest, so far as is consistent with his own statutory responsibilities.

Questions

1. Assess the argument that the growth of tribunals represents a "downgrading" of state sanctioned dispute resolution.

2. List the advantages and disadvantages of tribunals. What types of disputes do you think tribunals are best suited to (if any)?

3. If you were in charge of designing a new legal system, how would you go about determining which cases should be heard in courts and which in tribunals? Give a detailed explanation of the reasons for your choices.

4. What importance would you attach to the financial value of the claim, the seriousness of the alleged abuse, the needs of the litigants or a point of law in developing your new scheme?

5. Why are Abel-Smith and Stevens sceptical of the distinction between law and policy?

6. Do you think that tribunals and courts are roughly the same, or are they quite different from each other? Are they likely to become more similar in the post Leggatt era?

VI. Modernisation and the Recent Reform of the Court System

In the remaining section of this chapter we look at modernisation of the court system. One of the most striking features of the last decade has been the extensive process of reform which has been directed at both the criminal justice system and the civil justice system. We deal with each system in turn.

C. Reform of the criminal justice system

In recent years the Home Office has published a variety of papers aimed at reform of the criminal justice system. Examples include *Rebalancing the Criminal Justice System* (2006); *The Criminal Justice System: Simple, speedy, summary* (2006); the *Auld Review of the Criminal Courts*. In the first extract in this section, Bailey, Ching, Gunn and Ormerod explain the context of this reform agenda.

S.H. Bailey, Jane Ching, M.J. Gunn and David Ormerod, *Smith, Bailey and Gunn on the Modern English Legal System*, 4th edn (London: Sweet and Maxwell, 2002), pp.787–788:

"The recognition in the 1990s that miscarriages of justice had occurred in a series of high profile cases has led to a wealth of discussion of the aspects of the system that had contributed to them. Many related to the pre-trial stages, including the fabrication of evidence by the police, mistaken identification, unreliable work by forensic scientists, unreliable confessions, and non-disclosure of evidence. These matters were the subject of consideration by the Royal Commission on Criminal Justice (hereafter RCCJ) which was appointed in 1991. However, by the time the Commission reported in 1993 the government's central concern appeared to have reverted from the prevention of miscarriages of justice to the control of crime; and the RCCJ's Report itself, influenced as it was by the terms of reference drafted by government, did not have the prevention of miscarriages as its central organising theme. Its recommendations have been heavily criticised, and they certainly 'favoured the interests of the police and prosecution agencies more than those of suspects'. Nevertheless, its proposals continue to be influential in government legislation such as the Criminal Procedure and Investigation Act 1996.

Throughout the 1990s and into the new millennium, criminal justice reform continues to be driven by efficiency and crime control values, and increasingly by the influence of mangerialism and consumerism. Even taking account of the wide range of divers influences now brought to bear on the process, Packer's classic exposition of the two competing models of criminal justice—crime control and due process—serve a useful mechanism for evaluating the process. These and other, more sophisticated models, have been developed in an attempt to explain more effectively the interrelationships of the policies and principles at stake . . .

The government has unveiled its plan for overhaul of the criminal justice system generally and pre-trial criminal process will be significantly affected by the recommendations of the Auld *Review of the Criminal Courts*. This important Report examined the

> 'practices and procedures of, and the rules of evidence applied by the criminal courts at every level, with a view to ensuring that they deliver justice fairly, by streamlining all their processes, increasing their efficiency and strengthening the effectiveness of their relationships with others across the whole of the Criminal Justice System, and having regard to the interests of all parties including victims and witnesses, thereby promoting public confidence in the role of law'."

The response of the Government to the specific problem of miscarriages of justice led to the creation of the Criminal Cases Review Commission in 1997. Prior to it being established the Home Secretary dealt with applications from people claiming to be victims of miscarriages of justice. The commission now considers whether a conviction, finding of fact, verdict or sentence should be reviewed and can refer cases to the Court of Appeal where they need further consideration. In the period up to the end of February 2010 the commission had received a total of 12,451 applications and had made 447 referrals to the Court of Appeal. Nobles and Schiff explain how the need to establish the review commission was fuelled by a lack of confidence in the criminal courts.

Richard Nobles and David Schiff, "The Criminal Cases Review Commission: reporting success" (2001) 64 *Modern Law Review* 280 at 281–282:

"Setting up the Commission was a leading recommendation of the Royal Commission on Criminal Justice, a body whose own creation was announced on the day that the Birmingham Six appeal was upheld and their convictions quashed in 1991. That successful appeal followed the earlier successful appeal by the Guildford Four in 1989, and was followed in turn by successful appeals in a number of high profile cases: Maguire Seven; Tottenham Three; Cardiff Three, Stefan Kiszko, Judith Ward, Darvell brothers, Taylor sisters, and others. While each of these successful appeals was the result of specific grounds of appeal, and thus an acceptance by the Court of Appeal in each appeal that there had been an individual miscarriage of justice, press reporting on these cases was quite different. The media sought to link these successful appeals, and use them as evidence of a systemic failure of the English criminal justices system which, in the often repeated newspaper phrase of the time, was now itself 'on trial' While there was never a consensus as to the nature of this systemic failure, the certainty that the successful appeals were evidence of some general if submerged failures of criminal justice also led to the belief that there must be large numbers of miscarriages of justice waiting to be identified. The sense that the high-profile successful appeals represented a tip of some quite enormous iceberg was well evident in newspaper articles at the time, With influential journalists making this claim, it was not surprising that others repeated it:

‘[A] regrettable portion of those in prison are innocent of the crimes for which they were convicted.’

‘Waiting in the wings of the Court of Appeal is a legion of further, less notorious by equally shocking cases.’

Thus, if the task facing the Commission was to be read off from the newspaper articles that preceded its creation, it needed to deal with a potentially enormous number of miscarriages of justice. And this enormous number was a result of systemic failure whose exact nature, and the consequences of tackling it, had not been adequately identified or assessed. This statement of the Commission's task points immediately to the suspicion that it is an impossible one."

Questions

1. What can you find out about the various miscarriage of justice cases mentioned by Nobles and Schiff?

2. How do you think these could have been avoided?

D. Reform of the civil justice system

Concerns about the civil justice systems inefficiencies also intensified in the 1990s culminating with the release of the Woolf Report on *Access to Justice* and the Middleton Report which followed it. The background to these reforms is described by Darbyshire.

Penny Darbyshire, *Eddey on the English Legal System*, 7th edn (London: Sweet and Maxwell, 2001), pp.107–108:

"The problems of English civil procedure have been the subject of constant scrutiny throughout this century and much of the last. Prior to the Lord Chancellor's establishment of the Civil Justice Review in 1985, there had been no fewer than 63 reports, since the turn of the century on the same subject. With tedious and frustrating repetition, they all identify the same core problems so that the opening words of Chapter two of Lord Woolf's interim report, in 1995, give those of us who have been watching the legal system for some years more than a frisson of *dé-jà vu*: 'The process is too expensive, too slow and too complex.'

His Lordship quotes a number of famous judicial critics of the civil process who have all drawn attention to the fact that these problems militate against the provision of an accessible system of civil courts which is necessary if people are to be enabled to enforce their rights in civil law. Indeed, the very title of his Lordship's report, *Access to Justice*, seems like an ironic cliché, after years of concern over the lack of it.

The Civil Justice Review body reported in 1988. The review was remarkable for the breadth and depth of its scrutiny of the system, its radical approach and its success rate, in that many of its recommendations were soon translated into law, in the Courts and Legal Services Act 1990 and subsequent delegated legislation. Yet, despite the fact that its reforms were potentially the most radical since the Judicature Acts of 1893–95, they apparently did not solve those fundamental problems. No sooner had the dust settled on the new legislation than the two sides of the legal profession had established the Heilbron Committee, to produce a 1993 report on the continuing problems of civil justice and their proposals for dealing with them. The Lord Chancellor responded by commissioning Lord Woolf, when a Law Lord, to carry out yet another scrutiny of the system and suggest yet another list of proposed reforms."

Elliot and Quinn take up the story of reform from this point and describe the ills that were identified by the Woolf Report and the solutions that Lord Woolf and his team suggested to the problems.

C. Elliot and F. Quinn, *English Legal System*, 3rd edn (London: Longman, 2000) pp.355–356:

"In *Access to Justice: Final Report*, published in 1996, [Lord Woolf] stated that a civil justice system should:

-   be just in the results it delivers;

-   be fair in the way it treats litigants;

-   offer appropriate procedures at a reasonable cost;

-   deal with cases with reasonable speed;

- be understandable to those who use it;

- be responsive to the needs of those who use it;

- provide as much certainty as the nature of particular cases allows;

- be effective, adequately resourced and organized.

Lord Woolf concluded that the system at the time failed to achieve all these goals. It is possible that this failure is inevitable, as some of the aims conflict with others. A system based on cost-efficiency alone would make it difficult to justify claims for comparatively small sums, yet these cases are very important to the parties involved, and wide access to justice is vital. Promoting efficiency in terms of speed can also conflict with the need for fairness. Making the courts more accessible could lead to a flood of cases which would make it impossible to provide a speedy resolution and keep costs down. One practical example of the conflict between different aims is that the availability of legal aid to one party, one of the aims of widening access to justice, can put pressure on the other side if they are funding themselves, and so clash with the need for fairness. . . .

In the final analysis, it is for the Government to decide the balance they wish to strike, and how much they are prepared to spend on it. While conflicting interests may mean it is impossible to achieve a civil justice system that satisfies everyone, there were serious concerns that the civil justice system before April 1999 was giving satisfaction to only a small minority of users for a range of reasons which will be considered in turn. . . .

The civil justice system after April 1999
On 26 April 1999 new Civil Procedure Rules and accompanying Practice Directions came into force. The new rules apply to any proceedings commenced after that date. They constitute the most fundamental reform of the civil justice system this century, introducing the main recommendations of Lord Woolf in his final report, *Access to Justice*. He described his proposals as providing 'a new landscape for civil justice for the twenty-first century'. . . .

The reforms aim to eliminate unnecessary cost, delay and complexity in the civil justice system. The general approach of Lord Woolf is reflected in his statement: 'If "time and money are no object" was the right approach in the past, then it certainly is not today. Both lawyers and judges, in making decisions as to the conduct of litigation, must take into account more than they do at present, questions of cost and time and the means of the parties.' Lord Woolf has suggested that the reforms should lead to a reduction in legal bills by as much as 75 per cent, though it might also mean some lawyers would lose their livelihoods.

The ultimate goal is to change fundamentally the litigation culture. Thus, the first rule of the new Civil Procedure Rules lays down an overriding objective which is to underpin the whole system. This overriding objective is that the rules should enable the court to deal with cases 'justly'. This objective prevails over all other rules in case of a conflict. The parties and their legal representatives are expected to assist judges in achieving this objective. The Woolf report had heavily criticized practitioners, who were accused of manipulating the old system for their own convenience and causing delay and expense to both their clients and the users of the system as a whole. Lord Woolf felt that a change in attitude among the lawyers was vital for the new rules to succeed. According to rule 1.1(2):

'Dealing with a case justly includes, so far as is practicable—

a. ensuring that the parties are on an equal footing;
b. saving expense;
c. dealing with the case in ways which are proportionate—
    i.   to the amount of money involved;
    ii.   to the importance of the case;
    iii. to the complexity of the issues; and
    iv.   to the financial position of each party;

  d. ensuring that it is dealt with expeditiously and fairly; and

  e. allotting to it an appropriate share of the Court's resources, while taking into account the need to allot resources to other cases.'

The emphasis of the new rules is on avoiding litigation through pre-trial settlements. Litigation is to be viewed as a last resort, with the court having a continuing obligation to encourage and facilitate settlement. Lord Woolf had observed that it was strange that, although the majority of disputes ended in settlement, the old rules had been mainly directed towards preparation for trial. Thus the new rules put a greater emphasis on preparing cases for settlement rather than trial.

Case management

This is the most significant innovation of the 1999 reforms. Case management means that the court will be the active manager of the litigation. The main aim of this approach is to bring cases to trial quickly and efficiently. Traditionally it has been left to the parties and their lawyers to manage the cases. In 1995, the courts had made a move towards case management following a Practice Direction encouraging such methods, but it was only with the new Civil Procedure Rules that case management came fully into force. The new Rules firmly place the management of a case in the hands of the judges, with r.1.4 emphasizing that the court's duty is to take a proactive role in the management of each case. The judges are given considerable discretion in the exercise of their case management role. Lord Woolf does not feel that this will undermine the adversarial tradition, but he sees the legal professions fulfilling their adversarial functions in a more controlled environment. . . .

A proactive approach

Gone are the days when the court waited for the lawyers to bring the case back before it or allowed the lawyers to dictate without question the number of witnesses or the amount of costs incurred. In managing litigation the court must have regard to the overriding objective, set out in Part 1, which is to deal with cases justly. To fulfil this key objective of the reformed civil justice system, the court is required to:

- identify issues at an early stage;

- decide promptly which issues require full investigation and dispose summarily of the others;

- encourage the parties to seek alternative dispute resolution where appropriate;

- encourage the parties to cooperate with each other in the conduct of the procedures;

- help the parties to settle the whole or part of the case;

- decide the order in which issues are to be resolved;

- fix timetables or otherwise control the progress of the case;

- consider whether the likely benefits of taking a particular step will justify the cost of taking it;

- deal with a case without the parties' attendance at court if this is possible;

- make appropriate use of technology;

- give directions to ensure that the trial of a case proceeds quickly and efficiently."

The purported aims of the Woolf reforms were to reduce the delay, complexity and cost of civil litigation but they have also called into question a number of the adversarial conventions discussed earlier in this chapter. They have, for instance, undermined the autonomy of the parties and their advisers to run a case as they see fit. Moreover, the role of the judiciary has been strengthened. Since the introduction of the reforms, observers have witnessed much more proactive case management by a judiciary which has been empowered and encouraged to be much more interventionist in the run up to trial. Pre-action protocols now increase the power of the courts to regulate litigation behaviour by prescribing what should happen before proceedings have even been begun.

Other criticisms of the Woolf report have focused on its avowed aim to promote just settlements. We have already seen that the most common method for the resolution of disputes within the litigation process is settlement. It remains the case, however, that those who lodge a claim in the court system are still expected to prepare their case for litigation, in which they will state their opinions in an adversarial way, rather than from a standpoint of compromise. Despite its focus on early settlement, the Woolf Report may not result in changes to this litigation mindset.

Hazel Genn, "Access to just settlements: the case of medical negligence" in A.A.S. Zuckerman and Ross Cranston (eds) *Reform of Civil Procedure: Essays on "Access to Justice"* (Oxford: Clarendon Press, 1995), pp.393–395:

"The assumption of the proposed reforms is that through the twin principles of judicial case control and simplification of the procedures that facilitate adversarialism, problems of cost and delay will resolve themselves—settlements will occur earlier. One of the themes of the report is that 'the philosophy of litigation should be primarily to encourage early settlement of disputes'. The problem, however, resides in the means of promoting settlements. Attacking parties and their lawyers for the legitimate use of adversarial litigation tactics highlights the difficulty of achieving just settlements by means of court procedures. The rules of litigation are geared toward preparation for win or lose adjudication. They have not been designed to facilitate an efficient and relatively bloodless compromise between diametrically opposed positions. Will the new litigation 'tracks' and judicial managers adopt radically different rules designed primarily to promote settlement through bureaucratic case processing? Or might the new system simply represent a cut-down and speeded-up adversarial process which may exacerbate resource inequalities between the parties to the settlement process?

There is great variety in civil litigation: different types of disputes, different types of parties, and different configurations of parties. As a result it is not easy to generalise about the dynamics of litigation or to propose a litigation system appropriate to all. An instructive snippet of information which reinforces this point comes from a small survey of satisfaction with the civil justice system among corporate clients. Somewhat buried among the reported data showing widespread criticism of the length and complexity of the litigation process, frustration at delays and its implications for management time, there is one statistic which reveals that 77% of insurance defendants expressed satisfaction with the current litigation system. This, up to a point, speaks for itself. It suggests that the current system is operating to the satisfaction of at least some defendants with deep-pockets. What represents a problem or barrier to one party presents an opportunity to another."

More recently, in the 2008 Hamlyn Lectures, Genn suggests that some of the key goals of the Woolf reforms have not been achieved.

Hazel Genn, *Judging Civil Justice, The Hamlyn Lectures 2008* (Cambridge: Cambridge University Press, 2010), pp 55–58:

"Lord Woolf's solution to the perceived problems of civil justice was to promote settlement at the earliest moment and preferably without the issue of civil proceedings. The judiciary were to become case managers responsible for rationing procedure, guided by principles of efficiency, equality of arms and expedition. . . . The purpose of the new system was to provide a last rather than first resort for those in dispute. The intention was that cases should be settled privately and without the need to issue proceedings in court. Where proceedings had to be issued, cases should be settled as quickly as possible between the parties. Thus a principal solution to the notional crisis in civil justice was diversion of cases from the courts through early ADR and pre-action protocols. For those litigants who insisted on issuing proceedings in court, there would be proactive judicial case management, stripped-down procedures, reduction in orality, more emphasis on writing and strict timetables. Judges were given the power to divert cases to ADR and penalties could be imposed on litigants who 'unreasonably' insisted on going to trial rather than attempting ADR. By raising the financial limit on the small claims jurisdiction, a large proportion of county court business was pushed down into an informal, non-public procedure operated by District Judges in chambers, thus removing from visibility an enormous volume of judicial determinations.

Lord Woolf's intention was to reduce delay, complexity and cost in the civil justice system. The evidence suggests that post-issue delay has been reduced and that cases are being settled earlier. The concept of 'proportionality' in procedure has also been a constructive improvement to the operation of civil justice. However, the evidence also suggests that at least two of the objectives have not been met. The Civil Procedural Rules have become increasingly elaborate over the decade since they were introduced and the cost of litigation has risen. Indeed, in 2008, the head of civil justice, Sir Anthony Clarke MR, announced the appointment of Lord Justice Jackson to undertake a one-year fundamental review of the rules and principles governing the costs of civil litigation, commencing in January 2009. The objective of the review was 'to make recommendations in order to promote access to justice at proportionate cost'. The preliminary report of Lord Justice Jackson's costs review, published in May 2009, confirms the view that costs of litigation have increased:

> [I]t must be accepted that some of the cost increases since 1999 do appear to be consequential upon the Woolf reforms. Pre-action protocols and the requirements of the CPR [Civil Procedure Rules] have led to 'front loading' of costs. Also the detailed requirements of the CPR and the case management orders of courts cause parties to incur costs which would not have been incurred pre-April 1999. Where cases settle between issue and trial (and the vast majority of cases do so settle) the costs of achieving settlement are sometimes higher than before.

What the reforms have succeeded in doing, however, is removing cases from the justice system. . . . [T]he rate of issue has gone down in both the county court and the High Court and the number of trials has reduced. The only area of increase in judicial determination is in small claims, and the pressure here is clearly visible. While the courts may be dark, the offices of District Judges are heaving.

Although Lord Woolf did not talk about pressure on resources in his report, it is clear that this was a principal reason why the Lord Chancellor's Department commissioned the review. Whatever Lord Woolf's intention, and certainly he did not intend civil justice to be subsequently starved of resources, it has to be accepted that the terms of the argument and the language of the *Interim* and *Final Reports* were available to be used by government to support and justify squeezing resources for the civil courts. If settlement is the principal aim of civil justice, and private dispute resolution the new way of getting there, what matter if the civil courts are short of money?"

Questions

1. Do you find Genn's critique of the Woolf Report compelling?

2. To what extent should economic efficiency be the central goal of the civil justice system?

3. What do you think litigants want to achieve?

Useful website addresses

Courts Service, *http://www.hmcourts-service.gov.uk* [Accessed June 22, 2010]
Tribunals Service, *http://www.tribunalsservice.gov.uk* [Accessed June 22, 2010]
Administrative justice and tribunals council, *http://www.ajtc.gov.uk* [Accessed June 22, 2010]
Home Office, *http://www.homeoffice.gov.uk* [Accessed June 22, 2010]
Criminal Justice system portal, *http://www.cjsonline.org/home.html* [Accessed June 22, 2010]

Portal to sites of the key participants in the criminal justice system, *http://www.cjsonline.org/home.html* [Accessed June 22, 2010]

Office for Criminal Justice Reform, *http://www.cjsonline.gov.uk/the_cjs/ departments_of_the_cjs/ocjr/index.html* [Accessed June 22, 2010]

Criminal Procedure Rules Committee, *http://www.dca.gov.uk/procedurerules/ criminalpr_committee.htm* [Accessed June 22, 2010]

Civil procedure rules, *http://www.justice.gov.uk/civil/procrules_fin/* [Accessed June 22, 2010]

Civil Procedure Rules Committee, *http://www.justice.gov.uk/civil/procrules_fin/* [Accessed June 22, 2010]

Materials on the new Tribunals Service, *http://www.dca.gov.uk/legalsys/tribunals.htm* [Accessed June 22, 2010]

12

NON-ADJUDICATORY FORMS OF DISPUTE RESOLUTION

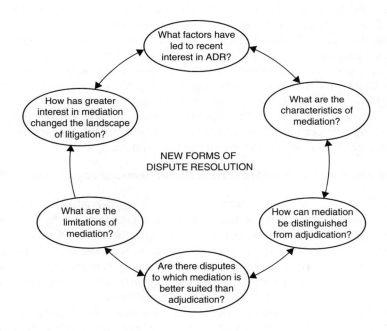

What factors have led to recent interest in ADR?

How has greater interest in mediation changed the landscape of litigation?

What are the characteristics of mediation?

NEW FORMS OF DISPUTE RESOLUTION

What are the limitations of mediation?

How can mediation be distinguished from adjudication?

Are there disputes to which mediation is better suited than adjudication?

In this chapter we continue our discussion of dispute resolution by looking at a range of alternatives to the courts which are currently being promoted by the government. By the end of this chapter, you should:

- understand what alternatives to adjudication exist;
- understand the various ideologies which underpin these methods of dispute resolution;
- be able to explain the key characteristics of mediation;
- be able to explain the concerns about these alternative forums which have been raised by academics.

The last two decades have witnessed unprecedented upheaval in the English legal system. In the last chapter we outlined some of the major changes which have been introduced in the way litigation is conducted and the additional efforts which are being made to resolve disputes before trial.

In this chapter we build on new understandings of the function of the legal system by looking at the increasing emphasis being placed on methods for the resolution of disputes other than trial or adjudication. Many of the changes we will be considering have been fuelled by concerns about the speed, efficiency and cost-effectiveness of litigation systems. But we will also be looking at changing ideologies of state-sanctioned dispute resolution and the burgeoning interest in non-adversarial approaches to disputes.

I. THE CONTEXT FOR REFORM

Although they are rarely discussed in conjunction with each other, changes to methods of dispute resolution in both the criminal and civil spheres bear some similarities. Whilst the Government reforms have largely been motivated by efficiency drives, policy makers have also been persuaded to instigate change in order to be more responsive to the needs of parties to disputes. Examples of this include the way in which party participation in the resolution of disputes is being encouraged through the mediation of civil and criminal cases and the involvement of the victim or claimant in the articulation of the impact of the damage they have suffered as a result of the crime committed. These shifts have encouraged intense debate among commentators from those who see the shift towards a "harmony ideology" as a serious threat to the public assertion of legal rights to those who feel that facilitating the meaningful participation of disputants in the resolution of their case is empowering and a victory for democratic process. In this chapter we will look at what is meant by alternatives to the adversarial process before going on to consider some of these debates in more detail. In the opening abstract, Lord Woolf reviews why the government has become so interested in alternatives to the adversarial process in the civil litigation system.

Lord Woolf, *Access to Justice: Interim Report* (*www.lcd.gov.uk*, June 1995):

"In recent years there has been, both in this country and overseas, a growth in alternative dispute resolution (ADR) and an increasing recognition of its contribution to the fair, appropriate and effective resolution of civil disputes. The fact that litigation is not the only means of achieving this aim, and may not in all cases be the best, is my main reason for including ADR in an Inquiry whose central focus is on improving access to justice through the courts. My second reason is to increase awareness still further, among the legal profession and the general public, of what ADR has to offer. Finally, it is also desirable to consider whether the various forms of ADR have any lessons to offer the courts in terms of practices and procedures.

From the point of view of the Court Service, ADR has the obvious advantage of saving scarce judicial and other resources. More significantly, in my view, it offers a variety of benefits to litigants or potential litigants. ADR is usually cheaper than litigation, and often produces quicker results. In some cases the parties will want to avoid the publicity associated with court proceedings. It may also be more beneficial for them, especially if they are involved in a continuing personal or business relationship, to choose a form of dispute resolution that will enable them to work out a mutually acceptable solution rather than submit to a legally correct adjudication which at least one party would inevitably find disappointing.

Despite these advantages I do not propose that ADR should be compulsory either as an alternative or as a preliminary to litigation. The prevalence of compulsory ADR in some United States jurisdictions is largely due to the lack of court resources for civil trials. Fortunately the problems in the civil justice system in this country, serious as they are, are not so great as to require a wholesale compulsory reference of civil proceedings to outside resolution.

In any event, I do not think it would be right in principle to erode the citizen's existing entitlement to seek a remedy from the civil courts, in relation either to private rights or to the breach by a public body of its duties to the public as a whole. I do, however, believe that the courts can and should play an important part . . . in providing information about the availability of ADR and encouraging its use in appropriate cases.

The scope of ADR

The various forms of ADR include some which resemble litigation in that they follow a relatively formal procedure and produce decisions which are binding on the parties, while others offer a considerably more flexible approach. ADR is used effectively in a wide variety of disputes, ranging from neighbours' quarrels to international commercial actions. Schemes may be court-annexed or independent of the court system, and may be used either before legal proceedings have begun or in the course of litigation. . . .

Developments overseas

The interest in ADR is worldwide. In common law systems, in particular, ADR schemes are being established and innovative experimentation is taking place. The extent of pro bono involvement of the legal profession in the United States is particularly impressive. In the course of preparing this report, I have been able to see some of these schemes at first hand and to discuss the operation of other schemes with those involved. All share an enthusiasm for the schemes with which they are involved and can usually quote impressive statistics to substantiate their effectiveness.

It should not necessarily be assumed, however, particularly in relation to the statistics, that the same results could be achieved within this jurisdiction. This is especially true of the schemes in the United States which are directed to achieving settlement of appeals. My attention was directed principally to those in New York, Washington DC and California. In each case, the models are very efficient and, according to the record, strikingly effective. In considering the results which are achieved, however, it has to be remembered that many of the appeals will be from decisions by juries and that there is a greater tendency to appeal in the United States than in this country. On the other hand, the cautious comments contained in the publication by the Director of the Institute for Civil Justice at the Rand Corporation as to the effectiveness of ADR must also be seen in context. She suggests that the findings of research into the reduction of cost to the public as a result of ADR are proving somewhat disappointing. That conclusion, however, is based on a situation where the existence of compulsory ADR at the court's expense attracts cases into the court system which would not otherwise be there. The result is that 'the aggregate cost to the court of providing arbitration hearings to thousands of cases may offset any public costs savings from reductions in the trial caseload'.

As long as the necessary care is exercised before translating the results experienced in other jurisdictions to what could be achieved here, there can be no doubt that there is an immense amount which would be of value to our court system which can be obtained by studying the initiatives in other jurisdictions. While what may be possible in the immediate future in this country may be limited, it is of great importance that we keep abreast with what is happening abroad, particularly in the United States, Australia and Canada. Fortunately, this is a subject to which the Judicial Studies Board is already directing attention. This should continue, if possible, on a more extensive scale."

Since the publication of Lord Woolf's report the new civil procedure rules have encouraged the use of mediation and empowered judges to direct cases to this alternative forum. As we saw in the last chapter, the objective of the new rules introduced in 1999 was to enable the courts to deal with cases through active case management by the judiciary. This included encouraging the parties to use an alternative dispute resolution procedure whether or not they were disposed to do so. Since the implementation of the rules there has been a significant drop in the number of claims being issued in the Queen's Bench Division of the High Court and the Centre for Effective Dispute Resolution has claimed that referrals from the courts to their mediation service have risen proportionally year on year. They predict that as the judiciary becomes more familiar and confident with the process that these figures will continue to rise. The judiciary has also supported the referral of cases to ADR by imposing cost sanctions on litigants who unreasonably refuse to engage in mediation; upholding the validity of mediated settlements; and enforcing contractual commitments to mediate.

In the extract from his report above, Lord Woolf makes much of the potential for mediation to improve the efficiency of the civil justice system and to make more effective use of judicial time. He also alludes to the claim that mediation does not just seek to achieve the same results as the court in a different way. Rather, the emphasis is on using a more participatory process to achieve qualitatively different outcomes. Many proponents of ADR have based their support on the claim that mediation is underpinned by an alternative ideology of dispute resolution. This more radical critique of the need for wider forms of "popular justice" is summarised in the following extract.

H. Brown and A. Marriot, *ADR Principles and Practice*, 1st edn (London: Sweet and Maxwell, 1996), pp.9–12:

"The references which are sometimes made to the 'ADR movement' and to the 'philosophy of ADR' both in the United Kingdom and the United States could create the impression that there is one single homogeneous group or school of thought guiding the development of ADR processes. While there are indeed supporters and protagonists of ADR, who could be viewed as comprising a movement, it is also a fact that these are drawn from disparate sources, with varying philosophies, cultures and practices. It is questionable whether there can be said to be one single philosophy of ADR, or a consensus that any one of these different approaches properly and authentically represents the 'true spirit' of ADR.

To establish whether and to what extent there is a philosophy of ADR, it may be helpful to examine ADR's main trends and its underlying objectives.

One of the motivations for ADR is commonly said to be the empowerment of the individual. Under traditional processes, dispute resolution is generally in the hands of lawyers, who use procedures and a language and reasoning of their own to resolve the issues for the parties, either by adjudication or by a settlement negotiated by the lawyers before trial. Empowerment of the individual is sometimes linked, especially by some involved in community mediation, with a move away from 'professionalisation'. The 'core of mediation' in the family context has been graphically described as 'reconnecting people to their own inner wisdom or common sense'.

Undoubtedly ADR processes, especially the mediation of inter-personal and family disagreements, commonly tend to help with the empowerment of individuals, giving them greater responsibility for the resolution of their own issues. Insofar as the processes are consensual (which accords with the prevalent view of ADR) the fact that parties need to reach their own resolution and do not depend on a third party to decide for them is itself empowering.

However, not all ADR involves empowerment to any significant extent: in some forms ADR may be a desirable, effective, cost-efficient and speedy form of dispute resolution; but it may not necessarily empower the disputants, other than leaving them with control over the outcome of their dispute, so far as they can jointly agree on this. There is indeed an argument that in some cases, where there are severe power imbalances between the parties, ADR is not empowering and may in fact be inappropriate. That argument . . . is a factor against which the empowerment notion should be viewed. As to the suggestion that ADR is empowering in that it represents a move away from professionalisation, this is countered by the fact that in many forms of ADR there are substantial contributions of skill, expertise and professionalism by the neutral as well as those who may be representing the parties. In any event, even those uneasy about professionalisation acknowledge that it is 'an ambiguous concept' which can refer to elements of professional activity perceived as dubious such as elitism, detachment and client disempowerment; or to those more positive and inherent features of professions, such as independence, training, responsibility, expertise and a commitment to appropriate values.

Another motivation for ADR is sometimes said to be the principle of 'co-operative problem solving'. This them underlies much of the theory of ADR and explains why much of the ADR literature . . . includes sections dealing with theories and strategies of negotiation, including in particular problem-solving theories of negotiation.

However, while experience shows that in many cases there is a shift during the ADR process to a more positive and collaborative approach to the resolution of the issues under negotiation, a significant proportion of parties in ADR cases may well be using the process as a means to an end in getting their case settled, without necessarily feeling any sense of being engaged in mutual problem solving. ADR does not depend for its effectiveness on the parties adopting a problem-solving approach. Such an approach can help to enhance the quality of settlements, but ADR processes are just as effective where the parties adopt positional bargaining, competitive negotiation, problem-solving modes or any permutation of these or any other approaches and strategies.

It is also often said that ADR is able to produce better outcomes than the traditional adversarial system. There are two reasons why this may be so. First, different kinds of disputes may need different kinds of approaches. If parties are not bound by the constraints of conventional litigation but can instead select a process, or permutation of processes, designed for their specific needs to enhance consensual resolution, then there must be an improved prospect of their finding better terms for the settlement of those issues. Secondly, mediation and other ADR forms involving more direct and intensive participation by the parties in settlement negotiations and the intervention of a skilled neutral facilitator will invariably tend to be more creative. There will be greater opportunities to establish the principles and detailed nuances of the settlement terms in a way which the court or an arbitrator could not possibly do, and which negotiations between the lawyers conducting the litigation would have considerable difficult in achieving."

Interest in mediation has not been limited to disputes in the sphere of civil justice. It has also been much debated in relation to the criminal justice system where it is commonly discussed in relation to "restorative justice". In the introductory section of his book on the topic, Gerry Johnstone summarises developments in the field.

Gerry Johnstone, *Restorative Justice: Ideas, values and debates* (Devon: Willan Publishing, 2002), pp.ix–x:

"In recent years, a new way of thinking about how we should view and respond to crime has emerged and is beginning to make significant inroads into criminal justice policy and practice. Called restorative justice, it revolves around the ideas that crime is, in essence, a violation of a *person* by another person (rather than a violation of legal rules); that in responding to a crime our primary concerns should be to make offenders aware of the harm they have caused, to get them to understand and meet their liability to repair such harm, and to ensure that further offences are prevented; that the form and amount of reparation from the offender to the victim and the measures to be taken to prevent re-offending should be decided collectively by offenders, victims and members of their communities through constructive dialogue in an informal and consensual process; and that efforts should be made to improve the relationship between the offender and victim and to reintegrate the offender into the law-abiding community.

During the past decade, restorative justice has been promoted—often with evangelistic fervour—as the way forward for criminal justice, which is allegedly failing to prevent crime and to provide victims and communities with a satisfactory experience of justice. These alleged failures are attributed, by restorative justice proponents, to the criminal justice system's adherence to a 'retributive' lens or paradigm, according to which offenders must be judicially punished and the state must take control of the process . . . Advocates have managed to persuade increasing numbers of scholars and practitioners working in the field of criminal justice that a move away from 'retributive justice' in the direction of restorative justice will solve the contemporary crisis in crime and punishment. Others, however, have greeted such ideas with a mixture of scepticism and distrust.

Such is the interest in restorative justice that there is now an abundance of literature—from a multitude of countries—explaining, describing, advocating or criticising it or specific aspects of it. For the uninitiated, working one's way through this complicated mass of literature is a daunting prospect, especially since—as Paul McCold 1998 demonstrates—there is a huge divergence of opinion regarding what is meant by the term 'restorative justice'."

Brown and Marriott continue this account of mediation in the criminal sphere by charting Home Office approaches to the topic.

H. Brown and A. Marriott, *ADR Principles and Practice*, 2nd edn (London: Sweet and Maxwell, 2002), pp.296–297:

"In the United Kingdom, interest in victim–offender reparation schemes developed in the 1970s. Compensation orders were introduced into the substantive law by the Criminal Justice Act, 1972. Community service schemes started around the same time sponsored by the Home Office, to help offenders re-integrate with their communities by carrying out acts of service. But it was only in the 1980s that actual reparation schemes began to be created. By then, there was an increasing awareness of victims' rights and needs, and the National Association of Victims Support Schemes had been launched. The Home Office established four experimental reparation schemes. These were in Coventry (funded by the Cadbury Trust, Martin Wright carried out a feasibility study, which was the first of its kind in England). Wolverhampton, Carlisle and Leeds.

Home Office interest in the experimental schemes moved towards reparation as an additional sanction of the court, rather than as a voluntary instrument of reconciliation. This was not approved by the experimental schemes. Home Office funding ended, and schemes found alternative sources of funding and support. Many of these developed into the victim–offender mediation programmes now in existence."

Restorative justice in the criminal justice system can take a number of different forms. It does not necessarily involve meetings with the offender. There can be face-to-face mediation if that is preferred, or indirect mediation; where the mediator liases between the victim and the offender at separate locations. The Criminal Justice service also encourages restorative conferences, including a wider group of people such as the young person's parents or friends. Sometimes restorative conferences are held even if the victim does not wish to attend, and the victim can have their views conveyed to the meeting by someone else if they wish. However the victim will always be consulted about whether and how they might be involved.

In their seminal account of mediation Bush and Folger provide four different accounts of the mediation "movement" which have been applied to developments in the criminal and civil justice fields. These help to streamline the various accounts and justifications for increased use of mediation into four main approaches.

R. Bush and J. Folger, *The Promise of Mediation* (San Francisco: Jossey-Bass, 1994), pp.15–24:

"While the growth of mediation in the past two decades is remarkable, what is even more striking is the extraordinary divergence of opinion about how to understand that growth and how to characterize the mediation movement itself. This divergence is so marked that there is no one accepted account of how the mediation movement evolved or what it represents. Instead, the literature of the field reveals several very different accounts or 'stories' of the movement, told by different authors and stressing different dimensions of the mediation process and its societal impacts. Thus, the movement is portrayed by some as a tool to reduce court congestion and provide 'higher quality' justice in individual cases, by others as a vehicle for organizing people and communities to obtain fairer treatment, and by still others as a covert means of social control and oppression. And some, including ourselves, picture the movement as a way to foster a qualitative transformation of human interaction. Indeed, these are the four main accounts of the mediation movement that run through the literature on mediation. We call them, respectively, the *Satisfaction Story* of the movement, the *Social Justice Story*, the *Oppression Story*, and the *Transformation Story*.

The fact that there are four distinct and divergent stories of the movement suggests two important points. On one level, it suggests that the mediation movement is not monolithic but pluralistic—that there are in fact different approaches to mediation practice, with varied impacts. The stories represent these different approaches. On a deeper level, the existence of divergent stories suggests that, while everyone sees the mediation movement as a means for achieving important societal goals, people differ over what goal is most important. The stories thus represent and support different goals, each of which is seen by some people as the most important one for the movement to fulfil.

Recounting the different stories of the movement is therefore a good way both to illustrate the diversity of mediation practice and also to identify the value choices implicit in varying approaches to practice. The following summary of the four stories presents each one as it might be told by its authors and adherents.

The Satisfaction Story

According to this story: 'The mediation process is a powerful tool for satisfying the genuine human needs of parties to individual disputes. Because of its flexibility, informality, and consensuality, mediation can open up the full dimensions of the problem facing the parties. Not limited by legal categories or rules, it can help reframe a contentious dispute as a mutual problem. Also, because of mediators' skills in dealing with power imbalances, mediation can reduce strategic manoeuvring and overreaching. As a result of these different features, mediation can facilitate collaborative, integrative problem solving rather than adversarial, distributive bargaining. It can thereby produce creative "win-win" outcomes that reach beyond formal rights to solve problems and satisfy parties' genuine needs in a particular situation. The mediation movement has employed these capabilities of the process to produce superior quality solutions to disputes of all kinds, in terms of satisfaction of parties' self-defined needs, for *all* sides.

Furthermore, in comparison to more formal or adversary processes, mediation's informality and mutuality can reduce both the economic and emotional costs of dispute settlement. The use of mediation has thus produced great *private* savings for disputants, in economic and psychic terms. Also, by providing mediation in many cases that would otherwise have gone to court, the mediation movement has also saved *public* expense. It has freed up the courts for other disputants who need them, easing the problem of delayed access to justice. In sum, the movement has led to more efficient use of limited private *and* public dispute resolution resources, which in turn means a greater overall satisfaction for individual "consumers" of the justice system.

This holds true for all the various contexts in which mediation has been used. Child custody mediation, for example, has produced better-quality results for both children and parents than litigated rulings. Small-claims mediation has resulted in higher party satisfaction with both process and outcome, and higher rates of compliance than litigation. Environmental and public policy mediation have produced creative and highly praised resolutions, while avoiding the years of delay and enormous expense that court action would have entailed. Moreover, mediation in these areas has reduced court caseloads and backlogs, facilitating speedier disposition of those cases that cannot be resolved without trial in court. In these and other kinds of disputes, mediation has produced more satisfaction for disputing parties than could have been provided otherwise.

The Satisfaction Story is widely told by a number of authors. Many are themselves mediators, either publicly employed or private practitioners or 'entrepreneurs'. Some are academics. Some who are both practitioners and teachers have been very influential in supporting this story of the movement. Also quite influential are the many judges and other justice system officials who tell this story, including former Chief Justice Warren Burger and many other judicial leaders.

The next two interpretations of the mediation movement, the Social Justice Story and the Transformation Story, differ somewhat from the Satisfaction Story. The Satisfaction Story claims to depict what has generally occurred in the use of mediation thus far, while the other two describe something that has admittedly occurred only in part thus far. In effect, these are 'minor' stories of the movement, but each is still seen by its adherents as representing the movement's most important potential.

The Social Justice Story

According to this story: 'Mediation offers an effective means of organizing individuals around common interests and thereby building stronger community ties and structures. This is important because affiliated individuals are especially subject to exploitation in this society and because more effective community organization can limit such exploitation and create more social justice. Mediation can support community organization in several ways. Because of its capacity for reframing issues and focusing on common interests, mediation can help individuals who think they are adversaries perceive a larger context in which they face a common enemy. As a result, mediation can strengthen the weak by helping establish alliances among them.

In addition, by its capacity to help parties solve problems for themselves, mediation reduces dependence on distant agencies and encourages self-help, including the formation of effective 'grass roots' community structures. Finally mediation treats legal rules as only one of a variety of bases by which to frame issues and evaluate possible solutions to disputes. Therefore, mediation can give groups more leverage to argue for their interests than they might have in formal legal processes. The mediation movement has used these capacities of the process, to some extent at least, to facilitate the organization of relatively powerless individuals into communities of interest. As a result, those common interests have been pursued more successfully, helping ensure greater social justice, and the individuals involved have gained a new sense of participation in civic life.

This picture applies to many, if not all, of the contexts in which mediation is used. Interpersonal neighborhood mediation has encouraged co-tenants or block residents, for example, to realize their common adversaries, such as landlords and city agencies, and to take joint action to pursue their common interests. Environmental mediation has facilitated the assertion of novel (and not strictly legal) claims by groups that have succeeded in redressing imbalances of power favoring land developers. Even mediation of consumer disputes has helped strengthen consumers' confidence in their ability to get complaints addressed, which has led to other forms of self-help and increased consumer power. In short, mediation has helped organize individuals and strengthen communities of interest in many different contexts—and could be used more widely for this purpose.

The Social Justice Story of the mediation movement has been told for a long time, though by a relatively small number of authors, usually people with ties to the tradition of grass-roots community organizing. . . . While the number of its adherents are few, this story has been told consistently from the earliest stages of the movement.

The third story, the Transformation story, focuses on some of the same features of the mediation process as the first two. However, it characterizes them, and especially their consequences, in distinct and quite different terms than the other stories.

The Transformation Story

According to this story: 'The unique promise of mediation lies in its capacity to transform the character of both individual disputants and society as a whole. Because of its informality and consensuality, mediation can allow parties to define problems and goals in their own terms, thus validating the importance of these problems and goals in the parties' lives. Further, mediation can support the parties' exercise of self-determination in deciding how, or even whether, to settle a dispute, and it can help the parties mobilize their own resources to address problems and achieve their goals. The mediation movement has (at least to some extent) employed these capabilities of the process to help disputing parties strengthen their own capacity to handle adverse circumstances of all kinds, not only in the immediate case but in future situations. Participants in mediation have gained a greater sense of self-respect, self-reliance, and self-confidence. This has been called the *empowerment* dimension of the mediation process.

In addition, the private, nonjudgmental character of mediation can provide disputants a nonthreatening opportunity to explain and humanize themselves to one another. In this setting, and with mediators who are skilled at enhancing interpersonal communications, parties often discover that they can feel and express some degree of understanding and concern for one another despite their disagreement. The movement has (again, to some extent) used this dimension of the process to help individuals strengthen their inherent capacity for relating with concern to the problems of others. Mediation has thus engendered, even between parties who start out as fierce adversaries, acknowledgment and concern for each other as fellow human beings. This has been called the *recognition* dimension of the mediation process.

While empowerment and recognition have been given only partial attention in the mediation movement thus far, a consistent and wider emphasis on these dimensions would contribute powerfully—incrementally and over time—to the transformation of individuals from fearful, defensive, and self-centered beings into confident, empathetic, and considerate beings, and to the transformation of society from a shaky truce between enemies into a strong network of allies.

This picture captures the potential of all branches of the mediation movement, not just certain areas in

which human relationships are considered important (implying that elsewhere they are not). Consumer mediation can strengthen and evoke mutual recognition between merchants and consumers, transforming both
the individuals involved and the character of commercial transactions and institutions. Divorce mediation can
strengthen and evoke recognition between men and women (even if as childless ex-spouses they will have
no further contact), changing both the people involved and the character of male-female interaction generally. Personal injury mediation can strengthen and evoke recognition between individuals who work for loss-
coverage institutions and individual accident victims, transforming both the persons involved and the character
of compensation processes and institutions in our society. In every area, mediation could, with sufficient energy
and commitment, help transform both individuals and society.

The Transformation Story of the mediation movement is not widely told in the published literature of the
field. . . . Nevertheless, beyond the world of the printed word, this story is given voice in informal discussions
among both academics and mediation practitioners. It is, as it were, the underground story of the movement,
often the motivating force behind practitioners' involvement. Perhaps it goes unstated because it is not easy to
articulate, or perhaps people are hesitant to articulate (or enact) it for fear of seeming too idealistic and imprac-
tical. Yet whenever the story *is* told, it generates a remarkably enthusiastic response, which suggests that it has
much more currency than its published expressions would indicate.

Here, then are three very different accounts of the mediation movement. Each of them expresses two different kinds of messages about the movement. On one level, each story is a description, purporting to recount
what the mediation movement has actually done and what its actual character is today (in whole or in part). On
another level, each story is a prescription, suggesting what the movement *should* do to fulfil what the story's
authors see as the most important societal goal or value that mediation can help achieve.

The final story of the movement differs from all the others. The first three all see positive effects of potentials in
the movement, although each sees them differently. The fourth, by contrast, sees only negative effects or potentials. It presents not a prescription for the movement but a warning against it. We call it the Oppression Story.

The Oppression Story

According to this story: 'Even if the movement began with the best of intentions, mediation has turned out
to be a dangerous instrument for increasing the power of the strong to take advantage of the weak. Because
of the informality and consensuality of the process, and hence the absence of both procedural and substantive rules, mediation can magnify power imbalances and open the door to coercion and manipulation by the
stronger party. Meanwhile, the posture of "neutrality" excuses the mediator from preventing this. Therefore, in
comparison to formal legal processes, mediation has often produced outcomes that are unjust, that is, dispro-
portionately and unjustifiably favorable to the stronger parties. Moreover, because of its privacy and informality,
mediation gives mediators broad strategic power to control the discussion, giving free rein to mediators' biases.
These biases can affect the framing and selection of issues, consideration and ranking of settlement options,
and many other elements that influence outcomes. Again, as a result, mediation has often produced unjust
outcomes.

Finally, since mediation handles disputes without reference to other, similar cases and without reference to
the public interest, it results in the "dis-aggregation" and privatization of class and public interest problems.
That is, the mediation movement has helped the strong to "divide and conquer". Weaker parties are unable to
make common cause and the public interest is ignored and undermined. In sum, the overall effect of the movement has been to neutralize social justice gains achieved by the civil rights, women's, and consumer's movements, among others, and to help re-establish the privileged position of the stronger classes and perpetuate
their oppression of the weaker.

This oppressive picture is found in all the movement's manifestations. Divorce mediation removes safeguards and exposes women to coercive and manipulative "bargaining" that results in unjust property and
custody agreements. Landlord-tenant mediation allows landlords to escape their obligations to provide
minimally decent housing, which results in substandard living conditions and unjust removals for tenants.
Employment discrimination mediation manipulates victims into accepting buy-offs and permits structural

racism and sexism to continue unabated in businesses and institutions. Even in commercial disputes between businesses, mediation allows the parties to strike deals behind closed doors that disadvantage consumers and others in ways that will never even come to light. In every area, the mediation movement has been used to consolidate the power of the strong and increase the exploitation and oppression of the weak.

The Oppression Story is clearly a different *kind* of story than the other three. Rather than offering a description of and prescription *for* the mediation movement, it sounds a warning *against* it. This story is almost as widely told as the Satisfaction Story, but by very different authors. . . . In general, many—although not all—writers and thinkers concerned with equality tend to interpret the mediation movement through the Oppression Story and to see it as a serious threat to disadvantaged groups."

II. The Characteristics of Mediation

Despite these differences in approach, most analysts continue to claim that a number of common threads generally run through most models of mediation. In the extract that follows, Brown and Marriott draw out a number of defining characteristics.

H. Brown and A. Marriott, *ADR Principles and Practice*, 2nd edn (London: Sweet and Maxwell, 2002), pp.128–131:

The use of a mediator

It may be trite, but mediation cannot take place without a mediator. Mediation brings a neutral third party into the dispute whose presence creates a new dynamic that does not exist when only the parties themselves or their representatives undertake direct negotiation. This element of third party intercession can be very helpful to the resolution process, but some traditional litigators find it difficult to accept. Edward de Bono in the introduction to his work *Conflicts: A Better way to Resolve Them* says that 'In any dispute the two opposing parties are logically incapable of designing a way out. There is a fundamental need for a third party role.'

The impartiality of the mediator

Mediator impartiality is fundamental to the mediation process. The mediator must have no interest in the outcome nor be associated or connected with any of the disputing parties in a way that would inhibit effective, even-handed intervention.

A distinction is sometimes drawn between 'impartiality' and 'neutrality'. There is a view that mediator neutrality implies that the mediator will not bring his or her personal values into the process. As this may be difficult if not impossible to achieve, some consider that 'neutrality' should not be offered unless the word 'neutral' is used specifically in relation to outcome rather than process. Generally, the concept of neutrality is given its everyday usage, which is defined in the Oxford dictionary as 'not helping or supporting either of two opposing sides, especially states at war or in dispute'. It is in this sense that neutrality is usually mentioned in an ADR context.

No authority to make a determination

If a mediator has authority to make any binding determination of the issues, that would be inconsistent with the notion of mediation. Mediators may, though, make decisions in the exercise of their management functions, which would not transgress this provision.

Authority derived from the parties

The mediator has no power or authority other than that given by the parties expressly or implicitly. If any party decides to withdraw power and authority from the mediator, that ends the mediation. If mediation is part of a court-annexed procedure, and the parties are compelled by the court to enter into it, they should nevertheless have the freedom to decide to end it without a resolution.

Any sanctions that may be imposed on parties for failing to settle in the course of mediation, such as the refusal of state funding for litigation, are likely to be geared to government budgetary considerations or the wish to reduce court lists rather than to the requirements of the mediation process.

Consensual resolution

The only binding outcome of mediation is one on which all parties agree. If the parties are unable to reach agreement on the resolution of their dispute, they will be free to have their issues dealt with in some other forum.

Resolution objective

Mediation has as its primary objective the resolution of differences between the disputants by negotiated agreement. Because of the need to reach agreement and because the process allows more ingenuity and nuances than is usually possible in the adversarial process, mediation aims for a resolution which maximises all parties' interests. (This is sometimes referred to as a 'win–win' outcome, as distinct from litigation, which is said to produce a 'win–lose' outcome.)

Facilitation of negotiation

The mediator's primary role is to assist the parties with their negotiations. All mediation involves some element of such facilitation, which is enhanced by the mediator's communication, negotiation and other skills. The mediator does not, however, negotiate with the parties, but rather assists them to negotiate with one another.

Providing a secure negotiating environment

Mediation should create conditions that are conducive to discussion, negotiation and the exploration of settlement options and possibilities. This applies to the physical arrangements, to the ambience which is created by the mediator, and to the ground rules regulating the process. Parties need to be able to negotiate freely, without fear, threat or harassment. It also includes the arrangements for confidentiality and evidentiary privilege.

Empowerment of the parties

In traditional adjudicatory processes, dispute resolution is generally in the hands of lawyers, who use procedures and a language and reasoning of their own to resolve the issues for the parties.

Empowerment means the increase in the parties' ability to make their own decisions and the corresponding reduction of their dependence on third parties including professional advisers. This arises in mediation because the parties are directly involved in the process and retain control over whether they wish to settle and on what terms. In some cases, particularly in family and inter-personal issues, the dynamic of the process, the way in which communications can be improved, and the attention given to power imbalances can all have an empowering effect on an individual party.

Empowerment is an important part of ADR, and to some, an essential one. This is true in the sense that parties will always have control over the outcome. However, the personal empowerment aspect may sometimes be minimal or virtually non-existent. For example, in commercial cases the parties may choose to be represented by lawyers in the mediation, or in family issues the couple may not seek empowerment but may merely wish to have help in sorting out practical matters.

Confidentiality

Although parties are free to agree that mediation is to be public or that the outcome is to be publicised in some way, one of the principles in all forms of mediation is that it is by nature a private and confidential process. The mediator will invariably offer confidentiality to the parties, who may be asked also to agree to mutual confidentiality.

No substitute for independent advice

Whatever model of mediation is followed, and whether or not an evaluation is made, a mediator will not ordinarily give advice to the parties, either individually or jointly, though information may well be provided. In mediation, parties are responsible for their own decisions, and where appropriate may need to take independent advice, whether on legal, technical or other issues, but not from the mediator.

Containment of escalation

Whereas the adversarial system has a tendency towards a competitive approach and confrontational communications, the mediation process tends to encourage a problem-solving approach, to facilitate communications and to allow for feelings to be expressed in a controlled and constructive forum. Consequently, mediation generally has the effect of containing escalation of issues and antagonism. This in turn means that the parties in disagreement who have a relationships with one another, whether business, family or personal, are generally more likely to sustain that relationship, or to vary or end it in a more co-operative way, by using mediation than through the adversarial process."

In the following extract Genn describes the format of a typical mediation of a civil dispute. In doing so she draws on her own evaluation of the Central London County Court mediation pilot scheme.

Hazel Genn, *Mediation in Action* (London: Calouste Gulbenkian Foundation, 1999), pp.23–25:

What happens in mediation
"Mediation sessions can take place in rooms in a court building, in the offices of a solicitor or barrister or other professional, or even in a hotel. The length of the mediation session tends to depend on the type of dispute and whether or not it is part of a court scheme. Disputes over relatively small sums of money or where the issues are not very complicated can usually be mediated in half a day, whereas in some large commercial disputes the mediation might last for more than a day. The Central London County Court limits its mediation sessions to three hours.

It is important for the mediation sessions to be in comfortable surroundings and to be conducted in an atmosphere that is informal but orderly. The mediator and disputing parties (and their legal or other representatives if present) are usually seated around a table. Mediators have different ways of seating people, but arrangements are generally informal to minimise any sense of confrontation. Sometimes mediators dispense with a table and have everyone sitting in a circle.

Preliminary joint meeting
The parties are usually welcomed at a preliminary joint meeting and congratulated on having taken the step of coming to mediate their dispute. The mediator may then give a little information about him- or herself before going on to explain how the session is going to proceed, what the role of the mediator will be and what the objectives are. He or she will stress that the process is entirely voluntary and that either party is free to leave at any time if they are unhappy with the process.

Sometimes the early stages of these introductory joint meetings can be somewhat tense, especially if it is the first time that the disputing parties have been face to face, or even spoken, since the beginning of the dispute and they feel awkward or embarrassed. The mediator has to reduce tension and create a calm and constructive atmosphere. Solicitors or other representatives, if present, can help by maintaining a courteous and professional approach. Most solicitors are extremely good at this.

The opening joint session is a very important opportunity for both parties to make clear to each other the most serious aspects of their grievance and to communicate exactly what it is that they are concerned about. The mediator will usually give each about fifteen minutes to summarise, in their own words and without interruption, the nature of their complaint against the other side. People tend to find that this opportunity is a very satisfying part of the process and helpful in reaching a compromise agreement to end the dispute.

However, there are some cases where relations between the parties are so bad that they do not want to be in the same room together. If this occurs, mediators will carry out the mediation without any joint sessions, and merely shuttle between the parties.

Private meetings
After the opening joint session each side goes into a separate room for private meetings with the mediator (together with their legal advisers or anyone else who is accompanying them). The mediator then begins a process of 'shuttle diplomacy', exploring with each party alternately the details of their case and discussing the strengths and weaknesses of their claim. Information given to the mediator during these private sessions is strictly confidential and he or she will only pass on information to the other side if given express permission to do so. During this process the mediator tries to establish where there is common ground between the parties

and to discover the scope for compromise, and will also try to identify the most important sticking points and to understand why the disputing parties take a different view of those points.

Usually after a period spent in private session the possibilities for agreement begin to emerge. The mediator will spend some time working out the exact terms of any agreement with each side to ensure that both sides are happy with them. This stage can often involve some intense bargaining, with the mediator acting as the go-between.

Concluding joint session

Once a broad agreement has been reached the mediator brings everyone back together for a final joint meeting to work out the details and to draft a document setting out the agreed terms for the disputing parties to sign. The mediator ends the mediation session by congratulating both sides on having reached a settlement and will often invite them to shake hands before they leave.

This final session can be crucially helpful in setting the tone for future relations between the parties and in laying grievances to rest. Even if the parties have not managed to reach an agreement, the mediator uses the final joint session to draw attention to the progress that has been made in clarifying the issues in dispute, and in moving closer to a settlement."

Genn also provides us with a case study of a dispute in which mediation proved to be successful.

Architect v client

"An architect had not received payment of his final bill for work carried out on a private flat. After asking for payment for a year and a half he finally issued court proceedings and the case was mediated. The architect, who had not consulted solicitors, accepted the court's offer of mediation because he did not feel that the money at stake (about £4,000) warranted legal fees, but on the other hand he said, 'it is not a sum of money I am prepared to let go. This has taken ages writing letters and it would take even longer if I went to court.'

The flat-owner's complaint was that the final bill had been much higher than expected, the quality of some of the work was poor and, because of lengthy building works, relations with neighbours had deteriorated. He said: 'This is a classic situation of communication breakdown. For a layman this was a very big project. Supporting walls had to be removed. There was a great deal of stress about the building project, but we went into it with our eyes open and took great care to take precautions. Our consultants and advisers were the best. We asked questions as we went along but no proper answers were given. They never apologised to us. Never once. The effect of that one single project has led to a whole lever-arch file of correspondence with our managing agents and we have been threatened with eviction by our landlord because the owners say that the building might fall down!'

During the course of the mediation an apology from the architect was read out to the flat-owner, which said: 'The plaintiff regrets any inconvenience and stress that has resulted to you and your family.' After this formal apology the parties managed to reach a settlement whereby the flat-owner paid £2,500 of the outstanding bill and both sides agreed that would be an end to litigation. In less than three hours the parties had managed to reach an agreement ending a dispute that had been going on for almost two years. At the end the architect said: 'I think mediation is a very good idea. It just short-circuits the whole business. Although I'm not happy with the outcome, the case was not financially worth pursuing further through the court. I haven't been to business school but even I know that!'"

In the extract below, Brown and Marriott give us a flavour of how mediation works in a criminal context.

H. Brown and A. Marriott, *ADR Principles and Practice*, 2nd edn (London: Sweet and Maxwell, 2002), pp.300–301:

Kinds of offences dealt with by mediation programmes

"The various victim–offender mediation schemes each have their own policy about the nature of the offence that can be brought to them. Many exclude serious violent and sexual offences, though some have no restrictions and may even gear themselves to cases that are more serious. Mediators will be careful to screen out parties who are too emotional or disturbed to handle direct meetings.

There may be a relationship between seriousness of offence and stage of proceedings at which it is brought into a scheme. A crime diverted before prosecution will tend to be less serious than one brought into the scheme following prosecution or sentence.

Offenders may be subject to an official caution, currently in the course of being prosecuted, or already sentenced. They will all have admitted guild: mediation is not appropriate where this is in dispute. They may be feeling remorse to variable extents prior to the meeting. Those with obviously cynical attitudes will not be accepted. One of the intentions of a meeting with the victim is to create a realisation of the personal harm caused and to encourage the offender to accept responsibility, so that some degree of change of attitude can be expected, often quite considerable, at least in the short term. The offender may be glad of the chance to apologise and to set the record straight, often also to offer reparation.

Some believe that it is in more serious cases, such as aggravated burglary or sexual assault, that victims have the most to gain from being able to express their feelings and come to some sort of resolution of the aftermath of the crime. Mediation has even been used in manslaughter and murder cases between the offender and relatives of the victim (usually some considerable time after the event). Mark Umbreit, writing about the transformative and healing power of mediation, observes that these powerful, if controversial to some, qualities of mediation have been observed in the use of mediation and dialogue in the United States between parents of murdered children and the murderer.

A significant proportion of crimes involving personal victims are committed by someone who is acquainted with the victim. A Home Office study showed that in half the cases it considered the victim and the offender already knew one another, at least by sight. Even if not, commonly they lived in the same neighbourhood, in either event creating the potential for dispute, especially in those cases where desire for revenge (by victim or offender) was a factor. Such situations offer opportunities for better understanding and reconciliation through mediation.

The Fife Young Offender Mediation Programme lists theft as the main crime brought into its scheme. Other offences mainly dealt with are vandalism, assault and road traffic offences. The Thames Valley Scheme specifies that only those offenders facing a caution are able to take part. The scheme is voluntary. Robinson suggests that 'police-based projects are inevitably concerned with less serious offences whilst court-based schemes can be expected to deal with the upper range of the magistrates' court caseload'.

Thames Valley Police provide a case study in their brochure of two drunken teenagers who smashed their way into a memorial hall in an Oxfordshire village in 1997. When arrested, both admitted the offence. Neither had previous convictions. The Parish Council initially wished to prosecute but agreed to participate in a conference. In the conference, the councillors outlined how the hall had become unusable and had closed down. Village groups had been affected. The young men's parents said how appalled they were at their sons' behaviour. The teenagers were very ashamed and offered to make amend by paying for the damage and helping by redecorating the hall. An agreement to this effect was signed, and the councillors, teenagers and their parents were all able to enter into discussions. The parish councillors said that they felt great satisfaction in having been able to participate. They and the local police were pleased with the outcome."

There are indications that more and more litigants are using mediation. Interestingly, a number of large City law firms, including some of the most traditional, have changed the name of their litigation departments in order to encompass arbitration and mediation. Provision for the mediation of consumer disputes which cannot be resolved at service level is becoming common. Government bodies have also taken a steer in these developments at national and international levels. In March 2001, the Lord Chancellor's Department (now the Ministry of Justice) announced that all government departments should seek to avoid litigation by using mediation and a year later the Office of Government Commerce published a dispute resolution guide for all those involved in the drafting of UK procurement contracts. In March 2005, a new National Mediation Helpline designed to identify an effective means to resolve disputes without going to court was launched which can help arrange mediation appointments with accredited independent mediators.

The value of mediation at all stages of the disputants' relationship is increasingly being discussed. Mediation agencies have reported being called in to help design dispute resolution clauses and to facilitate negotiations during the life of a contract where discussions have become stuck as opposed to when the relationship between the parties to the contract is effectively over. Policy makers have been keen to test the case for more extensive use of mediation in a wide range of settings and pilot schemes and evaluations continue to be funded. Recent examples include the Legal Services Commission Family Reduction pilot launched in 2009.

III. Critiques of Mediation

As we mentioned in the introduction to this chapter, increasing interest in mediation has also sparked intense debates about its disadvantages. Bush and Folger flagged this up in the extract above in which they refer to the "oppression story". A number of studies have, for instance, demonstrated that take up of mediation has been much lower than expected. One of the reasons given for this has been that lawyers remain sceptical about its benefits.

In her Hamlyn Lectures, Hazel Genn welcomed mediation schemes as an important supplement to courts but also cast doubt on some of the more ambitious claims made by its proponents.

Hazel Genn, *Judging Civil Justice, The Hamlyn Lectures 2008* (Cambridge: Cambridge University Press, 2010), pp 108–113:

"Unusually, and very helpfully, the government has invested quite heavily in evaluating a number of court-based mediation schemes. As a result there is a significant body of empirical evidence about the potential of mediation for resolving civil and commercial disputes. Most of these schemes followed a similar design. They were low cost, time limited (usually three hours) and held on court premises after the end of the normal court day (4.30–7.30 pm). Although the courts administered the schemes, the mediations themselves were undertaken by trained mediators.

First of all demand. All of the court-based schemes have demonstrated weak 'bottom-up' demand. This is particularly so for cases involving personal injury where the demand has been virtually non-existent. Since in most county courts personal injury cases account for more than half of the defended caseload, the failure to attract PI cases into mediation has been significant. Yet the overwhelming majority of PI cases settle without trial in any case. Although the value of mediation is generally compared with trial and adjudication, the challenge for mediation policy since the mid-1990s has been that it is seeking to encourage facilitated settlement in a system in which settlement is in any case the norm. Since most cases settle, mediation is principally offering accelerated settlement. But if one effect of the Woolf reforms has been to increase pre-action settlement, the those cases that go to court are likely to be the most contentious and therefore the least likely to be interested in mediation soon after the issue of proceedings.

Moreover, aside from sections of commercial practice, the profession is cautious about advising mediation and on the whole is not routinely recommending mediation. Although some might argue that this is because lawyers are mindful of their profits, it is also because they are still relatively unfamiliar with mediation. Lawyers responsible for the conduct of their cases find it difficult to envisage what value mediation might add to normal negotiation in a system that is in any case settlement dominated. Since most lawyers argue that their object in litigation is to achieve a settlement rather than go to trial, many consider that they are already 'doing mediation' themselves. The same considerations may apply to parties. Many business people who find themselves in the middle of a dispute are experienced negotiators and understandably believe that if they have not been able to negotiate a settlement, then a mediator is unlikely to be able to assist.

It is also true that, in the early stage of a dispute at least, many litigants are not ready to mediate civil disputes. They are not ready to compromise, which is what mediation largely demands. There are different reasons for claimants and defendants. Claimants do not want to mediate because they take their lawyer's advice, because they want 'justice' not compromise, because they believe they will win and because they want their 'day in court'. So an early invitation to mediate may not seem particularly attractive—although the evidence is that claimants have been more likely to accept offers to mediate than defendants.

Defendants have different reasons for not wanting to mediate. There are broadly two types of defendant—those who do not want to pay and those who cannot pay. In this first category are those who genuinely believe that they are not liable and who hope that if they refuse to pay, the claimant may become disheartened, exhausted or run out of money. In the second category are those who are impecunious and who are hoping that the case might collapse or who are simply putting off the moment when they will be ordered to pay. For both categories of defendant, delay is an advantage. So while the message of quick, cheap resolution may be attractive to some claimants, it is less so to the majority of defendants. Indeed, defendants can be brought to the mediation table only by a negative message—such as the threat of a financial penalty at trial for failing to agree to mediate.

And what have we learned about motivation to mediate? Why do litigants accept the opportunity to mediate once they have commenced court proceedings? It seems that the principal motivation for mediating is to avoid the anticipated cost, delay and discomfort of trial. It is not about reconciliation, or growth, or conflict resolution. It is because parties have been told and believe that mediating is a quicker and cheaper way of achieving some sort of remedy. More recently, an important motivating factor seems to have been concern to avoid the risk of *Dunnett v Railtrack* cost penalties.

As far as customer satisfaction is concerned, evaluations of court-annexed mediation schemes show high levels of satisfaction among those who *volunteer* to enter the process. What parties value is the informality of the process and the opportunity to be fully involved in the proceedings. They like the lack of legal technicality and the opportunity to be heard at the beginning of the proceedings. Parties like the speed of the process and, among businesses, the focus on commercial issues in the case. However, they do not like being pressured to settle and some complain that they felt under such pressure. The benefits of mediation are generally explained by comparison with the likely experience of the anticipated trial. This tendency to compare the experience with what might have happened at a trial is reinforced by the mediation process itself during which a principal tool for achieving settlement is to constantly remind parties of the 'danger' of not settling on the day and the unpleasantness that awaits them if they proceed through to trial.

On the question of speed and cost, analysis of large-scale data from court-based mediation schemes compared with control data provides no evidence to suggest any difference in case durations between mediated and non-mediated cases. The same analysis does, however, show that time-limited mediation can avoid trials in non-PI cases, either through immediate settlement or through bringing the parties closer to settlement so that they can settle before trial. The perceptions of mediators, parties and their lawyers is that successful mediation can save cost, but it is difficult to estimate how much, since, although the touchstone is always trial, the overwhelming majority of cases would not proceed to trial and would not therefore incur the costs of trial. It is also clear, however, that unsuccessful mediation may *increase* the costs for parties (estimated at between £1,500 and £2,000). And this fact raises serious questions for policies that seek to pressure parties to enter mediation unwillingly.

Analysis of the outcome of mediation in these court-based schemes show that the readiness of parties to mediate is an important factor in settlement. Put simply, cases are more likely to settle at mediation of the parties enter the process voluntarily rather than being pressured into the process. It seems clear that increased pressure to mediate depresses settlement rates. When people are forced to mediate, they may go through the motions without any intention of settling. They may use the opportunity to gain information about their opponent or to try to psyche out the opponent.

The other important lesson from mediation programmes for civil and commercial disputes is that most settlements involve simply a transfer of money. Only a small minority of settlements are in any way creative or provide something different from what would be available in court. It also seems clear that claimants significantly discount their claims in reaching mediated settlements. There is a price to pay in terms of substantive justice for early settlement."

Other evaluations of mediation schemes have also suggested that lack of demand for mediation from litigants and their representatives is a problem. Reflecting on her own evaluation of the Department of Health's Mediation pilot scheme, Mulcahy has suggested that much of the responsibility for the lack of take-up lies with the legal profession rather than their clients.

Linda Mulcahy, "Can leopards change their spots? An evaluation of the role of lawyers in medical negligence mediation" (2001) 8 *International Journal of the Legal Profession* 203:

"There have been a range of responses to this new environment. There is some evidence of resistance from the grass roots of the legal profession who see mediation as yet another new initiative in an ever changing and uncertain legal world. Globalisation, debate over rights of audience and judicial appointments, changes to legal aid, reform of complaints systems, the introduction of conditional fees have all transformed the last decade into a tumultuous period for legal practitioners. For litigators reeling from the changes to practice introduced by the Woolf reforms mediation provides a new threat, which as gatekeepers to many of the most recent pilot schemes, they still have the power to resist. Mediation is not a form of dispute resolution which is commonly used by High Street practitioners and not something which clients will automatically associate with them. This and fear of diversion of cases away from the courts has led to fears about the potential loss of fees. Firms of solicitors also have concerns that their levels of investment in litigation departments will prove to be misplaced. Some have expressed more principled objections to this open challenge to their monopoly. For this group the court room continues to be the most appropriate backdrop to settlement negotiations. In their view wholesale diversion of cases away from this forum brings with it a risk that too many cases will be decided by reference to the standards of the parties rather than the wider needs of the communities in which we live.

But whilst some members of the professional group have . . . remained . . . closed to such changes, others have proved . . . open to the threat to their shared world. This suggests that either they have embraced the alternative ideology of mediation or that they are buying time whilst they renegotiate the jurisdictional boundaries of their professional world. A considerable number of lawyers have undertaken training as mediators and many of the larger city firms are renaming their litigation departments to reflect a broader approach to dispute settlement. At national level elite members of the profession appear to have embraced mediation enthusiastically. The Law Society, Bar Council and the Lord Chancellor have all pledged their support for this form of dispute resolution. For some this is seen as an acknowledgement by the elite of the profession that there are serious failings in the traditional claims management system. Others have interpreted it as reflecting a proprietorial interest in mediation as a way of maintaining lawyers' professional status and dominance. The latter argument is convincing when one considers that the support of professional bodies has been contingent on lawyers playing a central role as mediators or representatives of the parties in state sponsored schemes. The Law Society has, for example, claimed regulatory control over the conduct of solicitors when they are acting as mediators rather than advisers or adversaries. Roberts has argued that giving public support for such innovation is an attempt by some members of the legal profession to secure or colonise new areas of work and stake a claim to be the only legitimate occupants of it. Reflecting on this array of responses it would seem that the mediation pilot scheme had the potential to create inter-professional rivalries between lawyers and mediators as well as intra-professional rivalries between those lawyers willing to embrace mediation because it preserves market share, those who accept the alternative ideology of mediation and those who see no point in supporting it at all.

It is my contention that at present these developments are little more than a skirmish at the edge of the professional world of lawyers. Legal activists have minimised the challenge posed by mediation by mobilising

during the planning stage of the pilot scheme. By helping to frame its parameters medical negligence specialists secured their inclusion in it. The majority came to understand and give meaning to mediation as an off-
shoot of the civil justice system which could be used in the rare cases in which solicitors are not able to achieve
settlement through bi-lateral negotiations. In this way mediation became an adjunct of the courts and litigation
system rather than an alternative to it. But the data presented also suggest that solicitors' confidence in their
ability to adapt to this new forum was often misplaced. Lawyers involved in the pilot scheme were more surprised by the informality of proceedings and the effect of the presence of their clients than they had anticipated.
Even more significant was the finding that participation in the scheme challenged the professional identity of
lawyers in ways that they did not anticipate. By focusing on the accounts of grievances provided by clients mediators forced them to reflect upon and justify the nature of their claim to a special knowledge and expertise. . . .

A challenging agenda?

Mediation challenges the professional identity of lawyers in a number of ways which increase as ADR processes
become more visible through their institutionalisation and promotion by government and court officials. The
first threat is that mediation can, and often does, take place without lawyers. Community and family mediation are excellent examples of this model. They are also reminders that although law and lawyers have become
inextricably linked in the popular imagination they do not have to co-exist. Some legal systems dispense with
lawyers and many lawyers in the West perform tasks which involve very little formal law. Anthropologists of
law constantly remind us that mediation is a folk concept which existed prior to the evolution of state law, legal
system and lawyer–litigators. In a modern context, the popularity of mediation in some settings has actually
been explained by a distrust of formalised law, lawyers and government agencies as tending to impose coercive, bureaucratic and 'outside' solutions on disputants. Reactions against state sanctioned dispute resolution
systems have also been fuelled by the conviction that the courts and lawyers are unresponsive to the needs
and interests of disadvantaged communities and a perception that legal rules are dogmatic, unpragmatic and
distant. For some mediation represents a radical alternative legality fuelled by the needs of the populace and
their call for greater participation in, and access to, justice. Whilst lawyers in the UK have secured a close association with law these alternative conceptualisations of law and lawyers provide us with a forceful reminder that
the legal profession need to remain sensitive to the need to justify their participation in dispute resolution.

The increased popularity of state-sanctioned mediation amongst politicians and civil servants has also
been construed as posing a threat to senior members of the legal profession. Commentators have argued that
in the final decades of the twentieth century the judiciary has been subjected to an unprecedented array of
reforms which could be seen as heralding the retreat of law from society. Mediation can be seen as a contemporary example of an increasingly bureaucratic state which constrains judicial autonomy by means of administrative case management and the regulation of funding. The creation of the NHS Litigation Authority, the
adoption of the medical negligence pre-action protocol, and recent reforms of legal aid are excellent examples
of the increase in the regulatory culture in a medico-legal context. The essence of this challenge is the demys-
tification of law. In contrast to the claims to abstract, exclusive and theoretical understanding of the rules,
signs and symbols of the law made by lawyers, such bureaucratisation of law has been viewed as encouraging
movement towards the rationalisation and compartmentalisation of knowledge.

It is also the case that by identifying the need for an alternative form of dispute resolution, proponents of
mediation are making a direct attack on the current litigation system and lawyers' ability to resolve cases efficiently and fairly. The ideology of co-operation espoused by mediators provides a justification for taking cases
out of an adversarial litigation system. Mediators involved in state sanctioned and private mediation schemes
compete for cases with litigators and judges. Prominent mediators and judges are often at pains to stress that
their functions should be viewed as symbiotic, that forward thinking practitioners aim for a form of dispute
resolution which best suits the parties and the case, rather than competing for the same cases. But empirical
studies have demonstrated that competitive strategies are rife. Emphasising the horrors of adjudication has
provided mediators with a powerful tool in their attempts to persuade disputants to select mediation instead of
court based adjudication.

Mediation also questions the relevance of lawyers' training and skills to effective dispute resolution. It has been repeatedly argued that academic and vocational legal education places too much emphasis on the courts, and in particular the upper courts, as the main forum where citizens' disputes are resolved. Legal training imbues graduates with an inappropriate fidelity to formal legality and the judiciary. Critics have, for instance, drawn attention to the lack of training in informal and conciliatory dispute resolution processes provided for fledgling lawyers. It has been suggested that the traditional law school curriculum inappropriately privileges an adversarial approach to disputes and pays undue attention to the case based method at the expense of more holistic or contextualised understandings of grievances. As Hunt has argued:

> ' "Thinking like lawyers" was a conceivable educational objective when the ideal model was that of mooting as a preparation for a career as an advocate. But this model embodies only a small part of what only a few graduates will end up doing. Once we recognise that lawyering is probably more about interviewing skills, negotiating strategies, financial and office management etc then the orthodox model is less than satisfactory.'

In short legal education pays 'endless attention to trees at the expense of forests', a situation which has led some to call for a radical rethinking of legal training and the role of lawyers.

Hunt's criticisms suggest that critics' concerns run deeper than arguments that current training programmes are incomplete. Mediation also undermines the claim of lawyers to classify disputes, to define the parameters of disputes and what constitutes successful process and outcome. Lawyers do much more than reproduce the arguments made by their clients. They play a pivotal role in the evolution of the grievances their clients present to them. They mould them and reinvent them as formal claims which are recognised by the legal system. The rhetorical accounts of common sense morality offered by disputants become generalised accounts of harm which fit into categories recognised by statute and case law. In a similar fashion, the desires of the clients are transformed into financial remedies. In the words of Felstiner and Sarat 'To fit into the system the client must reduce her conception of justice to what the law can provide'. Thus, the epistemological perspective of lawyers is a reductionist one. They place stress on the universal applicability of law and on the similarities in fact patterns rather than differences in the grievances recounted to them. The juridification of the client's account transforms the expert from the client's biographer to their autobiographer.

Within legal circles this change is considered to be an appropriate, indeed an essential, function of lawyers. The professional status of lawyers and their role in litigation is based on the contention that they are better able than the laity to interpret complex legal rules and to apply such abstract frameworks to the cases presented to them. Lawyers make a claim to represent clients because they are able to say things that their client can not because they lack eloquence or are too emotionally involved. They restrain clients from talking when they are likely to reveal too much about their case. Their distance from their clients and objectivity is a feature of their work which compares favourably with the unmanageable subjectivity of their client. Boon and Flood found this characteristic of their work to be positively celebrated by the profession. The disputant's grievance is not recognised in its entirety by the lawyer's interpretative framework leading them to routinely negate their client's understandings which are seen as sites of bias.

But the special knowledge claimed by lawyers is also a social construct. It reproduces and constitutes an order which keeps the expression of lay narratives in check. The mystery of the legal system serves to legitimate lawyers as translators but also provides incentives for them to constantly invent and recreate mystery. Viewed in this way law becomes a tool for the lawyer rather than a tool for the client. Bankowski and Mungham have argued that such control would be impossible to maintain if disputants were without fear and uncertainty. Their alienation from law is reinforced by their failure to speak for themselves. In the words of Bankowski and Mungham:

> '. . . the more the client knows, the less the lawyer is able to earn . . . a significant erosion of the monopoly of legal knowledge is not in the lawyer's interest either, for if this base begins to wither away then so does the claim of the lawyer to power and privileges in society.'

Mediation provides a direct challenge to this ordering. Mediators claim to take account of the disputant's narrative and the specificity of their grievance. They claim to privilege the client's story and encourage discussion of both legal and non-legal aspects of grievances. They place emphasise on achieving an outcome which is shaped by the disputants in accordance with their own meanings and objectives. Rather than placing grievances into existing categories commentators have suggested that the process provides important opportunities for norm creation and political debates about what constitutes a preferred standard, or at least acts as a rehearsal ground for the adaptation of norms. Mediators stress the importance of self determination and encourage the parties to mobilise their own resources in disputes resolution rather than relying on those of their lawyers or the state."

It is clear then, that a number of key issues in relation to mediation remain unresolved. In the following critique, Cappelletti hints at some of the wider concerns that academics have expressed about the process.

Mauro Cappelletti, "Alternative Dispute Resolution Processes within the Framework of the World-Wide Access-to-Justice Movement" (1993) 56 M.L.R. 282 at 283:

"[T]he search for alternatives has represented what Professor Bryant Garth and I happened to call 'the third wave' in the access-to-justice movement. Needless to say, there are here many hard questions and difficulties—perhaps contradictions . . . Among the hard questions to be faced, two stand out. First, what are the best kinds of institutions to be promoted? Possibilities include arbitration, mediation, conciliation and, of course, an array of simplified procedures as well as small claims courts. Second, which are the best kinds of persons to staff such institutions? These may include lay persons and, quite often . . . persons involved with and personally aware of the same kinds of interests and problems as the parties in the case. . . . Another hard question concerns the minimum standards and guarantees to be maintained even in these alternative kinds of adjudicatory organs and procedures. The risk, of course, is that the alternative will provide only a *second class justice* because, almost inevitably, the adjudicators in these alternative courts and procedures would lack, in part at least, those safeguards of independence and training that are present in respect of ordinary judges. And the procedures themselves might often lack, in part at least, those formal guarantees of procedural fairness which are typical of ordinary litigation."

Other authors have expressed concerns that by facilitating out of court settlement mediation takes cases away from the public arena of the court and in doing so leads to a privatisation of dispute resolution. In his leading article on the topic, Fiss takes up some of these concerns.

Owen M. Fiss, "Against settlement" (1984) 93 *Yale Law Journal* 1073 at 1075, 1076, 1078, 1085:

"In my view . . . the case for settlement rests on questionable premises. I do not believe that settlement as a generic practice is preferable to judgment or should be institutionalized on a wholesale and indiscriminate basis. It should be treated instead as a highly problematic technique for streamlining dockets. Settlement is for me the civil analogue of plea bargaining: Consent is often coerced; the bargain may be struck by someone without authority; the absence of a trial and judgment renders subsequent judicial involvement troublesome; and although dockets are trimmed, justice may not be done. Like plea bargaining, settlement is a capitulation to the conditions of mass society and should be neither encouraged nor praised.

The imbalance of power
By viewing the lawsuit as a quarrel between two neighbors, the dispute-resolution story . . . implicitly asks us to assume a rough equality between the contending parties. It treats settlement as the anticipation of the outcome of trial and assumes that the terms of settlement are simply a product of the parties' predictions of that outcome. In truth, however, settlement is also a function of the resources available to each party to finance the litigation, and those resources are frequently distributed unequally. Many lawsuits do not involve a property

dispute between two neighbors, or between AT&T and the government (to update the story), but rather concern a struggle between a member of a racial minority and a municipal police department over alleged brutality, or a claim by a worker against a large corporation over work-related injuries. In these cases, the distribution of financial resources, or the ability of one party to pass along its costs, will invariably infect the bargaining process, and the settlement will be at odds with a conception of justice that seeks to make the wealth of the parties irrelevant.

The disparities in resources between the parties can influence the settlement in three ways. First, the poorer party may be less able to amass and analyze the information needed to predict the outcome of the litigation, and thus be disadvantaged in the bargaining process. Second, he may need the damages he seeks immediately and thus be induced to settle as a way of accelerating payment, even though he realizes he would get less now than he might if he awaited judgment. All plaintiffs want their damages immediately, but an indigent plaintiff may be exploited by a rich defendant because his need is so great that the defendant can force him to accept a sum that is less than the ordinary present value of the judgment. Third, the poorer party might be forced to settle because he does not have the resources to finance the litigation, to cover either his own projected expenses, such as his lawyer's time, or the expenses his opponent can impose through the manipulation of procedural mechanisms such as discovery. It might seem that settlement benefits the plaintiff by allowing him to avoid the costs of litigation, but this is not so. The defendant can anticipate the plaintiff's costs if the case were to be tried fully and decrease his offer by that amount. The indigent plaintiff is a victim of the costs of litigation even if he settles. . . .

The absence of authoritative consent
The argument for settlement presupposes that the contestants are individuals. These individuals speak for themselves and should be bound by the rules they generate. In many situations, however, individuals are ensnared in contractual relationships that impair their autonomy: Lawyers or insurance companies might, for example, agree to settlements that are in their interests but are not in the best interests of their clients, and to which their clients would not agree if the choice were still theirs. But a deeper and more intractable problem arises from the fact that many parties are not individuals but rather organizations or groups. We do not know who is entitled to speak for these entities and to give the consent upon which so much of the appeal of settlement depends.

Some organizations, such as corporations or unions, have formal procedures for identifying the persons who are authorized to speak for them. But these procedures are imperfect: They are designed to facilitate transactions between the organization and outsiders, rather than to insure that the members of the organization in fact agree with a particular decision. Nor do they eliminate conflicts of interests. The chief executive officer of a corporation may settle a suit to prevent embarrassing disclosures about his managerial policies, but such disclosures might well be in the interest of the shareholders. The president of a union may agree to a settlement as a way of preserving his power within the organization; for that very reason, he may not risk the dangers entailed in consulting the rank and file or in subjecting the settlement to ratification by the membership. . . .

Justice rather than peace
The dispute-resolution story makes settlement appear as a perfect substitute for judgment, as we just saw, by trivializing the remedial dimensions of a lawsuit, and also by reducing the social function of the lawsuit to one of resolving private disputes: In that story, settlement appears to achieve exactly the same purpose as judgment—peace between the parties—but at considerably less expense to society. The two quarrelling neighbors turn to a court in order to resolve their dispute, and society makes courts available because it wants to aid in the achievement of their private ends or to secure the peace.

In my view, however, the purpose of adjudication should be understood in broader terms. Adjudication uses public resources, and employs not strangers chosen by the parties but public officials chosen by a process in which the public participates. These officials, like members of the legislative and executive branches, possess a power that has been defined and conferred by public law, not by private agreement. Their job is not to maximize the ends of private parties, nor simply to secure the peace, but to explicate and give force to the values embedded in authoritative texts such as . . . statutes: to interpret those values and to bring reality into accord with them. This duty is not discharged when the parties settle.

In our political system, courts are reactive institutions. They do not search out interpretive occasions, but instead wait for others to bring matters to their attention. They also rely for the most part on others to investigate and present the law and facts. A settlement will thereby deprive a court of the occasion, and perhaps even the ability, to render an interpretation. A court cannot proceed (or not proceed very far) in the face of a settlement. To be against settlement is not to urge that parties be 'forced' to litigate, since that would interfere with their autonomy and distort the adjudicative process; the parties will be inclined to make the court believe that their bargain is justice. To be against settlement is only to suggest that when the parties settle, society gets less than what appears, and for a price it does not know it is paying. Parties might settle while leaving justice undone."

Armstrong explains that in the context of the civil justice system the tension which Fiss describes, stems from two competing models of justice.

Nick Armstrong, "Making tracks" in A.A.S. Zuckerman and Ross Cranston (eds) *Reform of Civil Procedure: Essays on "access to justice"* (Oxford: Clarendon Press, 1995), p.97:

"The debate over the function of a civil justice system revolves around a tension between two different models of civil process: the 'dispute resolution' model and the 'policy implementation' model. Under the former, adjudication is understood simply as a method for peacefully resolving a conflict between private parties. The private interests are sovereign, and the state or public interest is limited to maximising the satisfaction of those interests in order to avoid forcible self-help. In other words, the interests of the parties must be realised, and the civil justice system must preserve its reputation of being capable of realising those interests, in order to create the incentives for disputants to use the court system: 'the rules of procedure should contain some carrots as well as sticks.' The provision of courts and legal services, or 'access to justice', may therefore be explained as 'civilisation's substitute for vengeance'.

The policy implementation model, by contrast, recognises a wider public interest. As well as observing the need to resolve the immediate dispute, this model also takes account of its potential effect on the future conduct of others. The existence of the private conflict becomes an opportunity to clarify and determine the standards by which society governs itself. Those standards include the Rule of Law, the maintenance of which transcends the interests of the private parties in order to achieve justice for those who are never involved in actual proceedings.

The difference between the two models, therefore, is one of emphasis between private and public interests. Under the dispute resolution model, the private interests of the parties take precedence; under the policy implementation model, they must sometimes yield to the wider public interest."

In response to the critics of mediation, Menkel-Meadow has replied that in the civil justice context:

Carrie Menkel-Meadow, "Lawyer negotiations: theories and realities—What we learn from mediation" (1993) 56 M.L.R. 361 at 369–370.

"[M]ost of these critiques ignore the fact that ours is a party-initiated system—one in which the parties may choose to remove their disputes from the formal legal system at any time should they choose to negotiate privately. Thus, the key to understanding the appropriateness of any negotiation process is whether justice is ill-served by the processes the parties choose, be they public litigation or private negotiation. Difficulties abound here—what are the appropriate baseline measures of what is a good settlement or fair process? Can the parties or their lawyers make an intelligent choice of process? Do they understand enough about the differences between and among processes? Are the lawyers sufficiently skilled at either negotiation or advocative activities or both to choose the process that will work most effectively for their clients? Most significantly, which processes will produce the 'best' solution?"

Menkel-Meadow's point is that it will require a more sophisticated analysis of particular cases to determine the merits of mediation. She suggests that there are no simple answers. This point is one to bear in mind as you examine the various perspectives on mediation which are the focus of the rest of this section.

IV. Feminist Perspectives on Mediation

Feminists have long considered the promises and perils of mediation and both have been the subject of considerable debate, especially in a family law context. The following two excerpts underscore both the possibilities and also the pitfalls of mediation in terms of advancing an alternative approach to law and dispute resolution. We start with the case *for* mediation.

Janet Rifkin, "Mediation from a feminist perspective: promise and problems" (1984) 2 *Law and Inequality* 21 at 21, 25:

"The interest in alternative dispute resolution is intensifying in this country and others as well. Programs offering mediation, arbitration, negotiation and conciliation services are proliferating throughout the United States, Canada, Australia and Western Europe. These programs may be court-related or community-based. In either case, the overt justifications for mediation programs are similar. Mediating conflict as a substitute for litigating disputes has been justified by two basic rationales: First, the formal court system is not suited to handle the range and number of disputes being brought to it. Second, the adversary process itself is not suited to resolve interpersonal disputes.

While mediation is flourishing, concern about the theory and practice of 'informal' justice is also increasing. Most of the criticisms focus on the manipulative potential of informal systems such as mediation. For example, critics suggest the bureaucratic logic that supports state legality is as much a part of the process in informal and non-bureaucratic settings as it is in the formal court of law. Critics also suggest that the state, faced with fiscal crisis, achieves spending cuts by resorting to informalization, accompanied by appeals to popular participation, consensual social life, and the struggle against bureaucracy. Others argue that mediation fosters the privatization of life—the cult of the personal—and denies the existence of irreconcilable structural conflicts between classes or between citizen and state. Finally, critics claim that mediation is detrimental to the interests of women, who, being less empowered, need both the formal legal system and aggressive legal representation to protect existing rights and pursue new legal safeguards.

Although these criticisms remain, the debate about mediation lacks a careful questioning of law and alternative dispute programs from a feminist perspective. For the most part, mediation's critics predicate their questions on the traditional view of law that litigation leads to social change and that the 'lawsuit' is the appropriate and most effective vehicle for challenging unfair social practices, for protecting individuals, and for delineating new areas of guaranteed 'rights.'

This dominant view leaves unchallenged the patriarchal paradigm of law as hierarchy, combat, and adversarialness; and, therefore, generates only a certain kind of questioning of mediation. This viewpoint has not asked whether and in what way alternative dispute resolution reflects a feminist analysis of law and conflict resolution, and whether in theory and practice mediation challenges or reinforces gender inequality in contemporary society.

My intention in this discussion is to articulate some of the questions basic to an understanding of the relationship between law, mediation and feminist inquiry. . . . What is not yet clearly developed is how mediation in theory reflects 'a new jurisprudence, a new relation between life and law.' Further, what is not yet known is whether in practice, mediating disputes reflects feminist jurisprudential differences from the male ideology of law or whether mediating simply reinforces the 'objective epistemology' of law. . . .

Mediation in practice operates as a process of discussion, clarification, and compromise aided by third party facilitators. It is a process in which the third party has no state-enforced power. A third party's power lies in the ability to persuade the parties to reach a voluntary settlement. It involves the creation of consensus between the parties in which the parties are brought together in an atmosphere of confidentiality to discover shared social and moral values as a means of coming to an agreement.

In mediation, the focus is not on formal and substantive rights. The emphasis is on the process by which the individual parties are encouraged to work out their own solution in a spirit of compromise. The intervention of a mediator turns the initial dyad of a dispute into a triadic interaction of some kind. However, the disputing parties retain their ability to decide whether or not to agree and accept proposals for an outcome irrespective of the source of the proposals. . . .

Although the mediator is a neutral intervenor with no self-interest, a mediator does become a negotiator. In that role the mediator inevitably brings to the process, deliberately or not, certain ideas, knowledge and assumptions. What a mediator can do is also affected by the particular context and the parties' expectations of mediation. . . .

The rhetoric of mediation rejects the 'objectivist epistemology' of the law. Theoretically, in mediation precedents, rules, and a legalized conception of facts are not only irrelevant but constrain the mediator's job of helping the parties to reorient their perception of the problem to the extent that an agreement can be reached. The legal rights of the parties are not central to the discussion which takes place in mediation. Again, in theory, the lack of focus in mediation on abstract legal rights contrasts with the emphasis on them in legal proceedings.

These differences, however, are clearer in theory than in practice. The following two case studies reflect this. . . .

Case study 1: separation and divorce

The participants in this study were a man and a woman who wanted to separate after fifteen years of marriage. They had three children aged six, eight, and ten. They had each retained separate counsel but after legal negotiations had broken down they decided to try mediation.

The woman came to the office first. The couple had agreed to separate ten months before but still occupied the same house. Relations were hostile and communication strained. The woman said that her children were not speaking to her and she felt that her husband was turning them against her. At the initial interview the woman said that the atmosphere among them—the lawyers, the children, and she and her husband—was so hostile that resolution of their marital dispute appeared impossible. She also indicated that she thought he needed 'help.'

The husband's interview verified her description. His anger and frustration were compounded because he had lost his job and was moving out of town within a month. He wanted to resolve the dispute before he moved. He also commented that she needed 'help.'

The following is a *summary* of their concerns:

Custody: *He* wanted custody of the children. *She* supported his having custody, but feared that she might never see them again. During the mediation she agreed to give him full custody of the children once assured of ample visitation rights.

Child Support: *He* would 'take care of his kids.' *She* was not in a position to support the children.

Alimony: *He* wasn't willing to give her alimony. *She* was uncertain of her financial needs but said that she wanted some financial help while looking for a job. She agreed to no alimony.

Property: The financial settlement involved an extensive and complex division of property. The main asset was their house. She agreed to accept a lump sum of money and twenty-five per cent of the net sale of the house over £80,000 in lieu of alimony.

Their attitudes and relationship with their lawyers became one of the most difficult and perhaps interesting aspects of this case. Both of their attorneys initially agreed that mediation might be useful. The man stated that he planned to drop his lawyer and represent himself in court if the mediation went well. His lawyer offered to put any final mediation agreement into legal language for presentation to the court. In the end, the man represented himself with his attorney's approval.

The woman came to the project with conflicting feelings about her lawyer. Although aware that she might gain financially with a formal, contested divorce, she feared the process could irreparably damage her relationship with her children. The case coordinator initially advised her to talk with her attorney about using mediation. She did so and her attorney agreed, with some reservations about her ability to protect her own interests. As the mediation proceeded, she was advised several times to consult with her attorney but the case coordinator suspected that she was not doing so.

In the end, her attorney rejected the final mediation agreement and told her it was impossible for him to represent her if she insisted on keeping the agreement as the divorce settlement. She chose to discontinue the relationship with her attorney and she, like her husband, represented herself in court proceedings. Her attorney was very upset and told the judge in her presence that he objected to her mediated settlement. The judge accepted the agreement after speaking with her at length.

Case study 2: sexual harassment

A twenty-five year old undergraduate woman was very troubled about what she described as sexual harassment by one of her professors. She claimed that he had made many inappropriate inquiries in class about the backgrounds of the women students, wanting to know about their boyfriends, their parties, and other similar matters. During a conversation with him regarding a research assistantship, he offered to drive her home. She consented to this and on the way, they stopped for a drink. During their conversation she learned the position would involve working closely with him. The conversation led to a discussion of personal matters and he told her of his unhappy marriage. Later on he mentioned that he was very attracted to her and would like to go to bed with her. She felt extremely uneasy and said that she would have to think about it.

The next day she went to his office and rejected his sexual proposal. He said that he was disappointed. Two weeks passed without any mention of the job. When she finally approached him, he told her the position was no longer available. She was upset and went to the department chair, who recommended that she consider mediation. She also spoke to the school's dean, who initially reacted with disbelief, but later believed the student after speaking to the professor. The dean told them both that he wanted the dispute worked out in mediation, but indicated that if he received another complaint he would dismiss the faculty member.

In a lengthy meeting with the mediation staff, the student learned that she could arrange for a more formal, potentially punitive process by requesting the administration to form an ad hoc hearing committee. She considered this alternative but requested mediation, claiming she did not want the professor fired. The professor also agreed to mediation.

During a four hour mediation session with the two parties, the student explained why the incident was so upsetting. The professor responded with tears and an apology. At the end of the mediation, they shook hands and both expressed satisfaction to the mediator. She said she mostly wanted the opportunity to make him hear her point of view. He said he understood and expressed appreciation at being spared the humiliation of a more public proceeding. She also expressed her relief at being able to avoid the pain of a public and more formalized hearing where her credibility might be subject to review and cross-examination. At the end of the mediation he apologized and offered her a job, which she rejected. He also promised not to penalize her by lowering her grade.

Summary

Although critics of mediation charge that it may keep the less powerful party from achieving equality and equal bargaining power, it is not so clear from these case studies how this operates in practice. These objections to mediation are inextricably tied to the view that the formal legal system offers both a better alternative and a greater possibility of achieving a fair and just resolution to the conflict. The general assumption that the lawyer can 'help' the client more meaningfully than a mediator is part of the problem with this view. In many instances, although new substantive rights or legal protections are realized, patterns of domination are reinforced by the lawyer-client relationship, in which the client is a passive recipient of the lawyer's expertise. This is particularly true for women clients, for whom patterns of domination are at the heart of the problem.

In both case studies, it can be argued that the pattern of *dominance* was affected. 'Dominance produces hierarchical arrangement of the partners, which is reflected in differences in such aspects of the relationship as freedom of movement, the utilization of resources, and rights and responsibilities.' In these situations, the women felt that the relationship of dominance had been altered and the hierarchy in the relationship had to some extent been altered. A transformation of the pattern of dominance will affect the power relationships as well.

Although mediation programs are proliferating, many questions remain. Why is the interest in alternatives intensifying? What kinds of disputes are best suited to mediation? Who should be mediators—lay persons, lawyers, or other professionals? What kind of training should mediators receive? Can mediation in practice alter the patterns of gender inequality in our society more effectively than formal law? Can the teaching of mediation begin to change and challenge the traditional approach to legal study? The answers to these questions may remain unclear, but if these issues are not addressed, mediation will simply become another popular 'technique' marketed as a panacea for a range of complex social problems."

Trina Grillo, who was a practising mediator as well as an academic was particularly concerned about *mandatory* mediation processes but also has reservations about mediation in general, and the dangers for women.

Trina Grillo, "The mediation alternative: process dangers for women" (1991) 100 *Yale Law Journal* 1545 at 1547, 1601, 1607:

"The western concept of law is based on a patriarchal paradigm characterized by hierarchy, linear reasoning, the resolution of disputes through the application of abstract principles, and the idea of the reasonable person. Its fundamental aspiration is objectivity, and to that end it separates public from private, form from substance, and process from policy. This objectivist paradigm is problematic in many circumstances, but never more so than in connection with a marital dissolution in which the custody of children is at issue, where the essential question for the court is what is to happen next in the family. The family court system, aspiring to the idea of objectivity and operating as an adversary system, can be relied on neither to produce just results nor to treat those subject to it respectfully and humanely.

There is little doubt that divorce procedure needs to be reformed, but reformed how? Presumably, any alternative should be at least as just, and at least as humane, as the current system, particularly for those who are least powerful in society. Mediation has been put forward, with much fanfare, as such an alternative. The impetus of the mediation movement has been so strong that in some states couples disputing custody are required by statute or local rule to undergo a mandatory mediation process if they are unable to reach an agreement on their own. Mediation has been embraced for a number of reasons. First, it rejects an objectivist approach to conflict resolution, and promises to consider disputes in terms of relationships and responsibility. Second, the mediation process is, at least in theory, cooperative and voluntary, not coercive. The mediator does not make a decision; rather, each party speaks for himself. Together they reach an agreement that meets the parties' mutual needs. In this manner, the process is said to enable the parties to exercise self-determination and eliminate the hierarchy of dominance that characterizes the judge/litigant and lawyer/client relationships. Third, since in mediation there are no rules of evidence or legalistic notions of relevancy, decisions supposedly may be informed by context rather than by abstract principle. Finally, in theory at least, emotions are recognized and incorporated into the mediation process. This conception of mediation has led some commentators to characterize it as a feminist alternative to the patriarchally inspired adversary system.

Whether mandatory mediation, required as part of court proceedings, fulfils these aspirations, or instead substitutes another objectivist, patriarchal, and even more damaging form of conflict resolution for its adversarial counterpart, is the subject of this Article. Many divorcing couples seem pleased with their mediation experiences. Indeed, studies have shown that mediation clients are more satisfied with their divorce outcomes than persons using the adversary system. Although there are significant methodological problems with each of these studies, the existence of substantial client satisfaction with some models of mediation cannot be completely discounted.

Nonetheless, I conclude that mandatory mediation provides neither a more just nor a more humane alternative to the adversarial system of adjudication of custody, and, therefore, does not fulfil its promises. In particular, quite apart from whether an acceptable result is reached, mandatory mediation can be destructive to many women and some men because it requires them to speak in a setting they have not chosen and often imposes a rigid orthodoxy as to how they should speak, make decisions, and be. This orthodoxy is imposed through subtle and not-so-subtle messages about appropriate conduct and about what may be said in mediation. It is an orthodoxy that often excludes the possibility of the parties' speaking with their authentic voices.

Moreover, people vary greatly in the extent to which their sense of self is 'relational'—that is, defined in terms of connection to others. If two parties are forced to engage with one another, and one has a more relational sense of self than the other, that party may feel compelled to maintain her connection with the other, even to her own detriment. For this reason, the party with the more relational sense of self will be at a disadvantage in a mediated negotiation. Several prominent researchers have suggested that, as a general rule, women have a more relational sense of self than do men, although there is little agreement on what the origin of this difference might be. Thus, rather than being a feminist alternative to the adversary system, mediation has the potential actively to harm women.

Some of the dangers of mandatory mediation apply to voluntary mediation as well. Voluntary mediation should not be abandoned, but should be recognized as a powerful process which should be used carefully and thoughtfully. Entering into such a process with one who has known you intimately and who now seems to threaten your whole life and being has great creative, but also enormous destructive, power. Nonetheless, it should be recognized that when two people themselves decide to mediate and then physically appear at the mediation sessions, that decision and their continued presence serve as a rough indication that it is not too painful or too dangerous for one or both of them to go on. . . .

As discussed earlier, several feminist scholars have suggested that women have a more 'relational' sense of self than do men. The most influential of these researchers, Carol Gilligan, describes two different, gendered modes of thought. The female mode is characterized by an 'ethic of care' which emphasizes nurturance, connection with others, and contextual thinking. The male mode is characterized by an 'ethic of justice' which emphasizes individualism, the use of rules to resolve moral dilemmas, and equality. Under Gilligan's view, the male mode leads one to strive for individualism and autonomy, while the female mode leads one to strive for connection with and caring for others. Some writers, seeing a positive virtue in the ethic of care, have applied Gilligan's work to the legal system. But her work has been criticized by others for its methodology, its conflation of biological sex with gender, and its failure to include race and class differences in its analysis. (Indeed, it is not likely that the male/female differences Gilligan notes are consistent across racial and class lines.) The 'ethic of care' has also been viewed as the manifestation of a system of gender domination. Nevertheless, it is clear that those who operate in a 'female mode'—whether biologically male or female—will respond more 'selflessly' to the demands of mediation.

Whether the ethic of care is to be enshrined as a positive virtue, or criticized as a characteristic not belonging to all women and contributing to their oppression, one truth emerges: many women see themselves, and judge their own worth, primarily in terms of relationships. This perspective on themselves has consequences for how they function in mediation.

Carrie Menkel-Meadow has suggested that the ethic of care can and should be brought into the practice of law—that the world of lawyering would look very different from the perspective of that ethic. Some commentators have identified mediation as a way to incorporate the ethic of care into the legal system and thereby modify the harshness of the adversary process. And, indeed, at first glance, mediation in the context of divorce might be seen as a way of bringing the woman-identified values of intimacy, nurturance, and care into a legal system that is concerned with the most fundamental aspects of women's and men's lives.

If mediation does not successfully introduce an ethic of care, however, but instead merely sells itself on that promise while delivering something coercive in its place, the consequences will be disastrous for a woman who embraces a relational sense of self. If she is easily persuaded to be cooperative, but her partner is not, she can only lose. If it is indeed her disposition to be caring and focused on relationships, and she has been rewarded for that focus and characterized as 'unfeminine' when she departs from it, the language of relationship, caring, and cooperation will be appealing to her and make her vulnerable. Moreover, the intimation that she is not being cooperative and caring or that she is thinking of herself instead of thinking selflessly of the children can shatter her self-esteem and make her lose faith in herself. In short, in mediation, such a woman may be encouraged to repeat exactly those behaviors that have proven hazardous to her in the past. . . .

It has been said that '[d]isputes are cultural events, evolving within a framework of rules about what is worth fighting for, what is the normal or moral way to fight, what kinds of wrongs warrant action, and what kinds of remedies are acceptable.' The process by which a society resolves conflict is closely related to its social structure. Implicit in this choice is a message about what is respectable to do or want or say, what the obligations are of being a member of the society or of a particular group within it, and what it takes to be thought of as a good person leading a virtuous life. In the adversary system, it is acceptable to want to win. It is not only acceptable, but expected, that one will rely on a lawyer and advocate for oneself without looking out for the adversary. The judge, a third party obligated to be neutral and bound by certain formalities, bears the ultimate responsibility for deciding the outcome. To the extent that women are more likely than men to believe in communication as a mode of conflict resolution and to appreciate the importance of an adversary's interests, this system does not always suit their needs.

On the other hand, under a scheme of mediation, the standards of acceptable behavior and desires change fundamentally. Parties are to meet with each other, generally without their lawyers. They are encouraged to look at each other's needs and to reach a cooperative resolution based on compromise. Although there are few restrictions on her role in the process, the mediator bears no ultimate, formal responsibility for the outcome of the mediation. In sum, when mediation is the prototype for dispute resolution, the societal message is that a good person—a person following the rules—cooperates, communicates, and compromises.

The glories of cooperation, however, are easily exaggerated. If one party appreciates cooperation more than the other, the parties might compromise unequally. Moreover, the self-disclosure that cooperation requires, when imposed and not sought by the parties, may feel and be invasive. Thus, rather than representing a change in the system to accommodate the 'feminine voice,' cooperation might, at least for the time being, be detrimental to their lives and the lives of their children. Under a system of forced mediation, women are made to feel selfish for wanting to assert their own interests based on their need to survive."

Questions

1. Do you find academic critiques of mediation compelling?

2. What is meant by the claim that mediation will bring about second class justice? Do you think such fears are justified?

3. According to Rifkin, in what ways does mediation exemplify a "new way of thinking about law"? In other words, how does the process of mediation differ from more formal and legalised methods of resolving disputes?

4. Do you think that mediation *necessarily* provides a preferable way of resolving disputes in cases involving domestic violence or abusive relationships? Are there advantages in these (and other) cases being resolved by the courts according to the "rule of law"?

5. Whose arguments do you find more convincing—Rifkin's or Grillo's? Should we avoid "grand theories" about the promise and dangers of mediation in favour of context specific analysis?

Useful website addresses

Victim Support, *http://www.victimsupport.com* [Accessed May 14, 2010]
Civil Mediation Council, *http://www.civilmediation.org* [Accessed May 13, 2010]
Chartered Institute of Arbitrators, *http://www.ciarb.org* [Accessed May 13, 2010]
Centre for Effective Dispute Resolution, *http://www.cedr.co.uk* [Accessed May 13, 2010]

Civil Justice Council, *http://www.civiljusticecouncil.gov.uk* [Accessed May 13, 2010]
National Mediation helpline *http://www.nationalmediationhelpline.com* [Accessed May 13, 2010]
National Family Mediation, *http://www.nfm.org.uk* [Accessed May 13, 2010]
Acas, *http://www.acas.org.uk* [Accessed May 13, 2010]

13

COMPARATIVE LEGAL METHODS AND SYSTEMS

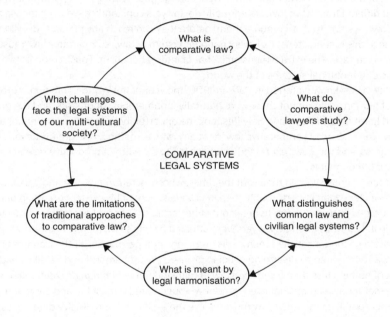

In this chapter, we look at legal method and system in a much broader context. The aim is for you to recognise how the legal traditions of other countries can enrich knowledge and understanding of your own. By the end of this chapter, you should:

- comprehend the meanings of comparative law;

- recognise the various ways in which legal systems and their traditions have been categorised and how those categories have changed over time;

- appreciate the importance of the civil law tradition in the law of the European Union;

- be able to assess the merits and disadvantages of legal harmonisation in the European Union;

- appreciate the diversity of legal systems in the world and the implications of that diversity for the definition of "law".

The belief that we can compare things rests upon two conflicting but fundamental assumptions. First, we assume that the things compared are the same (i.e. that they share something in common).

Second, we assume that the things compared are different (i.e. that they have some distinguishing features). These are the two assumptions of comparative law, and they are in constant tension.

The aim of this introductory extract is to provide you with a better understanding of the similarity and difference between legal traditions and systems. We begin, therefore, with some material on the meaning of "comparative law" and the establishment of comparative law as a discipline of study.

K. Zweigert and H. Kötz, *Introduction to Comparative Law*, 3rd edn (Oxford: Clarendon Press, 1998), pp.2–3, 15–16:

"Before we try to discover the essence, function, and aims of comparative law, let us first say what 'comparative law' means. The words suggest an intellectual activity with law as its object and comparison as its process. Now comparisons can be made between different rules in a single legal system, as, for example, between different paragraphs of the German Civil Code. If this were all that was meant by comparative law, it would be hard to see how it differed from what lawyers normally do: lawyers constantly have to juxtapose and harmonize the rules of their own system, that is, compare them, before they can reach any practical decision or theoretical conclusion. Since this is characteristic of every national system of law, 'comparative law' must mean more than appears on the surface. The extra dimension is that of internationalism. Thus, 'comparative law' is the comparison of the different legal systems of the world.

Comparative law as we know it started in Paris in 1900, the year of the World Exhibition. At this brilliant panorama of human achievement there were naturally innumerable congresses, and the great French Scholars Édouard Lambert and Raymond Saleilles took the opportunity to found an International Congress for Comparative Law. The science of comparative law, or at any rate its method, was greatly advanced by the occurrence of this Congress, and the views expressed at it have led to a wealth of productive research in this branch of legal study, young though it is.

The temper of the Congress was in tune with the times, whose increasing wealth and splendour had given everyone, scholars included, an imperturbable faith in progress. Sure of his existence, certain of its point and convinced of its success, man was trying to break out of his local confines and peaceably to master the world and all that was in it. Naturally enough, lawyers were affected by this spirit; merely to interpret and elaborate their own system no longer satisfied them. This outgoing spirit permeates all the Congress papers; the whole Congress was dominated by disarming belief in progress. What Lambert and Saleilles had in mind was the development of nothing less than a common law of mankind (*droit commun de l'humanité*). A world law must be created—not today, perhaps not even tomorrow—but created it must be, and comparative law must create it. As Lambert put it, comparative law must resolve the accidental and divisive differences in the laws of peoples at similar stages of cultural and economic development, and reduce the number of divergencies in law, attributable not to the political, moral, or social qualities of the different nations but to historical accident or to temporary or contingent circumstances.

Comparative law has developed continuously since then, despite great changes in man's attitude towards existence. The belief in progress, so characteristic of 1900, has died. World wars have weakened, if not destroyed, faith in world law. Yet despite a more sceptical way of looking at the world, the development and enrichment of comparative law has been steady. Comparative lawyers have come to know their field better, they have refined their methods and set their sights a little lower, but they remain convinced that comparative law is both useful and necessary. Scholars are more resistant to fashionable pessimism than people in other walks of life; they have no immediate aim, only the ultimate goal of discovering the truth. This is true also of research in comparative law; it has no immediate aim. But if one did want to adduce arguments of utility, comparative law must be at least as useful as it was, especially as technological developments since 1900 have made the world ever smaller and, to all appearances, national isolationism is on the wane. Furthermore, by the international exchanges which it requires, comparative law procures the gradual approximation of viewpoints, the abandonment of deadly complacency, and the relaxation of fixed dogma. It affords us a glimpse into the form and formation of legal institutions which develop in parallel, possibly in accordance with laws yet to be determined, and permits us to catch sight, through the differences in detail, of the grand similarities and so deepen our belief in the existence of a unitary sense of justice. . . .

It is beyond dispute today that the scholarly pursuit of comparative law has several significant functions. This emerges from a very simple consideration, that no study deserves the name of a science if it limits itself to phenomena arising within its national boundaries. For a long time lawyers were content to be insular in this sense, and to some extent they are so still. But such a position is untenable, and comparative law offers the only way by which law can become international and consequently a science.

In the natural and medical sciences, and in sociology and economics as well, discoveries and opinions are exchanged internationally. This is so familiar a fact that it is easy to forget its significance. There is no such thing as 'German' physics or 'British' microbiology or 'Canadian' geology. These branches of science are international, and the most one can say is that the contributions of the various nations to the different departments of world knowledge have been outstanding, average, or modest. But the position in legal science is astonishingly different. So long as Roman law was the essential source of all law on the Continent of Europe, an international unity of law and legal science did exist, and a similar unity, the unity of Common Law, can still be found, up to a point, in the English-speaking world. On the European continent, however, legal unity began to disappear in the eighteenth century as national codes were put in the place of traditional Roman law. The consequence was that lawyers concentrated exclusively on their own legislation, and stopped looking over the border. At a time of growing nationalism, this legal narcissism led to pride in the national system. Germans thought German law was the ark of the covenant, and the French thought the same of French law: national pride became the hallmark of juristic thought. Comparative law has started to put an end to such narrowmindedness.

The primary aim of comparative law, as of all sciences, is knowledge. If one accepts that legal science includes not only the techniques of interpreting the texts, principles, rules, and standards of a national system, but also the discovery of models for preventing or resolving social conflicts, then it is clear that the method of comparative law can provide a much richer range of model solutions than a legal science devoted to a single nation, simply because the different systems of the world can offer a greater variety of solutions than could be thought up in a lifetime by even the most imaginative jurist who was corralled in his own system. Comparative law is an 'école de vérité' which extends and enriches the 'supply of solutions' and offers the scholar of critical capacity the opportunity of finding the 'better solution' for his time and place.

Like the lively international exchange on legal topics to which it gives rise, comparative law has other functions which can only be mentioned here in the briefest way. It dissolves unconsidered national prejudices, and helps us to fathom the different societies and cultures of the world and to further international understanding; it is extremely useful for law reform in developing countries; and for the development of one's own system the critical attitude it engenders does more than local doctrinal disputes."

Questions

1. According to Zweigert and Kötz, how have the aims of comparative law changed?

2. What factors do the authors identify as having influenced the development of the functions of comparative law today? What other factors can you suggest?

3. How would you describe what "comparative law" means?

I. LEGAL SYSTEMS, CULTURES AND TRADITIONS

The authors of the previous extract referred to comparative law as a science with knowledge as its aim. To achieve this knowledge, however, we must first decide what it is that we are to study. Comparative lawyers have described the object of their inquiry in many different ways such as: legal systems, legal mentalities, legal traditions and legal cultures. Each of these categories helps bring the different goals of comparative law into perspective. The following extract should help you to understand the impact of these varied ways of identifying the object of comparative legal study.

J. Bell, *French Legal Cultures* (London: Butterworths, 2001), pp.6–7, 11–12, 14–16, 16–17:

"Tradition is an important part of culture, and especially the law. Law is a body of norms and practices which is handed down. The practice of preserving and developing a tradition gives rise to a legal community. Taking part in the tradition is the way one comes to understand the law from the legal point of view. A tradition connects norms, practices and people.

Hazareesingh suggests that 'a tradition is characteristically defined as the transmission of a relatively coherent body of knowledge or thought from one generation to the next'. Legal writers such as Krygier and Gerber concentrate on authoritative texts (statutes, reported cases and key doctrinal writings) as central to the legal tradition. Texts are handed on and become the focus of legal activity. The particular style and influences of the texts and the way these texts are treated and interpreted, are also important features of the legal tradition and make it distinctive. But it is also important to see both procedures and rituals as part of what is handed on. The way lawyers dress and perform legal acts helps to create the law as a way of life. The role of the notary in drawing up wills or marriage contracts in France, the layout of the courtroom and the roles which the different lawyers, advocats, greffiers and judges, perform in court is as much part of the French legal tradition as the Code civil or other received texts. Certainly both a body of principles and a set of practices form the basis for how continuity is preserved within the legal community. Grosso suggests that we should examine the 'experienced tradition', a substantive and continuing body of attitudes and activities which is not only handed on, but is lived out and serves as a basis for renewal. This is in contrast to the 'tradition as myth' or the 'sentimental tradition' which is a set of sentiments and attachments to a 'grand past' and aspirations for the future. The focus, as he suggests, is on the experience *from the legal point of view*, which perceives legal activity as a unity and as developing organically.

A tradition has to be transmitted and made accessible to each generation of participants. As a result, there has to be processes of conservation, of authenticating what is handed on and of interpretation. There is also a process of induction in the way by which new participants are formed to be able to make use of the tradition in a way that counts as legitimate. By all means, there is a legitimate activity of external criticism and interpretation. . . . But we are concerned . . . to explain the internal process of making sense of a legal argument. For this purpose, there are established ways in which interpretations can be accepted as valid. There are conventions within the legal community about what are appropriate arguments which support an interpretation—whether cases can be cited and from which courts, whether doctrinal legal writers can be cited as appropriate authorities. Education has an important role in the socialisation of participants into a culture. . . .

Comparative lawyers are agreed that it is not sufficient just to look at legal texts and rules to explain why legal systems are different. Cappelletti, Merryman and Perillo argued:

> '. . . a principle source of . . . differences lies quite outside the formal legal order. It is found in the pervading assumptions and attitudes, lay and professional, about law, in the generally accepted view of what law is, of what the legal process in the society should be, of how the legal process should be divided up among various official and unofficial agencies for making and administering the law. In a phrase, what gives the legal order character, individuality, a style of its own, is the prevailing legal outlook in the culture of which that legal order is an integral part.'

Even if there is agreement to go beyond the 'law in the books' for explanation, there is no agreement on how the concept of 'legal culture' can offer an explanatory framework.

In his seminal study, *Law and Society: an introduction*, Friedman distinguishes two different aspects of legal culture:

> '. . . legal culture refers to two rather different sets of attitudes and values: that of the general public (we can call this *lay* legal culture) and that of lawyers, judges and other professionals (we can call this *internal* legal culture).'

In his view, comparative lawyers tend to study this internal culture of a legal system, a lawyer's or a jurist's culture, rather than a general or social culture, the culture of the 'living law'. This he considers to be 'the marginal and arcane culture of lawyers in their formal training', the official law, which is the wrong focus of study for legal culture:

'Legal systems are not museums; they are tools, instruments, mechanisms; and those who use them are living people and living entities, grimly determined to float bonds, collect damages for auto accidents, merge with another company, avoid or minimize taxes, avoid or minimize prison, start or end a marriage, vindicate a reputation, go bankrupt, adopt a baby, or do any of the thousand things that people and institutions do by and through the law.'

. . . The concept of 'mentality' as an explanation of differences in cultural practices has become popular, particularly in France, since the work of Lévy-Bruhl. It is associated with a pre-logical set of perspectives on the world that shape action. Mentality offers a core explanation for ideas and practices. The concept has been much used by comparative lawyers. Zweigert and Kötz consider that a significant hallmark of a difference in a legal system is 'a distinctive mode of legal thinking' which they also characterise as 'mentality'. The concept has been developed further by Pierre Legrand. For him, a 'mentalité' is the 'collective mental programme' which contains the 'assumptions, attitudes, aspirations and antipathies' which provide the 'deep structures of legal rationality'.

Legrand focuses on the difference between common law and civil law, which he describes as a *primordial cleavage* in ways law is understood. There are radical differences in the nature of legal reasoning, the significance of systematisation, the character of rules, the role of facts, and the meaning of rights. Taken together, these represent a mapping of the world under the sway of culture. Such ideas shape the individual lawyer's mentalité. He considers that a particular mentality is so fundamental to the approach of civilian lawyers to law, that it constitutes a barrier to real harmonisation with common lawyers, even on the basis of common texts. Common lawyers just think differently about law. In this approach, mentalité describes a set of beliefs and interpretative ideas which shape an approach to action:

'I understand the notion of "culture" to mean the framework of intangibles within which an interpretative community operates, which has normative force for this community (even though not completely and coherently instantiated) and which, over the *longue durée*, determines the identity of a community as community.'

But there are voices which argue that such a single, macro explanation is unnecessary. Lloyd studied the scientific arguments of ancient Greece and ancient China, their styles of argument, their concepts and their products. He concludes that there are certain features that are common to all societies, such as the pursuit of logic, but there are other features of scientific argument that arise in a specific set of circumstances. Thus within a full set of beliefs, some features of a particular society are held in common with others, and some are specific. Lloyd's concern is how far there is a real difference in beliefs, and how far there are simply differences in the way those beliefs are presented and defended. Presentation depends on the availability of linguistic terms, and defence requires certain paradigms of convincing argument to be used more widely in society. He certainly notes a difference between Greece and China in the presentation of scientific argument. Chinese argument appealed to tradition and used a metaphorical form of language, while Greeks appealed to adversarial and legal forms of proof. But he does not think that the difference in presentation of reasoning demonstrates a difference in the form of scientific thought, since this can be explained by differences in the available and acceptable paradigms of argument and concepts in the two societies. He concludes that differences are best explained not in terms of some grand difference in scientific mentalities, but in the combination of more specific detailed differences of styles of inquiry and interpersonal exchanges. He concludes:

'. . . the appropriate framework within which we have to tackle the problems of interpretation that such examples [of diverse forms of investigation] present is provided by the complex interactions and tensions between a variety of competing ideas and assumptions on the aims, methods and subject-matter of those investigations. It is those ideas and assumptions, together with the contexts of communication in which they are embedded, that define what I have been calling divergent styles of inquiry, and nothing is to be gained from resorting to an appeal to one or more supposed underlying mentalities.'

Lloyd essentially argues that the concept of 'mentality' is too general. It fails to pay adequate attention to the complexity of the diverse individual approaches within a single society and to the way in which the situations of people in one society diverge from another society. His preference is for specific case-studies. Furthermore, he is concerned to explain the environmental conditions which facilitate the development and spread of certain views, rather than just to talk about a shared and global 'mentality' among a group of people.

Lloyd's own reductivist approach to mentality still talks of 'style' of inquiry and reasoning. For Zweigert and Kötz, the notion of 'style' is central to a distinction between legal systems, because it identifies not one single trait, but 'a congeries of particular features which the most diverse objects of study may possess' and which mark them out as belonging together. But again, this notion focuses attention on the ideological elements of a legal system—the key factors to be studied are the historical background of the legal system, its predominant mode of legal thought, its distinctive institutions, the kinds of legal sources it acknowledges, and its ideology. In other words, one is looking at a set of ideas and how they are conditioned. 'Style' is used by Markesinis to be essentially about presentation and ways of doing things, a superstructure, rather than something which defines the task in hand, hence his discussion of the style of judgments. I would want to go further and look at mentality and style as ways of describing more deeply rooted activities. The existence of particular styles of presentation may serve as evidence of difference in either a deep level of legal thought, or different traditions about how legal argumentation is presented. It can serve as an indicator that there is a different culture in operation."

Questions

1. How would you describe the difference between a legal tradition and a legal mentality? What distinction can be drawn between a legal tradition and a legal culture?

2. Which term (system, tradition, mentality, culture, style) best describes a set of legal institutions, procedures and rules?

3. It has been said that legal tradition relates the legal system to the culture of which it is an expression. Which aspects of the English legal system are particular expressions of English culture? Can you think of examples of how English attitudes about the nature and role of law are reflected in the English legal system?

II. "CARVING THE WORLD'S LAW UP" INTO INDIVIDUAL TRADITIONS

In order to compare legal traditions, we must first ask how we are going to distinguish between legal systems and must then choose the particular traits we wish to use in order to compare them. For example, to compare apples and oranges, we must first have decided to carve up the world of food in such a way that all fruit are grouped together (or perhaps all food that ripens naturally on trees). Once the fruit has been identified as the object of our comparison, we choose to compare particular traits that various fruits may have in common (e.g. the presence of vitamin C or an edible skin).

The division of the world into legal traditions or families has not remained stable. It has been affected by history and the proliferation of particular legal, political and social theories at specific periods of time. Thus, as we will see in the following extract, the breadth of comparative law today has been increased far beyond the three families of common law, civil law and socialist law into which classifications were traditionally organized.

H.P. Glenn, *Legal Traditions of the World: Sustainable diversity in law*, 2nd edn (Oxford: Oxford University Press, 2004), pp.344, 345–347, 348–349:

"Some very old, long-recognized traditions exist within other (major) traditions. There are endless, particular, chthonic legal traditions, as varied as the means of living harmoniously with the world. They have names, which are the names of chthonic peoples, such as Iroquois, or Aztec, or Masai. Talmudic law knows, among others, sephardic and ashkenazi traditions, and the traditions of orthodox, conservative and reform jewry. The civil law has known traditions of the ius civile, of the ius gentium, of Bartolus, of Cujas, of rhetoric, of constructive rationality, of dissent, of the nation-states which have each given to civil law a particular form of expression. Islamic law has its islams—sunni and shi'ite—and its schools—the Hanafi, Maliki, Shafi and Hanbali, and there are the regional variants, the accommodation—even incorporation—of local, informal, tradition. The common law has had its 'customs', its writs, its now-incorporated Equity, its tradition of judicial restraint (or activism, if you prefer) and now extends in diverse national form to many different societies. Hindu law too has its sadachara (the practice of virtue) and its schools—the Mitakshara and the Dayabhaga—and continues to float over, and govern, those who have their particular ways. Asia knows both li *and* fa, and neither of these places a premium on uniformity of execution; they appear compatible to some extent with both buddhist and taoist attitudes to legal ordering. . . .

There are also, arguably, the 'young traditions', the goslings of the traditional world, those which may (already) have been originated but which lack the accumulated 'pastness' which allows us to verify their staying power. These young, internal traditions seem to appear most often in traditions which value effort, originality or ijtihad, often along with aristotelian forms of logic. So we have the current shi'ite efforts to create a doctrine of the islamic state, or a contemporary legal cadre for islamic banking. The civil law world has known movements of 'libre recherche scientifique', of 'Freirecht' (both perhaps expired), of interest analysis ('Interessenjurisprudenz') and of 'alternative' forms of thinking law and commenting on law. In the effervescent common/civil law world which is the United States of America there are many movements in law, which may be a sign of intellectual strength or a sign of intellectual weakness. There is a movement which would analyse law in terms of its positive and utilitarian characteristics (law and economics); another which would subject it to feminist thought (feminist legal theory); another which would unmask its arbitrary and indeterminate methods (critical legal studies); another which would unearth its empirical assises (law and society); another which would situate it generally in postmodern society (postmodernism and law). Are these traditions *in* law, legal traditions, or do they represent something eventually antithetical to law, at least as it has (traditionally) been thought? We may eventually know. They are in any event presently internal to western law, though there are reflections of them (in varying strengths) in both common and civil law traditions.

There are also further, recognizable traditions which are not particular or internal to any given, larger tradition but which seem to run across many larger traditions. Casuistry is one such tradition, with deep and explicit roots in roman, talmudic, islamic and common laws (and perhaps hindu law, though there is the poetry). Nor would chthonic ways or Asian li stand opposed to casuistic thinking, though neither would track its exercise. Analogical reasoning or qiyas is also fundamental and explicit in traditions which seek to limit, subtly, judicial creativity (as in talmudic, islamic and common laws). Notions of inter-generational equity are very present in chthonic, hindu and Asian law, while contemporaneous notions of equity are explicit in both civil and common law, talmudic law ('acting inside the law') and islamic law. There is a tradition of constructive rationality in law, of ijtihad, most marked in western law (civil and common), the object of passionate debate in islamic law, of incredulity and scepticism elsewhere. Fundamentalism is a lateral tradition, in the name of particular gods, particular texts, particular principles (such as rights). There are also traditions of professional role—those of the adjudicator (decisor, iudex, judge, qadi) or, less frequently, of counsel (advocate, barrister, attorney or simple adviser). And there are the undefended, but practised, traditions of racism, of crime, of unthinking and spontaneous antagonism to the other, however defined. . . .

Western theory of tradition teaches that all tradition is normative, that is, that it provides a model, drawn from the past, as to how one should act. Legal traditions, of all traditions, should not depart from this general phenomenon, since law is perhaps the most normative of human endeavours. There are clear differences, however, amongst legal traditions in terms of the extent to which they claim to regulate human conduct. Chthonic law doesn't appear to regulate much, yet in proscribing all conduct incompatible with a recycling cosmos its normativity is unquestionable. Talmudic and islamic law regulate most of life; they are normative in all directions. The civil and common laws are laws of liberty; both have existed as optional, suppletive forms of social regulation, allowing some form of escape from congealed, chthonic patterns. In modern guise, they would both to some extent deny the normativity of their own pasts (reconstructed as fact), both directing attention to a more limited form of present law. Yet underlying notions of intellectual liberty, rights and institutional integrity are inherent and highly normative features of both, however notions of liberty and rights may contribute to present disruption. Hindu law allows a lot of choice, both individually and in terms of multiple informal traditions, yet no one who is hindu would escape some form of law recognized as hindu. Asian tradition rejects much formal law, but does so in favour of another type of normativity, one profoundly anchored, informally, in the past.

So in spite of some confusing signals, normativity is a constant feature of these legal traditions. Even in the western ones, where liberty is most prized, it is often constrained, and where it is not is assumes its own normativity—the obligation to be free and to exercise one's rights. The indecision of relativism is a problem external to these traditions; they do not acknowledge it. Relativism would be a problem, however, where legal traditions meet. It could be avoided by universalism—by insisting on the normativity in all cases of one's own tradition. If one refuses universalism, in the name of some form of tolerance, how does one avoid the indecision of relativism? How is this question dealt with, in the traditions?

Complex traditions

The legal traditions which have been examined all contain sub-traditions, either purely internal ones or lateral traditions. This appears to be another perspective of the multiplicity of traditions; the nest (like Russian dolls) within one another, such that the largest can even be said to be composed of a series of supporting, complementing, even recalcitrant, sub-traditions. *The largest, major traditions would therefore be large and major because of their complexity.* They succeed in bringing together, in the name of some important principle or being, a number of identifiable other traditions, providing some form of overarching cohesion."

Questions

1. Which legal traditions have been identified in the text?

2. Can you identify any traditions that have been left out? What does this say about the way in which Glenn has "carved up the world's law"?

III. COMPARING TWO TRADITIONS: COMMON AND CIVIL LAW

We now turn to a concrete example of the comparison of different legal traditions. In the following extracts, the authors have chosen to use common law and civil law traditions as their object of study. Each, however, focuses on different aspects of comparison. In the first text, by Farrar and Dugdale, the authors provide a brief overview of the two traditions and they make some broad conclusions about the differences between them. In the second text, Nicholas takes a particular example of the civil law in practice drawn from a text on the French law of contract. You should read both these extracts with a view to understanding what the authors identify as the similarities and differences between the common law and civil law traditions, as well as how these similarities and differences are reflected in the English common law and the French civil law systems.

J.D. Farrar and A.M. Dugdale, *Introduction to Legal Method*, 3rd edn (London: Sweet and Maxwell, 1990), pp.247–50:

The civilian tradition

"This is the oldest of the surviving traditions and can perhaps be traced to 450 BC, the date of the XII Tables in Rome which were a priestly codification of early Roman law.

It is the tradition of the original six member states of the EEC and Spain and Portugal together with their former colonies. It is the background to much of the early development of the EEC and indeed it has had a strong influence on the development of both public and private international law.

Roman law developed from a priestly system to a highly developed secular system through the influence of jurists (jurisconsults) who did not actually perform the function of a modern lawyer but wrote systematic treatises on particular branches of law. The law itself consisted of the *jus civile*, which only applied to citizens of the Roman empire, and the more flexible *jus gentium* which applied to non citizens. Both systems underwent considerable modification over centuries. In the sixth century AD the emperor Justinian arranged for the production of a Digest and codification of the law which assimilated the laws and doctrinal writings, eliminating conflict. Institutes were also prepared as a primer for law students. This mammoth work of rationalisation enabled Roman law to survive the decline and ultimate destruction of the Roman Empire. The Roman law tradition survived the Dark Ages and was studied in the medieval universities as the basis of rational principles of law.

However, it not only survived as a scholarly tradition, but also as a source of common law of nations at a time when Europe was subject to a multiplicity of local customs and laws. Voltaire reckoned that one changed one's laws as often as one changed one's horse in riding through eighteenth century France. In arriving at a just solution of mercantile disputes Roman law was often resorted to on the Continent. It also influenced the development of the canon law of the Christian Church and the movement towards the early conceptions of international law.

So, therefore, an important ingredient in the civilian tradition is the common inheritance of Roman law. However, a combination of the enlightenment of the eighteenth century and revolution created an impetus to modern codification. This was achieved in the Napoleonic period in France at the beginning of the nineteenth century, although Frederick the Great had attempted a less successful codification of parts of Prussian law in the eighteenth century. The Code Napoléon was a masterly codification of French customary law and Roman law as it stood at 1804. Directly and indirectly it was the blueprint for much European codification. Its basis was simple clear statements of law which left much unsaid. A different approach was adopted in the German codification measures of the end of the nineteenth century. Here the emphasis was on detail and a self contained code—every answer was to be found in the code itself. Most modern Civilian systems opt for one of these two models of codification although each system has areas of law which are not completely codified.

A further characteristic of Civilian systems is the high status accorded to doctrinal writings. While not a source of law as such they rank as high as or of higher status than judicial precedent as a guide to the interpretation of the codes. Where the law is codified the code is the definitive source. The status of judicial precedent is naturally less than in common law systems. It is not that precedent is unimportant in practice but that in theory its validity derives from the words of the code itself. Individual precedents are not binding. A body of precedent is regarded as good evidence of the true meaning of the code. . . .

Last, the Civilian tradition tends to employ more inquisitorial procedures with regard to fact finding than the common law and the whole of its procedure is administered by a career judiciary.

The Common Law tradition

. . . First, the common law, while slightly influenced by the form, did not receive the substance of the Roman law inheritance. It steadfastly resisted it for reasons which were partly political and partly professional. Roman law was linked with Catholicism and later with Stuart autocracy. England, unlike Scotland, developed its own professional structure and tradition from an early date. This was until remarkably recently outside the university framework. English law was not taught at the universities until the eighteenth century, but was the province of the Inns of Court and the profession. The history of legal education in the seventeenth and eighteenth century is rather appalling. Small parts of Roman law did influence some aspects of the common law, but this is mainly as a result of nineteenth century rationalisation.

Secondly, in spite of Bentham and the codification movement in the nineteenth century, the only area of codification has been in commercial law. . . .

Thirdly, as we have seen, although text books by living authors are now cited there is still less status accorded to doctrinal writing in the common law tradition. The status seems to depend *ad hominem* to a greater extent than in the civilian system and reflects perhaps the closed social world of the English judiciary.

Fourthly, the status of judicial precedent is much higher and it is an actual source of law. The standard of the judiciary in the common law world has been high and the process of ratiocination is more obvious in a common law judgment than in the bleak arrested style of a French judgment. As a continuing source, however, with the multiplication of reports the form of the law remains irrational and almost uncontrollable.

Fifthly, the terminology, but not necessarily the practice of interpretation, differs from the civilian tradition as we have seen.

Last, the common law tradition shows a marked preference for adversarial procedure before judges with forensic experience. The emphasis is perhaps more on justice than on truth."

B. Nicholas, *The French Law of Contract*, 2nd edn (Oxford: Clarendon Press, 1992), pp.1–23:

"French law belongs to that family of legal systems to which we attach the name of 'Civil law'. This family embraces the systems of continental Europe (or at least Western Europe), and also of Latin America and many other countries which derive their legal systems from continental Europe. The name is often criticized, especially by Civil lawyers themselves, because it refers to only one element in the tradition which unites those systems, and also because it ignores the differences which distinguish one from another. (In much the same way in ordinary life a stranger sees the resemblances between members of a family, while they themselves are more aware of their individuality). But the usage is inveterate among Common lawyers, and the name, if properly understood, does point to some important characteristics which the systems have in common and which are foreign to the Common law.

The origin of the name is clear. To the Romans the term *ius civile* had meant, at its widest, the law of a particular state, or more narrowly, the law of Rome herself. It was in accordance with this usage that Justinian's compilation of Roman law came to be known, after its rediscovery in the eleventh century, as the *Corpus Iuris Civilis*. And 'Civil law' thereafter meant the rediscovered Roman law. As this law was 'received' by the emergent states and cities of continental Europe as a *ius commune*, or common law, which was applied in default of, or to a varying extent in substitution for, the local law, it was natural that the English, whose courts had stood apart from this reception, should see in this common factor the identifying mark of the legal systems of the Continent. Nor did they habitually make any distinction between this contemporary Civil law and the historical law of Rome. Blackstone, for example, calls it 'the imperial law'.

During the past two hundred years, however, the justification for thus seeing the law of the Continent as predominantly Roman law in a modern context has diminished. The most important influence in this dwindling of the Roman element has been the movement for codification, the first great achievement of which was the enactment of Napoleon's *Code civil* in 1804. The codes which thereafter spread over Europe were important (in this context) in two ways. First, they cut the law off from its Roman roots, the *Corpus Iuris Civilis* could no long be cited as direct authority. If Roman rules were still applied, this was because they were embodied in the relevant code, and not (except as a matter of history) because they were to be found in the *Corpus Iuris*. Moreover, as Roman law disappeared from the courts, it took on a different appearance in the lecture room. The interest shifted from the task of interpreting the *Corpus Iuris* as a practical system to that of unearthing classical law. For that law lay buried beneath both the editorial work of Justinian and the heavy layer of interpretation and harmonization which had been elaborated by centuries of activity in the universities of Europe. 'Civil law' (or *ius commune*) was now seen to be not the same as Roman law.

This does not mean that there are no common elements in, say, French and German law which justify our still speaking of them as 'Civil law systems', but they are Civil law in a different sense. They belong to the Civil law because their methods of thought, their attitudes to law and its source, derive from the centuries in which the *ius commune*, Romanistic but not Roman, was created out of the materials in the *Corpus Iuris*. And those methods and attitudes were different, as we shall see, from those of the English Common law, which was nurtured in a quite other environment.

The Roman element, therefore, has dwindled since the coming of the codes. Its importance was indeed never as exclusive as the English use of the name 'Civil law' suggested. Apart from Canon law (which was Roman in spirit and, like Roman law, universal), there were everywhere two other elements: customary law and legislation. But these varied from one legal system to another, or even, in the case of customary law, from one local area to another, and it was natural for the Common lawyer to emphasize the universal element. Moreover, the non-Roman elements were mainly to be found in those areas of the law (the law of the family and of inheritance) which are everywhere most likely to be affected by differences of culture and of what one now calls 'policy'. The contribution of Roman law, on the other hand, was strongest in the parts which have, at least until recently, been most exclusively the handiwork of lawyers: the law of obligations (and especially the law of contract, which is the concern of this book), the law of property, and the general conceptual framework of the whole system. The advent of the codes, however (and this was the second way in which they diminished the Roman character of the systems to which they applied), unified and systematized the customary element, while the spirit of the times and the complexity of modern life has everywhere produced an ever-swelling volume of legislation only loosely related to the traditional Roman framework.

It is this framework which provides a link between the Common lawyer's use of 'Civil law' and the meaning which French lawyers give to *droit civil*. In its widest sense this denotes the whole of private law.

Characteristics of French law

The differences of method and attitude which have now to be identified derive, we have said, from the *ius commune*. For though important elements of French law come, as we have seen, from canon law, customary law, and legislation, the Common lawyer finds the principal differentiating characteristics of the system in the inheritance from this *ius commune*.

The heart of the matter is that the *ius commune* is a law of the book, elaborated in the universities, whereas the Common law is a law of the case, created by the courts. The *ius commune*, in theory at least, sprang fully formed from the *Corpus Iuris Civilis*, the function of the universities being that of interpretation. The Common law, on the other hand, is in a state of continuous creation and by its nature is never complete. Again, the *ius commune* was seen as universally valid, regardless of time or place. It was a set of rules for the conduct of life in society—rules which might or might not be applied in any particular court or jurisdiction. (Hence it is still true today that in the universities of the Continent law is studied by large numbers who will never go into practice.) The Common law, by contrast, is concerned to provide solutions to individual disputes, not to propound universal precepts; and it is expressed, in its traditional form, in terms of actions or remedies rather than of substantive rules. Insofar as nowadays it does think in terms of rules, those rules are seen as a generalization from the solutions of individual disputes, whereas for the Civil lawyer the rules logically precede the solutions. In short, for the Common law the beginning is the case, whereas for the *ius commune* the beginning is the book.

With the advent of the codes the character of the book changes, but the conception of law remains the same. The beginning is now the code or codes, not the *Corpus Iuris*, but the primacy of the written law remains. Law is still seen as a system, complete and intellectually coherent, composed of substantive rules. And the creative function is still that of interpretation, a function exercised in the first place by the universities. The decisions of the courts are, in conventional theory, merely an application of the enacted law. Some of these features need further examination in the particular context of French law.

(a) Primacy of legislation

In the conventional French analysis there are only two sources of law: legislation and custom. The latter is only interstitial and in the present context can be ignored. Law is primarily and characteristically a body of rules enacted by the state, to be found in the codes and, in ever-increasing measure, in legislation supplementary to the codes. Indeed, just as a Common lawyer will derive a general principle from particular cases, a French lawyer may, by what has been called 'amplifying induction', find in individual enactments evidence of a wider legislative intent which can be applied outside the area covered by the individual enactments. The Common lawyer's approach is quite different. For him law has characteristically been the unwritten law found in the decisions of the courts. It is true, of course, that legislation is the primary source in the sense that in case of conflict it will prevail, but it has traditionally been regarded as an inroad on or suspension of the Common law, which will revive when the legislation is repealed. Particular enactments will therefore be restrictively interpreted. So far from inferring a more general legislative intent, the Common lawyer will argue that if Parliament had intended to lay down a more general principle, it would have done so expressly.

This difference is reflected in a difference in the approach of the two systems to the interpretation of legislation (and, as a corollary, a difference in the style of drafting). The English courts, seeing legislation as an inroad on the basic unwritten law, interpret it restrictively, so as to minimize the inroad. This attitude would make no sense for the French lawyer for whom the basic law is itself legislation. In the period of the *ius commune*, when lawyers had to adapt the unchanging texts of the *Corpus Iuris* to the changing needs of society and to find a harmony in the rich discordance of these texts, they necessarily adopted a very free and creative method of interpretation. The method remains, and it is indeed in accord with the relatively subordinate position which is allotted to the judiciary by the French version of the separation of powers. Legislation is a manifestation of the will of the state and the function of the judiciary as an organ of the state is to give effect to that will.

This function is pre-supposed by the simplicity and brevity of French legislative drafting. The English draftsman tries to make his text 'judge-proof' by anticipating every eventuality, and he often in consequence produces a complex and technical formulation which only a lawyer can interpret. The French draftsman, by contrast, can rely on the collaboration of the courts, and his text is therefore limited to quite broad propositions. That this is true of the *Code civil* is well known (and it is a source of pride and confidence to the Frenchman that his law is presented in a simple and intelligible form) but even the necessarily more complex legislation of modern times may leave much to be filled in by interpretation.

(b) Character of the codes

If legislation is the characteristic form of law in France and the codes are the characteristic form of legislation, the *Code civil* is the characteristic code. The Napoleonic codification consisted of five codes, but the term *Code Napoléon* was reserved for the *Code civil* alone. And with justice. For the *Code civil* is the centre-piece to which the great influence of the whole codification is attributable.

A code in the strict sense is a systematic and complete statement of a body of law. In this sense the *Corpus Iuris Civilis* of Justinian is not a code. For though it is complete, it is not in any recognizable way systematic. The *Code civil* is systematic, though its system (which echoes, without entirely reproducing, that of the Institutes of Gaius and Justinian) is, as a piece of analysis, easily criticized; and it is a complete statement of the law governing relations between individuals (except insofar as these are governed by the *Code de commerce*) as that law was understood in 1804. We have seen, however, that even then the simplicity and brevity of its drafting left much to be supplied by interpretation, and it is now not complete in any sense. For the increasing complexity of modern life has called forth a large body of additional legislation. Some of this can be said merely to amplify the provisions of the Code, but by far the greater part is concerned with matters quite outside the area of the traditional *droit civil*. Codification, moreover, creates an expectation that all law will be presented in a systematic form, and a good deal of the additional legislation has itself been reduced to the form of subordinate codes. In England, by contrast, even in those areas of the law which are largely the creation of legislation, a systematic statement of the whole body of the law is not undertaken. At most, as in the Companies Act 1985, a consolidation of existing legislation is enacted, but this leaves the essential Common law foundations unstated; and when such a consolidation comes to be amended, as in the Companies Act 1989, no attempt is made to build the new legislation into the old. A codifying statute is a rarity, and the few which have been enacted deal in fact with areas of the law which were almost entirely judge-made. . . .

(d) Authority of case law

The courts of the *ancien régime* (the *parlements*) were one of the main objects of the hostility of the Revolution, not least because of their pretensions to a law-making function. The Constituent Assembly of 1790 took care that the new courts should be confined to the narrowly judicial function of applying the law in suits between private individuals (or, in criminal matters, between the state and the individual). They were to have no jurisdiction over the administration, and in exercising their proper function they were not to lay down general rules. They were even required to refer any matter of interpretation to the legislature. This was of course quite impracticable and remained a dead letter, but the prohibition against laying down general rules when deciding individual cases was repeated in article 5 of the *Code civil*. . . .

There is . . . no rule of binding precedent, but there is well-established practice that lower courts will normally follow the jurisprudence of the *Cour de cassation*. This leaves open, of course, the question of what constitutes a jurisprudence. It has often been said that the important difference in practice between the English and the French systems of precedent is that in England a single decision is sufficient, whereas in France authority attaches to what is called a *jurisprudence constante*, i.e. to a concordant series of decisions. But it is easy to point to single decisions which marked a new departure—and were immediately recognized as doing so. The significant distinction is rather between an *arrêt de principe* and an *arrêt d'espèce*, i.e. between a judgment which is intended to establish a principle (either because the case law has been uncertain or conflicting or because the court has decided to alter its previous jurisprudence) and one which, as an English lawyer might say, is to be confined to its own facts. This is not to suggest that all decisions are capable of being labelled as one or the other. The great majority of the vast number of *arrêts* rendered every year by the *Cour de cassation* are unremarkable decisions which merely augment an already well-established *jurisprudence constante* on the matter in issue. It is to the small residue of cases which do not fit into this category that the distinction applies. It is not, of course, a distinction which declares itself on the face of the *arrêt*, and its application is a matter of art as much as of science, but the reader of the French reports will acquire a part of the skill if he remembers that in a literary form as laconic as that of the French judgment, particularly as it is practised in the *Cour de cassation*, no word is wasted and none is unconsidered. For example, the formulation of the principle which constitutes the major premise of the judgment may be repeated unaltered through dozens or hundreds of cases, while the critical reader wonders at the increasingly forced interpretation of either the principle or the facts which is necessary in order to complete the syllogism, until finally a small alteration is made which so adjusts the principle that the forced interpretation is no longer necessary. Again, when the *jurisprudence* is uncertain or in disarray, a categorical statement of a general principle, particularly if it is placed at the beginning of the *arrêt* as what is called a *chapeau*, will be seen as the mark of the *arrêt de principe*.

There remains a very considerable difference in the methods by which in the two systems the principle established by a decision is identified. In the first example given above the alert reader will notice the change in formulation, but may well be left in doubt as to what it portends. The judgment itself will give him no assistance. If he is fortunate, this may be one of the rare cases in which the *conclusions* or the *rapport* are published. Otherwise he must interpret the change in the light of the *doctrine* on the subject, which will have discussed the difficulties presented by the previous cases. An attempt at such an interpretation will often be appended as a *note* to the report.

In an English judgment, on the other hand, the principle of the case is not encapsulated in a single carefully pruned and polished sentence. The decision of the case typically evolves from an examination of the previous cases and a discussion of how far the pattern set by those cases needs to be adapted to accommodate the new fact situation. The characteristic English intellectual device of 'distinguishing' is unknown in France, both because the form of the judgment provides no opportunity for it and because, at least in the *Cour de cassation*, the facts play a subordinate role, and may indeed be so elliptically stated as to be unintelligible without a reference to the decision of the court below. The reason for this is in part that the *Cour de cassation* is, as we have seen, concerned only with an examination of the proposition of law relied on by the court below, and in part that the courts as a whole still think of the judicial process as one of applying to the facts before them a rule established a priori. The cases are illustrations of principles rather than the material from which principles are drawn.

This attitude to facts lends considerable importance to the distinction between fact and law. Findings of fact are within the uncontrolled discretion of the court which tries the case (and this, on the French view of the nature of an appeal, includes the relevant *cour d'appel*). The *Cour de cassation* cannot interfere with this *pouvoir souverain du juge du fond* unless the interpretation of the primary facts is so unreasonable that it can be said to have 'denatured' them. From this it follows that the wider the area of what is categorized as fact, the more restricted will be the unifying power of the *Cour de cassation*. The view of cases as illustrations, which is an aspect of the tendency of a 'law of the book' to formulate broad rules, leaves a large area to fact. In the Common law, by contrast, since the law evolves from the cases, there is a constant tendency for fact to harden into law. Case-made rules are by their nature narrow. From time to time an act of judicial generalization, or perhaps the intervention of the legislature, will produce a broad rule or principle, but the process of producing small rules out of facts will then resume. . . .

Again, the *Code civil* lays down the broad rule that a mistake makes an agreement null if it concerns the 'substance' of the object to which the agreement relates. What constitutes 'substance' is a question of fact outside the control of the *Cour de cassation*, and since the form of the judgment given by the trial court does not require it to justify or explain its interpretation of the word, or to relate that interpretation to the interpretations implicit in other decisions of the same or other courts, there is here a very wide area open to judicial discretion. The French judge, supposedly confined and controlled by a clear written law, often in fact has a much freer hand than the English judge.

To put the matter in another way, in many areas French law is less detailed than English, even though the number of reported decisions is much larger. An English book on contract will be re-edited every four or five years and each new edition will embody many changes. Its French counterpart will probably be re-edited less often and the changes will be much less numerous. . . .

(f) Conceptualism and pragmatism

It is sometimes said that the Civil law is excessively conceptual or 'logical' or 'formalist', whereas the Common law is pragmatic and concrete. (A similar contrast is made, within the Common law between English law and American law.) This observation seems to bear two different meanings.

(i) It can mean that the Civil law will apply a given principle or concept 'logically' even though the practical consequences are unjust or inconvenient, whereas the Common law will abandon a principle if its consequences are unacceptable. More precisely this is a contrast not between logic and the lack of it, but between an approach which treats principles as having an immutable meaning (or at least is unwilling to re-examine the established interpretation in the light of its consequences), and one which acknowledges that meanings and interpretations change with circumstances. In other words, it is a contrast between an approach which speculates as to the correct conceptual analysis of a situation or relationship without advertising to the consequences which flow from that analysis (or without considering what policy may account for the attribution of those consequences which flow from that analysis) and an approach which acknowledges that principles and concepts are shorthand for practical consequences. For the realist or antiformalist cannot dispense with concepts without abandoning the element in law which ensures that like is treated alike; he can only insist that concepts be seen in the context of their consequences.

As far as French *jurisprudence* is concerned, the Common lawyer's view is encouraged by the form of the judgment, which gives no place to a consideration of practical consequences or of questions of 'policy'. It appears to treat principles as frozen in a single interpretation, whereas the English judgment makes plain the process by which convenience prevails over 'logic', or, more precisely, by which the previously accepted principle or interpretation is distinguished from one which can accommodate the argument from convenience. We have seen, however, that the form of the judgment does not correctly record the process by which the decision is reached.

As far as *doctrine* is concerned, the criticism was certainly well-founded in the nineteenth century, when the survival of eighteenth century natural law ideas, combined with an exclusive concentration on deriving the law from an examination of the words of the Code, did produce an attitude like that characterized above. Nor was this attitude confined to France. It was to be found even more markedly in German writing. And this in turn dominated the work of the contemporary English analytical jurists and the early English academic textbooks. It probably survived in Italy, where the isolation of doctrinal writing from the decisions of the courts and a general lack of interest in the application of principles to facts is still noticeable.

Present-day *doctrine*, particularly in the most recent works, is much more practically orientated than it used to be and devotes a great deal of attention to the decisions of the *Cour de cassation*, but it can still sometimes appear to the English lawyer to be examining a closed system. To some extent this is a mistaken impression, attributable to the different status of case law. As we have seen, the English lawyer, because he is constantly returning to the cases, is visibly rooting his principles and concepts in practical situations, whereas the French lawyer derives his principles and concepts primarily from the Code and legislation. That these principles and concepts are not reconcilable with *jurisprudence* is not, as it would be in England, a reason for abandoning them outright, though it is one ground for criticizing them. And to say that a principle is not rooted in the cases does not mean that it takes no account of practical considerations. What is true is that the emphasis in doctrinal writings is placed more on rational coherence and less on practical consequences than it is either in Common law writing, or, usually, in the *rapport* or *conclusions* presented to the courts.

(ii) This brings us to the second sense which can be borne by the observation which we are discussing. In this second sense the observation refers to the fact, which we have already noted, that the French *droit civil* is, ostensibly at least, a complete and coherent system, each part of which is capable of being related to every other part. As we can see from the many cross-references which editions of the *Code civil* provide, a French lawyer takes it for granted that one article can be interpreted in the light of another in a quite different part of the Code or in some subsequent legislation. This view of the law as a single, intellectually coherent system is common to all Civil law systems (it is carried to a far higher degree of generality by German law than by French) but it does not come readily to the mind of the Common lawyer. This is not, however, a matter of the presence or absence of logic or concepts, but of the scale on which each system thinks. English law thinks in pigeon-holes and rarely seeks to relate one pigeon-hole to another. This is the reason for its unease when it has to deal, for example, with the borderland between contract and tort. This relative lack of large-scale concepts reflects, of course, the primacy of the judge over the academic lawyer in the development of English law."

Questions

1. According to Farrar and Dugdale, what are the principal points of divergence between the common law and civilian traditions? What are the similarities?

2. What do Farrar and Dugdale mean by their statement that, in the common law tradition, "the emphasis is perhaps more on justice than on truth"?

3. How would a French judgment differ in style and content from an English judgment?

4. What is the role of doctrine in the civil law tradition?

5. It is sometimes claimed that common lawyers have a "bottom-up" approach to creating law, whereas civilians use a "top-down" approach. What does this mean?

IV. COMPARATIVE LAW AND A GLOBALISING LEGAL ORDER

Our story of comparative law began with the romantic hope of a group of lawyers for a common law of humanity which would encompass the world. But even at the Paris Congress of 1900 the importance of unification into a single legal system as an aim of comparative law was hotly debated. After more than a century, arguments still focus on the merits of a unified legal system as opposed to a diversity of legal traditions. In a world that is increasingly *globalised*, the issue of legal unification has become all the more important.

The importance placed on the study of legal *harmonisation* within the European Union makes this a very topical issue. The following extracts present diverse viewpoints as to the merits and the very possibility of legal harmonisation in the European Union.

B.S. Markesinis, "A Matter of Style" (1994) 110 L.Q.R. 607 at 625:

"In this lecture a number of differences have been noted between the style and contents of the English and German cases which can, ultimately, be traced to fundamental and interrelated decisions taken by these systems in the distant past. The English ones, of course, are well-known: a preference for procedure over principles of substantive law; a neglect of the academic component of the law; the appointment of judges from a small group of leading practitioners; and the adoption of the jury system with all the consequences this has had on procedure and presentation of legal argument. Known though these are, they may well be repeated here since two new developments are seriously affecting the second of the above-named factors and, indirectly, the law that is handed down by our courts. The developments to which I am referring are the greater interaction between English and continental European universities and the fact that nowadays in England a university training has become an essential ingredient of a legal (including judicial) career. These two developments are, I believe, to determine what we will 'take' in future years from continental systems and, also, what we might be able to 'give' them in exchange. . . .

If this development is now seen in the context of the even newer 'European' perspective—and by that I mean the growing significance for municipal law of the decisions of the European Courts in Luxembourg and Strasbourg and the growing contacts under Erasmus-type programmes—it can lead to the conclusion that it is no longer fanciful to predict a steady growth in the impact that European law and doctrine will have on ours. This may not affect the style of judgments—a main theme of this paper—indeed, I hope it does not! But it is bound to strengthen their doctrinal content—the second theme of this paper—combating the idea that because the tasks of judge and jurist are (in *some* respects) different *they must also be carried out in complete isolation from each other*. In this sense, too, the tide of European ideas will prove difficult to contain. The student of today, who will be the judge of tomorrow, will be unlikely to resist this influence since it will not be alien to him but, on the contrary, will have played a part in his formation and training.

But will the influence be one-sided? I think not and I hope not. If we do not remain in our shells we, too, can and will influence developments elsewhere. Moreover, I believe our *main* contribution may well be something of a paradox since it will come from our universities (which in historical terms were the junior partners in the development of our law) exporting the teaching techniques they have developed relying on the work of our judges. For, though statutory law is increasing in size and complexity, case law is still at the base of common law education. This and the tutorial system (to varying but, by comparison to continental universities, small numbers of students) are the distinctive features of our legal education. The political tradition of the European universities makes the second feature enviable but totally inimitable. But the first feature, coupled with the emergence of English as the new lingua franca of the western world, gives the common law a powerful instrument with which to make its own contribution to the transnational set of legal rules which many refer to as the new *jus commune*. Let me say just a few more words as to how this could come about.

Though certain features of the common law judgment may come to be imitated by foreign judges (and others rightly avoided), it would be foolish to predict any wholesale European importation of the model. But the study of English judgments is growing as more and more young lawyers from the continent of Europe spend short or longer periods of time in common law universities (the Oxford *Magister Juris* being, perhaps, one of the best illustrations). Though particular solutions of our law may often appeal to foreign lawyers, none, I think, return to their countries believing that our doctrinal analyses or theoretical constructions can ever equal theirs. But I do believe that they return to their base impressed by the common law decision, by its grammatical clarity, by the way it has revealed and discussed the issues that in their country are hidden by legal jargon, and—most importantly—by the way it is used as a tool for imparting further legal know-how. Here, I believe, we score heavily over continental models. And, I hope, we will exploit this strength in the context of many current, private and semi-public schemes aiming to draw up a European law curriculum or, even, design a European law school by becoming involved in such projects rather than rejecting them out of hand. For, behind these projects is not utopian idealism but the growing need *somehow* to harmonise teaching materials and interrelate legal cultures for the world of tomorrow in which lawyers will find themselves being as mobile as their clients. (And this is not mentioning the former eastern European countries which are looking westward for ideas for their legal education and for new laws which they need in order to cope with the new kind of economies that they have adopted.)

The English judgment—and the learning of law through studying the judgment—is, in short, along with our language, one of the two major implements at our disposal in the struggle for shaping the European legal culture of the next century. If we wish to have some impact on this new world we must be prepared to use them."

F. Werro "Notes on the purpose and aims of comparative law" (2001) 75 Tul. L. Rev. 1225 at 1230:

An Evaluation of the Difference between the American and the European Approaches

"Beyond the fact that comparative law in the United States was largely shaped by European immigrants and that this fact might be a source of discontent and doubt for contemporary Americans, it seems to me that the difference in attitude can also be explained from a more general point of view. One could venture two explanations. One is contemporary American intellectual leadership, and the other is the very way Americans and Europeans deal with law; this latter explanation explains perhaps in part the former. Let me briefly develop the second explanation.

The opposition between law as a science and law as a practical tool for solving conflicts remains valid in explaining the ways in which Europeans and Americans deal differently with comparative law. The European belief in law as a system, which one is only really able to understand if one is Kant's grandchild, on the one hand, and the American belief in law as a constantly evolving and overtly political method of dispute resolution, accompanied by a suspicion against any attempt of systematization or conceptualization, on the other hand, remains a distinction deeply rooted in lawyers' attitudes toward the law and thus toward comparative law. Another way of explaining this important difference in sensibility between (continental) Europeans and Americans should perhaps focus on the contrast between law as ultimately defined by a parliament after years of broad consultation with all possible interest groups and law as ultimately made in the courtroom with the understanding that majority votes should not restrain the judge's ability to shape fundamental principles. This difference also explains the differences in style in the teaching and training of future lawyers.

These differences should not be seen as absolute, but rather as influencing the varied emphases placed on doctrine versus practice at different levels of the legal edifice. For example, I do not believe that European lawyers have not understood the teachings of legal realism, even if it might look that way in most European classrooms. It is rather that legal realist considerations occur in a different place: not so much in the courts, but rather in the parliaments. In fact, I would think that lawmaking involves a wider range of people and interest groups in Europe than in the United States. Arguably, once the process is finished, there is less need than in the United States to debate the choice made. This explains in part why European studies tend to ignore the forces that shape the law; these forces are taken care of in advance. Thus, law gets taught as a finished and coherent product, rather than an ongoing, context-driven process.

Thus, to go back to our inquiry about the big questions in comparative law today, it is tempting to think that we need to take a differentiated view. We need to define the answer in accordance with our own context. In the United States, arguably, we need to take the concerns raised by the 1998 symposium seriously, and in some ways step out of the European shadow while taking full advantage of 'law and –ism'. In Europe, although regrettably in my view—a bit more 'law and –ism' as well as certain distrust for the pure grammar of the law in education would not hurt—we may want to satisfy ourselves with the idea that comparative law is doing well and serving essentially all the practical and doctrinal purposes it should be serving.

Yet having said this, I wonder if it is not the task of comparativists to try to define a common agenda. In a globalized world, one would think that there is much need for such an objective.

The phenomenon commonly referred to as globalization or other integrative processes triggers two questions that comparativists need more than ever to tackle: the first relates to the way in which one can acknowledge and integrate cultural diversity, and the second relates to the means of avoiding Western hegemony.

There may be many other questions linked to these two. For example, comparativists should study the risks of provincialism and parochialism, both on the part of minorities and on the part of hegemonic majorities. One major question appears to be how to put in place a better understanding amongst lawyers that law within the Western sense of the word is not the only way to define social norms of conduct.

The Need for Understanding Diversity

In a world driven by trends toward global law, the question of diversity has become essential. The need to define diversity and its proper boundaries arises more fundamentally than ever. To the extent that cultural diversity is a reality, law is bound to be defined in diversified terms.

It seems to me, however, that we are even less sure than ever before of what cultural diversity means and to what extent diversity should be reflected in legal choices. We run into this question in relation to World Trade Organization (WTO) issues for example. On a smaller scale, on a European level, we run into this question in relation to the project of unification of private law. Claiming 'the impossibility of legal transplants' is probably too extreme a position and betrays an exaggeration of cultural diversity, at least on the European level.

However, the statement that law and society are not in close relationship is also quite obviously an oversimplification. . . . both approaches need adjustment and corrections. To deny the possibility or the desirability of legal transplants seems to contradict the teachings of history and is at odds with the need for legal integration in certain geographic areas. It also assumes a degree of cultural diversity in Europe, for instance, that I fail to recognize. If diversity exists, it does not, in my view, reach a level of intensity that is necessarily relevant for legal integration, at least in certain areas of the law. Of course insisting on the nomadic or transplantable character of rules of law cannot mean that 'change in the law is independent from the workings of any social, historical, or cultural substratum'.

In other words, it appears that we need to find a middle road. While 'pain' is not 'bread' nor 'Brot', we might want to recognize that 'pain' is not 'pain' either, even in the same place, and that it might nevertheless be useful to treat all "pains" under the law in the same way. I do not wish to argue here the essential ingredients of the middle road. I think, however, that it is a necessity to define them. . . . if we want to make the European single market a reality, we need at least a common law of contracts. This may require an adaptation of legal education. I fail to see, however, why the European Principles of Contract Law would necessarily reduce European cultural diversity—whatever this evolving notion means—even if they were to become common law enacted by the European Parliament. I might use Pierre Legrand's eloquent but exaggerated views as a target. If we were to take his warnings as seriously as he expresses them, not only should we refuse the idea of a European civil code or of a European model law, but we should work toward abolishing all contemporary civil codes: they do not pay enough tribute to local culture.

Questioning Western Hegemony

The most important challenge in a globalized world seems to me related to the necessity to define the tools that will help prevent Western hegemonic thinking. We need to help lawyers acquire the means of nonchauvinistic legal thinking and work toward reducing nationalistic legal tendencies.

In an era of globalized trade and exchanges, it appears to be an absolute necessity to . . . safeguard competition in legal rules. To think that one country or one system has the monopoly of good ideas is not only naive and silly, but quite dangerous. Acknowledging the other as such . . . is a vital necessity. Nobody is entitled to be responsible for the well-being of the world. The North must acknowledge that it has to learn from the South as much as the West has to learn from the East. It might be that the WTO will have an impact on China. It may also very well be that China will change the WTO: we must prepare for that possibility and define mechanisms that help us fight chauvinism.

Comparativists are the first who must learn to change their attitudes so that they can teach their colleagues who deal only on the local level. Comparativists should define the appropriate tools for such an endeavor. I do not see that happening enough, and I think that this will be a problem if there is no improvement in the next century."

Efstathios Banakas, "The contribution of comparative law to the harmonization of European private law" in Andrew Harding and Esin Orucu *Comparative Law in the 21st Century* (London/ The Hague/New York: Kluwer, 2002) pp.184–185, 186–188, 189:

"The pace of Europeanization of legal life in the last few years in the European community must weigh heavily in answering the question of how culture-specific national legal systems still are. From universities to law firms, the European mix increases, and the European Courts in Luxembourg grow every day in confidence in laying foundations for common principles of European private law. Law students already have a European casebook on tort Law, and judges and practitioners a European textbook on contract Law. Several groups of European academics are at work developing common principles and rules on contract law (Lando group), tort (Vienna group), or, casting a wider net, a European Civil Code and the Common Core of European Civil Law (the Trento project). The European Academy in Trier is only one of many academic institutions offering a relentless programme of seminars in European private law, attended by practitioners of member states as part of their continuous education programme. What is the effect of all this on national legal cultures? This is an enormous question, of an enormous significance, which comparative lawyers in Europe must see as a big challenge.

The answer to that question will enlighten the debate of whether legal harmonization is a good or a bad thing for Europe, and whether it proceeds on the right path. For, whatever the political power of the market may be (and effecting the common market is the unique basis of harmonization of private law in the European Union at the present moment), the market, as the American experience shows, is only concerned with economic efficiency, and will not provide answers to wider questions of validity and value of legal rules and practices. It is difficult to foresee how far national legal cultures will be defended by national communities, against the onslaught of continuing European integration. There may be objectively little to regret, in terms of moral, artistic or other value, in the disappearance of national legal cultures in Europe. But there is evidence that in some member states other parallel [sic] to the national cultures, such as religion or literature are emerging as political flagships of resistance in support of national identity. And there is also evidence that certain bench-mark principles of national private law are now being defended as part of the constitutional fabric of member states, in anticipation of a further advance in harmonization, such as the French principle of *faute* or the English doctrine of public authority immunity in exercising discretion. More importantly perhaps, judges and practising lawyers in member states are increasingly unhappy with the scholarly rush to create a uniform theoretical basis of European private law. Private law is more than competition in the market or corporate and commercial trans-actions. It is also about intimate, very important aspects of personal life, that judges are convinced are better dealt with in the environment of local culture and tradition. There is evidence that in some members states judges and practising lawyers are already looking to their national governments for support in their defence of national legal culture against new Brussels initiatives. Could this be the beginning of the unfolding of the great process of harmonization of European private law? . . .

Civil codes in Europe have always been seen as important declarations of national legal identity, and the law of civil liability, the most dynamic part of civil law, has been the focus of efforts for distinctive national styles. Thus, in the two common law countries, United Kingdom and Ireland, the law of torts is jealously guarded as an idiosyncratic, judge-made branch of civil law with a practical and systematic importance unknown to Continental legal systems. The German Civil Code openly chose to differ from the Code Napoleon in its design of Liability for Unlawful Acts, after rejecting the idea of general clauses of liability similar to those of Articles 1382 *et seq.* CC, originally put forward in the first draft of the German Code produced by the first Commission. Germanic ideas of unlawfulness as an additional condition of delictual liability influenced, in different ways, the Spanish and Italian law of civil liability, both originally closer to the French, leading to separate development of the law by the courts in these two countries. The Greek and the Portuguese Civil Codes chose also their own ways of styling civil liability as important expressions of national legal culture, and the newest Dutch Civil Code ambitiously combined elements of all traditions. Extra-contractual liability, and its relation to other sources of civil liability such as breach of contract, has, in short, always been seen in the European legal systems as an issue of great intellectual, social and cultural importance, close to the definition of citizen's basic rights, reflecting the individual sensitivities of law and policy makers in different legal systems.

Despite the cultural resistance, it is true that a limited, piecemeal harmonization, of specific private law regimes, in areas that directly affect the operation of the common market or the free movement of persons and goods, has been agreed by Governments and attempted through Directives and Regulations. There have been a number of Directives and Draft Directives in diverse areas, such as: Product Liability for Defective Products, Consumer Protection, Consumer Credit, Package Travel, Holidays and Package Tours, Unfair Terms in Contracts, Proposal for a Directive on the Liability of Suppliers of Services, Proposal for a Directive on Liability for Injury caused by Waste.

But such areas apart, it is not immediately obvious whether there is the will, or, indeed, the need, for a systematic harmonization of private law in Europe, and the creation of a common European law. The question applies also to the broader issue of creating a European Civil Code, very much discussed among European politicians and academics recently. If there is a need, the will must be found. But present discussions and concerted efforts by various academic groups to formulate proposals for a European civil liability law or Civil Code, seem to put the cart before the horse in so much as they concentrate their efforts on how best to achieve harmonization, and much less on why such harmonization is needed. Are there any compelling reasons for harmonizing private law in Europe? . . .

A political ground for the harmonization of European private law can be found in the quest for a common European citizen's identity, a task that seems to be on its way to be confirmed as a political goal of the Union in the Charter of Human Rights, agreed in the European summit in Nice in December 2000. Uniform Human Rights can be seen as inevitably leading to uniform civil rights. If this is accepted, it will be a powerful argument for the harmonization of the law of civil liability in Europe. However, a number of Governments take a narrower view of the Charter, as addressing only the question of the protection of human rights internally in the Union, before Union organs and institutions, whereas others look at it as the first step of a constitutional restructuring of Europe, and an element of a common European identity to be projected also externally to the rest of the world.

To the extent that private law rules are more generous in their remedies in some countries than others, the equal treatment of all European national in the geographical area of the Union necessitates harmonization of national systems. Privacy is better protected at the present moment in Germany than in the United Kingdom, defamation is a more lucrative tort for a claimant in the United Kingdom than almost anywhere else. And citizens are compensated for disproportionate financial burdens imposed by *lawful* administrative action only in France. . . .

Common principles of European private law will be a sizeable transplant for all EU member states. As with all legal transplants, their introduction, survival and success depends on their reception in each country, first, by lawmakers (including judges) and other lawyers, practitioners and academics, and, second, by business interests, the insurance industry and the wider community. The experience from working with a group preparing a draft directive on the important issues of assessment of personal injury losses from car accidents has taught me that it is the reaction of the former group rather than the latter that is crucial.

In the light of the thesis advanced in this paper, that a common European private law must be forward looking, based on new principles, and not a conceptual legal syncretism of existing, and often outdated, national styles, it is important to educate and persuade national lawmakers and lawyers."

Questions

1. What is meant by the term "hegemony"? What does Werro mean when he refers to "Western hegemony"?

2. Do you think national legal cultures should be protected?

3. Do you think legal harmonisation "is a good or a bad thing for Europe"?

V. Postcolonialism and Postmodernism

In these final extracts, we bring our analysis "full circle" back to some of the questions with which we began this book. In earlier chapters, we considered the contribution of Lord Denning to statutory interpretation and judicial precedent. The extract from Harrington and Manji looks at his views on the development of African law in the period of decolonisation. Their analysis should also help you better to understand Denning's view of English common law and "Englishness" itself. Our final extract, by Menski, takes us back to our initial question, "What is law?", but it does so through the lens of Asian and African legal systems. Menski helps us to broaden our understanding, not just of our legal method and system, but of the meaning of "law".

John A. Harrington and Ambreena Manji, "'Mind with mind and spirit with spirit': Lord Denning and African legal systems" (2003) 30 *Journal of Law and Society* 376–99 at 389–392, 398:

"The obvious fragility of the rule of law in Lord Denning's Africa is connected with his understanding of the precise nature of the 'law' which was to 'rule' after independence. In his foreword to the *Journal of African Law* he noted somewhat sceptically that African law amounted 'at the moment to a jumble of pieces much like a jigsaw'. He identified the pieces as follows: those laws founded on the customs of African peoples; those based on the law of Islam; and those founded on English common law, on Roman–Dutch law or on Indian statutes. This legal plurality impeded the emergence of Africa 'into a great civilisation'. Accordingly, the key task of lawyers, and in particular of legal scholars, lay in sorting out the 'discordant pieces' and fitting them 'together into a single whole'. Even on completion of this task, however, African law would continue to betray its ersatz and hybrid nature. As he put it:

'The result is bound to be a patchwork but we should remember that a patchwork quilt of many colours can be just as serviceable as one of a single colour and it is often more admired because of the effort to make it.'

Here we see manifested the pragmatic and innovative approach to law for which Denning is well known. In an equivalent domestic context, he had already expressed a desire for greater uniformity between English and Scots law. He argued that the principles of Scots law, and indeed Scots lawyers themselves, had enriched English law and suggested that this 'intermingling' should be allowed to go forward 'so that we no longer have two separate systems of law but have the best of both'. In Britain as in Africa, Denning thus preferred a type of legal bricolage to an rationalistic or revolutionary law reform.

It was on the basis of this preference that he expressed his envy of the opportunities open to African lawyers. No doubt weary from his campaign against *stare decisis* and his lonely advocacy of a purposive approach to statutory interpretation, he commented that:

'In England the courts have little opportunity nowadays to develop the law. The principles are for the most part settled and static. No great change can be made here except by parliament and the work of lawyers is the dull routine of interpreting statutes. By contrast in Africa there is constructive work to be done on a grand scale.'

Like many an eager colonial officer before him, Denning seems to have viewed Africa as a realm of open possibility, a theatre of unconstrained self-assertion. On other occasions, however, he noted the inhospitable environment in which this jurisprudential freedom was to be realized. In a 1955 judgment concerning the tolls payable on the bridge linking Mombasa island with the Kenyan mainland he commented that:

> 'Just as with an English oak, so with the English common law. You cannot transplant it to the African continent and expect it to retain the tough character which it has in England. It will flourish indeed, but it needs careful handling.'

The turn to horticultural imagery is telling in this context. We can see in it the other side of what Dennis Klinck has called Lord Denning's pastoral vision. England, conceived of as a simple, but ordered garden, is juxtaposed here with its opposite: the African wilderness, uncontrolled and threateningly complex. Although both territories are characterized by a diversity of legal sources, as yet only in England has a successful integration of elements been achieved.

Denning's rhetoric is, thus, informed by an intensely particularistic conception of the common law as the innate sense of justice of the English people. Since it is organic and embodied, it amounts to what Michael Oakeshott called practical knowledge. As Denning wrote in *The Changing Law*: 'it is to be felt rather than to be seen and to be experienced rather than to be learnt . . . an atmosphere which springs out of our long experience and tradition.' This practical (or tacit) dimension is most clearly manifest in the British constitution and can be contrasted with the explicit or 'rationalist' approach taken in other countries. In Denning's view:

> 'The doctrine of Montesquieu about the separation of powers played a great part in the constitution of the United States. The doctrines of Rousseau about the rights of man are found reflected in the French constitution . . . But we English have always mistrusted philosophers and political theorists. We have no written constitution. We have worked out our constitution on purely practical grounds based on our own experience and needs.'

Similarly, the new states of West Africa were enshrining the fundamental principles of English law in their constitutions: they 'write down the principles which we have created through the ages'. Because of its particular and tacit nature English law could not be transmitted or transplanted directly to Africa. In the absence of an embodied local tradition, the law of the newly independent territories was only an abridged or derived version of its English antecedents."

Werner Menski, *Comparative Law in a Global Context*, 2nd edn (Cambridge: Cambridge University Press, 2006), pp.32, 33–35:

"Studying Asian and African legal systems from an internal perspective, attempting to understand 'from inside' how they are developed and function today, it becomes impossible to maintain a eurocentric, statist and purportedly universal set of assumptions about 'the law'. Perhaps that is why many people never even try to go that far. Herein, first of all, lies the central challenge for the comparative law teacher and legal theorist in the field of globalised legal education: the absence of any worldwide agreement, in theory as well as in practice, about the central object of globalised legal studies, namely 'the law' itself. Such definitional and ideological struggles are exacerbated by discrepancies between different religious systems and their competing truth claims. As in religious studies, it seems that, unless we agree to disagree about the basic ingredients of law itself and allow others the space to explain (and live) their culturally conditioned understandings of life and law, no real progress will be made in global legal debate.

In this context, academics often raise the objection of 'essentialising', stereotyping complex entities by emphasising one particular aspect of the whole. Allegedly this happens at the cost of fuller understanding or in disregard of flexibility of boundaries, and has caused enormous frustration in academic discourse. . . . However, provided one is aware of the fluidity of boundaries, what is wrong with demonstrating that a certain category or a particular legal system or legal rule is different from others and appears to have certain key characteristics?

Academics need such techniques to explain their thoughts. The deeper issue appears to be that the task of the comparatist in cherishing difference involves open-minded appreciation of 'the other', readiness to accept the other system as valid in its own right, thinking in open rather than closed basic categories. . . .

Many important questions arise. How are religion and society linked to law? Do Gods/gods or their human spokespersons make law? Are 'customs' to be treated as law? More specifically, do groups of people in a state have the right to determine their own rule systems if there are formal laws that they should follow? Do we treat such private law-making as evidence of lawlessness, even treason, or do we recognise it as a law-making process by social groups rather than states, and perhaps even by individuals? To what extent is this legitimate and still 'legal'? Does law really govern every moment of our lives, as legocentric approaches would claim? These are complex questions to which no universally agreed answers will ever be found because so much depends on one's perspectives and ideology. Simple eurocentric assumptions about 'law' cannot remain unquestioned in a sophisticated global educational environment. Law students in London or New York probably have quite different thoughts on such issues than budding lawyers in China, India, Namibia or elsewhere in the South. Even if we try to develop a working definition of law in the North/West, from the perspective of a traditional South African community leader, the legal world will look very different. Since the word 'law' is used to refer to a variety of concepts, we are offered a bewildering spectrum of definitional propositions from which to make a choice, in the knowledge that both the definitions and the choice are inescapably culture-bound and situation-specific.

Consequently, any attempt to answer the popular essay question whether law is a universal phenomenon is bedevilled from the start by the absence of consensus about methodology and the definition of 'law'. A narrow, state-centred approach would have to conclude that law is not a global phenomenon, as not all human societies (assuming we know what we mean by 'society') have formalised laws laid down by a state. Quite simply and logically, if one does not accept that customs can fall under 'law', then the conclusion inevitably becomes that not all human societies have law. Perhaps this logic is wrong? Do we really have lawless societies, and so-called 'primitive' people have no law? . . .

A more open approach to the definition of law than currently used in many debates would need to account for different forms of law in all human societies. Thus, in a so-called simple society, where no formal evidence of law exists and where no disputes may arise because everyone knows the basic rules and follows them to the satisfaction of others, there may be no visible evidence of law and of legal processes. A plurality-conscious analysis of law would nevertheless conclude that this society has its own laws, probably internalised to such an extent that nobody needs to write them down and apply them formally. Such a simple society still has a legal system, which perhaps includes the overriding principle that avoidance of disputes at all costs is the guiding principle or the 'golden rule'. So here, the 'rule of law' would be that there should be no recourse to formal law at all.

A globally valid analysis of 'law' needs to be sensitive to such informal and unwritten concepts, aware of many culture-specific and even personal idiosyncrasies. When one travels through Heathrow airport's Terminal 3 these days, one finds on the long walls of the walkways illustrations of common symbols with totally different culture-specific meanings abroad. Such thoughtful mental preparation for international travel indicates that such differences of meaning could become legally relevant when a particular cultural group assigns to some image, concept or human action specific negative or positive values. . . .

It is impossible for anyone to obtain a full mental map of all citizens of the world in their various life situations. Human life is just too complex; where do we stop? Do we prioritise the views of people in hour-long queues on congested roads in Mumbai's urban jungle over the assumptions carried by people who walk on foot every day through bushland to reach their place of work in the same jurisdiction? Do we make distinctions between rich and poor, rural and urban, dominant and servient, white and black, and so on? Yes, we do, all the time, reflecting the diversities of life. Applying law continuously involves making decisions that take account of different facts and circumstances and must, of necessity, involve consideration of socio-cultural elements. This even goes for commercial law, despite a strong belief that it is culture-neutral.

Legal science has moved through various modernising phases into a position where gradually the formal cosmopolitan law has become the dominant concept, often completely silencing lesser orders, little people and their local concerns. Since postmodern methodology involves a general re-questioning of all human activities, the task for legal scholarship is to build such realisations into a strong plurality-conscious methodology of global validity, focusing on the whole universe of legal phenomena . . . But what are legal phenomena? We are always thrown back to the conundrum of defining 'law'."

The issues raised above take yet another turn when studied within the context of a multi-cultural society. It has been argued that a major challenge facing the English legal system today is how to deal with the increasing tensions at the interface of secular and religious cultures within the same jurisdiction. The final extract in our book outlines the nature of some of the challenges facing us.

Ayelat Shachar, "Privatizing Diversity: A Cautionary Tale from Religious Arbitration in Family Law" (2008) 9 *Theoretical Inquiries in Law* 573 at 574–577:

"In discussions about citizenship, we repeatedly come across the modernist schema of privatizing identities: we are expected to act as undifferentiated citizens in the public sphere, but remain free to express our distinct cultural or religious identities in the private domain of family and communal life. Yet multiple tensions have exposed cracks in this privatizing identities formula: for instance, where precisely does the 'private' end and the 'public' begin? What happens when cultural and religious customs extend beyond the home into the spaces of our shared citizenship, such as the school, the workplace, or the voting booth? The recent debates surrounding the *hijab* (the headscarf worn by some Muslim women), which have engulfed courts and legislatures from Germany to France to Turkey, vividly illustrate these tensions.

We are also starting to see a new type of challenge on the horizon: namely, the request to 'privatize diversity' through alternative dispute resolution processes that permit parties to move their disputes from public courthouses into the domain of religious or customary sources of law and authority. The recent controversies in Canada and England related to the so-called Shari'a tribunals demonstrate the potential force of the storm to come. Acceptance of privatized diversity may indirectly make room for non-state norms to operate authoritatively within what are otherwise secular legal systems. It could also immunize such processes from the regulatory reach of statutory or constitutional norms of gender equality. These potentially far-reaching alterations to the legal system cannot be fully captured by the old and rigid vocabulary of 'private' versus 'public'; if anything, these changes challenge the very logic of this distinction. But what are the normative and prudential implications of this attempt to realign secular and religious law, public and private justice, citizenship and diversity? Who is likely to gain, and who may stand to lose from such changes? . . .

Although limiting intervention by the courts in cases where religious and civil world collide has a long history, the urgency of my plea for rethinking this approach is informed by the contemporary revival of demands for privatized diversity in Canada, England, and elsewhere. The reincarnation of this debate raises a slew of important questions for our conception of citizenship in contemporary societies in the context of a wider trend towards the privatization of justice in family law. Consider the following examples: should a court be permitted to enforce a civil divorce contract that also has a religious aspect, namely a promise by a Jewish husband to remove all barriers to remarriage by granting his wife the religious *get* (Jewish divorce decree)? Is it legitimate to establish private religious tribunals—as alternative dispute resolution (ADR) forums—in which consenting adults arbitrate family law disputes according to the parties' religious personal laws in lieu of the state's secular family laws? And, is there room for considerations of culture, religion, national-origin, or linguistic identity in determining a child's best interests in cases of custody, visitation, education, and so on? None of these examples are hypothetical. They represent real-life legal challenges raised in recent years by individuals and families who are seeking to redefine the place of culture and religion in their own private ordering, and, indirectly, in the larger polity as well.

Family law serves as a casebook illustration of these tensions. Take, for example, the situation of observant religious women who may wish—or feel bound—to follow the requirements of divorce according to their communities of faith, in addition to the rules of the state, in order to remove barriers to remarriage. Without the removal of such barriers, women's ability to build new families, if not their very membership status (or that of their children), may be adversely affected. This is particularly true for Muslim and Jewish women living in secular societies who have entered into the marital relationship through a religious ceremony—as permitted by law in many jurisdictions. For them, a civil divorce is merely part of the story; it does not, and cannot, dissolve the religious aspect of the relationship. Failure to recognize their 'split status' position—namely, that of being legally divorced according to state law, though still married according to their faith—may leave these women prey to abuse by recalcitrant husbands who are well aware of the adverse effect this situation has on their wives, as they fall between the cracks of the civil and religious jurisdictions.

Ignoring this multiplicity of affiliations may be compatible with an abstract public/private divide, but it misses the mark for these embedded individuals. Even the bulk of theoretical literature on multiculturalism seems to lose sight of this type of concern, engaging instead in intricate attempts to delineate the boundaries of *public, state-sponsored accommodation of diversity*. As if the public accommodation dilemma did not present enough of a hurdle for policymakers seeking to build a pluralist society, pressing at the edges is another, less easily categorized challenge, which I will here refer to, for the sake of clarity and simplicity, as *privatized diversity*. The main claim raised by advocates of privatized diversity is that what respect for religious freedom or cultural integrity requires is not inclusion in the public sphere, but exclusion from it. This leads to a demand that the state adopt a hands-off, non-interventionist approach, placing civil and family disputes with a religious or cultural aspect fully *outside* the official realm of equal citizenship."

Questions

1. Describe Lord Denning's view of "Africa" and its legal systems. How does it differ from his understanding of the English legal system?

2. How does the study of comparative law force us to question what "law" itself means? In other words, how might "we" "disagree about the basic ingredients of law itself"?

INDEX